TRAINING & REFERENCE

murach's Java programming

4th EDITION

Joel Murach

MIKE MURACH & ASSOCIATES, INC.

4340 N. Knoll Ave. • Fresno, CA 93722

www.murach.com • murachbooks@murach.com

Author: Joel Murach
Editor: Anne Boehm
Cover design: Zylka Design
Production: Maria Pedroza David

Books for Java programmers

Murach's Java Programming
Murach's Java Servlets and JSP

Books for database programmers

Murach's Oracle SQL and PL/SQL
Murach's MySQL
Murach's SQL Server for Developers

Books for web developers

Murach's HTML5 and CSS3
Murach's JavaScript and DOM Scripting
Murach's PHP and MySQL

Books for .NET programmers

Murach's C# 2010
Murach's ASP.NET 4 Web Programming with C# 2010
Murach's ADO.NET 4 Database Programming with C# 2010

Murach's Visual Basic 2010
Murach's ASP.NET 4 Web Programming with VB 2010
Murach's ADO.NET 4 Database Programming with VB 2010

Books for IBM mainframe programmers

Murach's OS/390 and z/OS JCL
Murach's Mainframe COBOL
Murach's CICS for the COBOL Programmer
DB2 for the COBOL Programmer, Part 1

Printed in the United States of America

10 9 8 7 6 5 4 3 2 1
ISBN: 978-1-890774-65-3

Contents

Expanded contents

Section 1 Essential Java skills

Section 4 GUI programming with Swing

Section 6 Advanced Java skills

Chapter 22 How to work with threads

Chapter 23 How to deploy an application

Introduction

Since its release in 1996, the Java language has established itself as one of the leading languages for object-oriented programming. Today, Java continues to be one of the most popular languages for application development, especially for web applications and for mobile applications like Android apps. And that's going to continue for many years to come, for several reasons.

First, developers can obtain Java and a wide variety of tools for working with Java for free. Second, Java code can run on any modern operating system. Third, Java's development has been guided largely by the Java community, and Sun Microsystems released most of Java as open source software in 2007. As a result, the Java platform is able to evolve according to the needs of the programmers who use the language. Although Sun was acquired by Oracle Corporation in 2010, Oracle has committed itself to supporting Java and the Java community.

Who this book is for

This book is for anyone who wants to learn the core features of the Java language. It works if you have no programming experience at all. It works if you have programming experience with another language. It works if you already know an older version of Java and you want to get up-to-speed with the latest version. And it works if you've already read three or four other Java books and still don't know how to develop a real-world application.

If you're completely new to programming, the prerequisites are minimal. You just need to be familiar with the operation of the platform that you're using. If, for example, you're developing programs using Windows on a PC, you should know how to use Windows to perform tasks like opening, saving, printing, closing, copying, and deleting files.

What version of Java this book supports

This book is designed to work with the Java Platform, Standard Edition 7 (Java SE 7) or later. This edition of Java includes the Java Development Kit (JDK). For marketing reasons, Oracle sometimes refers to this version of the JDK as JDK 7. However, from a developer's point of view, this version of the JDK is commonly referred to as version 1.7.

As you work with Java SE 7, please keep in mind that all Java versions are backwards-compatible. That means that everything in this book will also work with future versions of the JDK.

What operating systems this book supports

The Oracle web site provides the most current version of the JDK for the Windows, Linux, and Solaris operating systems. As this book goes to press, the Mac OS X operating system includes JDK 1.6, and there are some unofficial builds available for JDK 1.7. Before long, OS X will provide support for JDK 1.7. Until then, you can install an unofficial build as described in appendix B.

Since most Java development today is done under Windows, this book uses Windows to illustrate any platform-dependent procedures. However, whenever possible, we describe these procedures for other operating systems too. For example, appendix B shows how to install the software for this book on Mac OS X. However, if you're using another platform such as Linux or Solaris, you may need to search the Internet for more information about performing these platform-dependent procedures. Fortunately, if you use NetBeans as described in this book, there are very few platform-dependent procedures.

What IDE this book supports

This book shows you how to use the NetBeans IDE (Integrated Development Environment) to code, test, and debug applications. Although there are other excellent IDEs for working with Java, we decided to present NetBeans because we think it's the best IDE for getting started with Java. It's intuitive, easy to use, available for free, and it runs on all operating systems.

Even if you want to use another IDE such as Eclipse, we recommend that you use NetBeans to work with the applications presented in this book. Then, once you're done with this book, it should be easy for you to switch from NetBeans to another IDE. However, if you'd prefer to get started with another IDE right away, you can do that too. But first, you'll need to convert the NetBeans projects that are available from our web site so you can work with them in your preferred IDE.

How to get the software you need

You can download all of the software that you need for this book for free from the Internet. To make that easier for you, appendix A shows how to download and install the JDK as well as NetBeans on a PC. Similarly, appendix B shows how to download and install the JDK, NetBeans, and Derby on a Mac. That's all the software you need to start developing professional Java applications on your own.

What you'll learn in this book

Unlike competing books, this one focuses on the practical features that you'll need for developing professional Java applications. Here's a quick tour:

- In section 1, you'll quickly master the basics of the Java language. In chapter 1, you'll learn how to get started with NetBeans. In chapter 2, you'll learn how to write console applications that use the Scanner class to get input from the user. By the end of chapter 5, you'll know how to code applications that use custom methods to validate user input so they won't crash. And in chapter 6, you'll learn how to use NetBeans to thoroughly test and debug your applications.
- In section 2, you'll learn how to use Java for object-oriented programming. In chapter 7, you'll learn how to create and use your own classes, which is the basis for developing applications that are easier to test, debug, and maintain. Then, in chapters 8 through 10, you'll learn how to develop more sophisticated classes that use inheritance, interfaces, packages, type-safe enumerations, and the factory pattern. In addition, you'll learn how to use the three-tiered architecture that's the standard used by most professionals for designing and developing object-oriented, database applications.
- In section 3, you'll learn more of the core Java features that you'll use all the time. In chapters 11 through 14, for instance, you'll learn how to work with arrays, collections, dates, strings, and exceptions. Along the way, you'll learn how to use features such as enhanced for loops, typed collections, generics, and the StringBuilder class. You'll also learn how to use JDK 1.7 features such as the try-with-resources statement.
- In section 4, you'll learn how to use a built-in tool provided by NetBeans to develop graphical user interfaces (GUIs). We highly recommend this approach for getting started with GUI programming. First, you'll learn how to use Swing components to develop real-world GUI applications that handle events, validate data, and populate objects. Then, you'll learn how to develop applets, a special type of Java application that can be downloaded from the Internet and run within a web browser.
- Because storing data is critical to most applications, section 5 shows you how to store data in a file or database. In chapter 18, you'll learn how to work with text files and binary files, including random-access files. In chapter 19, you'll learn how to use an API known as StAX (the Streaming API for XML) that was introduced with JDK 1.6 to work with XML documents and files. In chapter 20, you'll learn how to work with the open-source Apache Derby database. And in chapter 21, you'll learn how to use JDBC to work with any database.
- In section 6, you'll learn some advanced Java skills. In chapter 22, you'll learn how to use threads so your applications can perform two or more tasks at the same time. Finally, in chapter 23, you'll learn how to deploy your finished applications using executable JAR files or Java Web Start.

Why you'll learn faster and better with this book

Like all our books, this one has features that you won't find in competing books. That's why we believe that you'll learn faster and better with our book than with any other. Here are just three of those features.

- To help you develop applications at a professional level, this book presents complete, non-trivial applications. For example, chapter 16 presents a Product Maintenance application that uses presentation classes, business classes, and data access classes. You won't find complete, real-world applications like this in other Java books even though studying these types of applications is the best way to master Java development.
- All of the information in this book is presented in our unique paired-pages format, with the essential syntax, guidelines, and examples on the right page and the perspective and extra explanation on the left page. This helps you learn more while reading less, and it helps you quickly find the information that you need when you use this book for reference.
- The exercises at the end of each chapter give you a chance to try out what you've just learned. They guide you through the development of some of the book's applications, and they challenge you to apply what you've learned in new ways. As a result, you'll gain valuable, hands-on experience in Java programming that will build both your skills and your confidence.

How our downloadable files make learning easier

To make learning easier, you can download the source code for all the applications presented in this book from our web site (www.murach.com). This source code includes the files and databases required by these applications. Then, you can view the complete code for these applications as you read each chapter; you can run these applications to see how they work; and you can copy portions of code for use in your own applications.

You can also download the source code that you need for doing the exercises in this book. That way, you don't have to start every exercise from scratch. This takes the busywork out of doing these exercises so you can get more practice in less time. For more information about these downloads, please see appendix A (Windows) and appendix B (Mac OS X).

Support materials for trainers and instructors

If you're a corporate trainer or a college instructor who would like to use this book for a course, we offer an Instructor's CD that includes: (1) a complete set of PowerPoint slides that you can use to review and reinforce the content of the book; (2) instructional objectives that describe the skills a student should have upon completion of each chapter; (3) the solutions to the exercises in this book; (4) projects that the students start from scratch; (5) solutions to those projects; and (6) test banks that measure mastery of those skills.

To learn more about this Instructor's CD and to find out how to get it, please go to our web site at www.murach.com and click the Trainers link or Instructors link. Or, if you prefer, you can call Kelly at 1-800-221-5528 or send an email to kelly@murach.com.

A companion book for web developers

Since web programming is one of the primary uses of Java, we also offer a book on web programming called *Murach's Java Servlets and JSP*. It shows you how to use Java servlets and JavaServer Pages as you develop professional web applications. As you read that book, you'll discover that Java web programming requires most of the skills that are presented in sections 1-3 of this book. That's why we see this book as the perfect companion for *Murach's Java Servlets and JSP*.

Please let us know how this book works for you

When we started the first edition of this book, our goals were (1) to teach you Java as quickly and easily as possible and (2) to teach you the practical Java concepts and skills that you need for developing real-world business applications. We've tried to improve on that with each subsequent edition, and as this fourth edition goes to press, we hope that the book is more effective than ever before. Many of the improvements have come from the feedback we've received from our readers, so if you have any comments about this book, we would appreciate hearing from you at murachbooks@murach.com.

Thanks for buying this book. We hope you enjoy reading it, and we wish you great success with your Java programming.

Joel Murach
Author

Anne Boehm
Editor

Section 1

Essential Java skills

This section gets you started quickly with Java programming. First, chapter 1 introduces you to Java applications and shows you how to use NetBeans to work with Java projects. Then, chapter 2 introduces you to the basic skills that you need for developing Java applications. When you complete these chapters, you'll be able to write, test, and debug simple applications of your own.

After that, chapter 3 presents the details for working with numeric data. Chapter 4 presents the details for coding control statements. Chapter 5 shows how to validate the data that's entered by the user. And chapter 6 shows how to thoroughly test and debug an application. These are the essential skills that you'll use in almost every Java application that you develop. When you finish these chapters, you'll be able to write solid programs of your own. And you'll have the background that you need for learning how to develop object-oriented programs.

1

How to get started with Java and NetBeans

Before you can begin learning the Java language, you need to install Java. In addition, you need to choose an IDE or a text editor for working with Java. For this book, we recommend that you use the NetBeans IDE. Appendix A of this book shows you how to install both Java and NetBeans on a Windows system, and appendix B shows you how to install them on a Macintosh OS X system. Then, this chapter shows how to use the NetBeans IDE to create and work with a Java application. But first, this chapter presents some background information about Java.

Introduction to Java

In 1996, Sun Microsystems released a new programming language called Java. Although Oracle bought Sun in 2010, Java remains one of the most widely used object-oriented programming languages.

Toolkits and platforms

Figure 1-1 describes all major releases of Java starting with version 1.0 and ending with version 1.7. Throughout Java's history, the terms *Java Development Kit* (*JDK*) and *Software Development Kit* (*SDK*) have been used to describe the Java toolkit. In this book, we'll use the term *JDK* since it's the most current and commonly used term. In addition, different numbering schemes have been used to indicate the version of Java. For example, Java 5.0 and Java 6 refer to versions 1.5 and 1.6 of Java. In this book, we'll use the 1.x style of numbering since this numbering is used by the documentation for Java.

With versions 1.2 through 1.5 of the JDK, the *Standard Edition* (*SE*) of Java was known as *Java 2 Platform, Standard Edition* (*J2SE*), and the *Enterprise Edition* (*EE*) was known as the *Java 2 Platform, Enterprise Edition* (*J2EE*). Since version 1.6 of the JDK, the Standard Edition of Java has been known as *Java SE*, and the Enterprise Edition is known as *Java EE*. This book shows how to use Java SE 7, but it should also work for earlier and future versions of Java. That includes Java SE 8, which is scheduled for release in late 2012.

How Java compares to C++ and C#

When Sun's developers created Java, they tried to keep the syntax for Java similar to the syntax for C++ so it would be easy for C++ programmers to learn Java. In addition, they designed Java so its applications can be run on any computer platform. In contrast, C++ needs to have a specific compiler for each platform. Java was also designed to automatically handle many operations involving the creation and destruction of memory. This is a key reason why it's easier to develop programs and write bug-free code with Java than with C++.

To provide these features, the developers of Java had to sacrifice some speed (or performance) when compared to C++. For many types of applications, however, Java's relative slowness is not an issue.

Microsoft's Visual C# language is similar to Java in many ways. Like Java, C# uses a syntax that's similar to C++ and that automatically handles memory operations. However, in practice, C# code only runs on Windows. Because of that, C# is a good choice for developing applications for a Windows-only environment. However, Java is a better choice if you need to develop cross-platform applications.

Java timeline

Year	Month	Event
1996	January	Sun releases Java Development Kit 1.0 (JDK 1.0).
1997	February	Sun releases Java Development Kit 1.1 (JDK 1.1).
1998	December	Sun releases the Java 2 Platform with version 1.2 of the Software Development Kit (SDK 1.2).
1999	August	Sun releases Java 2 Platform, Standard Edition (J2SE).
	December	Sun releases Java 2 Platform, Enterprise Edition (J2EE).
2000	May	Sun releases J2SE with version 1.3 of the SDK.
2002	February	Sun releases J2SE with version 1.4 of the SDK.
2004	September	Sun releases J2SE 5.0 with version 1.5 of the JDK.
2006	December	Sun releases Java SE 6 with version 1.6 of the JDK.
2010	April	Oracle buys Sun.
2011	July	Oracle releases Java SE 7 with version 1.7 of the JDK.

Operating systems supported by Java

Windows (XP, Vista, 7)

Linux

Solaris

Macintosh OS X

Java compared to C++ and C#

Feature	Description
Syntax	Java syntax is similar to C++ and C# syntax.
Platforms	Compiled Java code can be run on any platform that has a Java interpreter. Similarly, compiled C# code (MSIL) can be run on any system that has the appropriate interpreter. Currently, only Windows has an interpreter for MSIL. C++ code must be compiled once for each type of system that it is going to be run on.
Speed	C++ and C# run faster than Java, but Java is getting faster with each new version.
Memory	Both Java and C# handle most memory operations automatically, while C++ programmers must write code that manages memory.

Description

- Versions 1.2 through 1.4 of Java are called the *Software Development Kit (SDK).*
- Versions 1.5 through 1.7 of Java are called the *Java Development Kit (JDK).*

Note

- Java SE 8 with version 1.8 of the JDK is expected to be released late in 2012.

Figure 1-1 Introduction to Java

Applications, applets, and servlets

Figure 1-2 describes the three types of programs that you can create with Java. First, you can use Java to create *applications* that run directly on your computer. These are also known as *desktop applications*.

When you create these desktop applications, you can use a *graphical user interface* (*GUI*) to get user input and perform a calculation as shown at the top left of this figure. In chapter 15, you'll learn how to create these types of applications. Until then, you'll learn how to create another type of desktop application known as a *console application*. This type of application runs in the *console*, or *command prompt*, that's available from your operating system. An example of a console application is shown at the top right of this figure.

One of the unique characteristics of Java is that you can use it to create a special type of web-based application known as an *applet*. For instance, this figure shows an applet that works the same way as the applications above it. The main difference between an application and an applet is that an applet can be stored in an HTML page and can run inside a Java-enabled browser. As a result, you can distribute applets via the Internet or an intranet. In chapter 17, you'll learn how to create and deploy applets.

Although applets can be useful for creating a complex user interface within a browser, they have their limitations. First, you usually need to install a plug-in on each client machine, which isn't ideal for some types of applications. Second, since an applet runs within a browser on the client, it's not ideal for working with resources that run on the server, such as enterprise databases.

To provide access to enterprise databases, many developers use Java EE to create applications that are based on servlets. A *servlet* is a special type of Java application that runs on the server and can be called by a client, which is usually a web browser. This is also illustrated in this figure. Here, you can see that the servlet works much the same way as the applet. The main difference is that the code for the application runs on the server.

When a web browser calls a servlet, the servlet performs its task and returns the result to the browser, typically in the form of an HTML page. For example, suppose a browser requests a servlet that displays all unprocessed invoices that are stored in a database. Then, when the servlet is executed, it reads data from the database, formats that data within an HTML page, and returns the HTML page to the browser.

When you create a servlet-based application like the one shown here, all the processing takes place on the server and only HTML is returned to the browser. That means that anyone with an Internet or intranet connection, a web browser, and adequate security clearance can access and run a servlet-based application. Because of that, you don't need to install any special software on the client.

To make it easy to store the results of a servlet within an HTML page, the Java EE specification provides for *JavaServer Pages* (JSPs). Most developers use JSPs together with servlets when developing server-side Java applications. Although servlets and JSPs aren't presented in this book, we cover this topic in a companion book, *Murach's Java Servlets and JSP*. For more information about this book, please visit our web site at www.murach.com.

A GUI application and a console application

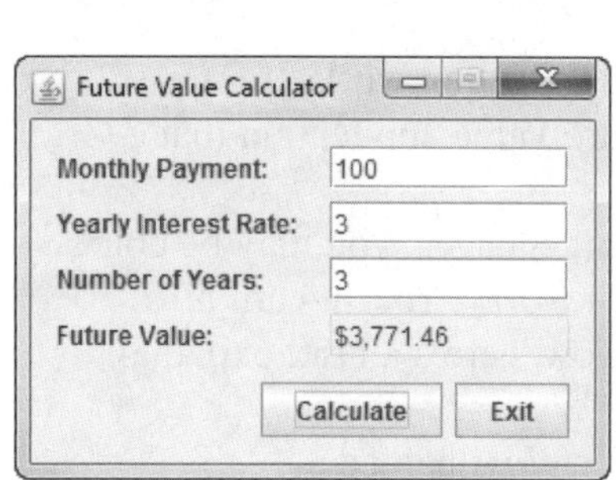

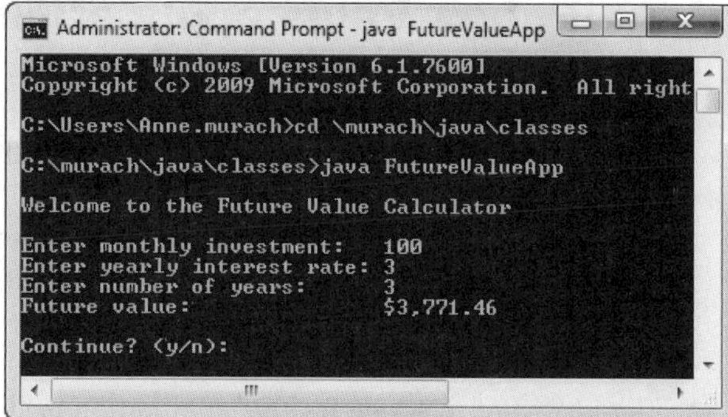

An applet

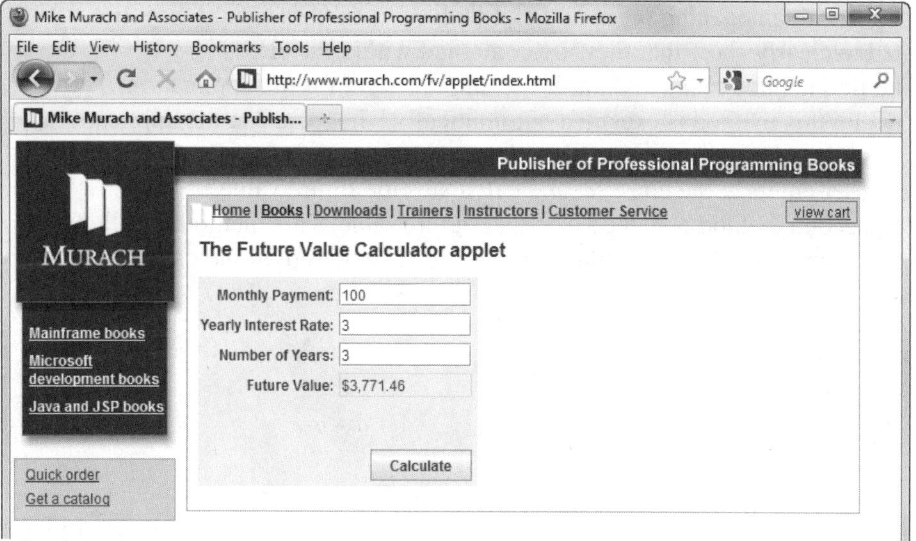

A servlet

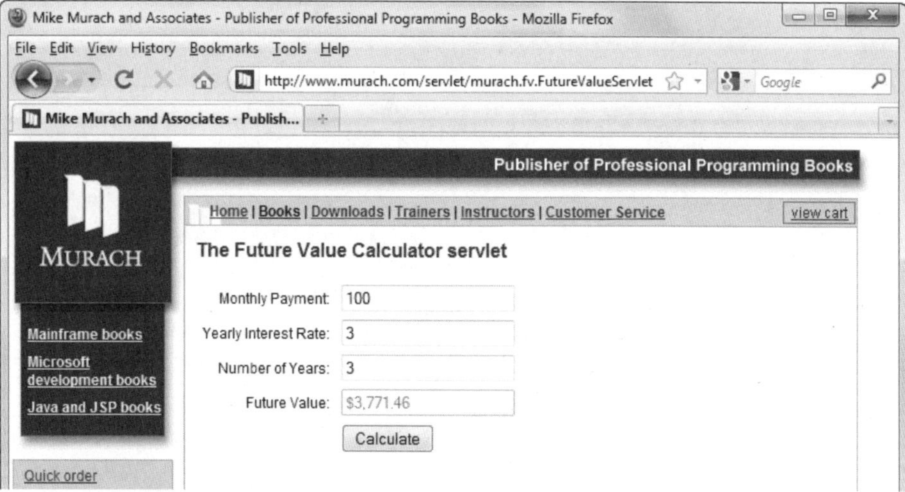

Figure 1-2 Applications, applets, and servlets

The code for the console version of the Future Value application

To give you an idea of how the code for a Java application works, figure 1-3 presents the code for the console version of the Future Value application that you saw in figure 1-2.

If you have experience with other programming languages, you may be able to understand much of this code already. If not, don't worry! You'll learn how all of this code works in the next few chapters. For now, here's a brief explanation of this code.

Most of the code for this application is stored in a *class* named FutureValueApp. This class begins with an opening brace ({) and ends with a closing brace (}). Within this class, two *methods* are defined. These methods also begin with an opening brace and end with a closing brace, and they are indented to clearly show that they are contained within the class.

The first method, named main, is the *main method* for the application. The code within this method is executed automatically when you run the application. In this case, the code displays the data the user sees on the console, accepts the data the user enters at the console, and calculates the future value.

The second method is named calculateFutureValue. This method is called from the main method and calculates the future value based on the data the user enters.

The code for the Future Value application

```
import java.util.Scanner;
import java.text.NumberFormat;

public class FutureValueApp
{
    public static void main(String[] args)
    {
        System.out.println("\nWelcome to the Future Value Calculator\n");

        Scanner sc = new Scanner(System.in);
        String choice = "y";

        while (choice.equalsIgnoreCase("y"))
        {
            // get the input from the user
            System.out.print("Enter monthly investment:   ");
            double monthlyInvestment = sc.nextDouble();
            System.out.print("Enter yearly interest rate: ");
            double interestRate = sc.nextDouble();
            System.out.print("Enter number of years:      ");
            int years = sc.nextInt();

            // calculate the future value
            double monthlyInterestRate = interestRate/12/100;
            int months = years * 12;
            double futureValue = calculateFutureValue(
                monthlyInvestment, monthlyInterestRate, months);

            // format and display the result
            NumberFormat currency = NumberFormat.getCurrencyInstance();
            System.out.println("Future value:               " +
                               currency.format(futureValue) + "\n");

            // see if the user wants to continue
            System.out.print("Continue? (y/n): ");
            choice = sc.next();
            System.out.println();
        }
    }

    private static double calculateFutureValue(double monthlyInvestment,
    double monthlyInterestRate, int months)
    {
        double futureValue = 0;
        for (int i = 1; i <= months; i++)
            futureValue = (futureValue + monthlyInvestment) *
                          (1 + monthlyInterestRate);
        return futureValue;
    }
}
```

Figure 1-3 The code for the console version of the Future Value application

How Java compiles and interprets code

When you develop a Java application, you create one or more *classes*. For each class, you write the Java statements that direct the operation of the class. Then, you use a Java tool to translate the Java statements into instructions that can be run by the computer. This process is illustrated in figure 1-4.

To start, you enter and edit the Java *source code* for a class. These are the Java statements like the ones you saw in figure 1-3 that tell the application what to do. Then, you use the *Java compiler* to compile the source code into a format known as Java *bytecodes*. At this point, the bytecodes can be run on any platform that has a *Java interpreter* to *interpret* (or translate) the Java bytecodes into code that can be understood by the underlying operating system.

Since Java interpreters are available for all major operating systems, you can run Java on most platforms. This is what gives Java applications their *platform independence*. In contrast, C++ requires a specific compiler for each type of platform that its programs are going to run on. When a platform has a Java interpreter installed on it, it can be considered an implementation of a *Java virtual machine* (*JVM*).

In addition, most modern web browsers can be Java enabled. This allows applets, which are bytecodes that are downloaded from the Internet or an intranet, to run within a web browser. To make this work, Sun developed (and Oracle now maintains) the *Java Plug-in*. This piece of software is similar to other browser plug-ins such as Apple QuickTime. It allows the browser to run the current version of the Java interpreter. You'll learn more about this in chapter 17.

How Java compiles and interprets code

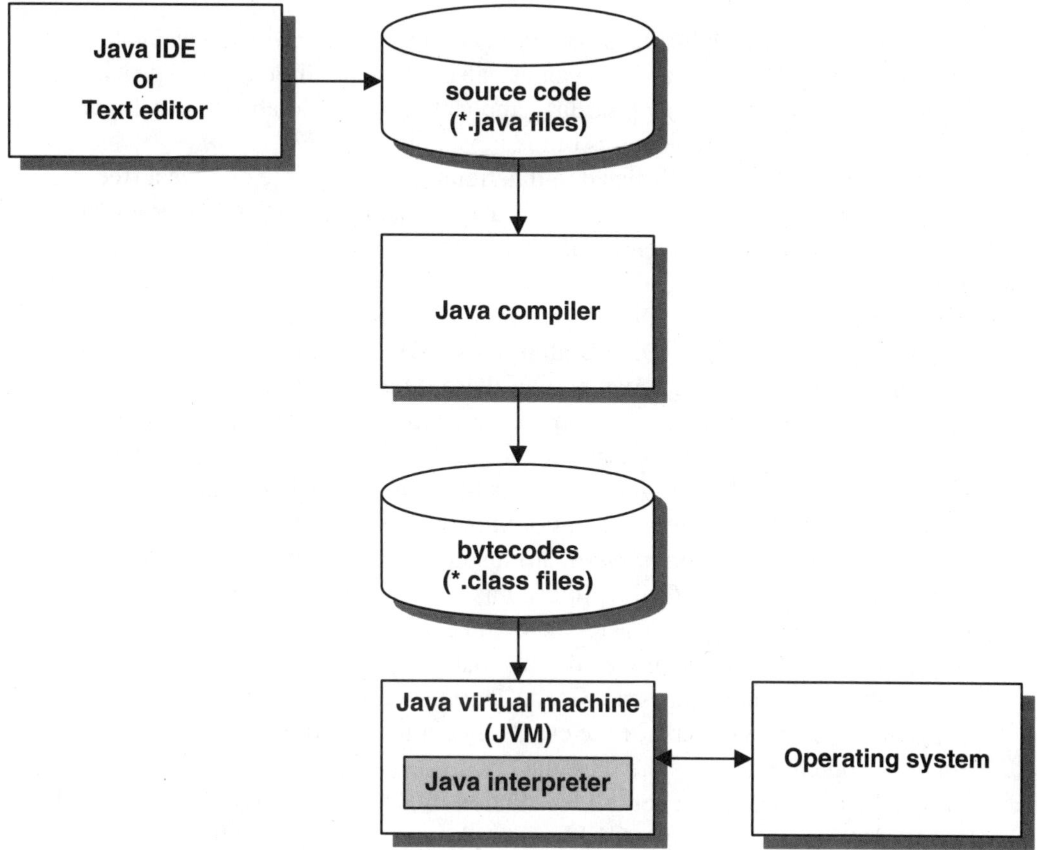

Description

- When you develop a Java application, you develop one or more *classes*.
- You can use a Java IDE or any text editor to create, edit, and save the *source code* for a Java class. Source code files have the *java* extension.
- The *Java compiler* translates Java source code into a *platform-independent* format known as Java *bytecodes*. Files that contain Java bytecodes have the *class* extension.
- The *Java interpreter* executes Java bytecodes. Since Java interpreters exist for all major operating systems, Java bytecodes can be run on most platforms. A Java interpreter is an implementation of a *Java virtual machine* (*JVM*).
- Most modern web browsers can be Java enabled. This lets applets run within these browsers. Oracle provides a tool known as the *Java Plug-in* that allows you to specify the version of the Java interpreter that you want to use.

Figure 1-4 How Java compiles and interprets code

Introduction to Java IDEs

To develop Java applications, you typically use an *Integrated Development Environment (IDE)*. Although you can use a simple text editor, an IDE provides features that can make developing Java applications considerably easier. Figure 1-5 describes some of the features of the most popular IDEs.

Note that all of the IDEs listed in this figure are either free or have a free edition. That makes them particularly attractive to students as well as programmers who are learning on their own. Most of these IDEs also run on all modern operating systems.

The first two IDEs listed in this figure, NetBeans and Eclipse, are arguably the two most popular Java IDEs. Both of these IDEs provide all of the features listed in this figure. For example, both of these IDEs help you complete your code and notify you of potential compile-time errors. They both automatically compile your code before you run it. And they both include a debugger that lets you perform standard debugging functions like setting breakpoints, stepping through code, and viewing the values of variables.

The default installation of NetBeans also provides a feature for building graphical user interfaces (GUIs). To use this GUI builder, you can drag controls onto a form on the design surface. Then, you can move, size, and align the controls and set properties of the controls that determine how they look. As you do this, the code that displays the GUI is automatically generated. Finally, you can generate event handlers for the events that you want to handle and then write the code that handles these events.

On the other hand, the default installation of Eclipse does not provide a GUI builder. However, several free GUI builder plug-ins are available for Eclipse. These GUI builders provide features similar to the GUI builder that's provided by NetBeans.

The last three IDEs listed in this figure aren't as popular as NetBeans and Eclipse. However, we have included them here to give you an idea of the wide range of IDE choices that are available for Java. In addition, other Java IDEs are available that aren't included here.

For this book, we recommend using NetBeans because we think it's more intuitive and easier to use than Eclipse, especially for beginners. Once you're done with this book, you can switch to whatever IDE you prefer. Fortunately, once you learn how to use one IDE, it's fairly easy to learn to use another one.

Popular Java IDEs

IDE	Description
NetBeans	A free, open-source IDE that runs on most modern operating systems.
Eclipse	A free, open-source IDE that runs on most modern operating systems.
IntelliJ IDEA	The Community Edition of this IDE is a free, open-source IDE that runs on most modern operating systems.
JCreator LE	The Lite Edition (LE) of this IDE is free, but the code is not open-source, and it only runs on Windows.
BlueJ	A free IDE that's designed for teaching Java to first-year students and runs on most modern operating systems.

Features provided by most IDEs

- A code editor with code completion and error detection.
- Automatic compilation of classes when you run the application.
- A debugger that lets you set breakpoints, step through code, and view the values of active variables.
- A GUI builder that lets you create graphical user interfaces by dragging controls onto a form, setting properties, and writing code that handles the events that are triggered when a user interacts with the form.

Description

- To develop Java applications, you typically use an *Integrated Development Environment* (*IDE*) like those listed above. All of these IDEs are either free or have free editions.

Figure 1-5 Introduction to Java IDEs

How to use NetBeans to work with existing projects

Now that you have some background information about Java, you're ready to start working with existing NetBeans projects. In particular, you're ready to learn how to open and run any of the applications for this book. You can download these applications from our web site as described in appendix A (Windows) or appendix B (Mac OS X).

Introduction to Java projects and the NetBeans IDE

Figure 1-6 shows the NetBeans IDE with an open Java project. In NetBeans, a *project* is a folder that contains all the files for an application. In this example, the project is named ch02_Invoice.

In the Projects window, you can see that the folder for the ch02_Invoice project contains two subfolders. The first one, named Source Packages, contains the source files for the application. The second one, named Libraries, contains the Java libraries that are used by the application. In this case, the application uses just the JDK 1.7 libraries, but you can add others.

Within the Source Packages folder, the source files can be organized into *packages*. In this case, no package was specified for the project, so the default package is used. When you develop simple applications like the one shown here, that's usually acceptable. For more complex applications, though, you'll want to use two or more packages as shown in chapter 10.

The application shown here consists of a single source file named InvoiceApp.java. You can see part of this file in the NetBeans *code editor*. You'll learn more about working with this code editor later in this chapter. For now, I just want to point out that this file defines a single class. Because this class contains the main method for the application, it's called the *main class*. When you run an application, the main method in the main class is executed by default.

NetBeans with a Java project open

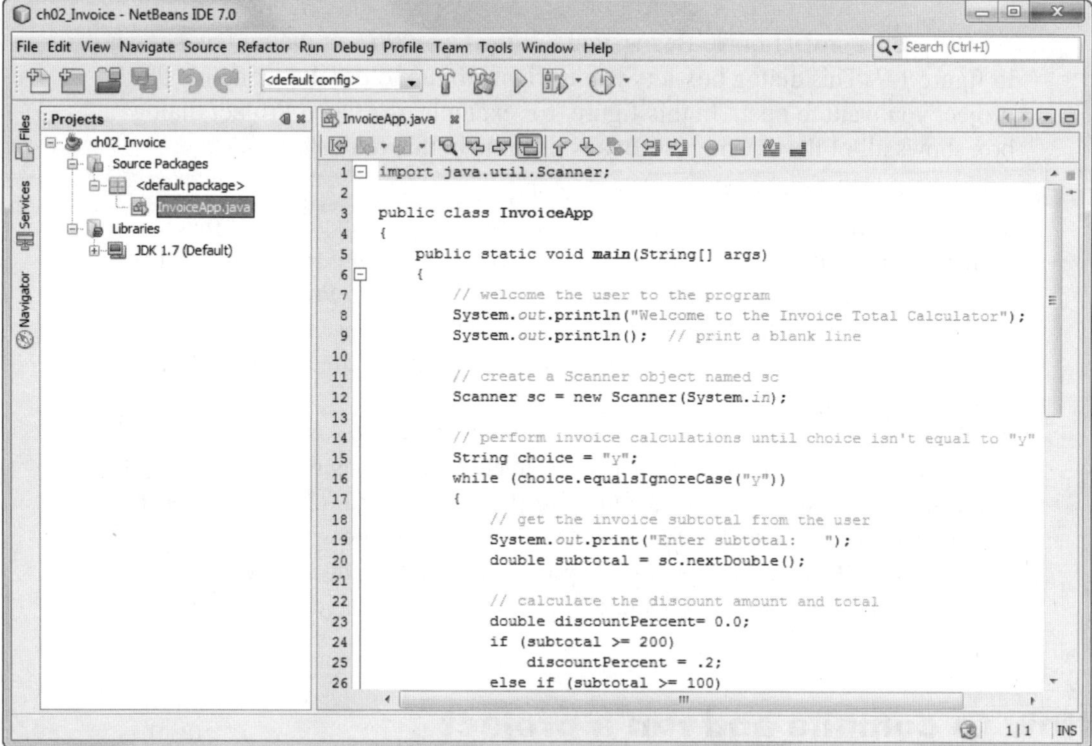

Description

- A NetBeans *project* consists of a top-level folder that contains the subfolders and files for an application.
- The Source Packages subfolder contains the .java files that make up the project. These files define *classes* that are later compiled into .class files.
- By default, a project consists of a single class that contains the *main method*. The main method is the starting point for the application, and the class that contains it is called the *main class*.
- The .java files that make up a project can be organized into one or more *packages*. If you don't specify a package for the main class when you create a project, it's stored in the default package.
- The Libraries subfolder contains the *libraries* that are available to your project. These libraries contain the Java classes that you can use in your projects. By default, you can use the classes in the JDK libraries.
- The folders, files, and libraries that make up a Java project are listed in the Projects window. If this window isn't visible, you can display it by using the Window→Projects command. Then, you can expand and collapse the nodes in this window by clicking on the plus and minus signs.
- You can display and work with the source code in a .java file in the *code editor window*. For details, see figure 1-11.

Figure 1-6 Introduction to Java projects and the NetBeans IDE

How to open, close, and delete a project

To open a project in NetBeans, you use the Open Project dialog box shown in figure 1-7. This dialog box lets you navigate to the folder that contains the project you want to open. In this figure, for example, the Open Project dialog box shows all of the existing NetBeans projects in this folder:

```
C:\murach\java\netbeans\book_apps
```

To clearly indicate when a folder contains a Java project, the Open Project dialog box displays a small coffee cup icon to the left of the folder name. Then, you select the project you want to open and click the Open Project button.

When you're done working with a project, you can close it to remove it from the Projects window. To do that, you can use one of the techniques described in this figure.

You can also delete a project if you decide that you no longer want to work with it in NetBeans. Before the project is deleted, NetBeans will prompt you to confirm the deletion. Then, by default, NetBeans deletes all of the files for the project except for the source files. That way, you can work with those files outside of NetBeans if you want to. If you want to delete the source files as well, you can select the "Also Delete Sources" option in the dialog box that's displayed.

How to compile and run a project

Figure 1-7 also describes how to compile and run a project. An easy way to run a project is to press F6. Then, if the project has been modified since the last time it was compiled, NetBeans automatically compiles the project and runs the main method in the main class.

If you want to compile a project without running it, you can use the Build command as described in this figure. You can also use the Clean and Build command to compile the project and remove any files that are no longer needed. This sometimes helps to get a project to work correctly after you have copied, moved, or renamed some of its files.

The dialog box for opening a project

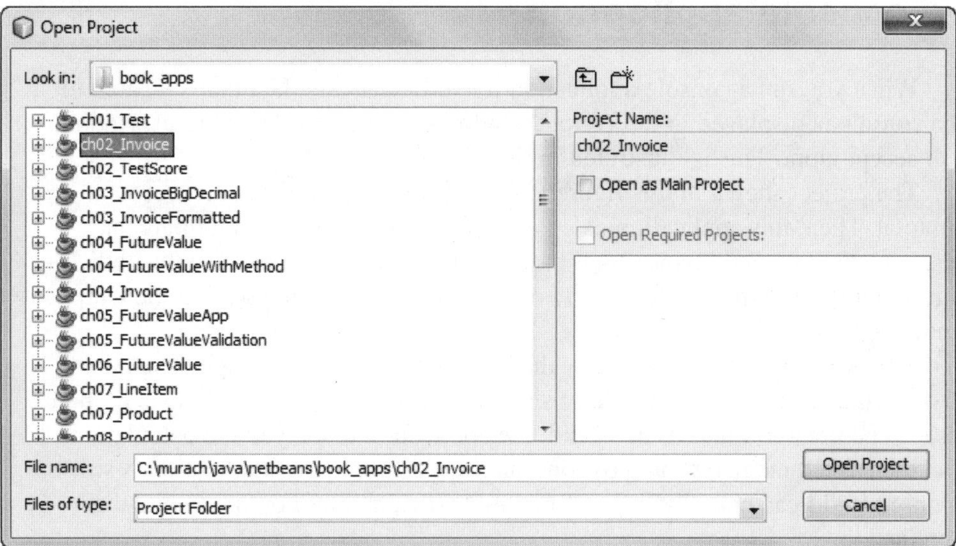

How to open, close, and delete a project

- To open a project, click the Open Project button in the toolbar or select the File→Open Project command. Then, use the Open Project dialog box that's displayed to locate and select the project and click the Open Project button.
- You can also open a project by using the File→Open Recent Project command and then selecting the project from the list that's displayed.
- To close a project, right-click on the project in the Projects window and select the Close command, or select the project and then use the File→Close Project command.
- To delete a project, right-click on the project in the Projects window and select the Delete command. When you do, you'll have the option of deleting just the files that NetBeans uses to manage the project or deleting all the folders and files for the project.

How to compile and run a project

- To run a project, press F6, use the Run→Run Project command, or click the Run Project button in the toolbar.
- When you run a project, NetBeans automatically compiles it. As a result, you usually don't need to compile a project separately.
- To compile a project without running it, you can right-click on the project in the Projects window and select the Build command.
- To delete all compiled files for a project and compile them again, you can right-click on the project and select the Clean and Build command. This removes files that are no longer needed and compiles the entire project.

Mac OS X note

- To enable right-clicking with Mac OS X, you can edit the system preferences for the mouse.

Figure 1-7 Basic skills for working with existing projects

How to use the Output window with a console application

When you run a console application in NetBeans, any data that's written to the console is displayed in the Output window. In addition, The Output window can accept input. This is illustrated in figure 1-8.

The project shown in this figure is for a simple application that accepts a subtotal. Then, this application calculates and displays the discount percent, discount amount, and invoice total based on that subtotal. You'll see the code for this application in the next chapter. For now, just focus on the data in the Output window.

Here, the application started by displaying a welcome message. Then, it displayed a prompt indicating that I should enter a subtotal. In response, I typed "100" and pressed Enter. When I did, the application displayed the calculations and then asked me if I wanted to continue. At this point, the application is still running, and I can enter "y" to perform another calculation or "n" to end the application.

When you're learning Java, it's common to create applications that use the console to display output and get input. Because of that, the first three sections of this book teach you Java using console applications. Then, section 4 of this book will teach you how to create modern applications with graphical user interfaces.

An application that uses the Output window for input and output

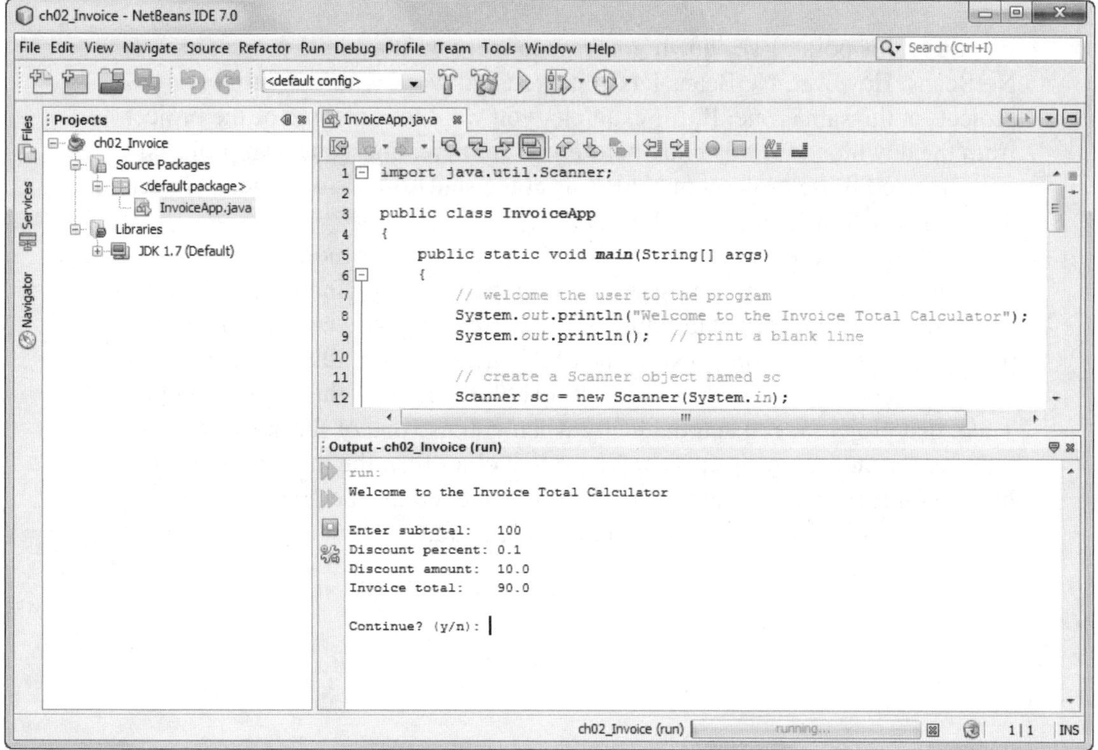

Description

- When you run an application that prints data to the console, that data is displayed in the Output window.
- When you run an application that requests input from the console, the Output window pauses to accept the input. Then, you can click in the Output window, type the input, and press the Enter key.
- In addition to displaying output and accepting input, the Output window can display other information. For example, it can display messages when the application is compiled, and it can display errors that are encountered when an application is run.

Figure 1-8 How to use the Output window with a console application

How to work with two or more projects

Up to this point, I've shown you how to work with a single project in NetBeans. However, NetBeans lets you open and work with two or more projects at the same time. If, for example, you want to run some of the projects from the download for this book before you start creating your own projects, you can open those projects in NetBeans at the same time. You'll get a chance to do that in the first exercise for this chapter.

Figure 1-9 presents the skills for working with two or more projects. To start, you can run a project by selecting it in the Projects window and then using the techniques you learned in figure 1-7. Alternatively, you can set one of the projects as the *main project* using one of the techniques in this figure. When you do that, NetBeans identifies the project by boldfacing it in the Projects window. Then, that project is run automatically when you use one of the standard techniques for running a project. To run a project other than the main project, you have to right-click on the project or the file that contains the main method for the project and select the Run or Run File command.

NetBeans with two open projects

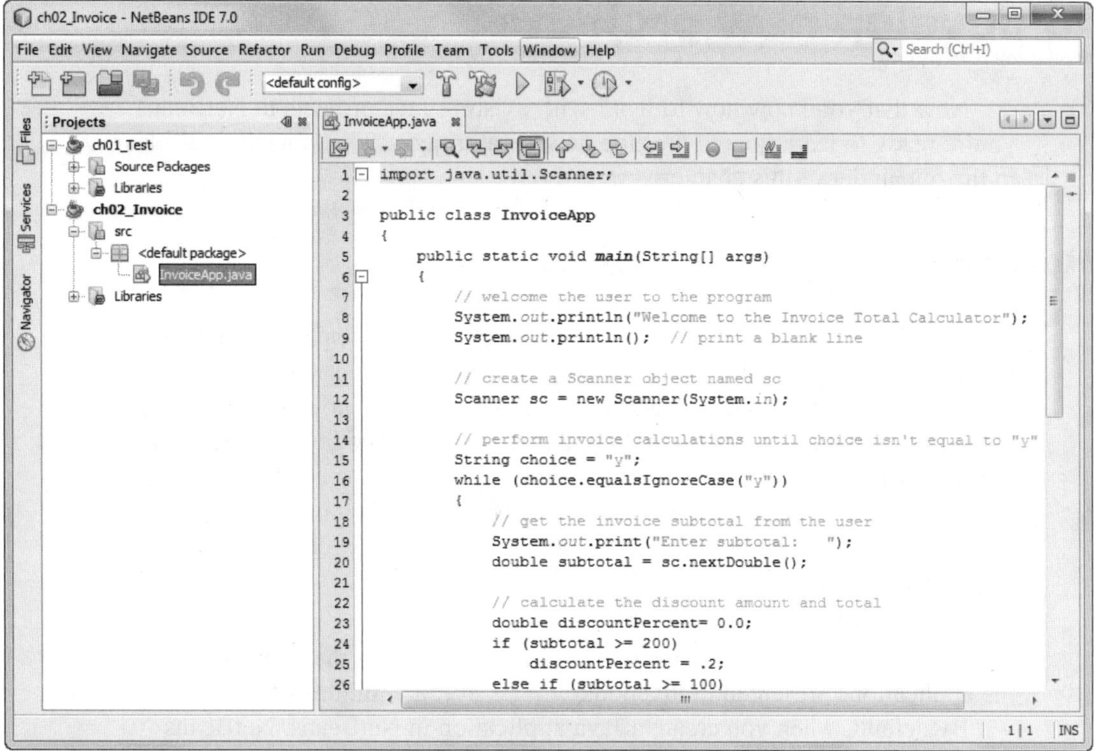

Description

- NetBeans lets you open and work with two or more projects at the same time.
- When you work with two or more projects, you can set one project as the *main project*. To do that, right-click on the project and select Set as Main Project. Or, when you open the project, select the Open as Main Project option.
- After you set a main project, you can run that project by pressing F6, by using the Run→Run Main Project command, or by clicking the Run Main Project button in the toolbar. The Run Main Project command and toolbar button replace the Run Project command and toolbar button when a main project is set.
- To run a project other than the main project, right-click on the project and select the Run command, or right-click on the file that contains the main method you want to run and select the Run File command.
- If you don't set a main project, you can run any project by selecting that project in the Projects window and then using standard techniques.

Figure 1-9 How to work with two or more projects

How to use NetBeans to develop new projects

Now that you know how to work with existing Java projects in NetBeans, you're ready to learn how to develop new Java projects. That's what you'll learn in the remainder of this chapter.

How to create a new project

Figure 1-10 presents the dialog boxes for creating a Java application. You use the New Project dialog box to choose the type of project you want to create. In most cases, you'll create a Java Application project as shown here. Then, when you click the Next button, NetBeans displays a New Java Application dialog box like the second one in this figure.

The New Java Application dialog box lets you enter a name and location for the project. In this figure, for example, the project name is "ch01_Test" and it will be stored in this folder:

```
C:\murach\java\netbeans\book_apps
```

If you install the source code for this book as described in the appendix, all of the applications presented in this book will be stored within this folder.

By default, when you create a Java application in NetBeans, NetBeans generates a main class with a main method. If that's not what you want, you can remove the check mark from the "Create Main Class" option. In most cases, though, you'll leave this option checked. Then, you can enter a name for the main class and, optionally, the package that contains it. For the project in this figure, for example, NetBeans suggested ch01_test.ch01_Test, where "ch01_test" is the name of the package and "ch01_Test" is the name of the class.

In this figure, I deleted the package name, and I changed the name of the class to TestApp. As a result, NetBeans created a project named ch01_Test that contains a main class named TestApp. Because I didn't specify a package name, this class is stored in the default package.

Like the Open Project dialog box you saw in figure 1-7, the New Java Application dialog box includes an option that determines if the new project is set as the main project. If you know that you want a project set as the main project when you create it, you should select this option. Otherwise, you can set the main project later using the technique you learned in figure 1-9.

When this dialog box is complete, you can click the Finish button to create the project and the class that contains the main method. Then, NetBeans creates a folder that corresponds with the project name, and it creates some additional files that it uses to configure the project.

The dialog boxes for creating a new project

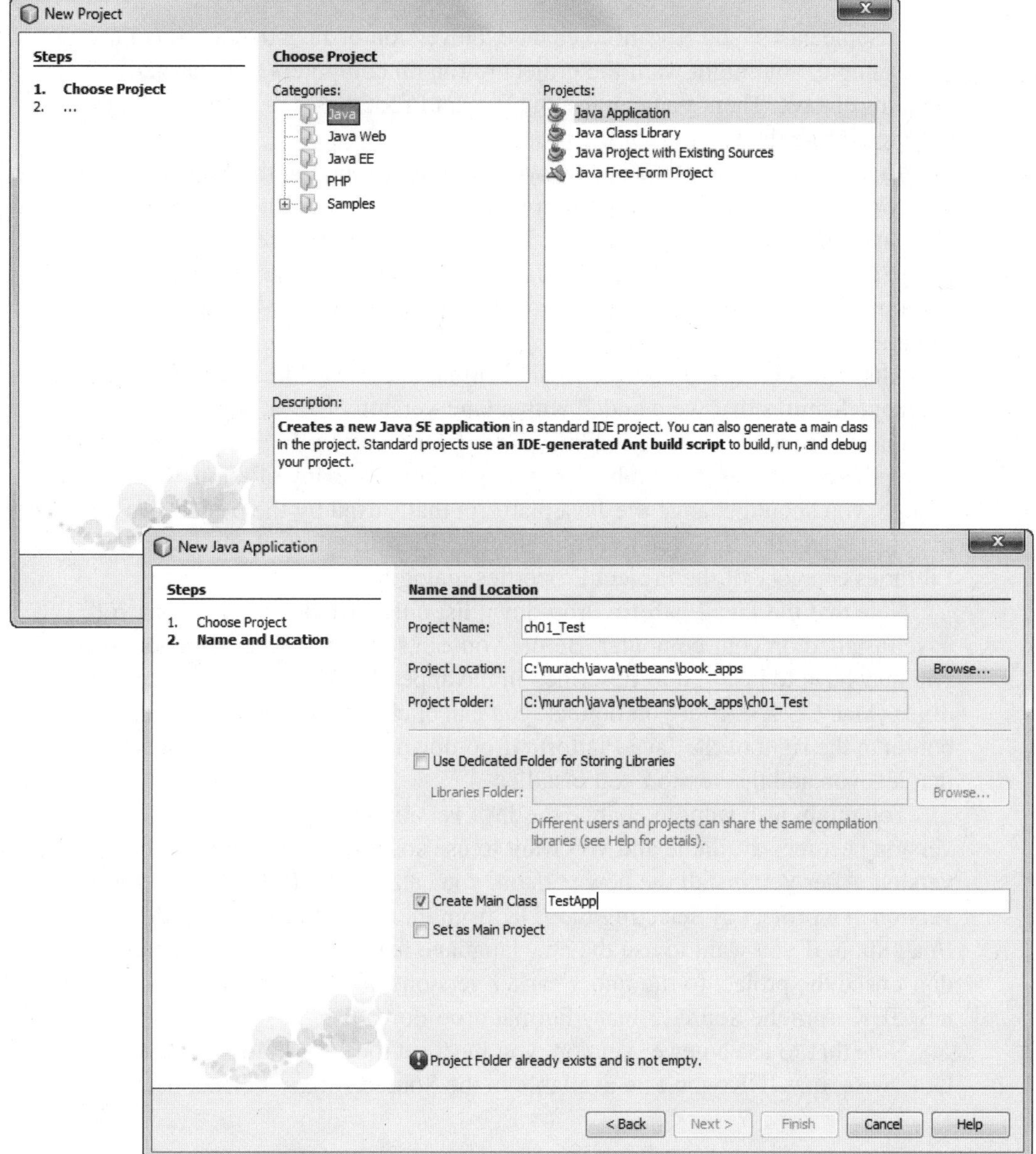

Description

- To create a new project, use the File→New Project command or click the New Project button in the toolbar to display the New Project dialog box. Then, select a project type, click the Next button and complete the dialog box that's displayed.
- To create a Java Application project, enter the project name and location and the name you want to use for the main class. You can also enter the name of the package that will contain the main class, but that's not necessary.

Figure 1-10 How to create a new project

How to set the Java version for a project

In some cases, you'll want to change the version of Java that a project uses. For example, you might want the project to run on computers with earlier versions of Java. Then, you can use the Project Properties dialog box in figure 1-11 to change the version for the project.

To use an earlier version of Java, you start by displaying the Sources category. Then, you select the version you want to use from the Source/Binary Format drop-down list. In this figure, I selected JDK 6. As a result, any language features that were added after Java 6 won't be available to the project. In addition, the bytecodes that are generated by the compiler for the project will run under Java 6 and later versions.

Although setting the Source/Binary Format option will keep you from using language features that were added with a later version of Java, it won't keep you from using features of the JDK libraries for later versions. In many cases, that's not a problem. If you want to be sure that you don't use any of the new features, though, you should change the Java platform that's used by the project. To do that, just select the JDK version from the Java Platform drop-down list in the Libraries category of the Project Properties dialog box.

Note that the Java Platform drop-down list only includes the versions you have installed on your computer. Before you can select a different version, then, you may have to install it as described in the appendix A (Windows) or appendix B (Mac OS X). After you do that, you can click the Manage Platforms button to the right of the Java Platform drop-down list to display a dialog box that lets you add the version you installed.

You might also want to change the Java version for a project if a newer version becomes available and you want to use some of the features of that version. After you install the new version, you can use the JDK libraries for that version in a project by selecting the JDK from the Java Platform drop-down list. In addition, if you want to use the new language features of that version and you don't need the project to run under earlier versions of Java, you can select the new JDK from the Source/Binary Format drop-down list.

Note that to use a newer version, you must set the Java Platform option first. Otherwise, that JDK won't be available in the Source/Binary Format list.

The Project Properties dialog box

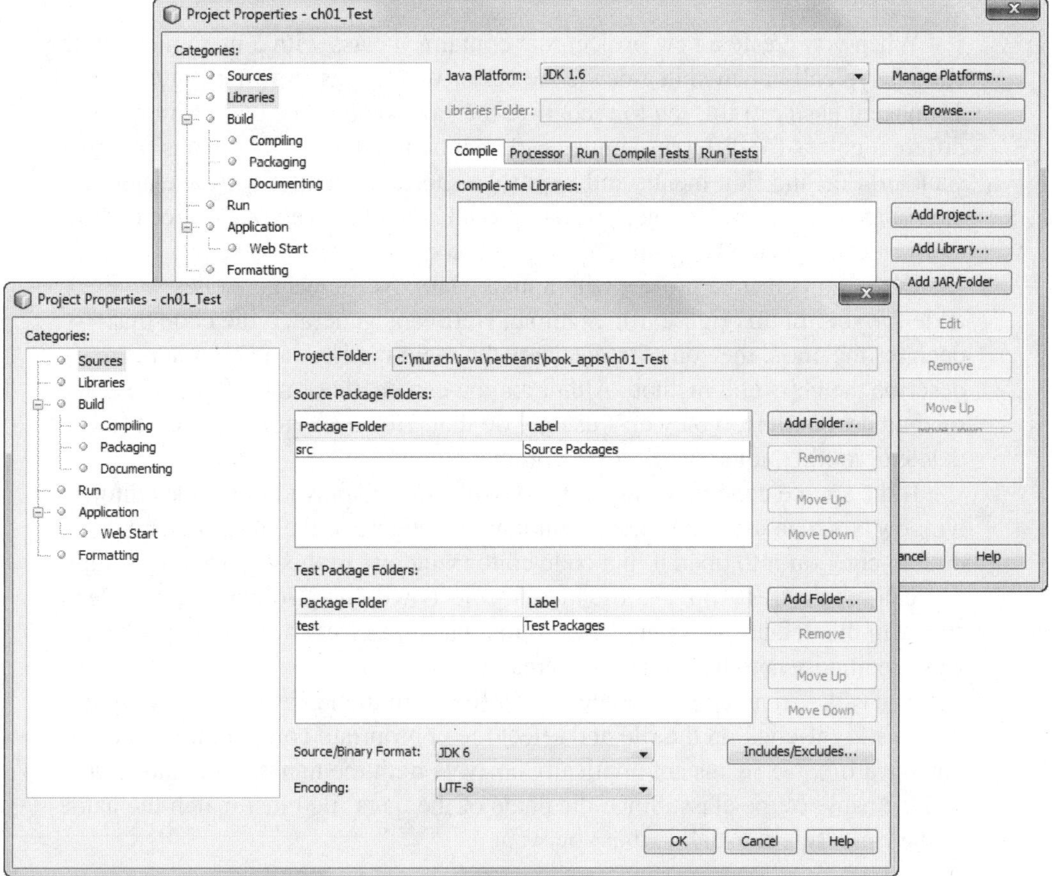

Description

- The Project Properties dialog box lets you set various properties that affect the project. To display this dialog box, right-click on the project in the Projects window and select the Properties command.
- To set the version of the Java language and compiled bytecodes the project uses, select the version from the Source/Binary Format drop-down list in the Sources category. Then, the compiled bytecodes for the project will run under this version of Java and later. In addition, the project can only use language features for the specified version of Java.
- To set the version of the JDK libraries that are available to the project, select the version from the Java Platform drop-down list in the Libraries category. Then, your project can only use the features that are available from that version of the JDK libraries. For this to work, the version of the JDK you want to use must be installed on your system.
- To be sure that the JDK libraries are compatible with the language features and bytecodes, select the same version of the JDK from the Java Platform and the Source/Binary Format drop-down lists.

Figure 1-11 How to set the Java version for a project

How to work with Java source code and files

When you create a new project that contains a class with a main method, the class is typically opened in a new code editor window as shown in figure 1-12. To make it easier to for you to recognize the Java syntax, the code editor uses different colors for different language elements. In addition, NetBeans provides standard File and Edit menus and keystroke shortcuts that let you save and edit the source code. For example, you can press Ctrl+S to save your source code, and you can use standard commands to cut, copy, and paste code.

When you create a project with a main class, NetBeans generates some code for you. In this figure, for example, NetBeans generated the code that declares the class, the code that declares the main method, and comments that describe the class and method. Although you can delete or modify the class and method declarations, you won't usually do that. However, you may want to delete or modify some or all of the comments.

If the source code you want to work with isn't displayed in a code editor window, you can use the Projects window to navigate to the .java file and then double-click on it to open it in a code editor window. In this figure, for example, you can see the TestApp.java file in the Projects window. Notice that this file is stored in the default package of the Source Packages folder, since no package was specified when the project was created.

You can also rename or delete a .java file from the Projects window. To do that, just right-click on the file and select the appropriate command. If you rename a file, NetBeans automatically changes both the name of the .java file and the name of the class. Since the name of the .java file must match the name of the class, this is usually what you want.

Net Bean's code editor with the starting source code for a project

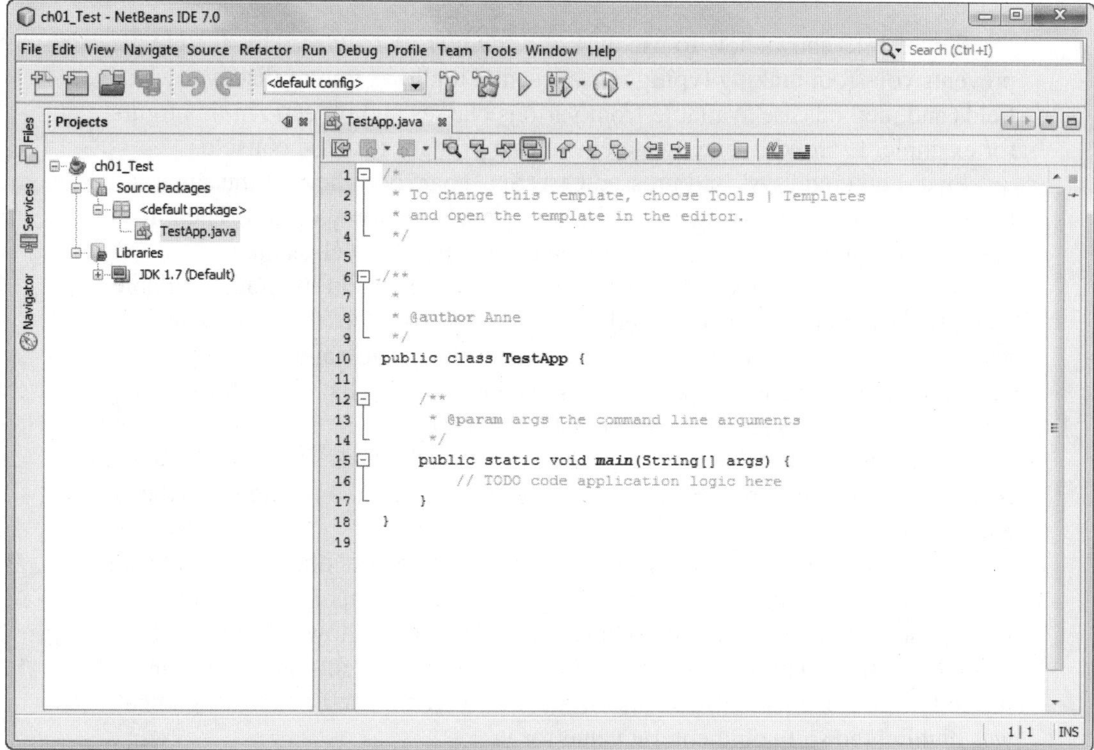

Description

- To open a .java file in the code editor, double-click on it in the Projects window. Then, you can use normal editing techniques to work with the source code.
- To collapse the code for a method or comment, click the minus sign (-) to its left. Then, a plus sign (+) appears to the left of the method or comment, and you can click the plus sign to display the code again.
- To save the source code for a file, use the File→Save command (Ctrl+S) or click the Save All Files button in the toolbar. This automatically compiles the file so it doesn't have to be compiled when the project is run.
- To rename a file, right-click on it, select the Refactor→Rename command, and enter the new name in the resulting dialog box.
- To delete a file, you can right-click on it, select the Delete command, and confirm the deletion in the resulting dialog box.

Figure 1-12 How to work with Java source code and files

How to use the code completion feature

Figure 1-13 shows how to use the *code completion feature*. This feature prevents you from making typing mistakes, and it allows you to discover what fields and methods are available from various classes and objects. In this figure, for example, I started to enter a statement that prints text to the console.

First, I entered "sys" and pressed Ctrl+Spacebar (both keys at the same time). This displayed a list with the System class as the only option. Then, I pressed the Enter key to automatically enter the rest of the class name.

Next, I typed a period. This displayed a list of fields and methods available from the System class. Then, I used the arrow keys to select the field named out and pressed the Enter key to automatically enter that field name.

Finally, I typed another period. This displayed a long list of method names. Then, I typed "pr" to scroll down the list to the methods that start with "pr", and I used the arrow keys to select one of the println methods as shown in the figure. At this point, I could press Enter to have NetBeans enter the method into the editor for me.

When you use code completion, it automatically enters opening and closing parentheses and arguments whenever they're needed. In this figure, for example, you can see that the println method that I've selected is followed by a set of parentheses that contains a string argument. When I inserted this method into the code editor, the parentheses and arguments were inserted and the argument was highlighted so I could enter a value for it.

The code completion feature can also make it easy for you to enter values for string variables. If you type a quotation mark to identify a string value, the code completion feature automatically enters both opening and closing quotation marks and places the cursor between the two. At this point, you can enter the text for the string.

If you experiment with the code completion feature, you'll quickly see when it helps you enter code more quickly and when it makes sense to enter the code yourself. In addition, you'll see that it helps you understand the kinds of fields and methods that are available to the various classes and objects that you're working with. This will make more sense as you learn about object-oriented programming in Java beginning in the next chapter.

The code editor with a code completion list

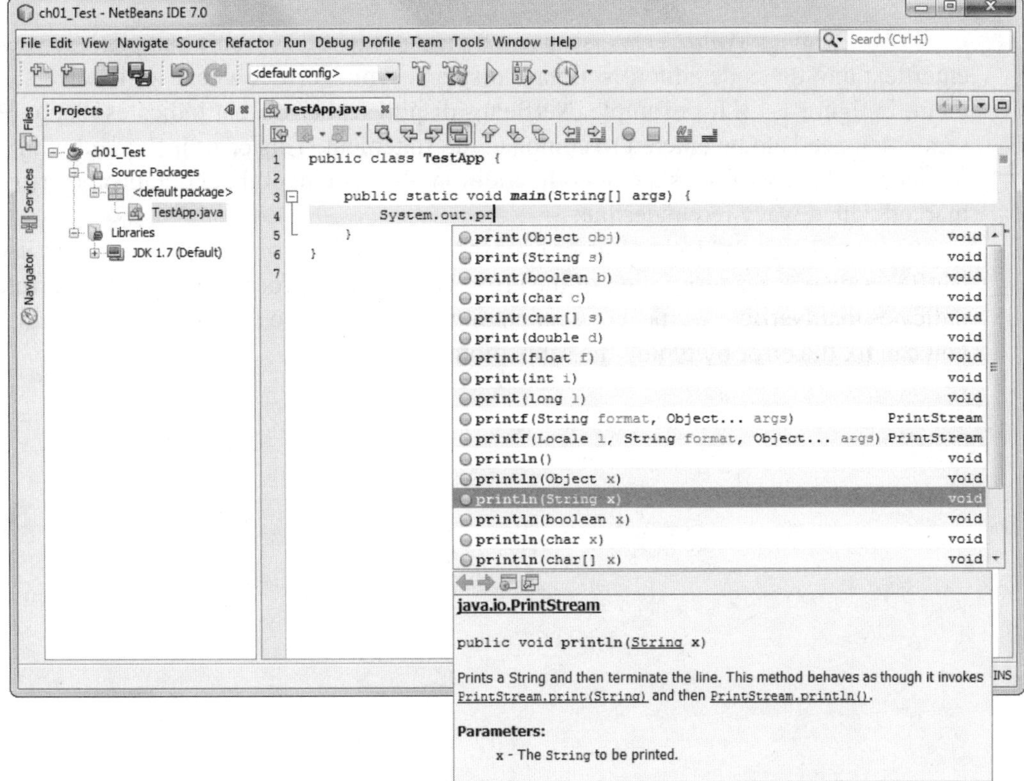

Description

- You can use the *code completion feature* to help you enter the names of classes and objects and select from the methods and fields that are available for a class or object.
- To activate the code completion feature for entering a class or object name, press Ctrl+Spacebar after entering one or more letters of the class or object name. Then, a list of all the classes and objects that start with those letters is displayed.
- To activate the code completion feature for a method or field of a class or object, enter a period after a class or object name. Then, a list of all the methods and fields for that class or object is displayed.
- To insert an item from a code completion list, select the item and then press the Enter key. If the item requires parentheses, they're added automatically. If the item requires one or more arguments, default values are added for those arguments and the first argument is highlighted so you can enter its value. Then, you can press the Tab key and enter the values for any remaining arguments.
- If you enter the opening quote for a string value, the code completion feature automatically adds the closing quote and places the cursor between the two quotes so you can enter a value.

How to detect and correct syntax errors

In NetBeans, a *syntax error* is caused by a statement that won't compile. As you enter text into the code editor, NetBeans displays syntax errors whenever it detects them. In figure 1-14, for example, NetBeans displays an error that indicates that a semicolon needs to be entered to complete the statement. This error is marked with a red icon to the left of the statement. In addition, the statement that contains the error is marked with a wavy red underline.

If you position the mouse cursor over the red error icon or over the statement itself, NetBeans displays a description of the error. In this figure, for example, the description indicates that NetBeans expects a semicolon at the end of the statement. As a result, you can fix the error by typing the semicolon.

The code editor with an error displayed

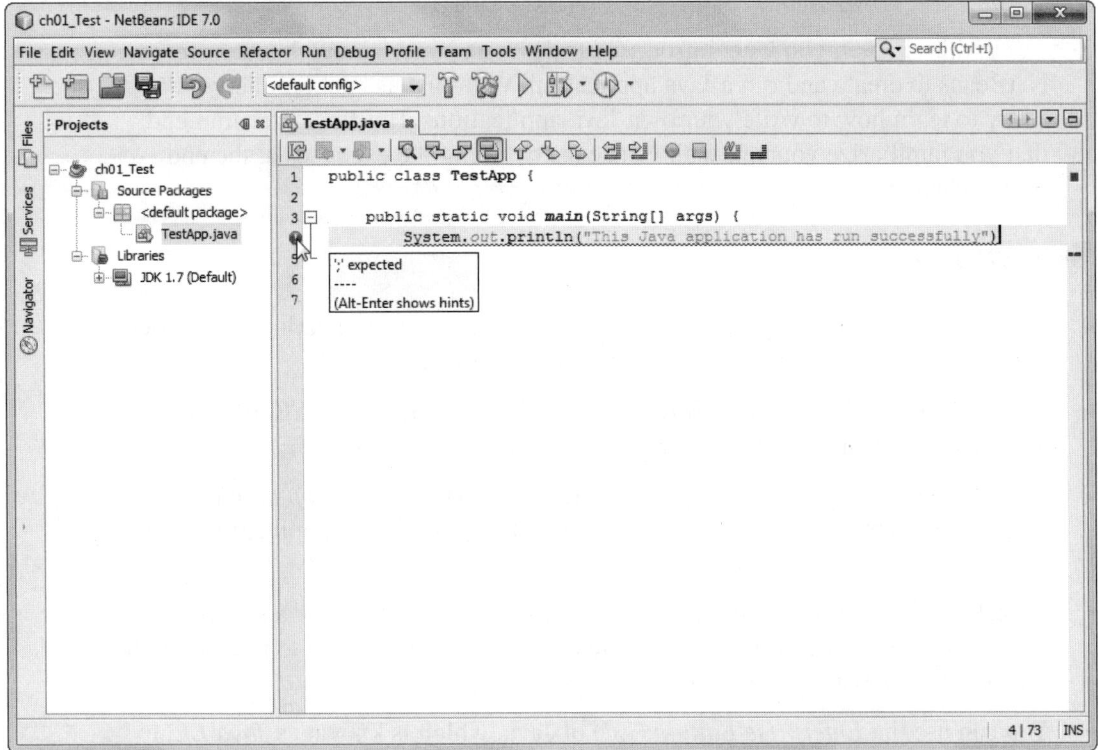

Description

- NetBeans often detects *syntax errors* as you enter code into the code editor.
- When NetBeans detects a syntax error, it displays a red error icon to the left of the statement in error and it places a red wavy line under the statement.
- To get more information about a syntax error, you can position the mouse pointer over the error icon. Or, you can move the cursor to the line that contains the error and press Alt+Enter.

Figure 1-14 How to detect and correct syntax errors

Perspective

In this chapter, you were introduced to Java, and you learned how to use NetBeans to create and run a Java application. With that as background, you're ready to learn how to write your own Java applications. But first, I recommend that you familiarize yourself with NetBeans by doing the exercises at the end of this chapter.

Summary

- You use the *Java Development Kit* (*JDK*) to develop Java applications. This used to be called the *Software Development Kit* (*SDK*) for Java.
- As of version 6, the *Standard Edition* (*SE*) of Java is called *Java SE*. In older versions, it was called the *Java 2 Platform, Standard Edition* (*J2SE*).
- You can use Java SE to create *applications* (also known as *desktop applications*) that run on your computer and a special type of Internet-based application known as an *applet*.
- A desktop application can use a *graphical user interface* (*GUI*) or a *console* to display output and get user input. Applications that use a console to interact with the user are known as *console applications*.
- You can use the *Enterprise Edition* (*EE*) of Java, which is known as *Java EE*, to create server-side applications using *servlets* and *JavaServer Pages* (*JSPs*).
- The *Java compiler* translates *source code* into a *platform-independent* format known as Java *bytecodes*.
- Any machine that has a Java interpreter installed on it can be considered an implementation of a *Java virtual machine* (*JVM*).
- An *Integrated Development Environment* (*IDE*) such as NetBeans can make working with Java easier.
- In NetBeans, a *project* is a folder that contains all of the files that make up an application.
- Java code is stored in *classes*. To organize multiple classes, you can store them in *packages*.
- The *main class* of an application is the class that contains the *main method*, which is the starting point of the application.
- If an application prints text to the *console*, NetBeans displays the text in the Output window. NetBeans also allows you to enter input into the Output window.
- When multiple projects are open, NetBeans identifies the *main project* by boldfacing its name in the Projects window.
- You can use the NetBeans *code editor* to enter and edit code. As you enter code, you can use the *code completion feature* to help you enter the names of classes and objects and select from fields and methods.

Before you do the exercises for this chapter

Before you do any of the exercises in this book, you need to install the JDK and NetBeans. In addition, you need to install the source code for this book from our web site (www.murach.com). See appendix A (Windows) or appendix B (Mac OS X) for details.

Exercise 1-1 Use NetBeans to open and run two projects

This exercise guides you through the process of using NetBeans to open and run two console applications.

Open and run the Invoice application

1. Start NetBeans. When the Start Page is displayed, review the information on its tabs. Then, close this page.
2. Open the project named ch01_ex1_Invoice. The project should be stored in this directory:
   `C:\murach\java\netbeans\ex_starts`
3. Open the InvoiceApp.java file in the code editor and review its code to get an idea of how this application works.
4. Press F6 to run the application. Enter a subtotal when you're prompted, and then enter "n" when you're asked if you want to continue.

Open and run the Test Score application

5. Open the project named ch01_ex2_TestScore. When you do, make sure to select the "Open as Main Project" option. Then, open the TestScoreApp.java file in the code editor and review its code.
6. Click the Run Project button in the toolbar to run the application. Enter one or more grades when you're prompted, and enter 999 to end the application.

Set the main project and run the applications again

7. Set the Invoice application as the main project. Then, press F6 to run this application. When you're done, end the application.
8. Right-click on the Test Score application and select the Run command to run this application. When you're done, end the application.
9. Close both projects.

Exercise 1-2 Use NetBeans to develop an application

This exercise guides you through the process of using NetBeans to enter, save, compile, and run a simple application.

Enter the source code and run the application

1. Start NetBeans if it isn't already open.
2. Select the File→New Project command from the NetBeans menu system. Then, use the resulting dialog boxes to create a Java Application project named ch01_Test that contains a main class named TestApp. Store the project in this directory:

   ```
   C:\murach\java\netbeans\ex_starts
   ```

3. Modify the generated code for the TestApp class so it looks like this (type carefully and use the same capitalization):

   ```
   public class TestApp
   {
       public static void main(String[] args)
       {
           System.out.println(
               "This Java application has run successfully.");
       }
   }
   ```

4. Press F6 to compile and run the application. This should display "This Java application has run successfully." in the Output window.

Use the code completion feature

5. Enter the statement that starts with System.out again, right after the first statement. This time, type "sys" and then press Ctrl+Spacebar. Then, use the code completion feature to select the System class, and complete the statement.
6. Enter this statement a third time, right after the second statement. This time, type System, enter a period, and select out from the list that's displayed. Then, enter another period, select println(String x), and complete the statement. You should now have the same statement three times in a row.
7. Run the application again to see that the message is displayed three times in a row in the Output window.

Introduce and correct a syntax error

8. In the code editor window, delete the semicolon at the end of the first println statement, and NetBeans will display an error icon to the left of the statement.
9. Correct the error, and NetBeans will remove the error icon.
10. Use the File→Save command (Ctrl+S) to save the changes.

2

Introduction to Java programming

Now that you know the basic skills for using NetBeans to work with Java projects, the quickest and best way to *learn* Java programming is to *do* Java programming. That's why this chapter shows you how to write complete Java programs that get input from a user, make calculations, and display output. When you finish this chapter, you should be able to write comparable programs of your own.

Basic coding skills

This chapter starts by introducing you to some basic coding skills. You'll use these skills for every Java program you develop.

How to code statements

The *statements* in a Java program direct the operation of the program. When you code a statement, you can start it anywhere in a coding line, you can continue it from one line to another, and you can code one or more spaces anywhere a single space is valid. In the first example in figure 2-1, the lines that aren't shaded are statements.

To end most statements, you use a semicolon. But when a statement requires a set of braces { }, it ends with the right brace. Then, the statements within the braces are referred to as a *block* of code. For example, the InvoiceApp class and the main method shown in this figure both contain a block of code.

To make a program easier to read, you should use indentation and spacing to align statements and blocks of code. This is illustrated by the program in this figure and by all of the programs and examples in this book.

How to code comments

Comments are used in Java programs to document what the program does and what specific blocks and lines of code do. Since the Java compiler ignores comments, you can include them anywhere in a program without affecting your code. In the first example in figure 2-1, the comments are shaded.

A *single-line comment* is typically used to describe one or more lines of code. This type of comment starts with two slashes (//) that tell the compiler to ignore all characters until the end of the current line. In the first example in this figure, you can see four single-line comments that are used to describe groups of statements. The other comment is coded after a statement. This type of comment is sometimes referred to as an *end-of-line comment*.

The second example in this figure shows how to code a *block comment*. This type of comment is typically used to document information that applies to a block of code. This information can include the author's name, program completion date, the purpose of the code, the files used by the code, and so on.

Although many programmers sprinkle their code with comments, that shouldn't be necessary if you write code that's easy to read and understand. Instead, you should use comments only to clarify code that's difficult to understand. In this figure, for example, an experienced Java programmer wouldn't need any of the single-line comments.

One problem with comments is that they may not accurately represent what the code does. This often happens when a programmer changes the code, but doesn't change the comments that go along with it. Then, it's even harder to understand the code because the comments are misleading. So if you change the code that you've written comments for, be sure to change the comments too.

An application consists of statements and comments

```
import java.util.Scanner;

public class InvoiceApp
{
    public static void main(String[] args)
    {
        // display a welcome message
        System.out.println("Welcome to the Invoice Total Calculator");
        System.out.println();  // print a blank line

        // get the input from the user
        Scanner sc = new Scanner(System.in);
        System.out.print("Enter subtotal:   ");
        double subtotal = sc.nextDouble();

        // calculate the discount amount and total
        double discountPercent = .2;
        double discountAmount = subtotal * discountPercent;
        double invoiceTotal = subtotal - discountAmount;

        // format and display the result
        String message = "Discount percent: " + discountPercent + "\n"
                       + "Discount amount:  " + discountAmount + "\n"
                       + "Invoice total:    " + invoiceTotal + "\n";
        System.out.println(message);
    }
}
```

A block comment that could be coded at the start of a program

```
/*
 * Author:  J. Murach
 * Purpose: This program uses the console to get a subtotal from the user,
 *          and it calculates the discount amount and total and displays them.
*/
```

Description

- Java *statements* direct the operations of a program, while *comments* are used to help document what the program does.
- You can start a statement at any point in a line and continue the statement from one line to the next. To make a program easier to read, you should use indentation and extra spaces to align statements and parts of statements.
- Most statements end with a semicolon. But when a statement requires a set of braces { }, the statement ends with the right brace. Then, the code within the braces can be referred to as a *block* of code.
- To code a *single-line comment*, type // followed by the comment. You can code a single-line comment on a line by itself or after a statement. A comment that's coded after a statement is sometimes called an *end-of-line comment*.
- To code a *block comment*, type /* at the start of the block and */ at the end. You can also code asterisks to identify the lines in the block, but that isn't necessary.

Figure 2-1 How to code statements and comments

How to create identifiers

As you code a Java program, you need to create and use *identifiers*. These are the names in the program that you define. In each program, for example, you need to create an identifier for the name of the program and for the variables that are used by the program.

Figure 2-2 shows you how to create identifiers. In brief, you must start each identifier with a letter, underscore, or dollar sign. After that first character, you can use any combination of letters, underscores, dollar signs, or digits.

Since Java is case-sensitive, you need to be careful when you create and use identifiers. If, for example, you define an identifier as CustomerAddress, you can't refer to it later as Customeraddress. That's a common coding error.

When you create an identifier, you should try to make the name both meaningful and easy to remember. To make a name meaningful, you should use as many characters as you need, so it's easy for other programmers to read and understand your code. For instance, netPrice is more meaningful than nPrice, and nPrice is more meaningful than np.

To make a name easy to remember, you should avoid abbreviations. If, for example, you use nwCst as an identifier, you may have difficulty remembering whether it was nCust, nwCust, or nwCst later on. If you code the name as newCustomer, though, you won't have any trouble remembering what it was. Yes, you type more characters when you create identifiers that are meaningful and easy to remember, but that will be more than justified by the time you'll save when you test, debug, and maintain the program.

For some common identifiers, though, programmers typically use just one or two lowercase letters. For instance, they often use the letters *i*, *j*, and *k* to identify counter variables. You'll see examples of this later in this chapter.

Notice that you can't create an identifier that is the same as one of the Java *keywords*. These 50 keywords are reserved by the Java language and are the basis for that language. To help you identify keywords in your code, Java IDEs display these keywords in a different color than the rest of the Java code. For example, NetBeans displays keywords in blue. As you progress through this book, you'll learn how to use almost all of these keywords.

Valid identifiers

```
InvoiceApp          $orderTotal     i
Invoice             _orderTotal     x
InvoiceApp2         input_string    TITLE
subtotal            _get_total      MONTHS_PER_YEAR
discountPercent     $_64_Valid
```

The rules for naming an identifier

- Start each identifier with a letter, underscore, or dollar sign. Use letters, dollar signs, underscores, or digits for subsequent characters.
- Use up to 255 characters.
- Don't use Java keywords.

Keywords

```
boolean     if          interface   class       true
char        else        package     volatile    false
byte        final       switch      while       throws
float       private     case        return      native
void        protected   break       throw       implements
short       public      default     try         import
double      static      for         catch       synchronized
int         new         continue    finally     const
long        this        do          transient   goto
abstract    super       extends     instanceof  null
```

Description

- An *identifier* is any name that you create in a Java program. These can be the names of classes, methods, variables, and so on.
- A *keyword* is a word that's reserved by the Java language. As a result, you can't use keywords as identifiers.
- When you refer to an identifier, be sure to use the correct uppercase and lowercase letters because Java is a case-sensitive language.

Figure 2-2 How to create identifiers

How to declare a class and a main method

In the last chapter, you learned that if you use NetBeans to create a project, it can generate a *main class* with a *main method* for the project. Although you saw the code for four different classes and three different main methods in chapter 1, figure 2-3 now presents the syntax for declaring any *class* or main method. Even if you use NetBeans, you should be familiar with this syntax.

To code a class, you begin with a *class declaration*. In the syntax for declaring a class, the boldfaced words are Java keywords, and the words that aren't boldfaced represent code that the programmer supplies. The bar (|) in this syntax means that you have a choice between the two items that the bar separates. In this case, the bar means that you can start the declaration with the public keyword or the private keyword.

The public and private keywords are *access modifiers* that control the *scope* of a class. Usually, a class is declared public, which means that other classes can access it. Later in this book, you'll learn when and how to use private classes.

After the public keyword and the class keyword, you code the name of the class using the basic rules for creating an identifier. When you do, it's a common coding convention to start every word within a class name with a capital letter and to use letters and digits only. We also recommend that you use a noun or a noun that's preceded by one or more adjectives for your class names.

After the class name, the syntax summary shows a left brace, the statements that make up the class, and a right brace. It's a good coding practice, though, to type your ending brace right after you type the starting brace to prevent missing braces. When you use NetBeans, the ending brace is automatically added after you type the starting brace and then press the Enter key.

The two InvoiceApp classes in this figure show how a class works. Notice that the only difference between the two classes is where the opening braces for the class and the block of code within the class are placed. Although either technique is acceptable, we've chosen to use the first technique for this book whenever possible.

Within a class, you code one or more *methods*, which are pieces of code that perform the actions of the application (they're similar to *functions* in some programming languages). As you know, the main method is a special kind of method that's automatically executed when the class that contains it is run. All Java programs contain a main method that starts the program.

To code a main method, you begin by coding a *main method declaration* within the class declaration as shown in the two InvoiceApp classes in this figure. Although I won't describe this declaration, you should know that all main method declarations are coded exactly as shown. You'll learn more about the keywords used by this declaration later in this book.

To make the structure of the main method clear, it's indented and its starting and ending braces are aligned so it's easy to see where the method begins and ends. Then, between the braces, you can see the one statement that this main method performs. This statement displays a message to the user, and you'll learn more about it later in this chapter.

The syntax for declaring a class

```
public|private class ClassName
{
    statements
}
```

The syntax for declaring a main method

```
public static void main(String[] args)
{
    statements
}
```

A public class named InvoiceApp that contains a main method

```
public class InvoiceApp                          // declare the class
{                                                // begin the class
    public static void main(String[] args)
    {
        System.out.println("Welcome to the Invoice Total Calculator");
    }
}                                                // end the class
```

The same class with different brace placement

```
public class InvoiceApp {                        // declare and begin the class
    public static void main(String[] args){
        System.out.println("Welcome to the Invoice Total Calculator");
    }
}                                                // end the class
```

The rules for naming a class

- Start the name with a capital letter.
- Use letters and digits only.
- Follow the other rules for naming an identifier.

Recommendations for naming a class

- Start every word within a class name with an initial cap.
- Each class name should be a noun or a noun that's preceded by one or more adjectives.

Description

- A Java application consists of one or more *classes* that start with a *class declaration*. You write the code for the class within the opening and closing braces of the declaration.
- The public and private keywords are *access modifiers* that control what parts of the program can use the class. Most classes are declared public, which means that the class can be used by all parts of the program.
- The file name for a class is the same as the class name with *java* as the extension.
- A *method* is a block of code that performs a task.
- Every Java application contains one *main method* that you can declare exactly as shown above. This is called the *main method declaration*.
- The statements between the braces in a main method declaration are run when the program is executed.

Figure 2-3 How to declare a class and a main method

How to work with numeric variables

In this topic, you'll learn how to work with numeric variables. This will introduce you to the use of variables, assignment statements, arithmetic expressions, and two of the eight primitive data types that are supported by Java. Then, you can learn all the details about working with the primitive data types in the next chapter.

How to declare and initialize variables

A *variable* is used to store a value that can change as a program executes. Before you can use a variable, you must *declare* its data type and name, and you must *assign* a value to it to *initialize* it. The easiest way to do that is shown in figure 2-4. Just code the data type, the variable name, the equals sign, and the value that you want to assign to the variable.

This figure also summarizes two of the eight Java *data types*. You can use the *int* data type to store *integers*, which are numbers that don't contain decimal places (whole numbers), and you can use the *double* data type to store numbers that contain decimal places. In the next chapter, you'll learn how to use the six other primitive data types, but these are the two that you'll probably use the most.

As you can see in the summary, the double data type can be used to store numbers with up to 16 *significant digits*. In case you aren't familiar with significant digits, they include any digit that identifies the precision of a number. That includes any non-zero digit as well as any zero digits between two non-zero digits and any zero digits at the end of a number with decimal places. For business applications, you'll rarely need to use numbers with more than 16 significant digits.

To illustrate the declaration of variables, the first example in this figure declares an int variable named scoreCounter with an initial value of 1. And the second example declares a double variable named unitPrice with an initial value of 14.95. When you assign values to double types, it's a good coding practice to include a decimal point, even if the initial value is a whole number. If, for example, you want to assign the number 29 to the variable, you should code the number as 29.0.

If you follow the naming recommendations in this figure as you name the variables, it will make your programs easier to read and understand. In particular, you should capitalize the first letter in each word of the variable name, except the first word, as in scoreCounter or unitPrice. This is commonly referred to as *camel notation*.

When you initialize a variable, you can assign a *literal* value like 1 or 14.95 to the variable as illustrated by the examples in this figure. However, you can also initialize a variable to the value of another variable as shown in the second example in this figure or to the value of an expression like the arithmetic expressions shown in the next figure.

Two of the eight primitive data types

Type	Description
`int`	Integers from -2,147,483,648 to 2,147,483,647.
`double`	Numbers with decimal places and up to 16 significant digits.

How to declare and initialize a variable in one statement

Syntax

```
type variableName = value;
```

Examples

```
int scoreCounter = 1;              // initialize an integer variable
double unitPrice = 14.95;          // initialize a double variable
```

How to code assignment statements

```
int quantity = 0;                  // initialize an integer variable
int maxQuantity = 100;             // initialize another integer variable

// two assignment statements
quantity = 10;                     // quantity is now 10
quantity = maxQuantity;            // quantity is now 100
```

Description

- A *variable* stores a value that can change as a program executes.
- Java provides for eight *primitive data types* that you can use for storing values in memory. The two that you'll use the most are the int and double data types. In the next chapter, you'll learn how to use the other primitive data types.
- The *int* data type is used for storing *integers* (whole numbers). The *double* data type is used for storing numbers that can have one or more decimal places.
- Before you can use a variable, you must *declare* its data type and *assign* an initial value to the variable. It's common to *initialize* integer variables to 0 and double variables to 0.0.
- An *assignment statement* assigns a value to a variable. This value can be a literal value, another variable, or an expression like the arithmetic expressions that you'll learn how to code in the next figure. If a variable has already been declared, the assignment statement doesn't include the data type of the variable.

Naming recommendations for variables

- Start variable names with a lowercase letter and capitalize the first letter in all words after the first word.
- Each variable name should be a noun or a noun preceded by one or more adjectives.
- Try to use meaningful names that are easy to remember.

Figure 2-4 How to declare and initialize variables

How to code assignment statements

After you declare a variable, you can assign a new value to it. To do that, you code an *assignment statement*. In a simple assignment statement, you code the variable name, an equals sign, and a new value. The new value can be a literal value or the name of another variable as shown in figure 2-4. Or, the new value can be the result of an expression like the arithmetic expressions shown in figure 2-5.

How to code arithmetic expressions

To code simple *arithmetic expressions*, you can use the four *arithmetic operators* that are summarized in figure 2-5. As the first group of statements shows, these operators work the way you would expect them to with one exception. If you divide one integer into another integer, any decimal places are truncated. In contrast, if you divide a double into a double, the decimal places are included in the result.

When you code assignment statements, it's common to code the same variable on both sides of the equals sign. For example, you can add 1 to the value of a variable named counter with a statement like this:

```
counter = counter + 1;
```

In this case, if counter has a value of 5 when the statement starts, it will have a value of 6 when the statement finishes. This concept is illustrated by the second and third groups of statements.

What happens when you mix integer and double variables in the same arithmetic expression? The integers are *cast* (converted) to doubles so the decimal places can be included in the result. To retain the decimal places, though, the result variable must be a double. This is illustrated by the fourth group of statements.

Although it's not shown in this figure, you can also code expressions that contain two or more operators. When you do that, you need to be sure that the operations are done in the correct sequence. You'll learn more about that in the next chapter.

The basic operators that you can use in arithmetic expressions

Operator	Name	Description
+	Addition	Adds two operands.
-	Subtraction	Subtracts the right operand from the left operand.
*	Multiplication	Multiplies the right operand and the left operand.
/	Division	Divides the right operand into the left operand. If both operands are integers, then the result is an integer.

Statements that use simple arithmetic expressions

```
// integer arithmetic
int x = 14;
int y = 8;
int result1 = x + y;          // result1 = 22
int result2 = x - y;          // result2 = 6
int result3 = x * y;          // result3 = 112
int result4 = x / y;          // result4 = 1

// double arithmetic
double a = 8.5;
double b = 3.4;
double result5 = a + b;       // result5 = 11.9
double result6 = a - b;       // result6 = 5.1
double result7 = a * b;       // result7 = 28.9
double result8 = a / b;       // result8 = 2.5
```

Statements that increment a counter variable

```
int invoiceCount = 0;
invoiceCount = invoiceCount + 1;                   // invoiceCount = 1
invoiceCount = invoiceCount + 1;                   // invoiceCount = 2
```

Statements that add amounts to a total

```
double invoiceAmount1 = 150.25;
double invoiceAmount2 = 100.75;
double invoiceTotal = 0.0;
invoiceTotal = invoiceTotal + invoiceAmount1;      // invoiceTotal = 150.25
invoiceTotal = invoiceTotal + invoiceAmount2;      // invoiceTotal = 251.00
```

Statements that mix int and double variables

```
int result9 = invoiceTotal / invoiceCount          // result9 = 125
double result10 = invoiceTotal / invoiceCount      // result10 = 125.50
```

Description

- An *arithmetic expression* consists of one or more *operands* and *arithmetic operators*.
- When an expression mixes the use of int and double variables, Java automatically *casts* the int types to double types. To retain the decimal places, the variable that receives the result must be a double.
- In the next chapter, you'll learn how to code expressions that contain two or more operators.

Figure 2-5 How to code arithmetic expressions

How to work with string variables

In the topics that follow, you'll learn some basic skills for working with strings. For now, these skills should be all you need for many of the programs you develop. Keep in mind, though, that many programs require extensive string operations. That's why chapter 13 covers strings in more detail.

How to create a String object

A *string* can consist of any letters, numbers, and special characters. To declare a string variable, you use the syntax shown in figure 2-6. Although this is much like the syntax for declaring a numeric variable, a string is an object that's created from the String class when a string variable is declared. Then, the String object refers to string data. When you declare a string variable, you must capitalize the String keyword because it is the name of a class, not a primitive data type.

In the next topic and in chapter 7, you'll learn more about classes and objects. For now, though, all you need to know is that string variables work much like numeric variables, except that they store string data instead of numeric data.

When you declare a String object, you can assign a *string literal* to it by enclosing the characters within double quotes. You can also assign an *empty string* to it by coding a set of quotation marks with nothing between them. Finally, you can use the null keyword to assign a *null value* to a String object. That indicates that the value of the string is unknown.

How to join and append strings

If you want to *join*, or *concatenate*, two or more strings into one, you can use the + operator. For example, you can join a first name, a space, and a last name as shown in the second example in figure 2-6. Then, you can assign that string to a variable. Notice that when concatenating strings, you can use string variables or string literals.

You can also join a string with a primitive data type. This is illustrated in the third example in this figure. Here, a variable that's defined with the double data type is appended to a string. When you use this technique, Java automatically converts the double value to a string.

You can use the + and += operators to *append* a string to the end of a string that's stored in a string variable. If you use the + operator, you need to include the variable on both sides of the = operator. Otherwise, the assignment statement will replace the old value with the new value instead of appending the old value to the new value. Since the += operator provides a shorter and safer way to append strings, this operator is commonly used.

The syntax for declaring and initializing a string variable

```
String variableName = value;
```

Example 1: How to declare and initialize a string

```
String message1 = "Invalid data entry.";
String message2 = "";
String message3 = null;
```

Example 2: How to join strings

```
String firstName = "Bob";                    // firstName is Bob
String lastName = "Smith";                   // lastName is Smith
String name = firstName + " " + lastName;    // name is Bob Smith
```

Example 3: How to join a string and a number

```
double price = 14.95;
String priceString = "Price: " + price;
```

Example 4: How to append one string to another with the + operator

```
firstName = "Bob";                    // firstName is Bob
lastName = "Smith";                   // lastName is Smith
name = firstName + " ";               // name is Bob followed by a space
name = name + lastName;               // name is Bob Smith
```

Example 5: How to append one string to another with the += operator

```
firstName = "Bob";                    // firstName is Bob
lastName = "Smith";                   // lastName is Smith
name = firstName + " ";               // name is Bob followed by a space
name += lastName;                     // name is Bob Smith
```

Description

- A *string* can consist of any characters in the character set including letters, numbers, and special characters like *, &, and #.
- In Java, a string is actually a String object that's created from the String class that's part of the Java *API* (*Application Programming Interface*). The API provides all the classes that are included as part of the JDK.
- To specify the value of a string, you can enclose text in double quotation marks. This is known as a *string literal*.
- To assign a *null value* to a string, you can use the null keyword. This means that the value of the string is unknown.
- To assign an *empty string* to a String object, you can code a set of quotation marks with nothing between them. This means that the string doesn't contain any characters.
- To *join* (or *concatenate*) a string with another string or a data type, use a plus sign. Whenever possible, Java will automatically convert the data type so it can be used as part of the string.
- When you *append* one string to another, you add one string to the end of another. To do that, you can use assignment statements.
- The += operator is a shortcut for appending a string expression to a string variable.

Figure 2-6 How to create and use strings

How to include special characters in strings

Figure 2-7 shows how to include certain types of special characters within a string. In particular, this figure shows how to include backslashes, quotation marks, and control characters such as new lines, tabs, and returns in a string. To do that, you can use the *escape sequences* shown in this figure.

As you can see, each escape sequence starts with a backslash. The backslash tells the compiler that the character that follows should be treated as a special character and not interpreted as a literal value. If you code a backslash followed by the letter *n*, for example, the compiler will include a new line character in the string. You can see how this works in the first example in this figure. If you omitted the backslash, of course, the compiler would just include the letter *n* in the string value. The escape sequences for the tab and return characters work similarly, as you can see in the second example.

To code a string literal, you enclose it in double quotes. If you want to include a double quote within a string literal, then, you must use an escape sequence. This is illustrated in the third example. Here, the \" escape sequence is used to include two double quotes within the string literal.

Finally, you need to use an escape sequence if you want to include a backslash in a string literal. To do that, you code two backslashes as shown in the fourth example. If you code a single backslash, the compiler will treat the next character as a special character. That will cause a compiler error if the character isn't a valid special character. And if the character is a valid special character, the results won't be what you want.

Common escape sequences

Sequence	Character
`\n`	New line
`\t`	Tab
`\r`	Return
`\"`	Quotation mark
`\\`	Backslash

Example 1: New line

String

```
"Code: JSPS\nPrice: $49.50"
```

Result

```
Code: JSPS
Price: $49.50
```

Example 2: Tabs and returns

String

```
"Joe\tSmith\rKate\tLewis"
```

Result

```
Joe     Smith
Kate    Lewis
```

Example 3: Quotation marks

String

```
"Type \"x\" to exit"
```

Result

```
Type "x" to exit
```

Example 4: Backslash

String

```
"C:\\java\\files"
```

Result

```
C:\java\files
```

Description

- Within a string, you can use *escape sequences* to include certain types of special characters.

Figure 2-7 How to include special characters in strings

How to use Java classes, objects, and methods

So far, you've learned how to create String objects from the String class in the Java API. As you develop Java applications, though, you need to use dozens of different Java classes and objects. To do that, you need to know how to create objects from Java classes, how to call Java methods, and how to import Java classes.

How to create objects and call methods

To use a Java *class*, you usually start by creating an *object* from the class. As the syntax in figure 2-8 shows, you do that by coding the Java class name, the name that you want to use for the object, an equals sign, the new keyword, and the Java class name again followed by a set of parentheses. Within the parentheses, you code any *arguments* that are required by the *constructor* of the object that's defined in the class.

In the examples, the first statement shows how to create a Scanner object named sc. The constructor for this object requires just one argument (System.in), which represents console input. In contrast, the second statement creates a Date object named now that represents the current date, but its constructor doesn't require any arguments. As you go through this book, you'll learn how to create objects with constructors that require two or more arguments, and you'll see that a single class can provide more than one constructor for creating objects.

When you create an object, you can think of the class as the template for the object. That's why the object can be called an *instance* of the class, and the process of creating the object can be called *instantiation*. Whenever necessary, you can create more than one object or instance from the class. For instance, you often use several String objects in a single program.

Once you've created an object from a class, you can use the *methods* of the class. To *call* one of these methods, you code the object name, a dot (period), and the method name followed by a set of parentheses. Within the parentheses, you code the arguments that are required by the method.

In the examples, the first statement calls the nextDouble method of the Scanner object named sc to get data from the console. The second statement calls the toString method of the Date object named now to convert the date and time that's stored in the object to a string. Neither one of these methods requires an argument, but you'll soon see some that do.

Besides methods that you can call from an object, some classes provide *static methods* that can be called directly from the class. To do that, you substitute the class name for the object name as illustrated by the third set of examples. Here, the first statement calls the toString method of the Double class, and the second statement calls the parseDouble method of the Double class. Both of these methods require one argument.

How to create an object from a class

Syntax

```
ClassName objectName = new ClassName(arguments);
```

Examples

```
Scanner sc = new Scanner(System.in);  // creates a Scanner object named sc
Date now = new Date();                // creates a Date object named now
```

How to call a method from an object

Syntax

```
objectName.methodName(arguments)
```

Examples

```
double subtotal = sc.nextDouble();    // get a double entry from the console
String currentDate = now.toString();  // convert the date to a string
```

How to call a static method from a class

Syntax

```
ClassName.methodName(arguments)
```

Examples

```
String sPrice = Double.toString(price);         // convert a double to a string
double total = Double.parseDouble(userEntry);   // convert a string to a double
```

Description

- When you create an *object* from a Java class, you are creating an *instance* of the *class*. Then, you can use the *methods* of the class by *calling* them from the object.
- Some Java classes contain *static methods*. These methods can be called directly from the class without creating an object.
- When you create an object from a class, the *constructor* may require one or more *arguments*. These arguments must have the required data types, and they must be coded in the correct sequence separated by commas.
- When you call a method from an object or a class, the method may require one or more arguments. Here again, these arguments must have the required data types and they must be coded in the correct sequence separated by commas.
- Although you can use the syntax shown in this figure to create a String object, the syntax in figure 2-6 is the preferred way to do that. Once a String object is created, though, you call its methods from the object as shown above.
- In this book, you'll learn how to use dozens of the Java classes and methods. You will also learn how to create your own classes and methods.

Figure 2-8 How to create objects and call methods

Incidentally, you can also use the syntax shown in this figure to create a String object. However, the preferred way to create a String object is to use the syntax shown in figure 2-6. Once a String object is created, though, you use the syntax in this figure to call one of its methods. You'll see examples of this later in this chapter.

In the pages and chapters that follow, you'll learn how to use dozens of classes and methods. For now, though, you just need to focus on the syntax for creating an object from a class, for calling a method from an object, and for calling a static method from a class. Once you understand that, you're ready to learn how to import the Java classes you need for your programs.

How to import Java classes

In the API for the Java SE, groups of related classes are organized into *packages*. In figure 2-9, you can see a list of some of the commonly used packages. Since the java.lang package contains the classes that are used in almost every Java program (such as the String class), this package is automatically made available to all programs.

To use a class from a package other than java.lang, though, you'll typically include an import statement for that class at the beginning of the program. If you don't, you'll still be able to use the class, but you'll have to qualify it with the name of the package that contains it each time you refer to it. Since that can lead to a lot of unnecessary typing, we recommend that you always code an import statement for the classes you use.

When you code an import statement, you can import a single class by specifying the class name, or you can import all of the classes in the package by typing an asterisk (*) in place of the class name. The first two statements in this figure, for example, import a single class, while the next two import all of the classes in a package. Although it requires less code to import all of the classes in a package at once, importing one class at a time clearly identifies the classes you're using.

As this figure shows, Java provides two different technologies for building a graphical user interface (GUI) that contains text boxes, command buttons, combo boxes, and so on. The older technology, known as the *Abstract Window Toolkit* (*AWT*), was used with versions 1.0 and 1.1 of Java. Its classes are stored in the java.awt package. Since version 1.2 of Java, though, a new technology known as *Swing* has been available. The Swing classes are stored in the javax.swing package. In general, many of the newer package names begin with javax instead of java. Here, the x indicates that these packages can be considered extensions to the original Java API.

In addition to the packages provided by the Java API, you can get packages from third party sources, either as open-source code or by purchasing them. For more information, check the Java web site. You can also create packages that contain classes that you've written. You'll learn how to do that in chapter 10.

Common packages

Package name	Description
`java.lang`	Provides classes fundamental to Java, including classes that work with primitive data types, strings, and math functions.
`java.text`	Provides classes to handle text, dates, and numbers.
`java.util`	Provides various utility classes including those for working with collections.
`java.io`	Provides classes to read data from files and to write data to files.
`java.sql`	Provides classes to read data from databases and to write data to databases.
`java.applet`	An older package that provides classes to create an applet.
`java.awt`	An older package called the *Abstract Window Toolkit* (AWT) that provides classes to create graphical user interfaces.
`java.awt.event`	A package that provides classes necessary to handle events.
`javax.swing`	A newer package called *Swing* that provides classes to create graphical user interfaces and applets.

The syntax of the import statement

```
import packagename.ClassName;
   or
import packagename.*;
```

Examples

```
import java.text.NumberFormat;
import java.util.Scanner;
import java.util.*;
import javax.swing.*;
```

How to use the Scanner class to create an object

With an import statement

```
Scanner sc = new Scanner(System.in);
```

Without an import statement

```
java.util.Scanner sc = new java.util.Scanner(System.in);
```

Description

- The API for the Java SE provides a large library of classes that are organized into *packages*.
- All classes stored in the java.lang package are automatically available to all Java programs.
- To use classes that aren't in the java.lang package, you can code an import statement as shown above. To import one class from a package, specify the package name followed by the class name. To import all classes in a package, specify the package name followed by an asterisk (*).
- If you don't code an import statement for a class, you must qualify the class name with the name of the package that contains it each time you refer to the class.

Figure 2-9 How to import Java classes

How to use the API documentation to research Java classes

If you refer back to figure 2-2, you can see that the Java language consists of just 50 keywords that you can master with relative ease. What's difficult about using Java, though, is mastering the hundreds of classes and methods that your applications will require. To do that, you frequently need to study the API documentation that comes with Java, and that is one of the most time-consuming aspects of Java programming.

Figure 2-10 summarizes some of the basic techniques for navigating through the API documentation. Here, you can see the start of the documentation for the Scanner class, which goes on for many pages. To get there, you click on the package name in the upper left frame and then on the class name in the lower left frame.

If you scroll through the documentation for this class, you'll get an idea of the scale of the documentation that you're dealing with. After a few pages of descriptive information, you come to a summary of the eight constructors for the class. After that, you come to a summary of the dozens of methods that the class offers. That in turn is followed by more detail about the constructors, and then by more detail about the methods.

At this point in your development, this is far more information than you can handle. That's why one of the goals of this book is to introduce you to the dozens of classes and methods that you'll use in most of the applications that you develop. Once you've learned those, the API documentation will make more sense to you, and you'll be able to use that documentation to research classes and methods that aren't presented in this book. To get you started with the use of objects and methods, figure 2-12 will show you how to use the Scanner class.

It's never too early to start using the documentation, though. So by all means use the documentation to get more information about the methods that are presented in this book and to research the other methods that are offered by the classes that are presented in this book. After you learn how to use the Scanner class, for example, take some time to do some research on that class. You'll get a chance to do that in exercise 2-4.

The documentation for the Scanner class

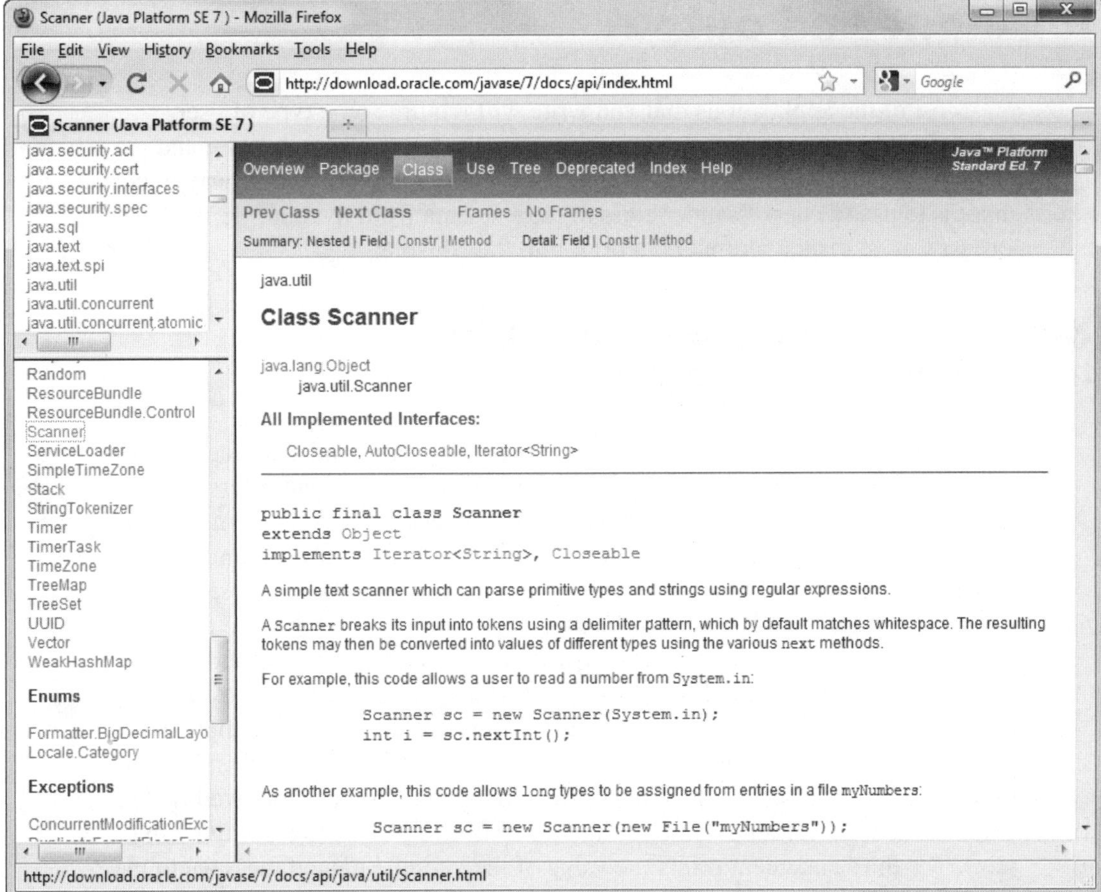

Description

- The Java SE API contains thousands of classes and methods that can help you do most of the tasks that your applications require.
- You can use a browser to view the Java SE API on the Internet by going to this address:
  `http://download.oracle.com/javase/7/docs/api/index.html`
- You can select the name of the package in the top left frame to display information about the package and the classes it contains. Then, you can select a class in the lower left frame to display the documentation for that class in the right frame.
- Once you display the documentation for a class, you can scroll through it or click on a hyperlink to get more information.
- To make it easier to access the API documentation, you should bookmark the index page. Then, you can easily redisplay this page whenever you need it.

Figure 2-10 How to use the API documentation to research Java classes

How to use the console for input and output

Most of the applications that you write will require some type of user interaction. In particular, most applications will get input from the user and display output to the user. Ever since version 1.5 of Java, the easiest way to get input is to use the new Scanner class to retrieve data from the console. And the easiest way to display output is to print it to the console.

How to use the System.out object to print output to the console

To print output to the *console*, you can use the println and print methods of the System.out object as shown in figure 2-11. Here, System.out refers to an instance of the PrintStream class. Because this object is created automatically by Java, you don't have to include code that creates it in your program.

Both the println and print methods accept a string argument that specifies the data to be printed. The only difference between the two is that the println method starts a new line after it displays the data, and the print method doesn't.

If you study the examples in this figure, you shouldn't have any trouble using these methods. For instance, the first statement in the first example uses the println method to print the words "Welcome to the Invoice Total Calculator" to the console. The second statement prints the string "Total: " followed by the value of the total variable (which is automatically converted to a string by this join). The third statement prints the value of the variable named message to the console. And the fourth statement prints a blank line since no argument is coded.

Because the print method doesn't automatically start a new line, you can use it to print several data arguments on the same line. For instance, the three statements in the second example use the print method to print "Total: ", followed by the total variable, followed by a new line character. Of course, you can achieve the same result with a single line of code like this:

```
System.out.println("Total: " + total);
```

This figure also shows an application that uses the println method to print seven lines to the console. In the main method of this application, the first four statements set the values for four variables. Then, the next seven statements print a welcome message, a blank line, the values for the four variables, and another blank line.

When you work with console applications, you should know that the appearance of the console may differ slightly depending on the operating system. Even if the console looks a little different, however, it should work the same.

Two methods of the System.out object

Method	Description
`println(data)`	Prints the data argument followed by a new line character to the console.
`print(data)`	Prints the data to the console without starting a new line.

Example 1: The println method

```
System.out.println("Welcome to the Invoice Total Calculator");
System.out.println("Total: " + total);
System.out.println(message);
System.out.println();           // print a blank line
```

Example 2: The print method

```
System.out.print("Total: ");
System.out.print(total);
System.out.print("\n");
```

Example 3: An application that prints data to the console

```
public class InvoiceApp
{
    public static void main(String[] args)
    {
        // set and calculate the numeric values
        double subtotal = 100;          // set subtotal to 100
        double discountPercent = .2;    // set discountPercent to 20%
        double discountAmount = subtotal * discountPercent;
        double invoiceTotal = subtotal - discountAmount;

        // print the data to the console
        System.out.println("Welcome to the Invoice Total Calculator");
        System.out.println();
        System.out.println("Subtotal:         " + subtotal);
        System.out.println("Discount percent: " + discountPercent);
        System.out.println("Discount amount:  " + discountAmount);
        System.out.println("Total:            " + invoiceTotal);
        System.out.println();
    }
}
```

The console output

```
Welcome to the Invoice Total Calculator

Subtotal:         100.0
Discount percent: 0.2
Discount amount:  20.0
Total:            80.0
```

Description

- Although the appearance of a console may differ from one system to another, you can always use the print and println methods to print data to the console.

Figure 2-11 How to use the System.out object to print output to the console

How to use the Scanner class to read input from the console

Figure 2-12 shows how you can use the Scanner class to read input from the console. To start, you create a Scanner object by using a statement like the one in this figure. Here, sc is the name of the Scanner object that is created and System.in represents console input, which is the keyboard. Like the System.out object, the System.in object is created by Java automatically. Because of that, you can use this object with a Scanner object whenever you want to get console input.

Once you've created a Scanner object, you can use the next methods to read data from the console. The method you use depends on the type of data you need to read. To read string data, for example, you use the next method. To read integer data, you use the nextInt method. To read double data, you use the nextDouble method. And to read all of the data on a line, you use the nextLine method.

The examples in this figure illustrate how these methods work. Here, the first statement gets a string and assigns it to a string variable named name. The second statement gets an integer and assigns it to an int variable named count. The third statement gets a double and assigns it to a double variable named subtotal. And the fourth statement reads any remaining characters on the line.

Each entry that a user makes is called a *token*, and a user can enter more than one token before pressing the Enter key. To do that, the user separates the entries by one or more space, tab, or return characters. This is called *whitespace*. Then, each next method gets the next token that has been entered. If, for example, you press the Enter key (a return character), type 100, press the Tab key, type 20, and press the Enter key again, the first token is 100 and the second one is 20.

If you want to get string data that includes whitespace, you can use the nextLine method. If, for example, the user enters "New York" and presses the Enter key, you can use the nextLine method to get the entire entry as a single string.

If the user doesn't enter the type of data that the next method is looking for, an error occurs and the program ends. In Java, an error like this is also known as an *exception*. If, for example, the user enters a double value but the nextInt method is used to get it, an exception occurs. In chapter 5, you'll learn how to prevent this type of error.

Although this figure only shows methods for working with String objects and int and double types, the Scanner class includes methods for working with most of the other data types that you'll learn about in the next chapter. It also includes methods that let you check what type of data the user entered. As you'll see in chapter 5, you can use these methods to avoid exceptions by checking the data type before you issue the next method.

The Scanner class

```
java.util.Scanner
```

How to create a Scanner object

```
Scanner sc = new Scanner(System.in);
```

Common methods of a Scanner object

Method	Description
`next()`	Returns the next token stored in the scanner as a String object.
`nextInt()`	Returns the next token stored in the scanner as an int value.
`nextDouble()`	Returns the next token stored in the scanner as a double value.
`nextLine()`	Returns any remaining input on the current line as a String object and advances the scanner to the next line.

How to use the methods of a Scanner object

```
String name = sc.next();
int count = sc.nextInt();
double subtotal = sc.nextDouble();
String cityName = sc.nextLine();
```

Description

- To create a Scanner object that gets input from the *console*, specify System.in in the parentheses.
- When one of the next methods of the Scanner class is run, the application waits for the user to enter data with the keyboard. To complete the entry, the user presses the Enter key.
- Each entry that a user makes is called a *token*. A user can enter two or more tokens by separating them with *whitespace*, which consists of one or more spaces, tab characters, or return characters.
- The entries end when the user presses the Enter key. Then, the first next, nextInt, or nextDouble method gets the first token; the second next, nextInt, or nextDouble method gets the second token; and so on. In contrast, the nextLine method gets all of the input or remaining input on the current line.
- If the user doesn't enter the type of data that the next method expects, an error occurs and the program ends. In Java, this type of error is called an *exception*. You'll learn more about this in chapter 5.
- Since the Scanner class is in the java.util package, you'll want to include an import statement whenever you use this class.

Note

- The Scanner class was introduced in version 1.5 of the JDK.

Figure 2-12 How to use the Scanner class to read input from the console

Examples that get input from the console

Figure 2-13 presents two examples that get input from the console. The first example starts by creating a Scanner object. Then, it uses the print method of the System.out object to prompt the user for three values, and it uses the next methods of the Scanner object to read those values from the console. Because the first value should be a string, the next method is used to read this value. Because the second value should be a double, the nextDouble method is used to read it. And because the third value should be an integer, the nextInt method is used to read it.

After all three values are read, a calculation is performed using the int and double values. Then, the data is formatted and the println method is used to display the data on the console. You can see the results of this code in this figure.

Unlike the first example, which reads one value per line, the second example reads three values in a single line. Here, the first statement uses the print method to prompt the user to enter three integer values. Then, the next three statements use the nextInt method to read those three values. This works because a Scanner object uses whitespace (spaces, tabs, or returns) to separate the data that's entered at the console into tokens.

Example 1: Code that gets three values from the user

```
// create a Scanner object
Scanner sc = new Scanner(System.in);

// read a string
System.out.print("Enter product code: ");
String productCode = sc.next();

// read a double value
System.out.print("Enter price: ");
double price = sc.nextDouble();

// read an int value
System.out.print("Enter quantity: ");
int quantity = sc.nextInt();

// perform a calculation and display the result
double total = price * quantity;
System.out.println();
System.out.println(quantity + " " + productCode
    + " @ " + price + " = " + total);
System.out.println();
```

The console after the program finishes

```
Enter product code: cshp
Enter price: 49.50
Enter quantity: 2

2 cshp @ 49.5 = 99.0
```

Example 2: Code that reads three values from one line

```
// read three int values
System.out.print("Enter three integer values: ");
int i1 = sc.nextInt();
int i2 = sc.nextInt();
int i3 = sc.nextInt();

// calculate the average and display the result
int total = i1 + i2 + i3;
int avg = total / 3;
System.out.println("Average: " + avg);
System.out.println();
```

The console after the program finishes

```
Enter three integer values: 99 88 92
Average: 93
```

Figure 2-13 Examples that get input from the console

How to code simple control statements

As you write programs, you need to determine when certain operations should be done and how long repetitive operations should continue. To do that, you code *control statements* like the if/else and while statements. This topic will get you started with the use of these statements, but first you need to learn how to write expressions that compare numeric and string variables.

How to compare numeric variables

Figure 2-14 shows how to code *Boolean expressions* that use the six *relational operators* to compare int and double data types. This type of expression evaluates to either true or false based on the result of the comparison, and the operands in the expression can be either variables or literals.

For instance, the first expression in the first set of examples is true if the value of the variable named discountPercent is equal to the literal value 2.3. The second expression is true if the value of subtotal is not equal to zero. And the sixth expression is true if the value of the variable named quantity is less than or equal to the value of the variable named reorderPoint.

Although you shouldn't have any trouble coding simple expressions like these, you must remember to code two equals signs instead of one for the equality comparison. That's because a single equals sign is used for assignment statements. As a result, if you try to code a Boolean expression with a single equals sign, your code won't compile.

When you compare numeric values, you usually compare values of the same data type. However, if you compare different types of numeric values, Java will automatically cast the less precise numeric type to the more precise type. For example, if you compare an int type to a double type, the int type will be cast to the double type before the comparison is made.

How to compare string variables

Because a string is an object, not a primitive data type, you can't use the relational operators to compare strings. Instead, you must use the equals or equalsIgnoreCase methods of the String class that are summarized in figure 2-14. As you can see, both of these methods require an argument that provides the String object or literal that you want to compare with the current String object.

In the examples, the first expression is true if the value in the string named userEntry equals the literal value "Y". In contrast, the second expression uses the equalsIgnoreCase method, so it's true whether the value in userEntry is "Y" or "y". Then, the third expression shows how you can use the not operator (!) to reverse the value of a Boolean expression that compares two strings. Here, the expression will evaluate to true if the lastName variable is *not* equal to "Jones". The fourth expression is true if the string variable named code equals the string variable named productCode.

Relational operators

Operator	Name	Description
`==`	Equality	Returns a true value if both operands are equal.
`!=`	Inequality	Returns a true value if the left and right operands are not equal.
`>`	Greater Than	Returns a true value if the left operand is greater than the right operand.
`<`	Less Than	Returns a true value if the left operand is less than the right operand.
`>=`	Greater Than Or Equal	Returns a true value if the left operand is greater than or equal to the right operand.
`<=`	Less Than Or Equal	Returns a true value if the left operand is less than or equal to the right operand.

Examples of conditional expressions

```
discountPercent == 2.3      // equal to a numeric literal
subtotal != 0               // not equal to a numeric literal
years > 0                   // greater than a numeric literal
i < months                  // less than a numeric variable
subtotal >= 500             // greater than or equal to a numeric literal
quantity <= reorderPoint    // less than or equal to a numeric variable
```

Two methods of the String class

Method	Description
equals(String)	Compares the value of the String object with a String argument and returns a true value if they are equal. This method makes a case-sensitive comparison.
equalsIgnoreCase(String)	Works like the equals method but is not case-sensitive.

Examples

```
userEntry.equals("Y")                  // equal to a string literal
userEntry.equalsIgnoreCase("Y")        // equal to a string literal
(!lastName.equals("Jones"))            // not equal to a string literal
code.equalsIgnoreCase(productCode)     // equal to another string variable
```

Description

- You can use the *relational operators* to compare two numeric operands and return a *Boolean value* that is either true or false.
- To compare two numeric operands for equality, make sure to use two equals signs. If you only use one equals sign, you'll code an assignment statement, and your code won't compile.
- If you compare an int with a double, Java will cast the int to a double.
- To test two strings for equality, you must call one of the methods of the String object. If you use the equality operator, you will get unpredictable results (more about this in chapter 4).

Figure 2-14 How to compare numeric and string variables

How to code if/else statements

Figure 2-15 shows how to use the *if/else statement* (or just *if statement*) to control the logic of your applications. This statement is the Java implementation of a control structure known as the *selection structure* because it lets you select different actions based on the results of a Boolean expression.

As you can see in the syntax summary, you can code this statement with just an if clause, you can code it with one or more else if clauses, and you can code it with a final else clause. In any syntax summary, the ellipsis (...) means that the preceding element (in this case the else if clause) can be repeated as many times as it is needed. And the brackets [ ] mean that the element is optional.

When an if statement is executed, Java begins by evaluating the Boolean expression in the if clause. If it's true, the statements within this clause are executed and the rest of the if/else statement is skipped. If it's false, Java evaluates the first else if clause (if there is one). Then, if its Boolean expression is true, the statements within this else if clause are executed, and the rest of the if/else statement is skipped. Otherwise, Java evaluates the next else if clause.

This continues with any remaining else if clauses. Finally, if none of the clauses contains a Boolean expression that evaluates to true, Java executes the statements in the else clause (if there is one). However, if none of the Boolean expressions are true and there is no else clause, Java doesn't execute any statements.

If a clause only contains one statement, you don't need to enclose that statement in braces. This is illustrated by the first statement in the first example in this figure. However, if you want to code two or more statements within a clause, you need to code the statements in braces. The braces identify the block of statements that is executed for the clause.

If you declare a variable within a block, that variable is available only to the other statements in the block. This can be referred to as *block scope*. As a result, if you need to access a variable outside of the block, you should declare it before the if statement. You'll see this illustrated by the program at the end of this chapter.

The syntax of the if/else statement

```
if (booleanExpression) {statements}
[else if (booleanExpression) {statements}] ...
[else {statements}]
```

Example 1: If statements without else if or else clauses

With a single statement

```
if (subtotal >= 100)
    discountPercent = .2;
```

With a block of statements

```
if (subtotal >= 100)
{
    discountPercent = .2;
    status = "Bulk rate";
}
```

Example 2: An if statement with an else clause

```
if (subtotal >= 100)
    discountPercent = .2;
else
    discountPercent = .1;
```

Example 3: An if statement with else if and else clauses

```
if (customerType.equals("T"))
    discountPercent = .4;
else if (customerType.equals("C"))
    discountPercent = .2;
else if (subtotal >= 100)
    discountPercent = .2;
else
    discountPercent = .1;
```

Description

- An *if/else statement*, or just *if statement*, always contains an if clause. In addition, it can contain one or more else if clauses, and a final else clause.
- If a clause requires just one statement, you don't have to enclose the statement in braces.
- If a clause requires more than one statement, you enclose the block of statements in braces.
- Any variables that are declared within a block have *block scope* so they can only be used within that block.

Figure 2-15 How to code if/else statements

How to code while statements

Figure 2-16 shows how to code a *while statement*. This is one way that Java implements a control structure know as the *iteration structure* because it lets you repeat a block of statements. As you will see in chapter 4, though, Java also offers other implementations of this structure.

When a while statement is executed, the program repeats the statements in the block of code within the braces *while* the expression in the statement is true. In other words, the statement ends when the expression becomes false. If the expression is false when the statement starts, the statements in the block of code are never executed.

Because a while statement loops through the statements in the block as many times as needed, the code within a while statement is often referred to as a *while loop*. Here again, any variables that are defined within the block have block scope, which means that they can't be accessed outside the block.

The first example in this figure shows how to code a loop that executes a block of statements while a variable named choice is equal to either "y" or "Y". In this case, the statements within the block get input from the console, process it, and display output. This is a common way to control the execution of a program, and you'll see this illustrated in detail in the next figure.

The second example shows how to code a loop that adds the numbers 1 through 4 and stores the result in a variable named sum. Here, a *counter variable* (or just *counter*) named i is initialized to 1 and the sum variable is initialized to zero before the loop starts. Then, each time through the loop, the value of i is added to sum and one is added to i. Because the value of i is 1 the first time through the loop, for example, 1 is added to sum so its value becomes 1. The second time through the loop, 2 is added to sum so its value becomes 3. The third time through the loop, 3 is added to sum so its value becomes 6. And the fourth time through the loop, 4 is added to sum so its value becomes 10. When the value of i becomes 5, though, the expression in the while statement is no longer true and the loop ends. The use of a counter like this is a common coding practice, and single letters like *i, j,* and *k* are commonly used as the names of counters.

When you code loops, you must be careful to avoid *infinite loops*. If, for example, you forget to code a statement that increments the counter variable in the second example, the loop will never end because the counter will never get to 5. Then, you have to cancel the application so you can debug your code. In NetBeans, you can do that by clicking on the Stop button that's available from the Output window when a console application is running.

The syntax of the while loop

```
while (booleanExpression)
{
   statements
}
```

Example 1: A loop that continues while choice is "y" or "Y"

```
String choice = "y";
while (choice.equalsIgnoreCase("y"))
{
    // get the invoice subtotal from the user
    Scanner sc = new Scanner(System.in);
    System.out.print("Enter subtotal:   ");
    double subtotal = sc.nextDouble();

    // the code that processes the user's entry goes here

    // see if the user wants to continue
    System.out.print("Continue? (y/n): ");
    choice = sc.next();
    System.out.println();
}
```

Example 2: A loop that calculates the sum of the numbers 1 through 4

```
int i = 1;
int sum = 0;
while (i < 5)
{
    sum = sum + i;
    i = i + 1;
}
```

Description

- A *while statement* executes the block of statements within its braces as long as the Boolean expression is true. When the expression becomes false, the while statement skips its block of statements so the program continues with the next statement in sequence.
- The statements within a while statement can be referred to as a *while loop*.
- Any variables that are declared in the block of a while statement have block scope.
- If the Boolean expression in a while statement never becomes false, the statement never ends. Then, the program goes into an *infinite loop*. In NetBeans, you can cancel an infinite loop by clicking on the Stop button in the Output window.

Figure 2-16 How to code while loops

Two illustrative applications

You have now learned enough about Java to write simple applications of your own. To show you how you can do that, this chapter ends by presenting two illustrative applications.

The Invoice application

In chapter 1, you saw how the console looks when displayed by NetBeans. Now, this figure shows the console in a platform-neutral format that's easy to read. This is the format that will be used to display console output for the rest of this book.

Figure 2-17 shows the console and code for an Invoice application. Although this application is simple, it gets input from the user, performs calculations that use this input, and displays the results of the calculations. It continues until the user enters anything other than "Y" or "y" in response to the Continue prompt.

The Invoice application starts by displaying a welcome message at the console. Then, it creates a Scanner object named sc that will be used in the while loop of the program. Although this object could be created within the while loop, that would mean that the object would be recreated each time through the loop, and that would be inefficient.

Before the while statement is executed, a String object named choice is initialized to "y". Then, the loop starts by getting a double value from the user and storing it in a variable named subtotal. After that, the loop uses an if/else statement to calculate the discount amount based on the value of subtotal. If, for example, subtotal is greater than or equal to 200, the discount amount is .2 times the subtotal (a 20% discount). If that condition isn't true but subtotal is greater than or equal to 100, the discount is .1 times the subtotal (a 10% discount). Otherwise, the discount amount is zero. When the if/else statement is finished, an assignment statement calculates the invoice total by subtracting discountAmount from subtotal.

At that point, the program displays the discount percent, discount amount, and invoice total on the console. Then, it displays a message that asks the user if he or she wants to continue. If the user enters "y" or "Y", the loop is repeated. Otherwise, the program ends.

Although this application illustrates most of what you've learned in this chapter, it has a couple of shortcomings. First, the numeric values that are displayed should be formatted with two decimal places since these are currency values. In the next chapter, you'll learn how to do that type of formatting.

Second, an exception will occur and the program will end prematurely if the user doesn't enter one valid double value for the subtotal each time through the loop. This is a serious problem that isn't acceptable in a professional program, and you'll learn how to prevent problems like this in chapter 5.

In the meantime, if you're new to programming, you can learn a lot by writing simple programs like the Invoice program. That will give you a chance to become comfortable with the coding for input, calculations, output, if/else statements, and while statements.

The console input and output for a test run

```
Welcome to the Invoice Total Calculator

Enter subtotal:   150
Discount percent: 0.1
Discount amount:  15.0
Invoice total:    135.0


Continue? (y/n):
```

The code for the application

```
import java.util.Scanner;

public class InvoiceApp
{
    public static void main(String[] args)
    {
        System.out.println("Welcome to the Invoice Total Calculator");
        System.out.println();  // print a blank line

        Scanner sc = new Scanner(System.in);

        // perform invoice calculations until choice isn't equal to "y" or "Y"
        String choice = "y";
        while (choice.equalsIgnoreCase("y"))
        {
            // get the invoice subtotal from the user
            System.out.print("Enter subtotal:   ");
            double subtotal = sc.nextDouble();

            // calculate the discount amount and total
            double discountPercent = 0.0;
            if (subtotal >= 200)
                discountPercent = .2;
            else if (subtotal >= 100)
                discountPercent = .1;
            else
                discountPercent = 0.0;

            double discountAmount = subtotal * discountPercent;
            double total = subtotal - discountAmount;

            // display the discount amount and total
            String message = "Discount percent: " + discountPercent + "\n"
                           + "Discount amount:  " + discountAmount + "\n"
                           + "Invoice total:    " + total + "\n";
            System.out.println(message);

            // see if the user wants to continue
            System.out.print("Continue? (y/n): ");
            choice = sc.next();
            System.out.println();
        }
    }
}
```

Figure 2-17 The Invoice application

The Test Score application

Figure 2-18 presents another Java application that will give you more ideas for how you can apply what you've learned so far. If you look at the console input and output for this application, you can see that it lets the user enter one or more test scores. To end the application, the user enters a value of 999. Then, the application displays the number of test scores that were entered, the total of the scores, and the average of the scores.

If you look at the code for this application, you can see that it starts by displaying the instructions for using the application. Then, it declares and initializes three variables, and it creates a Scanner object that will be used to get console input.

The while loop in this program continues until the user enters a test score that's greater than 100. To start, this loop gets the next test score. Then, if that test score is less than or equal to 100, the program adds one to scoreCount, which keeps track of the number of scores, and adds the test score to scoreTotal, which accumulates the total of the scores. The if statement that does this is needed, because you don't want to increase scoreCount and scoreTotal if the user enters 999 to end the program. When the loop ends, the program calculates the average score and displays the score count, total, and average.

To include decimal places in the score average, this program declares scoreTotal and averageScore as a double data types. Declaring scoreTotal as a double type causes the score average to be calculated with decimal places. Declaring the averageScore variable as a double type allows it to store those decimal places.

To allow statements outside of the while loop to access the scoreTotal and scoreCount variables, this program declares these variables before the while loop. If these variables were declared inside the while loop, they would only be available within that block of code and couldn't be accessed by the statements that are executed after the while loop. In addition, the logic of the program wouldn't work because these variables would be reinitialized each time through the loop.

Here again, this program has some obvious shortcomings that will be addressed in later chapters. First, the data isn't formatted properly, but you'll learn how to fix that in the next chapter. Second, an exception will occur and the program will end prematurely if the user enters invalid data, but you'll learn how to fix that in chapter 5.

The console input and output for a test run

```
Please enter test scores that range from 0 to 100.
To end the program enter 999.

Enter score: 90
Enter score: 80
Enter score: 75
Enter score: 999

Score count:   3
Score total:   245.0
Average score: 81.66666666666667
```

The code for the application

```
import java.util.Scanner;

public class TestScoreApp
{
    public static void main(String[] args)
    {
        System.out.println(
            "Please enter test scores that range from 0 to 100.");
        System.out.println("To end the program enter 999.");
        System.out.println();  // print a blank line

        // initialize variables and create a Scanner object
        double scoreTotal = 0.0;
        int scoreCount = 0;
        int testScore = 0;
        Scanner sc = new Scanner(System.in);

        // get a series of test scores from the user
        while (testScore <= 100)
        {
            // get the input from the user
            System.out.print("Enter score: ");
            testScore = sc.nextInt();

            // accumulate score count and score total
            if (testScore <= 100)
            {
                scoreCount = scoreCount + 1;
                scoreTotal = scoreTotal + testScore;
            }
        }

        // display the score count, score total, and average score
        double averageScore = scoreTotal / scoreCount;
        String message = "\n"
                       + "Score count:   " + scoreCount + "\n"
                       + "Score total:   " + scoreTotal + "\n"
                       + "Average score: " + averageScore + "\n";
        System.out.println(message);
    }
}
```

Figure 2-18 The Test Score application

How to test and debug an application

In chapter 1, you were introduced to errors that are detected by NetBeans as you enter code, called *syntax errors*. Because syntax errors keep an application from being compiled, they are also commonly referred to as *compile-time errors*. Once you've fixed the syntax errors, you're ready to test and debug the application as described in this topic. Then, in the next two chapters, you'll learn several more debugging techniques. And when you do the exercises, you'll get lots of practice testing and debugging.

How to test an application

When you *test* an application, you run it to make sure the application works correctly. As you test, you should try every possible combination of valid and invalid data to be certain that the application works correctly under every set of conditions. Remember that the goal of testing is to find errors, or *bugs*, not to show that an application works correctly.

As you test, you will encounter two types of bugs. The first type of bug causes a *runtime error* also known as a *runtime exception*. A runtime error causes the application to end prematurely, which programmers often refer to as "crashing" or "blowing up." In this case, an error message like the one in the first example in figure 2-19 is displayed, and this message shows the line number of the statement that was being executed when the error occurred.

The second type of bug produces inaccurate results when an application runs. These bugs occur due to *logic errors* in the source code. For instance, the second example in this figure shows output for the Test Score application. Here, the final totals were displayed and the application ended before any input was entered. This type of bug can be more difficult to find and correct than a runtime error.

How to debug an application

When you *debug* a program, you find the cause of the bugs, fix them, recompile, and test again. As you progress through this book and your programs become more complex, you'll see that debugging can be one of the most time-consuming aspects of programming.

To find the cause of runtime errors, you can start by finding the source statement that was running when the program crashed. You can usually do that by studying the error message that's displayed. In the first console in this figure, for example, you can see that the statement at line 20 in the main method of the InvoiceApp class was running when the program crashed. That's the statement that used the nextDouble method of the Scanner object, and that indicates that the problem is invalid input data. In chapter 5, you'll learn how to fix this bug.

To find the cause of incorrect output, you can start by figuring out why the application produced the output that it did. For instance, you can start by asking why the second application in this figure didn't prompt the user to enter any test scores. Once you figure that out, you're well on your way to fixing the bug.

A runtime error that occurred while testing the Invoice application

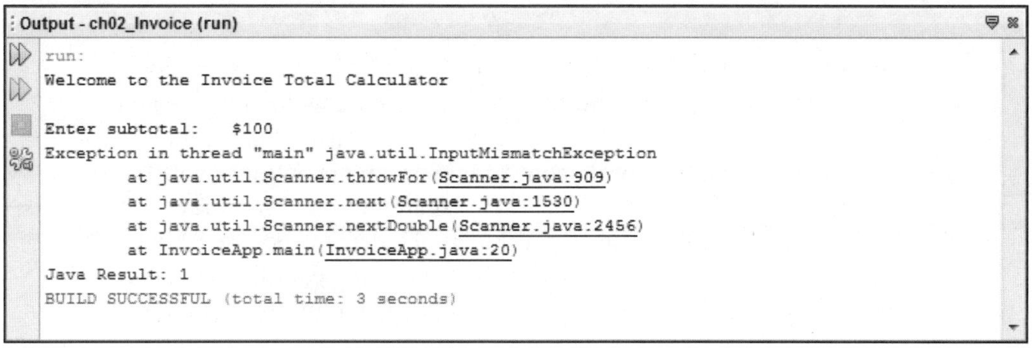

```
Output - ch02_Invoice (run)
run:
Welcome to the Invoice Total Calculator

Enter subtotal:   $100
Exception in thread "main" java.util.InputMismatchException
        at java.util.Scanner.throwFor(Scanner.java:909)
        at java.util.Scanner.next(Scanner.java:1530)
        at java.util.Scanner.nextDouble(Scanner.java:2456)
        at InvoiceApp.main(InvoiceApp.java:20)
Java Result: 1
BUILD SUCCESSFUL (total time: 3 seconds)
```

Incorrect output produced by the Test Score application

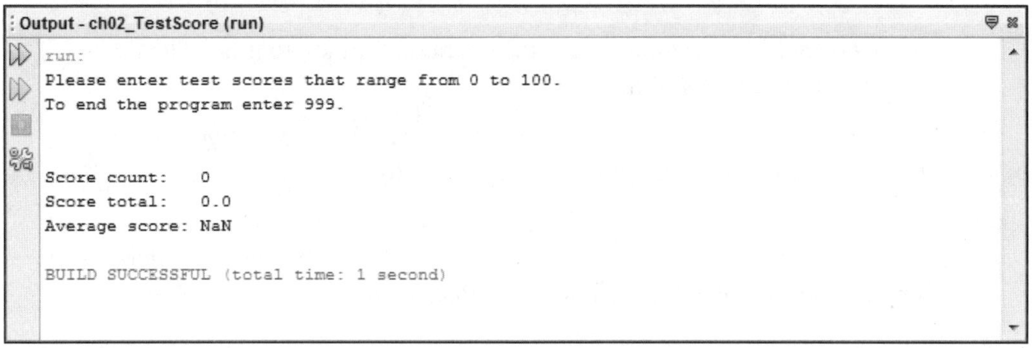

```
Output - ch02_TestScore (run)
run:
Please enter test scores that range from 0 to 100.
To end the program enter 999.


Score count:   0
Score total:   0.0
Average score: NaN

BUILD SUCCESSFUL (total time: 1 second)
```

Description

- A *syntax* or *compile-time error* occurs when a statement can't be compiled. Before you can test an application, you must fix the syntax errors.
- To *test* an application, you run it to make sure that it works properly no matter what combinations of valid and invalid data you enter. The goal of testing is to find the errors (or *bugs*) in the application.
- To *debug* an application, you find the causes of the bugs and fix them.
- One type of bug leads to a *runtime error* (also known as a *runtime exception*) that causes the program to end prematurely. This type of bug must be fixed before testing can continue.
- Even if an application runs to completion, the results may be incorrect due to *logic errors*. These bugs must also be fixed.

Debugging tips

- For a runtime error, go to the line in the source code that was running when the program crashed. In NetBeans, you can do that by clicking on the link to the line of source code. That should give you a strong indication of what caused the error.
- For a logical error, first figure out how the source code produced that output. Then, fix the code and test the application again.

Figure 2-19 How to test and debug an application

Perspective

The goal of this chapter has been to get you started with Java programming and to get you started fast. Now, if you understand how the Invoice and Test Score applications in figures 2-17 and 2-18 work, you've come a long way. You should also be able to write comparable programs of your own.

Keep in mind, though, that this chapter is just an introduction to Java programming. So in the next chapter, you'll learn the details about working with data. In chapter 4, you'll learn the details about using control statements. And in chapter 5, you'll learn how to prevent and handle runtime exceptions.

Summary

- The *statements* in a Java program direct the operation of the program. The *comments* document what the program does.
- You must code at least one public *class* for every Java program that you write. The *main method* of this class is executed when you run the class.
- *Variables* are used to store data that changes as a program runs, and you use *assignment statements* to assign values to variables. Two of the most common *data types* for numeric variables are the int and double types.
- A *string* is an object that's created from the String class, and it can contain any characters in the character set. You can use the plus sign to *join* a string with another string or a data type, and you can use assignment statements to *append* one string to another. To include special characters in strings, you can use *escape sequences*.
- When you use a *constructor* to create an *object* from a Java class, you are creating an *instance* of the class. There may be more than one constructor for a class, and a constructor may require one or more *arguments*.
- You *call* a *method* from an object and you call a *static method* from a class. A method may require one or more arguments.
- Before you use many of the classes in the Java *API*, you should code an import statement for the class or for the *package* that contains it.
- You can use the methods of a Scanner object to read data from the *console*, and you can use the print and println methods of the System.out object to print data to the console.
- You can code *if statements* to control the logic of a program based on the true or false values of *Boolean expressions*. You can code *while statements* to repeat a series of statements until a Boolean expression becomes false.
- *Testing* is the process of finding the errors or bugs in an application. *Debugging* is the process of locating and fixing the bugs.

Before you do the exercises for this chapter

If you haven't done it already, you should install and configure the JDK, the NetBeans IDE, and the source code for this book as described in the appendixes.

Exercise 2-1 Test the Invoice application

In this exercise, you'll test the Invoice application that's presented in figure 2-17. That will give you a better idea of how this program works.

1. Start the NetBeans IDE and open the project named ch02_ex1_Invoice. This project should be in this directory:

   ```
   C:\murach\java\netbeans\ex_starts
   ```

2. Open the file named InvoiceApp.java. Review the code for this file and note that NetBeans doesn't display any errors.
3. Test this application with valid subtotal entries like 50, 150, 250, and 1000 so it's easy to see whether or not the calculations are correct.
4. Test the application with a subtotal value like 233.33. This will show that the application doesn't round the results to two decimal places. But in the next chapter, you'll learn how to do that.
5. Test the application with an invalid subtotal value like $1000. This time, the application should crash. Study the error message that's displayed and determine which line of source code in the InvoiceApp class was running when the error occurred. Then, jump to this line by clicking on the link to it.
6. Restart the application, enter a valid subtotal, and enter 20 when the program asks you whether you want to continue. What happens and why?
7. Restart the application and enter two values separated by whitespace (like 1000 20) before pressing the Enter key. What happens and why?

Exercise 2-2 Modify the Test Score application

In this exercise, you'll modify the Test Score application that's presented in figure 2-18. That will give you a chance to write some code of your own.

1. Start NetBeans and open the project named ch02_ex2_TestScore that's in the ex_starts directory shown in the previous exercise.
2. Test this application with valid data to see how it works. Then, test the application with invalid data to see what will cause exceptions. Note that if you enter a test score like 125, the program ends, even though the instructions say that the program ends when you enter 999.

3. Open the file named TestScoreApp.java and modify the while statement so the program only ends when you enter 999. Then, test the program to see how this works.
4. Modify the if statement so it displays an error message like "Invalid entry, not counted" if the user enters a score that's greater than 100 but isn't 999. Then, test this change.

Exercise 2-3 Modify the Invoice application

In this exercise, you'll modify the Invoice application. When you're through with the modifications, a test run should look something like this:

```
Welcome to the Invoice Total Calculator

Enter subtotal:   100
Discount percent: 0.1
Discount amount:  10.0
Invoice total:    90.0

Continue? (y/n): y

Enter subtotal:   500
Discount percent: 0.25
Discount amount:  125.0
Invoice total:    375.0

Continue? (y/n): n

Number of invoices: 2
Average invoice:    232.5
Average discount:   67.5
```

1. Open the project named ch02_ex3_Invoice that's in the ex_starts directory. Then, open the file named InvoiceApp.java.
2. Modify the code so the application ends only when the user enters "n" or "N". As it is now, the application ends when the user enters anything other than "y" or "Y". To do this, you need to use a not operator (!) with the equalsIgnoreCase method. This is illustrated by the third example in figure 2-14. Then, compile this class and test this change by entering 0 at the Continue prompt.
3. Modify the code so it provides a discount of 25 percent when the subtotal is greater than or equal to 500. Then, test this change.
4. Modify the code so it displays the number of invoices, the average invoice amount, and the average discount amount when the user ends the program. Then, test this change.

Exercise 2-4 Use the Java API documentation

This exercise steps you through the Java API documentation for the Scanner, String, and Double classes. That will give you a better idea of how extensive the Java API is.

1. Open a browser and display the Java API documentation as described in figure 2-10.
2. Click the java.util package in the upper left frame and the Scanner class in the lower left frame to display the documentation for the Scanner class. Then, scroll through this documentation to get an idea of its scope.
3. Review the constructors for the Scanner class. The constructor that's presented in this chapter has just an InputStream object as its argument. When you code that argument, remember that System.in represents the InputStream object for the console.
4. Review the methods of the Scanner class with special attention to the next, nextInt, and nextDouble methods. Note that there are three next methods and two nextInt methods. The ones used in this chapter have no arguments. Then, review the has methods in the Scanner class. You'll learn how to use some of these methods in chapter 5.
5. Go to the documentation for the String class, which is in the java.lang package, and note that it offers a number of constructors. In this chapter, though, you learned the shortcut for creating String objects because that's the best way to do that. Now, review the methods for this class with special attention to the equals and equalsIgnoreCase methods.
6. Go to the documentation for the Double class, which is also in the java.lang package. Then, review the static parseDouble and toString methods that you'll learn how to use in the next chapter.

If you find the documentation difficult to follow, rest assured that you'll become comfortable with it before you finish this book. Once you learn how to create your own classes, constructors, and methods, it will make more sense.

3

How to work with data

In chapter 2, you learned how to use two of the eight primitive data types as you declared and initialized variables and coded assignment statements that used simple arithmetic expressions. Now, you'll learn all of the details that you need for working with variables and data types at a professional level.

Basic skills for working with data

In this topic, you'll learn about the six primitive data types that weren't presented in chapter 2. Then, you'll learn the fundamentals for working with all of the data types.

The eight primitive data types

Figure 3-1 shows the eight *primitive data types* provided by Java. You can use these eight data types to store six types of numbers, characters, and true or false values.

In chapter 2, you learned how to use the int data type for storing *integers* (whole numbers). But as this figure shows, you can also use three other data types for integers. If a value is too big for the int type, for example, you can use the *long* type. Although the use of the *short* and *byte* types is less common, you can use them when you're working with smaller integers and you need to save system resources.

In chapter 2, you also learned how to use the double data type for storing numbers with decimal places. But as this figure shows, you can also use the *float* data type for those numbers. The values in both of these data types are stored as *floating-point numbers* that can hold very large and very small values, but with a limited number of *significant digits*. For instance, the double type with its 16 significant digits provides for numbers like 12,345,678,901,234.56 or 12,345,678.90123456 or 12.34567890123456. Since the double type has more significant digits than the float type, you'll use the double type for most floating-point numbers.

To express the value of a floating-point number, you can use *scientific notation*. This lets you express very large and very small numbers in a sort of shorthand. To use this notation, you type the letter *e* or *E* followed by a power of 10. For instance, 3.65e+9 is equal to 3.65 times 10^9 (or 3,650,000,000), and 3.65e-9 is equal to 3.65 times 10^{-9} (or .00000000365).

You can use the *char* type to store one character. Since Java uses the two-byte *Unicode character set*, it can store practically any character from any language around the world. As a result, you can use Java to create programs that read and print Greek or Chinese characters. In practice, though, you'll usually work with the characters that are stored in the older one-byte *ASCII character set*. These characters are the first 256 characters of the Unicode character set.

Last, you can use the *boolean* type to store a true value or a false value. This data type is typically used to represent a condition that can be true or false.

The eight primitive data types

Type	Bytes	Use
`byte`	1	Very short integers from -128 to 127.
`short`	2	Short integers from -32,768 to 32,767.
`int`	4	Integers from -2,147,483,648 to 2,147,483,647.
`long`	8	Long integers from -9,223,372,036,854,775,808 to 9,223,372,036,854,775,807.
`float`	4	Single-precision, floating-point numbers from -3.4E38 to 3.4E38 with up to 7 significant digits.
`double`	8	Double-precision, floating-point numbers from -1.7E308 to 1.7E308 with up to 16 significant digits.
`char`	2	A single Unicode character that's stored in two bytes.
`boolean`	1	A *true* or *false* value.

Description

- A *bit* is a binary digit that can have a value of one or zero. A *byte* is a group of eight bits. As a result, the number of bits for each data type is the number of bytes multiplied by 8.
- *Integers* are whole numbers, and the first four data types above provide for integers of various sizes.
- *Floating-point numbers* provide for very large and very small numbers that require decimal positions, but with a limited number of *significant digits*. A *single-precision number* provides for numbers with up to 7 significant digits. A *double-precision number* provides for numbers with up to 16 significant digits.
- The *double* data type is commonly used for business programs because it provides the precision (number of significant digits) that those programs require.
- The *Unicode character set* provides for over 65,000 characters with two bytes used for each character.
- The older *ASCII character set* that's used by most operating systems provides for 256 characters with one byte used for each character. In the Unicode character set, the first 256 characters correspond to the 256 ASCII characters.
- A *boolean* data type holds a *true* or *false* value.

Technical notes

- To express the value of a floating-point number, you can use *scientific notation* like 2.382E+5, which means 2.382 times 10^5 (a value of 238,200), or 3.25E-8, which means 3.25 times 10^{-8} (a value of .0000000325). Java will sometimes use this notation to display the value of a float or double data type.
- Because of the way floating-point numbers are stored internally, they can't represent the exact value of the decimal places in some numbers. This can cause a rounding problem in some business applications. Later in this chapter, you'll learn how to use the BigDecimal class to solve these rounding problems.

Figure 3-1 The eight primitive data types

How to declare and initialize variables

In chapter 2, you learned how to *declare* and *initialize* a *variable*. This information is repeated in figure 3-2, but with some new information. In particular, it shows how to use separate statements to declare and initialize the variable. It also shows how to declare and initialize some of the data types that weren't presented in chapter 2.

Although you usually declare and initialize a variable in one statement, it occasionally makes sense to do it in two. For instance, you may want to declare a variable at the start of a coding routine without giving it a starting value because its value won't be set until later on.

The one-statement examples in this figure show how to declare and initialize various types of variables. Here, the third and fourth examples show how to assign values to the float and long types. To do that, you need to add a letter after the value. For a float type, you add an *f* or *F* after the value. For a long type, you add an *L*. You can also use a lowercase *l*, but it's not a good coding practice since the lowercase L can easily be mistaken for the number 1. If you omit the letter in one of these assignments, you'll get a compile-time error.

The fifth and sixth statements show how to assign an integer value that has seven digits. Although these statements assign the same value, the second statement uses underscores to separate each group of three digits. Since you can't use commas in numeric literals, you'll want to use underscores whenever that improves the readability of your code. And you can use this technique with all types of numeric literals including double, float, and long values. However, since this feature was introduced with version 1.7 of the JDK, you should only use it if you're sure your code will be run by version 1.7 or later.

The seventh example shows how you can use scientific notation as you assign a value to a variable. Then, the eighth and ninth examples show that you can assign a character to the char type by enclosing a character in single quotes or by supplying the integer that corresponds to the character in the Unicode character set. And the tenth example shows how to initialize a variable named valid as a boolean type with a false value.

The last example shows that you can declare and initialize two or more variables in a single statement. Although you may occasionally want to do this, it's usually better to declare and initialize one variable per statement. That way, it's easier to read your code and to modify it later on.

How to declare and initialize a variable in two statements

Syntax

```
type variableName;
variableName = value;
```

Example

```
int counter;                   // declaration statement
counter = 1;                   // assignment statement
```

How to declare and initialize a variable in one statement

Syntax

```
type variableName = value;
```

Examples

```
int counter = 1;               // initialize an int variable
double price = 14.95;          // initialize a double variable
float interestRate = 8.125F;   // F indicates a floating-point value
long numberOfBytes = 20000L;   // L indicates a long integer
int population = 1734323;      // initialize an int variable
int population = 1_734_323;    // underscores improve readability
double distance = 3.65e+9;     // scientific notation
char letter = 'A';             // stored as a two-digit Unicode character
char letter = 65;              // integer value for a Unicode character
boolean valid = false;         // where false is a keyword
int x = 0, y = 0;              // initialize 2 variables with 1 statement
```

Description

- A *variable* stores a value that can change as a program executes.
- Before you can use a variable, you must *declare* its data type and *initialize* it by assigning a value to it. As default values, it's common to initialize integer variables to 0, floating-point variables to 0.0, and boolean variables to false.
- To declare and initialize more than one variable for a single data type in a single statement, use commas to separate the assignments.
- To identify float values, you must type an *f* or *F* after the number. To identify long values, you must type an *l* or *L* after the number.

Naming conventions

- Start variable names with a lowercase letter and capitalize the first letter in all words after the first word.
- Try to use meaningful names that are easy to remember as you code.

Note

- The use of underscores in numeric literals was introduced in version 1.7 of the JDK.

Figure 3-2 How to declare and initialize variables

How to declare and initialize constants

A *constant* stores a value that can't be changed as the program executes. Most of the skills for declaring and initializing variables also apply to declaring and initializing constants. However, you begin the declaration statement for a constant with the *final* keyword. As a result, constants are sometimes called *final variables*. In addition, it's a common coding convention to use all uppercase letters for the name of a constant and to separate the words in the name with an underscore as shown in figure 3-3.

How to declare and initialize a constant

Syntax

```
final type CONSTANT_NAME = value;
```

Examples

```
final int DAYS_IN_NOVEMBER = 30;
final float SALES_TAX = .075F;
final double LIGHT_YEAR_MILES = 5.879e+12
```

Description

- A *constant* stores a value that cannot change as a program executes.
- The skills for initializing variables also apply to constants.

Naming conventions

- Capitalize all of the letters in constants and separate words with underscores.
- Try to use meaningful names that are easy to remember.

Figure 3-3 How to declare and initialize constants

How to code assignment statements and arithmetic expressions

In chapter 2, you learned how to code *assignment statements* that used simple *arithmetic expressions* to assign the value of the expression to a variable. These expressions used the first four *arithmetic operators* in figure 3-4. Now, this figure summarizes all of the Java arithmetic operators. These operators indicate what operations are to be performed on the *operands* in the expression, which can be either *literals* or variables.

In this figure, the first five operators work on two operands. As a result, they're referred to as *binary operators*. For example, when you use the subtraction operator (-), you subtract one operand from another.

In contrast, the last four operators work on one operand. As a result, they're referred to as *unary operators*. For example, you can code the negative sign operator (-) in front of an operand to reverse the value of the operand. Although you can also code the positive sign operator (+) in front of an operand, it doesn't change the value of the operand so it's rarely used as a unary operator.

While the addition (+), subtraction (-), and multiplication (*) operators are easy to understand, the division (/) and modulus (%) operators are more difficult. If you're working with integer data types, the division operator returns an integer value that represents the number of times the right operand will fit into the left operand. Then, the modulus operator returns an integer value that represents the remainder (which is the amount that's left over after dividing the left operand by the right operand). However, if you're working with non-integer data types, the division operator returns a value that uses decimal places to indicate the result of the division, and that's usually what you want.

When you code an increment (++) or decrement (--) operator, you can *prefix* the operand by coding the operator before the variable. Then, the increment or decrement operation is performed before the rest of the statement is executed. Conversely, you can *postfix* the operand by coding the operator after the variable. Then, the increment or decrement operation isn't performed until after the statement is executed.

Often, an entire statement does nothing more than increment a variable like this:

```
counter++;
```

Then, both the prefix and postfix forms will yield the same result. However, if you use the increment and decrement operators as part of a larger statement, you'll need to use the prefix and postfix forms of these operators to control when the operation is performed. More about that in a moment.

Since each char type is a Unicode character that has a numeric code that maps to an integer, you can perform some integer operations on char types. For instance, this figure shows an example of how you can use the increment operator to change the numeric value for a char variable from 67 to 68, which changes the character from *C* to *D*.

Arithmetic operators

Operator	Name	Description
+	Addition	Adds two operands.
-	Subtraction	Subtracts the right operand from the left operand.
*	Multiplication	Multiplies the right operand and the left operand.
/	Division	Divides the right operand into the left operand. If both operands are integers, then the result is an integer.
%	Modulus	Returns the value that is left over after dividing the right operand into the left operand.
++	Increment	Adds 1 to the operand (x = x + 1).
--	Decrement	Subtracts 1 from the operand (x = x - 1).
+	Positive sign	Indicates that the value is positive.
-	Negative sign	Changes a positive value to negative, and vice versa.

Examples of simple assignment statements

```
int x = 14;
int y = 8;
int result1 = x + y;        // result1 = 22
int result2 = x - y;        // result2 = 6
int result3 = x * y;        // result3 = 112
int result4 = x / y;        // result4 = 1
int result5 = x % y;        // result5 = 6
int result6 = -y + x;       // result6 = 6
int result7 = --y;          // result7 = 7, y = 7
int result8 = ++x;          // result8 = 15, x = 15

double a = 8.5;
double b = 3.4;
double result9 = a + b;     // result9 = 11.9
double result10 = a - b;    // result10 = 5.1
double result11 = a * b;    // result11 = 28.90
double result12 = a / b;    // result12 = 2.5
double result13 = a % b;    // result13 = 1.7
double result14 = -a + b;   // result14 = -5.1
double result15 = --a;      // result15 = 7.5
double result16 = ++b;      // result16 = 4.4

// character arithmetic
char letter1 = 'C';         // letter1 = 'C'  Unicode integer is 67
char letter2 = ++letter1;   // letter2 = 'D'  Unicode integer is 68
```

Description

- An *arithmetic expression* consists of *operands* and *arithmetic operators*. The first five operators above are called *binary operators* because they operate on two operands. The next four are called *unary operators* because they operate on just one operand.
- An *assignment statement* consists of a variable, an equals sign, and an expression. When the assignment statement is executed, the value of the expression is determined and the result is stored in the variable.

Figure 3-4 How to code assignment statements and arithmetic expressions

How to use the shortcut assignment operators

When coding assignment statements, it's common to code the same variable on both sides of the equals sign. This is illustrated by the first group of statements in figure 3-5. That way, you can use the current value of the variable in an expression and update the variable by assigning the result of the expression to it. You saw this illustrated in chapter 2.

Since it's common to write statements like this, the Java language provides the five shorthand *assignment operators* shown in this figure. Although these operators don't provide any new functionality, you can use them to write shorter code.

If, for example, you need to increment or decrement a variable by a value of 1, you can use a shortcut operator. For example:

```
month = month + 1;
```

can be coded with a shortcut operator as

```
month += 1;
```

which is equivalent to

```
month++;
```

Similarly, if you want to add the value of a variable named nextNumber to a summary field named sum, you can do it like this:

```
sum += nextNumber;
```

which is equivalent to

```
sum = sum + nextNumber;
```

The techniques that you use are mostly a matter of preference because the statements are easy to read and maintain however you code them.

Assignment operators

Operator	Name	Description
=	Assignment	Assigns a new value to the variable.
+=	Addition	Adds the operand to the starting value of the variable and assigns the result to the variable.
-=	Subtraction	Subtracts the operand from the starting value of the variable and assigns the result to the variable.
*=	Multiplication	Multiplies the operand by the starting value of the variable and assigns the result to the variable.
/=	Division	Divides the starting value of the variable by the operand and assigns the result to the variable. If the operand and the value of the variable are both integers, the result is an integer.
%=	Modulus	Derives the value that is left over after dividing the right operand by the value in the variable, and then assigns this value to the variable.

Statements that use the same variable on both sides of the equals sign

```
count = count + 1;          // count is increased by 1
count = count - 1;          // count is decreased by 1
total = total + 100.0;      // total is increased by 100.0
total = total - 100.0;      // total is decreased by 100.0
price = price * .8;         // price is multiplied by .8
sum = sum + nextNumber;     // sum is increased by value of nextNumber
```

Statements that use the shortcut operators to get the same results

```
count += 1;                 // count is increased by 1
count -= 1;                 // count is decreased by 1
total += 100.0;             // total is increased by 100.0
total -= 100.0;             // total is decreased by 100.0
price *= .8;                // price is multipled by .8
sum += nextNumber;          // sum is increased by the value of nextNumber
```

Description

- Besides the equals sign, Java provides for the five other *assignment operators* shown above. These operators provide a shorthand way to code common assignment operations.

How to work with the order of precedence

Figure 3-6 gives more information about coding arithmetic expressions. In particular, it gives the *order of precedence* of the arithmetic operations. This means that all of the prefixed increment and decrement operations in an expression are done first, followed by all of the positive and negative operations, and so on. If there are two or more operations at the same order of precedence, the operations are done from left to right.

Because this sequence of operations doesn't always work the way you want it to, you may need to override the sequence by using parentheses. Then, the expressions in the innermost sets of parentheses are done first, followed by the next sets of parentheses, and so on. Within the parentheses, though, the operations are done left to right by the order of precedence. In general, you should use parentheses to dictate the sequence of operations whenever there's any doubt about it.

The need for parentheses is illustrated by the first example in this figure. Because parentheses aren't used in the first expression that calculates the price, the multiplication operation is done before the subtraction operation, which gives an incorrect result. In contrast, because the subtraction operation is enclosed in parentheses in the second expression, this operation is performed before the multiplication operation, which gives a correct result.

The second example in this figure shows how parentheses can be used in a more complicated expression. Here, three sets of parentheses are used to calculate the current value of an investment account after a monthly investment amount is added to it, monthly interest is calculated, and the interest is added to it. If you have trouble following this, you can plug the initial values into the expression and evaluate it one set of parentheses at a time:

```
(5000 + 100) * (1 + (.12 / 12))
(5000 + 100) * (1 + .01)
5100 * 1.01
5151
```

If you have trouble creating an expression like this for a difficult calculation, you can often break the expression down into a series of statements. To illustrate, this figure shows another way to calculate the current value. Here, the first statement adds the monthly investment amount to the current value. The second statement calculates the monthly interest rate. The third statement calculates the monthly interest amount. And the fourth statement adds the interest to the current value. This not only takes away the need for parentheses, but also makes the code easier to read and debug.

The third example in this figure shows the differences between the use of prefixed and postfixed increment and decrement operators. With prefixed operators, the variable is incremented or decremented before the result is assigned. With postfixed operators, the result is assigned before the operations are done. Because this can get confusing, it's best to limit these operators to simple expressions.

The order of precedence for arithmetic operations

1. Increment and decrement
2. Positive and negative
3. Multiplication, division, and remainder
4. Addition and subtraction

Example 1: Code that calculates a discounted price

Using the default order of precedence

```
double discountPercent = .2;              // 20% discount
double price = 100;                       // $100 price
price = price * 1 - discountPercent;      // price = $99.8
```

Using parentheses that specify the order of precedence

```
price = price * (1 - discountPercent);  // price = $80
```

Example 2: Code that calculates the current value of a monthly investment

Using parentheses that specify the order of precedence

```
double currentValue = 5000;           // current value of investment account
double monthlyInvestment = 100;       // amount added each month
double yearlyInterestRate = .12;      // yearly interest rate

currentValue = (currentValue + monthlyInvestment) *
               (1 + (yearlyInterestRate/12));
```

Without using parentheses

```
currentValue += monthlyInvestment;                       // add investment
double monthlyInterestRate = yearlyInterestRate / 12;
double monthlyInterest = currentValue * monthlyInterestRate;
currentValue += monthlyInterest;                         // add interest
```

Example 3: Prefixed and postfixed increment and decrement operators

```
int a = 5;
int b = 5;
int y = ++a;      // a = 6, y = 6
int z = b++;      // b = 6, z = 5
```

Description

- Unless parentheses are used, the operations in an expression take place from left to right in the *order of precedence*.
- To specify the sequence of operations, you can use parentheses. Then, the operations in the innermost sets of parentheses are done first, followed by the operations in the next sets, and so on.
- When you use an increment or decrement operator as a *prefix* to a variable, the variable is incremented or decremented and then the result is assigned. But when you use an increment or decrement operator as a *postfix* to a variable, the result is assigned and then the variable is incremented or decremented.

Figure 3-6 How to work with the order of precedence

How to work with casting

As you develop Java programs, you'll frequently need to convert data from one data type to another. To do that, you use a technique called *casting*, which is summarized in figure 3-7.

As you can see, Java provides for two types of casting. *Implicit casts* are performed automatically and can be used to convert data with a less precise type to a more precise type. This is called a *widening conversion* because the new type is always wide enough to hold the original value. For instance, the first statement in this figure causes an integer value to be converted to a double value.

Java will also perform an implicit cast on the values in an arithmetic expression if some of the values have more precise data types than other values. This is illustrated by the next three statements in this figure. Here, the variables d, i, and j are used in an arithmetic expression. Notice that d is declared with the double data type, while i and j are declared with the int data type. Because of that, both i and j will be converted to double values when this expression is evaluated.

A *narrowing conversion* is one that casts data from a more precise data type to a less precise data type. With this type of conversion, the less precise data type may not be wide enough to hold the original value. In that case, you must use an *explicit cast*.

To perform an explicit cast, you code the data type in parentheses before the variable that you want to convert. When you do this, you should realize that you may lose some information. This is illustrated by the first example in this figure that performs an explicit cast. Here, a double value of 93.75 is cast to an int value of 93. An explicit cast is required in this example, however, because Java won't automatically cast a double value to an integer value since an integer value is less precise.

When you use explicit casting in an arithmetic expression, the casting is done before the arithmetic operations. This is illustrated by the last two examples of explicit casts. In the last example, two integer types are cast to double types before the division is done so the result will have decimal places if they are needed. Without explicit casting, the expression would return an integer value that would then be cast to a double.

When you code an explicit cast, an exception may occur at runtime if the JRE isn't able to perform the cast. As a result, you should use an explicit cast only when you're sure that the JRE will be able to perform the cast.

Although you typically cast between numeric data types, you can also cast between the int and char types. That's because every char value corresponds to an int value that identifies it in the Unicode character set. Since there's no possible loss of data, you can implicitly cast between these data types. However, if you prefer, you can also code these casts explicitly.

How implicit casting works

Casting from less precise to more precise data types

byte→short→int→long→float→double

Examples

```
double grade = 93;                  // convert int to double

double d = 95.0;
int i = 86, j = 91;
double average = (d+i+j)/3;         // convert i and j to double values
                                    // average = 90.666666...
```

How to code an explicit cast

Syntax

```
(type) expression
```

Examples

```
int grade = (int) 93.75;            // convert double to int (grade = 93)

double d = 95.0;
int i = 86, j = 91;
double average = ((int)d+i+j)/3;    // convert d to int value (average = 90)

double result = (double) i / (double) j;    // result has decimal places
```

How to cast between char and int types

```
char letterChar = 65;               // convert int to char (letterChar = 'A')
char letterChar2 = (char) 65;       // this works too
int letterInt = 'A';                // convert char to int (letterInt = 65)
int letterInt2 = (int) 'A';         // this works too
```

Description

- If you assign a less precise data type to a more precise data type, Java automatically converts the less precise data type to the more precise data type. This can be referred to as an *implicit cast* or a *widening conversion.*
- When you code an arithmetic expression, Java implicitly casts the less precise data types to the most precise data type.
- To code an assignment statement that assigns a more precise data type to a less precise data type, you must use parentheses to specify the less precise data type. This can be referred to as an *explicit cast* or a *narrowing conversion.*
- You can also use an explicit cast in an arithmetic expression. Then, the casting is done before the arithmetic operations.
- Since each char value has a corresponding int value, you can implicitly or explicitly cast between these types.

Figure 3-7 How to work with casting

How to use Java classes for working with data types

As you learned in chapter 2, Java provides hundreds of classes that include methods that you can use in your programs. Now, you'll learn about four of the classes that you'll use often when working with data types.

How to use the NumberFormat class

When you use numeric values in a program, you often need to format them. For example, you may want to apply a standard currency format to a double value. To do that, you need to add a dollar sign and commas and to display just two decimal places. Similarly, you may want to display a double value in a standard percent format. To do that, you need to add a percent sign and move the decimal point two digits to the right.

To do this type of formatting, Java provides the NumberFormat class, which is summarized in figure 3-8. Since this class is part of the java.text package, you'll usually want to include an import statement for this class before you begin working with it.

Once you import this class, you can call one of its static methods to return a NumberFormat object. As you learned in chapter 2, you can call static methods directly from a class. In other words, you code the name of the class, followed by the dot operator, followed by the method. For instance, the first example calls the static getCurrencyInstance method directly from the NumberFormat class.

Once you use a static method to return a NumberFormat object, you can call non-static methods from that object. To do that, you code the name of the object, followed by the dot operator, followed by the method. For instance, the first example calls the non-static format method from the NumberFormat object named currency. This returns a string that consists of a dollar sign plus the value of the price variable with two decimal places. In this format, negative numbers are enclosed in parentheses.

The second example shows how to format numbers with the percent format. The main difference between the first and second examples is that you use the getPercentInstance method to create a NumberFormat object that has the default percent format. Then, you can use the format method of this object to format a number as a percent. In this format, negative numbers have a leading minus sign.

The third example shows how to format numbers with the number format, and how to set the number of decimal places for a NumberFormat object. Here, the format is changed from the default of three decimal places to just one decimal place. In this format, negative numbers also have a leading minus sign.

The fourth example shows how you can use one statement to create a NumberFormat object and use its format method. Although this example accomplishes the same task as the second example, it doesn't create a variable for the NumberFormat object that you can use later in the program. As a result, you should only use code like this when you need to format just one number.

The NumberFormat class

```
java.text.NumberFormat
```

Three static methods of the NumberFormat class

Method	Returns a NumberFormat object that ...
`getCurrencyInstance()`	Has the default currency format ($99,999.99).
`getPercentInstance()`	Has the default percent format (99%).
`getNumberInstance()`	Has the default number format (99,999.999).

Three methods of a NumberFormat object

Method	Description
`format(anyNumberType)`	Returns a String object that has the format specified by the NumberFormat object.
`setMinimumFractionDigits(int)`	Sets the minimum number of decimal places.
`setMaximumFractionDigits(int)`	Sets the maximum number of decimal places.

Example 1: The currency format

```
double price = 11.575;
NumberFormat currency = NumberFormat.getCurrencyInstance();
String priceString = currency.format(price);         // returns $11.58
```

Example 2: The percent format

```
double majority = .505;
NumberFormat percent = NumberFormat.getPercentInstance();
String majorityString = percent.format(majority);    // returns 50%
```

Example 3: The number format with one decimal place

```
double miles = 15341.253;
NumberFormat number = NumberFormat.getNumberInstance();
number.setMaximumFractionDigits(1);
String milesString = number.format(miles);           // returns 15,341.3
```

Example 4: Two NumberFormat methods that are coded in one statement

```
String majorityString = NumberFormat.getPercentInstance().format(majority);
```

Description

- You can use one of the three static methods of the NumberFormat class to create a NumberFormat object. Then, you can use the methods of that object to format one or more numbers.
- When you use the format method, the result is automatically rounded by using a rounding technique called half-even. This means that the number is rounded up if the preceding digit is odd, but the extra decimal places are truncated if the preceding digit is even.
- Since the NumberFormat class is in the java.text package, you'll want to include an import statement when you use this class.

Figure 3-8 How to use the NumberFormat class

When you use the format method of a NumberFormat object, the numbers are automatically rounded using a technique called *half-even*. This technique rounds up if the preceding digit is odd, but rounds down if the preceding digit is even. If, for example, the currency format is used for a value of 123.455, the formatted result is $123.46, which is what you would expect. But if the value is 123.445, the result is $123.44. Although this is okay for many applications, it can cause problems in others. You'll learn more about this later in this chapter.

How to use the Math class

The Math class provides a few dozen methods for working with numeric data types. Some of the most useful ones for business applications are presented in figure 3-9.

The first group of examples shows how to use the round method. Here, the first statement rounds a double type to a long type, and the second statement rounds a float type to an int type. Note, however, that this method only rounds to an integer value so it's not that useful.

The second group of examples shows how to use the pow method to raise the first argument to the power of the second argument. This method returns a double value and accepts two double arguments. However, since Java automatically converts any arguments of a less precise numeric type to a double, the pow method accepts all of the numeric types. In this example, the first statement is equal to 2^2, the second statement is equal to 2^3, and the third and fourth statements are equal to 5^2.

In general, the methods of the Math class work the way you would expect. Sometimes, though, you may need to cast numeric types to get the methods to work the way you want them to. For example, the pow method returns a double type. So if you want to return an int type, you need to cast the double type to an int type as shown in the fourth pow example.

The third group of examples shows how to use the sqrt method to get the square root of a number, and the fourth group shows how to use the max and min methods to return the greater or lesser of two values. If you study these examples, you shouldn't have any trouble understanding how they work.

The fifth group of examples shows how to use the random method to generate random numbers. Since this method returns a random double value greater than or equal to 0.0 and less than 1.0, you can return any range of values by multiplying the random number by another number. In this example, the first statement returns a random double value greater than or equal to 0.0 and less than 100.0. Then, the second statement casts this double value to a long data type. A routine like this can be useful when you want to generate random values for testing a program.

If you have the right mathematical background, you shouldn't have any trouble using these or any of the other Math methods. If you've taken a course in trigonometry, for example, you should be able to understand the trigonometric methods that the Math class provides.

The Math class

```
java.lang.Math
```

Common static methods of the Math class

Method	Description
`round(floatOrDouble)`	Returns the closest long value to a double value or the closest int value to a float value. The result has no decimal places.
`pow(number, power)`	Returns a double value of a double argument (number) that is raised to the power of another double argument (power).
`sqrt(number)`	Returns a double value that's the square root of the double argument.
`max(a, b)`	Returns the greater of two float, double, int, or long arguments.
`min(a, b)`	Returns the lesser of two float, double, int, or long arguments.
`random()`	Returns a random double value greater than or equal to 0.0 and less than 1.0.

Example 1: The round method

```
long result = Math.round(1.667);        // result is 2
int result = Math.round(1.49F);         // result is 1
```

Example 2: The pow method

```
double result = Math.pow(2, 2);         // result is 4.0 (2*2)
double result = Math.pow(2, 3);         // result is 8.0 (2*2*2)
double result = Math.pow(5, 2);         // result is 25.0 (5 squared)
int result = (int) Math.pow(5, 2);      // result is 25 (5 squared)
```

Example 3: The sqrt method

```
double result = Math.sqrt(20.25);       // result is 4.5
```

Example 4: The max and min methods

```
int x = 67;
int y = 23;
int max = Math.max(x, y);               // max is 67
int min = Math.min(x, y);               // min is 23
```

Example 5: The random method

```
double x = Math.random() * 100;    // result is a value >= 0.0 and < 100.0
long result = (long) x;            // converts the result from double to long
```

Description

- You can use the static methods of the Math class to perform common arithmetic operations. This figure summarizes the methods that are the most useful for business applications.
- When a method requires one or more arguments, you code them between the parentheses, separating multiple arguments with commas.
- In some cases, you need to cast the result to the data type that you want.

Figure 3-9 How to use the Math class

How to use the Integer and Double classes

Figure 3-10 shows how to use a few of the constructors and static methods that are provided by the Integer and Double classes. Since these classes can be used to create objects that wrap around the primitive types, they are sometimes referred to as *wrapper classes*. Wrapper classes also exist for the other six primitive data types.

The first group of statements in this figure shows how to create Integer and Double objects that can store int and double data types. This is useful when you want to provide an int or double data type as an argument to a method, but the method requires that the argument be an object, not a data type. You'll see how this works in a later chapter. Once you create an Integer or Double object, you can use any of the methods of these classes to work with the data it contains.

Note, however, that these classes also provide static methods that you can use without creating objects. For instance, the second group of statements in this figure shows how to use the static toString method to convert a primitive type to a string. Here, the first statement converts the int variable named counter to a string and returns the value to a string variable named counterString. The second statement converts the double variable named price to a string and returns that value to the string variable named priceString.

Similarly, the third group of statements shows how to use the static parse methods to convert strings to primitive types. Here, the first statement uses the parseInt method of the Integer class to convert a string to an int data type. The second statement uses the parseDouble method of the Double class to convert a string to a double data type. Once these statements have been executed, you can use the quantity and price variables in arithmetic expressions.

But what happens if the string contains a non-numeric value like "ten" that can't be parsed to an int or double type? In that case, the parseInt or parseDouble method will cause a runtime error known as an exception. Using Java terminology, you can say that the method will *throw an exception*. In chapter 5, you'll learn how to *catch* the exceptions that are thrown by these methods.

Constructors for the Integer and Double classes

Constructor	Description
`Integer(int)`	Creates an Integer object from an int data type.
`Double(double)`	Creates a Double object from a double data type.

Two static methods of the Integer class

Method	Description
`parseInt(stringName)`	Attempts to convert the String object that's supplied as an argument to an int type. If successful, it returns the int value. If unsuccessful, it throws an exception.
`toString(intName)`	Converts the int value that's supplied as an argument to a String object and returns that String object.

Two static methods of the Double class

Method	Description
`parseDouble(stringName)`	Attempts to convert the String object that's supplied as an argument to a double type. If successful, it returns the double value. If unsuccessful, it throws an exception.
`toString(doubleName)`	Converts the double value that's supplied as an argument to a String object and returns that String object.

How to create Integer and Double objects

```
Integer quantityIntegerObject = new Integer(quantity);
Double priceDoubleObject = new Double(price);
```

How to use static methods to convert primitive types to String objects

```
String counterString = Integer.toString(counter);
String priceString = Double.toString(price);
```

How to use static methods to convert String objects to primitive types

```
int quantity = Integer.parseInt(quantityString);
double price = Double.parseDouble(priceString);
```

Description

- The Integer and Double classes are known as *wrapper classes* since they can be used to construct Integer and Double objects that contain (wrap around) int and double values. This can be useful when you need to pass an int or double value to a method that only accepts objects, not primitive data types.
- The Integer and Double classes also provide static methods that you can use for converting values from these data types to strings and vice versa.
- If the parseInt and parseDouble methods can't successfully parse the string, they will cause an error to occur. In Java terminology, this is known as *throwing an exception*. You'll learn how to handle or *catch* exceptions in chapter 5.
- Every primitive type has a wrapper class that works like the Integer and Double classes.

Figure 3-10 How to use the Integer and Double classes

The formatted Invoice application

To illustrate some of the skills you've just learned, figure 3-11 shows the console and code for an enhanced version of the Invoice application that was presented in chapter 2. This time, the application does a few more calculations and formats the results before displaying them. You can see the results for one user entry in the console that's in this figure.

The code for the application

The shaded code in this figure identifies the primary changes to the Invoice application of the last chapter. First, two new values are calculated. Sales tax is calculated by multiplying the total before tax by the SALES_TAX_PCT constant that's declared and initialized at the beginning of the main method. And the invoice total is calculated by adding the sales tax to the total before tax.

Second, currency and percent objects are created by using the methods of the NumberFormat class. Then, the format methods of these objects are used to format the five values that have been calculated by this application. This shows how one currency object can be used to format two or more values. The result of each use of the format method is a string that is added to the message that eventually gets displayed.

Although this application is now taking on a more professional look, you should remember that it still has some shortcomings. First, it doesn't handle the exception that's thrown if the user doesn't enter a valid number at the console. You'll learn how to fix that problem in chapter 5. Second, because of the way rounding works with the NumberFormat methods, the results may not always come out the way you want them to. You'll learn more about that next.

The console for the formatted Invoice application

```
Enter subtotal:    150.50
Discount percent:  10%
Discount amount:   $15.05
Total before tax:  $135.45
Sales tax:         $6.77
Invoice total:     $142.22

Continue? (y/n):
```

The code for the formatted Invoice application

```
import java.util.Scanner;
import java.text.NumberFormat;

public class InvoiceApp {
    public static void main(String[] args) {

        final double SALES_TAX_PCT = .05;

        Scanner sc = new Scanner(System.in);
        String choice = "y";
        while (choice.equalsIgnoreCase("y")) {
            // get the input from the user
            System.out.print("Enter subtotal:    ");
            double subtotal = sc.nextDouble();

            // calculate the results
            double discountPercent = 0.0;
            if (subtotal >= 100)
                discountPercent = .1;
            else
                discountPercent = 0.0;
            double discountAmount = subtotal * discountPercent;
            double totalBeforeTax = subtotal - discountAmount;
            double salesTax = totalBeforeTax * SALES_TAX_PCT;
            double total = totalBeforeTax + salesTax;

            // format and display the results
            NumberFormat currency = NumberFormat.getCurrencyInstance();
            NumberFormat percent = NumberFormat.getPercentInstance();
            String message =
                "Discount percent: " + percent.format(discountPercent) + "\n"
              + "Discount amount:  " + currency.format(discountAmount) + "\n"
              + "Total before tax: " + currency.format(totalBeforeTax) + "\n"
              + "Sales tax:        " + currency.format(salesTax) + "\n"
              + "Invoice total:    " + currency.format(total) + "\n";
            System.out.println(message);

            // see if the user wants to continue
            System.out.print("Continue? (y/n): ");
            choice = sc.next();
            System.out.println();
        }
    }
}
```

Figure 3-11 The formatted Invoice application

A bug in the arithmetic

The console at the top of figure 3-12 shows more output from the Invoice application in figure 3-11. But wait! The results for a subtotal entry of 100.05 don't add up. If the discount amount is $10.00, the total before tax should be $90.05, but it's $90.04. What's going on?

How to debug the application

To analyze data problems like this, you can add *debugging statements* to a program like the ones in figure 3-12. These statements display the unformatted values of the result fields so you can see what they are before they're formatted. This is illustrated by the console at the bottom of this figure, which shows the results for the same entries as the ones in the console at the top of this figure.

If you look at the unformatted results, you can easily see what's going on. Because of the way NumberFormat rounding works, the discount amount value of 10.005 and the total before tax value of 90.045 aren't rounded up. However, the invoice total value of 94.54725 is rounded up. With this extra information, you know that everything is working the way it's supposed to, even though you're not displaying the results you want.

Although an error like this may be acceptable in some applications, it is unacceptable in most business applications. And for those applications, you need to provide solutions that deliver the results that you want. (Imagine getting an invoice that didn't add up!)

One solution is to write your own code that does the rounding so you don't need to use the NumberFormat class to do the rounding for you. As you go through this book, you'll learn how to use classes and methods that will help you do that. However, that still doesn't deal with the fact that some decimal fractions can't be accurately represented by floating-point numbers. To solve that problem as well as other data problems, the best solution is to use the BigDecimal class that you'll learn about next.

The console with an arithmetic bug

```
Enter subtotal:    100.05
Discount percent: 10%
Discount amount:   $10.00
Total before tax: $90.04
Sales tax:         $4.50
Invoice total:     $94.55

Continue? (y/n):
```

Debugging statements that can be added to the code

```
String debugMessage = "\nUNFORMATTED RESULTS\n"
                    + "Discount percent: " + discountPercent + "\n"
                    + "Discount amount:  " + discountAmount + "\n"
                    + "Total before tax: " + totalBeforeTax + "\n"
                    + "Sales tax:        " + salesTax + "\n"
                    + "Invoice total:    " + total + "\n"
                    + "\nFORMATTED RESULTS";
System.out.println(debugMessage);
```

The console with debugging information

```
Enter subtotal:    100.05

UNFORMATTED RESULTS
Discount percent: 0.1
Discount amount:  10.005
Total before tax: 90.045
Sales tax:        4.50225
Invoice total:    94.54725

FORMATTED RESULTS
Discount percent: 10%
Discount amount:  $10.00
Total before tax: $90.04
Sales tax:        $4.50
Invoice total:    $94.55

Continue? (y/n):
```

How to use the BigDecimal class

The BigDecimal class is designed to solve two types of problems that are associated with floating-point numbers. First, the BigDecimal class can be used to exactly represent decimal numbers. Second, it can be used to work with numbers that have more than 16 significant digits.

The constructors and methods

Figure 3-13 summarizes a few of the constructors that you can use with the BigDecimal class. These constructors accept an int, double, long, or string argument and create a BigDecimal object from it. Because floating-point numbers are limited to 16 significant digits and because these numbers don't always represent decimal numbers exactly, it's often best to create BigDecimal objects from strings rather than doubles.

Once you create a BigDecimal object, you can use its methods to work with the data. In this figure, for example, you can see some of the BigDecimal methods that are most useful in business applications. Here, the add, subtract, multiply, and divide methods let you perform those operations. The compareTo method lets you compare the values in two BigDecimal objects. And the toString method lets you convert the value of a BigDecimal object to a string.

This figure also includes the setScale method, which lets you set the number of decimal places (*scale*) for the value in a BigDecimal object as well as the rounding mode. For example, you can use the setScale method to return a number that's rounded to two decimal places like this:

```
salesTax = salesTax.setScale(2, RoundingMode.HALF_UP);
```

In this example, RoundingMode.HALF_UP is a value in the RoundingMode enumeration that's summarized in this figure. The scale and rounding mode arguments work the same for the divide method.

Enumerations are similar to classes, and you'll learn more about them in chapter 10. For now, you can code the rounding mode as HALF_UP because it provides the type of rounding that is normal for business applications. However, you need to import the RoundingMode enumeration at the start of the application unless you want to qualify the rounding mode like this:

```
java.math.RoundingMode.HALF_UP
```

If you look at the API documentation for the BigDecimal class, you'll see that it provides several other methods that you may want to use. This class also provides many other features that you may want to become more familiar with.

The BigDecimal class

`java.math.BigDecimal`

Constructors of the BigDecimal class

Constructor	Description
`BigDecimal(int)`	Creates a new BigDecimal object with the specified int value.
`BigDecimal(double)`	Creates a new BigDecimal object with the specified double value.
`BigDecimal(long)`	Creates a new BigDecimal object with the specified long value.
`BigDecimal(String)`	Creates a new BigDecimal object with the specified String object. Because of the limitations of floating-point numbers, it's often best to create BigDecimal objects from strings.

Methods of the BigDecimal class

Methods	Description
`add(value)`	Returns the value of this BigDecimal object after the specified BigDecimal value has been added to it.
`compareTo(value)`	Compares the value of the BigDecimal object with the value of the specified BigDecimal object and returns -1 if less, 0 if equal, and 1 if greater.
`divide(value, scale, rounding-mode)`	Returns the value of this BigDecimal object divided by the value of the specified BigDecimal object, sets the specified scale, and uses the specified rounding mode.
`multiply(value)`	Returns the value of this BigDecimal object multiplied by the specified BigDecimal value.
`setScale(scale, rounding-mode)`	Sets the scale and rounding mode for the BigDecimal object.
`subtract(value)`	Returns the value of this BigDecimal object after the specified BigDecimal value has been subtracted from it.
`toString()`	Converts the BigDecimal value to a string.

The RoundingMode enumeration

`java.math.RoundingMode`

Two of the values in the RoundingMode enumeration

Values	Description
`HALF_UP`	Round towards the "nearest neighbor" unless both neighbors are equidistant, in which case round up.
`HALF_EVEN`	Round towards the "nearest neighbor" unless both neighbors are equidistant, in which case round toward the even neighbor.

Description

- The BigDecimal class provides a way to perform accurate decimal calculations in Java. It also provides a way to store numbers with more than 16 significant digits.

Figure 3-13 The constructors and methods for the BigDecimal class

How to use BigDecimal arithmetic

Figure 3-14 shows how you can use BigDecimal arithmetic in the Invoice application. To start, look at the console output when BigDecimal is used. As you can see, this solves both the rounding problem and the floating-point problem so it now works the way you want it to.

To use BigDecimal arithmetic in the Invoice application, you start by coding an import statement that imports all of the classes and enumerations of the java.math package. This includes both the BigDecimal class and the RoundingMode enumeration. Then, you use the constructors and methods of the BigDecimal class to create the BigDecimal objects, do the calculations, and round the results when necessary.

In this figure, the code starts by constructing BigDecimal objects from the subtotal and discountPercent variables, which are double types. To avoid conversion problems, though, the toString method of the Double class is used to convert the subtotal and discountPercent values to strings that are used in the BigDecimal constructors.

Since the user may enter subtotal values that contain more than two decimal places, the setScale method is used to round the subtotal entry after it has been converted to a BigDecimal object. However, since the discountPercent variable only contains two decimal places, it isn't rounded. From this point on, all of the numbers are stored as BigDecimal objects and all of the calculations are done with BigDecimal methods.

In the statements that follow, only discount amount and sales tax need to be rounded. That's because they're calculated using multiplication, which can result in extra decimal places. In contrast, the other numbers (total before tax and total) don't need to be rounded because they're calculated using subtraction and addition. Once the calculations and rounding are done, you can safely use the NumberFormat objects and methods to format the BigDecimal objects for display.

When working with BigDecimal objects, you may sometimes need to create one BigDecimal object from another BigDecimal object. However, you can't supply a BigDecimal object to the constructor of the BigDecimal class. Instead, you need to call the toString method from the BigDecimal object to convert the BigDecimal object to a String object. Then, you can pass that String object as the argument of the constructor as illustrated by the last statement in this figure.

Is this a lot of work just to do simple business arithmetic? Relative to some other languages, you would have to say that it is. In fact, it's fair to say that this is a weakness of Java. However, once you get the hang of working with the BigDecimal class, you should be able to solve floating-point and rounding problems with ease.

The Invoice application output when BigDecimal arithmetic is used

```
Enter subtotal:    100.05
Subtotal:          $100.05
Discount percent: 10%
Discount amount:   $10.01
Total before tax: $90.04
Sales tax:         $4.50
Invoice total:     $94.54

Continue? (y/n):
```

The import statement that's required for BigDecimal arithmetic

```
import java.math.*;  // imports all classes and enumerations in java.math
```

The code for using BigDecimal arithmetic in the Invoice application

```
// convert subtotal and discount percent to BigDecimal
BigDecimal decimalSubtotal = new BigDecimal(Double.toString(subtotal));
decimalSubtotal = decimalSubtotal.setScale(2, RoundingMode.HALF_UP);
BigDecimal decimalDiscountPercent =
    new BigDecimal(Double.toString(discountPercent));

// calculate discount amount
BigDecimal discountAmount =
    decimalSubtotal.multiply(decimalDiscountPercent);
discountAmount = discountAmount.setScale(2, RoundingMode.HALF_UP);

// calculate total before tax, sales tax, and total
BigDecimal totalBeforeTax = decimalSubtotal.subtract(discountAmount);
BigDecimal salesTaxPercent = new BigDecimal(SALES_TAX_PCT);
BigDecimal salesTax = salesTaxPercent.multiply(totalBeforeTax);
salesTax = salesTax.setScale(2, RoundingMode.HALF_UP);
BigDecimal total = totalBeforeTax.add(salesTax);
```

How to create a BigDecimal object from another BigDecimal object

```
BigDecimal total2 = new BigDecimal(total.toString());
```

Description

- With this code, all of the result values are stored in BigDecimal objects, and all of the results have two decimal places that have been rounded correctly when needed.
- Once the results have been calculated, you can use the NumberFormat methods to format the values in the BigDecimal objects without any fear of rounding problems. However, the methods of the NumberFormat object limits the results to 16 significant digits.

Figure 3-14 How to use BigDecimal arithmetic

Perspective

If this chapter has succeeded, you should now be able to work with whatever primitive data types you need in your applications. You should be able to use the NumberFormat, Math, Double, and Integer classes whenever you need them. And you should be able to use the BigDecimal class to solve the problems that are associated with floating-point numbers.

Summary

- Java provides eight *primitive data types* to store *integer*, *floating-point*, *character*, and *boolean* values.
- *Variables* store data that changes as a program runs. *Constants* store data that doesn't change as a program runs. You use *assignment statements* to assign values to variables.
- You can use *arithmetic operators* to form *arithmetic expressions*, and you can use some *assignment operators* as a shorthand for some types of arithmetic expressions.
- Java can *implicitly cast* a less precise data type to a more precise data type. Java also lets you *explicitly cast* a more precise data type to a less precise data type.
- You can use the NumberFormat class to apply standard currency, percent, and number formats to any of the primitive numeric types.
- You can use the static methods of the Math class to perform mathematical operations such as rounding numbers and calculating square roots.
- You can use the constructors of the Double and Integer *wrapper classes* to create objects that wrap double and int values. You can also use the static methods of these classes to convert strings to numbers and vice versa.
- You can use the constructors of the BigDecimal class to create objects that store decimal values that aren't limited to 16 significant digits. Then, you can use the methods of these objects to do the calculations that your programs require.

Exercise 3-1 Test the Invoice application

In this exercise, you'll test the formatted Invoice application that's presented in figure 3-11.

1. Open the project named ch03_ex1_InvoiceFormatted that's in the ex_starts directory. Then, review the code for this project.
2. Run the application and test it. As you test the application, enter the two subtotal values that are shown in figures 3-11 and 3-12 to see how the program works and to see what the problems are.
3. To better understand what is happening, add debugging statements like those in figure 3-12 so the program displays two sets of data for each entry: first the unformatted output, then the formatted output. When you add debugging statements, you should try to do it in a way that makes them easy to remove when you're through debugging.
4. Test the application again with a range of entries so you clearly see what the data problems are when you study the unformatted and formatted results.

Exercise 3-2 Modify the Test Score application

In this exercise, you'll use some of the skills that you learned in this chapter to modify the Test Score application.

1. Open the project named ch03_ex2_TestScore that's in the ex_starts directory. Then, review the code for this project and run it until you understand how it works.
2. Use the += operator to increase the scoreCount and scoreTotal variables. Then, test this to make sure that it works.
3. As the user enters test scores, use the methods of the Math class to keep track of the minimum and maximum scores. When the user enters 999 to end the program, display these scores at the end of the other output data. Now, test these changes to make sure that they work. (This step can be challenging if you're new to programming, but you'll learn a lot by doing it.)
4. Change the variable that you use to total the scores from a double to an int data type. Then, use casting to cast the score count and score total to doubles as you calculate the average score and save that average as a double. Now, test that change.
5. Use the NumberFormat class to round the average score to one decimal place before displaying it at the end of the program. Then, test this change. Note that the rounding method that's used doesn't matter in a program like this.

Exercise 3-3 Create a new application

In this exercise, you'll develop an application that will give you a chance to use the arithmetic skills you learned in this chapter. This application asks the user to enter a file size in megabytes (MB) and a download speed in megabytes per second. Then, it calculates how long it takes to download that file. The output from this application should look something like this:

```
Welcome to the Download Time Estimator

Enter file size (MB): 800
Enter download speed (MB/sec): 1

This download will take approximately 0 hours 13 minutes 20 seconds

Continue? (y/n): n
```

1. Start a new project named ch03_ex3_DownloadTime that contains a class named DownloadTimeApp that has a main method.
2. Add the code that gets input from the user and displays output. To do that, you can copy code from another similar application and modify it so it's appropriate for this application.
3. Add the code that calculates the hours, minutes, and seconds needed to download the specified file size at the specified download speed. To do that, start by calculating the download time in seconds and then rounding that value to an integer. Then, divide the total seconds by the number of seconds in an hour to get the number of hours, and divide the remaining seconds by the number of seconds in a minute to get the number of minutes. Note that this application only calculates an approximate value, so you don't need to use BigDecimal arithmetic.
4. Test the application to make sure it works correctly.

Exercise 3-4 Use BigDecimal arithmetic

This exercise has you modify the Test Score application so it uses BigDecimal arithmetic.

1. Open the project named ch03_ex4_TestScore in the ex_starts directory.
2. Modify the code so it uses BigDecimal arithmetic to calculate the average test score with the result rounded to one decimal place. Note that because the scoreCount and scoreTotal variables are ints, you don't need to create the BigDecimal objects from strings.
3. Test this change with a range of values to make sure it works.

4

How to code control statements

In chapter 2, you learned how to code simple if and while statements to control the execution of your applications. Now, you'll learn more about coding these statements. You'll learn how to code the other control statements that Java offers. And you'll learn how to code your own static methods, which will help you divide your applications into manageable parts.

How to code Boolean expressions

In chapter 2, you learned how to code the *Boolean expressions* that control the operation of your control statements. These are expressions that evaluate to either true or false. To start, this topic repeats some of the information that you learned before, but in a larger context.

How to compare primitive data types

Figure 4-1 shows how to use the six *relational operators* to code a Boolean expression that compares *operands* that are primitive data types. In a Boolean expression, an operand can be a literal, a variable, an arithmetic expression, or a keyword such as true or false.

The first three expressions in this figure use the equality operator (==) to test if the two operands are equal. To use this operator, you must code two equals signs instead of one. That's because a single equals sign is used for assignment statements. As a result, if you try to code a Boolean expression with a single equals sign, your code won't compile.

The next expression uses the inequality operator (!=) to test if a variable is not equal to a numeric literal. The two expressions after that use the greater than operator (>) to test if a variable is greater than a numeric literal and the less than operator (<) to test if one variable is less than another. And the two expressions after that use the greater than or equal operator (>=) and less than or equal operator (<=) to compare operands.

The last two expressions in this figure illustrate that you don't need the == or != operator when you use a boolean variable in an expression. That's because, by definition, a boolean variable evaluates to a boolean value. As a result,

```
isValid == true
```

is the same as

```
isValid
```

and

```
!isValid
```

is the same as

```
isValid == false
```

Although the first and last expressions may be easier for a beginning programmer to understand, the second and third expressions are commonly used by professional programmers.

When comparing numeric values, you usually compare values of the same data type. However, if you compare different types of numeric values, Java will automatically cast the less precise numeric type to the more precise type. For example, if you compare an int type to a double type, the int type will be cast to the double type before the comparison is made.

Relational operators

Operator	Name	Description
`==`	Equality	Returns a true value if both operands are equal.
`!=`	Inequality	Returns a true value if the left and right operands are not equal.
`>`	Greater Than	Returns a true value if the left operand is greater than the right operand.
`<`	Less Than	Returns a true value if the left operand is less than the right operand.
`>=`	Greater Than Or Equal	Returns a true value if the left operand is greater than or equal to the right operand.
`<=`	Less Than Or Equal	Returns a true value if the left operand is less than or equal to the right operand.

Examples of Boolean expressions

```
discountPercent == 2.3    // equal to a numeric literal
letter == 'y'             // equal to a char literal
isValid == false          // equal to the false value

subtotal != 0             // not equal to a numeric literal

years > 0                 // greater than a numeric literal
i < months                // less than a variable

subtotal >= 500           // greater than or equal to a numeric literal
quantity <= reorderPoint  // less than or equal to a variable

isValid                   // isValid is equal to true
!isValid                  // isValid is equal to false
```

Description

- You can use the relational operators to create a Boolean expression that compares two operands and returns a boolean value that is either true or false.
- If you compare two numeric operands that are not of the same type, Java will convert the less precise operand to the type of the more precise operand before doing the comparison.
- By definition, a boolean variable evaluates to a boolean value of true or false.

Figure 4-1 How to compare primitive data types

How to compare strings

As you learned in chapter 2, a string is an object, not a primitive data type, so you can't use the relational operators to compare strings. Instead, you must use the equals or equalsIgnoreCase method of the String class as shown by the expressions at the start of figure 4-2.

Both of these methods require an argument that provides the String object or literal that you want to compare with the current object. The difference between the two is that the equals method is case-sensitive while the equalsIgnoreCase method is not.

If you call the equals or equalsIgnoreCase method from a string that contains a null, however, Java will throw an exception. To avoid that, you can use the equality operator (==) or the inequality operator (!=) to check whether a string contains a null before you use the equals or equalsIgnoreCase method. This is illustrated by the last two expressions at the start of this figure.

The next block of code shows what happens when you test two strings for equality with the == operator. Here, the code asks you to enter values for two different strings. No matter what values you enter, though, the equals comparison that follows will be false. If, for example, you enter "abc" for both strings, the equals test will be false.

That's because all object variables are *reference types*, which means that they don't actually contain the data like primitive types do. Instead, reference types refer to (or point to) the data, which is held in another area of internal storage. For these types, the equality and inequality operators test to see whether the variables refer to the same object. If they do, they're considered equal. But if they refer to two different objects, they're considered unequal, even if the objects contain the same values.

What happens if you issue this statement?

```
string1 = string2;
```

The variable named string1 now refers to the same data that string2 refers to. As a result, the Boolean expression

```
string1 == string2
```

will be true because both variables will refer to the same object.

This just makes the point that you shouldn't use the equality and inequality operators to test whether two strings have the same values because these operators don't work that way. Since all objects are reference types, this holds true for other types of objects too. As a result, you'll learn other ways to test objects for equality as you progress through this book.

Two methods of the String class

Method	Description
`equals(String)`	Compares the current String object with the String object specified as the argument and returns a true value if they are equal. This method makes a case-sensitive comparison.
`equalsIgnoreCase(String)`	Works like the equals method but is not case-sensitive.

Expressions that compare two string values

```
firstName.equals("Frank")              // equal to a string literal
firstName.equalsIgnoreCase("Frank")    // equal to a string literal
firstName.equals("")                   // equal to an empty string

!lastName.equals("Jones")              // not equal to a string literal
!code.equalsIgnoreCase(productCode)    // not equal to another string variable

firstName == null                      // equal to a null value
firstName != null                      // not equal to a null value
```

Code that tests whether two strings refer to the same object

```
Scanner sc = new Scanner(System.in);
System.out.print("Enter string1: ");
String string1 = sc.next();
System.out.print("Enter string2: ");
String string2 = sc.next();

if (string1 == string2)        // this will be false no matter what you enter
    System.out.println("string1 = string2");
else
    System.out.println("string1 not = string2");
```

Description

- To test two strings to see whether they contain the same string values, you must call one of the methods of the String object.
- To test whether a string is null, you can use the equality operator (==) or the inequality operator (!=) with the null keyword.
- A string object is a *reference type*, not a primitive data type. That means that a string variable doesn't contain the data like a primitive type does. Instead, a string variable refers to (or points to) the data, which is in another location of computer memory.
- If you use the equality or inequality operator to compare two string variables, Java tests to see whether the two strings refer to the same String object. If they do, the expression is true. If they don't, it's false.

Technical note

- Because Java stores string literals in pools to reduce duplication, the equality and inequality tests for strings may not work as shown above when two String objects are assigned the same literal value.

Figure 4-2 How to compare strings

How to use the logical operators

Figure 4-3 shows how to use the *logical operators* to code a Boolean expression that consists of two or more Boolean expressions. For example, the first expression uses the && operator. As a result, it evaluates to true if both the first expression *and* the second expression evaluate to true. Conversely, the second expression uses the || operator. As a result, it evaluates to true if either the first expression *or* the second expression evaluate to true.

When you use the && and || operators, the second expression is only evaluated if necessary. Because of that, these operators are sometimes referred to as the *short-circuit operators*. To illustrate, suppose the value of subtotal in the first example is less than 250. Then, the first expression evaluates to false. That means that the entire expression will return a false value. As a result, the second expression is not evaluated. Since this is more efficient than always evaluating both expressions, you'll want to use these operators most of the time.

However, there may be times when you want to evaluate both expressions regardless of the value that's returned by the first expression. For example, there may be times when the second expression performs an operation such as incrementing a variable or calling a method. In that case, you can use the & and | operators to make sure that the second expression is evaluated.

You can also use multiple logical operators in the same expression as illustrated by the fifth example. Here, the && and || operators connect three expressions. As a result, the entire expression is true if the first *and* second expressions are true *or* the third expression is true.

When you code this type of expression, the expression is evaluated from left to right based on this order of precedence: arithmetic operations first, followed by relational operations, followed by logical operations. For logical operations, And operations are performed before Or operations. If you need to change this sequence or if there's any doubt about the order of precedence, you can use parentheses to clarify or control this evaluation sequence.

If necessary, you can use the ! operator to reverse the value of an expression. However, this can create code that's difficult to read. As a result, you should avoid using the ! operator whenever possible. For example, instead of coding

```
!(subtotal < 100)
```

you can code

```
subtotal >= 100
```

Both expressions perform the same task, but the second expression is easier to read.

Logical operators

Operator	Name	Description
&&	And	Returns a true value if both expressions are true. This operator only evaluates the second expression if necessary.
||	Or	Returns a true value if either expression is true. This operator only evaluates the second expression if necessary.
&	And	Returns a true value if both expressions are true. This operator always evaluates both expressions.
|	Or	Returns a true value if either expression is true. This operator always evaluates both expressions.
!	Not	Reverses the value of the expression.

Examples

```
subtotal >= 250 && subtotal < 500
timeInService <= 4 || timeInService >= 12

isValid == true & counter++ < years
isValid == true | counter++ < years

(subtotal >= 250 && subtotal < 500) || isValid == true

!(counter++ >= years)
```

Description

- You can use the *logical operators* to create a Boolean expression that combines two or more Boolean expressions.
- Since the && and || operators only evaluate the second expression if necessary, they're sometimes referred to as *short-circuit operators* and are slightly more efficient than the & and | operators.
- By default, Not operations are performed first, followed by And operations, and then Or operations. These operations are performed after arithmetic operations and relational operations.
- You can use parentheses to change the sequence in which the operations will be performed or to clarify the sequence of operations.

Figure 4-3 How to use the logical operators

How to code if/else and switch statements

In chapter 2, you were introduced to the if/else statement, but this topic will expand on that. This topic will also present the switch statement.

How to code if/else statements

Figure 4-4 reviews the use of the *if/else statement* (or just *if statement*). This is Java's implementation of the *selection structure*.

When an if statement is executed, Java begins by evaluating the Boolean expression in the if clause. If it's true, the statements within this clause are executed and the rest of the if/else statement is skipped. If it's false, Java evaluates the first else if clause (if there is one). Then, if its Boolean expression is true, the statements within this else if clause are executed, and the rest of the if/else statement is skipped. Otherwise, Java evaluates the next else if clause.

This continues with any remaining else if clauses. Finally, if none of the clauses contains a Boolean expression that evaluates to true, Java executes the statements in the else clause (if there is one). If none of the Boolean expressions are true and there is no else clause, Java doesn't execute any statements.

Although the syntax indicates that the statements for an if, else if, or else clause must be coded within braces, the braces are optional if the clause contains a single statement. That's the case in the first example in this figure. In contrast, braces are required for the if and else if clauses in the second example.

Whenever you code a set of braces in Java, you are explicitly defining a *block* of code that may contain one or more statements. Then, any variables that are declared within those braces have *block scope*. In other words, they can't be accessed outside of that block. As a result, if you want to access a variable outside of the block, you must declare it before the block. This is illustrated by both the first and second examples.

When coding if statements, it's a common practice to code one if statement within another if statement. This is known as *nesting* if statements, and it's illustrated by the third example in this figure. When you nest if statements, it's a good practice to indent the nested statements and their clauses since this allows the programmer to easily identify where each nested statement begins and ends. In this figure, for example, Java only executes the nested statement if the customer type is "R". Otherwise, it executes the statements in the outer else clause.

Another good coding practice is to code the conditions with a logical structure and in a logical sequence. If necessary, you can also add comments to your code so it's easier to follow. As always, the easier your code is to read and understand, the easier it is to test, debug, and maintain.

The syntax of the if/else statement

```
if (booleanExpression) {statements}
[else if (booleanExpression) {statements}] ...
[else {statements}]
```

Example 1: An if statement with else if and else clauses

```
double discountPercent = 0.0;
if (subtotal >= 100 && subtotal < 200)
    discountPercent = .1;
else if (subtotal >= 200 && subtotal < 300)
    discountPercent = .2;
else if (subtotal >= 300)
    discountPercent = .3;
else
    discountPercent = 0.05;
```

Example 2: An if statement that contains two blocks of code

```
double discountPercent = 0.0;
String shippingMethod = "";
if (customerType.equals("R"))
{                                           // start block
    discountPercent = .1;
    shippingMethod = "UPS";
}                                           // end block
else if (customerType.equals("C")
{                                           // start block
    discountPercent = .2;
    shippingMethod = "Bulk";
}                                           // end block
else
    shippingMethod = "USPS";
```

Example 3: Nested if statements

```
if (customerType.equals("R"))
{
    if (subtotal >= 100)                    // begin nested if
        discountPercent = .2;
    else
        discountPercent =.1;                // end nested if
}
else
    discountPercent = .4;
```

Description

- If a clause in an if/else statement contains just one statement, you don't have to enclose the statement in braces. You can just end the clause with a semicolon. However, this statement can't declare a variable or it won't compile.
- If a clause requires more than one statement, you must enclose the *block* of statements in braces. Then, any variable that is declared within the block has *block scope* so it can only be used within that block.

Figure 4-4 How to code if/else statements

How to code switch statements

Figure 4-5 shows how to work with the *switch statement*. This is the Java implementation of a control structure known as the *case structure*, which lets you code different actions for different cases. The switch statement can sometimes be used in place of an if statement with else if clauses.

Prior to version 1.7 of Java, the switch statement could only be used with expressions that evaluate to an integer. As a result, in early versions of Java, the switch statement had limited use. However, with version 1.7 and later, the switch statement can also be used with expressions that evaluate to a string.

To code a switch statement, you start by coding the switch keyword followed by a switch expression that evaluates to one of the integer types or to a string. After the switch expression, you can code one or more *case labels* that represent the possible values of the switch expression. Then, when the switch expression matches the value specified by the case label, the statements after the label are executed.

You can code the case labels in any sequence, but you should be sure to follow each label with a colon. Then, if the label contains one or more statements, you can code a *break statement* after them to jump to the end of the switch statement. Otherwise, the execution of the program *falls through* to the next case label and executes the statements in that label. The *default label* is an optional label that identifies the statements to execute if none of the case labels are executed.

The first example shows how to code a switch statement that sets the description for a product based on the value of an int variable named productID. Here, the first case label assigns a value of "Hammer" to the productDescription variable if productID is equal to 1. Then, the break statement exits the switch statement. Similarly, the second case label sets the product description to "Box of Nails" if productID is equal to 2 and then exits the switch statement. If productID is equal to something other than 1 or 2, the default case label is executed. Like the other two case labels, this one sets the value of the productDescription variable and then exits the switch statement.

The second example works like the first example, but the switch statement evaluates the value of a String variable named productCode. Here, the first case label assigns a value of "Hammer" to the productDescription variable if productCode is equal to "hm01". Since the switch statement is case-sensitive, this case label is only executed if the productCode variable stores a string with the exact same capitalization. For example, this case isn't executed if productCode is equal to "HM01". Similarly, the second case label sets the product description to "Box of Nails" if productCode is equal to "bn03".

The syntax of the switch statement

```
switch (switchExpression)
{
    case label1:
        statements
        break;
    [case label2:
        statements
        break;] ...
    [default:
        statements
        break;]
}
```

Example 1: A switch statement that uses an integer

```
switch (productID)
{
    case 1:
        productDescription = "Hammer";
        break;
    case 2:
        productDescription = "Box of Nails";
        break;
    default:
        productDescription = "Product not found";
        break;
}
```

Example 2: A switch statement that uses a string

```
switch (productCode)
{
    case "hm01":
        productDescription = "Hammer";
        break;
    case "bn03":
        productDescription = "Box of Nails";
        break;
    default:
        productDescription = "Product not found";
        break;
}
```

Description

- Prior to version 1.7 of Java, the switch statement could only be used with an expression that evaluated to one of these integer types: char, byte, short, or int.
- Starting with version 1.7 of Java, the switch statement can also be used with string expressions. Then, the switch statement uses the equals method of the String object to compare the strings. As a result, the strings in switch statements are case-sensitive.
- The switch statement transfers control to the appropriate *case label*. If control isn't transferred to one of the case labels, the optional *default label* is executed.

Figure 4-5 How to code switch statements (part 1 of 2)

The third example in figure 4-5 shows how to code a switch statement that sets a day variable to "weekday" or "weekend" depending on the value of the integer in the variable named dayOfWeek. Here, the case labels for 2, 3, 4, and 5 don't contain any statements, so execution falls through to the case label for 6. As a result, day is set to "weekday" for any of those values. Similarly, whenever dayOfWeek equals 1 or 7, day is set to "weekend".

Although a break statement is coded at the end of the last case label in this example, you should know that it isn't required. If you omit this break statement, program execution automatically falls through to the statement that follows the switch statement. However, it's generally considered a good programming practice to code a break statement at the end of the last case label. That way, if you add a new case label after the last case label, your switch statement still works correctly. Similarly, if you move the last case label so it occurs earlier in the switch statement, it still works correctly.

When you code switch statements, you can nest one statement within another. You can also nest if/else statements within switch statements and switch statements within if/else statements. Here again, you should try to code the statements with a logical structure that is relatively easy to understand. If necessary, you can also add comments that clarify the logic of your code.

Example 3: A switch statement that falls through case labels

```
switch (dayOfWeek)
{
    case 2:
    case 3:
    case 4:
    case 5:
    case 6:
        day = "weekday";
        break;
    case 1:
    case 7:
        day = "weekend";
        break;
}
```

Description

- If a case label doesn't contain a break statement, code execution will *fall through* to the next label. Otherwise, the break statement ends the switch statement.
- The case labels can be coded in any sequence.

Figure 4-5 How to code switch statements (part 2 of 2)

An enhanced version of the Invoice application

To give you a better idea of how if/else statements can be used, figure 4-6 presents another enhanced version of the Invoice application. This time, the console prompts the user for two entries: customer type and subtotal.

In this application, if the user enters "R" or "C" for the customer type, the discount percent changes depending on the value of the subtotal. If, for example, the customer type is "R" and the subtotal is greater than or equal to 250, the discount percent is .2. Or, if the customer type is "C" and the subtotal is less than 250, the discount percent is .2.

Here, you can see that the conditions are coded in a logical order. For instance, the expressions in the nested if statement for customer type "R" go from a subtotal that's less than 100, to a subtotal that's greater than or equal to 100, to a subtotal that's greater than or equal to 250. That covers all of the possible subtotals from the smallest to the largest. Although you could code these conditions in other sequences, this sequence makes it easy to tell that all possibilities have been covered.

The console

```
Enter customer type (r/c): r
Enter subtotal:   100
Discount percent: 10%
Discount amount:  $10.00
Total:            $90.00

Continue? (y/n):
```

The code

```
import java.text.NumberFormat;
import java.util.Scanner;

public class InvoiceApp
{
    public static void main(String[] args)
    {
        Scanner sc = new Scanner(System.in);
        String choice = "y";

        while (!choice.equalsIgnoreCase("n"))
        {
            // get the input from the user
            System.out.print("Enter customer type (r/c): ");
            String customerType = sc.next();
            System.out.print("Enter subtotal:   ");
            double subtotal = sc.nextDouble();

            // get the discount percent
            double discountPercent = 0.0;
            if (customerType.equalsIgnoreCase("R"))
            {
                if (subtotal < 100)
                    discountPercent = 0;
                else if (subtotal >= 100 && subtotal < 250)
                    discountPercent = .1;
                else if (subtotal >= 250)
                    discountPercent = .2;
            }
            else if (customerType.equalsIgnoreCase("C"))
            {
                if (subtotal < 250)
                    discountPercent = .2;
                else
                    discountPercent = .3;
            }
            else
                discountPercent = .1;

            // the code to calculate, format, and display results goes here

            // the code to see if the user wants to continue goes here
        }
    }
}
```

Figure 4-6 The enhanced Invoice application

How to code loops

In chapter 2, you learned how to code while statements and while loops. Now, you'll review the coding for those loops and learn how to code two other Java statements that implement the *iteration structure*.

How to code while and do-while loops

Figure 4-7 shows how to use the *while statement* to code a *while loop*. Then, it shows how to code a *do-while loop*. The difference between these types of loops is that the Boolean expression is evaluated at the beginning of a while loop and at the end of a do-while loop. As a result, the statements in a while loop are executed zero or more times while the statements in a do-while loop are always executed at least once.

When coding while and do-while loops, it's common to use a *counter variable* to execute the statements in the loop a certain number of times. The first loop in this figure, for example, uses an int counter variable named i that's initialized to 1. Then, the last statement in the loop increments the counter variable with each iteration of the loop. As a result, the first statement in this loop will be executed as long as the counter variable is less than or equal to 36. As I've mentioned earlier, it is a common coding practice to name counter variables with single letters like *i, j,* and *k.*

Most of the time, you can use either of these two types of loops to accomplish the same task. For instance, the first example in this figure uses a while loop to calculate the future value of a series of monthly payments at a specified interest rate, and the second example uses a do-while loop to perform the same calculation.

When you code loops, it's important to remember that the code within a loop has block scope. As a result, any variables that are declared within the loop can't be used outside of the loop. That's why the variables that are needed outside of the loops in this figure have been declared outside of the loop. That way, you can use these variables after the loop has finished executing.

It's also important to avoid *infinite loops*. If, for example, you forget to code a statement that increments the counter variable, the loop will never end. Then, in NetBeans, you can stop the loop by clicking on the Stop button that's displayed in the Output window.

The syntax of the while loop

```
while (booleanExpression)
{
   statements
}
```

A while loop that calculates a future value

```
int i = 1;
int months = 36;
while (i <= months)
{
    futureValue = (futureValue + monthlyPayment) *
        (1 + monthlyInterestRate);
    i++;
}
```

The syntax of the do-while loop

```
do
{
   statements
}
while (booleanExpression);
```

A do-while loop that calculates a future value

```
int i = 1;
int months = 36;
do
{
    futureValue = (futureValue + monthlyPayment) *
        (1 + monthlyInterestRate);
    i++;
}
while (i <= months);
```

Description

- In a *while loop*, the condition is tested before the loop is executed. In a *do-while loop*, the condition is tested after the loop is executed.
- A while or do-while loop executes the block of statements within the loop as long as its Boolean expression is true.
- If a loop requires more than one statement, you must enclose the statements in braces. This identifies the block of statements that are executed by the loop, and any variables or constants that are declared in that block have block scope.
- If a loop requires just one statement, you don't have to enclose the statement in braces. However, that statement can't declare a variable or it won't compile.
- If the condition at the start of a while statement or at the end of a do-while statement never becomes false, the statement never ends. Then, the program goes into an *infinite loop*. In NetBeans, you can cancel an infinite loop by clicking on the Stop button in the Output window.

Figure 4-7 How to code while and do-while loops

How to code for loops

Figure 4-8 shows how to use the for statement to code *for loops*. This type of loop is useful when you need to increment or decrement a counter that determines how many times the loop is going to be executed.

To code a for loop, you start by coding the for keyword followed by three expressions enclosed in parentheses and separated by semicolons. The first expression is an initialization expression that gives the starting value for the counter variable. This expression can also declare the counter variable, if necessary. The second expression is a Boolean expression that determines when the loop will end. And the third expression is an increment expression that determines how the counter is incremented or decremented each time the loop is executed.

The first example in this figure shows how to use these expressions. First, the initialization expression declares the counter variable that's used to determine the number of loops and assigns an initial value to it. In this example, the counter variable is an int type named i, and it's initialized to 0. Next, a Boolean expression specifies that the loop will be repeated as long as the counter is less than 5. Then, the increment expression increments the counter by 1 at the end of each repetition of the loop.

Since the two loops in this example store the counter variable followed by a space in a string, this code stores the numbers 0 to 4 in a string variable like this:

```
0 1 2 3 4
```

Notice that you can code this loop using a single statement or a block of statements. If you use more than one statement, though, you must enclose those statements in braces.

The second example calculates the sum of 8, 6, 4, and 2. Here, the sum variable is declared before the loop so it will be available outside of the loop. Within the parentheses of the for loop, the initialization expression initializes the counter variable to 8, the Boolean expression indicates that the loop will end when the counter variable is no longer greater than zero, and the increment expression uses an assignment operator to subtract 2 from the counter variable with each repetition of the loop. Within the loop, the value of the counter variable is added to the value that's already stored in the sum variable. As a result, the final value for the sum variable is 20.

The third example shows how to code a loop that calculates the future value for a series of monthly payments. Here, the loop executes one time for each month. If you compare this example with the examples in the previous figure, you can see how a for loop improves upon a while or do-while loop when a counter variable is required.

The syntax of the for loop

```
for (initializationExpression; booleanExpression; incrementExpression)
{
    statements
}
```

Example 1: A for loop that stores the numbers 0 through 4 in a string

With a single statement

```
String numbers = "";
for (int i = 0; i < 5; i++)
    numbers += i + " ";
```

With a block of statements

```
String numbers = "";
for (int i = 0; i < 5; i++)
{
    numbers += i;
    numbers += " ";
}
```

Example 2: A for loop that adds the numbers 8, 6, 4, and 2

```
int sum = 0;
for (int j = 8; j > 0; j -= 2)
{
    sum += j;
}
```

Example 3: A for loop that calculates a future value

```
for (int i = 1; i <= months; i++)
{
    futureValue = (futureValue + monthlyPayment) *
        (1 + monthlyInterestRate);
}
```

Description

- A *for loop* is useful when you need to increment or decrement a counter that determines how many times the loop is executed.
- Within the parentheses of a for loop, you code an initialization expression that gives the starting value for the counter, a Boolean expression that determines when the loop ends, and an increment expression that increments or decrements the counter.
- The loop ends when the Boolean expression is false.
- If necessary, you can declare the counter variable before the for loop. Then, this variable will be in scope after the loop finishes executing.

Figure 4-8 How to code for loops

The Future Value application

Now that you've learned the statements for coding loops, figure 4-9 presents an application that uses a for loop within a while loop. As the console for this application shows, the user starts by entering the values for the monthly payment that will be made, the yearly interest rate, and the number of years the payment will be made. Then, for each group of entries, the application calculates and displays the future value.

If you look at the code for this application, you can see that it uses a while loop to determine when the program will end. Within this loop, the program first gets the three entries from the user. Next, it converts these entries to the same time unit, which is months. To do that, the number of years is multiplied by 12, and the yearly interest rate is divided by 12. Besides that, the yearly interest rate is divided by 100 so it will work correctly in the future value calculation.

Once those variables are prepared, the program enters a for loop that calculates the future value. When the loop finishes, the program displays the result and asks whether the user wants to continue.

Because this application doesn't validate the user's entries, it will crash if the user enters invalid data. But you'll learn how to fix that in the next chapter. Otherwise, this application works the way you would want it to. In this case, rounding isn't an issue because the result is rounded just one time after the future value loop has finished.

Because it can be hard to tell whether an application with a loop is producing the right results, it often makes sense to add debugging statements within the loop while you're testing it. For instance, you could add this statement to the Future Value application as the last statement in the loop:

```
System.out.println("Debug: " + i + "     " + futureValue);
```

Then, one line will be displayed on the console each time through the loop so you can check to make sure that the calculations for the first few months are accurate. You will also be able to tell at a glance whether the loop was executed the right number of times.

The console

```
Enter monthly investment:    100
Enter yearly interest rate: 3
Enter number of years:      3
Future value:               $3,771.46

Continue? (y/n): y
```

The code

```
import java.util.Scanner;
import java.text.NumberFormat;

public class FutureValueApp
{
    public static void main(String[] args)
    {
        Scanner sc = new Scanner(System.in);
        String choice = "y";
        while (!choice.equalsIgnoreCase("n"))
        {
            // get the input from the user
            System.out.print("Enter monthly investment:    ");
            double monthlyInvestment = sc.nextDouble();
            System.out.print("Enter yearly interest rate: ");
            double interestRate = sc.nextDouble();
            System.out.print("Enter number of years:      ");
            int years = sc.nextInt();

            // convert yearly to monthly values and initialize future value
            double monthlyInterestRate = interestRate/12/100;
            int months = years * 12;
            double futureValue = 0.0;

            // use a for loop to calculate the future value
            for (int i = 1; i <= months; i++)
            {
                futureValue =
                    (futureValue + monthlyInvestment) *
                    (1 + monthlyInterestRate);
            }

            // format and display the result
            NumberFormat currency = NumberFormat.getCurrencyInstance();
            System.out.println("Future value:               "
                                  + currency.format(futureValue));
            System.out.println();

            // see if the user wants to continue
            System.out.print("Continue? (y/n): ");
            choice = sc.next();
            System.out.println();
        }
    }
}
```

Figure 4-9 The Future Value application

How to code nested loops

Like if and switch statements, you can also nest loops. In the last figure, for example, you saw a for loop that calculates a future value nested within a while loop that determines when the program ends. Now, figure 4-10 shows how to nest a for loop within another for loop. Notice that as with all nested statements, the nested for loops are indented to clearly show how they're related.

The example in this figure shows how to use three levels of nested for loops to display a table of future value calculations. Here, the amount of the monthly investment is set to $100, the interest rate varies from 5.0% to 6.5%, and the number of years varies from 2 years to 4 years. Before the nested for loops are executed, another for loop adds the headings to the string that will hold the table.

The outermost for loop iterates through the years (4, 3, and 2), adding one row for each year to the table string. To do that, the code within this loop starts by adding the year to the string that will hold the data for the row. Then, the next for loop iterates through the four interest rates (5%, 5.5%, 6%, and 6.5%). The code within this loop uses the innermost for loop to calculate the future value for each interest rate. Then, the result of each calculation is appended to the row string. When this loop is finished, the outermost loop appends the row string to the table string and clears the row string so it can be used again in the next iteration of the loop. After all three loops are finished, the println method prints the table string to the console.

As you review this code, you might notice that spaces are used to align the data in the columns. Although it would be possible to use tab characters to align the columns, that doesn't always work the way you want. To explicitly control alignment, then, you should use spaces.

The console

```
Monthly Payment: 100.0

         5.0%          5.5%          6.0%          6.5%
4     $5,323.58     $5,379.83     $5,436.83     $5,494.59
3     $3,891.48     $3,922.23     $3,953.28     $3,984.64
2     $2,529.09     $2,542.46     $2,555.91     $2,569.45
```

Nested loops that print a table of future values

```
// get the currency and percent formatters
NumberFormat currency = NumberFormat.getCurrencyInstance();
NumberFormat percent = NumberFormat.getPercentInstance();
percent.setMinimumFractionDigits(1);

// set the monthly payment to 100 and display it to the user
double monthlyPayment = 100.0;
System.out.println("Monthly Payment: " + monthlyPayment);
System.out.println();

// declare a variable to store the table
String table  = "       ";

// fill the first row of the table
for (double rate = 5.0; rate < 7.0; rate += .5)
{
    table += percent.format(rate/100) + "         ";
}
table += "\n";

// loop through each row
for (int years = 4; years > 1; years--)
{
    // append the years variable to the start of the row
    String row = years + "    ";
    // loop through each column
    for (double rate = 5.0; rate < 7.0; rate += .5)
    {
        // calculate the future value for each rate
        int months = years * 12;
        double monthlyInterestRate = rate/12/100;
        double futureValue = 0.0;
        for (int i = 1; i <= months; i++)
        {
            futureValue =
                (futureValue + monthlyPayment) *
                (1 + monthlyInterestRate);
        }
        // add the calculation to the row
        row += currency.format(futureValue) + "    ";
    }
    table += row + "\n";
    row = "";
}

System.out.println(table);
```

Figure 4-10 How to code nested loops

How to code break and continue statements

When you code loops, you usually want them to run to completion. Occasionally, though, an application may require that you jump out of a loop. To do that, you can use the break or continue statement.

How to code break statements

Figure 4-11 shows how to use the break statement and the labeled break statement to exit loops. If you need to exit the current loop, you can code a break statement. If you need to exit another loop in a set of nested loops, you can use the labeled break statement.

The first example shows how you can use the break statement to exit from an inner loop. Here, a while loop that generates random numbers is nested within a for loop. Notice that the Boolean expression for the while loop has been set to true. Because of that, this loop would execute indefinitely without a statement that explicitly jumps out of the loop. In this case, a break statement is used to exit from the loop when the random number that's generated is greater than 7. Then, control is returned to the for loop, which is executed until its Boolean expression is satisfied.

The second example shows how you can use the labeled break statement to exit an outer loop from an inner loop. To use a labeled break statement, you code a *label* for the loop that you want to exit. Then, to break out of the outer loop, you just type the break statement followed by the name of the label. This will transfer control to the statement that follows the outer loop.

The syntax of the break statement

```
break;
```

Example 1: A break statement that exits the inner loop

```
for (int i = 1; i < 4; i++)
{
    System.out.println("Outer " + i);
    while (true)
    {
        int number = (int) (Math.random() * 10);
        System.out.println("    Inner " + number);
        if (number > 7)
            break;

    }
}
```

The syntax of the labeled break statement

```
break labelName;
```

The structure of the labeled break statement

```
labelName:
loop declaration
{
    statements
    another loop declaration
    {
        statements
        if (conditionalExpression)
        {
            statements
            break labelName;
        }
    }
}
```

Example 2: A labeled break statement that exits the outer loop

```
outerLoop:
for (int i = 1; i < 4; i++)
{
    System.out.println("Outer " + i);
    while (true)
    {
        int number = (int) (Math.random() * 10);
        System.out.println("    Inner " + number);
        if (number > 7)
            break outerLoop;
    }
}
```

Description

- To jump to the end of the current loop, you can use the break statement.
- To jump to the end of an outer loop from an inner loop, you can label the outer loop and use the labeled break statement. To code a *label*, type the name of the label and a colon before a loop.

Figure 4-11 How to code break statements

How to code continue statements

Figure 4-12 shows how to use the continue statement and the labeled continue statement. These statements work similarly to the break statements, but they jump to the beginning of a loop instead of the end of a loop. Like the break statements, you can use the unlabeled version of the statement to work with the current loop, and you can use the labeled version of the statement to work with nested loops.

The first example uses a for loop to generate 9 random numbers ranging in value from 0 to 10. Then, if the random number is less than or equal to 7, the continue statement jumps to the beginning of the loop. As a result, the println method that comes after the continue statement is only executed if the random number is greater than 7.

The second example uses nested for loops to print the prime numbers that are less than 20. In case you're not familiar with prime numbers, a prime number is an integer greater than 1 that can only be divided by 1 and itself. For example, 7 is a prime number because it can only be divided by 1 and 7. In contrast, 9 is not a prime number because it can be divided by 3 in addition to 1 and 9.

To identify the prime numbers, the outer loop in this example iterates through the numbers 2 through 19. Then, the inner loop iterates through the numbers 2 to the counter in the outer loop minus 1. In other words, it looks for a number other than 1 and the counter itself that will divide the number. To do that, the modulus operator is used to get the remainder of the counter from the outer loop divided by the counter from the inner loop. If the remainder equals 0, it indicates that the number can be divided by another number and is therefore not a prime number. In that case, the continue statement causes control of the program to jump to the top of the outer loop, and the outer loop continues with the next number. If the remainder doesn't equal 0 at any point in the inner loop, though, it indicates that the number is a prime number. Then, the last statement in the outer loop prints the number to the console.

The syntax of the continue statement

```
continue;
```

Example 1: A continue statement that jumps to the beginning of a loop

```
for (int j = 1; j < 10; j++)
{
    int number = (int) (Math.random() * 10);
    System.out.println(number);
    if (number <= 7)
        continue;
    System.out.println("This number is greater than 7");
}
```

The syntax of the labeled continue statement

```
continue labelName;
```

The structure of the labeled continue statement

```
labelName:
loop declaration
{
    statements
    another loop declaration
    {
        statements
        if (conditionalExpression)
        {
            statements
            continue labelName;
        }
    }
}
```

Example 2: A labeled continue statement that jumps to the beginning of the outer loop

```
outerLoop:
for (int i = 2; i < 20; i++)
{
    for (int j = 2; j < i-1; j++)
    {
        int remainder = i % j;
        if (remainder == 0)
            continue outerLoop;
    }
    System.out.println(i);
}
```

Description

- To skip the rest of the statements in the current loop and jump to the top of the current loop, you can use the continue statement.
- To skip the rest of the statements in the current loop and jump to the top of a labeled loop, you can add a label to the loop and use the labeled continue statement.
- To code a label, type the name of the label and a colon before a loop.

Figure 4-12 How to code continue statements

How to code and call static methods

So far, you've learned how to code applications that consist of a single method, the static main method that's executed automatically when you run a class. Now, you'll learn how to code and call other static methods. That's one way to divide the code for an application into manageable parts.

How to code static methods

Figure 4-13 shows how to code a *static method*. To start, you code an *access modifier* that indicates whether the method can be called from other classes (public) or just the class that it's coded in (private). Next, you code the static keyword to identify the method as a static method.

After the static keyword, you code a return type that identifies the type of data that the method will return. That return type can be either a primitive data type or a class like the String class. If the method doesn't return any data, you code the void keyword.

After the return type, you code a method name that indicates what the method does. A common coding convention is to use camel notation and to start each method name with a verb followed by a noun or by an adjective and a noun, as in calculateFutureValue.

After the method name, you code a set of parentheses. Within the parentheses, you declare the *parameters* that are required by the method. If a method doesn't require any parameters, you can code an empty set of parentheses as shown by the first example. And if a method requires more than one parameter, you separate them with commas as shown by the second example. Later on, when you call the method, you pass values to these parameters.

At this point, you code a set of braces that contains the statements that the method will execute. If the method is going to return a value, these statements must include a *return statement* that identifies the variable or object to be returned. This is illustrated by the calculateFutureValue method in this figure.

When you code the method name and parameter list of a method, you form the *signature* of the method. As you might expect, each method must have a unique signature. However, you can code two or more methods with the same name but with different parameters. This is known as *overloading* a method, and you'll learn more about that in chapter 7.

How to call static methods

Figure 4-13 also shows how to *call* a public or private static method that's coded within the same class. This is just like calling a static method from a Java class, but you don't need to code the class name. Then, if the method requires *arguments*, you code the arguments within parentheses, separating each argument with a comma. Otherwise, you code an empty set of parentheses.

Notice that if you pass arguments, those arguments must be in the same order as the parameters in the method. The arguments and parameters must also

The basic syntax for coding a static method

```
public|private static returnType methodName([parameterList])
{
   statements
}
```

A static method with no parameters and no return type

```
private static void printWelcomeMessage()
{
    System.out.println("Hello New User");
}
```

A static method with three parameters that returns a double value

```
public static double calculateFutureValue(double monthlyInvestment,
double monthlyInterestRate, int months)
{
    double futureValue = 0.0;
    for (int i = 1; i <= months; i++)
    {
        futureValue = (futureValue + monthlyInvestment)
            * (1 + monthlyInterestRate);
    }
    return futureValue;
}
```

The syntax for calling a static method that's in the same class

```
methodName([argumentList])
```

A call statement with no arguments

```
printWelcomeMessage();
```

A call statement that passes three arguments

```
double futureValue = calculateFutureValue(investment, rate, months);
```

Description

- To allow other classes to access a method, use the public *access modifier*. To prevent other classes from accessing a method, use the private modifier.
- To code a method that returns data, code a return type in the method declaration and code a *return statement* in the body of the method. The return statement ends the execution of the method and returns the specified value to the calling method.
- Within the parentheses of a method, you can code an optional *parameter list* that contains one or more *parameters* that consist of a data type and name. These are the values that must be passed to the method when it is called.
- The name of a method along with its parameter list form the *signature* of the method, which must be unique.
- When you call a method, the *arguments* in the *argument list* must be in the same order as the parameters in the parameter list defined by the method, and they must have compatible data types. However, the names of the arguments and the parameters don't need to be the same.

Figure 4-13 How to code and call static methods

have compatible data types. That means that an argument and parameter must have the same data type, or the parameter must have a more precise data type than the argument so the argument can be implicitly cast to that type. To refresh your memory on implicit casting, you can refer back to figure 3-7 in chapter 3.

In practice, the terms *parameter* and *argument* are often used interchangeably. In this book, however, we'll use the term *parameter* to refer to the variables of a method declaration, and we'll use the term *argument* to refer to the variables that are passed to a method.

The Future Value application with a static method

To illustrate the use of static methods, figure 4-14 presents another version of the Future Value application. This time, the application uses a static method to calculate the future value. This method requires three arguments, and it includes the for loop that processes those arguments. When the loop finishes, the return statement returns the future value to the main method.

To use the static method, the main method prepares the three arguments so they're all in month units. Then, it calls the static method and passes the three arguments to it. This simplifies the main method and illustrates how static methods can be used to divide a program into manageable components.

In this case, the statement that calls the method passes arguments that have the same variable names as the parameters of the method. Although this isn't necessary, it makes the code easier to follow. What is necessary, though, is that the arguments be passed in the same sequence as the parameters and have compatible data types.

In the next chapter, you'll see other ways that static methods can be used. Then, in chapter 7, you'll see how static methods can be coded with the public keyword so they can be accessed by other classes. For now, though, you can code all of your static methods with the private access modifier.

The code

```
import java.util.Scanner;
import java.text.NumberFormat;

public class FutureValueApp
{
    public static void main(String[] args)
    {
        Scanner sc = new Scanner(System.in);
        String choice = "y";
        while (!choice.equalsIgnoreCase("n"))
        {
            // get the input from the user
            System.out.print("Enter monthly investment:   ");
            double monthlyInvestment = sc.nextDouble();
            System.out.print("Enter yearly interest rate: ");
            double interestRate = sc.nextDouble();
            System.out.print("Enter number of years:      ");
            int years = sc.nextInt();

            // convert yearly values to monthly values
            double monthlyInterestRate = interestRate/12/100;
            int months = years * 12;

            // call the future value method
            double futureValue = calculateFutureValue(
                monthlyInvestment, monthlyInterestRate, months);

            // format and display the result
            NumberFormat currency = NumberFormat.getCurrencyInstance();
            System.out.println("Future value:               "
                             + currency.format(futureValue));
            System.out.println();

            // see if the user wants to continue
            System.out.print("Continue? (y/n): ");
            choice = sc.next();
            System.out.println();
        }
    }

    //  a static method that requires three arguments and returns a double
    private static double calculateFutureValue(double monthlyInvestment,
    double monthlyInterestRate, int months)
    {
        double futureValue = 0.0;
        for (int i = 1; i <= months; i++)
        {
            futureValue =
                (futureValue + monthlyInvestment) *
                (1 + monthlyInterestRate);
        }
        return futureValue;
    }
}
```

Figure 4-14 The Future Value application with a static method

Perspective

If this chapter has succeeded, you should now be able to use if, switch, while, do-while, and for statements. These are the Java statements that implement the selection, case, and iteration structures, and they provide the logic of an application. You should also be able to code and call your own static methods, which will help you divide your programs into manageable parts.

Summary

- You can use the *relational operators* to create *Boolean expressions* that compare primitive data types and return true or false values, and you can use the *logical operators* to connect two or more Boolean expressions.
- To determine whether two strings are equal, you can call the equals and equalsIgnoreCase methods from a String object.
- You can use *if/else statements* and *switch statements* to control the logic of an application, and you can *nest* these statements whenever necessary.
- You can use *while*, *do-while*, and *for loops* to repeatedly execute one or more statements until a Boolean expression evaluates to false, and you can nest these statements whenever necessary.
- You can use *break statements* to jump to the end of the current loop or a labeled loop, and you can use *continue statements* to jump to the start of the current loop or a labeled loop.
- To code a *static method*, you code an access modifier, the static keyword, its return type, its name, and a *parameter* list. Then, to return a value, you code a *return statement* within the method.
- To call a static method that's in the same class as the main method, you code the method name followed by an *argument* list.

Exercise 4-1 Test the Future Value application

In this exercise, you'll test the Future Value application that's presented in figure 4-9 in this chapter.

1. Open the project named ch04_ex1_FutureValue that's stored in the ex_starts directory. Then, test it with valid data to see how it works.
2. To make sure that the results are correct, add a debugging statement within the for loop that calculates the future value. This statement should display the month and future value each time through the loop. Then, test the program with simple entries like 100 for monthly investment, 12 for yearly interest (because that's 1 percent each month), and 1 for year. When the debugging data is displayed, check the results manually to make sure they're correct.

Exercise 4-2 Enhance the Invoice application

In this exercise, you'll modify the nested if/else statements that are used to determine the discount percent for the Invoice application in figure 4-6. Then, you'll code and call a static method that determines the discount percent.

Open the application and change the if/else statement

1. Open the project named ch04_ex2_Invoice that's stored in the ex_starts directory. Then, run the application to see how it works.
2. Change the if/else statement so customers of type "R" with a subtotal that is greater than or equal to $250 but less than $500 get a 25% discount and those with a subtotal of $500 or more get a 30% discount. Next, change the if/else statement so customers of type "C" always get a 20% discount. Then, test the application to make sure this works.
3. Add another customer type to the if/else statement so customers of type "T" get a 40% discount for subtotals of less than $500, and a 50% discount for subtotals of $500 or more. Then, test the application.
4. Check your code to make sure that no discount is provided for a customer type code that isn't "R", "C", or "T". Then, fix this if necessary.

Code and call a static method that determines the discount percent

5. Code a static method named getDiscountPercent that has two parameters: customer type and subtotal. To do that efficiently, you can move the appropriate code from the main method of the application into the static method and make the required modifications.
6. Add code that calls the static method from the body of the application. Then, test to make sure that it works.

Exercise 4-3 Enhance the Test Score application

In this exercise, you'll enhance the Test Score application so it uses a while or a do-while loop plus a for loop. After the enhancements, the console for a user's session should look something like this:

```
Enter the number of test scores to be entered: 5

Enter score 1: 75
Enter score 2: 80
Enter score 3: 75
Enter score 4: 880
Invalid entry, not counted
Enter score 4: 80
Enter score 5: 95

Score count:   5
Score total:   405
Average score: 81
Minimum score: 75
Maximum score: 95

Enter more test scores? (y/n): y

Enter the number of test scores to be entered: 3

Enter score 1: 85
Enter score 2: 95
Enter score 3: 100

Score count:   3
Score total:   280
Average score: 93.3
Minimum score: 85
Maximum score: 100

Enter more test scores? (y/n):
```

1. Open the project named ch04_ex3_TestScore that's stored in the ex_starts directory. Then, run the application to see how it works.
2. Change the while statement to a do-while statement, and test this change. Does this work any better than the while loop?
3. Enhance the program so it uses a while or do-while loop that lets the user enter more than one set of test scores. When you do that, be sure to move the declarations for the variables inside the loop so these variables are initialized each time through the loop. Test the application to make sure it works.
4. Add code at the beginning of the while or do-while loop that asks the user how many test scores are going to be entered. Then, use this number in a for loop to get that many test score entries from the user. When the for loop ends, the program should display the summary data for the test scores. Test these enhancements.
5. If you didn't already do it, make sure that the code in the for loop doesn't count an invalid entry. In that case, an error message should be displayed and the counter should be decremented by one. Now, test to make sure this works.

5

How to validate input data

In the last three chapters, you learned how to code applications that get input from a user and perform calculations based on that input. However, if the user enters data that the application can't handle, an exception will occur and the application will crash.

Now, you'll learn how to validate the input data before processing it so problems like that won't occur. But first, you'll learn the basic skills for handling exceptions caused by invalid data. These are essential skills when you're developing professional applications.

How to handle exceptions

To prevent your applications from crashing, you can write code that handles exceptions when they occur. This is known as *exception handling*, and it plays an important role in most applications.

How exceptions work

When an application can't perform an operation, Java *throws* an *exception*. An exception is an object that's created from one of the classes in the Exception hierarchy such as the ones shown in figure 5-1. Exception objects represent errors that have occurred, and they contain information about those errors. One of the most common causes of exceptions is invalid input data.

The Exception class that's at the top of the exception hierarchy defines the most general type of exception. The RuntimeException class is a *subclass* of the Exception class that defines a more specific type of exception. Similarly, the NoSuchElementException and IllegalArgumentException classes are subclasses of the RuntimeException class that define even more specific types of exceptions. Since the RuntimeException class represents exceptions that occur at runtime, none of the exceptions shown in this figure are checked by the compiler. In chapter 14, you'll learn about another type of exception that is checked by the compiler.

A well-coded application will *catch* any exceptions that are thrown and handle them. Exception handling can be as simple as notifying users that they must enter valid data. Or, for more serious exceptions, it may involve notifying users that the application is being shut down, saving as much data as possible, cleaning up resources, and exiting the application as smoothly as possible.

When you're testing an application, it's common to encounter exceptions that haven't been handled. For a console application, this will typically cause information about the exception to be displayed at the console. This information usually includes the name of the exception class, a brief message that describes the cause of the exception, and a *stack trace*. In this figure, for example, you can see the information that's displayed when the user enters an invalid double value for the Invoice application.

As you can see in this example, a stack trace is a list of the methods that were called before the exception occurred. These methods are listed in the reverse order from the order in which they were called. Each method includes a line number, which can help you find the statement that caused the exception in your source code. The stack trace in this figure, for example, indicates that line 20 of the main method of the InvoiceApp class threw an exception when it called the nextDouble method of the Scanner class.

One common situation where you'll need to handle exceptions is when you convert string data to numeric data. If, for example, the nextInt or nextDouble method of the Scanner class can't convert the data the user enters to the correct data type, an InputMismatchException is thrown. Similarly, a NumberFormatException is thrown when a value of one data type can't be

Some of the classes in the Exception hierarchy

```
Exception
    RuntimeException
        NoSuchElementException
            InputMismatchException
        IllegalArgumentException
            NumberFormatException
        ArithmeticException
        NullPointerException
```

The console after an InputMismatchException has been thrown

```
Enter subtotal:   $100
Exception in thread "main" java.util.InputMismatchException
    at java.util.Scanner.throwFor(Scanner.java:909)
    at java.util.Scanner.next(Scanner.java:1530)
    at java.util.Scanner.nextDouble(Scanner.java:2456)
    at InvoiceApp.main(InvoiceApp.java:20)
```

Four methods that might throw an exception

Class	Method	Throws
Scanner	nextInt()	InputMismatchException
Scanner	nextDouble()	InputMismatchException
Integer	parseInt(String)	NumberFormatException
Double	parseDouble(String)	NumberFormatException

Description

- An *exception* is an object that contains information about an error that has occurred. When an error occurs in a method, the method *throws* an exception.
- If an exception is thrown when you're testing a console application, some information about the exception, including its name and stack trace, is displayed at the console.
- A *stack trace* is a list of the methods that were called before the exception occurred. The list appears in reverse order, from the last method called to the first method called.
- All exceptions are *subclasses* of the Exception class. The Exception class represents the most general type of exception. Each successive layer of subclasses represents more specific exceptions.
- The class for an exception is usually stored in the same package as the class whose methods throw that type of exception. For instance, the InputMismatchException class is stored in the java.util package along with the Scanner class.

Figure 5-1 How exceptions work

converted to another data type. This exception can be thrown by the parseDouble method of the Double class or the parseInt method of the Integer class.

The class for an exception is usually stored in the same package as the class that has the methods that throw that type of exception. For instance, the InputMismatchException is thrown by the Scanner class, so the class for this exception is stored in the java.util package along with the Scanner class. As a result, if your application is going to use this exception object, it should import java.util.InputMismatchException or all of the classes in the java.util package.

How to catch exceptions

To catch and handle exceptions, you use the *try statement* shown in figure 5-2. First, you code a try clause that contains a block of one or more statements that may cause an exception. Then, you code a catch clause immediately after the try clause. This clause contains the block of statements that will be executed if an exception is thrown by a statement in the try block. Since this block contains the code that handles the exception, it is known as an *exception handler*.

The example in this figure shows how you might use a try statement in the Invoice application. Here, the nextDouble method of the Scanner class is coded within a try clause, and a catch clause is coded for the InputMismatchException. Then, if the user enters a non-numeric value for the subtotal, the nextDouble method will throw an InputMismatchException and the code in the catch block will be executed. To catch that exception, though, the application must either import the class for that exception, or it must qualify the name of the class with the name of the package that contains it.

In this case, the catch block starts by calling the next method of the Scanner object to discard the incorrectly entered value. That way, the scanner won't try to retrieve this value the next time the nextDouble method is called. This is necessary because the nextDouble method isn't completed if an exception occurs. After this value is discarded, the second statement displays an error message. And finally, the continue statement jumps to the beginning of the loop, which causes the application to prompt the user to enter another subtotal. Of course, this assumes that the try/catch statement is coded within a while loop like the one shown in the next figure.

The catch block in this example will only be executed if the InputMismatchException is thrown. Since this exception is the only exception that's likely to be thrown in the try block, this is the clearest way to catch this exception. If you wanted the catch clause to catch other exceptions as well, however, you could name an exception higher up in the Exception hierarchy. For example, if you wanted to catch any runtime exception, you could code this catch clause:

```
catch (RuntimeException e)
```

And if you wanted to catch any exception, you could code this catch clause:

```
catch (Exception e)
```

You'll learn more about how this works in chapter 14.

The syntax for the try statement

```
try { statements }
catch (ExceptionClass exceptionName) { statements }
```

Two ways to import the InputMismatchException class

```
import.java.util.InputMismatchException;
import.java.util.*;
```

A try statement that catches an InputMismatchException

```
double subtotal = 0.0;
try
{
    System.out.print("Enter subtotal:   ");
    subtotal = sc.nextDouble();
}
catch (InputMismatchException e)
{
    sc.next();       // discard the incorrectly entered double
    System.out.println("Error! Invalid number. Try again.\n");
    continue;        // jump to the top of the loop
}
```

Console output

```
Enter subtotal:   $100
Error! Invalid number. Try again.

Enter subtotal:
```

Description

- In a *try statement* (or *try/catch statement*), you code any statements that may throw an exception in a *try block*. Then, you can code a *catch block* that will handle any exceptions that may occur in the try block.
- When an exception occurs, any remaining statements in the try block are skipped and the statements in the catch block are executed.
- Any variables or objects that are used in both the try and catch blocks must be declared before the try and catch blocks so both the try and catch blocks can access them.
- If you use a catch block to catch a specific type of exception, you should also import the package that contains that exception class.

The Future Value application with exception handling

Figure 5-3 presents an improved version of the Future Value application that was presented in the last chapter. This version uses a try statement that's coded within the while loop to catch any exceptions that might be thrown when data is retrieved from the user.

To start, this application begins with an import statement that imports all of the classes in the java.util package. This includes the Scanner class and the InputMismatchException class. As a result, this application can use a Scanner object to get user input from the console, and it can catch the InputMismatchException object that may be thrown by the methods of the Scanner class.

To catch exceptions, all of the statements that get numeric input are coded within a try block. Then, if the user enters data with an invalid numeric format, the three statements in the catch block will be executed. The first statement uses the next method to discard the invalid entry. Then, the second statement displays a message that indicates that the entry is not a valid number. And finally, the continue statement causes execution to continue at the top of the while loop. That way, the user is prompted repeatedly until valid data is entered for all three values.

Although this technique works, it has two shortcomings. First, the user must start entering values from the beginning each time an exception is thrown even if some of the values were valid. Second, the application displays a generic error message that isn't as descriptive or helpful as it could be. Later in this chapter, you'll learn how to fix both of these shortcomings.

The code for the Future Value application with exception handling

```
import java.util.*;
import java.text.NumberFormat;

public class FutureValueExceptionApp
{
    public static void main(String[] args)
    {
        System.out.println("Welcome to the Future Value Calculator\n");
        Scanner sc = new Scanner(System.in);
        String choice = "y";
        while (choice.equalsIgnoreCase("y"))
        {
            double monthlyInvestment = 0.0;
            double interestRate = 0.0;
            int years = 0;
            try
            {
                System.out.print("Enter monthly investment:   ");
                monthlyInvestment = sc.nextDouble();
                System.out.print("Enter yearly interest rate: ");
                interestRate = sc.nextDouble();
                System.out.print("Enter number of years:      ");
                years = sc.nextInt();
            }
            catch (InputMismatchException e)
            {
                sc.next();      // discard the invalid number
                System.out.println("Error! Invalid number. Try again.\n");
                continue;       // jump to the top of the loop
            }

            double monthlyInterestRate = interestRate/12/100;
            int months = years * 12;
            double futureValue = calculateFutureValue(
                monthlyInvestment, monthlyInterestRate, months);

            NumberFormat currency = NumberFormat.getCurrencyInstance();
            System.out.println("Future value:               "
                             + currency.format(futureValue) + "\n");
            System.out.print("Continue? (y/n): ");
            choice = sc.next();
            System.out.println();
        }
    }

    private static double calculateFutureValue(double monthlyInvestment,
    double monthlyInterestRate, int months)
    {
        double futureValue = 0;
        for (int i = 1; i <= months; i++)
            futureValue = (futureValue + monthlyInvestment) *
                          (1 + monthlyInterestRate);
        return futureValue;
    }
}
```

Figure 5-3 The Future Value application with exception handling

How to validate data

Although you can use the try statement to catch and handle an exception caused by invalid data, it's usually best to prevent exceptions from being thrown whenever that's possible. To do that, you can use a technique called *data validation*. Then, when an entry is invalid, the application displays an error message and gives the user another chance to enter valid data. This is repeated until all the entries are valid.

How to prevent exceptions from being thrown

Figure 5-4 presents four methods of the Scanner class that you can use to prevent exceptions from being thrown. For instance, the first example in this figure illustrates how you can use the hasNextDouble method to check if the user has entered a string that can be converted to a double type. To do that, the hasNextDouble method is coded as the condition on an if statement. If this condition is true, the nextDouble method is called to retrieve the value.

If the condition on the if statement isn't true, it means that the user entered an invalid double value. In that case, the nextLine method is used to discard the entire line that the user entered. Then, an error message is displayed and the continue statement jumps to the beginning of the loop. This assumes, of course, that the if statement is coded within a loop like the while loop shown in figure 5-3.

When writing code like this, you might think that you could use the next method to discard the string that the user enters. However, if the user enters two or more strings, the next method will only discard the first string. Then, when the continue statement jumps to the top of the loop, if the next string can be converted to a double, the nextDouble method will read that string without prompting the user for a new value. Since that's not what you want, you'll typically use the nextLine method instead of the next method to discard all the remaining values.

In the last chapter, you learned that if you call the equals or equalsIgnoreCase method from a string that contains a null, Java will throw an exception. Specifically, Java will throw a NullPointerException. To prevent this exception from being thrown, you can use code like that shown in the second example. To start, this code checks the value of a variable named customerType. If it isn't null, the code that follows calls the equals method. If it is null, no processing is performed. Later in this book, you'll see why this type of code is often necessary.

Since code that checks user input without using exception handling runs faster than code that uses exception handling, you should avoid using exception handling to check user input whenever possible. In general, it's considered a good practice to use exception handling only when the situation is truly exceptional. For example, it's not exceptional that a user would accidentally enter a non-numeric value for a subtotal. As a result, you should use the methods of the Scanner class to prevent these types of exceptions whenever possible.

Methods of the Scanner class you can use to validate data

Method	Description
`hasNext()`	Returns true if the scanner contains another token.
`hasNextInt()`	Returns true if the scanner contains another token that can be converted to an int value.
`hasNextDouble()`	Returns true if the scanner contains another token that can be converted to a double value.
`nextLine()`	Returns any remaining input on the current line as a String object and advances the scanner to the next line.

Example 1: Code that prevents an InputMismatchException

```
double subtotal = 0.0;
System.out.print("Enter subtotal:   ");
if (sc.hasNextDouble())
{
    subtotal = sc.nextDouble();
}
else
{
    sc.nextLine();     // discard the entire line
    System.out.println("Error! Invalid number. Try again.\n");
    continue;          // jump to the top of the loop
}
```

Console output

```
Enter subtotal:   $100
Error! Invalid number. Try again.

Enter subtotal:
```

Example 2: Code that prevents a NullPointerException

```
if (customerType != null)
{
    if (customerType.equals("R"))
        discountPercent = .4;
}
```

Description

- The hasXxx methods of the Scanner class let you check whether additional data is available at the console and whether that data can be converted to a specific data type. You can use these methods to prevent an exception from being thrown when one of the next methods is called.
- You can use the nextLine method to retrieve and discard any additional data that the user enters on a line that isn't required by the application.
- When your code prevents an exception from being thrown, it runs faster than code that catches and then handles the exception.

Figure 5-4 How to prevent exceptions from being thrown

How to validate a single entry

When a user enters data in a console application, you may want to perform several types of data validation. In particular, it's common to perform the two types of data validation for numeric entries that are illustrated in figure 5-5.

First, if the application requires that the user enter a number at the prompt, you can use one of the has methods of the Scanner class to check that the string value the user entered can be converted to the appropriate numeric data type. Second, if the application requires that the user enter a number within a specified range, you can use if/else statements to check that the number falls within that range. This is known as *range checking*.

To repeat this checking until all the entries on the form are valid, you can use a while loop like the one shown in this figure. This loop is executed repeatedly as long as the value of a boolean variable named isValid is false. Then, within the while loop, the first if/else statement checks whether the user entered a double value. If so, the nextDouble method is used to retrieve that value, and the isValid variable is set to true. If not, an error message is displayed.

If the value the user entered is valid, the second if/else statement checks the value to see if it is greater than 0 and less than 10000. If so, the data is valid and the while loop ends. Otherwise, an appropriate error message is displayed, and the isValid variable is set to false so the while loop will repeat.

In this code, the nextLine method is called after the first if/else statement to discard any unnecessary or invalid entries. For example, if the user enters

```
100 dollars
```

the nextDouble method converts 100 to a double value, and the nextLine method reads past the "dollars" string. Then, because the String object that's returned by the nextLine method isn't assigned to a variable, it's discarded. Similarly, if the user enters an invalid double value, it's discarded by the nextLine method.

Since all characters in a string are valid, you don't need to check string variables for that type of validity. In some cases, though, you need to check whether the characters that a string contains are acceptable to the application. If, for example, the user is asked to enter a one-character code that should only be R, C, or T, the application should check to make sure the user has entered one of those characters. That's easily done with an if statement.

Although this figure only shows how to check data that the user has entered at a command prompt, the same principles apply to other types of applications. In section 4, for example, you'll see how these principles can be used to validate entries for an application that uses a graphical user interface.

Code that gets a valid double value within a specified range

```
Scanner sc = new Scanner(System.in);
double subtotal = 0.0;
boolean isValid = false;
while (isValid == false)
{
    // get a valid double value
    System.out.print("Enter subtotal:   ");
    if (sc.hasNextDouble())
    {
        subtotal = sc.nextDouble();
        isValid = true;
    }
    else
    {
        System.out.println("Error! Invalid number. Try again.");
    }
    sc.nextLine();  // discard any other data entered on the line

    // check the range of the double value
    if (isValid == true && subtotal <= 0)
    {
        System.out.println("Error! Number must be greater than 0.");
        isValid = false;
    }
    else if (isValid == true && subtotal >= 10000)
    {
        System.out.println("Error! Number must be less than 10000.");
        isValid = false;
    }
}
```

Description

- When a user enters data, that data usually needs to be checked to make sure that it is valid. This is known as *data validation.*
- When an entry is invalid, the program needs to display an error message and give the user another chance to enter valid data. This needs to be repeated until the entry is valid. One way to code this type of validation routine is to use a while loop.
- Two common types of validity checking for a numeric entry are (1) to make sure that the entry has a valid numeric format, and (2) to make sure that the entry is within a valid range (known as *range checking*).

Figure 5-5 How to validate an entry

How to use generic methods to validate an entry

Almost all professional applications need to validate two or more entries. Instead of writing code that validates a specific entry then, it often makes sense to create generic methods like the ones shown in figure 5-6. These methods perform the same types of validation shown in the previous figure, but they work for any double entry instead of for a specific entry.

In this figure, the getDouble method checks to be sure that the user enters a double value. This method accepts two parameters: a Scanner object and a String object that contains the text for the prompt. Then, this method displays the prompt to the user and, if the user enters a valid double value, it uses the scanner to read that value. Finally, the return statement returns the value to the calling method.

The getDoubleWithinRange method accepts four parameters. The first two parameters are the same as those used by the getDouble method. The second two parameters contain doubles that identify the range of values that are accepted by the application. Within the while loop for this method, the first statement passes the Scanner object and the prompt string to the getDouble method to get a double value from the user. Then, the if/else statement that follows checks if the double value returned by the getDouble method falls within the specified range. If so, the while loop ends and the double value is returned to the calling method. Otherwise, the getDouble method is called again until the user enters a value within the valid range.

Note that the public keyword is used as the access modifier for both of these methods. That way, the methods can be accessed and used by other classes. You'll learn more about that in chapter 7. If you're only going to use the methods within one class, though, the access modifier can be coded as private.

Once you understand how the getDouble and getDoubleWithinRange methods work, you can code methods for other numeric types. For example, you can code a getInt method that uses the hasNextInt method to be sure that the user enters a valid int value at the prompt. Similarly, you can code a getIntWithinRange method to check that an int value is within a specified range.

The code at the bottom of this figure shows how to call these methods to make sure a valid double value has been entered at the Subtotal prompt. The first statement creates the Scanner object that's needed by the getDouble method. Then, the second statement calls the getDouble method to get a valid double value for the subtotal. The third statement uses the getDoubleWithinRange method to get a valid double value for a subtotal that is greater than 0 and less than 10000. This shows that you can call the getDouble method directly if you don't need to check the range. If you need to check the range, however, you can call the getDoubleWithinRange method, which calls the getDouble method for you.

A method that gets a valid numeric format

```
public static double getDouble(Scanner sc, String prompt)
{
    double d = 0.0;
    boolean isValid = false;
    while (isValid == false)
    {
        System.out.print(prompt);
        if (sc.hasNextDouble())
        {
            d = sc.nextDouble();
            isValid = true;
        }
        else
        {
            System.out.println("Error! Invalid number. Try again.");
        }
        sc.nextLine();     // discard any other data entered on the line
    }
    return d;
}
```

A method that checks for a valid numeric range

```
public static double getDoubleWithinRange(Scanner sc, String prompt,
double min, double max)
{
    double d = 0.0;
    boolean isValid = false;
    while (isValid == false)
    {
        d = getDouble(sc, prompt);  // call the getDouble method
        if (d <= min)
        {
            System.out.println(
                "Error! Number must be greater than " + min + ".");
        }
        else if (d >= max)
        {
            System.out.println(
                "Error! Number must be less than " + max + ".");
        }
        else
            isValid = true;
    }
    return d;
}
```

Code that uses these methods to return two valid double values

```
Scanner sc = new Scanner(System.in);
double subtotal1 = getDouble(sc, "Enter subtotal: ");
double subtotal2 = getDoubleWithinRange(sc, "Enter subtotal: ", 0, 10000);
```

Description

- Because most applications need to check more than one type of entry for validity, it often makes sense to create and use generic methods for data validation.

Figure 5-6 How to use generic methods to validate an entry

The Future Value application with data validation

Figure 5-3 presented a version of the Future Value application that used a try statement to catch the most common exceptions that might be thrown. Now, you'll see an improved version of this application that uses generic methods to validate the user entries. This code prevents the most common exceptions from being thrown, and it provides more descriptive messages to the user.

The console

Figure 5-7 shows the console display when the user enters invalid data for the improved version of the Future Value application. Here, the error messages have been highlighted so you can see them more easily. For example, the first error message is displayed if the user doesn't enter a valid double value for the monthly investment. The second error message is displayed if the user enters a value that's out of range for the interest rate. And the third error message is displayed if the user doesn't enter a valid integer value for the years.

The Data Entry section in this figure uses descriptive error messages to identify the problems to the user, and it doesn't require that the user re-enter values that have already been successfully entered. In addition, it only uses the first value the user enters on a line, which is usually what you want. All other values are discarded.

After the user completes the Data Entry section, the Future Value application calculates the future value and displays it along with the user's entries in the Formatted Results section. This makes it easy to see what valid values the user entered, which is useful if the user has entered one or more invalid entries in the Data Entry section.

The console for the Future Value application

```
Welcome to the Future Value Calculator


DATA ENTRY
Enter monthly investment: $100
Error! Invalid decimal value. Try again.
Enter monthly investment: 100 dollars
Enter yearly interest rate: 120
Error! Number must be less than 30.0.
Enter yearly interest rate: 12.0
Enter number of years: one
Error! Invalid integer value. Try again.
Enter number of years: 1

FORMATTED RESULTS
Monthly investment:       $100.00
Yearly interest rate:     12.0%
Number of years:          1
Future value:             $1,280.93

Continue? (y/n):
```

Description

- The Data Entry section gets input from the user and displays an appropriate error message if the user enters an invalid numeric format or a number that's outside the valid range.
- The Formatted Results section displays the data that was entered by the user along with the future value in a format that's easy to read.

Figure 5-7 The console for the Future Value application with data validation

The code

Figure 5-8 shows the code for this version of the Future Value application. On page 1, you can see the code for the main method. Because this code is similar to code you've already seen, you shouldn't have any trouble understanding how it works. The biggest difference is that it uses methods named getDoubleWithinRange and getIntWithinRange to validate the data entered by the user. In this case, the monthly investment must be a double that's greater than 0 and less than 1000, the yearly interest rate must be a double that's greater than 0 and less than 30, and the number of years must be an int that's greater than 0 and less than 100. Then, the application will be able to calculate the future value for any values within these ranges.

The getDouble and getDoubleWithinRange methods shown on page 2 of this listing are the ones presented in figure 5-6. As a result, if you have any trouble understanding how these methods work, you may want to review that figure. The getInt and getIntWithinRange methods on page 3 work like the getDouble and getDoubleWithinRange methods except that they validate an int value instead of a double value. Note that all four of these methods, as well as the calculateFutureValue method, are coded with the public access modifier so they can be accessed from other classes.

As you review this code, notice how each method performs a specific task. For example, the getDouble and getInt methods prompt the user for an entry, validate the entry, and return the valid entry. Similarly, the calculateFutureValue method performs a calculation and returns the result. This is a good design because it leads to code that's reusable and easy to maintain. For example, you can use the getDouble and getInt methods with any console application that gets double or int values from the user. Although you can copy these methods from one application to another, you can also store them in classes that you can access from any application. You'll learn how to do that in chapter 7.

The code for the Future Value application with data validation Page 1

```
import java.util.*;
import java.text.*;

public class FutureValueApp
{
    public static void main(String[] args)
    {
        System.out.println("Welcome to the Future Value Calculator\n");

        Scanner sc = new Scanner(System.in);
        String choice = "y";
        while (choice.equalsIgnoreCase("y"))
        {
            System.out.println("DATA ENTRY");
            double monthlyInvestment = getDoubleWithinRange(sc,
                "Enter monthly investment: ", 0, 1000);
            double interestRate = getDoubleWithinRange(sc,
                "Enter yearly interest rate: ", 0, 30);
            int years = getIntWithinRange(sc,
                "Enter number of years: ", 0, 100);

            double monthlyInterestRate = interestRate/12/100;
            int months = years * 12;
            double futureValue = calculateFutureValue(
                monthlyInvestment, monthlyInterestRate, months);

            NumberFormat currency = NumberFormat.getCurrencyInstance();
            NumberFormat percent = NumberFormat.getPercentInstance();
            percent.setMinimumFractionDigits(1);

            String results =
                  "Monthly investment:\t"
                      + currency.format(monthlyInvestment) + "\n"
                + "Yearly interest rate:\t"
                      + percent.format(interestRate/100) + "\n"
                + "Number of years:\t"
                      +  years + "\n"
                + "Future value:\t\t"
                      + currency.format(futureValue) + "\n";

            System.out.println();
            System.out.println("FORMATTED RESULTS");
            System.out.println(results);

            System.out.print("Continue? (y/n): ");
            choice = sc.next();
            sc.nextLine();      // discard any other data entered on the line
            System.out.println();
        }
    }
```

The code for the Future Value application with data validation Page 2

```
public static double getDoubleWithinRange(Scanner sc, String prompt,
double min, double max)
{
    double d = 0.0;
    boolean isValid = false;
    while (isValid == false)
    {
        d = getDouble(sc, prompt);
        if (d <= min)
            System.out.println(
                "Error! Number must be greater than " + min + ".");
        else if (d >= max)
            System.out.println(
                "Error! Number must be less than " + max + ".");
        else
            isValid = true;
    }
    return d;
}

public static double getDouble(Scanner sc, String prompt)
{
    double d = 0.0;
    boolean isValid = false;
    while (isValid == false)
    {
        System.out.print(prompt);
        if (sc.hasNextDouble())
        {
            d = sc.nextDouble();
            isValid = true;
        }
        else
        {
            System.out.println(
                "Error! Invalid decimal value. Try again.");
        }
        sc.nextLine();  // discard any other data entered on the line
    }
    return d;
}
```

Figure 5-8 The code for the Future Value application with data validation (part 2 of 3)

The code for the Future Value application with data validation Page 3

```
    public static int getIntWithinRange(Scanner sc, String prompt,
    int min, int max)
    {
        int i = 0;
        boolean isValid = false;
        while (isValid == false)
        {
            i = getInt(sc, prompt);
            if (i <= min)
                System.out.println(
                    "Error! Number must be greater than " + min + ".");
            else if (i >= max)
                System.out.println(
                    "Error! Number must be less than " + max + ".");
            else
                isValid = true;
        }
        return i;
    }

    public static int getInt(Scanner sc, String prompt)
    {
        int i = 0;
        boolean isValid = false;
        while (isValid == false)
        {
            System.out.print(prompt);
            if (sc.hasNextInt())
            {
                i = sc.nextInt();
                isValid = true;
            }
            else
            {
                System.out.println(
                    "Error! Invalid integer value. Try again.");
            }
            sc.nextLine();  // discard any other data entered on the line
        }
        return i;
    }

    public static double calculateFutureValue(double monthlyInvestment,
    double monthlyInterestRate, int months)
    {
        double futureValue = 0;
        for (int i = 1; i <= months; i++)
        {
            futureValue =
                (futureValue + monthlyInvestment) *
                (1 + monthlyInterestRate);
        }
        return futureValue;
    }
}
```

Figure 5-8 The code for the Future Value application with data validation (part 3 of 3)

Perspective

Now that you've completed this chapter, you should be able to write console applications that validate the input data that's entered by the users and catch any exceptions that occur. As a result, the applications should never crash. That, of course, is the way professional applications should work.

At this point, you've learned a complete subset of Java, and you know how to use some of the methods in a few of the classes in the Java API. But there's a lot more to Java programming than that. In particular, you need to learn how to create your own classes that have their own methods. That's the essence of object-oriented programming, and that's what you'll learn in the next section of this book. But first, you'll learn how to test and debug an application.

Summary

- An *exception* is an object that's created from the Exception class or one of its *subclasses*. This object contains information about an error that has occurred.
- The *stack trace* is a list of methods that were called before an exception occurred.
- You can code a *try statement* to create an *exception handler* that will *catch* and handle any exceptions that are *thrown*. This is known as *exception handling*.
- *Data validation* refers to the process of checking input data to make sure that it's valid.
- *Range checking* refers to the process of checking an entry to make sure that it falls within a certain range of values.

Exercise 5-1 Add validation to the Invoice application

In this exercise, you'll add code to the Invoice application that validates the data the user enters. That includes exception handling code as well as specific data validation methods.

1. Open the project named ch05_ex1_Invoice in the ex_starts directory. Then, test the application to see how it works.
2. As you test the application, enter an invalid customer type code to see what happens. Then, enter an invalid subtotal entry like $1000 to see what happens when the application crashes.

Validate the customer type code

3. Modify the application so it will only accept customer type codes r and c. It should also discard any extra entries on the customer type line. If the user enters an invalid code, the application should display an error message and

ask the user to enter a valid code. This should be done before the user enters a subtotal. Then, test this enhancement.

4. Code a static method named getValidCustomerType that does the validation of step 3. This method should include one parameter that receives a Scanner object, and it should return a valid customer type code. The method should get an entry from the user, check it for validity, display an error message if it's invalid, and discard any other user entries whether or not the entry is valid. This method should continue getting user entries until one is valid. The easiest way to add the code for this method is to copy the code you wrote in step 3.
5. Modify the application so it uses this method. Then, test this enhancement.

Validate the subtotal

6. Add a try statement that catches any InputMismatchException that the nextDouble method of the Scanner class might throw. The catch block should display an error message and issue a continue statement to jump to the beginning of the while loop. It should also discard the invalid entry and any other entries on the line. For this to work, you'll need to import the InputMismatchException class, and you'll need to declare the subtotal variable before the try statement so it can be used outside that statement. Test this enhancement.
7. Code a static method named getValidSubtotal that uses the hasDouble method of the Scanner class to validate the subtotal entry so the InputMismatchException won't occur. This method should require one parameter that receives a Scanner object, and it should return a valid subtotal. This method should get an entry from the user, check that it's a valid double value, check that it's greater than zero and less than 10000, display appropriate error messages if it isn't valid, and discard any other user entries whether or not the entry is valid. This should continue until the method gets a valid subtotal entry.
8. Modify the code within the try statement so it uses this method. Then, test this enhancement so you can see that an InputMismatchException is no longer caught by the catch block.

Discard any extra entries for the Continue prompt

9. Run the application again. When the Continue prompt is displayed, enter two or more values to see what happens.
10. Modify the code so the application works right even if the user enters two or more values when asked if he wants to continue. To do that, you need to discard any extra entries. Then, test this enhancement.

At this point, the application should be bulletproof. It should only accept valid entries for customer type and subtotal, and it should work even if the user makes two or more entries for a single prompt.

Exercise 5-2 Add validation to the Test Score application

In this exercise, you'll add data validation to a variation of the Test Score application that you worked on in previous chapters. To do that, you'll use generic methods that you can copy from the Future Value application. This will show you that generic validation methods can be used in a wide range of applications.

1. Open the project named ch05_ex2_TestScore in the ex_starts directory. Then, run the application to see how it works. Note that it crashes if you enter an invalid integer for a score or if you enter "y" followed by another value at the prompt that asks if you want to enter another score. Note also that it allows invalid scores such as 150.
2. Open the ch05_FutureValueValidation project in the book_apps directory. Then, copy the generic getInt and getIntWithinRange methods from that application and paste them into the TestScoreApp class.
3. Use the getInt and getIntWithinRange methods to validate that each score ranges from 1 through 100. Then, test this enhancement.
4. Add code that discards any extra entries at the prompt that asks if you want to enter another score. Then, test the application to make sure that it is bulletproof.

6

How to test and debug an application

As you develop a Java application, you need to test it to make sure that it performs as expected. Then, if you encounter any problems, you need to debug the application to locate the cause of the problems. This chapter shows how to do both.

Basic skills for testing and debugging

When you *test* an application, you run it to make sure that it works correctly. As you test the application, you try every possible combination of input data and user actions to be certain that the application works in every case. In other words, the goal of testing is to make an application fail.

When you *debug* an application, you fix the errors (*bugs*) that you discover during testing. Each time you fix a bug, you test again to make sure that the change that you made didn't affect any other aspect of the application.

Typical test phases

When you test an application, you typically do so in phases. Figure 6-1 lists three common test phases.

In the first phase, you test the user interface. For a console application, that means you should make sure that the console displays the correct text and prompts the user for the correct data. For an application with a graphical user interface, that means you should visually check the controls to make sure they're displayed properly with the correct text. Then, you should make sure that all the keys and controls work correctly. For instance, you should test the Tab and Enter keys as well as the operation of check boxes and drop-down lists.

In the second phase, you test the application with valid data. To start, you can enter data that you would expect a user to enter. Then, you should enter valid data that tests all of the limits of the application.

In the third phase, you try to make the application fail by testing every combination of invalid data and user action that you can think of. That should include random actions like pressing the Enter key or clicking the mouse at the wrong time.

The three types of errors

Three types of errors can occur as you test an application. These errors are described in figure 6-1.

Syntax errors, also called *compile-time errors*, prevent your application from compiling and running. This type of error is the easiest to find and fix. If you use an IDE like NetBeans, it automatically detects syntax errors as you type and gives you suggestions for how to fix them.

Unfortunately, some errors can't be detected until you run an application. These errors are known as *runtime errors*, and they throw *exceptions* that stop the execution of an application.

Even if an application runs without throwing exceptions, it may contain *logic errors* that prevent the application from working correctly. This type of error is often the most difficult to find and correct. For example, the Future Value application in this figure has a logic error. Can you tell what it is?

The Future Value application with a logic error

```
Welcome to the Future Value Calculator

DATA ENTRY
Enter monthly investment: 100
Enter yearly interest rate: 3
Enter number of years: 3

FORMATTED RESULTS
Monthly investment:        $100.00
Yearly interest rate:      3.0%
Number of years:           3
Future value:              $6,517.42

Continue? (y/n):
```

The goal of testing

- To find all errors before the application is put into production.

The goal of debugging

- To fix all errors before the application is put into production.

Three test phases

- Check the user interface to make sure that it works correctly.
- Test the application with valid input data to make sure the results are correct.
- Test the application with invalid data or unexpected user actions. Try everything you can think of to make the application fail.

The three types of errors that can occur

- *Syntax errors* violate the rules for how Java statements must be written. These errors, also called *compile-time errors*, are caught by the NetBeans IDE or the Java compiler before you run the application.
- *Runtime errors* don't violate the syntax rules, but they throw *exceptions* that stop the execution of the application.
- *Logic errors* are statements that don't cause syntax or runtime errors, but produce the wrong results. In the Future Value application shown above, the future value isn't correct, which is a logic error.

Description

- To *test* a Java application, you run it to make sure that it works properly no matter what combinations of valid or invalid data you enter.
- When you *debug* an application, you find and fix all of the errors (*bugs*) that you find when you test the application.

Figure 6-1 An introduction to testing and debugging

Common Java errors

Figure 6-2 presents some of the coding errors that are commonly made as you write a Java application. If you study this figure, you'll have a better idea of what to watch out for. And if you did the exercises for the first five chapters, you've probably experienced some of these errors already.

The code at the top of this figure is the start of the code for the static getDouble method of the Future Value application, but with four errors introduced. The first error is that a data type has not been declared for the variable named d. Unlike some other languages, Java requires that you declare the data type for all variables.

The second error is a missing semicolon at the end of the statement that declares the variable named isValid. As you know, Java requires a semicolon at the end of every statement unless the statement contains a block of code that's enclosed in braces.

The third error is a missing closing parenthesis at the end of the condition for the if statement. Remember that every opening parenthesis, brace, or quotation mark must have a closing parenthesis, brace, or quotation mark.

The fourth error is that the statement that calls the nextDouble method from the Scanner object named sc uses improper capitalization. For this statement, "NextDouble" should be "nextDouble" since Java is case-sensitive.

This figure also describes the problem that Java has with floating-point arithmetic. As you can see in the example near the bottom of this figure, floating-point arithmetic can produce strange results even with simple calculations. This is the same problem that was described at the end of chapter 3, so you should already be aware of it and know how to use the BigDecimal class to fix it.

Code that contains errors

```
public static double getDouble(Scanner sc, String prompt)
{
    d = 0.0;                           // no data type declared
    boolean isValid = false            // missing semicolon at end of statement
    while (isValid == false)
    {
        System.out.print(prompt);
        if (sc.hasNextDouble()         // missing closing parenthesis
        {
            d = sc.NextDouble();       // improper capitalization
            isValid = true;
        }
        else
        {
            System.out.println("Error! Invalid decimal value. Try again.");
        }
        sc.nextLine();
    }
    return d;
}
```

Common syntax errors

- Misspelling keywords.
- Forgetting to declare a data type for a variable.
- Forgetting an opening or closing parenthesis, bracket, brace, or comment character.
- Forgetting to code a semicolon at the end of a statement.
- Forgetting an opening or closing quotation mark.

Problems with identifiers

- Misspelling or incorrectly capitalizing an identifier.
- Using a reserved word, global property, or global method as an identifier.

Problems with values

- Not checking that a value is the right data type before processing it. For example, you expect the user to enter a number, but he or she enters a non-numeric value instead.
- Using one equals sign instead of two when testing numeric and Boolean values for equality.
- Using two equals signs instead of the equals or equalsIgnoreCase method to test two strings for equality.

A problem with floating-point arithmetic

- The double data type uses floating-point numbers that can lead to arithmetic errors. For example, 0.2 + 0.7 is 0.8999999999999999.
- One way around this is to use the BigDecimal class as described at the end of chapter 3.

Figure 6-2 Common Java errors

A simple way to trace code execution

When you *trace* the execution of an application, you add statements to your code that display messages or variable values at key points in the code. You typically do this to help find the cause of a logic error.

If, for example, you can't figure out why the future value that's calculated by the Future Value application is incorrect, you can insert println statements into the code for the application as shown in figure 6-3. Here, the first println statement prints a message that indicates that the calculateFutureValue method is starting. Then, the next three println statements print the values of monthlyInvestment, monthlyInterestRate, and months variables. Finally, the last println statement prints the value of the counter variable and the futureValue variable each time through the for loop. That should help you determine where the calculation is going wrong. Then, when you find and fix the problem, you can remove the println statements.

When you use this technique, you usually start by adding just a few println statements to the code. Then, if that doesn't help you solve the problem, you can add more. This works well for simple applications, but it creates extra work for you because you have to add statements to your code and remove them later.

In the next few figures, you'll learn how to use NetBeans to debug an application without having to add or remove statements. Since this is usually easier than adding and removing statements, you'll rarely need to use the technique shown in this figure. However, it can be useful in some cases.

Code that uses println statements to trace execution

```
public static double calculateFutureValue(double monthlyInvestment,
double monthlyInterestRate, int months)
{
    System.out.println("starting calculateFutureValue method...");
    double futureValue = 0;
    System.out.println("monthlyInvestment: " + monthlyInvestment);
    System.out.println("monthlyInterestRate: " + monthlyInterestRate);
    System.out.println("months: " + months);
    for (int i = 1; i <= months; i++)
    {
        futureValue =
            (futureValue + monthlyInvestment) *
            (1 + monthlyInterestRate);
        System.out.println("month " + i + " futureValue: " + futureValue);
    }
    return futureValue;
}
```

The data that's printed to the console

```
starting calculateFutureValue method...
monthlyInvestment: 100.0
monthlyInterestRate: 0.03
months: 36
month 1 futureValue: 103.0
month 2 futureValue: 209.09
month 3 futureValue: 318.3627
month 4 futureValue: 430.913581
month 5 futureValue: 546.84098843
...
...
```

Description

- A simple way to *trace* the execution of an application is to insert println statements at key points in the code that print messages to the console.
- The messages that are printed to the console can indicate what code is being executed, or they can display the values of variables.
- When you see an incorrect value displayed, there is a good chance that the application contains a logic error between the current println statement and the previous one.

Figure 6-3 A simple way to trace code execution

How to use NetBeans to debug an application

As you test applications, you will encounter errors that are commonly referred to as bugs. When that happens, you must find and fix those errors using a process known as *debugging*. Fortunately, NetBeans includes a powerful tool called a *debugger* that can help you find and fix these errors.

How to set and remove breakpoints

The first step in debugging an application is to figure out what is causing the bug. To do that, it's often helpful to view the values of the variables at different points in the application's execution. This will help you determine the cause of the bug, which is critical to debugging the application.

The easiest way to view the variable values as an application is executing is to set a *breakpoint* as shown in figure 6-4. To do that, you click on the line number to the left of the line of code. Then, the breakpoint is marked by a red square. Later, when you run the application with the debugger, execution will stop just prior to the statement at the breakpoint. Then, you will be able to view the variables that are in scope at that point in the application. You'll learn more about that in the next figure.

When debugging, it's important to set the breakpoint before the line in the application that's causing the bug. Often, you can figure out where to set a breakpoint by reading the runtime exception that's displayed when your application crashes. Sometimes, though, you will have to experiment before finding a good location to set a breakpoint.

After you set the breakpoint, you need to run the application with the debugger. To do that, you can use the Debug Project/Debug Main Project button that's available from the toolbar (just to the right of the Run Project/Run Main Project button). If you encounter any problems, try right-clicking on the .java file that contains the main method and selecting the Debug File command to run the application with the debugger.

Note that once you set a breakpoint, it remains set until you remove it. That's true even if you close the project and exit from NetBeans. To remove a breakpoint, you can click on its icon.

A code editor window with a breakpoint

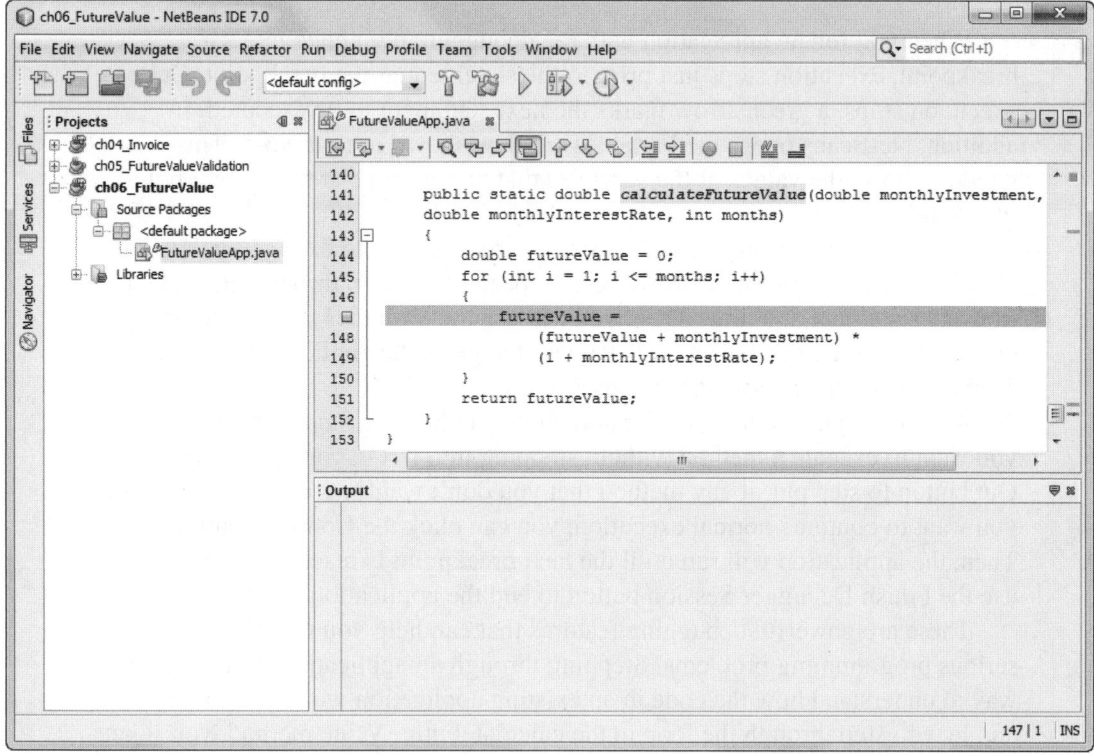

Description

- A *breakpoint* causes program execution to stop before the line that contains the breakpoint is executed.
- To set a breakpoint for a line, open the code editor for the class and click on the line number. The breakpoint is identified by a small red square that's placed to the left of the line of code.
- To remove a breakpoint, click on the breakpoint icon.
- You can set and remove breakpoints either before you start debugging or while you're debugging. In most cases, you'll set at least one breakpoint before you start debugging.
- To start debugging for the main project, click the Debug Main Project button on the toolbar. If a single project is open and it's not set as the main project, the name of this button is Debug Project.
- You can also start debugging by right-clicking on a project and selecting the Debug command or by right-clicking on the file that contains the main method you want to run and selecting the Debug File command.

Figure 6-4 How to set and remove breakpoints

How to step through code

When you run an application with the debugger and it encounters a breakpoint, execution stops just prior to the statement at the breakpoint. Once execution stops, a green arrow marks the next statement to be executed. In addition, NetBeans opens the Variables window shown in figure 6-5. This window shows the values of the variables that are in scope at the current point of execution.

NetBeans also displays the Debug toolbar while you're debugging. You can click the Step Into button on this toolbar repeatedly to step through an application one statement at a time. Then, you can use the Variables window to observe exactly how and when the variable values change as the application executes. That can help you determine the cause of a bug.

As you step through an application, you can click the Step Over button if you want to execute a method without stepping into it. Or, you can use the Step Out button to step out of any method that you don't want to step through. When you want to continue normal execution, you can click the Continue button. Then, the application will run until the next breakpoint is reached. Or, you can use the Finish Debugger Session button to end the application's execution.

These are powerful debugging features that can help you find the cause of serious programming problems. Stepping through an application is also a good way to understand how the code in an existing application works. If, for example, you step through the loop in the calculateFutureValue method, you'll get a better idea of how that loop works.

How to inspect variables

When you set breakpoints and step through code, the Variables window automatically displays the values of the variables that are in scope. In figure 6-5, the execution point is in the calculateFutureValue method of the FutureValueApp class. Here, the Variables window shows the values of the three parameters that are passed to the method (monthlyInvestment, monthlyInterestRate, and months) and two local variables that are declared within the method (futureValue and i).

For numeric variables and strings, the value of the variable is shown in the Variables window. However, when an object such as one that's created from the Scanner class is displayed in the Variables window, it doesn't display the values of its variables automatically. Instead, it displays a plus sign to the left of the object name. Then, you can view the values for the object by clicking on that plus sign to expand it.

In the next chapter, you'll learn how to create objects from classes that you define. Then, if the code within one of these objects is executing, you'll see a variable named *this* in the Variables window. This is a keyword that's used to refer to the current object, and you can expand it to view the values of the variables that are defined by the object. That will make more sense when you start to learn about object-oriented programming in the next chapter.

A debugging session

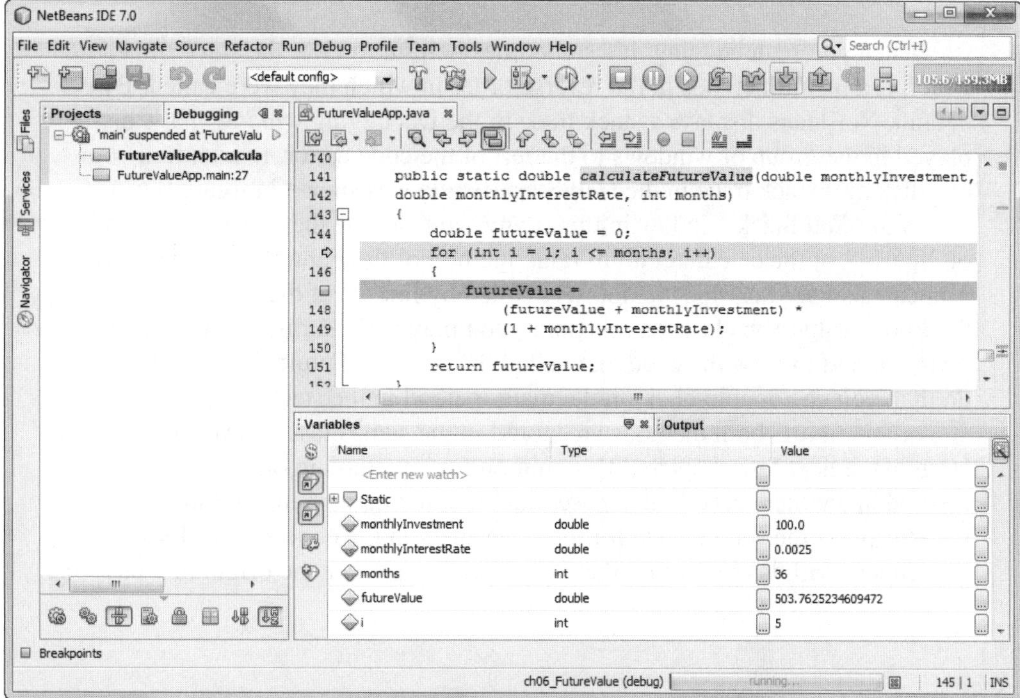

Some of the buttons on the Debug toolbar

Button	Keyboard shortcut	Description
Step Over	F7	Steps through the code one statement at a time, skipping over called methods.
Step Into	F8	Steps through the code one statement at a time, including statements in called methods.
Step Out	Ctrl+F7	Finishes executing the code in the current method and returns to the calling method.
Continue	F5	Continues execution until the next breakpoint.
Finish Debugger Session	Shift+F5	Ends the application's execution.

Description

- When a breakpoint is reached, program execution is stopped before the line is executed.
- The arrow in the bar at the left side of the code editor window shows the line that will be executed next.
- The Variables window shows the values of the variables that are in scope for the current method. This window is displayed by default when you start a debugging session. If you close it, you can open it again using the Window→Debugging→Variables command.
- If a variable in the Variables window refers to an object, you can view the values for that object by clicking the plus sign to the left of the object name to expand it.
- You can use the buttons on the Debug toolbar to control the execution of an application.

Figure 6-5 How to step through code and inspect variables

How to inspect the stack trace

When you're debugging, it's sometimes helpful to view the *stack trace*, which is a list of methods in the reverse order in which they were called. By default, NetBeans displays a stack trace in the Debugging window that's displayed in the group of windows to the left of the code editor. In addition, you can display a stack trace in the Call Stack window as shown in figure 6-6.

In the Call Stack window in this figure, you can see that code execution is on line 147 of the calculateFutureValue method of the FutureValueApp class. You can also see that this method was called by line 27 of the main method of the FutureValueApp class. At this point, you may want to display line 27 of the main method to view the code that called the calculateFutureValue method. To do that, you can double-click on the main method in the stack trace.

In this figure, both methods are stored in the same class. However, as you'll learn in the next few chapters, it's common for a method in one class to call a method in another class. In that case, double-clicking on a method in the stack trace displays the source code for the other class in the code editor. If you experiment with is, you'll find that it can help you locate the origin of a bug.

A debugging session with the Call Stack window displayed

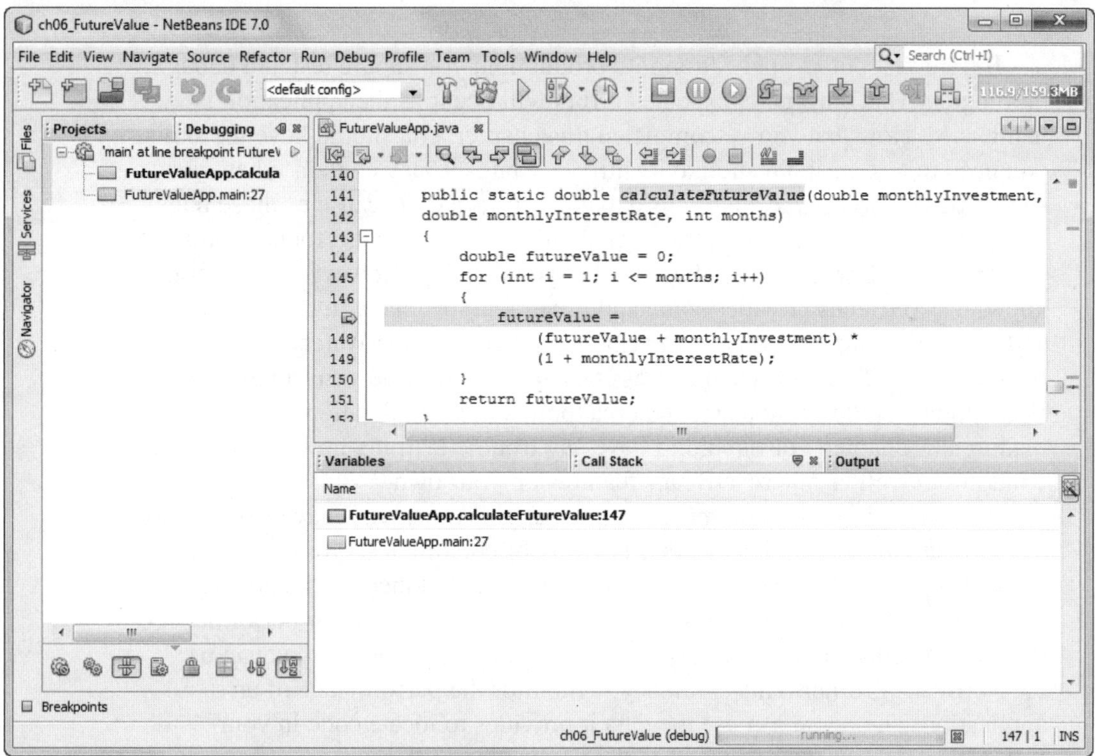

Description

- A *stack trace* is a list of the methods that have been called in the reverse order in which they were called.
- By default, NetBeans displays a stack trace in the Debugging window that's included in the group of windows at the left side of the IDE.
- You can also display a stack trace in the Call Stack window, which appears in the group of windows below the code editor. You can display this window by selecting the Window→Debugging→Call Stack command.
- To jump to a line of code in the code editor that's displayed in the stack trace, double-click on that line in the stack trace.

Figure 6-6 How to inspect the stack trace

Perspective

Before you put an application into production, you should test and debug it thoroughly. That way, no unexpected errors will occur as the application is being used. Now that you've completed this chapter, you should have the skills you need to test an application to identify any bugs it may contain. Then, you should be able to use the NetBeans debugger to locate the cause of those bugs.

The skills presented in this chapter should give you a solid foundation for testing and debugging any application that you develop. However, you should know that NetBeans provides some additional features that you can use to test and debug your applications. For example, you can use the Watches window to list the values of variables and expressions you specify, and you can use the Breakpoints window to manage the breakpoints in an application. After reading this chapter, you shouldn't have any trouble learning how to use these windows as well as other NetBeans features on your own.

As you begin to develop more complex applications, you may also want to learn about unit testing. Unit testing is a way of creating tests for individual units of source code such as methods to make sure that they work correctly.

As you test an application, you may also run into memory or performance-related problems. To help identify the source of these problems, you can use the NetBeans Profiler. This tool lets you monitor the performance of an application. Then, you can use the data it provides to locate code in your application that can be optimized so the application will run more efficiently.

Summary

- To *test* an application, you run it to make sure that it works properly no matter what combinations of valid or invalid data you enter.
- When you *debug* an application, you find and fix all of the errors (*bugs*) that you find when you test the application.
- *Syntax errors* violate the rules for how Java statements must be written. These errors are detected by the NetBeans IDE or the Java compiler before you can run the application.
- *Runtime errors* occur after you run an application. These types of errors throw *exceptions* that stop the execution of the application.
- *Logic errors* don't cause the application to crash, but they prevent it from working correctly.
- A simple way to *trace* the execution of an application is to insert println statements at key points in the code.
- NetBeans includes a powerful tool known as a *debugger* that can help you find and fix these errors.

- You can set a *breakpoint* on a line of code to stop code execution just before that line of code. Then, you can step through the code and view the values of the variables as the code executes.
- A *stack trace* is a list of methods in the reverse order in which they were called.

Exercise 6-1 Test and debug the Invoice application

This exercise guides you through the process of using NetBeans to test and debug an application.

Test the Invoice application with invalid data

1. Open the ch06_ex1_Invoice project, and test the Invoice application with an invalid subtotal like $1000 (enter the dollar sign too). This should cause the application to crash with a runtime error and to display an error message in the Output window.
2. Study the error message, and note the line number of the statement in the InvoiceApp class that caused the crash. Then, click on the link to that line of code. This should open the InvoiceApp.java file in the code editor and highlight the line of code that caused the crash. Based on this information, you should be able to figure out that the application crashed because $1000 isn't a valid double value. By now, you should know how to fix this type of problem.

Set a breakpoint and step through the application

3. Set a breakpoint on this line of code:
   ```
   double discountPercent = 0.0;
   ```
4. Make sure that the ch06_ex1_InvoiceApp project is set as the main project. Then, click on the Debug Main Project button in the toolbar. This runs the project with the debugger on.
5. Click the Output tab to display the Output window and enter a value of 100 for the subtotal when prompted by the application. When you do, the application runs to the breakpoint and stops.
6. Click the Variables tab to display the Variables window and note that the choice and subtotal variables have been assigned values.
7. Click the Step Into button in the toolbar repeatedly to step through the application one statement at a time. After each step, review the values in the Variables window to see how they have changed. Note how the application steps through the if/else statement based on the subtotal value.
8. Click the Continue button in the toolbar to continue the execution of the application.
9. Display the Output window again. Then, enter "y" to continue and enter a value of 50 for the subtotal.

10. Display the Variables window again and inspect the values of the variables.
11. Click the Step Over button in the toolbar repeatedly to step through the application one statement at a time. After each step, review the values in the Variables window to see how they have changed.
12. When you're done inspecting the variables, click the Finish Debugger Session button to end the application. This should give you some idea of how useful the NetBeans debugging tools can be.

Exercise 6-2 Test and debug the Future Value application

In this exercise, you'll use NetBeans to find and fix syntax errors and a logic error in the Future Value application.

Use NetBeans to correct the syntax errors

1. Open the ch06_ex2_FutureValue project, and then display the FutureValueApp.java file. Note that the getDouble method in this file contains syntax errors.
2. Use NetBeans to find and fix the errors.

Use println statements to trace code execution

3. Scroll down to the calculateFutureValue method, and add a println statement within the loop that prints the value of the month and the future value each time the loop is executed.
4. Run the application to see how the println statement works. Review the values that are displayed in the Output window, and notice that that the future value increases by too much each month.
5. Comment out the println statement so it no longer prints messages to the Output window.

Step through the application

6. In the calculateFutureValue method, set a breakpoint on the statement that calculates the future value.
7. Run the application and enter values when prompted. The application should stop at the breakpoint.
8. Experiment with the Step Into, Step Over, and Step Out buttons as you step through the code of the application. At each step, notice the values that are displayed in the Variables window and use them to find the logic error.
9. When you're done experimenting, click on the Finish Debugger Session button and remove the breakpoint.
10. Fix the logic error and then run the application again to be sure it produces correct results.

Section 2

Object-oriented programming with Java

In the first section of this book, you learned how to use classes that are provided as part of the Java API. For instance, you learned how to use the Math class to perform common arithmetic operations, and you learned how to use the NumberFormat class to format numeric values. That's one part of object-oriented programming.

Besides the classes provided by the API, though, you can create your own classes. That's the other part of object-oriented programming, and that's what the four chapters in this section teach you to do. Specifically, chapter 7 shows you how to create your own classes. Chapter 8 shows you how to use inheritance, one of the most important features of object-oriented programming. Chapter 9 shows you how to use interfaces. And chapter 10 presents other object-oriented skills.

Because each of the chapters in this section builds on the previous chapters, you should read these chapters in sequence. In addition, you should read all of the chapters in this section before going on to sections 3, 4, or 5. That's because many of the chapters in these sections rely on your knowledge of inheritance and interfaces.

7

How to define and use classes

This chapter shows you how to create and use your own classes in Java applications. Here, you'll learn how to create classes that include regular fields and methods as well as classes that contain static fields and methods. In addition, you'll see two complete applications that use several user-defined classes.

When you complete this chapter, you'll start to see how creating your own classes can help simplify the development of an application. As a bonus, you'll have a better understanding of how the Java API works.

An introduction to classes

The topics that follow introduce you to the concepts that you need to know before you create your own classes. That includes how you'll use classes in a typical business application, how the fields and methods of a class can be encapsulated within the class, and how a class relates to its objects.

How classes can be used to structure an application

Figure 7-1 shows how you can use classes to simplify the design of a business application using a *multi-layered architecture*, also called a *multi-tiered architecture*. In a multi-layered application, the classes that perform different functions of the application are separated into two or more layers, or tiers.

A *three-tiered* application architecture like the one shown in this figure consists of a presentation layer, a middle layer, and a database layer. In practice, the middle layer is sometimes eliminated and its functions split between the database and presentation layers. On the other hand, the design of some applications further develops the middle layer into additional layers.

The classes in the *presentation layer* handle the details of the application's user interface. So far, all of the applications you've seen have been console applications. In these applications, most of the presentation layer is handled by the main method, which may call methods of other classes. In section 4, though, you'll learn how to write Java applications that display a graphical user interface (GUI) that consists of multiple windows called frames. In these applications, a separate class is usually created for each frame displayed by the application.

The classes of the *database layer* are responsible for all of the database access that's required by the application. These classes typically include methods that connect to the database and retrieve, add, update, and delete information from the database. Then, the other layers can call these methods to access the database. Although we refer to this layer as the database layer, it can also contain classes that work with data that's stored in files.

The *middle layer* provides an interface between the database layer and the presentation layer. This layer often includes classes that correspond to business entities (for example, products and customers). It may also include classes that implement business rules, such as discount or credit policies. The classes in this tier are often referred to as *business classes*, and the objects that are created from these classes are often called *business objects*.

One advantage of developing applications with a tiered architecture is that it allows the work to be spread among members of a development team. For example, one group of developers might work on the database layer, another group on the middle layer, and still another group on the presentation layer.

Another advantage is that it allows classes to be shared among applications. In particular, the classes that make up the database and middle layers can be stored in packages that can be used by more than one project. You'll learn how to work with packages in chapter 10.

The architecture of a three-tiered application

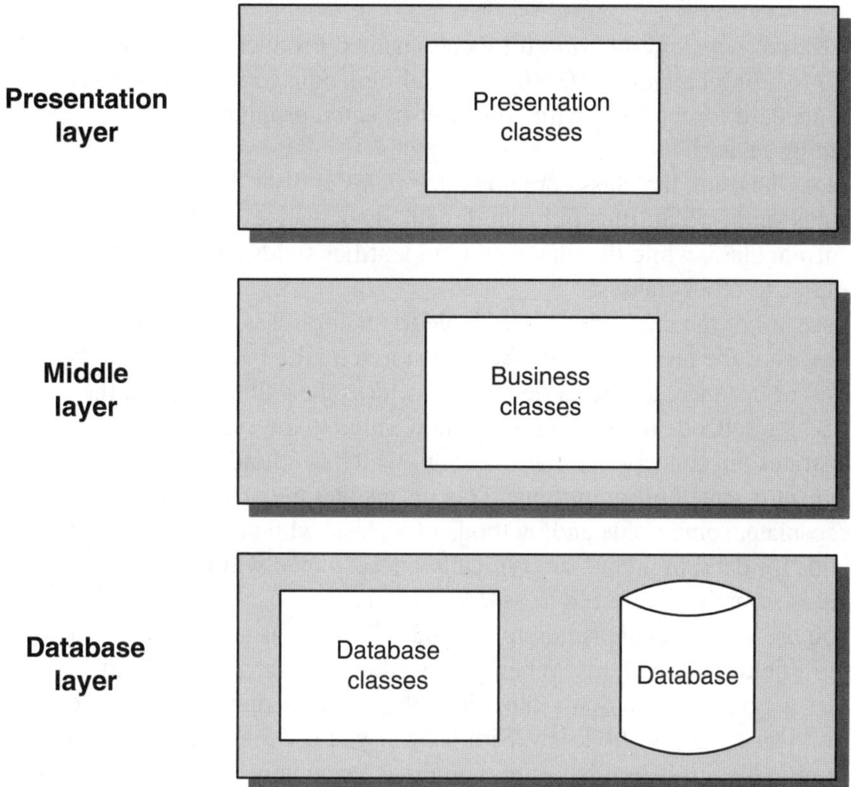

Description

- To simplify development and maintenance, many applications use a *three-tiered architecture* to separate the application's user interface, business rules, and database processing. Classes are used to implement the functions performed at each layer of the architecture.
- The classes in the *presentation layer* control the application's user interface. For a console application, the presentation layer typically consists of a class with a main method and any other classes related to console input and output. For a GUI application, the user interface typically consists of one class for each window (called a *frame* in Java) that makes up the GUI.
- The classes in the *database layer* handle all of the application's data processing.
- The classes in the *middle layer*, which is sometimes called the *business rules layer*, act as an interface between the classes in the presentation and database layers. Sometimes, these classes correspond to business entities, such as customers or products, and sometimes these classes implement business rules, such as discount or credit policies. Often, the classes in this layer are referred to as *business classes*, and the objects created from them are called *business objects*.
- The classes that make up each layer are often stored in packages that can be shared among applications. For more information, see chapter 10.

Figure 7-1 How classes can be used to structure an application

How encapsulation works

Figure 7-2 shows a *class diagram* for a class named Product. This diagram uses *Unified Modeling Language* (*UML*), a modeling language that has become the industry standard for working with all object-oriented programming languages including Java.

In this class diagram, the class contains three *fields* and seven *methods*. Here, the minus sign (-) identifies fields and methods that are available only within the current class, while the plus sign (+) identifies fields and methods that are available to other classes.

In this case, all of the methods are available to other classes, but none of the fields are. However, the methods make the data stored by the fields available to other classes. For instance, the getCode method returns the value stored in the code field, and the setCode method assigns a new value to the code field.

This illustrates the concept of *encapsulation*, which is a fundamental concept of object-oriented programming. This means that the programmer can *hide*, or encapsulate, some fields and methods of a class, while *exposing* others. Since the fields (or data) of a class are typically encapsulated within a class, encapsulation is sometimes referred to as *data hiding*.

When you use a class, encapsulation lets you think of it as a black box that provides useful fields and methods. When you use the parseInt method of the Integer class, for example, you don't know how the method converts a string to an integer, and you don't need to know. Similarly, if you use the getPrice method of the Product class in this figure, you don't know how the method works, and you don't need to know.

This also means that you can change the code for a method within a class without affecting the classes that use the method. For instance, you can change the code for the getPrice method without changing the classes that use that method. This makes it easier to upgrade or enhance an application because you only need to change the classes that need upgrading.

A class diagram for the Product class

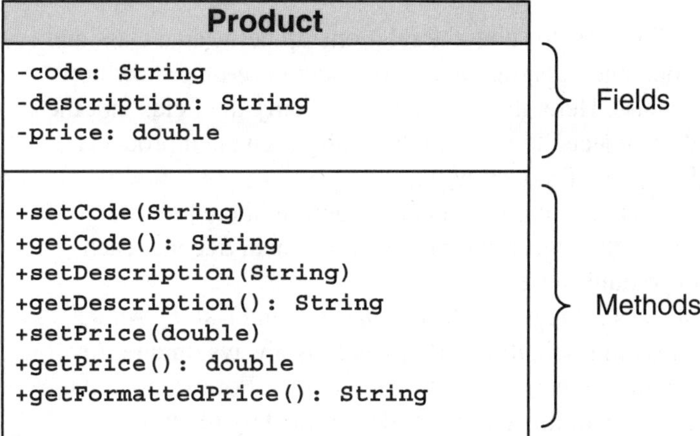

Description

- The *fields* of a class store the data of a class.
- The *methods* of a class define the tasks that a class can perform. Often, these methods provide a way to work with the fields of a class.
- *Encapsulation* is one of the fundamental concepts of object-oriented programming. This means that the class controls which of its fields and methods can be accessed by other classes. As a result, the fields in the class can be hidden from other classes, and the methods in a class can be modified or improved without changing the way that other classes use them.

UML diagramming notes

- *UML* (*Unified Modeling Language*) is the industry standard used to describe the classes and objects of an object-oriented application.
- The minus sign (-) in a UML *class diagram* marks the fields and methods that can't be accessed by other classes, while the plus sign (+) marks the fields and methods that can be accessed by other classes.
- For each field, the name is given, followed by a colon, followed by the data type.
- For each method, the name is given, followed by a set of parentheses. If a method requires parameters, the data type of each parameter is listed in the parentheses. Otherwise, the parentheses are left empty, and the data type of the value that's going to be returned is given after the colon.

Figure 7-2 How encapsulation works

The relationship between a class and its objects

Figure 7-3 uses UML diagrams to show the relationship between a class and its objects. In this figure, one class diagram and two *object diagrams* show how objects are created from a class. Here, the diagrams show only the fields, not the methods, of the class and its objects. In this case, two objects named product1 and product2 are created from the Product class.

Although an object diagram is similar to a class diagram, there are two differences. First, the name of the object diagram is underlined. Second, each field in an object diagram contains a value.

Once an *instance* of a class is created, it has an *identity* and a *state*. An object's identity is its address in internal memory, which is always unique. An object's state refers to the values that are stored by the object. For example, the states of the two Product objects in this figure are determined by the three values that they hold. As a program executes, the state of an object may change, but the identity of the object won't.

The relationship between a class and its objects

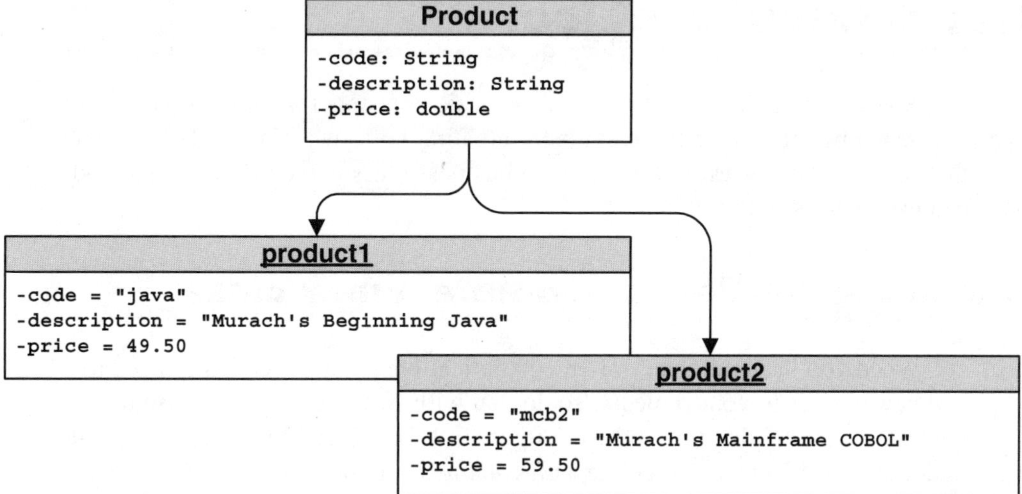

Description

- A *class* can be thought of as a template from which *objects* are made.
- An *object diagram* provides the name of the object and the values of the fields.
- Once an *instance* of a class is created, it has an *identity* (a unique address) and a *state* (the values that it holds). Although an object's state may change throughout a program, its identity never does.

How to code a class that defines an object

Now that you've learned some of the basic concepts for using classes, you're ready to learn the basic skills for creating your own classes. In the topics that follow, you'll learn how to create a business class named Product that you can use to work with products.

How to use NetBeans to create a new class

When you develop object-oriented applications, you'll frequently need to add new classes to your projects. To do that with NetBeans, you can use the New Java Class dialog box shown in figure 7-4. In this figure, for example, this dialog box is being used to create a class named Product.

Notice here that a package isn't specified for the class. Because of that, the class will be stored in the default package. Although it's typically a good idea to use packages to organize the classes in an application, this chapter and the next two chapters will focus on creating and using classes. Then, in chapter 10, you'll learn how to create and use packages.

When you complete the New Java Class dialog box, NetBeans creates a file that will store the Java code for the class. For the Product class in this figure, that file will be named Product.java. NetBeans also generates the starting code for the class as shown in this figure. Note that the name of the class matches the name of the file, which is required. In addition, the public *access modifier* is used so the class can be accessed from other classes.

By default, NetBeans places the opening brace for a class it creates on the same line as the class declaration. However, if you prefer to have the opening brace on its own line, you should know that you can change how this code is generated. To do that, you can use the Tools→Option command as described in this figure.

The dialog box for creating a new Java class

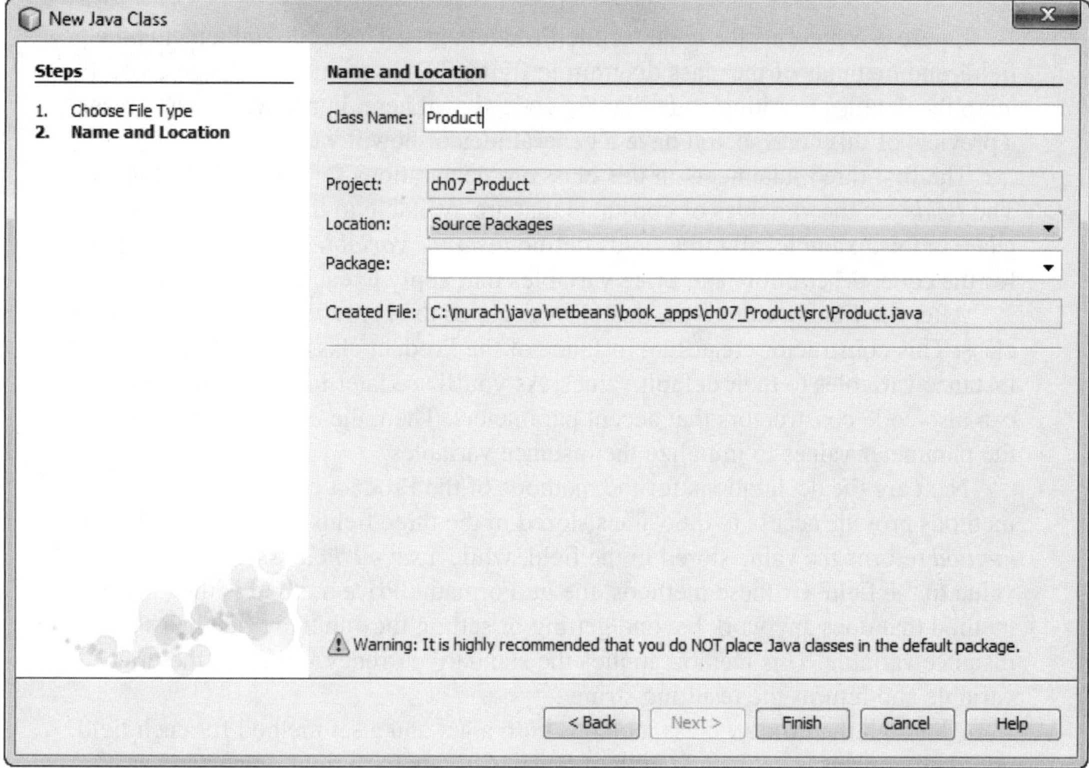

The code that's generated for the Product class

```
public class Product {

}
```

Description

- To create a new class, right-click on the package where you want to add the class, select the New→Java Class command, and respond to the resulting dialog box. At the least, you should enter a name for the class in the Class Name text box.
- Although this dialog box encourages you to select a package for the class, this isn't required. If you don't select a package for the class, NetBeans will store the class in the default package. To learn how to create and use packages, see chapter 10.
- You can change a NetBeans option so the opening brace for a class is on its own line rather than on the same line as the class declaration. To do that, use the Tools→Options command, click the Editor button at the top of the Options dialog box that's displayed, display the Formatting tab, select Java from the Language drop-down list, and select Braces from the Category drop-down list. Then, select New Line from the Class Declaration drop-down list.

Figure 7-4 How to use NetBeans to create a new class

The code for the Product class

Figure 7-5 presents the code for the Product class. This code implements the fields and methods of the class diagram in figure 7-2. In the next six pages, you'll learn the details of writing code like the code shown here. For now, I'll just present a preview of this code so you have a general idea of how it works.

The first three statements in this class are declarations for the fields of the class. The *fields* are the variables or constants that are available to the class and its objects. In this example, all three fields define *instance variables*, which store the data for the code, description, and price variables that apply to each Product object.

After the field declarations, this class declares the *constructor* of the Product class. This constructor creates an instance of the Product class and initializes its instance variables to their default values. As you'll see later in this chapter, you can also code constructors that accept parameters. Then, the constructor can use the parameter values to initialize the instance variables.

Next are the declarations for the methods of the Product class. In this class, the methods provide access to the values stored in the three fields. For each field, a *get method* returns the value stored in the field, while a *set method* assigns a new value to the field. Of these methods, the getFormattedPrice method is the only method that does any work beyond getting or setting the value provided by the instance variable. This method applies the standard currency format to the price variable and returns the resulting string.

Although the Product class includes both a get and a set method for each field, you don't always have to code both of these methods for a field. In particular, it's common to code just a get method for a field so that its value can be retrieved but not changed. This can be referred to as a *read-only field*. Although you can also code just a set method for a field, that's uncommon.

The private and public keywords determine which *members* of a class are available to other classes. Since all of the instance variables of the Product class use the private keyword, they are only available within that class. The constructor and the methods, however, use the public keyword. As a result, they are available to all classes. Keep in mind, though, that you can include both public and private instance variables and methods in any class.

By the way, this class follows the three coding rules that are required for a *JavaBean*. First, it includes a constructor that requires no arguments. Second, all of the instance variables are private. Third, it includes get and set methods for all instance variables that you want to be able to access. As you progress with Java, you'll find many advantages to creating classes that are also JavaBeans. For example, if you develop JavaServer Pages (JSPs) for a web application, you can use special JSP tags to create a JavaBean and to access its get and set methods.

Now that you've seen the code for the Product class, you might want to consider how it uses encapsulation. First, the three fields are hidden from other classes because they're declared with the private keyword. In addition, all of the code contained within the constructor and methods is hidden. Because of that, you can change any of this code without having to change the other classes that use this class.

The Product class

```
import java.text.NumberFormat;

public class Product
{
    // the instance variables
    private String code;
    private String description;
    private double price;

    // the constructor
    public Product()
    {
        code = "";
        description = "";
        price = 0;
    }

    // the set and get methods for the code variable
    public void setCode(String code)
    {
        this.code = code;
    }
    public String getCode()
    {
        return code;
    }

    // the set and get methods for the description variable
    public void setDescription(String description)
    {
        this.description = description;
    }
    public String getDescription()
    {
        return description;
    }

    // the set and get methods for the price variable
    public void setPrice(double price)
    {
        this.price = price;
    }
    public double getPrice()
    {
        return price;
    }

    // a custom get method for the price variable
    public String getFormattedPrice()
    {
        NumberFormat currency = NumberFormat.getCurrencyInstance();
        return currency.format(price);
    }
}
```

Figure 7-5 The code for the Product class

How to code instance variables

Figure 7-6 shows how to code the instance variables that define the types of data that are used by the objects that are created from a class. When you declare an instance variable, you should use an access modifier to control its accessibility. If you use the private keyword, the instance variable can be used only within the class that defines it. In contrast, if you use the public keyword, the instance variable can be accessed by other classes. You can also use other access modifiers that give you finer control over the accessibility of your instance variables. You'll learn about those modifiers in the chapters that follow.

This figure shows four examples of declaring an instance variable. The first example declares a variable of the double type. The second one declares a variable of the int type. The third one declares a variable that's an object of the String class. And the last one declares an object from the Product class...the class that you're learning how to code right now.

Although instance variables work like regular variables, they must be declared within the class body, but not inside methods or constructors. That way, they'll be available throughout the entire class. In this book, all of the instance variables for a class are declared at the beginning of the class. However, when you read through code from other sources, you may find that the instance variables are declared at the end of the class or at other locations within the class.

The syntax for declaring instance variables

```
public|private primitiveType|ClassName variableName;
```

Examples

```
private double price;
private int quantity;
private String code;
private Product product;
```

Where you can declare instance variables

```
public class Product
{
    //common to code instance variables here
    private String code;
    private String description;
    private double price;

    //the constructors and methods of the class
    public Product(){}
    public void setCode(String code){}
    public String getCode(){ return code; }
    public void setDescription(String description){}
    public String getDescription(){ return description; }
    public void setPrice(double price){}
    public double getPrice(){ return price; }
    public String getFormattedPrice(){ return formattedPrice; }

    //also possible to code instance variables here
    private int test;
}
```

Description

- An instance variable may be a primitive data type, an object created from a Java class such as the String class, or an object created from a user-defined class such as the Product class.
- To prevent other classes from accessing instance variables, use the private keyword to declare them as private.
- You can declare the instance variables for a class anywhere outside the constructors and methods of the class.

Figure 7-6 How to code instance variables

How to code constructors

Figure 7-7 shows how to code a constructor for a class. When you code one, it's a good coding practice to assign a value to all of the instance variables of the class as shown in the four examples. You can also include any additional statements that you want to execute within the constructor. For instance, the fourth example ends by calling two different get methods from the current class.

When you code a constructor, you must use the public access modifier and the same name, including capitalization, as the class name. Then, if you don't want to accept arguments, you must code an empty set of parentheses as shown in the first example. On the other hand, if you want to accept arguments, you code the parameters for the constructor as shown in the next three examples. When you code the parameters for a constructor, you must code a data type and a name for each parameter. For the data type, you can code a primitive data type or the class name for any class that defines an object.

The second example shows a constructor with three parameters. Here, the first parameter is a String object named code; the second parameter is a String object named description; and the third parameter is a double type named price. Then, the three statements within the constructor use these parameters to initialize the three instance variables of the class.

In this example, the names of the parameters are the same as the names of the instance variables. As a result, the constructor must distinguish between the two. To do that, it uses the this keyword to refer to the instance variables of the current object. You'll learn about other ways you can use this keyword later in this chapter.

The third example works the same as the second example, but it doesn't need to use the this keyword because the parameter names aren't the same as the names of the instance variables. In this case, though, the parameter names aren't very descriptive. As a result, the code in the second example is easier for other programmers to read than the code in the third example.

The fourth example shows a constructor with one parameter. Here, the first statement assigns the first parameter to the first instance variable of the class. Then, the second statement calls a method of a class named ProductDB to get a Product object for the specified code. Finally, the last two statements call methods of the Product object, and the values returned by these methods are assigned to the second and third instance variables.

When you code a constructor, the class name plus the number of parameters and the data type for each parameter form the *signature* of the constructor. You can code more than one constructor per class as long as each constructor has a unique signature. For example, the first two constructors shown in this figure have different signatures so they could both be coded within the Product class. This is known as *overloading* a constructor.

If you don't code a constructor, Java will create a *default constructor* that doesn't accept any parameters and initializes all instance variables to null, zero, or false. If you code a constructor that accepts parameters, though, Java won't create this default constructor. So if you need a constructor like that, you'll need to code it explicitly. To avoid this confusion, it's a good practice to code all of

The syntax for coding constructors

```
public ClassName([parameterList])
{
    // the statements of the constructor
}
```

Example 1: A constructor that assigns default values

```
public Product()
{
   code = "";
   description = "";
   price = 0.0;
}
```

Example 2: A custom constructor with three parameters

```
public Product(String code, String description, double price)
{
    this.code = code;
    this.description = description;
    this.price = price;
}
```

Example 3: Another way to code the constructor shown above

```
public Product(String c, String d, double p)
{
    code = c;
    description = d;
    price = p;
}
```

Example 4: A constructor with one parameter

```
public Product(String code)
{
    this.code = code;
    Product p = ProductDB.getProduct(code);
    description = p.getDescription();
    price = p.getPrice();
}
```

Description

- The constructor must use the same name and capitalization as the name of the class.
- If you don't code a constructor, Java will create a *default constructor* that initializes all numeric types to zero, all boolean types to false, and all objects to null.
- To code a constructor that has parameters, code a data type and name for each parameter within the parentheses that follow the class name.
- The name of the class combined with the parameter list forms the *signature* of the constructor. Although you can code more than one constructor per class, each constructor must have a unique signature.
- In the second and fourth examples above, the this keyword is used to refer to an instance variable of the current object.

Figure 7-7 How to code constructors

your own constructors. That way, it's easy to see which constructors are available to a class, and it's easy to check the values that each constructor uses to initialize the instance variables.

How to code methods

Figure 7-8 shows how to code the methods of a class. To start, you code an access modifier. Most of the time, you can use the public keyword to declare the method so it can be used by other classes. However, you can also use the private keyword to hide the method from other classes.

After the access modifier, you code the return type for the method, which refers to the data type that the method returns. After the return type, you code the name of the method followed by a set of parentheses. Within the parentheses, you code the parameter list for the method. Last, you code the opening and closing braces that contain the statements of the method.

Since a method name should describe the action that the method performs, it's a common coding practice to start each method name with a verb. For example, methods that set the value of an instance variable usually begin with *set*. Conversely, methods that return the value of an instance variable usually begin with *get*. These types of methods are typically referred to as *accessors* because they let you access the values of the instance variables. Methods that perform other types of tasks also begin with verbs such as print, save, read, and write.

The first example shows how to code a method that doesn't accept any parameters or return any values. To do that, it uses the void keyword for the return type and it ends with a set of empty parentheses. When this method is called, it prints the instance variables of the Product object to the console, separating each instance variable with a pipe character (|).

The next three examples show how to code methods that return data. To do that, these methods specify a return type, and they include a return statement to return the appropriate variable. When coding a method like this, you must make sure that the return type that you specify matches the data type of the variable that you return. Otherwise, your code won't compile.

In the fourth example, the getFormattedPrice method uses a NumberFormat object to apply standard currency formatting to the double variable named price. This also converts the double variable to a String object. Then, the return statement returns the String object to the calling method.

The fifth and sixth examples show two possible ways to code a set method. In the fifth example, the method accepts a parameter that has the same name as the instance variable. As a result, the assignment statement within this method uses the this keyword to identify the instance variable. In the sixth example, the parameter has a different name than the instance variable. As a result, the assignment statement doesn't need to use the this keyword. Since the parameter name for both examples are descriptive, both of these examples work equally well.

The syntax for coding a method

```
public|private returnType methodName([parameterList])
{
   // the statements of the method
}
```

Example 1: A method that doesn't accept parameters or return data

```
public void printToConsole()
{
    System.out.println(code + "|" + description +  "|" + price);
}
```

Example 2: A get method that returns a string

```
public String getCode()
{
   return code;
}
```

Example 3: A get method that returns a double value

```
public double getPrice()
{
   return price;
}
```

Example 4: A custom get method

```
public String getFormattedPrice()
{
    NumberFormat currency = NumberFormat.getCurrencyInstance();
    return currency.format(price);
}
```

Example 5: A set method

```
public void setCode(String code)
{
    this.code = code;
}
```

Example 6: Another way to code a set method

```
public void setCode(String productCode)
{
    code = productCode;
}
```

Description

- To allow other classes to access a method, use the public keyword. To prevent other classes from accessing a method, use the private keyword.
- To code a method that doesn't return data, use the void keyword for the return type. To code a method that returns data, code a return type in the method declaration and code a return statement in the body of the method.
- When you name a method, you should start each name with a verb. It's a common coding practice to use the verb *set* for methods that set the values of instance variables and to use the verb *get* for methods that return the values of instance variables. These methods are typically referred to as set and get *accessors*.

Figure 7-8 How to code methods

How to overload methods

Figure 7-9 shows how to overload a method, which is similar to overloading a constructor. When you overload a method, you code two or more methods with the same name, but with unique combinations of parameters. In other words, you code methods with unique signatures.

For a method signature to be unique, the method must have a different number of parameters than the other methods with the same name, or at least one of the parameters must have a different data type. Note that the names of the parameters aren't part of the signature. So using different parameter names isn't enough to make the signatures unique. Also, the return type isn't part of the signature. As a result, you can't create two methods with the same name and parameters but different return types.

The purpose of overloading is to provide more than one way to invoke a given method. For example, this figure shows three versions of the printToConsole method. The first one accepts a String parameter named sep that's used to separate the code, price, and description of a Product object. Then, it prints the resulting string to the console.

The second method doesn't accept a parameter that specifies the separator string. Instead, it separates the code, price, and description with the pipe character. To do that, it calls the first printToConsole method and passes the pipe character to it. Although I could have just called the println method to print the line, calling an overloaded method can often prevent code duplication.

The third method accepts a String parameter for the separator along with a boolean parameter that indicates whether to print a blank line after printing the data to the console. This method begins by passing the sep parameter to the first printToConsole method. Then, it uses an if statement to determine whether to print a blank line.

When you refer to an overloaded method, the number of arguments you specify and their types determine which version of the method is executed. The three statements in this figure that call the printToConsole method illustrate how this works. Because the first statement doesn't specify an argument, it causes the second version of the printToConsole method to be executed. In contrast, the second statement specifies a String argument of four blank spaces and a boolean argument of true. As a result, it will cause the third version of the printToConsole method to be executed. Finally, the third statement specifies a single String argument, which causes the first version of the printToConsole method to be executed.

Example 1: A method that accepts one argument

```
public void printToConsole(String sep)
{
    System.out.println(code + sep + description + sep + price);
}
```

Example 2: An overloaded method that provides a default value

```
public void printToConsole()
{
    printToConsole("|");     // this calls the method in the first example
}
```

Example 3: An overloaded method with two arguments

```
public void printToConsole(String sep, boolean printLineAfter)
{
    printToConsole(sep);     // this calls the method in the first example
    if (printLineAfter)
        System.out.println();
}
```

Code that calls these methods

```
Product p = ProductDB.getProduct("java");

p.printToConsole();
p.printToConsole("    ", true);
p.printToConsole("    ");
```

The console

```
java|Murach's Beginning Java 2|49.5
java    Murach's Beginning Java  49.5

java    Murach's Beginning Java  49.5
```

Description

- When you create two or more methods with the same name but with different parameter lists, the methods are overloaded. It's common to use overloaded methods to provide two or more versions of a method that work with different data types or that supply default values for omitted parameters.

How to use the this keyword

In figures 7-7 and 7-8, you saw how to use the this keyword to refer to an instance variable from a constructor or method. You can also use this keyword to call methods of the current object, to pass the current object to another method, and to call another constructor of the current class from the current constructor. Figure 7-10 shows you how to use this keyword.

The first line of the syntax summary shows how to refer to an instance variable of the current object. The second and third lines show how to call a constructor or method of the same class. And the fourth and fifth lines show how to pass the current object to a method of the object and to a static method of a class.

Since Java implicitly supplies the this keyword for all instance variables and methods, you don't usually need to code this keyword when referring to instance variables or methods. However, the first example is an exception to this rule. Here, the code, description, and price parameters in the constructor have the same names as the code, description, and price instance variables. As a result, you need to use the this keyword to explicitly identify the instance variables. Of course, another approach would be to change the parameter names so they aren't the same as the instance variable names.

The second example shows how to call the getPrice method of the current object. In this case, the this keyword isn't necessary because it would be added implicitly. However, it does make it clear that the getPrice method is a method of the current object.

The third example shows how to call another constructor in the same class. Specifically, this constructor uses the this keyword to call the constructor in the first example, and it passes three default values to it. This is an easy way to overload a constructor so it provides default values for missing parameters.

The fourth example shows how to use the this keyword to pass the current object to a method. In this example, a method named print sends the current object to the println method of the System.out object. As a result, the println method will print a representation of the current object to the console.

The fifth example works like the fourth example, but it shows that you can use the this keyword to pass the current object to a static method. In this case, a method named save saves the current object by calling the static saveProduct method of the ProductDB class.

The syntax for using the this keyword

```
this.variableName // refers to an instance variable of the current object
this(argumentList); // calls another constructor of the same class
this.methodName(argumentList) // calls a method of the current object
objectName.methodName(this) // passes the current object to a method
ClassName.methodName(this) // passes the current object to a static method
```

Example 1: How to refer to instance variables

```
public Product(String code, String description, double price)
{
    this.code = code;
    this.description = description;
    this.price = price;
}
```

Example 2: How to refer to methods

```
public String getFormattedPrice()
{
    NumberFormat currency = NumberFormat.getCurrencyInstance();
    return currency.format(this.getPrice);
}
```

Example 3: How to call a constructor

```
public Product()
{
    this("", "", 0.0);
}
```

Example 4: How to send the current object to a method

```
public void print()
{
    System.out.println(this);
}
```

Example 5: How to send the current object to a static method

```
public void save()
{
    ProductDB.saveProduct(this);
}
```

Description

- Since Java implicitly uses the this keyword for instance variables and methods, you don't need to explicitly code it unless a parameter has the same name as an instance variable.
- If you use the this keyword to call another constructor, the statement must be the first statement in the constructor.

Figure 7-10 How to use the this keyword

How to use NetBeans to work with classes

Figure 7-11 shows how NetBeans can make it easier to work with classes. To start, after you enter the private fields for a class, you can use NetBeans to generate the get and set methods for those fields. To do that, you use the Encapsulate Fields dialog box shown in this figure. As you can see, this dialog box lists all the private fields and lets you select what methods you want to generate for each field. It also lets you set several options that control how the methods are generated.

When you use the Encapsulate Fields dialog box, the get and set methods for a field are formatted like this by default:

```
public String getCode() {
    return code;
}

public void setCode(String code) {
    this.code = code;
}
```

Just as you can when you create a class, though, you can change the code that's generated for a method so the opening brace is on its own line. To do that, you select the New Line option from the Method Declaration drop-down list in the Options dialog box. For more information about displaying this option, see figure 7-4.

Once you've created a class, you can use the Navigator window shown in this figure to jump to any member of the class. To do that, just double-click on the member name. Although the usefulness of this feature isn't obvious for a simple class like the Product class, it can be helpful for classes with more members.

The NetBeans window for the Product application

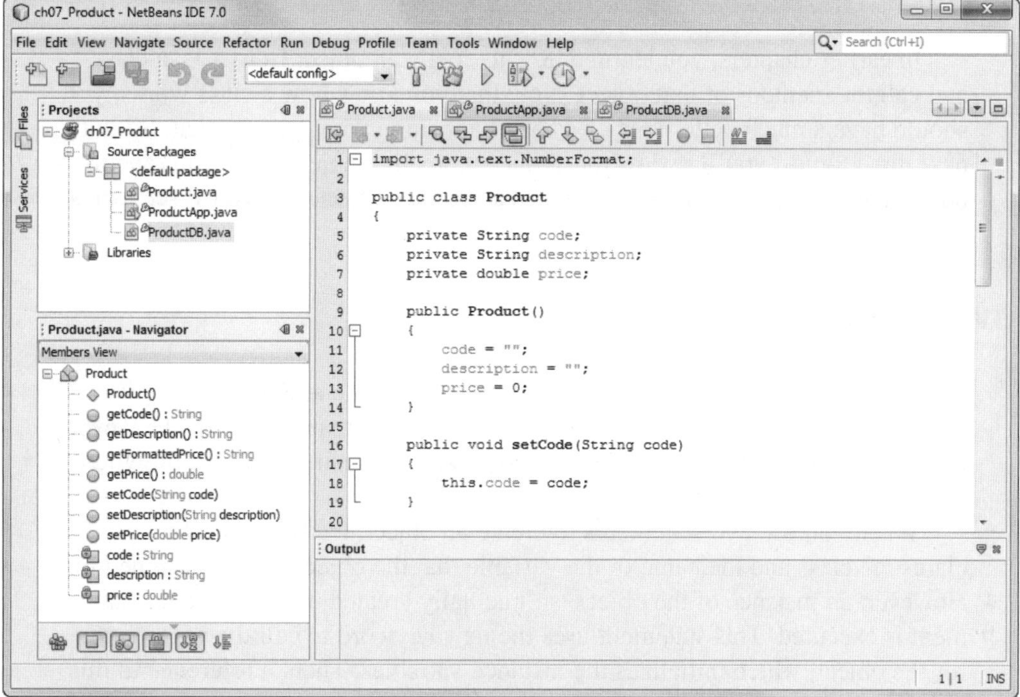

The dialog box for generating get and set methods

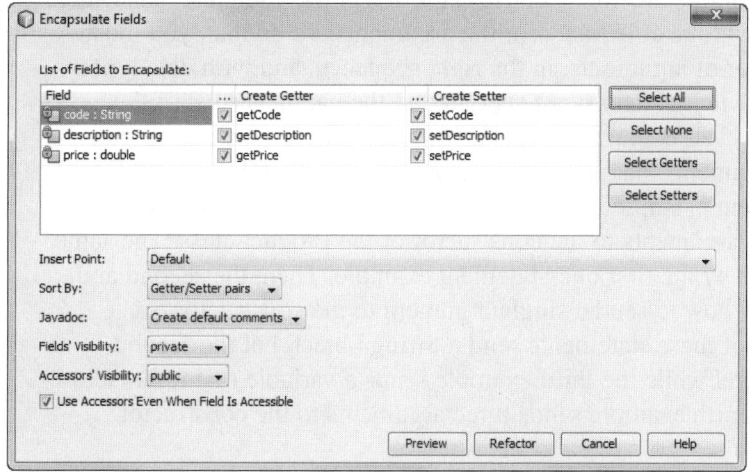

Description

- To generate get and set methods for one or more field, select the Refactor→Encapsulate Fields command and respond to the resulting dialog box.
- The Navigator window lists all the members of the currently selected class. To display this window, click on its tab at the left side of the IDE, or use the Window→Navigating→Navigator command. To jump to a member, double-click on it in the Navigator window.

Figure 7-11 How to use NetBeans to work with classes

How to create and use an object

In earlier chapters, you learned how to create an object from a Java class and call the methods of that object. Now that you know how a class works, you should have a much better idea of what's happening when you do that. So in the next three topics, you'll review the skills for creating objects and using methods. Then, you'll see a class that creates a Product object, and you'll see a class that uses that object.

How to create an object

Figure 7-12 shows how to create an object with one and with two statements. Most of the time, you'll use one statement to create an object. However, as you'll see later in this book, certain types of coding situations require you to create an object with two statements.

When you use two statements to create an object, the first statement declares the class and the name of the variable that the object will be assigned to. However, an instance of the object isn't actually created until the second statement is executed. This statement uses the new keyword to call the constructor for the object, which initializes the instance variables. Then, a reference to this object is assigned to the variable. At this point, you can use the variable to refer to the object.

When you send arguments to the constructor of a class, you must make sure that the constructor will be able to accept the arguments. To do that, you must send the right number of arguments, in the right sequence, and with data types that are compatible with the data types specified in the parameter list of the constructor. When a class contains more than one constructor, the constructor that matches the arguments that are sent is the constructor that will be executed.

The two-statement example in this figure creates a new Product object without passing any arguments to the constructor of the Product class. The same task is accomplished by the first one-statement example. Then, the second and third examples show how to send a single argument to the constructor of the Product class. Both of these statements send a String object, but the second example sends a literal while the third example sends a variable that refers to a String object. The fourth example sends three arguments to the constructor.

How to create an object in two statements

Syntax

```
ClassName variableName;
variableName = new ClassName(argumentList);
```

Example with no arguments

```
Product product;
product = new Product();
```

How to create an object in one statement

Syntax

```
ClassName variableName = new ClassName(argumentList);
```

Example 1: No arguments

```
Product product = new Product();
```

Example 2: One literal argument

```
Product product = new Product("java");
```

Example 3: One variable argument

```
Product product = new Product(productCode);
```

Example 4: Three arguments

```
Product product = new Product(code, description, price);
```

Description

- To create an object, you use the new keyword to create a new instance of a class. Each time the new keyword creates an object, Java calls the constructor for the object, which initializes the instance variables for the object.
- After you create an object, you assign it to a variable. When you do, a reference to the object is stored in the variable. Then, you can use the variable to refer to the object.
- To send arguments to the constructor, code the arguments between the parentheses that follow the class name. To send more than one argument, separate the arguments with commas.
- When you send arguments to the constructor, the arguments must be in the sequence called for by the constructor and they must have data types that are compatible with the data types of the parameters for the constructor.

Figure 7-12 How to create an object

How to call the methods of an object

Figure 7-13 shows how to call the methods of an object. By now, you should be familiar with the basic syntax for calling a method, so this figure should just be review. To start, you type the object name followed by the dot operator and the method name. Then, if the method requires arguments, you code the argument list between the parentheses, separating multiple arguments with commas. Otherwise, you code an empty set of parentheses.

The first two examples show two ways to call methods that don't return any data. The first example doesn't send an argument, while the second example sends an argument named productCode. In this case, the argument is a variable that represents a String object, but the argument could also be a literal value such as "java". Either way, you need to send the right number of arguments, and the data types of those arguments must be compatible with the data types specified in the parameter list of the method.

The third and fourth examples show how to call a method that returns a value and assigns that value to a variable. In the third example, the getPrice method doesn't have any arguments, but it does return a value. Then, that value is assigned to a double variable named price. In the fourth example, the getFormattedPrice method sends a boolean variable as an argument that indicates whether a dollar sign should be included in the formatted value. This is a variation of the getFormattedPrice method you saw back in figure 7-5. Like that method, this method returns a string that is then stored in a string variable.

The fifth example shows how to call a method within an expression. Here, the expression includes a call to the getCode method, which returns a String object. Then, that String object is joined with three string literals, and the result is assigned to another String object.

How to call a method

Syntax

```
objectName.methodName(argumentList)
```

Example 1: Sends and returns no arguments

```
product.printToConsole();
```

Example 2: Sends one argument and returns no arguments

```
product.setCode(productCode);
```

Example 3: Sends no arguments and returns a double value

```
double price = product.getPrice();
```

Example 4: Sends an argument and returns a String object

```
String formattedPrice = product.getFormattedPrice(includeDollarSign);
```

Example 5: A method call within an expression

```
String message = "Code: " + product.getCode() + "\n\n"
               + "Press Enter to continue or enter 'x' to exit:";
```

Description

- To call a method that doesn't accept arguments, type an empty set of parentheses after the method name.
- To call a method that accepts arguments, enter the arguments between the parentheses that follow the method name. Here, the data type of each argument must be compatible with the data type that's specified by the method's parameters.
- To code more than one argument, separate the arguments with commas.
- If a method returns a value, you can code an assignment statement to assign the return value to a variable. Here, the data type of the variable must be compatible with the data type of the return value.

Figure 7-13 How to call the methods of an object

How primitive types and reference types are passed to a method

Figure 7-14 shows the difference between passing *primitive types* to a method and passing *reference types* (objects) to a method. In both cases, the value of the variable is passed to the method rather than the variable itself. Since a primitive type variable stores the actual value of the variable, though, that means that the method can't change the value of the variable directly. In contrast, a reference type variable stores a reference to the object. Because of that, the method has access to the object and can change the values of its variables.

The first example shows how this works when a primitive data type is passed to a method that increases the value of the variable by 10%. In this case, the increasePrice method uses a return statement to return the increased value. Then, the code that calls this method reassigns the return value to the original variable. In other words, the method works with the value of the variable, but it can't modify the value in the variable itself.

The second example shows how this works when a reference type is passed to a method. Here, the increasePrice method accepts a Product object. Notice that the return type for this method is void, so no value is returned by the method. Instead, the getPrice and setPrice methods of the Product class are used to get and set the quantity variable. In other words, the method refers to the object and its data so that data is actually changed by the method.

In practice, you usually don't need to know how values are passed to methods. Most of the time, you won't need to modify a value that's stored in a parameter. Occasionally, though, you do need to be aware of the differences in how you work with primitive types and object types. When you do, you can refer back to this figure to refresh your memory.

Example 1: A primitive type that's passed to a method

A method that changes the value of a double type

```
static double increasePrice(double price) // returns a double
{
    return price *= 1.1;
}
```

Code that calls the method

```
double price = 49.5;
price = increasePrice(price);          // reassignment statement
System.out.println("price: " + price);
```

Result

```
price: 54.45
```

Example 2: An object type that's passed to a method

A method that changes a value stored in a Product object

```
static void increasePrice(Product product)  // no return value
{
    double price = product.getPrice();
    product.setPrice(price *= 1.1);
}
```

Code that calls the method

```
Product product = ProductDB.getProduct("java");
System.out.println("product.getPrice(): " + product.getPrice());
increasePrice(product);                  // no reassignment necessary
System.out.println("product.getPrice(): " + product.getPrice());
```

Result

```
product.getPrice(): 49.5
product.getPrice(): 54.45
```

Description

- When a *primitive type* is passed to a method, the method receives the value of the variable. That means the method can't change the value of the variable directly. Instead, the method must return a new value that gets stored in the variable.
- When a *reference type* (an object) is passed to a method, the method also receives the value of the variable. Because an object variable contains a pointer to the object, though, the method can change the data in the object. That means that a new value doesn't need to be returned by the method.

Figure 7-14 How primitive types and reference types are passed to a method

A ProductDB class that creates a Product object

Figure 7-15 presents a database class named ProductDB that provides the data processing required by an application that displays the data for a product. This class consists of a single static method named getProduct that returns a Product object based on the product code that's passed to it.

The code within the getProduct method starts by creating a Product object. If you look back to figure 7-5, you'll see that this causes the code and description fields to be set to empty strings and the price to be set to zero.

After the Product object is created, its setCode method is called to assign the product code that was passed to the getProduct method to the code field of this object. Next, the getProduct method uses an if/else statement to determine what values are assigned to the description and price fields of the Product object depending on the value of the product code. Notice that the setDescription and setPrice methods of the Product object are used to set these values. Also notice that if the product code doesn't match any of the specified products, this method sets the description to "Unknown" and it leaves the price at its default value of zero. Finally, this method returns the Product object.

Because this class doesn't retrieve the data for a product from a file or database, it isn't realistic. However, it does simulate the processing that would be done by a class like this. In fact, you could use code like this to test the basic functions of an application before you add the code that works with a file or database. In section 5 of this book, you'll learn how to implement a class like this so it gets the required data from a file or a database.

The ProductDB class

```
public class ProductDB
{
    public static Product getProduct(String productCode)
    {
        // create the Product object
        Product p = new Product();

        // fill the Product object with data
        p.setCode(productCode);
        if (productCode.equalsIgnoreCase("java"))
        {
            p.setDescription("Murach's Beginning Java");
            p.setPrice(49.50);
        }
        else if (productCode.equalsIgnoreCase("jsps"))
        {
            p.setDescription("Murach's Java Servlets and JSP");
            p.setPrice(49.50);
        }
        else if (productCode.equalsIgnoreCase("mcb2"))
        {
            p.setDescription("Murach's Mainframe COBOL");
            p.setPrice(59.50);
        }
        else
        {
            p.setDescription("Unknown");
        }
        return p;
    }
}
```

Notes

- The ProductDB class provides the database layer that creates a Product object and gets the data for it from a file or database. In this case, though, the ProductDB class just simulates the processing that would be done by a database class.
- In a more realistic application, the database class would use the product code to retrieve the data for a product from a file or database and then fill the Product object with that data. It would also include methods for adding new products and for modifying and deleting existing products. You'll learn how to code classes like this in section 5.

Figure 7-15 A ProductDB class that returns a Product object

A ProductApp class that uses a Product object

Figure 7-16 presents a ProductApp class that uses the ProductDB class and the Product object it creates. As you can tell from the console at the top of this figure, this application prompts the user for a product code. Then, it retrieves and displays the description and price of that product.

The ProductApp class shown here contains the main method for the application, which means that this method is executed when the application starts. To make it easy to tell which class of an application contains the main method, it's common to add a suffix to the class name. In this book, we use "App" as the suffix as you've seen in all the applications we've presented to this point.

The main method in this class is similar to the other ones that you've seen. It uses a loop to retrieve and display the product data for each product code the user enters. The code that uses the Product class in this loop is highlighted. The first statement calls the getProduct method of the ProductDB class to create a Product object named product. Notice here that except for the capitalization, the object and class have the same name. That's possible because Java is a case-sensitive language.

Once the Product object is created and initialized, this program displays the product's description and price. To get that information, it calls the getDescription and getFormattedPrice methods of the Product object.

The console

```
Welcome to the Product Selector

Enter product code: java

SELECTED PRODUCT
Description: Murach's Beginning Java
Price:       $49.50

Continue? (y/n):
```

The ProductApp class

```
import java.util.Scanner;

public class ProductApp
{
    public static void main(String args[])
    {
        // display a welcome message
        System.out.println("Welcome to the Product Selector");
        System.out.println();

        // display 1 or more products
        Scanner sc = new Scanner(System.in);
        String choice = "y";
        while (choice.equalsIgnoreCase("y"))
        {
            // get the input from the user
            System.out.print("Enter product code: ");
            String productCode = sc.next();  // read the product code
            sc.nextLine();  // discard any other data entered on the line

            // get the Product object
            Product product = ProductDB.getProduct(productCode);

            // display the output
            System.out.println();
            System.out.println("SELECTED PRODUCT");
            System.out.println("Description: " + product.getDescription());
            System.out.println("Price:       " + product.getFormattedPrice());
            System.out.println();

            // see if the user wants to continue
            System.out.print("Continue? (y/n): ");
            choice = sc.nextLine();
            System.out.println();
        }
    }
}
```

Note

- This class contains the main method that provides the entry point for the Product application. In this book, we've used the suffix "App" to identify this type of class.

Figure 7-16 A ProductApp class that uses a Product object

How to code and use static fields and methods

In chapters 2 and 3, you learned how to call static methods from some of the classes in the Java API. In chapter 4, you learned how to code static methods in the same class as the main method. Now, you'll learn how to code static fields and methods in a separate class and how to call them from other classes.

How to code static fields and methods

Figure 7-17 shows how to code *static fields* and *static methods*. While instance variables and regular methods belong to an object that's created from a class, static fields and static methods belong to the class itself. As a result, they're sometimes called *class fields* and *class methods*.

The top of this figure shows how to code static fields. In short, you use a syntax that's similar to the syntax for a regular variable or constant. However, you use the static keyword so the variable or constant belongs to the class, not the object. Then, you supply an initial value for the variable or constant. Typically, the static variables of a class are declared with private access, but the static constants of a class are declared with public access. That way, other classes can access and use these constants.

The first example shows how to code a class that contains one static field and a static method. The static field is a constant that stores the number of months per year. The static method is similar to the calculateFutureValue method that you learned how to code in chapter 4. However, this method uses the static field named MONTHS_IN_YEAR, and it is coded in a separate class named FinancialCalculations. Note that since this class doesn't contain any non-static fields or methods, you don't need to code a constructor for this class.

The second example shows how you can add a static variable and a static method to the Product class. In this example, a static variable named objectCount counts the number of Product objects that are created from the Product class. This variable is declared as private so no other class can access it directly. Then, the constructor increments the static variable each time a new object is created from this class. Finally, the static getObjectCount method returns the static objectCount variable.

When you code a class that mixes regular fields and methods with static fields and methods, it's a good practice to keep your fields and methods organized. To do that, you can group your fields and methods by type (instance or static; variable or constant) and by access modifier (private or public). To illustrate, the second example lists all instance variables in a group, followed by the single static variable. For small classes, grouping fields and methods like this isn't critical. However, as your classes get longer, grouping can make your code easier to read and maintain.

How to declare static fields

```
private static int numberOfObjects = 0;
private static double majorityPercent = .51;
public static final int DAYS_IN_JANUARY = 31;
public static final float EARTH_MASS_IN_KG = 5.972e24F;
```

Example 1: A class that contains a static constant and a static method

```
public class FinancialCalculations
{
    public static final int MONTHS_IN_YEAR = 12;

    public static double calculateFutureValue(double monthlyPayment,
        double yearlyInterestRate, int years)
    {
        int months = years * MONTHS_IN_YEAR;
        double monthlyInterestRate = yearlyInterestRate/MONTHS_IN_YEAR/100;
        double futureValue = 0;
        for (int i = 1; i <= months; i++)
            futureValue = (futureValue + monthlyPayment) *
                (1 + monthlyInterestRate);
        return futureValue;
    }
}
```

Example 2: The Product class with a static variable and a static method

```
public class Product
{
    private String code;
    private String description;
    private double price;

    private static int objectCount = 0; // declare a static variable

    public Product()
    {
        code = "";
        description = "";
        price = 0;
        objectCount++;                   // update the static variable
    }

    public static int getObjectCount()  // get the static variable
    {
        return objectCount;
    }
   ...
```

Description

- You can use the static keyword to code *static fields* and *static methods*. Since static fields and static methods belong to the class, not to an object created from the class, they are sometimes called *class fields* and *class methods*.
- When you code a static method, you can only use static fields and fields that are defined in the method. You can't use instance variables in a static method because they belong to an instance of the class, not to the class as a whole.

Figure 7-17 How to code static fields and methods

How to call static fields and methods

Figure 7-18 shows how to call static fields and methods. As you would expect, you use the same syntax for calling static fields and methods from your own classes as you would for calling static fields and methods from the Java API.

To call a static field, you just code the class name, followed by the dot operator, followed by the field name. To illustrate, the first statement calls the PI field from the Math class. This field returns a double value for *pi*, which is the ratio of the circumference of a circle to its diameter. Then, the second statement calls the MONTHS_IN_YEAR field from the FinancialCalculations class in the previous figure.

The third statement shows how to call an objectCount field from the Product class. If you declare this static field as public in the Product class, you can use code like this to directly get or set this int value, which represents the number of objects that have been created from the Product class. However, if you declare this static field as private as shown in the previous figure, you can only use static methods to get or set its value. And if you only declare a get method, the field is a read-only field.

To call a static method, you code the class name, followed by the dot operator, followed by the name of the static method and a pair of parentheses. Within the parentheses, you code the arguments required by the method (if any). To illustrate, the first statement in the static method examples calls the static getCurrencyInstance method of the NumberFormat class. This method doesn't take any arguments, and it returns a NumberFormat object. The second statement calls the static parseInt method of the Integer class. This method takes a string argument, converts it to an int value, and returns that value. And the third statement uses the static pow method of the Math class to return the squared value of a variable named r.

The fourth statement calls the static calculateFutureValue method from the FinancialCalculations class described in the previous figure. This method accepts three arguments and returns the future value that's calculated based on the three arguments. Then, the eighth statement calls the static getObjectCount method of the Product class. This method returns the value stored in the static objectCount field.

The last statement in this figure shows how you can use both a static field and a static method in an expression. Here, the value that's returned by the static pow method of the Math class is multiplied by the static PI field of the Math class. Then, the result is assigned to a double variable named area.

Although the examples in this figure call static fields and methods from the classes that contain them, you can also call a static field or method from an object created from the class that contains it. For example, you can call the getObjectCount method from a Product object named product like this:

```
int productCount = product.getObjectCount();
```

To make it clear that a field or method is static, however, we recommend that you always call it from the class.

The syntax for calling a static field or method

```
className.FINAL_FIELD_NAME
className.fieldName
className.methodName(argumentList)
```

How to call static fields

From the Java API

```
Math.PI
```

From a user-defined class

```
FinancialCalculations.MONTHS_IN_YEAR
Product.objectCount   // if objectCount is declared as public
```

How to call static methods

From the Java API

```
NumberFormat currency = NumberFormat.getCurrencyInstance();
int quantity = Integer.parseInt(inputQuantity);
double rSquared = Math.pow(r, 2);
```

From user-defined classes

```
double futureValue = FinancialCalculations.calculateFutureValue(
    monthlyPayment, yearlyInterestRate, years);
int productCount = Product.getObjectCount();
```

A statement that calls a static field and a static method

```
double area = Math.PI * Math.pow(r, 2);  // pi times r squared
```

Description

- To call a static field, type the name of the class, followed by the dot operator, followed by the name of the static field.
- To call a static method, type the name of the class, followed by the dot operator, followed by the name of the static method, followed by a set of parentheses. If the method requires arguments, code the arguments within the parentheses, separating multiple arguments with commas.

Figure 7-18 How to call static fields and methods

How to code a static initialization block

When it takes more than one statement to initialize a static field, you can use a *static initialization block* to initialize the field as shown in figure 7-19. To start, you just code the static keyword followed by braces. Then, you code the statements of the block within the braces. The statements in this block are executed when the class is loaded, which happens when you call one of the class constructors or static methods.

In the example in this figure, the ProductDB class contains a static initialization block that executes several statements that initialize the static Connection object. This object is used by some of the static methods in the class to connect to a database. Since a static initialization block runs as soon as any method of the class is called, this makes the Connection object available to the rest of the methods in the class.

For now, don't worry if you don't understand the code in the static block. The point is that it takes several statements to initialize the static Connection object. You'll learn more about these statements and how to connect to a database in chapter 21.

When to use static fields and methods

Now that you know how to code static fields and methods, you may wonder when to use them and when to use regular fields and methods. In general, when you need to create objects from a class, you should use regular fields and methods. That way, you can create several objects from a class, and each object has its own data in its own instance variables. Then, you can use the methods of each object to process that data.

In contrast, if you just need to perform a single task like a calculation, you can use a static method. Then, you send the method the arguments it needs, and it returns the result that you need without ever creating an object. As you progress through this book, you'll see many examples that will give you a better idea of when static fields and methods are appropriate.

The syntax for coding a static initialization block

```
public class className
{
    // any field declarations

    static
    {
        // any initialization statements for static fields
    }

    // the rest of the class
```

A class that uses a static initialization block

```
public class ProductDB
{
    private static Connection connection;    // static variable

    // the static initialization block
    static
    {
        try
        {
            String url = "jdbc:mysql://localhost:3306/MurachDB";
            String user = "root";
            String password = "sesame";
            connection = DriverManager.getConnection(url, user, password);
        }
        catch (Exception e)
        {
            System.err.println("Error connecting to database.");
        }
    }

    // static methods that use the Connection object
    public static Product get(String code){}
    public static boolean add(Product product){}
    public static boolean update(Product product){}
    public static boolean delete(String code){}
}
```

Description

- To initialize the static variables of a class, you typically code the values in the declarations. If, however, a variable can't be initialized in a single statement, you can code a *static initialization block*.
- When a class is loaded, Java initializes all static variables and constants of the class. Then, it executes all static initialization blocks in the order in which they appear. (A class is loaded when one of its constructors or static methods is called.)

Figure 7-19 How to code a static initialization block

The Line Item application

The topics that follow present a Line Item application that calculates the total price for an invoice line item entered by the user. As you'll see, this application is more complex than the Product application you saw earlier in this chapter. As a result, it should give you a better feel for what you can do when you divide your applications into classes. It also illustrates how easy it is to use business and database classes in two or more applications.

The console

Figure 7-20 shows the console for the Line Item application. This application starts by prompting the user to enter a product code. Then, it prompts the user to enter a quantity for that product. Finally, it displays the data for the line item that's retrieved and calculated by the application.

The class diagrams

Figure 7-20 also shows the classes used by the Line Item application. Here, the Product and ProductDB classes that you saw earlier are used again without any changes. Since you're already familiar with those classes, I'll focus on the other classes in this diagram.

The LineItem class defines three instance variables named product, quantity, and total. The product variable holds the Product object that's created by the ProductDB class based on the product code the user enters. The quantity variable holds the quantity the user enters. And the total variable holds the value that results by multiplying the quantity by the price of the product.

The LineItem class also defines seven methods. The first five are the get and set methods that provide access to the instance variables. In contrast, the private calculateTotal method is used by the getTotal method to calculate the line item total based on the quantity and price. The last method, getFormattedTotal, is similar to the getFormattedPrice method of the Product class. It applies the currency format to the line item total and returns it as a string.

The Validator class contains methods that are similar to the generic validation methods you saw in chapter 5. It includes methods for validating string, integer, and double input. You'll see the details of how these methods work in a minute.

Before I go on, you should notice the arrows between the ProductDB and Product classes and the LineItem and Product classes. This is a UML standard that's used to indicate that one class uses another. In this case, both the ProductDB and LineItem classes use the Product class. As you'll see in a minute, all of the classes shown here are also used by the class that contains the main method for the Line Item application.

The console

```
Welcome to the Line Item Calculator

Enter product code: java
Enter quantity:     2

LINE ITEM
Code:         java
Description: Murach's Beginning Java
Price:        $49.50
Quantity:     2
Total:        $99.00


Continue? (y/n):
```

The class diagrams

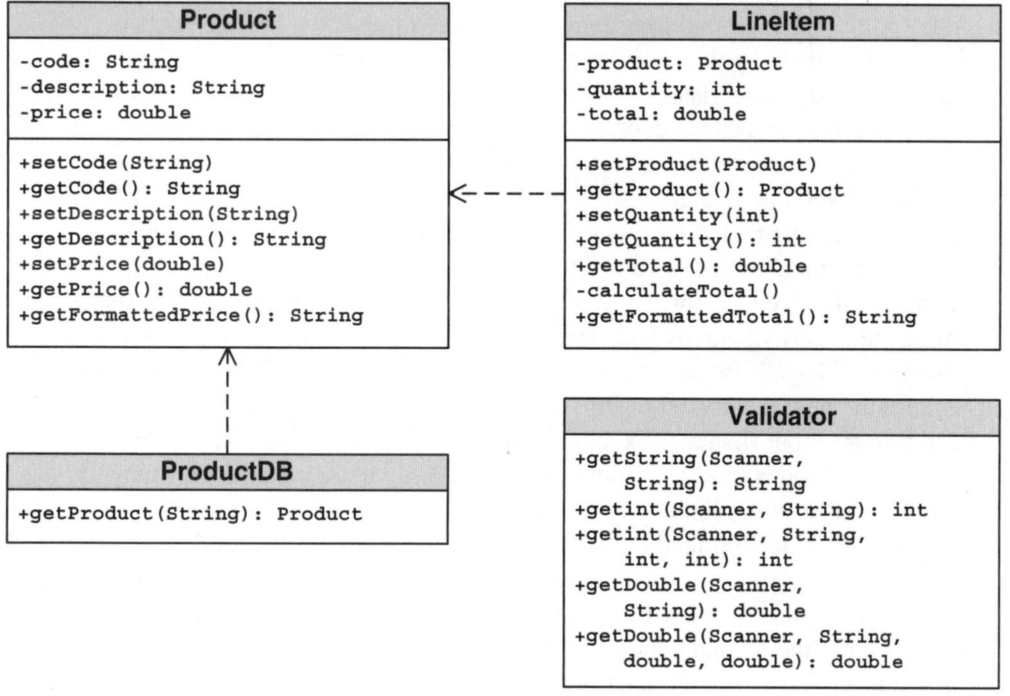

Description

- The Line Item application accepts a product code and quantity from the user, creates a line item using that information, and displays the result to the user.
- The Validator class is used to validate the data the user enters.
- The three instance variables of the LineItem class are used to store a Product object, the quantity, and the line item total. The get and set methods are used to get and set the values of these variables. The calculateTotal method is used to calculate the line item total, and the getFormattedTotal method is used to format the total as a currency value.

Figure 7-20 The console and the class diagrams for the Line Item application

The code for the classes

Figure 7-21 shows the code for the LineItemApp class. This class contains the main method that gets the input from the user and displays the output to the user. To get the input, this method uses the static getString and getInt methods of the Validator class to get a valid product code and quantity.

After the main method gets valid user entries, it calls the getProduct method of the ProductDB class to get a Product object that corresponds to the product code that was entered by the user. Then, it creates a new LineItem object from the LineItem class. Next, it uses the set methods of the LineItem object to set the Product object and the quantity. Finally, this application uses the get methods of the Product and LineItem objects to get the output that's displayed.

Since you've already seen the Product and ProductDB classes, you shouldn't have much trouble understanding how the code in the LineItemApp class works. To understand it completely, however, you need to understand the code for the Validator and LineItem classes that's presented in the next two figures. As a result, you may want to refer back to this figure after you've had a chance to study these classes.

Figure 7-22 shows the code for the Validator class. This class contains five static methods: one getString method, two overloaded getInt methods, and two overloaded getDouble methods.

The getString method accepts a Scanner object and a string that prompts the user for input and returns a valid String value. This method uses the next method of the Scanner object to read the data that the user enters. Notice that, unlike the generic methods you saw in chapter 5 for validating numeric data, this method doesn't include code to prevent an InputMismatchException. That's because the next method stores the data that's retrieved from the console as a string, so an InputMismatchException isn't possible. After the next method, the nextLine method is used to retrieve and discard any extra data the user may have entered at the console.

After the getString method are two methods named getInt. These methods work the same as the getInt and getIntWithinRange methods you saw in chapter 5. In this case, though, they have the same name so they are overloaded. Notice, however, that the second getInt method still calls the first getInt method to get a valid integer from the user. That way, this code doesn't have to be repeated in the second method.

Although they're not used by the Line Item application, the Validator class also includes two methods named getDouble. As you can see on page 2 of the code listing for this class, these methods provide the same functions as the getDouble and getDoubleWithinRange methods you saw in chapter 5, but this time they are overloaded methods. By including these methods, the Validator class can be used by any application that requires the user to enter a double type.

The LineItemApp class

```
import java.util.Scanner;

public class LineItemApp
{
    public static void main(String args[])
    {
        // display a welcome message
        System.out.println("Welcome to the Line Item Calculator");
        System.out.println();

        Scanner sc = new Scanner(System.in);
        String choice = "y";
        while (choice.equalsIgnoreCase("y"))
        {
            // get the input from the user
            String productCode = Validator.getString(sc,
                "Enter product code: ");
            int quantity = Validator.getInt(sc,
                "Enter quantity:     ", 0, 1000);

            // get the Product object
            Product product = ProductDB.getProduct(productCode);

            // create the LineItem object and set its fields
            LineItem lineItem = new LineItem();
            lineItem.setProduct(product);
            lineItem.setQuantity(quantity);

            // display the output
            System.out.println();
            System.out.println("LINE ITEM");
            System.out.println("Code:        " + product.getCode());
            System.out.println("Description: " + product.getDescription());
            System.out.println("Price:       " + product.getFormattedPrice());
            System.out.println("Quantity:    " + lineItem.getQuantity());
            System.out.println("Total:       " +
                lineItem.getFormattedTotal() + "\n");

            // see if the user wants to continue
            choice = Validator.getString(sc, "Continue? (y/n): ");
            System.out.println();
        }
    }
}
```

Description

- After the user enters a valid product code and quantity, the getProduct method of the ProductDB class is called to get a Product object for the product with that code. Then, a new line item object is created with that product and quantity.
- The getCode, getDescription, and getFormattedPrice methods of the Product object are used to get the code, description, and price fields so they can be displayed at the console. The getQuantity and getFormattedTotal methods of the LineItem class are used to get the quantity and total.

Figure 7-21 The code of the LineItemApp class

The Validator class

Page 1

```
import java.util.Scanner;

public class Validator
{
    public static String getString(Scanner sc, String prompt)
    {
        System.out.print(prompt);
        String s = sc.next();  // read the user entry
        sc.nextLine();  // discard any other data entered on the line
        return s;
    }

    public static int getInt(Scanner sc, String prompt)
    {
        int i = 0;
        boolean isValid = false;
        while (isValid == false)
        {
            System.out.print(prompt);
            if (sc.hasNextInt())
            {
                i = sc.nextInt();
                isValid = true;
            }
            else
            {
                System.out.println(
                    "Error! Invalid integer value. Try again.");
            }
            sc.nextLine();  // discard any other data entered on the line
        }
        return i;
    }

    public static int getInt(Scanner sc, String prompt,
    int min, int max)
    {
        int i = 0;
        boolean isValid = false;
        while (isValid == false)
        {
            i = getInt(sc, prompt);
            if (i <= min)
                System.out.println(
                    "Error! Number must be greater than " + min + ".");
            else if (i >= max)
                System.out.println(
                    "Error! Number must be less than " + max + ".");
            else
                isValid = true;
        }
        return i;
    }
```

Figure 7-22 The code of the Validator class (part 1 of 2)

The Validator class **Page 2**

```
    public static double getDouble(Scanner sc, String prompt)
    {
        double d = 0;
        boolean isValid = false;
        while (isValid == false)
        {
            System.out.print(prompt);
            if (sc.hasNextDouble())
            {
                d = sc.nextDouble();
                isValid = true;
            }
            else
            {
                System.out.println(
                    "Error! Invalid decimal value. Try again.");
            }
            sc.nextLine();  // discard any other data entered on the line
        }
        return d;
    }

    public static double getDouble(Scanner sc, String prompt,
    double min, double max)
    {
        double d = 0;
        boolean isValid = false;
        while (isValid == false)
        {
            d = getDouble(sc, prompt);
            if (d <= min)
                System.out.println(
                    "Error! Number must be greater than " + min + ".");
            else if (d >= max)
                System.out.println(
                    "Error! Number must be less than " + max + ".");
            else
                isValid = true;
        }
        return d;
    }
}
```

Description

- This class is part of the presentation layer for a console application. It can be called from the application's main method.

Figure 7-22 The code of the Validator class (part 2 of 2)

Figure 7-23 shows the LineItem class that defines a line item for an invoice. Like the Product class, the LineItem class defines a business object in the application's middle tier. If you review the code for this object, you shouldn't have any trouble understanding how it works.

As you can see, this class contains a constructor that initializes the instance variables to default values. Notice here that the product variable is initialized to a new Product object with default values. Although you could also assign a null value to the product variable, we don't recommend that. If you do assign a null, you'll get a NullPointerException if you try to use the variable before you assign an object to it.

After the constructor, the next five methods provide get and set methods for the three instance variables. These methods simply set or return the value of the corresponding instance variable. Note that the getTotal method calls the calculateTotal method to calculate the line item total. This method calls the getPrice method of the Product object to get the price of the product, multiplies the price by the quantity, and assigns the result to the total instance variable. The last method, getFormattedTotal, returns the line item total formatted as currency. To do that, it calls the getTotal method to calculate and return the total.

The LineItem class

```
import java.text.NumberFormat;

public class LineItem
{
    private Product product;
    private int quantity;
    private double total;

    public LineItem()
    {
        this.product = new Product();
        this.quantity = 0;
        this.total = 0;
    }

    public void setProduct(Product product)
    {
        this.product = product;
    }

    public Product getProduct()
    {
        return product;
    }

    public void setQuantity(int quantity)
    {
        this.quantity = quantity;
    }

    public int getQuantity()
    {
        return quantity;
    }

    public double getTotal()
    {
        this.calculateTotal();
        return total;
    }

    private void calculateTotal()
    {
        total = quantity * product.getPrice();
    }

    public String getFormattedTotal()
    {
        NumberFormat currency = NumberFormat.getCurrencyInstance();
        return currency.format(this.getTotal());
    }
}
```

Figure 7-23 The code of the LineItem class

Perspective

Now that you've completed this chapter, you may be wondering why you should go to the extra effort of dividing an application into classes. The answer is twofold. First, dividing the code into classes makes it easier to use the classes in two or more applications. For example, any application that needs to work with product data can use the Product class. Second, using classes helps you separate the business logic and database processing of an application from the presentation elements. That can simplify the development of the application and make the application easier to maintain and enhance later on.

In this chapter, though, you've just learned the basic skills for creating and using classes. As you will soon see, there's a lot more to creating classes than what's presented here. And that's what the next three chapters are going to show you.

Summary

- In a *three-tiered architecture*, an application is separated into three layers. The *presentation layer* consists of the user interface. The *database layer* consists of the database and the database classes that work with it. And the *middle layer* provides an interface between the presentation layer and the database layer. Its classes are often referred to as *business classes*.
- The *Unified Modeling Language* (*UML*) is the standard modeling language for working with object-oriented applications. You can use UML *class diagrams* to identify the *fields* and *methods* of a class.
- *Encapsulation* lets you control which fields and methods within a class are *exposed* to other classes. When fields are encapsulated within a class, it's called *data hiding*.
- Multiple *objects* can be created from a single *class*. Each object can be referred to as an *instance* of the class.
- The data that makes up an object can be referred to as its *state*. Each object is a separate entity with its own state.
- A *field* is a variable or constant that's defined at the class level. An *instance variable* is a field that's allocated when an object is instantiated. Each object has a separate copy of each instance variable.
- Every class that contains instance variables has a *constructor* that initializes those variables.
- When you code the methods of a class, you often code public *get* and *set methods*, called *accessors*, that provide access to the fields of the class.
- If you want to code a method or constructor that accepts arguments, you code a list of *parameters* between the parentheses for the constructor or method. For each parameter, you must include a data type and a name.

- When coding a class, you can use the this keyword to refer to the current object.
- When Java passes a *primitive type* to a method, it passes the value of the variable so the variable can't be changed directly. When Java passes an object (a *reference type*) to a method, the value it passes is a reference to the object so the method can change the values of the object's variables.
- The name of a method or constructor combined with the list of parameter types is known as the *signature* of the method or constructor. You can *overload* a method or constructor by coding different parameter lists for constructors or methods that have the same name.
- When you use a class that contains only *static fields*, *static methods*, and *static initialization blocks*, you don't create an object from the class. Instead, you call these fields and methods directly from the class.

Exercise 7-1 Enhance the Line Item application

This exercise guides you through the process of testing and enhancing the Line Item application that is presented in this chapter.

1. Open the project named ch07_ex1_LineItem that's in the ex_starts directory. Then, review the code for the LineItemApp, Validator, Product, LineItem, and ProductDB classes.
2. Run the project and test it with valid codes like "java", "jsps", and "mcb2" to make sure that this application works correctly. Then, test it with an invalid code to see how that works.
3. Add another product to the ProductDB class. Its code should be "txtp", its description should be "TextPad", and its price should be $20.00. Then, test the application again with the new product code. This shows that you can make a change to a class without affecting the other classes that use it.
4. Modify the methods for the Validator class so they are regular methods instead of static methods. Then, add a constructor to the Validator class that takes zero arguments.
5. Modify the LineItemApp class so it creates a Validator object named v from the Validator class. Then, use the Validator object to call the methods of the Validator class.
6. Run the project and test it to make sure it works the same.

Exercise 7-2 Enhance the Future Value application

This exercise guides you through the process of modifying the Future Value application so it uses classes that provide static methods.

1. Open the project named ch07_ex2_FutureValue that's stored in the ex_starts directory. Then, review the code for the FutureValueApp class.
2. Start a new class named Validator in the same package as the FutureValueApp class. Then, move the getDouble, getDoubleWithinRange, getInt, and getIntWithinRange methods from the FutureValueApp class to the Validator class. For this to work, you will also need to add an import statement for the Scanner class to the Validator class.
3. Change the name of the getDoubleWithinRange method to getDouble, and change the name of the getIntWithinRange method to getInt. This overloads the getDouble and getInt methods.
4. Modify the FutureValueApp class so it uses the methods in the Validator class. Then, run the application to make sure that it still works correctly.
5. Start a new class named FinancialCalculations and save it in the same package as the other classes. Then, move the calculateFutureValue method from the FutureValueApp class to the FinancialCalculations class, and make sure that the method is public.
6. Modify the FutureValueApp class so it uses the static calculateFutureValue method that's stored in the FinancialCalculations class. Then, run the application to make sure that it still works properly.

Exercise 7-3 Use objects in the Invoice application

In this exercise, you'll create an Invoice class and construct objects from it as you convert the Invoice application to an object-oriented application.

1. Open the project named ch07_ex3_Invoice that's in the ex_starts directory. Then, review the code for the InvoiceApp and Validator classes, and run the project to see how this application works.
2. Start a new class named Invoice and save it in the same package as the other classes. Then, write the code for this class as described here, copying the code from the InvoiceApp class whenever that makes sense:
   - Include two private fields for the customer type and subtotal entered by the user.
   - Include a single constructor that accepts the customer type and subtotal as parameters.
   - Include a get method that returns the subtotal as a double value. In addition, include get methods that calculate and return double values for the discount percent, discount amount, and total.
   - Include get methods that return formatted string values for the subtotal, discount percent, discount amount, and total. These methods should call the other get methods to get the values to be formatted.
   - Include a get method that returns a string that contains the full name for a customer type.
3. Modify the code in the InvoiceApp class so it creates an Invoice object. Then, call the methods of the Invoice object to display the formatted values for the Invoice, and delete any code that is no longer needed. That should simplify the InvoiceApp class considerably.
4. Test this application to make sure that it works the way it did in step 1.

8

How to work with inheritance

Inheritance is one of the key concepts of object-oriented programming. It lets you create a class that's based on another class. As you'll see in this chapter, inheritance is used throughout the classes of the Java API. In addition, you can use it in the classes that you create.

An introduction to inheritance

Inheritance allows you to create a class that's based on another class. When used correctly, inheritance can simplify the overall design of an application. The following topics present an introduction to the basic concepts of inheritance.

How inheritance works

Figure 8-1 illustrates how inheritance works. When inheritance is used, a *subclass* inherits the fields, constructors, and methods of a *superclass*. Then, the objects that are created from the subclass can use these inherited members. The subclass can also provide its own members that *extend* the superclass, and it can *override* methods of the superclass by providing replacement definitions for them.

The two classes shown in this figure illustrate how this works. Here, the superclass is javax.swing.JFrame. That's the Java API class that you can use to create a GUI window, which is called a *frame*. As this figure shows, this class has several public fields and methods, such as the HIDE_ON_CLOSE field and the setTitle method. This class has many more methods than the ones shown here, though. This figure only shows a few representative ones.

The subclass in this figure is the ProductFrame class, and the diagram lists two groups of members for this class. The first group shows the code that uses fields and methods that are inherited from the superclass. This sets some basic attributes of the frame, such as the title, location, and size. The second group includes two new methods that have been added to the subclass.

Incidentally, in this book, we'll primarily use superclass to refer to a class that another class inherits, and we'll use subclass to refer to a class that inherits another class. However, a superclass can also be called a *base* or *parent class*, and a subclass can also be called a *derived* or *child class*.

How inheritance works

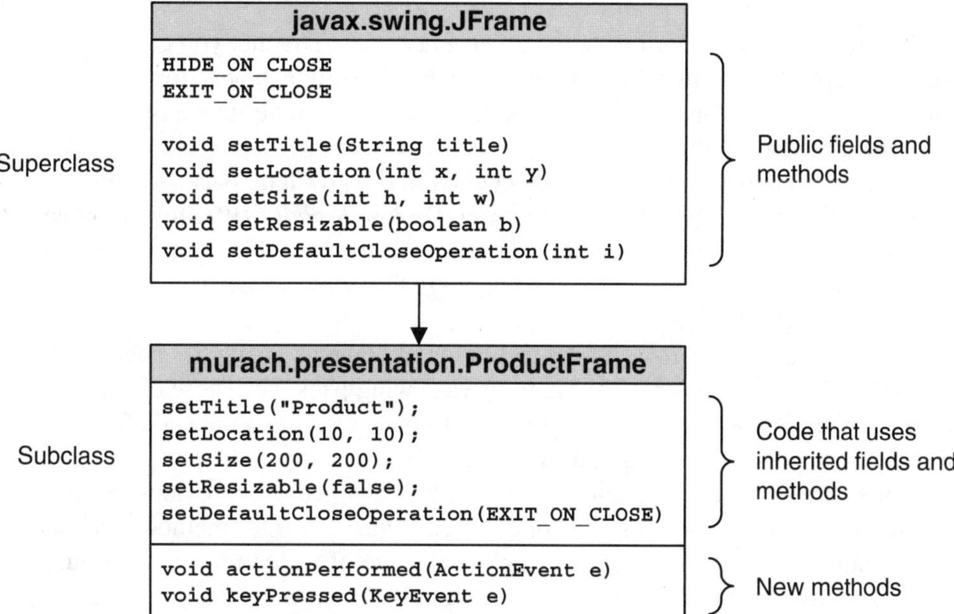

Description

- *Inheritance* lets you create a new class based on an existing class. Then, the new class *inherits* the fields, constructors, and methods of the existing class.
- A class that inherits from an existing class is called a *derived class, child class,* or *subclass.* A class that another class inherits is called a *base class, parent class,* or *superclass.*
- A subclass can *extend* the superclass by adding new fields, constructors, and methods to the superclass. It can also *override* a method from the superclass with its own version of the method.
- To create a new window (called a *frame* in Java), you can code a class that inherits the JFrame class that's in the javax.swing package. Then, your frame will inherit all the fields and methods that are available to this class. Once you inherit the JFrame class, you can write code that uses the inherited fields and methods, you can add controls to the frame, and you can extend the frame by coding new fields and methods.

Figure 8-1 How inheritance works

How the Java API uses inheritance

Figure 8-2 shows a portion of the *inheritance hierarchy* that you can use to create a graphical user interface that uses windows, buttons, labels, text boxes, combo boxes, and so on. This illustrates how extensively inheritance is used throughout the Java API.

To start, all classes inherit the Object class in the java.lang package. Then, the Java API uses the classes in the *Abstract Window Toolkit* (*AWT*) to define the classes for various GUI components. These classes are stored in the java.awt package. However, they are an older technology that was primarily used with versions 1.0 and 1.1 of Java.

Since version 1.2 of Java, a GUI technology known as *Swing* has been available. These classes are stored in the javax.swing package. These classes inherit classes in the java.awt package so they can use some of the code from these classes while improving and extending this code.

For example, the Component class in the java.awt package provides features that are common to all frames and controls. This class provides methods such as setLocation and setSize that set the location and size of the component. Because these methods are provided by the Component class, they are available to all awt and swing components. That includes frames and the components that you place on frames such as buttons, labels, text boxes, and so on.

When you work with a class that inherits other classes, it's important to know that it can use fields and methods from any of the classes in its inheritance hierarchy. For example, the JFrame class can use fields and methods from the Frame, Window, Container, Component, and Object classes.

The shaded classes in this figure are the GUI components that you'll learn about in section 4 of this book. All of these classes are derived indirectly from the Component class. However, the JComponent class is the direct parent of the swing controls for buttons, text boxes, labels, and so on. Similarly, the Frame class is the direct parent of the swing frame.

For now, don't worry if you don't completely understand this figure. You'll learn all about using the JFrame class and the controls in the javax.swing package in section 4. The main point is that inheritance is a feature that's used extensively within the Java API.

The inheritance hierarchy for Swing forms and controls

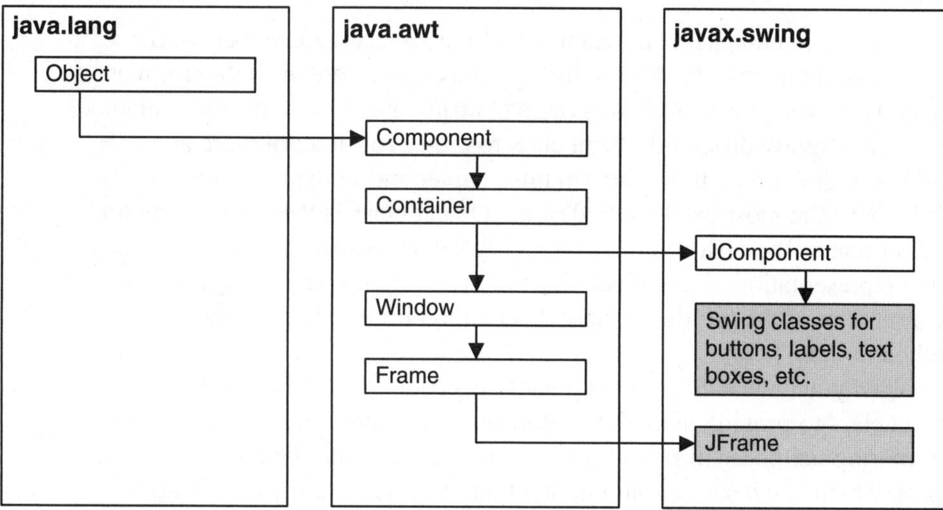

Description

- The Java API uses inheritance extensively in its own classes, so you often need to know what the *inheritance hierarchy* is as you use these classes. For example, you need to know that all classes ultimately inherit the Object class in the java.lang package.
- All *Swing* classes, which are stored in the javax.swing package, inherit the Component and Container classes in the java.awt package. This package contains the *Abstract Window Toolkit* (*AWT*) classes.
- A class can use the fields and methods of any of its superclasses. For example, the JFrame class can use the fields and methods provided by the Frame, Window, Container, Component, and Object classes.

Figure 8-2 How the Java API uses inheritance

How the Object class works

Figure 8-3 summarizes the methods of the java.lang.Object class. Since every class automatically inherits these methods, they are available from every object. However, since subclasses often override these methods, these methods may work slightly differently from class to class. You'll learn more about working with these methods later in this chapter and in the next chapter.

Perhaps the most-used method of the Object class is the toString method. That's because the Java compiler implicitly calls this method when it needs a string representation of an object. For example, when you supply an object as the argument of the println method, this method implicitly calls the toString method of the object.

When you code a class, you typically override the toString method of the Object class to provide more detailed information about the object. Otherwise, the toString method will return the name of the class and the *hash code* of the object, which is a hexadecimal number that indicates the object's location in memory.

Unlike C++ and other languages that require you to manage memory, Java uses a mechanism known as the *garbage collector* to automatically manage memory. When the garbage collector determines that the system is running low on memory and that the system is idle, it frees the memory for any objects that don't have any more references to them. Before it does that, though, it calls the finalize method for each of those objects.

Although you can code a more specific finalize method for an object, that's generally not a good idea. Since you can't tell when the garbage collector will call this method, you can't be assured that your finalize method will be executed before the program terminates. Therefore, you shouldn't rely on the finalize method to handle any timely tasks.

On the other hand, if you were to write code for an object that uses non-Java calls to allocate memory, you should code a method for that object that releases those resources. Otherwise, Java won't free this memory, and you will create a "memory leak." If, for example, you code a method named "dispose" that releases all non-Java resources for an object, you can call that method whenever you need to free those resources.

The Object class

```
java.lang.Object
```

Methods of the Object class

Method	Description
`toString()`	Returns a String object containing the class name, followed by the @ symbol, followed by the hash code for this object. If that's not what you want, you can override this method as shown in figure 8-6.
`equals(Object)`	Returns true (boolean) if this object points to the same location in memory as the specified object. Otherwise, it returns false, even if both objects contain the same data. If that's not what you want, you can override the equals method as shown in figure 8-15.
`getClass()`	Returns a Class object that represents the type of this object. For more information, see figure 8-13.
`clone()`	Returns a copy of this object as an Object object. Before you can use this method, you must implement the Cloneable interface as shown in the next chapter.
`hashCode()`	Returns the hash code (int) for this object.
`finalize()`	Called by the garbage collector when the garbage collector determines that there are no more references to the object.

Description

- The Object class in the java.lang package is the superclass for all classes. In other words, every class inherits the Object class or some other class that ultimately inherits the Object class. As a result, the methods defined by the Object class are available to all classes.
- When creating classes, it's a common practice to override the toString and equals methods so they work appropriately for each class. For example, the toString method might return a value that uniquely identifies an object. And the equals method might compare two objects to see if their instance variables are equal.
- The *hash code* for an object is a hexadecimal number that identifies the object's location in memory.
- In general, you don't need to override the finalize method for an object, even though its default implementation doesn't do anything. That's because the *garbage collector* automatically reclaims the memory of an object whenever it needs to. Before it does that, though, it calls the finalize method of the object.

Figure 8-3 How the Object class works

How to use inheritance in your applications

In figure 8-1, you saw one way that you can use inheritance in your business applications. That is, you can create classes that inherit classes defined by the Java API. But it's also common to create classes that inherit classes that you define. This is illustrated in figure 8-4.

The inheritance hierarchy in this figure shows how you might use inheritance to create two classes that represent similar types of objects. In this case, the objects are different types of products—books and software—and the Product class is a superclass that defines the methods that are common to these objects. Then, the subclasses that define the Book and Software objects inherit all of the public methods of the Product class. In addition, each class adds a couple of methods that are unique to the class. In particular, the Book class adds the getAuthor and setAuthor methods, and the Software class adds the getVersion and setVersion methods.

An important aspect of inheritance is that you can use a subclass as an argument or return value for any method that is designed to work with the superclass. For example, if a method accepts a Product object, you can also pass a Book or a Software object to it. You'll see how this works in a moment.

Business classes for a Product Maintenance application

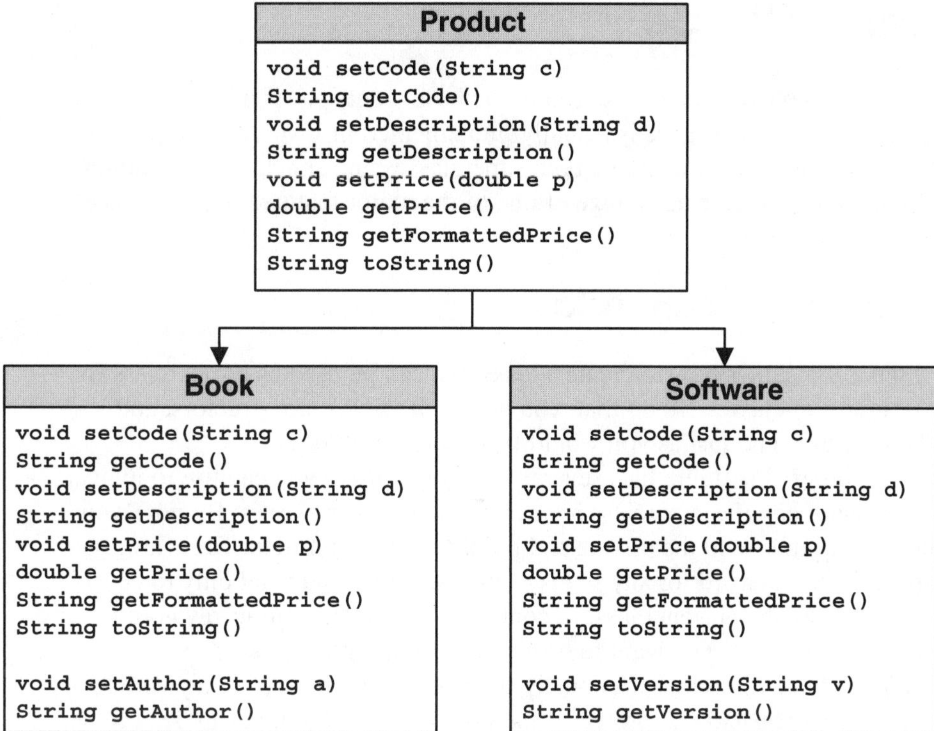

Description

- You can use inheritance in your applications to create generic superclasses that implement common elements of related subclasses. For example, if you need separate classes to represent distinct types of products, you can create a Product superclass. Then, you can create a separate subclass for each type of product that inherits the Product class.
- It's also common to create classes that inherit from classes that are defined by the Java API. For example, you might create a ProductFrame class that inherits the JFrame class as shown in figure 8-1.
- When you inherit a class, you can use the subclass whenever an instance of the superclass is called for. For example, if the Book class inherits the Product class as shown above, a Book object can be used whenever a Product object is called for.

Figure 8-4 How to use inheritance in your applications

Basic skills for working with inheritance

Now that you've been introduced to the basic concepts of inheritance, you're ready to see how inheritance is actually implemented in Java. In the topics that follow, you'll learn how to create both superclasses and subclasses. In addition, you'll learn how to take advantage of one of the major features of inheritance, called polymorphism.

How to create a superclass

Figure 8-5 shows how to create a class that can be used as a superclass for one or more subclasses. To do that, you define the fields, constructors, and methods of the class just as you would for any other class.

The table in this figure lists several *access modifiers* you can use to indicate whether members of a superclass are accessible to other classes. By now, you should be familiar with the private and public access modifiers. To review, you use the private keyword for any fields or methods that you want only to be available within the current class. In contrast, you use the public keyword for any fields or methods that you want to be available to all other classes.

Beyond that, you may occasionally want to use the protected keyword to code *protected members*. A protected member is a member that can be accessed within the defining class, any class in the same package, and any class that inherits the defining class, but not by any other class. This lets subclasses access certain parts of the superclass without exposing those parts to other classes. For example, the Product class in this figure includes a static field named count that has protected access. As a result, any subclass of the Product class can access this field, regardless of whether the subclass is in the same package as the Product class. You'll see an example of how to use a field like this in the next figure.

You can also code a field or method without an access modifier. Then, the classes in the same package will be able to access the field or method, but classes in other packages won't be able to do that.

The Product class shown in this figure includes a toString method that overrides the toString method of the java.lang.Object class. This method returns a string that includes the code, description, and price for the product. As a result, any subclasses of this class can use this toString method. Or, they can override the toString method to provide their own code for that method.

When you override a method, it's generally considered a good practice to add an *annotation* to the method in the subclass to clearly indicate that the method in the subclass overrides the method in the superclass. An annotation is a standard way to provide information about your code that can be used by the compiler, the JRE, and other software development tools. In this figure, for example, an @Override annotation is coded above the toString method.

Although this annotation isn't required, it's helpful for two reasons. First, the compiler can use this information to make sure that the toString method correctly

Access modifiers

Keyword	Description
`private`	Available within the current class.
`public`	Available to classes in all packages.
`protected`	Available to classes in the same package and to subclasses.
no keyword coded	Available to classes in the same package.

An annotation for overriding a method

```
@Override
// method declaration goes here
```

The code for the Product superclass

```
import java.text.NumberFormat;

public class Product
{
    private String code;
    private String description;
    private double price;
    protected static int count = 0;    // a protected static variable

    public Product()
    {
        code = "";
        description = "";
        price = 0;
    }

    // get and set accessors for the code, description, and price
    // instance variables

    @Override
    public String toString()
    {
        return "Code:        " + code + "\n" +
               "Description: " + description + "\n" +
               "Price:       " + this.getFormattedPrice() + "\n";
    }

    public static int getCount()   // create public access for the
    {                              // count variable
        return count;
    }
}
```

Description

- *Access modifiers* specify the accessibility of the members declared by a class. *Protected members* are accessible to the current class, to other classes in the same package, and to subclasses.
- An *annotation* is a standard way to provide information about your code. When you override a method, you can add the @Override annotation to the method.

Figure 8-5 How to create a superclass

overrides the toString method in the superclass. If it doesn't, the compiler can generate an error. Second, other programmers can use this information to easily see that this method overrides a method in the superclass.

How to create a subclass

Figure 8-6 shows how to create a subclass. To indicate that a class is a subclass, you follow the class name on the class declaration with the extends keyword and the name of the superclass that the subclass inherits. For example, the code for the Book class shown in this figure specifies that the Book class extends the Product class. In other words, the Book class is a subclass of the Product class.

After you declare the subclass, you can extend the functionality of the superclass by adding fields, constructors, and methods. In this figure, for example, you can see that the Book class adds a new instance variable and a new constructor. It also adds new setAuthor and getAuthor methods, and it overrides the toString method defined by the Product class.

The constructor for the Book subclass starts by using the super keyword to call the default constructor of the Product class. This initializes the code, description, and price fields. Next, the author field is assigned a default value of an empty string. Finally, the count field, which was declared in the superclass with protected access, is incremented.

To override a method of the superclass, you just code a method with the same signature as the method in the superclass. In this case, the toString method of the Book class overrides the toString method of the Product class. This method accepts no parameters and returns a string. The code within this method uses the super keyword to call the toString method of the Product class. This method returns a string representation of the Product object. Then, this code appends the author's name to this string. Finally, it returns the string. As you review this code, note that the toString method of the Book class is clearly marked with the @Override annotation.

The syntax for creating subclasses

To declare a subclass

```
public class SubclassName extends SuperClassName{}
```

To call a superclass constructor

```
super(argumentList)
```

To call a superclass method

```
super.methodName(argumentList)
```

The code for a Book subclass

```
public class Book extends Product
{
    private String author;

    public Book()
    {
        super();  // call constructor of Product superclass
        author = "";
        count++;  // update the count variable in the Product superclass
    }

    public void setAuthor(String author)
    {
        this.author = author;
    }

    public String getAuthor()
    {
        return author;
    }

    @Override
    public String toString()  // override the toString method
    {
        return super.toString() +     // call method of Product superclass
            "Author:      " + author + "\n";
    }
}
```

Description

- You can directly access fields that have public or protected access in the superclass from the subclass.
- You can extend the superclass by adding new fields, constructors, and methods to the subclass.
- You can override methods in the superclass by coding methods in the subclass that have the same signatures as methods in the superclass.
- You use the super keyword to call a constructor or method of the superclass. If necessary, you can call constructors or methods that pass arguments to the superclass.

Figure 8-6 How to create a subclass

How polymorphism works

Polymorphism is one of the most important features of object-oriented programming and inheritance. As figure 8-7 shows, polymorphism lets you treat objects of different types as if they were the same type by referring to a superclass that's common to both objects. For example, consider the Book and Software classes that were presented in figure 8-4. Because these classes inherit the Product class, objects created from these classes can be treated as if they were Product objects.

One benefit of polymorphism is that you can write generic code that's designed to work with a superclass. Then, you can use that code with instances of any class that's derived from the superclass. For example, suppose you have a ProductDB class with an addRecord method that accepts a Product object as a parameter. Because the Book and Software classes are both derived from the Product class, the addRecord method will work with Book and Software objects.

The examples in this figure illustrate how polymorphism works. To start, the first three examples show the toString methods for the Product, Book, and Software classes. The Book version of the toString method adds the author's name to the end of the string that's returned by the toString method of the Product class. Similarly, the Software version adds the version number to the end of the string that's returned by the toString method of the Product class.

Then, the last example shows how polymorphism works with these classes. This code begins by creating an instance of the Book class, assigning it to a variable named b, and assigning values to its instance variables. After that, it creates an instance of the Software class, assigns it to a variable named s, and assigns values to its instance variables.

Next, a variable named p of type Product is declared, and the Book object is assigned to it. Then, the toString method of the Product class is called. When the JRE sees that the p variable refers to a Book object and that this object contains an overridden version of the toString method, it calls the overridden version of this method.

This example finishes by doing the same thing with the Software object. First, this Software object is assigned to the Product variable. Then, the toString method defined by the Product class is called, which causes the toString method of the Software class to be executed.

The key to polymorphism is that the decision of what method to call is based on the inheritance hierarchy at runtime. This can be referred to as *late binding*. At compile time, the compiler simply recognizes that a method with the specified signature exists.

Three versions of the toString method

The toString method in the Product superclass

```
public String toString()
{
    return "Code:        " + code + "\n" +
           "Description: " + description + "\n" +
           "Price:       " + this.getFormattedPrice() + "\n";
}
```

The toString method in the Book class

```
public String toString()
{
    return super.toString() +
        "Author:      " + author + "\n";
}
```

The toString method in the Software class

```
public String toString()
{
    return super.toString() +
        "Version:     " + version + "\n";
}
```

Code that uses the overridden methods

```
Book b = new Book();
b.setCode("java");
b.setDescription("Murach's Beginning Java");
b.setPrice(49.50);
b.setAuthor("Steelman");

Software s = new Software();
s.setCode("txtp");
s.setDescription("TextPad");
s.setPrice(27.00);
s.setVersion("4.7.3");

Product p;
p = b;
System.out.println(p.toString());  // calls toString from the Book class
p = s;
System.out.println(p.toString());  // calls toString from the Software class
```

Description

- *Polymorphism* is a feature of inheritance that lets you treat objects of different subclasses that are derived from the same superclass as if they had the type of the superclass. If, for example, Book is a subclass of Product, you can treat a Book object as if it were a Product object.
- If you access a method of a superclass object and the method is overridden in the subclasses of that class, polymorphism determines which method is executed based on the object's type. For example, if you call the toString method of a Product object, the toString method of the Book class is executed if the object is a Book object.

Figure 8-7 How polymorphism works

The Product application

Now that you've learned how to code superclasses and subclasses, the following topics present a version of the Product application that uses inheritance. This version of the application uses the Book and Software classes that were described in figure 8-4. In addition, it uses a ProductDB class that can return two distinct types of products: books and software.

The console

Figure 8-8 shows the console for this version of the Product application. As you can see, this application works much like the one you saw in chapter 7. However, there are three main differences. First, this application displays an additional piece of information about each product, which varies depending on whether the product is a book or software. In particular, it displays an author for a book and a version number for software. Second, this application displays a count of the total number of objects it has created. Third, if the user enters an invalid product code, the application displays an appropriate error message.

The console for the Product application

```
Welcome to the Product Selector

Enter product code: java

Code:        java
Description: Murach's Beginning Java
Price:       $49.50
Author:      Andrea Steelman

Product count: 1

Continue? (y/n): y

Enter product code: txtp

Code:        txtp
Description: TextPad
Price:       $27.00
Version:     4.7.3

Product count: 2

Continue? (y/n): y

Enter product code: xxxx

No product matches this product code.

Product count: 2

Continue? (y/n):
```

Description

- This version of the Product application handles two types of products: books and software.
- If you enter the product code for a book, the information about the product includes an author.
- If you enter the product code for software, the information about the product includes a version number.

Figure 8-8 The console for the Product application

The ProductApp class

Figure 8-9 shows the code for this version of the ProductApp class. This code is similar to the code for the ProductApp class that was presented in chapter 7. However, in this version of the application, the product that's returned by the getProduct method of the ProductDB class is handled a little differently. That's possible because this method has been modified so it returns a null if the user enters an invalid product code. Otherwise, it returns a Book or Software object that corresponds to the product code. Note, however, that regardless of whether a Book or a Software object is returned, the object is stored in a Product variable.

The next statement tests the Product variable. If it contains a null, an error message is displayed. Otherwise, the println method is used to print the object that this variable refers to. If the object is a book, this causes the toString method of the Book class to be called to get its string representation. If it's software, it causes the toString method of the Software class to be called. In other words, this statement uses polymorphism to determine which method to call. If you look back to figure 8-8, you can see the differences in the information that's displayed by these two methods.

In this application, the product code that's entered by the user determines whether a Book object or a Software object is created. As a result, at compile time, the application doesn't know which version of the toString method it will call. At runtime, however, the JRE can determine what type of object has been returned, and it can call the appropriate method.

The code for the ProductApp class

```
import java.util.Scanner;

public class ProductApp
{
    public static void main(String args[])
    {
        // display a welcome message
        System.out.println("Weclome to the Product Selector");
        System.out.println();

        // perform 1 or more selections
        Scanner sc = new Scanner(System.in);
        String choice = "y";
        while (choice.equalsIgnoreCase("y"))
        {
            System.out.print("Enter product code: ");
            String productCode = sc.next();  // read the product code
            sc.nextLine();  // discard any other data entered on the line

            // get the Product object
            Product p = ProductDB.getProduct(productCode);

            // display the output
            System.out.println();
            if (p != null)
                System.out.println(p);
            else
                System.out.println("No product matches this product code.\n");

            System.out.println("Product count: " + Product.getCount() + "\n");

            // see if the user wants to continue
            System.out.print("Continue? (y/n): ");
            choice = sc.nextLine();
            System.out.println();
        }
    }
}
```

Figure 8-9 The code for the ProductApp class

The Product, Book, and Software classes

Figures 8-10 and 8-11 show the code for the Product superclass and its two subclasses, Book and Software. The Product class is shown in figure 8-10. Since you saw most of the code for this class in figure 8-5, you shouldn't have any trouble understanding how it works.

Similarly, the Book class shown in figure 8-11 is identical to the Book class presented in figure 8-6. The Software class shown in figure 8-11 works like the Book class. After it extends the Product class, it declares a private instance variable named version. Next, it provides a parameterless constructor that creates a new Software object with default values and increments the count variable that was defined in the Product class. Finally, it provides setVersion, getVersion, and toString methods.

The toString method of the Software class overrides the toString method of the Product class. However, it uses the super keyword to call the toString method of the Product class, which returns a string that includes the code, price, and description. Then, it appends information about the software version to the end of this string.

The ProductDB class

Figure 8-12 shows the code for the getProduct method of the ProductDB class, which returns the Book and Software objects used by the Product application. Here, the return type for the getProduct method is a Product object. Since the Book and Software classes are subclasses of the Product class, this method can return both Book and Software objects.

Within the getProduct method, the first statement declares a Product variable named p and assigns a null value to it. Then, if the user doesn't enter a product code that matches a product, this null value will be returned.

If the product code that's passed to this method matches one of the valid book codes, a new Book object is created. Then, the instance variables for that object are set depending on the book code. Finally, that Book object is assigned to the Product variable.

If, on the other hand, the product code that's passed to this method matches the code for a software product, a new Software object is created and its instance variables are set. Then, that Software object is assigned to the Product variable. Although only one valid software product is included in this example, additional products could have been included. In that case, a nested if statement like the one for the Book objects would have been used.

The last statement in this method returns the Product variable to the calling method. In this case, the calling method is the main method of the ProductApp class. Because the Product variable can contain either a Book object, a Software object, or a null, it can then be processed as shown in figure 8-9.

The code for the Product class

```
import java.text.NumberFormat;

public class Product
{
    private String code;
    private String description;
    private double price;
    protected static int count = 0;

    public Product() {}

    public void setCode(String code)
    {
        this.code = code;
    }
    public String getCode(){
        return code;
    }

    public void setDescription(String description)
    {
        this.description = description;
    }
    public String getDescription()
    {
        return description;
    }

    public void setPrice(double price)
    {
        this.price = price;
    }
    public double getPrice()
    {
        return price;
    }
    public String getFormattedPrice()
    {
        NumberFormat currency = NumberFormat.getCurrencyInstance();
        return currency.format(price);
    }

    @Override
    public String toString()
    {
        return "Code:        " + code + "\n" +
               "Description: " + description + "\n" +
               "Price:       " + this.getFormattedPrice() + "\n";
    }

    public static int getCount()
    {
        return count;
    }
}
```

Figure 8-10 The code for the Product class

The code for the Book class

```
public class Book extends Product
{
    private String author;

    public Book()
    {
        super();
        author = "";
        count++;
    }

    public void setAuthor(String author)
    {
        this.author = author;
    }
    public String getAuthor()
    {
        return author;
    }

    @Override
    public String toString()
    {
        return super.toString() + "Author:      " + author + "\n";
    }
}
```

The code for the Software class

```
public class Software extends Product
{
    private String version;

    public Software()
    {
        super();
        version = "";
        count++;
    }

    public void setVersion(String version)
    {
        this.version = version;
    }
    public String getVersion()
    {
        return version;
    }

    @Override
    public String toString()
    {
        return super.toString() + "Version:     " + version + "\n";
    }
}
```

Figure 8-11 The code for the Book and Software classes

The code for the ProductDB class

```
public class ProductDB
{
    public static Product getProduct(String productCode)
    {
        // In a more realistic application, this code would
        // get the data for the product from a file or database
        // For now, this code just uses if/else statements
        // to return the correct product data

        Product p = null;

        if (productCode.equalsIgnoreCase("java") ||
           productCode.equalsIgnoreCase("jsps") ||
           productCode.equalsIgnoreCase("mcb2"))
        {
            Book b = new Book();
            if (productCode.equalsIgnoreCase("java"))
            {
                b.setCode(productCode);
                b.setDescription("Murach's Beginning Java");
                b.setPrice(49.50);
                b.setAuthor("Andrea Steelman");
            }
            else if (productCode.equalsIgnoreCase("jsps"))
            {
                b.setCode(productCode);
                b.setDescription("Murach's Java Servlets and JSP");
                b.setPrice(49.50);
                b.setAuthor("Andrea Steelman");
            }
            else if (productCode.equalsIgnoreCase("mcb2"))
            {
                b.setCode(productCode);
                b.setDescription("Murach's Mainframe COBOL");
                b.setPrice(59.50);
                b.setAuthor("Mike Murach");
            }
            p = b; // set Product variable equal to the Book object
        }
        else if (productCode.equalsIgnoreCase("txtp"))
        {
            Software s = new Software();
            s.setCode("txtp");
            s.setDescription("TextPad");
            s.setPrice(27.00);
            s.setVersion("4.7.3");
            p = s; // set Product variable equal to the Software object
        }
        return p;
    }
}
```

More skills for working with inheritance

Now that you've learned the basics of inheritance and you've seen an application that uses it, you're ready to learn some additional techniques that are often required when you work with inheritance. That includes getting information about an object's type, casting objects, and comparing objects.

How to get information about an object's type

When Java runs an application, it uses a class named Class to keep track of all of the objects that it loads. For each object that it loads, Java creates a Class object that contains information about the object. This is sometimes referred to as *runtime type identification* (*RTTI*). Although the getName method is the most commonly used method of a Class object, this class and other related classes contain hundreds of methods that let you get a wide range of information about an object at runtime.

Figure 8-13 shows how you can use a Class object to get information about an object's type. To start, you call the getClass method of an object to return a Class object for that object. This works because the getClass method is a member of the Object class, so it's inherited by every object. Once you have the Class object, you can use its methods to get information about the object's type. For example, you can use the getName method to get a string that contains the name of its class.

The first example in this figure shows how this works. Here, the first statement creates a Book object and assigns it to a Product variable named p. Then, the second statement calls the getClass method to return a Class object that contains information about the object that's referred to by this variable. Finally, the third statement calls the getName method of the Class object to get the name of the class, and it displays it at the console. As you can see, the getClass method determines that the object that's stored in this variable is really a Book object even though the variable named p has a type of Product.

The second example in this figure shows how you can code an if statement to test an object's type. This example calls the getClass method from the variable named p to return a Class object. Then, it calls the getName method from the Class object that's returned to get a string object. Finally, it uses the equals method to see if the name of the class is equal to "Book".

The code in this example doesn't assign the Class and String objects returned by the getClass and getName methods to variables. Instead, it calls one method directly from another method. In other words, the code in this example is a more concise way of writing this code:

```
Class c = p.getClass();
String s = c.getName();
if (s.equals("Book"))
```

If you don't need to use the variables, though, there's no reason to create them.

The Class class

```
java.lang.Class
```

Common method

Method	Description
`getName()`	Returns a String object for the name of this Class object.

Example 1: Code that displays an object's type

```
Product p = new Book();  // create a Book object and assign it to a Product
                         // variable
Class c = p.getClass();  // get the Class object for the product
System.out.println("Class name: " + c.getName()); // print the object type
```

The console

```
Class name: Book
```

Example 2: Code that tests an object's type

```
Product p = new Book();  // create a Book object
if (p.getClass().getName().equals("Book"))
    System.out.println("This is a Book object");
```

The console

```
This is a Book object
```

Example 3: An easier way to test an object's type

```
Product p = new Book();  // create a Book object
if (p instanceof Book)
    System.out.println("This is a Book object");
```

The console

```
This is a Book object
```

Description

- Every object has a getClass method that returns a Class object that corresponds to the object's type.
- You can use the methods of the Class class to obtain information about any object, such as its name.
- The method shown above is only one of the more than 90 properties and methods of the Class class.
- You can use the instanceof operator to check if an object is an instance of a particular class.

Figure 8-13 How to get information about an object's type

Instead of using a class object to test an object's type, you can use the instanceof keyword. This is illustrated in the third example in figure 8-13. If you compare this code with the code in the second example, I think you'll agree that this is a much easier way to check if an object is an instance of a particular class.

How to cast objects

Another potentially confusing aspect of using inheritance is knowing when to cast inherited objects explicitly. The basic rule is that Java can implicitly cast a subclass to its superclass, but you must use explicit casting if you want to treat a superclass object as one of its subclasses. Figure 8-14 illustrates how this works.

To start, the first group of statements creates a Book object, assigns this object to a Book variable named b, and assigns values to the object's instance variables. Then, the second group of statements shows how you can cast a subclass to its superclass without explicitly coding a cast. The first statement in this group casts the Book object to a new Product variable named p. Since this cast goes up the inheritance hierarchy (from more data to less), you don't need to explicitly code the cast.

Once you perform a cast like this, you can't call methods that are specific to the subclass. For example, once you cast a Book object to a Product object, you can't call the setAuthor method of the Book object. However, you can call methods of the Product class such as the setDescription method.

The third group of statements shows how to explicitly cast a superclass to a subclass. Since this cast goes down the inheritance hierarchy (from less data to more), you need to code the class name within parentheses in the assignment statement before you code the name of the object you're casting. Here, the first statement casts a Product object to a Book object. This works because the Product object is actually the Book object that was created in the first group of statements. This makes all methods of the Book object available again and doesn't cause any of the data in the original Book object to be lost.

The fourth group of statements shows a cast that will cause a ClassCastException to be thrown. Here, the first statement creates a Product object. Then, the second statement attempts to cast this object to the Book type. Since the Product variable named p2 refers to an instance of the Product class, not an instance of the Book class, an exception will be thrown when this statement is executed.

Casting examples that use the Product and Book classes

```
Book b = new Book();
b.setCode("java");
b.setDescription("Murach's Beginning Java");
b.setAuthor("Andrea Steelman");
b.setPrice(49.50);

Product p = b;              // cast Book object to a Product object
p.setDescription("Test"); // OK - method in Product class
//p.setAuthor("Test");      // not OK - method not in Product class

b = (Book) p;               // cast the Product object back to a Book object
b.setAuthor("Test");        // OK - method in Book class

Product p2 = new Product();
Book b2 = (Book) p2;        // will throw a ClassCastException because
                            // p2 is a Product object not a Book object
```

Description

- Java can implicitly cast a subclass to a superclass. As a result, you can use a subclass whenever a reference to its superclass is called for. For example, you can specify a Book object whenever a Product object is expected because Book is a subclass of Product.
- You must explicitly cast a superclass object when a reference to one of its subclasses is required. For example, you must explicitly cast a Product object to Book if a Book object is expected. This only works if the Product object is a valid Book object. Otherwise, a ClassCastException will be thrown.
- Casting affects the methods that are available from an object. For example, if you store a Book object in a Product variable, you can't call the setAuthor method because it's defined by the Book class, not the Product class.

How to compare objects

Figure 8-15 shows how the equals method of the Object class works. In short, this method checks whether two variables refer to the same object, not whether two variables hold the same data. Since that's not usually the behavior you want when comparing objects for equality, many classes in the API, such as the String class, override this method. When you code your own classes, you'll often want to override this method too.

The first two examples in this figure show how the equals method of the Object class works when the Product class doesn't override the equals method. In the first example, the first two statements create two variables that refer to the same object. Since both variables point to the same location in memory, the expression that uses the equals method to compare these variables evaluates to true. In the second example, though, the first two statements create two objects that contain the same data. However, since these objects are stored at different locations in memory, the expression that uses the equals method to compare the variables that point to these objects evaluates to false. But that's usually not what you want.

The third example shows how to code an equals method in the Product class that overrides the equals method of the Object class. To start, this method uses the same signature as the equals method of the Object class, which returns a boolean value and accepts a parameter of the Object type. Then, an if statement uses the instanceof operator to make sure that the passed object is an instance of the Product class. If so, it casts the Object parameter to a Product object. Then, an if statement compares the three instance variables stored in the Product object with the instance variables stored in the current object. If all instance variables are equal, this statement returns true. Otherwise, it returns false. As a result, the first two examples in this figure will return a true value if the Product class contains this method.

The fourth example shows how to code an equals method in the LineItem class you saw in the last chapter. The code for this method works the same as the code for the equals method of the Product class. However, because a LineItem object contains a Product object, the equals method of the LineItem class uses the equals method of the Product class. As a result, you must code an equals method for the Product class before this method will work.

How the equals method of the Object class works

Example 1: Both variables refer to the same object

```
Product product1 = new Product();
Product product2 = product1;
if (product1.equals(product2))              // expression returns true
```

Example 2: Both variables refer to different objects that store the same data

```
Product product1 = new Product();
Product product2 = new Product();
if (product1.equals(product2))              // expression returns false
```

How to override the equals method of the Object class

Example 3: The equals method of the Product class

```
@Override
public boolean equals(Object object)
{
    if (object instanceof Product)
    {
        Product product2 = (Product) object;
        if
        (
            code.equals(product2.getCode()) &&
            description.equals(product2.getDescription()) &&
            price == product2.getPrice()
        )
            return true;
    }
    return false;
}
```

Example 4: The equals method of the LineItem class

```
@Override
public boolean equals(Object object)
{
    if (object instanceof LineItem)
    {
        LineItem li = (LineItem) object;
        if
        (
            product.equals(li.getProduct()) &&
            quantity == li.getQuantity()
        )
            return true;
    }
    return false;
}
```

Description

- To test if two objects point to the same location in memory, you can use the equals method of the Object class.
- To test if two objects store the same data, you can override the equals method in the subclass so it tests whether all instance variables in the two objects are equal.

Figure 8-15 How to compare objects

How to work with the abstract and final keywords

The last two topics of this chapter show how you can require or restrict the use of inheritance in the classes you create by using the abstract and final keywords.

How to work with the abstract keyword

An *abstract class* is a class that can't be instantiated. In other words, you can't create an object directly from an abstract class. Instead, you can code a class that inherits an abstract class, and you can create an object from that class.

Figure 8-16 shows how to work with abstract classes. To declare an abstract class, you include the abstract keyword in the class declaration as shown in the Product class at the top of this figure. Within an abstract class, you can use the abstract keyword to code *abstract methods*. For example, the Product class shown here includes an abstract method named getDisplayText that returns a string. The declaration for this method includes the abstract keyword, it ends with a semicolon, and no method body is coded.

When you include abstract methods in an abstract class, you must override them in any class that inherits the abstract class. This is illustrated in the second example in this figure. Here, you can see that a class named Book that inherits the Product class overrides the abstract getDisplayText method that's defined by that class.

At this point, you may be wondering why you would use abstract classes. To help you understand, consider the Product application that's presented in this chapter. This application uses two types of product objects: Book objects and Software objects. However, there's nothing to stop you from creating instances of the Product class as well. As a result, the Product class hierarchy actually allows for three types of objects: Book objects, Software objects, and Product objects.

If that's not what you want, you can declare the Product class as an abstract class. Then, you can't create instances of the Product class. Instead, the Product class can only be used as the superclass for other classes. In addition, if you want to make sure that both the Book and Software classes implement the getDisplayText method, you can declare this method as abstract in the Product class.

Note that this doesn't mean that you can't declare variables of an abstract type. It only means that you can't use the new keyword with an abstract type to create an instance of the type. For example, if you declare the Product class as an abstract class, you can still declare a Product variable that holds Book or Software objects. But you can't use the new keyword with the Product class to create a Product object.

An abstract Product class

```
public abstract class Product
{
    private String code;
    private String description;
    private double price;

    // regular constructors and methods for instance variables

    @Override
    public String toString()
    {
        return "Code:        " + code + "\n" +
               "Description: " + description + "\n" +
               "Price:       " + this.getFormattedPrice() + "\n";
    }

    abstract String getDisplayText();  // an abstract method
}
```

A class that inherits the abstract Product class

```
public class Book extends Product
{
    private String author;

    // regular constructor and methods for the Book class

    @Override
    public String getDisplayText()  // implement the abstract method
    {
        return super.toString() +
            "Author:      " + author + "\n";
    }
}
```

Description

- An *abstract class* is a class that can be inherited by other classes but that you can't use to create an object. To declare an abstract class, code the abstract keyword in the class declaration.
- An abstract class can contain fields, constructors, and methods just like other superclasses. In addition, an abstract class can contain abstract methods.
- To create an *abstract method*, you code the abstract keyword in the method declaration and you omit the method body. Abstract methods cannot have private access. However, they may have protected or default access (no access modifier).
- When a subclass inherits an abstract class, all abstract methods in the abstract class must be overridden in the subclass.
- An abstract class doesn't have to contain abstract methods. However, any class that contains an abstract method must be declared as abstract.

Figure 8-16 How to work with the abstract keyword

How to work with the final keyword

Figure 8-17 shows how to use the final keyword to declare *final classes, final methods*, and *final parameters*. You can use this keyword whenever you want to make sure that no one will override or change your classes, methods, or parameters. When you declare a final class, other programmers won't be able to create a subclass from your class. When you declare a final method, other programmers won't be able to override that method. And when you declare a final parameter, other programmers won't be able to assign a new value to that parameter.

Why would you want to use final classes, methods, or parameters? First, for design reasons, you may not want other programmers to be able to change the behavior of a method or a class. Second, Java can execute final classes, methods, and parameters slightly faster than regular methods.

When should you use final classes and methods? For the sake of efficiency, you can use a final class or method whenever you're sure that no one else will want to inherit your class or override your methods. Often, though, it's hard to know when that's true. In addition, the performance gain is slight. As a result, you should avoid using final classes and methods unless you're certain that no one else will benefit by extending your class or by overriding a method in your class.

The first example shows how to declare a final class. This example declares the Book class that inherits the Product class as final. When you declare a final class like this, all methods in the class automatically become final methods.

The second example shows how to declare a final method. Since this method is in the Software class, which hasn't been declared as final, the class can still be inherited by other classes. However, any class that inherits the Software class won't be able to override the getVersion method.

The third example shows how you can declare final parameters when you're coding a method. Since you would rarely want to assign a new value to the variable that's supplied by the parameter, you can almost always declare parameters as final. However, the performance gain is slight, and the extra keyword clutters the code. As a result, you may or may not want to use final parameters, depending on the type of project that you're working on.

In most cases, you'll declare an entire class as final rather than declaring specific methods as final. Because of that, you typically won't need to worry about whether individual methods of a class are final. If you ever encounter final methods, however, you should now understand how they work.

Example 1: A final class

```
public final class Book extends Product
{
    // all methods in the class are automatically final
}
```

Example 2: A final method

```
public final String getVersion()
{
    return version;
}
```

Example 3: A final parameter

```
public void setVersion(final String version)
{
    // version = "new value"; // not allowed
    this.version = version;
}
```

Description

- To prevent a class from being inherited, you can create a *final class* by coding the final keyword in the class declaration.
- To prevent subclasses from overriding a method of a superclass, you can create a *final method* by coding the final keyword in the method declaration. In addition, all methods in a final class are automatically final methods.
- To prevent a method from assigning a new value to a parameter, you can code the final keyword in the parameter declaration to create a *final parameter*. Then, if a statement in the method tries to assign a new value to the parameter, the compiler will report an error.
- Coding the final keyword for classes and methods can result in a minor performance improvement for your application because the compiler doesn't have to allow for inheritance and polymorphism. As a result, it can generate more efficient code.

Figure 8-17 How to work with the final keyword

Perspective

Conceptually, this is one of the most difficult chapters in this book. Although the basic idea of inheritance isn't that difficult to understand, the complications of polymorphism, overriding, casting, and abstract and final classes are enough to make inheritance a difficult topic. So if you find yourself a bit confused right now, don't be disheartened. It will become clearer as you actually use the techniques you've learned here and see them used in the Java API.

The good news is that you don't have to understand every nuance of how inheritance works to use it. In fact, since all classes automatically inherit the Object class, you've already been using inheritance without even knowing it. Now that you've completed this chapter, though, you should have a better understanding of how the Java API works. In addition, you should have a better idea of how you can use inheritance to improve the design of your own classes.

Summary

- *Inheritance* lets you create a new class based on an existing class. The existing class is called the *superclass*, *base class*, or *parent class*, and the new class is called the *subclass*, *derived class*, or *child class*.
- A subclass inherits all of the fields and methods of its superclass. The subclass can *extend* the superclass by adding its own fields and methods, and it can *override* a method with a new version of the method.
- All classes inherit the java.lang.Object class, which provides methods such as toString, equals, and getClass.
- You can use *access modifiers* to limit the accessibility of the fields and methods declared by a class. *Protected members* can be accessed only by classes in the same package or by subclasses.
- An *annotation* is a standard way to provide information about your code to other software tools and developers. When you override a method, it's generally considered a good practice to add the @Override annotation to the method.
- In a subclass, you can use the super keyword to access the fields, constructors, and methods of the superclass.
- *Polymorphism* is a feature of inheritance that lets you treat subclasses as though they were their superclass.
- You can call the getClass method from any object to get a Class object that contains information about that object.
- You can use the instanceof operator to check if an object is an instance of a particular class.

- Java can implicitly cast a subclass type to its superclass type, but you must use explicit casting to cast a superclass type to a subclass type.
- *Abstract classes* can be inherited by other classes but can't be used to create an object. Abstract classes can include *abstract methods* that must be implemented by subclasses.
- You can use the final keyword to declare *final classes*, *final methods*, and *final parameters*. No class can inherit a final class, no method can override a final method, and no statement can assign a new value to a final parameter.

Exercise 8-1 Look at a class that inherits the JFrame class

This exercise lets you view and run a class that inherits the javax.swing.JFrame class.

1. Open the project named ch08_ex1_ProductFrame that's stored in the ex_starts directory. Review the code in the ProductFrame class, and notice how it inherits the JFrame class and calls methods inherited from this class. In addition, note that this class contains a main method that creates an instance of the ProductFrame class and displays that instance.
2. Run this project. This should display a frame. When you click on its close button, the frame should close. In section 4, you'll learn more about working with frames like this one. In particular, you'll learn how to add components such as buttons, labels, and text boxes.
3. Use the documentation from the Java API documentation to research the methods of the JFrame class that are called by this code. Then, add comments to the code to indicate which class the method is inherited from.
4. Use your research from step 3 to determine which class inherited by the JFrame class declares the setVisible method. Then, import that class and modify the code in the main method so the frame variable is declared as that type rather than as a JFrame type. Run the application to verify that it still works properly.

Exercise 8-2 Create a Product application that uses inheritance

In this exercise, you'll create a Product application like the one presented in this chapter that uses inheritance. However, you will add an additional kind of product: compact discs.

Create a new subclass named CompactDisc

1. Open the project named ch08_ex2_Product that's in the ex_starts directory. Then, review the code.
2. Add a class named CompactDisc that inherits the Product class. This new class should work like the Book and Software classes, but it should include public get and set methods for a private instance variable named artist. In addition, its toString method should append the artist name to the end of the string.

Modify the ProductDB class so it returns a CompactDisc object

3. Modify the ProductDB class so it creates at least one CompactDisc object. For example, this object might contain the following information:

```
Code:         sgtp
Description:  Sgt. Pepper's Lonely Hearts Club Band
Price:        $15.00
Artist:       The Beatles
```

Add a protected variable

4. Open the Product class and change the access modifier for the count variable from public to protected.
5. Run the application to make sure that it works correctly and that the count is maintained properly.

Exercise 8-3 Use the abstract and final keywords

In this exercise, you'll change the Product class in the Product application to an abstract class to see how that works, and you'll add an abstract method and implement it in the Book, Software, and CompactDisc subclasses. Then, you'll change the Book class to a final class to see that a final class can't be inherited, and you'll create a final method to see that it can't be overridden.

Change the Product class to an abstract class

1. Open the project named ch08_ex3_Product that's in the ex_starts directory. Then, review the code.
2. Add the abstract keyword to the Product class declaration.

3. Open the ProductApp class, and add this statement before the statement that calls the getProduct method:

```
Product pTest = new Product();
```

4. If you're using NetBeans, a syntax error should be displayed indicating that the Product class is declared as abstract and cannot be instantiated. If this error isn't displayed, save or compile the ProductApp class so it is displayed.
5. Delete the statement you just added. Then, run the application to make sure it works.

Add an abstract method to the Product class

6. Add an abstract method named getDisplayText to the Product class. This method should accept no parameters, and it should return a String object. Then, compile this class.
7. Rename the toString methods in the Book and Software classes to getDisplayText.
8. Modify the ProductApp class so it calls the getDisplayText method of a product instead of the toString method. Then, run the application to be sure it works correctly.

Change the Book class to a final class

9. Add the final keyword to the Book class declaration.
10. Create a class named UsedBook that inherits the Book class. You don't need to include any code in the body of this class. If you're using NetBeans, a syntax error should be displayed indicating that the Book class can't be inherited because that class is final. If this error isn't displayed, save or compile the Book and UsedBook classes so it is displayed.

Add a final method

11. Remove the final keyword from the Book class declaration. Then, add the final keyword to the getDisplayText method of the Book class.
12. Add a getDisplayText method to the UsedBook class to override the getDisplayText method of the Book class. Code this method so it returns an empty string. If you're using NetBeans, a syntax error should be displayed indicating that the getDisplayText method can't be overridden because that method is final. If this message isn't displayed, save or compile the Book and UsedBook classes so it is displayed.
13. Remove the final keyword from the getDisplayText method of the Book class. Now, no syntax errors should be displayed. If you get a warning about the @Override annotation, though, add this annotation to the getDisplayText method of the UsedBook class.

Exercise 8-4 Code an equals method

In this exercise, you'll add an equals method to the Product and LineItem classes that you can use to compare the instance variables of two objects.

1. Open the project named ch08_ex4_EqualsTest in the ex_starts directory. This application creates and compares two Product objects and two LineItem objects using the equals method. Review this code to see how it works.
2. Run the project. Since the equals method isn't overridden in the Product or LineItem class, the output from this application should indicate that the comparisons are based on object references and not the data the objects contain.
3. Open the Product class, and add an equals method like the one shown in figure 8-15. Then, run the project again. This time, the output should indicate that the products are being compared based on their data and not their references.
4. Repeat step 3 for the LineItem class. This time, the comparisons for both the products and line items should be based on their data.

9

How to work with interfaces

The Java API defines hundreds of interfaces. Although most of them are intended for use by other classes in the API, you may need to use a few of these interfaces in your own applications. You'll learn how to use one of these interfaces, Cloneable, in this chapter. In addition, you'll learn how to create and use your own interfaces. As you'll see, interfaces are similar to abstract classes, but they have several advantages that make them easier to create and more flexible to use.

An introduction to interfaces

In some object-oriented programming languages, such as C++, a class can inherit more than one class. This is known as *multiple inheritance*. Although Java doesn't support multiple inheritance, it does support a special type of coding element known as an *interface*. An interface provides many of the advantages of multiple inheritance without some of the problems that are associated with it.

A simple interface

Figure 9-1 illustrates how you create and use an interface. Here, the first example shows the code for a simple interface named Printable. This code is similar to the code that defines a class and would be stored in a file named Printable.java. However, the code for an interface uses the interface keyword instead of the class keyword and contains only abstract methods.

The second example shows a Product class that *implements* the Printable interface. To implement the Printable interface, the declaration for the Product class uses the implements keyword followed by the name of the interface. Then, the body of the Product class implements the print method that's specified by the Printable interface.

The third example shows that a Product object that implements the Printable interface can be stored in a variable of the Printable type. In other words, an object created from a Product class that implements the Printable interface is both a Product object and a Printable object. As a result, you can use this object anywhere a Printable object is expected. You'll learn more about how this works later in this chapter.

Example 1: A Printable interface that defines a print method

```
public interface Printable
{
    public abstract void print();
}
```

Example 2: A Product class that implements the Printable interface

```
import java.text.NumberFormat;

public class Product implements Printable
{
    private String code;
    private String description;
    private double price;

    public Product(String code, String description, double price)
    {
        this.code = code;
        this.description = description;
        this.price = price;
    }

    // get and set methods for the fields

    public void print()  // implement the Printable interface
    {
        System.out.println("Code:           " + code);
        System.out.println("Description:    " + description);
        System.out.println("Price:          " + this.getFormattedPrice());
    }
}
```

Example 3: Code that uses the print method of the Product class

```
Printable product =
    new Product("java", "Murach's Beginning Java", 49.50);
product.print();
```

Resulting output

```
Code:           java
Description:    Murach's Beginning Java
Price:          $49.50
```

Description

- An *interface* defines a set of public methods that can be implemented by a class. The interface itself doesn't provide any code to implement the methods. Instead, it provides the method signatures.
- A class that *implements* an interface must provide an implementation for each method defined by the interface.
- An interface can also define public constants. Then, those constants are available to any class that implements the interface.

Figure 9-1 A simple interface

Interfaces compared to abstract classes

At this point, you might be wondering how an interface compares to an abstract class. Figure 9-2 illustrates the similarities and differences. It also lists some of the advantages of each.

To start, both abstract classes and interfaces can contain abstract methods and static constants, and neither can be instantiated. However, an abstract class can also contain other types of fields, and it can define static and regular methods. In this respect, abstract classes are more powerful than interfaces.

A more important difference between abstract classes and interfaces is that a class can only inherit one other class—abstract or not—but it can implement more than one interface. This gives interfaces an important advantage over abstract classes. In short, interfaces are how Java provides some of the features of multiple inheritance.

To illustrate, suppose you want to create several types of products, such as books, software, and compact discs, and you want each type of product to have a print method that prints information about the product that's appropriate for the product type. You could implement this hierarchy using inheritance, with an abstract Product class at the top of the hierarchy and Book, Software, and CompactDisc classes that extend the Product class. Then, the Product class would provide features common to all products, such as a product code, description, and price. In addition, the Product class would declare an abstract print method, and the Book, Software, and CompactDisc classes would provide their own implementations of this method.

The drawback of this approach is that there are undoubtedly other objects in the applications that use these classes that can be printed as well. For example, objects such as invoices and customers have information that can be printed. Obviously, these objects wouldn't inherit the abstract Product class, so they'd have to define their own print methods.

In contrast, if you created a Printable interface like the one in this figure, it could be implemented by any class that represents an object that can be printed. One advantage of this is that it ensures consistency within the application by guaranteeing that any printable object will be printed using a method named print. Without the interface, some printable objects might use a method called print, while others might use methods with names like display or show.

More importantly, an interface defines a Java type, so any object that implements an interface is marked as that interface type. As a result, an object that's instantiated from a Book class that extends the Product class and implements the Printable interface is not only an object of type Book and of type Product, but also an object of type Printable. That means you can use the object, or any other object that implements the Printable interface, wherever a Printable type is called for. You'll see examples of this later in this chapter.

An abstract class compared to an interface

Abstract class	Interface
Variables Constants Static variables Static constants	Static constants
Methods Static methods Abstract methods	Abstract methods

Example 1: A Printable interface

```
public interface Printable
{
    public abstract void print();
}
```

Example 2: A Printable abstract class

```
public abstract class Printable
{
    public abstract void print();
}
```

Advantages of an abstract class

- An abstract class can use instance variables and constants as well as static variables and constants. Interfaces can only use static constants.
- An abstract class can define regular methods that contain code as well as abstract methods that don't contain code. An interface can only define abstract methods.
- An abstract class can define static methods. An interface can't.

Advantages of an interface

- A class can only directly inherit one other class, but it can directly implement multiple interfaces.
- Any object created from a class that implements an interface can be used wherever the interface is accepted.

Figure 9-2 Interfaces compared to abstract classes

Some interfaces of the Java API

Almost every package in the Java API includes one or more interfaces. If you look in the API documentation, you'll see that the names of the interfaces are italicized. This makes it easy to differentiate between classes and interfaces.

To give you an idea of what some of the interfaces in the API do, figure 9-3 lists a few of the interfaces that you may need to use in your applications. The first table lists two general-purpose Java interfaces: Cloneable and Comparable. Of these interfaces, the one you're most likely to implement is Cloneable.

The Cloneable interface lets you identify objects that can safely use the clone method of the Object class. Since this interface contains no constants or methods, it is known as a *tagging interface*. Later in this chapter, you'll see an example of how to implement this interface for the Product and LineItem classes.

The Comparable interface provides a standard way for an object to compare itself with another object. However, most business classes don't have any real basis for determining whether one instance of the class is greater than or less than another. For example, how would you determine whether one product object is greater than or less than another product object? By comparing the product codes? The price? The amount of inventory on hand? One situation where you may need to use the comparable interface, however, is if you want to sort the elements in an array. You'll see an example of how to do that in chapter 11.

The second table lists several interfaces that are used for developing graphical user interfaces. As you'll learn in section 4, a graphical user interface is a window that contains graphical components such as buttons, labels, and text boxes. A user can use a graphical user interface to interact with an application. To do that, the application must "listen" for events that occur on the window and its components. And that's where the interfaces shown in this figure come into play.

Some interfaces in the java.lang package

Interface	Methods	Description
`Cloneable`	None	An interface that identifies the object as safe for cloning. When using this interface, it's recommended to override the protected clone method of the Object class.
`Comparable`	`int compareTo(Object o)`	Compares objects.

Some interfaces in the java.util and java.awt.event packages

Interface	Methods	Description
`EventListener`	None	An interface that identifies the object as an event listener.

`WindowListener`	`void windowActivated(WindowEvent e)`
	`void windowClosed(WindowEvent e)`
	`void windowClosing(WindowEvent e)`
	`void windowDeactivated(WindowEvent e)`
	`void windowDeiconified(WindowEvent e)`
	`void windowIconified(WindowEvent e)`
	`void windowOpened(WindowEvent e)`
		A type of event listener that listens for events that occur during a window's life.

`ActionListener`	`void actionPerformed(ActionEvent e)`	A type of event listener that listens for events that occur on GUI components such as text boxes, buttons, and combo boxes.

Description

- The Java API defines many interfaces that you can implement in your classes. In this chapter, you'll see an example of a class that implements the Cloneable interface.
- Since the Cloneable interface doesn't contain any methods and is primarily used to identify an interface as being safe for cloning, it's known as a *tagging interface*. Similarly, the EventListener interface is a tagging interface that identifies an interface as a type of EventListener.
- The WindowListener and ActionListener interfaces inherit the EventListener interface.
- This table only lists the most important members of each interface. For a complete description of these interfaces and a list of their members, see the documentation for the Java API.

Figure 9-3 Some interfaces of the Java API

How to work with interfaces

Now that you have an idea of what interfaces do, you're ready to learn the details of coding and implementing them.

How to code an interface

Figure 9-4 shows how to code an interface. To start, you code the public keyword, followed by the interface keyword, followed by the name of the interface. When you name an interface, it's common to end the name with a suffix of "able" or "er". For example, as you saw in figure 9-3, the Java API uses names like Cloneable, Comparable, EventListener, ActionListener, and so on.

The first example in this figure shows the code for the Printable interface. This interface contains a single abstract method named print that doesn't accept any arguments or return any data. As with all abstract methods, you don't code braces at the end of the method. Instead, you code a semicolon immediately after the parentheses.

The second example shows the code for an interface named ProductWriter. This interface contains three abstract methods: addProduct, updateProduct, and deleteProduct. All thrcc of these methods accept a Product object as an argument and return a boolean value that indicates whether the operation was successful.

The third example shows how to code an interface that defines constants. In this case, an interface named DepartmentConstants defines three constants that map departments to integer values. You'll see how you can use constants like these in the next figure.

When you code an abstract method in an interface, you don't have to use the public and abstract keywords. That's because Java automatically supplies these keywords for all methods. Similarly, Java automatically supplies the public, static, and final keywords for constants. However, you can code these keywords if you think that they help clarify the code.

The fourth example shows the code for the Cloneable interface, which is a tagging interface. To code a tagging interface, you code an interface that doesn't contain any constants or methods. When a class implements a tagging interface, it often indicates that the class conforms to specifications made by that interface. For example, implementing the Cloneable interface in a class indicates that the class can be cloned. You'll learn more about how that works later in this chapter.

The syntax for declaring an interface

```
public interface InterfaceName
{
    type CONSTANT_NAME = value;                    // declares a field
    returnType methodName([parameterList]);        // declares a method
}
```

Example 1: An interface that defines one method

```
public interface Printable
{
    void print();
}
```

Example 2: An interface that defines three methods

```
public interface ProductWriter
{
    boolean addProduct(Product p);
    boolean updateProduct(Product p);
    boolean deleteProduct(Product p);
}
```

Example 3: An interface that defines constants

```
public interface DepartmentConstants
{
    int ADMIN = 1;
    int EDITORIAL = 2;
    int MARKETING = 3;
}
```

Example 4: A tagging interface with no members

```
public interface Cloneable
{
}
```

Description

- Declaring an interface is similar to declaring a class except that you use the interface keyword instead of the class keyword.
- In an interface, all methods are automatically declared public and abstract, and all fields are automatically declared public, static, and final. Although you can code the public, abstract, and final keywords, they're optional.
- Interface methods can't be static.

Figure 9-4 How to code an interface

How to implement an interface

Figure 9-5 shows how to code a class that implements an interface. To do that, you code the implements keyword after the name of the class followed by the names of one or more interfaces separated by commas. In this figure, for example, you can see a class named Employee that implements both the Printable and DepartmentConstants interfaces.

A class that implements an interface must implement all of the methods defined by that interface. For example, because the Employee class implements the Printable interface, it must implement the print method declared by that interface. If this method isn't implemented, the class won't compile.

When a class implements an interface, it can use any of the constants defined by that interface. For example, since the Employee class implements the DepartmentConstants interface, this class can use the ADMIN, EDITORIAL, and MARKETING constants that are defined by that interface. In this example, the if statement in the print method uses these constants to determine what department name is included in the output.

To use a constant from an interface that's implemented by a class, you can code the name of the constant without any qualification as shown in this figure. If you want to, however, you can also code the name of the interface that defines the constant, followed by the dot operator, followed by the name of the constant. While this makes it clear where the value of the constant is stored, it also results in more code. Because of that, the interface name is typically omitted when referring to constants.

The syntax for implementing an interface

```
public class ClassName implements Interface1[, Interface2]...{}
```

A class that implements two interfaces

```
import java.text.NumberFormat;

public class Employee implements Printable, DepartmentConstants
{
    private int department;
    private String firstName;
    private String lastName;
    private double salary;

    public Employee(int department, String lastName, String firstName,
        double salary)
    {
        this.department = department;
        this.lastName = lastName;
        this.firstName = firstName;
        this.salary = salary;
    }

    public void print()
    {
        NumberFormat currency = NumberFormat.getCurrencyInstance();
        System.out.println("Name:\t" + firstName + " " + lastName);
        System.out.println("Salary:\t" + currency.format(salary));

        String dept = "";
        if (department == ADMIN)
            dept = "Administration";
        else if (department == EDITORIAL)
            dept = "Editorial";
        else if (department == MARKETING)
            dept = "Marketing";

        System.out.println("Dept:\t" + dept);
    }
}
```

Description

- To declare a class that implements an interface, you use the implements keyword. Then, you provide an implementation for each method defined by the interface.
- If you forget to implement a method that's defined by an interface that you're implementing, the compiler will issue an error message.
- A class that implements an interface can use any constant defined by that interface.

Figure 9-5 How to implement an interface

How to inherit a class and implement an interface

Figure 9-6 shows how to code a class that inherits another class and implements an interface. In particular, this figure shows how the Book class that you learned about in the previous chapter can inherit the Product class and implement the Printable interface. To do that, the declaration for the Book class uses the extends keyword to indicate that it inherits the Product class. Then, it uses the implements keyword to indicate that it implements the Printable interface. Finally, the Book class implements the print method specified by the Printable interface. As a result, an object created from the Book class can be used anywhere a Book, Product, or Printable object is required.

In figure 9-1, you saw a Product class that implements the Printable interface. If the Book class inherits this version of the Product class, it automatically implements the Printable interface, and it can use the print method implemented by the Product class. If you want to, however, you can include the implements keyword on the declaration for the Book class to clearly show that this class implements the Printable interface. In that case, though, you don't need to implement the print method since it's already implemented in the Product class. However, you can override this method.

The syntax for inheriting a class and implementing an interface

```
public class SubclassName extends SuperclassName implements Interface1
    [, Interface2]...{}
```

A Book class that inherits Product and implements Printable

```
public class Book extends Product implements Printable
{
    private String author;

    public Book(String code, String description, double price,
        String author)
    {
        super(code, description, price);
        this.author = author;
    }

    public void setAuthor(String author)
    {
        this.author = author;
    }

    public String getAuthor()
    {
        return author;
    }

    public void print()     // implement the Printable interface
    {
        System.out.println("Code:\t" + super.getCode());
        System.out.println("Title:\t" + super.getDescription());
        System.out.println("Author:\t" + this.author);
        System.out.println("Price:\t" + super.getFormattedPrice());
    }
}
```

Description

- A class can inherit another class and also implement one or more interfaces.
- If a class inherits another class that implements an interface, the subclass automatically implements the interface. However, you can code the implements keyword in the subclass for clarity.
- If a class inherits another class that implements an interface, the subclass has access to any methods of the interface that are implemented by the superclass and can override those methods.

Figure 9-6 How to inherit a class and implement an interface

How to use an interface as a parameter

Figure 9-7 shows how to code a method that uses an interface as the type for one of its parameters. When you do that, the statement that calls the method can pass any object that implements the interface to the method. Then, the method can call any of the methods that are defined by the interface and implemented by the object. You can use this type of code to create a flexible design that provides for processing objects created from different classes.

The first example in this figure shows a method named printMultiple that accepts two parameters. The first parameter is an object that implements the Printable interface, and the second parameter is an integer value that specifies the number of times to print the first parameter. Since the first parameter specifies Printable as the type, the printMultiple method doesn't know what type of object it will get, but it does know that the object will contain a print method. As a result, the code in the body of the method can call the print method.

In the second example, the printMultiple method is used to print two copies of a Product object to the console. This works because the Product class implements the Printable interface. Here, the first statement creates the Product object and assigns it to a variable of the Product type. Then, the second statement uses the printMultiple method to print two copies of the Product object.

The third example shows that you can also declare a variable using an interface as the type. Then, you can assign any object that implements the interface to the variable, and you can pass the variable to any method that accepts the interface as a parameter. As you can see, this code yields the same result as the second example, but it clearly shows that the Product object implements the Printable interface.

Example 1: A method that accepts a Printable object

```
private static void printMultiple(Printable p, int count)
{
    for (int i = 0; i < count; i++)
        p.print();
}
```

Example 2: Code that passes a Product object to the method

```
Product product = new Product("java", "Murach's Beginning Java", 49.50);
printMultiple(product, 2);
```

Resulting output

```
Code:           java
Description:    Murach's Beginning Java
Price:          $49.50
Code:           java
Description:    Murach's Beginning Java
Price:          $49.50
```

Example 3: Code that passes a Printable object to the method

```
Printable product = new Product("java", "Murach's Beginning Java", 49.50);
printMultiple(product, 2);
```

Resulting output

```
Code:           java
Description:    Murach's Beginning Java
Price:          $49.50
Code:           java
Description:    Murach's Beginning Java
Price:          $49.50
```

Description

- You can declare a parameter that's used by a method as an interface type. Then, you can pass any object that implements the interface to the parameter.
- You can also declare a variable as an interface type. Then, you can assign an instance of any object that implements the interface to the variable, and you can pass the variable as an argument to a method that accepts the interface type.

Figure 9-7 How to use an interface as a parameter

How to use inheritance with interfaces

Figure 9-8 shows how one interface can inherit other interfaces. To start, this figure presents three interfaces that don't use inheritance: ProductReader, ProductWriter, and ProductConstants. Then, it presents a ProductDAO interface that inherits the first three interfaces. This interface is named ProductDAO because it defines an object that provides data access for products. In other words, DAO stands for "Data Access Object." This is a common pattern and naming convention, so you may see it used in other applications you work on.

When an interface inherits other interfaces, any class that implements that interface must implement all of the methods declared by that interface and the inherited interfaces. For example, if a class implements the ProductDAO interface, it must implement all of the methods defined by the ProductReader and ProductWriter classes. If it doesn't, the class must be declared as abstract so that no objects can be created from it.

When a class implements an interface that inherits other interfaces, it can use any of the constants stored in the interface or any of its inherited interfaces. For example, any class that implements the ProductDAO interface can use any of the constants in the ProductConstants interface.

When a class implements an interface that inherits other interfaces, you can use an object created from that class anywhere any of interfaces in the inheritance hierarchy are expected. If a class implements the ProductDAO interface, for example, an object created from that class can be passed to a method that accepts a ProductReader as a parameter. That's because any class that implements the ProductDAO interface must also implement the ProductReader interface.

The syntax for declaring an interface that inherits other interfaces

```
public interface InterfaceName
    extends InterfaceName1[, InterfaceName2]...
{
     // the constants and methods of the interface
}
```

Example 1: A ProductReader interface

```
public interface ProductReader
{
    Product getProduct(String code);
    String getProductsString();
}
```

Example 2: A ProductWriter interface

```
public interface ProductWriter
{
    boolean addProduct(Product p);
    boolean updateProduct(Product p);
    boolean deleteProduct(Product p);
}
```

Example 3: A ProductConstants interface

```
public interface ProductConstants
{
    int CODE_SIZE = 4;
    int DESCRIPTION_SIZE = 40;
}
```

Example 4: A ProductDAO interface that inherits these three interfaces

```
public interface ProductDAO
    extends ProductReader, ProductWriter, ProductConstants
{
}
```

Description

- An interface can inherit one or more other interfaces by specifying the inherited interfaces in an extends clause.
- An interface can't inherit a class.
- A class that implements an interface must implement all the methods declared by the interface as well as all the methods declared by any inherited interfaces unless the class is defined as abstract.
- A class that implements an interface can use any of the constants declared in the interface as well as any constants declared by any inherited interfaces.

Figure 9-8 How to use inheritance with interfaces

How to use NetBeans to work with interfaces

Figure 9-9 shows how NetBeans can make it easier to work with interfaces. To start, you can create an interface using a technique similar to the one you use to create a class. Then, NetBeans generates the declaration for the interface, and you can enter the constants and methods for the interface.

When coding a class that implements an interface, you can automatically generate all the method declarations for the interface. To do that, you click the yellow light bulb icon that appears to the left of the class declaration when you enter the implements keyword followed by the name of an interface. This displays a menu with the "Implement all abstract methods" command as shown in this figure. Then, you can select this command to generate the method declarations for the interface. In this figure, for example, NetBeans generated the method declarations that implement the ProductDAO interface. This saves you time and eliminates coding errors.

In the generated code, each method contains a single statement that throws an exception that indicates that the method is not supported yet. At this point, you can delete this statement and write the code that implements the method. For more information about the statement that throws the exception, see chapter 14.

A class that implements the ProductDAO interface

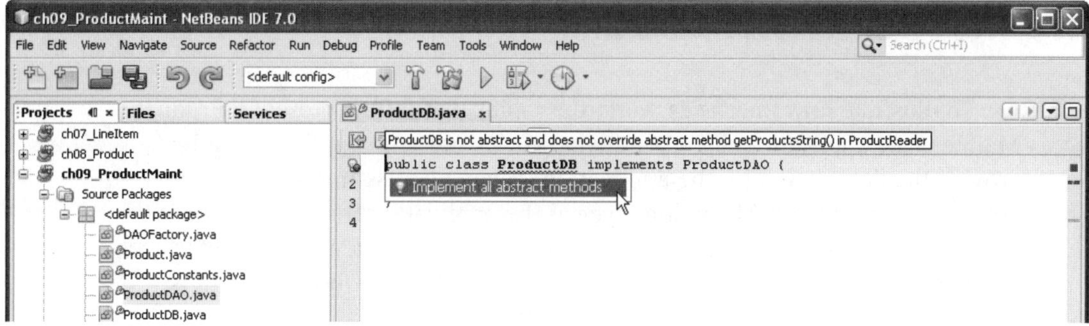

The code that's generated by NetBeans

```
public class ProductDB implements ProductDAO {

    @Override
    public Product getProduct(String code) {
        throw new UnsupportedOperationException("Not supported yet.");
    }

    @Override
    public String getProductsString() {
        throw new UnsupportedOperationException("Not supported yet.");
    }

    @Override
    public boolean addProduct(Product p) {
        throw new UnsupportedOperationException("Not supported yet.");
    }

    @Override
    public boolean updateProduct(Product p) {
        throw new UnsupportedOperationException("Not supported yet.");
    }

    @Override
    public boolean deleteProduct(Product p) {
        throw new UnsupportedOperationException("Not supported yet.");
    }
}
```

Description

- To add an interface to a project, right-click on the package you want to add the interface to, select the New→Java Interface command, and use the resulting dialog box to enter a name for the interface.
- When coding a class that implements an interface, you can automatically generate all the method declarations for the interface. To do that, create a new class as described in chapter 7, use the implements keyword to identify the interface, click on the light bulb icon in the left margin, and select the "Implement all abstract methods" command.

Figure 9-9 How to use NetBeans to work with interfaces

A Product Maintenance application that uses interfaces

To illustrate how interfaces work, the topics that follow present a Product Maintenance application that uses the interfaces presented in figure 9-8 to provide the data access for the application. When you use interfaces like this, you can separate the presentation layer of the application from the database layer. That's because the presentation layer only needs to know what interfaces the data access object implements. It doesn't need to know how the data is stored or processed.

The class diagram

Figure 9-10 shows the class diagram for the Product Maintenance application. Notice that the main class for the application, ProductMaintApp, uses the ProductDAO interface. As you saw in the last figure, the ProductDAO interface inherits the ProductConstants, ProductWriter, and ProductReader interfaces.

Because ProductDAO is an interface, it can't directly provide the data access functions for the application. That's where the ProductTextFile class comes in. It implements the ProductDAO interface by saving and retrieving product data from a text file. Notice, however, that there's no arrow going from the ProductMaintApp class to the ProductTextFile class. That's because the ProductMaintApp class isn't aware of the specific class that provides the data access. It only knows that the class it uses for data access implements the ProductDAO interface.

The key to this application is the DAOFactory class. As you'll see in a minute, this class has a single method named getProductDAO that returns an object that implements the ProductDAO interface. Then, after the ProductMaintApp class calls the getProductDAO method to get the ProductDAO object, it uses the methods of that object to handle the data access for the application. In short, the DAOFactory class insulates the ProductMaintApp class from the database layer of the application. This design pattern, called the *factory pattern*, is commonly used to provide flexibility in the application's database layer.

In this application, the getProductDAO method of the DAOFactory class returns an instance of the ProductTextFile class, which implements the ProductDAO interface with a text file. Because it uses the factory pattern, though, this implementation can easily be changed to a binary file, XML file, or a database such as MySQL, Oracle, or Microsoft SQL Server. To do that, you just provide another class that implements the ProductDAO interface, and you change the one statement in the DAOFactory class so it returns an object for that class. Since those are the only classes that need to be changed, the factory pattern is commonly used when the implementation details are likely to change.

The class diagram for the Product Maintenance application

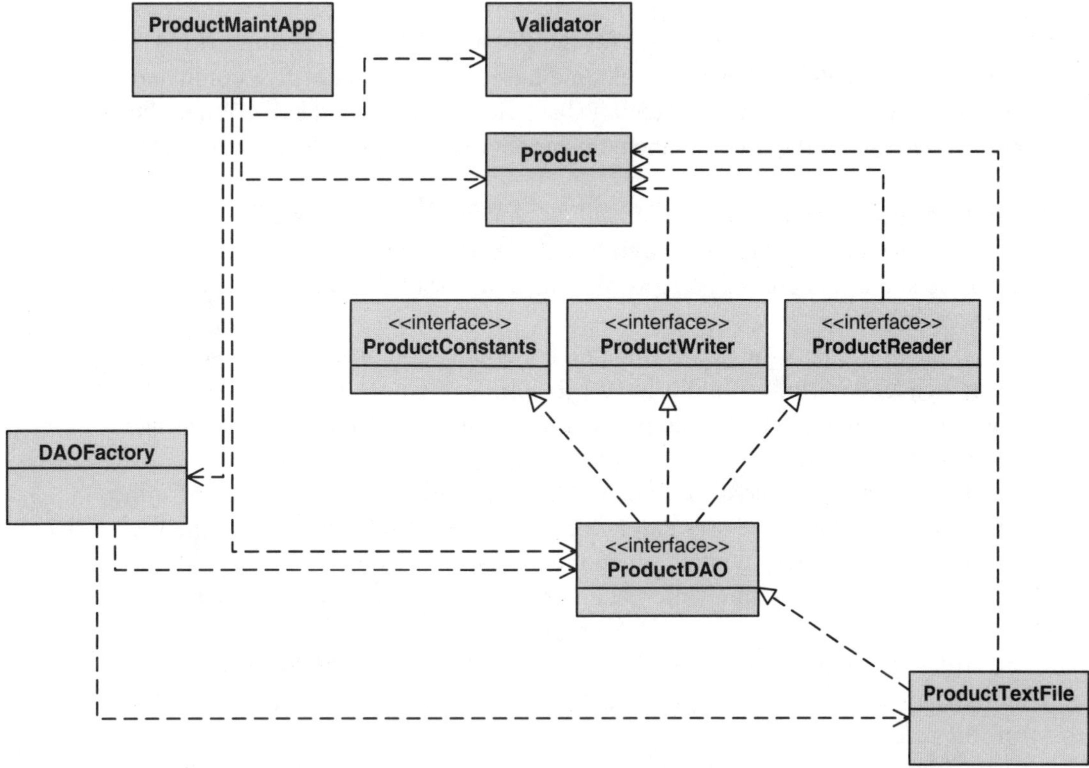

Classes and interfaces used by the Product Maintenance application

Class	Description
Product	A class that defines the Product object.
Validator	A class that provides methods that get and validate user input.
ProductConstants	An interface that defines the constants used by the application.
ProductWriter	An interface that defines the methods that write the Product data.
ProductReader	An interface that defines the methods that read the Product data.
ProductDAO	An interface that inherits the ProductConstants, ProductReader, and ProductWriter interfaces.
ProductTextFile	A class that implements the ProductDAO interface.
DAOFactory	A class that maps the ProductDAO interface to the ProductTextFile object. This is the only linkage between the ProductTextFile object and the rest of the application.
ProductMaintApp	A class that contains the main method for the application.

Figure 9-10 The class diagram for the Product Maintenance application

The console

Figure 9-11 shows the console for the Product Maintenance application. To start, this application displays a welcome message and a list of five commands that are recognized by the application (list, add, del, help, and exit). When the user enters one of these commands, this application performs the appropriate action.

If the user enters the list command, the application displays a list of all the products that are currently stored in the file. A user might use this command after the add or del command to verify that a product has been added or deleted from the file.

If the user enters the add command, the application prompts the user to enter a code, description, and price for the product. Once the user makes these entries, the application adds the product to the file and displays an appropriate message to the user.

If the user enters the del command, the application prompts the user for the product's code. Once the user enters a code for a product that exists in the file, the application deletes the product and displays an appropriate message. However, if the user enters an invalid code, the application displays a message that indicates that the product couldn't be found.

If the user enters the help command, the application displays the menu of commands again. This command may come in handy if the menu has scrolled off the screen.

Although it's not shown here, alternate commands are provided for the delete and help commands. For example, the user can enter either "del" or "delete" to delete a product. Similarly, the user can enter either "help" or "menu" to display the menu of commands.

To exit from this application, the user enters the exit command. Then, the application displays a goodbye message and ends.

The console for the Product Maintenance application

```
Welcome to the Product Maintenance application

COMMAND MENU
list     - List all products
add      - Add a product
del      - Delete a product
help     - Show this menu
exit     - Exit this application

Enter a command: list

PRODUCT LIST
java     Murach's Beginning Java                              $49.50
jsps     Murach's Java Servlets and JSP                       $49.50
cshp     Murach's C#                                          $49.50
mcb2     Murach's Mainframe COBOL                             $59.50

Enter a command: del

Enter product code to delete: cshp

Murach's C# has been deleted.

Enter a command: add

Enter product code: txtp
Enter product description: TextPad 7.4
Enter price: 20

TextPad 7.4 has been added.

Enter a command: list

PRODUCT LIST
java     Murach's Beginning Java                              $49.50
jsps     Murach's Java Servlets and JSP                       $49.50
mcb2     Murach's Mainframe COBOL                             $59.50
txtp     TextPad 7.4                                          $20.00

Enter a command: exit

Bye.
```

Description

- When this application first starts, it displays a menu of the commands the user can enter. When the user enters one of these commands, the appropriate processing is performed. Otherwise, an error message is displayed.

The DAOFactory class

Figure 9-12 shows the DAOFactory class. This class contains one static method named getProductDAO that returns a ProductDAO object. In this case, the ProductDAO object is an instance of the ProductTextFile class. That's possible because the ProductTextFile class implements the ProductDAO interface. In fact, the two lines of code within this method could be condensed into this single line of code:

```
return new ProductTextFile();
```

The ProductTextFile class

Figure 9-12 also presents an outline of the ProductTextFile class. Because this class implements the ProductDAO interface, it must implement the methods defined by the ProductReader and ProductWriter interfaces that this interface inherits. You can see the declarations for the five methods defined by these interfaces in this figure.

Since an interface can only define non-static methods, all of the methods in the ProductTextFile class are also non-static. As a result, the ProductTextFile class includes a constructor. When you create an object from this class, this constructor initializes the fields defined by the class. Then, you can call any of the methods from the ProductTextFile object.

If you look back at figure 9-8, you can see that the ProductConstants interface defines two constants: CODE_SIZE and DESCRIPTION_SIZE. Because the ProductDAO interface also inherits this interface, the ProductTextFile class can use these constants. These constants can be used in the getProductsString method to set the maximum number of characters that are displayed for the code and description fields. That way, the columns in the product list that's returned by this method can be aligned.

Because the code for implementing the methods shown in this figure uses some techniques that haven't been presented yet, it isn't shown here. In particular, the methods in this class use some of the techniques for working with collections that are covered in chapter 12, and they use some of the techniques for working with text files that are covered in chapter 18. If you're curious to see how this works, you can look ahead to chapter 18 to see a similar ProductTextFile class. You will also get a chance to review the code for this class when you do exercise 9-2. For now, though, you can focus on using the methods of this ProductTextFile class rather than on the implementation details.

The code for the DAOFactory class

```
public class DAOFactory
{
    public static ProductDAO getProductDAO()
    {
        ProductDAO pDAO = new ProductTextFile();
        return pDAO;
    }
}
```

The code for the ProductTextFile class

```
public class ProductTextFile implements ProductDAO
{
    // field declarations

    public ProductTextFile()
    {
        // code that initializes the fields
    }

    //***********************************************
    // Implement the ProductReader interface
    //***********************************************
    public Product getProduct(String code)
    {
        // code that returns a Product
    }

    public String getProductsString()
    {
        // code that returns a String that lists all products

        // this code can use the CODE_SIZE and DESCRIPTION_SIZE
        // constants from the ProductConstants interface
        // to align the product data
    }

    //***********************************************
    // Implement the ProductWriter interface
    //************************************************
    public boolean addProduct(Product p)
    {
        // code that adds a Product
    }

    public boolean deleteProduct(Product p)
    {
        // code that deletes a Product
    }

    public boolean updateProduct(Product p)
    {
        // code that updates a Product
    }
}
```

Figure 9-12 The DAOFactory and ProductTextFile classes

The ProductMaintApp class

Figure 9-13 shows the code for the ProductMaintApp class. To start, this class declares two static class variables. The first one is for a ProductDAO variable named productDAO that's set to a null. The second one is for a Scanner variable named sc that's also set to a null. Because these variables are defined at the class level, they are available to all the methods in the ProductMaintApp class.

After the main method displays a welcome message, the second group of statements assigns objects to the productDAO and sc variables. To get a ProductDAO object, the getProductDAO method of the DAOFactory class is called. This method actually returns a ProductTextFile object, but since the code that creates this object is in the DAOFactory class, the ProductMaintApp class has no direct knowledge of this. Instead, all of the methods of the ProductMaintApp class use the ProductDAO object.

Once the class variables have been set, the main method calls the displayMenu method that's shown on page 2 of this listing. This method displays a list of commands that are recognized by the Product Maintenance application. As a result, this list is displayed when the program starts to remind the user what commands are available.

After the main method displays the command menu, it enters a while loop. Within this loop, the application uses the getString method of the Validator class you saw in chapter 7 to prompt the user for a command until the user enters the exit command. When the user enters this command, the application displays a goodbye message and exits. If the user enters an invalid command, the program displays an error message. Otherwise, the program calls a method to perform the requested function.

The code for the ProductMaintApp class — Page 1

```
import java.util.Scanner;

public class ProductMaintApp
{
    // declare two class variables
    private static ProductDAO productDAO = null;
    private static Scanner sc = null;

    public static void main(String args[])
    {
        System.out.println(
            "Welcome to the Product Maintenance application\n");

        // set the class variables
        productDAO = DAOFactory.getProductDAO();
        sc = new Scanner(System.in);

        // display the command menu
        displayMenu();

        // perform 1 or more actions
        String action = "";
        while (!action.equalsIgnoreCase("exit"))
        {
            // get the input from the user
            action = Validator.getString(sc, "Enter a command: ");
            System.out.println();

            if (action.equalsIgnoreCase("list"))
                displayAllProducts();
            else if (action.equalsIgnoreCase("add"))
                addProduct();
            else if (action.equalsIgnoreCase("del") ||
                     action.equalsIgnoreCase("delete"))
                deleteProduct();
            else if (action.equalsIgnoreCase("help") ||
                     action.equalsIgnoreCase("menu"))
                displayMenu();
            else if (action.equalsIgnoreCase("exit"))
                System.out.println("Bye.\n");
            else
                System.out.println("Error! Not a valid command.\n");
        }
    }
```

Figure 9-13 The ProductMaintApp class (part 1 of 2)

If the user enters the list command, the displayAllProducts method is executed. This method displays a list of the products that are stored in the file. To do that, it calls the getProductsString method of the productDAO object to get a string that contains a list of the products. Then, it prints this string to the console.

If the user enters the add command, the addProduct method is executed. This method uses methods of the Validator class to get a valid product code, description, and price from the user. For this application, though, a new method has been added to this class. This method, named getLine, uses the nextLine method of the Scanner class to get an entire line of data. It's used to validate the description the user enters. That's necessary because the description may consist of more than one word.

After the data has been gathered from the user, the addProduct method creates a Product object and sets its values. Then, it calls the addProduct method of the productDAO object to add the product to the file. Finally, this method displays a message to confirm that the product was successfully added.

If the user enters the del or delete command, the deleteProduct method is executed. This method uses the getString method of the Validator class to get a product code from the user. Then, it calls the getProduct method of the productDAO object to get a Product object that contains the data for the specified product. If no product is found with the specified product code, the Product variable, p, is set to null. In that case, a message is displayed to indicate that no product with that product code was found. Otherwise, the Product object is passed to the deleteProduct method of the productDAO object to delete the product from the file. Finally, a message is displayed that indicates that this product has been deleted from the database.

This page of code shows that the linkage between the database layer and the presentation layer is minimal. In other words, none of the methods of the ProductTextFile class are called directly from the ProductMaintApp class. Instead, the ProductMaintApp class calls methods of the ProductDAO interface, which is implemented by the ProductTextFile class. As a result, it's easy to substitute another data storage mechanism. To do that, you can code another class that implements the ProductDAO interface. Then, you can modify the single line of code in the DAOFactory class that maps the ProductDAO interface to the appropriate implementing class. For example, you could code a class named ProductMySQL that stores product data in a MySQL database. Or, you could code a class named ProductXMLFile that stores the product data in an XML file.

This approach has some advantages and disadvantages. On the upside, this approach makes it easy to switch between data storage mechanisms. On the downside, this approach requires more code in the form of interfaces, and it increases the conceptual complexity of an application. As a result, if you're certain that you won't need to provide for other data storage mechanisms, you may want to keep things simple and call methods of the classes in the database layer directly. However, if you need to provide for varying data storage mechanisms, you may want to use interfaces as shown here.

The code for the ProductMaintApp class — Page 2

```
    public static void displayMenu()
    {
        System.out.println("COMMAND MENU");
        System.out.println("list     - List all products");
        System.out.println("add      - Add a product");
        System.out.println("del      - Delete a product");
        System.out.println("help     - Show this menu");
        System.out.println("exit     - Exit this application\n");
    }

    public static void displayAllProducts()
    {
        System.out.println("PRODUCT LIST");
        System.out.println(productDAO.getProductsString());
    }

    public static void addProduct()
    {
        String code = Validator.getString(sc, "Enter product code: ");
        String description = Validator.getLine(
            sc, "Enter product description: ");
        double price = Validator.getDouble(sc, "Enter price: ");

        Product product = new Product();
        product.setCode(code);
        product.setDescription(description);
        product.setPrice(price);
        productDAO.addProduct(product);

        System.out.println();
        System.out.println(description + " has been added.\n");
    }

    public static void deleteProduct()
    {
        String code = Validator.getString(sc,
            "Enter product code to delete: ");

        Product p = productDAO.getProduct(code);

        System.out.println();
        if (p != null)
        {
            productDAO.deleteProduct(p);
            System.out.println(p.getDescription()
                + " has been deleted.\n");
        }
        else
        {
            System.out.println("No product matches that product code.\n");
        }
    }
}
```

Figure 9-13 The ProductMaintApp class (part 2 of 2)

How to implement the Cloneable interface

Occasionally, you may need to *clone* an object. When you clone an object, you create a new instance of the object that contains all the same data as the first object. To do that, you can call the clone method of the Object class. But first, you must implement the Cloneable interface that's in the java.lang package to tell the compiler that it's safe to use this method.

A Product class that implements the Cloneable interface

Figure 9-14 shows how to code a Product class that can be cloned. First, the Product class implements the Cloneable interface. This allows the Product class to call the clone method of the Object class. However, the clone method of the Object class has protected access. As a result, this method will only be available to subclasses and classes in the same package. To give public access to this method, the Product class overrides the clone method of the Object class and gives it public access. Then, the clone method of the Product class uses the super keyword to call the clone method of thc Objcct class. This clones the product, which is then returned to the calling method.

Because the clone method of the Object class throws a CloneNotSupportedException, you must either throw or catch this exception when you override this method. In this example, you can see that the clone method in the Product class throws this exception. You'll learn more about throwing exceptions in chapter 14.

The code that uses the clone method of the Product class shows how the clone method works. Here, the first group of statements creates a Product object and fills it with data. Then, the next statement uses the clone method to make a copy of the Product object. Since the clone method returns an Object type, this method casts the Object type to a Product type. At this point, the p1 and p2 variables both refer to their own copies of a Product object. As a result, you can change the price in one Product object without also changing the price in the other Product object.

By the way, it's a common mistake to try to clone an object using code like this:

```
Product p2 = p1;
```

However, this simply assigns the reference to an object that's stored in one variable to another variable. In other words, after executing this statement, both variables will refer to the same Product object. As a result, if you change the price in one variable, the price will also be changed in the other variable.

A Product class that implements the Cloneable interface

```
public class Product implements Cloneable
{
    private String code;
    private String description;
    private double price;

    // the code for the constructor and methods

    @Override
    public Object clone() throws CloneNotSupportedException
    {
        return super.clone();
    }
}
```

Code that uses the clone method of the Product class

```
// create a new product
Product p1 = new Product();
p1.setCode("java");
p1.setDescription("Murach's Beginning Java");
p1.setPrice(49.50);

// clone the product
Product p2 = (Product) p1.clone();

// change a value in the cloned product
p2.setPrice(44.50);

// print the results
System.out.println(p1);
System.out.println(p2);
```

The result

```
Code:        java
Description: Murach's Beginning Java
Price:       $49.50

Code:        java
Description: Murach's Beginning Java
Price:       $44.50
```

Description

- You can use the clone method of the Object class to *clone* a user-defined class only if the user-defined class implements the Cloneable interface.
- Since the clone method in the Object class has protected access, it is only available to subclasses and other classes in the same package. To make this method available to all classes, you can override the clone method of the Object class with a clone method that has public access.
- The clone method returns an Object type.
- The clone method of the Object class throws a CloneNotSupportedException.

Figure 9-14 A Product class that implements the Cloneable interface

A LineItem class that implements the Cloneable interface

The Product class that you saw in the previous figure contains only a primitive type (double) and two *immutable* objects (String). A String object is immutable because its value can't be changed. Instead, when you assign a new value to a string variable, the original String object is deleted and it's replaced with a new String object that contains the new value. To clone an object like this, you can simply call the clone method of the Object class.

In contrast, if a class contains *mutable* objects (objects that can be changed), the clone method of the Object class may not work properly. In that case, you'll need to override this method when you implement the Cloneable interface to be sure it works. Figure 9-15 shows how this works.

At the top of this figure, you can see a LineItem class that implements the Cloneable interface. Since this class contains an instance variable of a mutable object (a Product object), you must clone both the LineItem object and the Product object. So the first statement in the clone method clones the LineItem object by calling the clone method of the Object class. Because this method returns an Object type, that object is cast to a LineItem so it can be stored in a LineItem variable. At this point, you have two LineItem objects, but they both point to the same Product object.

To clone the Product object, the second statement calls the clone method of that object. Then, the object that's returned by that method is cast to a Product object and stored in a Product variable. The third statement assigns this object to the Product instance variable. At this point, each LineItem object points to its own copy of the Product object. As a result, this clone method will work properly for a LineItem object.

The code that uses the clone method of the LineItem class shows how this works. This code starts by creating a Product object and filling it with data. Then, it creates a LineItem object, supplying the data for the line item to the constructor. Next, the clone method of the LineItem object is called to clone the line item. To illustrate that both the line item and the product it contains have been cloned, the next two statements change the quantity of the second line item and the price of the product stored in that line item. Then, the last two statements print both LineItem objects to the console so you can see that the changes were applied only to the second line item and product.

A LineItem class that implements the Cloneable interface

```
public class LineItem implements Cloneable
{
    private Product product;
    private int quantity;
    private double total;

    // the code for the constructors and methods

    @Override
    public Object clone() throws CloneNotSupportedException
    {
        LineItem li = (LineItem) super.clone();
        Product p = (Product) product.clone();
        li.setProduct(p);
        return li;
    }
}
```

Code that uses the clone method of the LineItem class

```
Product p1 = new Product();
p1.setCode("java");
p1.setDescription("Murach's Beginning Java");
p1.setPrice(49.50);

LineItem li1 = new LineItem(p1, 3);

// clone the line item
LineItem li2 = (LineItem) li1.clone();

// change values in the cloned LineItem and its Product object
li2.setQuantity(2);
li2.getProduct().setPrice(44.50);

// print the results
System.out.println(li1);
System.out.println(li2);
```

The result

```
Code: java
Description: Murach's Beginning Java
Price: $49.50
Quantity: 3
Total: $148.50

Code: java
Description: Murach's Beginning Java
Price: $44.50
Quantity: 2
Total: $89.00
```

Description

- To clone an object that contains an instance variable for a *mutable object*, you need to override the clone method and manually clone that object.

Figure 9-15 A LineItem class that implements the Cloneable interface

Perspective

In this chapter, you've learned how to use interfaces and how they can be used to improve the design of an application. That means that you should now be able to implement all types of classes that are commonly used in business applications. In the next chapter, though, you'll learn some additional object-oriented skills that will round out your knowledge of object-oriented programming.

Summary

- An *interface* is a special type of coding element that can contain static constants and abstract methods. Although a class can only inherit one other class, it can *implement* more than one interface.
- To implement an interface, a class must implement all the abstract methods defined by the interface. An interface can also inherit other interfaces, in which case the implementing class must also implement all the methods of the inherited interfaces.
- An interface defines a Java type. Because of that, you can use an object that's created from a class that implements an interface anywhere that interface is expected.
- When you *clone* an object, you make an identical copy of the object.
- Before you can use the clone method of the Object class, you need to implement the Cloneable interface. Then, you can override the clone method so it is public and so it works correctly with *mutable* objects.

Exercise 9-1 Create and work with interfaces

In this exercise, you'll create and implement the DepartmentConstants interface presented in this chapter. You'll also create and implement an interface named Displayable that's similar to the Printable interface.

Create the interfaces

1. Open the project named ch09_ex1_DisplayableTest in the ex_starts directory.
2. Add an interface named DepartmentConstants that contains the three constants shown in figure 9-4.
3. Add an interface named Displayable. This interface should contain a single method named getDisplayText that returns a String.

Implement the interfaces

4. Edit the Product class so it implements the Displayable interface. The getDisplayText method in this class should format a string that can be used to display the product information.

5. Edit the Employee class so it implements the DepartmentConstants and Displayable interfaces. The getDisplayText method in this class should work like the one in the Product class, and it should use the constants in the DepartmentConstants interface to include the department name in the return value.

Use the classes that implement the interfaces

6. Open the DisplayableTestApp class and add code to it that creates an Employee object, assigns it to a Displayable variable, and displays the information in the Employee object at the console. To get the information for an employee, you'll need to use the getDisplayText method of the Displayable interface.
7. Run the application to make sure that it displays the employee information.
8. Repeat steps 6 and 7 for a Product object.

Use an interface as a parameter

9. Open the DisplayableTestApp class and add a method with this signature:

   ```
   private static String displayMultiple(Displayable d, int count)
   ```

   Write the code for this method so it returns a string that contains the Displayable parameter the number of times specified by the int parameter.
10. Modify the code in the main method so it uses the displayMultiple method to display the employee information once and the product information twice.
11. Run the application to make sure it works correctly.

Exercise 9-2 Add an update function to the Product Maintenance application

In this exercise, you'll review the Product Maintenance application presented in this chapter. Then, you'll add an update function to this application.

Review and run the application

1. Open the project named ch09_ex2_ProductMaintenance in the ex_starts directory.
2. Review the code in each file to see how it works.
3. Run the application and try each of its functions. When you're comfortable with how it works, exit from the application.

Modify the application so it includes an update function

4. Add code to the ProductMaintApp class that lets the user update an existing product. To do that, you'll need to add an update command to the list of commands, you'll need to add an updateProduct method that provides for updating a product, and you'll need to add an else if clause to the if statement in the main method that executes the updateProduct method if the user enters the update command.

5. The updateProduct method should start by getting a valid product code from the user. Then, it should ask the user if he wants to update the product's description or price. Depending on the user's response, it should then accept a new description or price from the user. Finally, it should call the updateProduct method of the ProductDAO object to update the product and print a line that indicates the update operation that was performed.
6. Run the ProductMaintApp class to make sure it works correctly.

Exercise 9-3 Implement the Cloneable interface

In this exercise, you'll implement the Cloneable interface for the Product and LineItem classes.

1. Open the project named ch09_ex3_CloneableTest in the ex_starts directory. Display the ProductCloneApp class and review its code. Note that this class contains an error because the clone method has protected access in the Object class and isn't available from the Product class.
2. Implement the Cloneable interface for the Product class. When you do, the ProductCloneApp class should no longer display an error.
3. Run the ProductCloneApp class to make sure it works correctly. To do that, you can right-click on this class and select the Run File command.
4. Repeat steps 1 through 3 for the LineItemCloneApp and LineItem classes.

10

Other object-oriented programming skills

In this chapter, you'll learn some other skills that are related to object-oriented programming. In particular, you'll learn how to create and use your own packages, how to document the classes in a package, how to create and use your own enumerations, and how to store two or more classes in one .java file.

How to work with packages

To make it easy for you to find and access classes, the Java API organizes its classes into *packages*. This allows you to import just the classes and packages that an application needs. Now, you'll learn how to organize your own classes into packages.

Packages provide two main advantages. First, when a project contains a large number of classes, packages can provide some logical structure to your application and make it easier to find the classes that you're looking for. Second, packages provide a way to avoid naming conflicts between classes. This is particularly important if you make your classes available to other programmers.

An introduction to packages

Figure 10-1 shows the directories and files of the Line Item application presented in chapter 7 after packages have been used to organize the classes in that application. Here, the ch10_LineItem\src directory contains the subdirectories for each package. Then, each subdirectory contains the classes for a package. For example, the murach\business directory stores the Product and LineItem classes that define the business objects for this application.

When you name a package, you can use any name you want. However, if you want to make sure that the name of your package is unique, it's considered a good practice to start the name with your Internet domain name in reverse. For example, since our Internet domain name is murach.com, all packages created by our company would begin with com.murach.

Even if you don't follow this convention, you should avoid using a generic name that might be used by someone else. For example, a package name of business is too generic. However, murach.business is specific enough that it's unlikely to conflict with any other package names. For this book, I decided to use just murach as the first level of the package name to clearly identify the company that created these packages. Then, you can use the second level to organize the packages within the first level.

Once you store a class in the correct directory, you must code a package statement at the beginning of the class. This statement consists of the package keyword followed by the name of the package. In this figure, for example, the LineItem, Product, and ProductDB classes each begin with a package statement that corresponds with the directory that contains the class. Although you can code comments before the package statement, that's not usually necessary.

If a class is stored in a package, it can't be accessed from classes in other packages without qualifying it with the package name. As a result, you typically import the class to make it easier to refer to. This works the same for the packages and classes that you create as it does for the classes of the Java API. In this figure, for example, the ProductDB class imports all the classes in the murach.business package. As a result, the ProductDB class can use the Product class, which is a member of this package, without qualification.

The directories and files for an application that uses packages

```
ch10_LineItem\src
    murach
        business
            LineItem.java
            Product.java
        database
            ProductDB.java
        lineitem
            LineItemApp.java
        presentation
            Validator.java
```

The LineItem class

```
package murach.business;

import java.text.NumberFormat;

public class LineItem {...}
```

The Product class

```
package murach.business;

import java.text.NumberFormat;

public class Product {...}
```

The ProductDB class

```
package murach.database;

import murach.business.*;

public class ProductDB {...}
```

Description

- A *package* can store one or more classes. A package can also store interfaces, although we'll just focus on classes in this chapter.
- Each package name corresponds with a directory that has the same name. The names you use should be unique to prevent conflicts with other packages.
- When you organize an application into packages, it's common to store all the classes in packages other than the default package. That includes the class that contains the main method for the application, which is often stored in a directory with a name that's similar to the application name.
- When you store a class in a package, the first statement of the class must be a package statement that specifies the name of the package.
- After the package statement, you can code the import statements for the class. These statements work the same for the packages and classes that you create as they do for the packages and classes of the Java API.

Figure 10-1 An introduction to packages

How to use NetBeans to work with packages

When you work with packages, you need to make sure that the name of the package corresponds with the name of the directory for the package. If you have to do this manually, it can quickly become a tedious task. Fortunately, NetBeans handles this for you automatically.

When a project contains packages, you can use the Projects window to navigate through the packages for the project. To do that, you can click on the plus and minus signs to the left of the packages to expand or collapse them. In figure 10-2, for example, the Projects window displays the four packages for the Line Item application that were described in the previous figure.

To get started with packages, you can add a new package to a project as described in this figure. As you do that, remember that package names correspond to the directories and subdirectories that are used to store the source code for the packages. If these directories and subdirectories don't already exist, they're created when you create the packages.

Once you've created packages for your application, NetBeans automatically adds the necessary package statement to any new class that you add to a package. In addition, if you rename a package, NetBeans automatically renames the corresponding directories and modifies the package statements for all classes in the package. Similarly, if you move a class from one package to another, NetBeans can modify the package statement for that class. In short, when you use NetBeans to work with packages, it automatically takes care of most of the details for you.

A NetBeans project that contains multiple packages

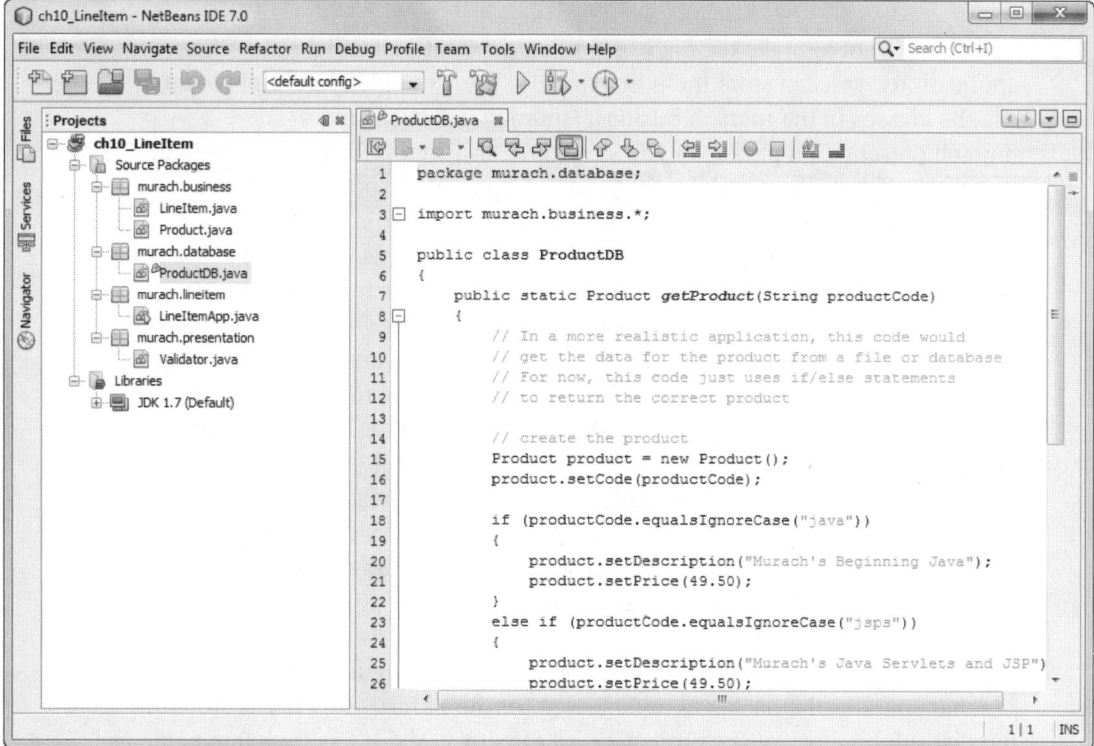
ch10_LineItem - NetBeans IDE 7.0
File Edit View Navigate Source Refactor Run Debug Profile Team Tools Window Help
Search (Ctrl+I)
<default config>
Projects
ch10_LineItem
Source Packages
murach.business
LineItem.java
Product.java
murach.database
ProductDB.java
murach.lineitem
LineItemApp.java
murach.presentation
Validator.java
Libraries
JDK 1.7 (Default)
ProductDB.java
package murach.database;
import murach.business.*;
public class ProductDB
{
public static Product getProduct(String productCode)
{
// In a more realistic application, this code would
// get the data for the product from a file or database
// For now, this code just uses if/else statements
// to return the correct product
// create the product
Product product = new Product();
product.setCode(productCode);
if (productCode.equalsIgnoreCase("java"))
{
product.setDescription("Murach's Beginning Java");
product.setPrice(49.50);
}
else if (productCode.equalsIgnoreCase("jsps"))
{
product.setDescription("Murach's Java Servlets and JSP")
product.setPrice(49.50);
1 | 1
INS

Description

- To navigate through existing packages, use the Projects window to expand or collapse the packages within a project.
- To add a new package to a project, right-click on the project name or the Source Packages folder in the Projects window, select the New→Java Package command, and enter the name of the package in the resulting dialog box. This creates a directory, if necessary, as well as a subdirectory within that directory.
- If you specify a package when you add a new class and that package doesn't already exist, it's automatically created for you.
- To remove a package from a project, right-click on the package and select the Delete command from the resulting menu. This deletes the directory for the package and all subdirectories and files within that directory.
- If you add a new class to a package, NetBeans automatically adds the necessary package statement to the class.
- To rename a package, use the Refactor→Rename command. Then, NetBeans automatically modifies the package statement.
- To move a class from one package to another, drag it in the Projects window. Then, click the Refactor button in the Move Class dialog box that's displayed so NetBeans modifies the package statement.

Figure 10-2 How to use NetBeans to work with packages

How to use NetBeans to work with libraries

If you want to make the packages of an application available to other applications, you can store them in a *library*. For example, you might want to use the classes in the murach.business, murach.database, and murach.presentation packages you saw in the last figure from other applications that work with product and line item data. Figure 10-3 shows how to use NetBeans to create a library that stores packages like this.

To start, you create a project that contains just the packages and classes that you want to include in the library. One way to do that is to copy an existing project that contains the packages and classes you want and then delete any packages and classes from that project that you don't want to include in the library. To create the ch10_MurachLib project shown in this figure, for example, I copied the ch10_LineItem project shown in figure 10-2. Then, I renamed that project and deleted the Murach.lineitem package from it.

Another way to create a project for a library is to create a new Java Application project without a main class. Then, you can open another project that contains the packages and classes that you want to include in the library. Finally, you can copy those packages from the existing project and then paste them into the new project.

After you create the project, you compile it to create a *Java Archive* (*JAR*) *file* that contains the packages and classes for the library. This file is stored in the dist subdirectory of the project's root directory, and it has the same name as the project. In some cases, you'll want to copy the JAR file to the project's src subdirectory. That will prevent other developers from modifying the file, and it will ensure that the file will always be moved with the project. Note that the JAR file doesn't include the source code (.java files) by default. Instead, it only includes the .class files, which is usually what you want.

This figure also shows how to use a library after you create it. To do that, you start by creating or opening the project that will use the library. Then, you add the JAR file for the library to the project's Libraries folder. In this figure, for example, the project named ch10_Product uses the library that's stored in the ch10_MurachLib.jar file. Finally, you add import statements for these packages to the classes that use them. The ProductApp class shown in this figure, for example, imports all the classes from all three packages that are available from the library.

When you create a library that will be used by other applications, you typically store it in a central location. In addition, you typically give the JAR file a name that identifies its contents. For example, you might give the ch10_MurachLib.jar file a name like murach.jar. That will make it easier for other programmers to use.

A NetBeans project that uses a library

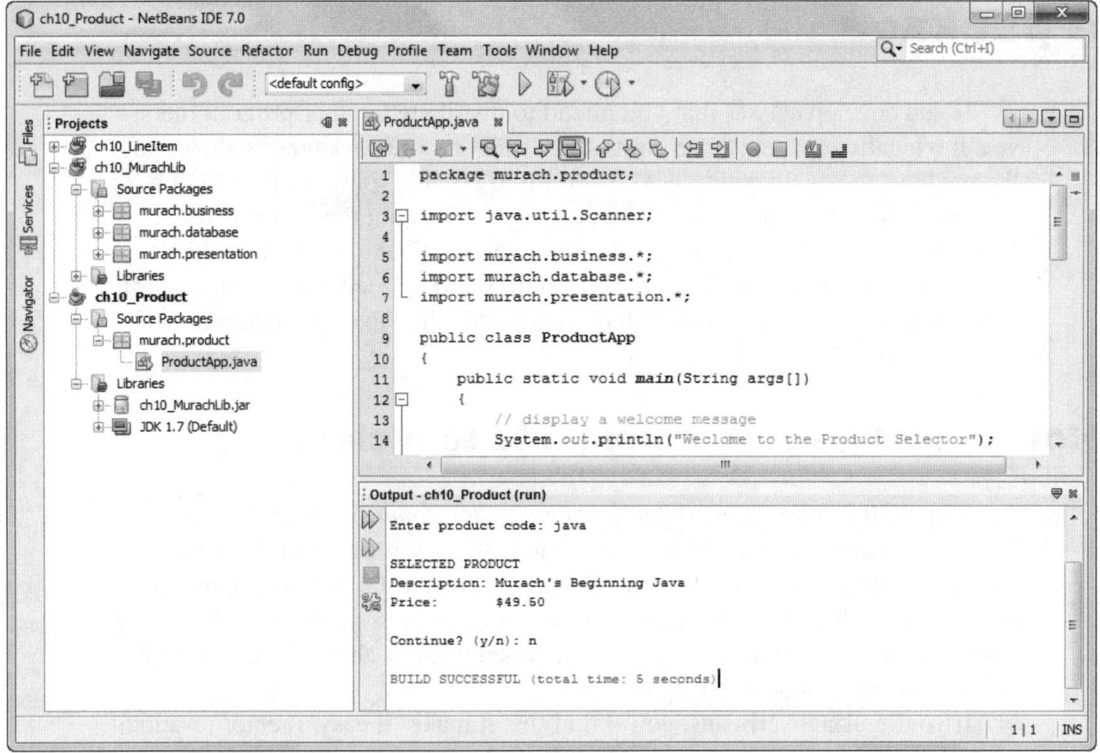
ch10_Product - NetBeans IDE 7.0
File Edit View Navigate Source Refactor Run Debug Profile Team Tools Window Help
Search (Ctrl+I)
<default config>
Projects
ch10_LineItem
ch10_MurachLib
Source Packages
murach.business
murach.database
murach.presentation
Libraries
ch10_Product
Source Packages
murach.product
ProductApp.java
Libraries
ch10_MurachLib.jar
JDK 1.7 (Default)
ProductApp.java
package murach.product;
import java.util.Scanner;
import murach.business.*;
import murach.database.*;
import murach.presentation.*;
public class ProductApp
{
public static void main(String args[])
{
// display a welcome message
System.out.println("Weclome to the Product Selector");
Output - ch10_Product (run)
Enter product code: java
SELECTED PRODUCT
Description: Murach's Beginning Java
Price: $49.50
Continue? (y/n): n
BUILD SUCCESSFUL (total time: 5 seconds)

How to create a library

1. Create a project that contains just the packages and classes that you want to include in the library.
2. Right-click on the project and select the Build command to compile the project. Then, NetBeans automatically creates a JAR file for the project and it stores it in the dist subdirectory for the project.

How to use a library

1. Create or open the project that will use the library.
2. Right-click on the Libraries directory and select the "Add JAR/Folder" command. Then, use the resulting dialog box to select the JAR file for the library.
3. Code the import statements for the packages and classes in the library that you want to use. Then, you can use the classes stored in those packages.

Description

- A *library* can store one or more packages that each contains one or more classes.
- When you create a library using NetBeans, the library is stored in a *Java Archive (JAR) file*.
- After you create a library, you can make it available to other programmers by storing it in a central location.

Figure 10-3 How to use NetBeans to work with libraries

How to use javadoc to document a package

If you develop classes that you intend to distribute to other programmers, you'll typically organize those classes into one or more packages as shown in the previous topics. In addition, you'll want to provide some documentation for your classes so other programmers can easily learn about the fields, constructors, and methods of those classes. Fortunately, the JDK includes a utility named javadoc that makes it easy to generate HTML-based documentation for your classes. This documentation looks and works like the documentation for the Java API.

How to add javadoc comments to a class

Figure 10-4 shows how to add simple *javadoc comments* to a class. A javadoc comment begins with /** and ends with */. Within a javadoc comment, any additional asterisks are ignored. Because of that, asterisks are commonly used as shown here to set the comments off from the rest of the code. For these comments to work, though, they must be coded directly above the class, field, constructor, or method that they describe.

If you're using NetBeans, you'll find that it makes it easy to enter javadoc comments. To do that, you enter a slash (/) followed by two or more asterisks on a blank line before the code for a class, field, constructor, or method. Then, when you press the Enter key, NetBeans generates the starting comment for the class or its member. That includes one line with a single asterisk where you can start entering the comment, followed by a line with the */ characters that end the comment. It can also include one or more of the javadoc tags you'll learn about in the next figure.

The Product class with javadoc comments

```
package murach.business;

import java.text.NumberFormat;

/************************************************************
 * The Product class represents a product and is used by
 * the LineItem and ProductDB classes.
************************************************************/
public class Product
{
    private String code;
    private String description;
    private double price;

    /***********************************************************
     * Creates a new Product with default values.
     ***********************************************************/
    public Product()
    {
        code = "";
        description = "";
        price = 0;
    }

    /***********************************************************
     * Sets the product code to the specified String.
     ***********************************************************/
    public void setCode(String code)
    {
        this.code = code;
    }

    /***********************************************************
     * Returns a String that represents the product code.
     ***********************************************************/
    public String getCode()
    {
        return code;
    }

    ...
```

Description

- A *javadoc comment* begins with /** and ends with */, and asterisks within the comment are ignored. You can use javadoc comments to describe a class and its public and protected fields, constructors, and methods.
- A comment should be placed immediately above the class or member it describes. For a class, that means that the comment must be placed after any import statements.
- If you enter a slash (/) followed by two or more asterisks on a blank line before the code for a class, field, constructor, or method in NetBeans, NetBeans generates beginning javadoc comments. That includes comments with some of the javadoc tags you'll learn about in the next figure.

Figure 10-4 How to add javadoc comments to a class

How to use HTML and javadoc tags in javadoc comments

To help format the information that's displayed in the documentation for a class, you can include HTML and javadoc tags in your javadoc comments as shown in figure 10-5. The *HTML tag* you're most likely to use is the <code> tag. This tag can be used to display text in a monospaced font. In the Product class in this figure, for example, this tag is used to format the name of each class that's referred to in the class comment, and it's used to format the name of any object that's referred to in the other comments. Although it's not shown here, this tag is also commonly used to format references to primitive types.

The four *javadoc tags* shown here should be self-explanatory. You typically use the @author and @version tags in the class comment to document the author and current version of the class. Note that by default, this information isn't displayed in the documentation that's generated. Although you can specify that you want to include this information when you generate the documentation, that's usually not necessary.

You use the @param tag to describe a parameter that's accepted by a constructor or public method. In this figure, for example, you can see that a @param tag is used to document the code parameter used by the setCode method. Similarly, if a method returns a value, you can use the @return tag to describe that value. In this figure, the @return tag is used to document the String that's returned by the getCode method.

In addition to the tags shown here, you should realize that additional HTML and javadoc tags are available. For example, you can use the <i> tag to italicize text, and you can use the <b> tag to boldface text. To create a hyperlink, you can use the javadoc @see tag. For more information on this tag and other javadoc tags, see the online documentation for the javadoc utility.

Common HTML tag used to format javadoc comments

HTML tag	Description
`<code></code>`	Displays the text between these tags with a monospaced font.

Common javadoc tags

Javadoc tag	Description
@author	Identifies the author of the class. Not displayed by default.
@version	Describes the current version of the class. Not displayed by default.
@param	Describes a parameter of a constructor or method.
@return	Describes the value that's returned by a method.

The Product class with comments that use HTML and javadoc tags

```
package murach.business;

/******************************************************************
 * The <code>Product</code> class represents a product and is used
 * by the <code>LineItem</code> and <code>ProductDB</code> classes.
 * @author Joel Murach
 * @version 1.0.0
 ******************************************************************/
public class Product {
    private String code;
    private String description;
    private double price;

    /**************************************************************
     * Creates a <code>Product</code> with default values.
     **************************************************************/
    public Product(){
        code = "";
        description = "";
        price = 0;
    }

    /**************************************************************
     * Sets the product code to the specified <code>String</code>.
     * @param code A <code>String</code> for the product code.
     *************************************************************/
    public void setCode(String code){
        this.code = code;
    }

    /**************************************************************
     * Returns a <code>String</code> that represents the product code.
     * @return A <code>String</code> for the product code.
     *************************************************************/
    public String getCode(){
        return code;
    }

    ...
```

Figure 10-5 How to use HTML and javadoc tags in javadoc comments

How to use NetBeans to generate documentation

After you add javadoc comments to the classes of a project, you can use NetBeans to generate the documentation for those classes as described in figure 10-6. After it generates the documentation, NetBeans displays it in your default web browser as shown here. Then, you can review this documentation to be sure that it contains all the necessary information.

By default, NetBeans stores the documentation for a project in the dist\javadoc subdirectory of the project's root directory. This documentation consists of a number of files and subdirectories. Note that if you generate documentation for a project and the dist\javadoc directory already contains documentation, NetBeans overwrites the old files with the new ones, which is usually what you want.

How to view the documentation for a package

You can use a web browser to view the documentation for user-defined classes the same way that you view the documentation for the Java API. The main difference is that the index.html file for user-defined classes is stored somewhere on your hard drive. In figure 10-6, for example, the documentation is stored in this directory:

```
C:\murach\java\netbeans\book_apps\ch10_LineItem\dist\javadoc
```

Here, I selected the murach.business package from the upper left frame. When I did that, the two classes in that package were listed in the lower left frame. Then, when I selected the Product class, the documentation for that class was displayed in the right frame.

The documentation for the Product class indicates that the Product class is in the murach.business package. It also includes a brief description of the Product class, which was generated from the javadoc comment for the class. Next, it provides a summary of the constructors and methods of the class that are available to other classes, along with the descriptions I provided. If this class contained public or protected fields, the documentation would also include a summary of those fields. Finally, the documentation includes details of all the fields, constructors, and methods in the summaries. This is where you'll see any information provided with @param and @return tags.

Note that the documentation doesn't expose the code that is encapsulated within the class. As a result, the documentation makes it easy for other programmers to use your classes without knowing the details of how they're coded.

The API documentation that's generated for the Product class

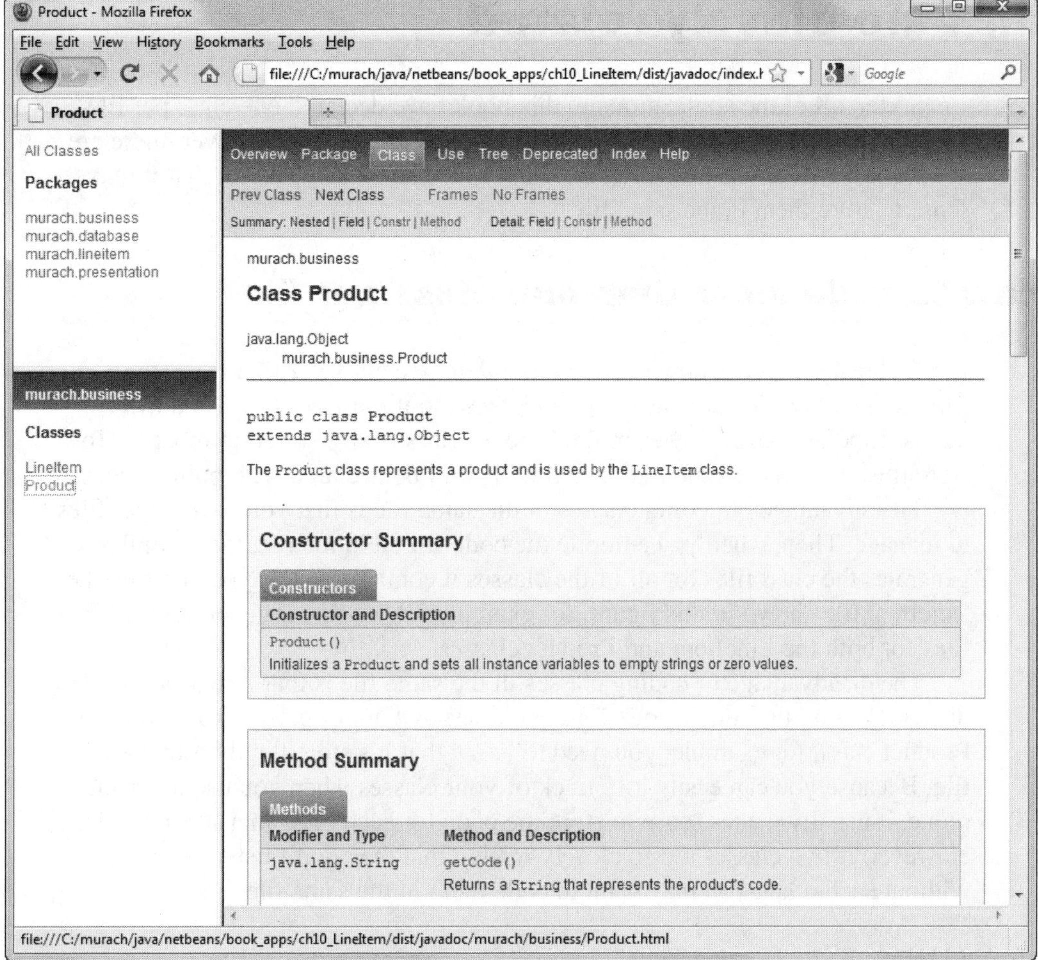

Description

- To generate or view the documentation for a project from NetBeans, you can right-click on the project in the Projects window and select the "Generate Javadoc" command. When you do, NetBeans generates the Java documentation for the project and displays it in the default web browser.
- By default, NetBeans stores the documentation for a project in a subdirectory named dist\javadoc that's subordinate to the project's root directory.
- If the project already contains documentation, NetBeans overwrites existing files without any warning.
- You can view the generated documentation by starting a web browser and navigating to the index.html file that's created in the dist\javadoc directory.

Figure 10-6 How to generate and view the documentation for a package

How to code classes that are closely related

So far, all of the applications in this book have declared one class per file. Most of the time, that's how you want to code your classes. However, there are some coding situations in which two classes are so closely related that it makes sense to store them in the same file.

How to code more than one class per file

Figure 10-7 shows how to code more than one class per file. Here, the LineItem class is declared as the public class, so it must be stored in a file named LineItem.java. However, the Product class is also stored in this file. To store this class in the LineItem.java file, it can't be declared with public access.

The advantage of coding classes in the same file is that you have fewer files to manage. Then, when you compile the code stored in the file, the compiler generates the class files for all of the classes it contains. When you compile the LineItem file shown in this figure, for example, the compiler generates the class files for both the LineItem and Product classes.

The disadvantage of coding classes in the same file is that it makes it more difficult to find the source code for the classes that aren't public. To modify the Product class, for example, you need to know that it's stored in the LineItem file. Because you can easily lose track of your classes when you use this technique, it usually makes sense to store the code for each class in a separate file. However, if two classes are so closely related that they don't make sense without each other, you may want to code them in the same file.

Two classes declared within a file named LineItem.java

```
import java.text.NumberFormat;

public class LineItem
{
    private Product product;
    private int quantity;
    private double total;
    .
    .
    .
}

class Product
{
    // body of Product class
}
```

The class files that are generated when the code above is compiled

```
LineItem.class
Product.class
```

Description

- When you code two or more classes in the same file, you can only have one public class in the file, and that class should be declared first.
- The name of a file that contains two or more classes must be the same as the name of the public class.

Figure 10-7 How to code more than one class per file

An introduction to nested classes

You can code *nested classes* whenever you need to code a class that only makes sense within the context of another class. Most of the time, you won't need to use nested classes. Because of that, I'll just introduce you to them here.

Figure 10-8 shows the syntax and principles for coding nested classes. After you code the *outer class*, you can code *inner classes* and *static inner classes*. Since these types of classes are members of the outer class, they're sometimes called *member classes*.

The outer class in the first example in this figure works the same as the rest of the classes that you've been working with throughout this book. It must be declared public, and it must be stored in a file that has the same name as the class. Then, it can contain instance variables, static variables, constructors, methods, and static methods.

The first nested class shows the types of data that you can use in an inner class. Since an inner class has direct access to all private variables and methods of the outer class, you may want to use an inner class for some closely related classes. However, an inner class can't contain any static variables or methods.

The second nested class shows the types of data that you can use in a static inner class. Unlike regular inner classes, static inner classes are independent of the outer class. In fact, you can create an instance of the static inner class without referring to the outer class. As a result, static inner classes can't access any of the instance variables or methods of the outer class. However, they can access the static variables and methods of the outer class. Note that you can only code a static class within another class.

The second example in this figure shows how you can nest a class within a method. In this case, the class is known as a *local class* because it can only be called from within the method.

If you compile the code for these examples, the compiler generates the classes shown in this figure. Here, a dollar sign ($) separates the outer class and inner class names. This clearly shows that the inner classes are nested within the outer class.

Example 1: Two classes nested within another class

```
public class OuterClassName
{
    // can contain instance variables and methods
    // can contain static variables and methods
    class InnerClassName
    {
        // can contain instance variables and methods
        // can't contain static variables or methods
        // can access all variables and methods of OuterClass
    }
    static class StaticInnerClassName
    {
        // can contain instance variables and methods
        // can contain static variables and methods
        // can access static variables and methods of OuterClass
        // can't access instance variables or methods of OuterClass
    }
}
```

The class files generated for this class

```
OuterClassName.class
OuterClassName$InnerClassName.class
OuterClassName$StaticInnerClassName.class
```

Example 2: A class nested within a method

```
public class ClassName
{
    // code for the outer class
    public void methodName()
    {
        class InnerClassName
        {
            // code for the inner class
        }
        // code for the method
    }
}
```

The class files generated for this class

```
ClassName.class
ClassName$InnerClassName.class
```

Description

- A *nested class* is a class that's coded within the block of code for another class.
- When you nest classes, the *outer class* must be declared public and must have the same name as the file name of the class.
- Within an outer class, you can nest *inner classes* and *static inner classes*. Since the inner classes are members of the outer class, they are sometimes called *member classes*.
- A class can also be nested inside a method or any other type of block. These types of classes are sometimes called *local classes*.

Figure 10-8 An introduction to nested classes

How to work with enumerations

An *enumeration* is a set of related constants that define a type. Enumerations were introduced with JDK 1.5. In chapter 3, you learned how to use the RoundingMode enumeration of the Java API to set the rounding mode for a BigDecimal object. Now, you'll learn how to create and use your own enumerations.

How to declare an enumeration

Figure 10-9 shows how to declare an enumeration. To do that, you code the public keyword, followed by the enum keyword, followed by the name of the enumeration. Then, within the enumeration, you code the names of one or more constants, separating each name with a comma.

Internally, each constant within the enumeration is assigned an integer value beginning with zero. For instance, in the ShippingType enumeration shown in the first example in this figure, the UPS_NEXT_DAY constant has a value of zero, the UPS_SECOND_DAY constant has a value of one, and so on. In most cases, though, you won't use these integer values.

When coding your own enumerations, it's common to store them in a separate file. That way, the enumeration is available to all classes within the current package. However, you can also store your enumerations in the same file as a related class, and you can nest enumerations within a class. This works just like it does for classes.

How to use an enumeration

The next three examples in figure 10-9 show how you can use an enumeration. The second example shows that you can declare a variable as an enumeration type. Then, you can assign a constant in that enumeration to the variable. In this case, the UPS_SECOND_DAY constant is assigned to a ShippingType variable named secondDay.

The third example shows a getShippingAmount method that accepts a ShippingType enumeration as a parameter. Then, the code within the method compares the constant that's passed to the method with two of the constants in the enumeration to determine the shipping amount.

The fourth example shows a statement that calls the getShippingAmount method. This statement passes the UPS_SECOND_DAY constant of the ShippingType enumeration to the getShippingAmount method.

The statement that's commented out in the fourth example illustrates that you can't use an integer, or any other type, in place of an enumeration even though the constants in the enumeration are assigned integer values. In other words, enumerations are *type-safe*. In contrast, if you didn't code the constants in an enumeration, you could use the constant name or its value wherever the constant is expected. This is one of several reasons that enumerations are generally preferred to constants.

The syntax for declaring an enumeration

```
public enum EnumerationName
{
    CONSTANT_NAME1[,
    CONSTANT_NAME2]...
}
```

Example 1: An enumeration that defines three shipping types

```
public enum ShippingType
{
    UPS_NEXT_DAY,
    UPS_SECOND_DAY,
    UPS_GROUND
}
```

Example 2: A statement that uses the enumeration and one of its constants

```
ShippingType secondDay = ShippingType.UPS_SECOND_DAY;
```

Example 3: A method that uses the enumeration as a parameter type

```
public static double getShippingAmount(ShippingType st)
{
    double shippingAmount = 2.99;
    if (st == ShippingType.UPS_NEXT_DAY)
        shippingAmount = 10.99;
    else if (st == ShippingType.UPS_SECOND_DAY)
        shippingAmount = 5.99;
    return shippingAmount;
}
```

Example 4: A statement that calls the method

```
double shippingAmount = getShippingAmount(ShippingType.UPS_SECOND_DAY);
// double shippingAmount2 = getShippingAmount(1); // Wrong type, not allowed
```

Description

- An *enumeration* contains a set of related constants. The constants are defined with the int type and are assigned values from 0 to the number of constants in the enumeration minus 1.
- An enumeration defines a type. Because of that, you can't specify another type where an enumeration type is expected. That means that enumerations are *type-safe*.
- To add an enumeration to a project using NetBeans, right-click on the package you want to add the enumeration to and select the New→Other command. Select Java Enum as the file type from the dialog box that's displayed, click the Next button, and use the resulting dialog box to enter a name for the enumeration.

Figure 10-9 How to declare and work with enumerations

How to enhance an enumeration

Most of the time, the skills presented in figure 10-9 are the only ones you'll need for working with enumerations. You should know, however, that you can override methods that an enumeration inherits from the java.lang.Object and java.lang.Enum classes. You can also add your own methods. When you do that, you may want to use methods of the enumeration constants. Two of those methods are shown at the top of figure 10-10.

This figure also shows an enhanced version of the ShippingType enumeration. This enumeration includes a toString method that overrides the toString method of the Enum class. Without this method, the toString method of the Enum class would return the name of the constant.

In this example, a semicolon is coded following the constants of the enumeration. This semicolon lets the compiler know that there are no more constants. Then, the toString method uses a series of if/else statements to return an appropriate string for each constant in the enumeration. To do that, it begins by using the ordinal method to return an int value for the constant. Then, it compares that value to integer values and returns a string that's appropriate for the current constant.

How to work with static imports

In addition to enumerations, JDK 1.5 introduced a new feature known as *static imports*. This feature lets you simplify references to the constants in an enumeration. Figure 10-10 shows how.

To use the static import feature, you begin by coding a static import statement. This statement is similar to a regular import statement, but you code the static keyword after the import keyword, and you typically use the wildcard character (*) to import all of the constants of an enumeration. In this figure, for example, the static import statement specifies that all of the constants in the ShippingType enumeration in the murach.business package should be imported. (This assumes that the ShippingType enumeration has been stored in the murach.business package as described earlier in this chapter.)

Once you code a static import statement, you no longer need to code the name of the enumeration that contains the constants. For example, after you import the ShippingType enumeration, you no longer need to code the ShippingType qualifier when you refer to a constant in this enumeration. In this figure, for example, you can see a statement that refers to the UPS_GROUND constant of this enumeration.

In addition to using static imports to import enumerations, you can use them to import the static fields and methods of a class. For example, you could use a static import to import all the static fields and methods of the java.lang.Math class. Then, you could refer to those fields and methods without qualification.

Although you can save some typing by using static imports, they often result in code that's more difficult to read. That's because it may not be obvious where the constants, fields, and methods that an application refers to are stored. As a result, you should use static imports only when they don't cause confusion.

Two methods of an enumeration constant

Method	Description
`name()`	Returns a String for the enumeration constant's name.
`ordinal()`	Returns an int value that corresponds to the enumeration constant's position.

How to add a method to an enumeration

An enumeration that overrides the toString method

```
public enum ShippingType
{
    UPS_NEXT_DAY,
    UPS_SECOND_DAY,
    UPS_GROUND;

    @Override
    public String toString()
    {
        String s = "";
        if (this.ordinal() == 0)
            s = "UPS Next Day (1 business day)";
        else if (this.ordinal() == 1)
            s = "UPS Second Day (2 business days)";
        else if (this.ordinal() == 2)
            s = "UPS Ground (5 to 7 business days)";
        return s;
    }
}
```

Code that uses the toString method

```
ShippingType ground = ShippingType.UPS_GROUND;
System.out.println("toString: " + ground.toString() + "\n");
```

Resulting output

```
toString: UPS Ground (5 to 7 business days)
```

How to work with static imports

How to code a static import statement

```
import static murach.business.ShippingType.*;
```

The code above when a static import is used

```
ShippingType ground = UPS_GROUND;
System.out.println("toString: " + ground.toString() + "\n");
```

Description

- All enumerations inherit the java.lang.Object and java.lang.Enum classes and can use or override the methods of those classes or add new methods.
- By default, the toString method of an enumeration constant returns the same string as the name method.
- You can use a *static import* to import all of the constants of an enumeration or all of the static fields and methods of a class.

Figure 10-10 How to enhance an enumeration and work with static imports

Perspective

Now that you've finished this chapter, you should be able to package and document your classes so other programmers can use them. You should also be able to apply the appropriate technique for coding classes that are closely related, and you should be able to create and work with enumerations. With these skills, you'll be able to implement the classes, interfaces, and enumerations that are commonly used in business applications.

Summary

- You can use *packages* to organize the classes in your application. Then, you can use import statements to make the classes in that package available to other classes.
- You can use a *library* to make packages and classes available to other applications. When you use NetBeans to create a library, it's stored in a *Java Archive* (*JAR*) *file*.
- You can use *javadoc comments* to document a class and its fields, constructors, and methods. Then, you can generate HTML-based documentation for your class.
- When two or more classes are closely related, it sometimes makes sense to store them all in one file or to *nest* them.
- You can use an *enumeration* to define a set of related constants as a type. Then, you can use the constants in the enumeration anywhere the enumeration is allowed.
- You can use *static imports* to import the constants of an enumeration or the static fields and methods of a class. Then, you can refer to the constants, fields, and methods without qualification.

Exercise 10-1 Work with packages and libraries

This exercise guides you through the process of using packages to organize the classes of an application, and it gives you a chance to work with a library.

Review a project that uses packages

1. Open the project named ch10_ex1_LineItem that's in the ex_starts directory, and notice that this project is organized into packages.
2. Review the code for each of the classes, and note that the package statement for each class corresponds with the package directories that are shown in the Projects window.

3. Review the subdirectories and files of this directory:

   `ex_starts\ch10_ex1_LineItem\src`

   Note that these subdirectories and files correspond with the packages and classes for this project.

Work with packages

4. Add a new package named murach.test to the project.
5. Move the LineItemApp class from the murach.lineitem package to the murach.test package. When the Move Class dialog box is displayed, click the Refactor button so that NetBeans automatically modifies the package statement for this class.
6. Delete the package named murach.lineitem.
7. Rename the murach.database package to murach.db. Note that NetBeans automatically renames the directory that corresponds with this package and modifies the package statement for the class that's stored in this package.
8. Open the ProductDB class and comment out its import statement. If you're using NetBeans, this will cause syntax errors that indicate that the ProductDB class can't find the Product class. To fix this, uncomment the import statement.
9. Run the project to make sure it's working correctly.

Create a library

10. Use the Build command to compile the project. Then, look in the file system and note that the ch10_ex1_LineItem\dist subdirectory contains a JAR file named ch10_ex1_LineItem.jar.
11. Rename the JAR file to murach.jar.

Use a library

12. Copy the murach.jar file into the ch10_ex1_Product\src directory. Then, open the project named ch10_ex1_Product and review the code in the ProductApp class.
13. Delete the murach.business, murach.database, and murach.presentation packages, but not the murach.product package. If you're using NetBeans, this will cause syntax errors in the ProductApp class that indicate that the packages in the import statements and the Product, ProductDB, and Validator classes can't be found.
14. Add the library that's stored in the murach.jar file to the project's Libraries folder. Note that the ProductApp class still can't find the ProductDB class.
15. Modify the import statement for the ProductDB class so it works correctly. Hint: You modified the name of this package earlier in this exercise.
16. Run this project to make sure it works correctly.

Exercise 10-2 Document some code

This exercise guides you through the process of using NetBeans to add javadoc comments to the Validator class and to generate the API documentation for all the murach packages.

1. Open the project named ch10_ex2_LineItem that's stored in the ex_starts directory.
2. Open the Product class that's in the murach.business package. Then, view the javadoc comments that have been added to this class. Note that these comments don't include the @param or @return tags.
3. Open the LineItem class that's in the murach.business package. Note that a single javadoc comment has been added at the beginning of this class.
4. Open the Validator class that's in the murach.presentation package. Then, add javadoc comments to this class and each of its methods. Make sure to include @param and @return tags for all of its methods.
5. Generate the documentation for the project. This should automatically open the documentation in a web browser.
6. View the documention for the LineItem class so you can see the documentation that's generated for a class by default.
7. View the documentation for the Product class. Note that the details for the methods don't include a description of the parameters or return values.
8. View the documentation for the Validator class. Note that the details for the methods include the descriptions of the parameters and return values. Then, close your browser.
9. Navigate to the dist\javadoc directory for the project and view the files for this directory. Then, open the index.html page in your browser. Note that it displays the documentation for the project.

Exercise 10-3 Code more than one class per file

In this exercise, you'll combine the code for two classes into a single file.

1. Open the project named ch10_ex3_Classes that's stored in the ex_starts directory. Review the code for the Customer and Address classes.
2. Cut the code from the Address class and paste it at the end of the Customer class. Delete the public modifier from the declaration of the Address class, and save the file.
3. Delete the Address.java file. At this point, the project should only contain the Customer.java file.

4. Compile the Customer class. Then, view the files in the build\classes subdirectory of the project. This subdirectory should contain .class files for both the Customer and Address classes. This shows that the Customer.java file now stores two classes.

Exercise 10-4 Create and use an enumeration

In this exercise, you'll create an enumeration and then use it in a test application.

1. Open the project named ch10_ex4_Enumeration that's in the ex_starts directory.
2. Create an enumeration named CustomerType. This enumeration should contain constants that represent three types of customers: retail, trade, and college.
3. Open the CustomerTypeApp class. Then, add a method to this class that returns a discount percent (.10 for retail, .30 for trade, and .20 for college) depending on the CustomerType variable that's passed to it.
4. Add code to the main method that declares a CustomerType variable, assigns one of the customer types to it, gets the discount percent for that customer type, and displays the discount percent. Run the application to be sure that it works correctly.
5. Add a statement to the main method that displays the string returned by the toString method of the customer type. Then, run the application again to see the result of this method.
6. Add a toString method to the CustomerType enumeration. This method should return a string that contains "Retail customer," "Trade customer," or "College customer" depending on the customer type. Run the application one more time to view the results of the toString method.

Section 3

More Java essentials

This section consists of four chapters that show you how to use more of the core Java features. Chapter 11 presents the concepts and techniques you need to know to work with arrays. Chapter 12 shows you how to work with collections as well as a feature that was introduced with Java 5 called generics. Chapter 13 presents the most important skills for working with dates and strings. And chapter 14 provides additional information about handling exceptions.

Except for chapter 12, each chapter in this section is treated as an independent unit. Because of that, you can read these chapters in any sequence you like. If, for example, you want to learn more about handling exceptions, you can read chapter 14 next. Or, if you want to learn about using dates and strings, you can read chapter 13 next. However, chapter 12 assumes that you know how to work with arrays, so you'll want to read chapter 11 before reading this chapter.

Once you've read chapters 11 and 12, which present skills that are critical to most Java applications, you can skip ahead to the remaining sections. If, for example, you want to learn how to develop a graphical user interface, you can skip to section 4. Or, if you want to learn how to store the data for your business objects in a file or database, you can skip to section 5. As you read those sections, you can skip back to the chapters in this section whenever necessary. For instance, since exception handling becomes more complicated when you store data in a database, you'll want to read chapter 14 before you read chapter 21.

11

How to work with arrays

In this chapter, you'll learn how to work with arrays, which are important in many types of Java applications. For example, you can use a sales array to hold the sales amounts for each of the 12 months of the year. Then, you can use that array to perform calculations on those amounts. In this chapter, you'll learn the basic concepts and techniques for working with arrays.

Basic skills for working with arrays

In the topics that follow, you'll learn how to use an array to work with primitive types or objects. First, you'll learn how to create an array. Next, you'll learn how to assign values to an array. Then, you'll see some examples that show how to work with arrays.

How to create an array

An *array* is an object that contains one or more items called *elements*, each of which is a primitive type such as an int or a double or an object such as a String or a custom type. All of the elements in an array must be of the same type. Thus, an int array can contain only integers, and a double array can contain only doubles. Note, however, that an array can contain elements that are derived from the array's base type. As a result, if you declare an array of type Object, the array can contain any type of object because all Java classes are ultimately derived from the Object class.

The *length* (or *size*) of an array indicates the number of elements that it contains. In Java, arrays have a fixed length. So once you create an array, you can't change its length. If your application requires that you change the length of an array, you should consider using one of the collection classes described in chapter 12 instead of an array.

Figure 11-1 shows several ways to create an array. To start, you must declare a variable that will be used to refer to the array. Then, you instantiate an array object and assign it to the variable. You can use separate statements to declare the array variable and instantiate the array, or you can declare the variable and instantiate the array in a single statement.

Notice that when you declare the array variable, you use an empty set of brackets to indicate that the variable is an array. You can code these brackets after the variable name or after the array type. Most programmers prefer to code the empty brackets after the array type to indicate that the array is an array of a particular type, but either technique is acceptable.

When you instantiate an array, you use another set of brackets to indicate the number of elements in the array. If you know the size of the array at compile time, you can code the number of elements as a literal or as a constant of type int. If you won't know the size of the array until run time, you can use a variable of type int to specify its size.

The first three examples show how to declare an array of double types. The first example simply declares an array variable without instantiating an array. The second example instantiates an array that holds four doubles and assigns it to the array variable declared in the first example. The third example combines these two statements into a single statement that both declares and instantiates the array.

The other group of examples in this figure shows other ways to create arrays. The first two examples in this group create arrays of String and Product objects. And the last two examples use a constant and a variable to provide the length for an array of String objects.

The syntax for declaring and instantiating an array

Two ways to declare an array

```
type[] arrayName;
type arrayName[];
```

How to instantiate an array

```
arrayName = new type[length];
```

How to declare and instantiate an array in one statement

```
type[] arrayName = new type[length];
```

Examples of array declarations

Code that declares an array of doubles

```
double[] prices;
```

Code that instantiates an array of doubles

```
prices = new double[4];
```

Code that declares and instantiates an array of doubles in one statement

```
double[] prices = new double[4];
```

Other examples

An array of String objects

```
String[] titles = new String[3];
```

An array of Product objects

```
Product[] products = new Product[5];
```

Code that uses a constant to specify the array length

```
final int TITLE_COUNT = 100;          // array size set at compile time
String[] titles = new String[TITLE_COUNT];
```

Code that uses a variable to specify the array length

```
Scanner sc = new Scanner(System.in);
int titleCount = sc.nextInt();        // array size not set until runtime
String[] titles = new String[titleCount];
```

Description

- An *array* can store more than one primitive type or object. An *element* is one of the items in an array.
- To create an array, you must declare a variable of the correct type and instantiate an array object that the variable refers to. You can declare and instantiate the array in separate statements, or you can combine the declaration and instantiation into a single statement.
- To declare an array variable, you code a set of empty brackets after the type or the variable name. Most programmers prefer coding the brackets after the array type.
- To instantiate an array, you use the new keyword and specify the *length*, or *size*, of the array in brackets following the array type. You can specify the length by coding a literal value or by using a constant or variable of type int.
- When you instantiate an array of primitive types, numeric types are set to zeros and boolean types to false. When you create an array of objects, they are set to nulls.

Figure 11-1 How to create an array

How to assign values to the elements of an array

Figure 11-2 shows how to assign values to the elements of an array. As the syntax at the top of this figure shows, you refer to an element in an array by coding the array name followed by an *index* in brackets. The index must be an int value starting at 0 and ending at one less than the size of the array. In other words, an index of 0 refers to the first element in the array, 1 refers to the second element, 2 refers to the third element, and so on.

The first three examples in this figure show how to assign values to the elements in an array by coding one statement per element. The first example creates an array of 4 double values, then assigns a literal value to each element. In this example, the first element holds the value 14.95, the second holds 12.95, the third holds 11.95, and the fourth holds 9.95. The second example creates an array that holds String objects and initializes the strings. And the third example creates an array that holds Product objects and initializes those objects.

If you specify an index that's outside of the range of the array, Java will throw an ArrayIndexOutOfBoundsException. For instance, the commented out line at the end of the first example in this figure refers to the element with index number 4. Because this array has only four elements, however, this statement would cause an ArrayIndexOutOfBoundsException. Although you can catch this exception, it's better to write your code so it avoids using indexes that are out of bounds. You'll see examples of code like that in the next figure.

The syntax and examples at the bottom of this figure show how to create an array and assign values to the elements of the array in one statement. Here, you declare the array variable as usual. Then, you use the special assignment syntax to assign the initial values. With this syntax, you simply list the values you want assigned to the array within braces following the equals sign. Then, the number of values you list within the braces determines the size of the array that's created. The last three examples show how to use this special syntax to create the same arrays that were created by the first three examples in this figure.

The syntax for referring to an element of an array

```
arrayName[index]
```

Examples that assign values by accessing each element

Code that assigns values to an array of double types

```
double[] prices = new double[4];
prices[0] = 14.95;
prices[1] = 12.95;
prices[2] = 11.95;
prices[3] = 9.95;
//prices[4] = 8.95;  // this would throw ArrayIndexOutOfBoundsException
```

Code that assigns values to an array of String types

```
String[] names = new String[3];
names[0] = "Ted Lewis";
names[1] = "Sue Jones";
names[2] = "Ray Thomas";
```

Code that assigns objects to an array of Product objects

```
Product[] products = new Product[2];
products[0] = new Product("java");
products[1] = new Product("jsps");
```

The syntax for creating an array and assigning values in one statement

```
type[] arrayName = {value1, value2, value3, ...};
```

Examples that create an array and assign values in one statement

```
double[] prices = {14.95, 12.95, 11.95, 9.95};
String[] names = {"Ted Lewis", "Sue Jones", "Ray Thomas"};
Product[] products = {new Product("java"), new Product("jsps")};
```

Description

- To refer to the elements in an array, you use an *index* that ranges from zero (the first element in the array) to one less than the number of elements in the array.
- If you specify an index that's less than zero or greater than the upper bound of the array, an ArrayIndexOutOfBoundsException will be thrown when the statement is executed.
- You can instantiate an array and provide initial values in a single statement by listing the values in braces. The number of values you provide determines the size of the array.

Figure 11-2 How to assign values to the elements of an array

How to use for loops with arrays

For loops are commonly used to process the elements in an array one at a time by incrementing an index variable. Figure 11-3 shows how to process an array using a for loop.

The syntax at the top of this figure shows how to use the length field to return the length of an array. Since length is a field rather than a method, you don't need to include parentheses after it. The length field returns an int value that represents the length of the array. You'll typically use this value in the Boolean expression of a for loop to stop the loop after the last element has been processed.

The first example in this figure shows how to create an array of 10 int values and fill it with the numbers 0 through 9. Here, an int variable named i is used in the for loop both to index the array and to assign a value to each element in the array. Since the same variable is used to index the array and assign the element values, the value that's stored within each element is equal to the index for the element.

The second example shows how you can use a for loop to print the contents of an array to the console. Here, an array of doubles named prices is created with initial values. Then, a for loop is used to access each element of the array. The single statement within the loop prints the value of each element in the array to the console as shown.

The third example shows how you can use a for loop to calculate the average of the prices array. This example assumes you've already created the prices array as shown in the previous example. Then, it uses a for loop to add the value of each array element to a variable named sum. When the for loop finishes, sum contains the total of all the prices in the array. Then, the average is calculated by dividing this total by the number of elements in the array.

The fourth example shows another way to calculate the average value for the prices array. In this example, the normal iterator expression of the for loop (i++) is replaced with an expression that adds the current element to the sum variable and increments the index variable. As a result, no statement is required within the loop. Because we think this type of clever coding obscures the purpose of the loop, we don't recommend you use it. However, you may see this type of coding in other applications, so you should be familiar with how it works.

The syntax for getting the length of an array

```
arrayName.length
```

Example 1: Code that puts the numbers 0 through 9 in an array

```
int[] values = new int[10];
for (int i = 0; i < values.length; i++)
{
   values[i] = i;
}
```

Example 2: Code that prints an array of prices to the console

```
double[] prices = {14.95, 12.95, 11.95, 9.95};
for (int i = 0; i < prices.length; i++)
{
   System.out.println(prices[i]);
}
```

The console output

```
14.95
12.95
11.95
9.95
```

Example 3: Code that computes the average of the array of prices

```
double sum = 0.0;
for (int i = 0; i < prices.length; i++)
{
   sum += prices[i];
}
double average = sum / prices.length;
```

Example 4: Another way to compute the average in a for loop

```
double sum = 0.0;
for (int i = 0; i < prices.length; sum += prices[i++]);
average = sum / prices.length;
```

Description

- You can use the length field of an array to determine how many elements are defined for the array.
- For loops are often used to process each element in an array.

Figure 11-3 How to use for loops with arrays

How to use enhanced for loops with arrays

In addition to the standard for loop, JDK 1.5 introduced an *enhanced for loop* that's designed especially for working with arrays and collections. The enhanced for loop is sometimes called a *foreach loop* because it's used to process each element in an array or collection. Figure 11-4 shows how this loop works.

As the syntax at the top of this figure shows, the enhanced for loop doesn't use separate expressions to initialize, test, and increment a counter variable like the for loop does. Instead, it declares a variable that will be used to refer to each element of the array. Then, within the loop, you can use this variable to access each array element.

To understand how this works, the first example in this figure shows how you can use an enhanced for loop to print the elements of an array of doubles. This example performs the same function as the second example in figure 11-3. In the enhanced for loop version, a variable named price is used to access each element in the prices array. Then, the statement within the for loop simply prints the price variable to the console. Notice that because the enhanced for loop keeps track of the current element automatically, no indexing is required.

The second example shows how to use an enhanced for loop to calculate the average value in the prices array. This example performs the same function as the third example in figurc 11-3. Again, no indexing is required since the enhanced for loop automatically indexes the array.

The syntax of the enhanced for loop

```
for (type variableName : arrayName)
{
    statements
}
```

Example 1: Code that prints an array of prices to the console

```
double[] prices = {14.95, 12.95, 11.95, 9.95};
for (double price : prices)
{
   System.out.println(price);
}
```

The console output

```
14.95
12.95
11.95
9.95
```

Example 2: Code that computes the average of the array of prices

```
double sum = 0.0;
for (double price : prices)
{
   sum += price;
}
double average = sum / prices.length;
```

Description

- Version 1.5 of the JDK introduced a new form of the for loop called an *enhanced for loop*. The enhanced for loop simplifies the code required to loop through arrays. The enhanced for loop is sometimes called a *foreach loop* because it lets you process each element of an array.
- Within the parentheses of an enhanced for loop, you declare a variable with the same type as the array followed by a colon and the name of the array.
- With each iteration of the loop, the variable that's declared by the for loop is assigned the value of the next element in the array.

Note

- You can also use foreach loops to work with collections. See chapter 12 for details.

Figure 11-4 How to use enhanced for loops with arrays

More skills for working with arrays

Now that you've learned the basic skills for creating and working with arrays, you're ready to learn some additional skills for working with arrays. So in this topic, you'll learn how to use the Arrays class, the Comparable interface, and the System class to work with arrays. You'll also learn how to create a second variable to refer to an existing array.

The methods of the Arrays class

The Arrays class of the java.util package contains several static methods that you can use to compare, sort, and search arrays. In addition, you can use this class to assign a value to one or more elements of an array. Figure 11-5 describes these methods.

As you can see, you can use the fill method to assign a value to all or part of an array. You can use the equals method to compare two arrays to check whether they contain the same number of elements with the same values stored within each element. You can use the copyOf and copyOfRange methods to copy all or part of an array to another array. And you can use the sort method to sort all or part of an array. Note, however, that if you want to sort objects that are created from classes that you defined, such as the Product class, you must implement the Comparable interface as shown in figure 11-7. Note also that the copyOf and copyOfRange methods were introduced with JDK 1.6 and won't work with earlier versions of Java. You'll see an example that uses these methods in figure 11-8.

The last method in this summary is the binarySearch method, which lets you search for an element with a specific value and return its index. Before you can use this method, though, you must use the sort method to sort the array.

You can supply an array of primitive types or an array of objects as the array argument for any of the methods, and you can supply any primitive type or object as the value argument. However, you must make sure that the value type matches the array type. In addition, when you supply an index argument, you must make sure that the index falls within the bounds of the array. Otherwise, the method will throw an exception.

The Arrays class

`java.util.Arrays`

Static methods of the Arrays class

Method	Description
`fill(arrayName, value)`	Fills all elements of the specified array with the specified value.
`fill(arrayName, index1, index2, value)`	Fills elements of the specified array with the specified value from the index1 element to, but not including, the index2 element.
`equals(arrayName1, arrayName2)`	Returns a boolean true value if both arrays are of the same type and all of the elements within the arrays are equal to each other.
`copyOf(arrayName, length)`	Copies the specified array, truncating or padding with default values as necessary so the copy has the specified length.
`copyOfRange(arrayName, index1, index2)`	Copies the specified range of the specified array into a new array.
`sort(arrayName)`	Sorts the elements of an array into ascending order.
`sort(arrayName, index1, index2)`	Sorts the elements of an array into ascending order from the index1 element to, but not including, the index2 element.
`binarySearch(arrayName, value)`	Returns an int value for the index of the specified value in the specified array. Returns a negative number if the specified value is not found in the array. For this method to work properly, the array must first be sorted by the sort method.

Description

- All of these methods accept arrays of primitive data types and arrays of objects for the arrayName argument, and they all accept primitive types and objects for the value argument.
- All of the index arguments for these methods must be int types. If an index argument is less than zero or greater than one less than the length of the array, the method will throw an ArrayIndexOutOfBoundsException.
- If you use the sort method on an array of objects created from a user-defined class, such as the Product class, the class must implement the Comparable interface as shown in figure 11-7.
- The copyOf and copyOfRange methods were introduced with JDK 1.6. As a result, they won't work with older versions of the JDK.

Figure 11-5 The methods of the Arrays class

Code examples that work with the Arrays class

Figure 11-6 presents several examples that illustrate how the methods of the Arrays class work. The first example shows how to use the fill method to assign a value to all of the elements in an array of int values. Here, the first statement creates an array of 5 int values. By default, this statement automatically initializes each element to 0. Then, the second statement uses the fill method of the Arrays class to set all five values to 1.

The second example shows how to use the fill method to fill just part of an array. Here, the second and third arguments for the method indicate that elements 1, 2, and 3 should be filled with a value of 100. This use of indexes is a little peculiar, since the index that specifies the end of the range to be filled is actually one greater than the end of the range. Thus, to fill elements 1 through 3, you specify 1 as the starting index and 4 as the ending index.

The third example shows how to use the equals method to compare two arrays. Here, the first two statements create two arrays of String objects. Both arrays have two elements with identical values. Then, an if statement uses the equality operator (==) to test whether the arrays are equal. The equality operator doesn't actually compare the values of the elements in these arrays, however. Instead, it tests whether the two array variables refer to the same array object. As a result, this comparison returns false. Next, an if statement uses the equals method of the Arrays class to compare the arrays. Because this method compares the values of each of the elements in the arrays, this comparison returns true.

The fourth example shows how to use the sort method to sort an array of int values. Here, the first statement creates an unsorted array of integers from 0 to 9, and the second statement uses the sort method to sort these values. After the sort, a for loop prints the contents of the array so you can see that the array has been sorted.

The fifth example shows how to use the binarySearch method. Here, the first statement creates an array of unsorted strings. Then, the second statement uses the sort method to sort this array. For strings, this will result in the array being sorted alphabetically from A to Z. As a result, the binarySearch method used in the third statement will return a value of 2, which means that the string is the third element of the array.

Example 1: Code that uses the fill method

```
int[] quantities = new int[5];
Arrays.fill(quantities, 1);           // all elements are set to 1
```

Example 2: Code that uses the fill method to fill 3 elements in an array

```
int[] quantities = new int[5];
Arrays.fill(quantities, 1, 4, 100);  // elements 1, 2, and 3 are set to 100
```

Example 3: Code that uses the equals method

```
String[] titles1 = {"War and Peace", "Gone With the Wind"};
String[] titles2 = {"War and Peace", "Gone With the Wind"};

if (titles1 == titles2)
    System.out.println("titles1 == titles2 is true");
else
    System.out.println("titles1 == titles2 is false");

if (Arrays.equals(titles1, titles2))
    System.out.println("Arrays.equals(titles1, titles2) is true");
else
    System.out.println("Arrays.equals(titles1, titles2) is false");
```

The console output

```
titles1 == titles2 is false
Arrays.equals(titles1, titles2) is true
```

Example 4: Code that uses the sort method

```
int[] numbers = {2,6,4,1,8,5,9,3,7,0};
Arrays.sort(numbers);
for (int num : numbers)
{
    System.out.print(num + " ");
}
```

The console output

```
0 1 2 3 4 5 6 7 8 9
```

Example 5: Code that uses the sort and binarySearch methods

```
String[] productCodes = {"mcbl", "jsps", "java"};
Arrays.sort(productCodes);
int index = Arrays.binarySearch(productCodes, "mcbl");    // sets index to 2
```

Figure 11-6 Code examples that work with the Arrays class

How to implement the Comparable interface

You can only use the sort method of the Arrays class to sort an array of objects when the class for those objects implements the Comparable interface. As a result, when you code your own classes, you need to implement the Comparable interface for any class that you need to sort. To do that, you must provide an implementation of the compareTo method of this interface. Figure 11-7 shows how you can do this for a simple Item class.

The code at the top of this figure shows how the Comparable interface is defined by the Java API. This interface provides a single method named compareTo that accepts an Object as an argument. This method should return a negative number if the current object is less than the passed object, 0 if the two objects are equal, and a positive number if the current object is greater than the passed object.

The Item class in this figure begins by declaring two private instance variables named number and description, a constructor that accepts values for these fields, and methods that return the values of these fields. Then, it provides a compareTo method that compares Item objects based on the values of the number fields. In other words, two items are considered equal if they have the same item number.

The compareTo method begins by casting the object passed to it to an Item object. Then, it uses if statements to compare the item numbers and determine whether to return -1, 0, or 1. These values are used by the sort method to determine if the current object is less than, equal to, or greater than the object it's being compared to.

The code example after the Item class shows how you can sort an array of Item objects. Here, an array of three Item objects is created. Then, the sort method of the Arrays class is used to sort the array. Finally, an enhanced for loop is used to print the contents of the array. As you can see in the resulting output, the array is printed in item number sequence even though the array elements were created in a different sequence.

In this example, the objects are compared based on a numeric field. Because of that, you can use the greater than and less than operators to determine if one object is greater than or less than another. If you want to compare two objects based on a string field, however, you can't do that using these operators. Instead, you need to use the compareTo method of the String class. You'll learn more about how to use this method in chapter 13.

The Comparable interface defined in the Java API

```
public interface Comparable {
   int compareTo(Object obj);
}
```

An Item class that implements the Comparable interface

```
public class Item implements Comparable {
    private int number;
    private String description;

    public Item(int number, String description) {
        this.number = number;
        this.description = description;
    }

    public int getNumber() {
        return number;
    }

    public String getDescription() {
        return description;
    }

    @Override
    public int compareTo(Object o) {
        Item i = (Item) o;
        if (this.getNumber() < i.getNumber())
            return -1;
        if (this.getNumber() > i.getNumber())
            return 1;
        return 0;
    }
}
```

Code that sorts an array of Item objects

```
Item[] items = new Item[3];
items[0] = new Item(102, "Duct Tape");
items[1] = new Item(103, "Bailing Wire");
items[2] = new Item(101, "Chewing Gum");
Arrays.sort(items);
for (Item i : items)
    System.out.println(i.getNumber() + ": " + i.getDescription());
```

The console output

```
101: Chewing Gum
102: Duct Tape
103: Bailing Wire
```

Description

- You can use the sort method of the Arrays class to sort an array of objects only if the class that defines those objects implements the Comparable interface. To implement this interface, a class must define the compareTo method.
- The compareTo method must return -1 if the current object is less than the passed object, 0 if the objects are equal, and 1 if the current object is greater than the passed object.

Figure 11-7 How to implement the Comparable interface

How to create a reference to an array

The first example in figure 11-8 shows how to create a *reference* to an array by assigning an array variable to an existing array. Here, the grades variable and the percentages variable both refer to the same array. As a result, any change to the grades variable will be reflected by the percentages variable and vice versa. For instance, the third statement in this example sets percentages[1] to 70.2. Then, the last statement prints grades[1]. Because the percentages and grades variables actually refer to the same array, this statement prints the value 70.2.

Once you create an array, you can't change its size. However, you can use an existing array variable to refer to a larger or smaller array. When you do this, the reference to the original array is dropped, a new array is created, and the array variable is set to refer to the new array. For instance, suppose you create an array that contains 5 elements. Then, later in the program, you realize that you want that array to have 20 elements. To do this, you just reuse the array variable as shown in the second example and create a new array of 20 elements. When you do, any values you stored in the original 5-element array will be lost.

How to copy an array

Figure 11-8 also shows how to copy an array. The easiest way to do that is to use the static copyOf or copyOfRange method as shown in the third and fourth examples. Then, each array variable will point to its own copy of the array, and any changes that are made to one array won't affect the other array.

The third example shows how to use the copyOf method to make a copy of an entire array. Here, the length argument is set to the length of the grades array. As a result, this example copies all of the elements of the grades array into the percentages array. However, if you specified a larger number for the length argument, the percentages array would be padded with extra elements with a default value of zero. Or, if you specified a smaller number for the length argument, the extra elements in the percentages array would be truncated.

The fourth example shows how to use the copyOfRange method to copy parts of one array into other arrays. Here, the first statement creates an array of four double values, and the second statement sorts these values from lowest to highest. Next, the third statement creates an array that can hold two double values and copies the two lowest values into it. Then, the fourth statement creates an array that can hold two double values and copies the two highest values into it.

The copyOf and copyOfRange methods were introduced with JDK 1.6. If you're using a version of Java prior to that, you can create a copy of an array by using the arraycopy method of the System class as shown in the fifth and sixth examples. To use the arraycopy method, you specify the five arguments shown in the figure. First, you specify the source array and the starting index. Next, you specify the target array and the starting index. Then, you specify the total number of elements to copy. When you use the arraycopy method, the target array must already exist, and it must be large enough to hold the number of elements that you're copying. In addition, both arrays must be of the same type.

How to create a reference to an array

Example 1: Code that creates a reference to an array

```
double[] grades = {92.3, 88.0, 95.2, 90.5};
double[] percentages = grades;
percentages[1] = 70.2;                          // changes grades[1] too
System.out.println("grades[1]=" + grades[1]);   // prints 70.2
```

Example 2: Code that reuses an array variable

```
double[] grades = new double[5];
grades = new double[20]
```

How to copy an array with JDK 1.6 or later

Example 3: Code that copies the values of an array

```
double[] grades = {92.3, 88.0, 95.2, 90.5};
double[] percentages = Arrays.copyOf(grades, grades.length);
percentages[1] = 70.2;                         // doesn't change grades[1]
System.out.println("grades[1]=" + grades[1]);  // prints 88.0
```

Example 4: Code that copies part of one array into another array

```
double[] grades = {92.3, 88.0, 95.2, 90.5};
Arrays.sort(grades);
double[] lowestGrades = Arrays.copyOfRange(grades, 0, 2);
double[] highestGrades = Arrays.copyOfRange(grades, 2, 4);
```

How to copy an array prior to JDK 1.6

The syntax of the arraycopy method of the System class

```
System.arraycopy(fromArray, intFromIndex, toArray, intToIndex, intLength);
```

Example 5: Code that copies the values of an array

```
double[] grades = {92.3, 88.0, 95.2, 90.5};
double[] percentages = new double[grades.length];
System.arraycopy(grades, 0, percentages, 0, grades.length);
percentages[1] = 70.2;                         // doesn't change grades[1]
System.out.println("grades[1]=" + grades[1]);  // prints 88.0
```

Example 6: Code that copies part of one array into another array

```
double[] grades = {92.3, 88.0, 95.2, 90.5};
Arrays.sort(grades);
double[] lowestGrades = new double[2];
System.arraycopy(grades, 0, lowestGrades, 0, 2);
double[] highestGrades = new double[2];
System.arraycopy(grades, 2, highestGrades, 0, 2);
```

Description

- To create a *reference* to an existing array, code an assignment statement like the one shown in the first example. Then, two variables will point to the same array in memory.
- To copy the elements of one array into another with JDK 1.6 or later, use the copyOf or copyOfRange methods of the Arrays class. Prior to JDK 1.6, use the arraycopy method of the System class.
- When you copy an array, the new array must be the same type as the source array.

Figure 11-8 How to refer to and copy arrays

How to work with two-dimensional arrays

So far, this chapter has shown how to work with an array that uses one index to store a single set of elements. You can think of that as a *one-dimensional array*. Now, you'll learn how to work with *two-dimensional arrays* that use two indexes to store data. You can think of a two-dimensional array as a table made up of rows and columns where each element in the array is at the intersection of a row and column.

If you're familiar with array processing in other languages such as C++ or even Visual Basic, you may be surprised to discover that Java doesn't directly support two-dimensional arrays in the same way those languages do. Instead, Java implements a two-dimensional array as an *array of arrays* where each element of the first array is itself an array. Although the syntax is different, the effect is nearly the same.

How to work with rectangular arrays

Figure 11-9 shows how to create and use the simplest type of two-dimensional array, called a *rectangular array*. In a rectangular array, each row has the same number of columns. For example, a 5x10 array consists of an array of five elements, each of which is a 10-element array. If you think of this rectangular array as a table, the 5-element array represents the table's rows, and each 10-element array represents the columns for one of the rows.

The syntax and code at the top of this figure show how to create a rectangular array. As you can see, you specify two sets of empty brackets following the array type. Then, you specify the number of rows and columns when you instantiate the array. Thus, the code example shown here declares and instantiates a rectangular array with 3 rows, each with 2 columns.

To refer to an element in a rectangular array, you specify two index values in separate sets of brackets. The first value refers to the row index, and the second value refers to the column index. Thus, numbers[1][0] refers to row 2, column 1 of the numbers array.

You can also create a rectangular array and assign values to its elements using a single statement. To do that, you use the same shorthand notation you use for one-dimensional arrays. However, you code each element of the array as a separate array as shown in this figure. Here, the numbers array is assigned three elements, each of which is a two-element array with the values {1, 2}, {3, 4}, and {5, 6}.

The last example in this figure shows how to use nested for loops to process the elements of a rectangular array. Here, the outer for loop uses the variable i to index the rows of the array, and numbers.length is used to determine the number of rows in the array. Then, the inner for loop uses the variable j to index the columns, and numbers[i].length is used to determine the number of columns in each row.

How to create a rectangular array

The syntax for creating a rectangular array

```
type[][] arrayName = new type[rowCount][columnCount];
```

A statement that creates a 3x2 array

```
int[][] numbers = new int[3][2];
```

How to assign values to a rectangular array

The syntax for referring to an element of a rectangular array

```
arrayName[rowIndex][columnIndex]
```

The indexes for a 3x2 array

```
[0][0]          [0][1]
[1][0]          [1][1]
[2][0]          [2][1]
```

Code that assigns values to the array

```
numbers[0][0] = 1;
numbers[0][1] = 2;
numbers[1][0] = 3;
numbers[1][1] = 4;
numbers[2][0] = 5;
numbers[2][1] = 6;
```

Code that creates a 3x2 array and initializes it in one statement

```
int[][] numbers = { {1,2} {3,4} {5,6} };
```

How to use nested for loops to process a rectangular array

Code that processes a rectangular array with nested for loops

```
int[][] numbers = { {1,2}, {3,4}, {5,6} };
for (int i = 0; i < numbers.length; i++)
{
    for (int j = 0; j < numbers[i].length; j++)
        System.out.print(numbers[i][j] + "  ");
    System.out.print("\n");
}
```

The console output

```
1  2
3  4
5  6
```

Description

- *Two-dimensional arrays* use two indexes and allow data to be stored in a table that consists of rows and columns. This can also be thought of as an *array of arrays* where each row is a separate array of columns.
- A *rectangular array* is a two-dimensional array whose rows all have the same number of columns.
- Although it's rarely necessary, you can extend this two-dimensional syntax to work with arrays that have more than two dimensions.

Figure 11-9 How to work with rectangular arrays

Although it's not shown in figure 11-9, you should realize that you can also use nested foreach loops to work with rectangular arrays. To do that, you declare an array variable in the outer for loop that you can use to refer to the rows in the array. Then, you declare a variable in the inner for loop that you can use to refer to the columns in each row. For example, figure 11-10 uses nested foreach loops to work with another type of two-dimensional array called a jagged array.

How to work with jagged arrays

A *jagged array* is a two-dimensional array in which the rows contain unequal numbers of columns. This is possible because each row of a two-dimensional array is actually a separate one-dimensional array, and Java doesn't require that each of these arrays be the same size. Figure 11-10 shows how to work with jagged arrays.

When you instantiate a jagged array, you specify the number of rows but not the number of columns. Then, you instantiate the array for each row separately, specifying as many columns as are necessary for that row. To illustrate, the first statement in the first example in this figure creates a jagged array named numbers that has 3 rows. Then, the next three statements create arrays of 10, 15, and 20 elements for the three rows of the numbers array.

The second example in this figure shows how you can initialize a jagged array using the shorthand notation. Here, a jagged array of strings is created with three rows. The first row contains three elements, the second row contains four elements, and the third row contains two elements.

In the third example, a jagged array of type int is created with four rows. Then, a for loop cycles through the rows and creates a different number of elements for each column array. The first time through the loop, i will be equal to 0 so the length of the array will be set to 1. The second time through the loop, i will be equal to 1 so the length of the array will be set to 2. And so on.

For each column array, another for loop is used to initialize the element values. This loop uses a variable named j to index the columns. A variable named number is used to assign a value to each column. This variable is incremented within this for loop. As a result, the first row will have one element with the value 0. The second row will have two elements with the values 1 and 2. The third row will have three elements with the values 3, 4, and 5. And so on.

The fourth example in this figure uses nested for loops to print the contents of the array created in the third example. Here, each row is printed on a separate line so you can clearly see the number of elements it contains.

The fifth example shows how you can use nested foreach loops to produce the same output. In this example, the outer for loop accesses each element in the pyramid array as an array of int values named row. Then, the inner for loop accesses each element in the row array as an int value named col.

The syntax for creating a jagged array

```
type[][] arrayName = new type[rowCount][];
```

Example 1: Code that creates a jagged array of integers

```
int[][] numbers = new int[3][];
numbers[0] = new int[10];
numbers[1] = new int[15];
numbers[2] = new int[20];
```

Example 2: Code that creates and initializes a jagged array of strings

```
String[][] titles = {{"War and Peace", "Wuthering Heights", "1984"},
                     {"Casablanca", "Wizard of Oz", "Star Wars", "Birdy"},
                     {"Blue Suede Shoes", "Yellow Submarine"}};
```

Example 3: Code that creates and initializes a jagged array of integers

```
int number = 0;
int[][] pyramid = new int[4][];
for (int i = 0; i < pyramid.length; i++)
{
    pyramid[i] = new int[i+1];
    for (int j = 0; j < pyramid[i].length; j++)
        pyramid[i][j] = number++;
}
```

Example 4: Code that prints the contents of the jagged array of integers

```
for (int i = 0; i < pyramid.length; i++)
{
   for (int j = 0; j < pyramid[i].length; j++)
      System.out.print(pyramid[i][j] + " ");
   System.out.print("\n");
}
```

The console output

```
0
1 2
3 4 5
6 7 8 9
```

Example 5: Code that uses foreach loops to print a jagged array

```
for (int[] row : pyramid)
{
    for (int col : row)
        System.out.print(col + " ");
    System.out.print("\n");
}
```

Description

- A *jagged array* is a two-dimensional array whose rows have different numbers of columns. When you create a jagged array, you specify the number of rows in the array, but you leave the size of each column array unspecified and set it later.

Figure 11-10 How to work with jagged arrays

Perspective

Now that you've finished this chapter, you should know how to work with one-dimensional and two-dimensional arrays. Although you'll use arrays in many applications, they may not always provide the functionality you need. In that case, you can use a more advanced data structure called a collection. You'll learn how to work with collections in the next chapter.

Summary

- An *array* is a special type of object that can store more than one primitive data type or object. The *length* (or *size*) of an array is the number of *elements* that are stored in the array. The *index* is the number that is used to identify any element in the array.
- For loops are often used to process arrays. Version 1.5 of the JDK introduced a new type of for loop, called an *enhanced for loop* or a *foreach loop*, that lets you process each element of an array without using indexes.
- You can use the Arrays class to fill, compare, copy, sort, and search arrays. You can use an assignment statement to create a second *reference* to the same array.
- To provide for sorting a user-defined class, that class must implement the Comparable interface.
- A *one-dimensional array* provides for a single list or column of elements so just one index value is required to identify each element. In contrast, a *two-dimensional array*, or an *array of arrays*, can be used to organize data in a table that has rows and columns. As a result, two index values are required to identify each element.
- A two-dimensional array can be *rectangular,* in which case each row has the same number of columns, or *jagged,* in which case each row has a different number of columns.

Exercise 11-1 Use a one-dimensional array

In this exercise, you can get some practice using one-dimensional arrays.

1. Open the project named ch11_ex1_ArrayTest in the ex_starts directory. Then, open the ArrayTestApp class.
2. Create a one-dimensional array of 99 double values. Then, use a for loop to add a random number from 0 to 100 to each element in the array. To do that, use the random method of the Math class to get a double value between 0.0 and 1.0 and multiply it by 100.
3. Use an enhanced for loop to sum the values in the array. Then, calculate the average value and print that value on the console followed by a blank line. Next, test this code.

4. Use the sort method of the Arrays class to sort the values in the array, and print the median value (the 50th value) on the console followed by a blank line. Then, test this enhancement.
5. Print the 9th value of the array on the console and every 9th value after that. Then, test this enhancement.

Exercise 11-2 Use a rectangular array

This exercise guides you through the process of adding a rectangular array to the Future Value application. This array will store the values for up to ten of the calculations that are performed. When the program ends, it will print a summary of those calculations that looks something like this:

```
Future Value Calculations

Inv/Mo. Rate    Years   Future Value
$100.00 8.0%    10      $18,416.57
$125.00 8.0%    10      $23,020.71
$150.00 8.0%    10      $27,624.85
```

1. Open the project named ch11_ex2_FutureValue in the ex_starts directory. Then, review the code and run the application to make sure it works correctly.
2. Declare variables at the beginning of the main method for a row counter and a rectangular array of strings that provides for 10 rows and 4 columns.
3. After the code that calculates, formats, and displays the results for each calculation, add code that stores the formatted values as strings in the next row of the array. (Hint: You need to use the toString method of the Integer class to store the years value.)
4. Add code to display the elements in the array at the console when the user indicates that the program should end. The output should be formatted as shown above and should only include the rows that contain data. Then, test the program by making up to 10 future value calculations.

Exercise 11-3 Sort an array of user-defined objects

In this exercise, you'll modify a Customer class so it implements the Comparable interface. Then, you'll sort an array of objects created from this class.

1. Open the project named ch11_ex3_SortedCustomers in the ex_starts directory. Then, review the code in the Customer and SortedCustomersApp classes.
2. Add code to the Customer class to implement the Comparable interface. The compareTo method you create should compare the email field of the current customer with the email field of another customer. To do that, you can't use the > and < operators because the email field is a string. Instead, you'll need to use the compareToIgnoreCase method of the String class. This method compares

the string it's executed on with the string that's passed to it as an argument. If the first string is less than the second string, this method returns a negative integer. If the first string is greater than the second string, it returns a positive integer. And if the two strings are equal, it returns 0.

3. Add code to the SortedCustomersApp class that creates an array of Customer objects that can hold 3 elements, and create and assign Customer objects to those elements. Be sure that the email values you assign to the objects aren't in alphabetical order. Sort the array.
4. Code a foreach loop that prints the email, firstName, and lastName fields of each Customer object on a separate line.
5. Test the program until you're sure it works correctly.

Exercise 11-4 Work with a deck of cards

In this exercise, you'll write an application that uses a variety of arrays and for loops to work with a deck of cards. If you can complete this exercise, you can be sure that you have a solid grasp of the skills presented in this chapter.

1. Open the project named ch11_ex4_CardDeck in the ex_starts directory. Then, open the CardDeckApp class.
2. Create an array whose elements hold the first initial of the four different suits in a card deck. Declare another array that can hold a representation of the cards in a deck of cards without jokers. Both of these arrays should be declared at the class level so they can be accessed by all the methods you'll add to this project.
3. Write a method to load the card array, one suit at a time. (Use the numbers 11, 12, and 13 to represent Jacks, Queens, and Kings respectively, and use the number 1 to represent Aces.) Write another method to print the cards in the array. Print each suit on a separate line by processing the cards array in 4 groups of 13 cards each. Separate the cards in each suit by a space. Call these two methods from the main method. Test the application to be sure the array is loaded and printed properly.
4. Write a method that shuffles the deck of cards. To do that, this method should get a number between 1 and 51 by multiplying the result of the random function by 50, converting it to an integer, and adding 1. Then, it should switch each card in the deck with the card that is the given number of cards after it (if there is one). This should be repeated 100 times to shuffle the deck thoroughly. Call this method from the main method, followed by the method that prints the cards array. Test the application to be sure that the cards are shuffled.
5. Declare a rectangular array at the class level that represents fours hands of cards with five cards each. Write a method that loads this array by dealing cards from the cards array. Be sure to deal one card at a time to each hand. Write a method that prints the hands, separating the cards in each hand by a space and printing each hand on a separate line. Test the application to be sure that the cards are dealt properly.

12

How to work with collections and generics

In this chapter, you'll learn how to work with collections. As you'll see, collections are similar to arrays but provide more advanced features. Along with collections, you'll learn how to use generics, a feature that was introduced with Java 1.5 that lets you specify the type of objects that can be stored in a collection. Because this chapter assumes that you already know how to work with arrays, you should read chapter 11 before reading this chapter.

An introduction to Java collections

Like an array, a *collection* is an object that can hold one or more other objects. However, unlike arrays, collections aren't a part of the Java language itself. Instead, collections are classes that are provided with the Java API. In the topics that follow, you'll learn how collections compare to arrays, you'll learn about the interfaces and classes in the Java collection hierarchy, and you'll learn about a Java 1.5 feature called generics that make collections easier to work with.

A comparison of arrays and collections

Figure 12-1 presents a brief comparison of arrays and collections. As you can see, both arrays and collections can be used to store multiple occurrences of objects such as strings. You can also use arrays or collections to store objects created from user-defined classes such as Customer or Product. In addition, some collection classes—most notably the ArrayList class—actually use an array to store data. As a result, a collection based on the ArrayList class behaves much like an array.

Although arrays and collections have some similarities, they also have many differences. One important difference is that arrays are fixed in size. That means that if you initially create an array with 100 elements and then discover that you need to add 101 elements, you must create a new array large enough to hold 101 elements, copy the 100 elements from the first array to the new array, and then discard the original array. In contrast, collections are designed so they can grow in size. When you create a collection, you don't specify the maximum size of the collection. Instead, you simply add as many elements to the collection as you want. Then, the collection will expand automatically to hold the elements you add.

Another difference between arrays and collections is that arrays can store primitive types, but collections can only store objects. Because of that, you have to use wrapper classes to store primitive types such as integers and doubles in a collection. You'll see examples of that later in this chapter.

Finally, you typically use indexes to work with the elements in an array, but you don't usually need to use indexes to work with the elements in a collection. This is illustrated in the two examples in this figure. Here, the first example stores three values in an array and then displays those values. The second example does the same thing using a collection created from the ArrayList class. Instead of using indexes to add the three values, the collection example uses the add method of the ArrayList class. However, both examples use an enhanced for loop to print the elements of the collection.

By the way, you shouldn't worry if you don't understand all of the code in the second example. You'll learn the details of working with the ArrayList class and some of the other collection classes later in this chapter. This example is simply meant to illustrate some of the differences between working with arrays and collections.

How arrays and collections are similar

- Both can store multiple occurrences of objects.
- Some collection types (such as ArrayList) use arrays internally to store data.

How arrays and collections differ

- An array is a Java language feature. Collections are classes in the Java API.
- Collection classes have methods that perform operations that arrays don't provide.
- Arrays are fixed in size. Collections are variable in size.
- Arrays can store primitive types. Collections can't.
- Indexes are almost always required to process arrays. Collections are usually processed without using indexes.

Example 1: Code that uses an array

```
String[] codes = new String[3];
codes[0] = "mcb2";
codes[1] = "java";
codes[2] = "jsps";
for (String s : codes)
    System.out.println(s);
```

Example 2: Code that uses a collection

```
ArrayList<String> codes = new ArrayList<String>();
codes.add("mcb2");
codes.add("java");
codes.add("jsps");
for (String s : codes)
    System.out.println(s);
```

Description

- A *collection* is an object that can hold other objects. Collections are similar to arrays, but are more flexible to use and are more efficient than arrays for many applications.

Figure 12-1 A comparison of arrays and collections

An overview of the Java collection framework

Figure 12-2 shows a simplified map of the Java *collection framework*. This framework consists of a hierarchy of interfaces and classes. Here, the shaded boxes represent interfaces that define the basic collection types. The unshaded boxes represent classes that implement the collection interfaces.

The collection framework provides two main types of collections represented by two distinct class hierarchies. The first hierarchy begins with an interface named Collection. A *collection* is simply an object that can hold one or more objects. The Set and List interfaces inherit the Collection interface and define two distinct types of collections. A *set* is a collection of unique objects. In most cases, sets are also unordered. That means that sets don't retain information about the order of elements added to the set.

On the other hand, a *list* is an ordered collection of objects. A list always maintains some sort of order for the objects it contains. Depending on the type of list, the order might simply be the order in which the items were added to the list, or it might be a sorted order based on a key value. In addition, lists allow duplicate elements.

The second main type of collection is called a *map*, and it's defined by the Map interface. A map is similar to a collection, but its elements consist of *key-value pairs* in which each value element is associated with a unique key element. Each key must be associated with one and only one value. For example, a map might be used to store Customer objects mapped to customer numbers. In that case, the customer numbers are the keys and the Customer objects are the values. Note that even though the Map interface doesn't inherit the Collection interface, the term *collection* is often used to refer to both collections and maps.

Although Java provides more than 30 classes that implement the List, Set, or Map interface, you don't need to know how to use them all. The second table in this figure lists the five collection classes you'll probably use most often. Once you learn how to use these five classes, you shouldn't have much trouble learning how to use other collection classes if the need arises.

The ArrayList class implements an *array list*, which works much like a standard array. In fact, the ArrayList class uses an array internally to store the entries you add to the array list. The ArrayList class provides efficient access to the individual elements in the list. However, inserting an element into the middle of an array list can be inefficient because all of the elements after the insertion point must be moved to accommodate the inserted element.

The LinkedList class is an implementation of the List interface that uses a special structure called a *linked list* to store the list's elements. Each element in a linked list contains pointers to the elements immediately before and immediately after it. As a result, an element can be inserted into the middle of a linked list efficiently by simply adjusting the pointers in the elements before and after the inserted element. However, the elements in a linked list can't be retrieved as efficiently as the elements in an array list.

Because ArrayList and LinkedList are the two most commonly used classes in the collection framework, much of this chapter focuses on those two classes.

The collection framework

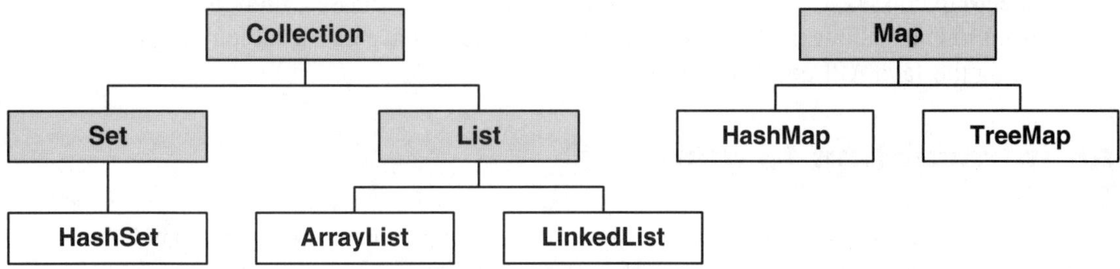

Collection interfaces

Interface	Description
Collection	Defines the basic methods available for all collections.
Set	Defines a type of collection in which no duplicate elements are allowed.
List	Defines a type of collection that maintains the order in which elements were added to the list.
Map	Defines a map, which is similar to a collection but holds one or more key value pairs instead of simple elements. Each key-value pair consists of a key that uniquely dentifies an entry and a value that provides data associated with a particular key.

Common collection classes

Class	Description
ArrayList	Works much like an array, but can be easily expanded to accommodate new elements. Very efficient for accessing individual elements in random sequence, but inserting elements into the middle of the list can be inefficient.
LinkedList	Similar to an array list, but with more features. Less efficient than an array list for accessing elements randomly, but more efficient when inserting items into the middle of the list.
HashSet	Stores a set of unique values based on a *hash code*. Duplicates are not allowed. Objects you add to a hash set must implement a method called hashCode to generate a hash code for the object, which is used to ensure uniqueness.
HashMap	Similar to a hash set, but is based on the Map interface rather than the Set interface. As a result, a hash map stores key-value pairs whose keys must be unique.
TreeMap	Stores key-value pairs in a special arrangement called a *tree*. Entries in a tree map are automatically maintained in key sequence.

Description

- The Java *collection framework* is interface based, which means that each class in the collection implements one of the interfaces defined by the collection framework.
- The collection framework consists of two class hierarchies: Collection and Map. Collections store individual objects as elements. Maps store pairs of key objects and value objects in a way that lets you retrieve a value object based on its key.
- Although there are many classes in the Java collection framework, the most commonly used classes are the ArrayList, LinkedList, HashSet, HashMap, and TreeMap classes.

Figure 12-2 The Java collection framework and classes

However, you'll also learn the basic skills for working with the HashMap and TreeMap classes. If you want to learn more about these classes, though, or you want to learn about the HashSet class, you shouldn't have any trouble doing that using the Java API documentation.

An introduction to generics

Prior to Java 1.5, the elements of a collection were defined as type Object. As a result, you could store any type of object as an element in a collection. At first, this flexibility might seem like an advantage. But with it comes two disadvantages. First, there's no way to guarantee that only objects of a certain type are added to a collection. For example, you can't limit an ArrayList so it can hold only Product objects. Second, you must use casting whenever you retrieve an object from a collection. That's because an element can be any type of object. For example, to retrieve a Product object from a collection, you must cast the object to a Product.

Java 1.5 introduced a new feature called *generics* that addresses these two problems. The generics feature lets you specify the element type for a collection. Then, Java can ensure that only objects of the specified type are added to the collection. And any objects you retrieve from the collection are automatically cast to the correct type.

Figure 12-3 shows how the generics feature works. To specify a type when you declare a collection, you code the type in angle brackets immediately following the name of the collection class (such as ArrayList or LinkedList). Prior to Java 1.7, you had to do this twice: once when you use the collection class to declare the collection, and again when you use the constructor of the collection class to create an instance of the collection. As I'll explain in a moment, though, Java 1.7 introduced a feature that lets you simplify this code.

The first example shows a statement that declares and instantiates an instance of an array list collection named codes that will hold String objects. Here, <String> is specified following the ArrayList class name to indicate that the elements of the array list must be String objects. The second and third examples are similar, but they create collections that can hold integers and Product objects.

In the second example, a *wrapper class* is specified as the type instead of the primitive type. That's necessary because a collection can only hold objects, not primitive types. But if you declare a collection with a wrapper type, you can store values of the related primitive type in that collection.

If you're using Java 1.7 or later, you can omit the type from the brackets that follow the constructor as long as the compiler can infer the type from the context. This is illustrated in the fourth example in this figure, which works the same as the first example. Because this feature simplifies your code, I'll use it in most of the remaining examples in this chapter.

You can also create your own classes that use generics. To do that, you specify one or more type variables in angle brackets following the class name as shown in the fifth example. Here, the type variable is specified as E. Then, you can use this variable within the class anywhere you would normally specify a type. You'll learn more about how this works later in this chapter.

The syntax for specifying the type of elements in a collection

```
CollectionClass<Type> collectionName = new CollectionClass<Type>();
```

Example 1: A statement that creates an array list of type String

```
ArrayList<String> codes = new ArrayList<String>();
```

Example 2: A statement that creates an array list of integers

```
ArrayList<Integer> numbers = new ArrayList<Integer>();
```

Example 3: Code that creates a linked list of type Product

```
LinkedList<Product> products;
products = new LinkedList<Product>();
```

The syntax for using type inference with JDK 1.7 or later

```
CollectionClass<Type> collectionName = new CollectionClass<>();
```

Example 4: A statement that creates an array list of type String

```
ArrayList<String> codes = new ArrayList<>();
```

The syntax for declaring a class that uses generic types

```
public class ClassName<TypeVariable [,TypeVariable]...>{}
```

Example 5: A class statement for a class that implements a queue

```
public class GenericQueue<E>{}
```

Description

- *Generics* refers to a feature introduced with Java 1.5 that lets you create typed collections. A *typed collection* is a collection that can hold only objects of a certain type.
- To declare a variable that refers to a typed collection, you list the type in angle brackets (<>) following the name of the collection class.
- When you use a constructor for a typed collection, you can specify the type variable in angle brackets following the constructor name. The type variable can't be a primitive type such as int or double, but it can be a wrapper class such as Integer or Double. It can also be a user-defined class.
- Beginning with Java 1.7, you can omit the type from within the brackets that follow the constructor if the compiler can infer the type from the context. This empty set of brackets is known as the *diamond operator*.
- If you do not specify a type for a collection, the collection can hold any type of object. However, the Java compiler will issue warning messages whenever you access the collection to warn you that type checking can't be performed for the collection.
- To create a *generic class* that lets you specify type information, specify one or more *type variables* in angle brackets following the class name on the class statement. Then, you can use the type variable within the class anywhere you would normally specify a type.

Figure 12-3 An introduction to generics

How to use the ArrayList class

The ArrayList class is one of the most commonly used Java collection classes. The following topics present an overview of this class along with several examples of how you can use it.

The ArrayList class

Figure 12-4 presents an overview of the ArrayList class, which is used to create a type of collection called an *array list*. An array list uses an array internally to store elements, so an array list is similar to an array in many ways. However, unlike an array, you can change the capacity of an array list after you've created it. In fact, an array list automatically adjusts its size as you add elements to it. So you don't have to write any special code to make sure that you don't exceed the capacity of an array list.

If adding an object to an array list causes the list to exceed the current capacity of the internal array, the ArrayList class automatically increases the capacity of the internal array. The documentation for the ArrayList class says that the method used to determine the new capacity of the array is unspecified. However, an examination of the source code for the ArrayList class reveals that the size of the internal array is increased by 50% plus 1. So, for example, if the current capacity of an array list is 1000, the array list will be expanded to a capacity of 1501.

Unfortunately, increasing the capacity of an array list is not an efficient operation, especially if the array list is large. First, the ArrayList class must create a new array of the expanded size. Then, the elements of the old array must be copied to the new array. Finally, the old array must be removed from memory.

The ArrayList class includes a constructor that lets you specify the initial capacity of the array list. If you don't provide this value, the array list is given a default capacity of 10 elements. Because expanding an array list is inefficient, you should always specify an appropriate initial capacity whenever you create an array list.

All three constructors in this figure show that the ArrayList class can be used to create a typed collection. This is indicated by the E that's enclosed in angle brackets following the class name. A capital letter E is the standard way of representing the type of elements that are stored in a collection.

The ArrayList class also has several methods that let you work with an array list. The ones you'll use most often are the add method, which lets you add an object to the list, and the get method, which lets you retrieve an object using an index. You'll find code examples of these and several other methods of the ArrayList class in the next figure.

The ArrayList class

`java.util.ArrayList`

Constructors of the ArrayList class

Constructor	Description
`ArrayList<E>()`	Creates an empty array list with an initial capacity of ten objects of the specified type.
`ArrayList<E>(intCapacity)`	Creates an empty array list with the specified capacity.
`ArrayList<E>(Collection)`	Creates an array list containing the elements of the specified collection.

Common methods of the ArrayList class

Method	Description
`add(object)`	Adds the specified object to the end of the list.
`add(index, object)`	Adds the specified object at the specified index position.
`clear()`	Removes all elements from the list.
`contains(object)`	Returns true if the specified object is in the list.
`get(index)`	Returns the object at the specified index position.
`indexOf(object)`	Returns the index position of the specified object.
`isEmpty()`	Returns true if the list is empty.
`remove(index)`	Removes the object at the specified index position.
`remove(object)`	Removes the specified object.
`set(index, object)`	Sets the element at the specified index to the specified object.
`size()`	Returns the number of elements in the list.
`toArray()`	Returns an array containing the elements of the list.

Description

- An *array list* is a collection that's similar to an array, but can change its capacity as elements are added or removed. The ArrayList class uses an array to store the elements it contains.
- You can specify the type of elements to be stored in the array list by naming a type in angle brackets.
- You can specify the size of an array list when you create it, or you can let the array list default to an initial capacity of 10 elements.
- The capacity of an array list automatically increases whenever necessary.

Figure 12-4 The ArrayList class

Code examples that work with array lists

Figure 12-5 shows four code examples that use the ArrayList class. The first example creates an ArrayList of type String and adds three string values to it. Notice that the third call to the add method specifies an index value of 0. As a result, the string "warp" will be added as the first element in the array list, and the strings that were added before it ("mbdk" and "citr") will be moved down in the list.

Next, this example uses a standard for loop to print the elements in the array list. Inside the loop, the get method is called to retrieve each element by its index. Then, the println method is called to display the element. The resulting output shows the three strings in the order they're stored in the list.

The second example shows an alternate way to display the values in a collection. To do that, you simply specify the name of the collection in the println method. This implicitly calls the collection's toString method, which returns a string that lists the value of each element. Because the values are all listed on the same line and enclosed in brackets, this technique is useful only for collections with just a few elements.

The third example shows how to replace or delete elements in an array list. First, the set method is called to change the value of the element at index 1 to "wuth." Then, the remove method is used to delete the element whose value is "warp." Finally, the remove method is used to delete the element whose index is 1.

In the output for this example, you can see that the only remaining element in the collection is "wuth." You might be wondering why that element remains, since the element at index 1 was deleted by the third statement in this example. The reason is that the second statement deleted the element whose value is "warp." This element was at index 0, so when it was deleted, the elements after element 0 were moved up 1 position. As a result, element 1 ("wuth") was moved to element 0 and element 2 ("citr") was moved to element 1. Then, the third statement deleted "citr", not "wuth."

The fourth example shows code that works with an array list of type Integer. If you're new to Java, there's probably nothing remarkable about this example. However, if you've worked with collections in older versions of Java, you'll notice that no special coding is required to add int values to an array of Integers. That's because versions 1.5 and later of Java automatically convert int values to Integer values and vice versa using a technique called *autoboxing*. In previous versions of Java, you had to call the constructor of the Integer class to create a new Integer object with the desired value. You'll see an example of this later in this chapter when we present techniques for working with legacy collections.

Example 1: Code that uses an array list of type String

```
// create an array list of type String
ArrayList<String> codes = new ArrayList<>();
// add three strings
codes.add("mbdk");
codes.add("citr");
codes.add(0, "warp");
// print the array list
for (int i =0; i < codes.size(); i++)
{
    String code = codes.get(i);
    System.out.println(code);
}
```

Resulting output

```
warp
mbdk
citr
```

Example 2: Another way to display the contents of a collection

```
System.out.println(codes);
```

Resulting output

```
[warp, mbdk, citr]
```

Example 3: Code that replaces and deletes objects

```
codes.set(1, "wuth");
codes.remove("warp");
codes.remove(1);
System.out.print(codes);
```

Resulting output

```
[wuth]
```

Example 4: Code that uses an array list of type Integer

```
ArrayList<Integer> numbers = new ArrayList<>();
numbers.add(1);
numbers.add(2);
numbers.add(3);
System.out.println(numbers);
```

Resulting output

```
[1, 2, 3]
```

Description

- When you use generics to create a collection that holds a wrapper type, the compiler automatically converts the primitive type to its wrapper type and vice versa using a technique called *autoboxing*.

Figure 12-5 Code examples that work with array lists

An Invoice application that uses an array list

The topics that follow present an Invoice application that lets the user enter one or more line items. This is similar to the Line Item application you've seen in earlier chapters, but the Invoice application stores the line items in an array list within an Invoice object.

An overview of the Invoice application

As figure 12-6 shows, the Invoice application lets the user enter a product code and quantity for one or more line items. As each line item is entered, the application adds it to the invoice and asks if the user wants to enter another line item. When the user is finished entering line items, the application displays a list of the line items for the invoice. Then, it displays the total for all the invoices and ends.

The Invoice application uses six classes. The first four classes listed in this figure were presented in chapter 7. If you want to refresh your memory on how those classes work, you can refer back to that chapter to see the code for these classes. In this chapter, I'll present the code for the two new classes used by this application: the Invoice class, which represents the invoice entered by the user, and the InvoiceApp class, which contains the main method for the application.

As this figure shows, the Invoice class has one constructor (which accepts no parameters) and four methods. The addItem method adds a LineItem object to the invoice. The line item is stored within the Invoice object in an array list that can be accessed via the getLineItems method. The getInvoiceTotal method returns a double that's the sum of the totals for all the line items in the invoice. And the getFormattedTotal method returns this same value with a currency format.

Note that this application lets the user enter just one invoice, and it doesn't save the invoice when the application ends. A more realistic application would process more than one invoice, and the invoices would be saved to a file or database. In addition, the Invoice object would include additional information such as information about the customer, an invoice number, invoice date, and so on. The point of this application, though, is just to illustrate the use of an ArrayList.

Console output for the Invoice application

```
Welcome to the invoice application.

Enter product code: java
Enter quantity:     1
Another line item? (y/n): y

Enter product code: jsps
Enter quantity:     2
Another line item? (y/n): n

Code    Description                       Price   Qty     Total
----    -----------                       -----   ---     -----
java    Murach's Beginning Java           $49.50  1       $49.50
jsps    Murach's Java Servlets and JSP    $49.50  2       $99.00

                                          Invoice total:  $148.50
```

Classes used by the Invoice application

Name	Description
Product	Represents a Product object.
ProductDB	Provides a getProduct method that retrieves the Product object for a specified product code.
Validator	Provides methods that accept and validate user input.
LineItem	Represents an invoice line item, which includes a Product object, a quantity, and a total.
Invoice	Represents a single invoice. The line items are represented by an array list.
InvoiceApp	Contains the main method for the Invoice application.

The constructor and methods for the Invoice class

Constructor	Description
`Invoice()`	Creates an empty invoice.
Method	**Description**
`void addItem(LineItem lineItem)`	Adds the specified line item to the invoice.
`ArrayList getLineItems()`	Returns an ArrayList object that contains the line items for the invoice.
`double getInvoiceTotal()`	Returns a double that contains the sum of the totals for the line items in the invoice.
`String getFormattedTotal()`	Returns a String that contains the invoice total formatted as currency.

Description

- The user enters a product code and quantity for each line item to be added to the invoice. When the user indicates that all of the line items have been entered, the application displays each line item on a separate line along with the total for the invoice.
- The Product, ProductDB, Validator, and LineItem classes are described in chapter 7.

Figure 12-6 An overview of the Invoice application

The code for the Invoice class

Figure 12-7 presents the code for the Invoice class. This class defines one instance variable, which is an array list of LineItem objects named lineItems. This array list is used to store the line items for the invoice. The default constructor for the Invoice class instantiates the lineItems array list but doesn't add any line items to it.

The addItem method accepts a LineItem object as a parameter. This method consists of a single line that calls the add method of the lineItems array list to add the line item to the array list.

The getLineItems method provides access to the lineItems array list. Notice that the return type for this method (ArrayList<LineItem>) specifies the generic type of the array list that's returned to the caller. If you omitted the type here, the class would not compile correctly.

The getInvoiceTotal method uses an enhanced for loop to process each LineItem element in the lineItems array list. Within this loop, the getTotal method is called for the current line item, and the result is added to the invoiceTotal variable. Then, the invoiceTotal variable is used as the method's return value.

Finally, the getFormattedTotal method uses the NumberFormat class to format the invoice total as a currency string. Notice that this method calls the getInvoiceTotal method to get the invoice total. That way, the getFormattedTotal method doesn't duplicate the code used to calculate the invoice total.

The code for the Invoice class

```
import java.text.NumberFormat;
import java.util.ArrayList;

public class Invoice
{
    // the instance variable
    private ArrayList<LineItem> lineItems;

    // the constructor
    public Invoice()
    {
        lineItems = new ArrayList<>();
    }

    // a method that adds a line item
    public void addItem(LineItem lineItem)
    {
        this.lineItems.add(lineItem);
    }

    // the get accessor for the line item collection
    public ArrayList<LineItem> getLineItems()
    {
        return lineItems;
    }

    // a method that gets the invoice total
    public double getInvoiceTotal()
    {
        double invoiceTotal = 0;
        for (LineItem lineItem : this.lineItems)
        {
            invoiceTotal += lineItem.getTotal();
        }
        return invoiceTotal;
    }

    // a method that returns the invoice total in currency format
    public String getFormattedTotal()
    {
        NumberFormat currency = NumberFormat.getCurrencyInstance();
        return currency.format(this.getInvoiceTotal());
    }
}
```

Figure 12-7 The code for the Invoice class

The code for the InvoiceApp class

Figure 12-8 shows the code for the InvoiceApp class, the main class for the Invoice application. First, it displays a welcome message. Then, it calls a method named getLineItems to get the line items for the invoice. Finally, it calls a method named displayInvoice to display the invoice's line items and total. Because both of these methods need access to the invoice data entered by the user, an Invoice object named invoice is declared at the class level. That way, the getLineItems method can add line items to the invoice and the displayInvoice method can retrieve the line items and calculate the invoice total.

The getLineItems method uses a while loop to let the user enter one or more line items. Within the while loop, the Scanner class and the Validator class are used to get a valid product code and quantity from the user. Then, the getProduct method of the ProductDB class is called to get a Product object for the code entered by the user. Next, the getLineItems method calls the addItem method of the invoice object to add the line item to the invoice. Because the addItem method accepts a LineItem object, a new instance of the LineItem class is created using the Product object and the quantity entered by the user.

After the line item has been added to the invoice, the user is asked whether he or she wants to enter another line item. The reply is saved in the choice variable, which is used to control the while loop.

The displayInvoice method is called when the user has finished entering line items. This method uses an enhanced for loop to process the line items. This for loop calls the getLineItems method of the invoice object to get an array list of LineItem objects. Then, it calls the getProduct method of the line item object to get the Product object for each line item so its code, name, and price can be displayed. After all the line items are displayed, the displayInvoice method calls the getFormattedTotal method of the invoice object to get the total of all the invoices in currency format. Then, this value is displayed at the console.

The code for the InvoiceApp class

```
import java.util.Scanner;

public class InvoiceApp
{
    public static Invoice invoice = new Invoice();

    public static void main(String args[])
    {
        System.out.println("Welcome to the invoice application.\n");
        getLineItems();
        displayInvoice();
    }

    public static void getLineItems()
    {
        Scanner sc = new Scanner(System.in);
        String choice = "y";
        while (choice.equalsIgnoreCase("y"))
        {
            // get the input from the user
            String productCode = Validator.getString(sc,
                "Enter product code: ");
            int quantity = Validator.getInt(sc,
                "Enter quantity:      ", 0, 1000);

            Product product = ProductDB.getProduct(productCode);
            invoice.addItem(new LineItem(product, quantity));

            // see if the user wants to continue
            choice = Validator.getString(sc, "Another line item? (y/n): ");
            System.out.println();
        }
     }

    public static void displayInvoice()
    {
        System.out.println("Code\tDescription\t\t\tPrice\tQty\tTotal");
        System.out.println("----\t-----------\t\t\t-----\t---\t-----");
        for (LineItem lineItem : invoice.getLineItems())
        {
            Product product = lineItem.getProduct();
            String s = product.getCode()
                + "\t" + product.getDescription()
                + "\t" + product.getFormattedPrice()
                + "\t" + lineItem.getQuantity()
                + "\t" + lineItem.getFormattedTotal();
            System.out.println(s);
        }
        System.out.println("\n\t\t\t\t\tInvoice total:\t"
            + invoice.getFormattedTotal() + "\n");
    }
}
```

Figure 12-8 The code for the InvoiceApp class

How to use the LinkedList class

The LinkedList class is similar to the ArrayList class, but it provides more features and uses a different technique to store its data. The topics that follow describe the LinkedList class and show some code examples that illustrate how you can use this class.

The LinkedList class

Figure 12-9 presents an overview of the LinkedList class, which creates a special type of list called a *linked list*. Unlike an array list, a linked list doesn't use an array to store its elements. Instead, the elements you add to a linked list are stored as separate objects. Each list element is stored along with a pointer to the object that precedes it and the object that follows it. As a result, the LinkedList class can use these pointers to navigate through the entire list.

Because the entries for a linked list aren't stored in an array, inserting an element into the middle of a linked list is more efficient than inserting an element into the middle of an array list. To insert an element into the middle of an array list, all of the elements that follow the insertion point must be moved down in the list. The more elements in the array list and the closer to the beginning of the array the insertion point is, the longer it takes to insert the element. In contrast, an element can be inserted into the middle of a linked list by simply adjusting the previous and next pointers for the elements that precede and follow the insertion point.

There is a trade-off to this efficiency, however. Although a linked list can be updated more quickly than an array list, it can't be accessed as quickly. Because all of the elements in an array list are stored in adjacent memory locations, access to those elements is fast. In contrast, access to the elements in a linked list is relatively slow because the pointers for the elements must be used.

For example, suppose you use the get method to access the 500th element in a linked list with more than 1,000 elements. To do that, the get method begins by accessing the first element in the list to get the pointer to the second element. It then accesses the second element to get a pointer to the third element. This process continues until the 500th element has been retrieved. In other words, to access a particular element in a linked list, all of the elements that precede it must be accessed.

Actually, the get method first checks to see if the element being retrieved is closer to the first or last element in the list. If the element is closer to the last element, the search for the element begins at the last element and proceeds backwards until the desired element is located.

When you develop a Java application that calls for a list, you should carefully consider whether to implement the collection using the ArrayList class or the LinkedList class. This is especially important if the list will contain a large number of elements. The larger the list, the more important the performance trade-offs of using an array list or a linked list become. In many cases, though, you'll use a linked list simply because you need the additional features that the LinkedList class provides.

The LinkedList class

`java.util.LinkedList`

A constructor for the LinkedList class

Constructor	Description
LinkedList<E>()	Creates an empty linked list using the specified type.

Common methods of the LinkedList class

Method	Description
add(object)	Adds the specified object to the list.
add(index, object)	Adds the specified object at the specified index position.
addFirst(object)	Adds the specified object to the beginning of the list.
addLast(object)	Adds the specified object to the end of the list.
clear()	Removes all elements from the list.
contains(object)	Returns true if the specified object is in the list.
get(index)	Returns the object at the specified index position.
getFirst()	Returns the first element in the list.
getLast()	Returns the last element in the list.
indexOf(object)	Returns the index position of the specified object.
peek()	Returns but doesn't remove the first element in the list.
offer(object)	Attempts to add the specified object to the end of the list. Returns true if the object was added. Returns false if the object is rejected.
poll()	Returns and removes the first element from the list. Returns null if the list is empty.
remove()	Returns and removes the first element from the list. Throws NoSuchElementException if the list is empty.
remove(index)	Removes and returns the object at the specified index position.
remove(object)	Removes the specified object.
removeFirst()	Removes and returns the first element of the list.
removeLast()	Removes and returns the last element of the list.
set(index, object)	Replaces the element at the specified index position with the specified object.
size()	Returns the number of elements in the list.
toArray()	Returns an array containing the elements of the list.

Description

- A *linked list* is a collection that's similar to an array list. However, the LinkedList class doesn't use an array to store its elements. Instead, each element in the list contains pointers that are used to refer to adjacent elements.
- You can specify the type of elements the linked list can contain by listing the type in angle brackets.
- The LinkedList class contains methods that let you perform more advanced operations than the ArrayList class.

Figure 12-9 The LinkedList class

Code examples that work with linked lists

Figure 12-10 shows four code examples that demonstrate the basic techniques for working with linked lists. The first example creates a linked list of type String and uses the add method to add three strings to the list. Then, it uses the println method to display the contents of the linked list by implicitly calling the list's toString method. As you can see, the last string that was added is displayed first because it was added at index position 0. Then, the other two strings are displayed in the order in which they were added to the list.

The second example shows code that uses the addFirst and addLast methods to add entries to the beginning and end of the list. As you can see in the console output for this example, the string added by the addFirst method appears first, followed by the three strings that were added in the first example, followed by the string that was added by the addLast method.

The third example shows code that uses an enhanced for loop to process all of the elements in the linked list. Note that you could also process the list using a standard for loop with an index variable and the get method. However, processing a linked list with an enhanced for loop is more efficient than processing it with a standard for loop. That's because the enhanced for loop is able to efficiently use the pointers stored with each list entry to access the next element in the list. For example, to move from the 100th element to the 101st element, the enhanced for loop simply uses the pointer to the next element. In contrast, the get method must start at the beginning of the list each time an element is accessed.

The fourth example shows code that uses the removeFirst and removeLast methods to retrieve and remove the first and last elements from the list. Notice that after these methods have been called, the list consists of just the three elements that were added in the first example.

Example 1: Code that creates a linked list of type String

```
// create a linked list of type String
LinkedList<String> codes = new LinkedList<>();

// add three strings
codes.add("mbdk");
codes.add("citr");
codes.add(0, "warp");

System.out.println(codes);
```

Resulting output

```
[warp, mbdk, citr]
```

Example 2: Code that adds elements to the beginning and end of the list

```
codes.addFirst("wuth");
codes.addLast("wooz");

System.out.println(codes);
```

Resulting output

```
[wuth, warp, mbdk, citr, wooz]
```

Example 3: Code that uses an enhanced for loop to process the list

```
for (String s : codes)
    System.out.println(s);
```

Resulting output

```
wuth
warp
mbdk
citr
wooz
```

Example 4: Code that retrieves the first and last elements of the list

```
String firstString = codes.removeFirst();
String lastString = codes.removeLast();
System.out.println(firstString);
System.out.println(lastString);
System.out.println(codes);
```

Resulting output

```
wuth
wooz
[warp, mbdk, citr]
```

Figure 12-10 Code examples that work with linked lists

A class that uses a linked list to implement a generic queue

As figure 12-11 shows, a *queue* is a type of collection that lets you access elements on a first-in, first-out basis. Queues are used in many different types of data processing applications. For example, orders that are entered online at a web site are often queued so that they're processed in the order in which they were received.

A queue supports two basic operations: *push*, which adds an entry to the end of the queue, and *pull,* which retrieves the entry that's at the front of the queue. Note that whenever you pull an entry, the entry is removed from the queue. As a result, all of the other entries in the queue move up one position in the queue.

The LinkedList class provides the basic operations you need to implement a queue. The addLast method provides the push operation, and the removeFirst method provides the pull operation. Although the LinkedList class provides many other operations, most aren't used for queues.

The code in the first example in this figure shows a class that implements a simple queue based on the LinkedList class. Here, the class creates a linked list as a private class variable. Then, it exposes three methods: push, which calls the addLast method of the LinkedList class; pull, which calls the removeFirst method; and size, which calls the size method. When you use this class, all other features of the LinkedList class are effectively hidden.

Notice that the declaration for this class includes a type variable named E. This allows for any type of object to be stored in the queue. As you can see, this type variable is used when the linked list is created, it's used as the parameter type for the push method, and it's used as the return type for the pull method. So, for example, if the user specifies String for the queue type, the GenericQueue class creates a linked list of type String. In addition, the push method accepts a String parameter and the pull method returns a String value.

The second example shows how this works. The code in this example starts by creating a queue that stores strings. Then, it calls the push method three times to add three entries to the queue. Next, it uses the println method to display the number of entries in the queue. To do that, it calls the size method. Finally, it uses a while loop to pull and print each entry. This loop executes as long as the size method of the queue indicates that there is at least one more entry in the queue.

Basic methods of a class that implements a generic queue

Method	Description
push(element)	Adds the specified element to the end of the queue.
pull()	Retrieves and removes an element from the front of the queue.
size()	Returns the number of elements in the queue.

Example 1: Code for a GenericQueue class that implements a queue

```
import java.util.LinkedList;

public class GenericQueue<E>
{
    private LinkedList<E> list = new LinkedList<>();

    public void push(E item)
    {
        list.addLast(item);
    }

    public E pull()
    {
        return list.removeFirst();
    }

    public int size()
    {
        return list.size();
    }
}
```

Example 2: Code that uses the GenericQueue class

```
GenericQueue<String> q1 = new GenericQueue<>();
q1.push("Item One");
q1.push("Item Two");
q1.push("Item Three");
System.out.println("The queue contains " + q1.size() + " items");
while (q1.size() > 0)
    System.out.println(q1.pull());
System.out.println("The queue now contains " + q1.size() + " items");
```

Resulting output

```
The queue contains 3 items
Item One
Item Two
Item Three
The queue now contains 0 items
```

Description

- A *queue* is a first-in, first-out collection. To implement a queue, you can use a linked list as shown above.
- A class that implements a queue is typically declared with a type variable that's used to specify the type of objects the queue will hold.

Figure 12-11 A class that uses a linked list to implement a generic queue

An enhanced version of the Invoice application

The following topics present an enhanced version of the Invoice application that was presented earlier in this chapter. This version illustrates one way to use a linked list in an application.

An overview of the enhanced Invoice application

Figure 12-12 shows the operation of the enhanced Invoice application. This version is similar to the version that was presented in figures 12-6 through 12-8. However, in addition to letting the user enter several line items for each invoice, it lets the user enter more than one invoice. These invoices are saved in a queue created using the GenericQueue class that was shown in figure 12-11. When the user finishes entering invoices, the application displays one line for each invoice that lists the invoice number and the invoice total. Then, it displays a total for all of the invoices.

Because the Invoice class doesn't provide for an invoice number, this application simply assigns sequential numbers to the invoices, starting with 1 for the first invoice entered. In addition, it doesn't save the invoice numbers with the invoices. Although I could have created another version of the Invoicc class for this application that included an invoice number, that would have unnecessarily complicated the code without illustrating any additional features of the LinkedList class.

This application uses several classes in addition to the InvoiceApp class that's presented in the next figure. You saw the GenericQueue class in the last figure, and you saw the Invoice class in figure 12-7. The other classes—LineItem, Product, ProductDB, and Validator—are identical to the versions that were shown in chapter 7.

Console output for the enhanced Invoice application

```
Welcome to the invoice application.


Enter line items for invoice 1
Enter product code: java
Enter quantity:     1
Another line item? (y/n): n

Another invoice? (y/n): y


Enter line items for invoice 2
Enter product code: jsps
Enter quantity:     2
Another line item? (y/n): n

Another invoice? (y/n): n

You entered the following invoices:

Number  Total
------  -----
1       $49.50
2       $99.00
Total for all invoices: $148.50
```

Description

- This version of the Invoice application lets the user enter more than one invoice. The invoices are stored in a queue created from the GenericQueue class that was presented in figure 12-11.
- When the user has finished entering invoices, the application displays the invoice number and total for each invoice. Then, the application displays the total for all the invoices that were entered.
- The Invoice application assigns an invoice number to each invoice, starting with 1 for the first invoice entered. However, the invoice number isn't stored as a part of the Invoice object.

Figure 12-12 An overview of the enhanced Invoice application

The code for the InvoiceApp class

Figure 12-13 shows the code for the InvoiceApp class of the enhanced Invoice application. This code begins by declaring a static variable named invoices that will be used to store the invoices entered by the user. This variable is created from the GenericQueue class, and the type for the queue is specified as Invoice. As a result, the queue can be used for storing Invoice objects.

This class also declares an Invoice variable named invoice. This variable will be used to refer to the invoice that's currently being entered by the user. Notice that this statement doesn't instantiate an Invoice object. Instead, a new Invoice object will be instantiated each time the user indicates that there's another invoice to be entered.

After it displays a welcome message, the main method calls the getInvoices method. This method uses a while loop to get invoices from the user until the user indicates there are no more invoices to be entered. This loop begins by instantiating a new Invoice object and displaying a message that indicates the invoice number to be entered. Then, it calls the getLineItems method to get all of the line items for the invoice. The getLineItems method is almost identical to the getLineItems method you saw in figure 12-8, so I won't explain its operation here.

After the user has entered all of the line items for an invoice, the getInvoices method adds the invoice to the invoices collection by calling the push method. Then, it asks if the user wants to enter another invoice and increments the invoice number variable.

Code for the InvoiceApp class

Page 1

```
import java.util.Scanner;
import java.text.NumberFormat;

public class InvoiceApp
{
    private static GenericQueue<Invoice> invoices
        = new GenericQueue<>();

    private static Invoice invoice;

    private static Scanner sc;

    public static void main(String args[])
    {
        System.out.println("Welcome to the invoice application.\n");
        getInvoices();
        displayInvoices();
    }

    public static void getInvoices()
    {
        sc = new Scanner(System.in);
        int invoiceNumber = 1;
        String anotherInvoice = "y";
        while (anotherInvoice.equalsIgnoreCase("y"))
        {
            invoice = new Invoice();
            System.out.println("\nEnter line items for invoice "
                + invoiceNumber);
            getLineItems();
            invoices.push(invoice);

            // see if the user wants to continue
            anotherInvoice = Validator.getString(sc,
                "Another invoice? (y/n): ");
            System.out.println();
            invoiceNumber++;
        }
    }
```

Figure 12-13 The code for the InvoiceApp class (part 1 of 2)

When the user indicates there are no more invoices to enter, control returns to the main method. Then, this method calls the displayInvoices method to display information for each invoice. This method uses a while loop that executes as long as the size method of the invoices collection indicates that there is at least one more invoice in the queue. Variables named invoiceNumber and batchTotal are used to keep track of the invoice numbers and totals for the invoices that were entered. Within the loop, the pull method is called to retrieve each Invoice object from the queue. Next, the println method is called to display the invoice number and the total for the invoice, the invoice number is incremented, and the invoice total is added to the batchTotal variable. After all of the invoices have been displayed, the batchTotal value is formatted and displayed.

Code for the InvoiceApp class **Page 2**

```
    public static void getLineItems()
    {
        String anotherItem = "y";
        while (anotherItem.equalsIgnoreCase("y"))
        {
            // get the input from the user
            String productCode = Validator.getString(sc,
                "Enter product code: ");
            int quantity = Validator.getInt(sc,
                "Enter quantity:      ", 0, 1000);

            Product product = ProductDB.getProduct(productCode);
            invoice.addItem(new LineItem(product, quantity));

            // see if the user wants to continue
            anotherItem = Validator.getString(sc,
                "Another line item? (y/n): ");
            System.out.println();
        }
    }

    public static void displayInvoices()
    {
        System.out.println("You entered the following invoices:\n");
        System.out.println("Number\tTotal");
        System.out.println("------\t-----");
        double batchTotal = 0;
        int invoiceNumber = 1;
        while (invoices.size() > 0)
        {
            Invoice invoice = invoices.pull();
            System.out.println(invoiceNumber + "\t"
                + invoice.getFormattedTotal());
            invoiceNumber++;
            batchTotal += invoice.getInvoiceTotal();
        }
        NumberFormat currency = NumberFormat.getCurrencyInstance();
        System.out.println("Total for all invoices: "
            + currency.format(batchTotal));
    }
}
```

Figure 12-13 The code for the InvoiceApp class (part 2 of 2)

How to work with maps

The next two topics show you how to work with two classes that implement the Map interface: HashMap and TreeMap. These classes let you create collections in which objects can be accessed by using a key value. The main difference between a *hash map* and a *tree map* is that the entries in a hash map are not stored in any particular sequence, while the entries in a tree map are automatically sorted by key value.

The HashMap and TreeMap classes

Figure 12-14 presents the HashMap and TreeMap classes. Both of these classes implement the Map interface, which defines the basic behavior of a map. A *map* is a collection whose elements are pairs of keys and values. For example, you might use a map to store a collection of Product objects that can be accessed by a product code. In that case, the keys would be product codes and the values would be Product objects.

Unlike the other collections you've seen in this chapter, you specify two types when you declare and instantiate a map. The first, identified as K in the figure, represents the type of the map's keys. The second, identified as V, is the type of the map's objects. Typically, the key is a simple type such as String or Integer and the value is a user-defined type such as Product or Customer.

Like other collections, you use the get method to retrieve an object from a map. The get method accepts a single parameter that represents the key value for the object you want to retrieve. Then, the get method returns the value object that corresponds to the specified key. If the key isn't in the map, the get method returns null.

Although it's unlikely, it's possible for a key value to be in the map, but for the value associated with the key to be null. In that case, the get method will return null. Because of that, a null can mean that either the key isn't in the map, or the key is in the map but the value object associated with the key is null. To distinguish between these possibilities, you can use the containsKey method. This method returns true if the key is in the map and false if it isn't.

Unlike other types of collections, maps don't have an add method. Instead, the Map interface uses a method called put to add an element to a map. The put method accepts two arguments that represent the key and value. If the key is already in the map, the put method replaces the existing value.

Each element of a map implements an interface called Map.Entry. As this figure shows, this interface provides two methods that you can use to get the key and value for an entry: getKey and getValue. You'll see examples of how this interface is used in the next figure.

In case you're interested, a hash map and a tree map use different data structures to store their elements. A hash map uses a data structure called a *hash table*, and a tree map uses a structure called a *red-black tree*. The details of how these structures work are beyond the scope of this book. But if you're interested, you can search the internet for these structures by name.

The HashMap and TreeMap classes

```
java.util.HashMap
java.util.TreeMap
```

Common constructors of the HashMap and TreeMap classes

Constructor	Description
`HashMap<K,V>()`	Creates an empty HashMap using the specified types for the keys and values.
`TreeMap<K,V>()`	Creates an empty TreeMap using the specified types for the keys and values.

Common methods of the HashMap and TreeMap classes

Method	Description
`clear()`	Removes all entries from the map.
`containsKey(key)`	Returns true if the specified key is in the map.
`containsValue(value)`	Returns true if the specified value is in the map.
`entrySet()`	Returns a set of all the entries in the map as Map.Entry objects.
`get(key)`	Returns the value for the entry with the specified key. Returns null if the key isn't found.
`put(key, value)`	Adds an entry with the specified key and value, or replaces the value if an entry with the key already exists.
`remove(key)`	Removes the entry with the specified key.
`size()`	Returns the number of entries in the map.

Common methods of the Map.Entry interface

Method	Description
`getKey()`	Returns the key for the map entry.
`getValue()`	Returns the value for the map entry.

Description

- A *map* is a collection that contains values that are associated with keys. The two most commonly used classes that implement maps are HashMap and TreeMap.
- The main difference between a hash map and a tree map is that a tree map automatically maintains entries in order based on the key values. In contrast, a hash map doesn't maintain its entries in sorted order. If an application doesn't require that the entries be kept in order, a hash map is often more efficient than a tree map.
- Each entry of a map implements the Map.Entry interface in the java.util.Map package. You can use two of the methods provided by this interface to get the key and value for an entry.

Note

- You can use a custom class for the key objects of a hash map. To do that, the class must override the hashCode and equals methods inherited from Object. For more information, see the Java documentation.

Figure 12-14 The HashMap and TreeMap classes

Code examples that work with hash maps and tree maps

Figure 12-15 shows two code examples that work with maps. The only difference between these two examples is that the first one uses the HashMap class and the second one uses the TreeMap class. Other than the line that creates the map, the code for these two examples is identical. However, the resulting output is different.

Both examples start by declaring and creating a map named books. This map will be used to store book titles that are associated with codes. Because both the book titles and the book codes are strings, this statement specifies String for both the key and value type. Note that this code uses the diamond operator that was introduced with Java 1.7 in the constructor for both classes. As a result, the compiler automatically infers the correct types for the key and value.

The next three statements use the put method to add three entries to the map. Then, an enhanced for loop is used to display the entries in the map. Notice that the element type in this loop is Map.Entry. As a result, the statement within the loop can use the getKey and getValue methods of the Map.Entry interface to get the key and value objects for an entry. After this loop is executed, the get method is used to get the title of the book whose code is "mbdk" and that title is displayed at the console.

Notice in the resulting output for the first example that the books in the hash map aren't stored in key sequence. In addition, they aren't stored in the order in which they were added to the map. Instead, their positions in the collection are determined by a hashing function that converts the key values to index values. In contrast, the output for the second example shows that the books in the tree map are stored in key sequence.

Example 1: Code that uses a hash map

```
// create an empty hash map
HashMap<String,String> books = new HashMap<>();

// add three entries
books.put("wooz", "Wizard of Oz");
books.put("mbdk", "Moby Dick");
books.put("wuth", "Wuthering Heights");

// print the entries
for (Map.Entry book : books.entrySet())
    System.out.println(book.getKey() + ": " + book.getValue());

// print the entry whose key is "mbdk"
System.out.println("\nCode mbdk is " + books.get("mbdk"));
```

Resulting output

```
wuth: Wuthering Heights
mbdk: Moby Dick
wooz: Wizard of Oz

Code mbdk is Moby Dick
```

Example 2: Code that uses a tree map

```
// create an empty tree map
TreeMap<String,String> books = new TreeMap<>();

// add three entries
books.put("wooz", "Wizard of Oz");
books.put("mbdk", "Moby Dick");
books.put("wuth", "Wuthering Heights");

// print the entries
for (Map.Entry book : books.entrySet())
    System.out.println(book.getKey() + ": " + book.getValue());

// print the entry whose key is "mbdk"
System.out.println("\nCode mbdk is " + books.get("mbdk"));
```

Resulting output

```
mbdk: Moby Dick
wooz: Wizard of Oz
wuth: Wuthering Heights

Code mbdk is Moby Dick
```

Figure 12-15 Code examples that work with hash maps and tree maps

How to work with legacy collections

Java's collection classes have gone through several major overhauls over the years. Originally, Java included just a few collection classes, and they weren't very powerful. In the topics that follow, you'll be introduced to these classes. That way, you'll be familiar with them if you ever encounter code that uses them. In addition, you'll learn how to work with the classes in the collection framework without using generics. You'll see code like this in any application that was written before Java 1.5.

An introduction to legacy collection classes

Figure 12-16 presents a brief introduction to Java legacy collection classes. These classes are called *legacy classes* because although they are no longer the preferred classes, they are widely used in existing Java applications. Note that these classes have not been deprecated, so they are still fully supported by the Java API. However, you should use the newer collection framework classes for new application development.

The Vector class works much like the ArrayList class. In fact, the ArrayList class is in many ways simply an improved version of the Vector class. The HashTable class is an older class that has been replaced by the HashMap class. And the Stack class has been replaced by the LinkedList class.

The code example in this figure shows how to create a simple *vector*, add some string values to it, and display its contents using a for loop. If you compare this example with the first example in figure 12-5 that works with an array list, you'll find that they're similar. One difference is that the first statement in this figure declares the codes variable as a vector rather than as an array list. Another difference is that the object that's returned by the get method must be cast from the Object type to the String type.

Legacy collection classes

Class	Description
Vector	Provides features similar to the more powerful ArrayList class.
HashTable	Provides features similar to the more powerful HashMap class.
Stack	A type of Vector that implements a *stack*, which is a last-in, first-out list. The LinkedList class is now the preferred class for implementing a stack.

Code that uses a vector

```
// create a vector
Vector codes = new Vector();

// add three strings
codes.add("mbdk");
codes.add("citr");
codes.add(0, "warp");

// print the vector
for (int i =0; i < codes.size(); i++)
{
    String code = (String)codes.get(i);
    System.out.println(code);
}
```

Resulting output

```
warp
mbdk
citr
```

Description

- The collection hierarchy was introduced with Java 1.2. For compatibility reasons, Java still supports older collection classes such as Vector, HashTable, and Stack. However, you should avoid using these classes for new program development.
- The classes listed in this figure aren't deprecated. They are still fully supported as part of the Java API.
- The Vector class was the most commonly used legacy collection class. Because the newer ArrayList class is an improved version of the Vector class, the code used to work with a *vector* is similar to the code used to work with an array list.

Figure 12-16 An introduction to legacy collection classes

How to use an untyped collection

Figure 12-17 shows how to work with a collection whose type isn't specified. This type of collection, called an *untyped collection*, holds elements of type Object. This is the only type of collection that was available before Java 1.5.

The code at the top of this figure shows how you work with an untyped array list. After creating the array list, this code creates three Product objects and adds them to the list. Then, it uses a for loop to display the products. Within the for loop, the get method is used to retrieve each product. Because the array list is untyped, the get method returns an object of type Object. Then, this object must be cast to a Product object.

Although you can use code like this in applications you develop with Java 1.5 or later, you're encouraged to use generics instead to create typed collections. In fact, if you use an untyped collection with Java 1.5 or later, the compiler generates a warning message like the one shown in this figure for the class that uses the untyped collection. Because this is only a warning message, the code will still compile and execute. If you ever see a message like this one, however, you should consider modifying your code to use a typed collection.

Code that stores strings in an untyped array list

```
// create an untyped array list
ArrayList products = new ArrayList();

// add three productss
products.add(new Product("dctp", "Duct Tape", 4.95));
products.add(new Product("blwr", "Bailing Wire", 14.95));
products.add(new Product("cgum", "Chewing Gum", 0.95));

// print the array list
for (int i = 0; i < products.size(); i++)
{
    Product p = (Product)products.get(i);
    System.out.println(p.getCode() + "\t" + p.getDescription() + "\t"
        + p.getFormattedPrice());
}
```

The compiler warning generated by the above code

```
Note: C:\murach\java\ch12_tester\src\Main.java uses unchecked or
unsafe operations.
Note: Recompile with -Xlint:unchecked for details.
```

Resulting output

```
dctp    Duct Tape       $4.95
blwr    Bailing Wire    $14.95
cgum    Chewing Gum     $0.95
```

Description

- Code written before Java 1.5 uses *untyped collections*, which don't use generics to specify the element type.
- Untyped collections hold elements of type Object. No special coding is required to add objects to an untyped collection. However, you must typically use a cast to retrieve objects from an untyped collection.
- Versions 1.5 and later of the Java compiler generate a warning message whenever you add an element to an untyped collection.

Figure 12-17 How to use an untyped collection

How to use wrapper classes with untyped collections

Figure 12-18 shows another complication of working with untyped collections. In short, until Java 1.5, you couldn't add primitive data types directly to a collection. That's because the methods that add elements to a collection take an Object type as a parameter and, in Java, primitive types aren't derived from the Object class.

The solution to this problem is to use wrapper classes to create objects that contain the primitive values you want to add to the collection. Once you do that, the wrapper object can be stored in the collection.

The first example in this figure shows how this works. The code in this example creates instances of the Integer class to add three integer values to an untyped array list. If it had specified the integer values directly as arguments to the add method, the compiler would have generated an error.

To retrieve a primitive value from a collection, you can cast the retrieved value to the wrapper type as shown in the second example. Here, the result of the get method is cast to an Integer and then assigned to an int variable and displayed. Again, if you tried to assign the result of the get method to an int variable without casting, the compiler would have generated an error.

Wrapper classes for primitive types

Primitive type	Wrapper class
byte	Byte
short	Short
int	Integer
long	Long
float	Float
double	Double
char	Char
boolean	Boolean

Example 1: Code that adds integers to an untyped array list

```
ArrayList numbers = new ArrayList();

numbers.add(new Integer(1));
numbers.add(new Integer(2));
numbers.add(new Integer(3));
```

Example 2: Code that retrieves integers from the array list

```
for (int i = 0; i < numbers.size(); i++)
{
    int number = (Integer)numbers.get(i);
    System.out.println(number);
}
```

Resulting output

```
1
2
3
```

Description

- Because untyped collections hold elements of type Object, they can't hold primitive types. As a result, you must use wrapper classes to store primitive types in a collection.
- To add a primitive type to an untyped collection, create an instance of the appropriate wrapper class and pass the value you want it to hold to the constructor of that class.
- To retrieve an element that holds a primitive type, cast the element to the wrapper type. Because wrapper types can automatically be converted to their corresponding primitive types, you can assign the wrapper type to a primitive type variable without any explicit casting.

Figure 12-18 How to use wrapper classes with untyped collections

Perspective

Now that you've finished this chapter, you should know how to work with array lists and linked lists, the two most commonly used Java collections. You should also know how to use hash maps and tree maps to work with collections that store key-value pairs. Finally, you should know how to work with legacy collections in case you ever come across older programs that use them.

However, you should also understand that the interfaces and classes for working with collections that were presented in this chapter only begin to scratch the surface of what's available from the Java API. Many other classes for working with collections have become available with versions 1.5 and 1.6 of Java, and each of these classes provides functionality that's useful in certain situations. As a result, if the collections presented in this chapter don't provide the functionality that your program requires, there's a good chance that the Java API already includes a collection that provides this functionality. To find the collection that you need and to learn how it works, you can start by looking in the documentation for the java.util package. Then, you can use many of the same skills that were presented in this chapter to work with the collection.

Summary

- A *collection* is an object that's designed to store other objects.
- The two most commonly used collection classes are ArrayList and LinkedList. An *array list* uses an array internally to store its data. A *linked list* uses a data structure with next and previous pointers.
- The *generics* feature, which became available with Java 1.5, lets you specify the type of elements a collection can store. This feature also lets you create *generic classes* that work with variable data types.
- The *diamond operator*, which became available with Java 1.7, allows you to code an empty set of brackets (<>) in the constructor of a typed collection instead of having to code the type within those brackets.
- A *map* is a collection that contains key-value pairs.
- The two most commonly used map classes are HashMap and TreeMap. The main difference between these two types of maps is that a *tree map* maintains its entries in key sequence and a *hash map* does not.
- Code that was written before Java 1.5 used *untyped collections*, which hold elements of type Object. To retrieve an element from an untyped collection, you typically have to use casting. To store primitive types in an untyped collection, you have to use *wrapper classes*.

Exercise 12-1 Use an array list

This exercise will guide you through the process of adding an array list to the Future Value application. This array list will store the values for each calculation that is performed. When the program ends, it will print a summary of those calculations that looks something like this:

```
Future Value Calculations

Inv/Mo. Rate    Years   Future Value
$100.00 8.0%    10      $18,416.57
$125.00 8.0%    10      $23,020.71
$150.00 8.0%    10      $27,624.85
```

1. Open the project named ch12_ex1_FutureValue in the ex_starts directory. Then, review the code for this application and run it to make sure it works correctly.
2. Declare a variable at the beginning of the main method for an array list that stores strings.
3. After the code that calculates, formats, and displays the results for each calculation, add code that formats a string with the results of the calculation and then stores the string in the array list.
4. Add code to display the elements in the array list at the console when the user indicates that the program should end. Then, test the program by making at least 3 future value calculations.

Exercise 12-2 Use a linked list

In this exercise, you'll create a Future Value application that's similar to the one described in the previous exercise. However, this application will use a linked list and display the calculations in the reverse order.

1. Open the project named ch12_ex2_FutureValue that's stored in the ex_starts directory. Then, review the code for this application and run it to make sure it works correctly.
2. Declare a variable at the beginning of the main method for a linked list that stores strings.
3. After the code that calculates, formats, and displays the results for each calculation, add code that formats a string with the results of the calculation and then stores the string in the linked list.
4. Add code to display the elements in the linked list at the console when the user indicates that the program should end. This code should retrieve the elements of the linked list in reverse order. To do that, you'll need to use methods of the LinkedList class. Then, test the program by making at least 3 future value calculations.

Exercise 12-3 Create a stack

In this exercise, you'll create a class called GenericStack that uses a linked list to implement a stack, which is a collection that lets you access entries on a first-in, last-out basis. Then, you'll create another class that uses the GenericStack class. The GenericStack class should implement these methods:

Method	Description
push(element)	Adds an element to the top of the stack.
pop()	Returns and removes the element at the top of the stack.
peek()	Returns but does not remove the element at the top of the stack.
size()	Returns the number of entries in the stack.

Create the GenericStack class

1. Open the project named ch12_ex3_GenericStack that's in the ex_starts directory.
2. Create a new class named GenericStack that specifies a type variable that provides for generics.
3. Declare a linked list that will hold the elements in the stack. Then, use the linked list to implement the methods shown above.

Create a class that uses the GenericStack class

4. Open the GenericStackApp class. Then, declare a generic stack at the beginning of the main method that will store String objects.
5. Add code to the main method that uses the push method to add at least three items to the stack. After each item is added, display its value at the console (you'll need to use a string literal to do this). Then, use the size method to return the number of items in the stack and display that value.
6. Use the peek method to return the first item and display that item, and use the size method to return the number of items again and display that value.
7. Use the pop method to return each item, displaying it as it's returned, and display the number of items one more time.
8. Run the project. If it works correctly, your output should look something like this:

```
Push: Apples
Push: Oranges
Push: Bananas
The stack contains 3 items

Peek: Bananas
The stack contains 3 items

Pop: Bananas
Pop: Oranges
Pop: Apples
The stack contains 0 items
```

13

How to work with dates and strings

In section 1 of this book, you learned some basic skills for working with strings. In this chapter, you'll learn more about working with strings, and you'll learn how to work with dates. Because you'll use dates and strings in many of the applications that you develop, you should know how to use all of the skills presented in this chapter.

How to work with dates and times

Although Java doesn't have a primitive data type for working with dates and times, it does have several classes that you can use to work with dates and times. In this topic, you'll learn how to create objects that store dates and times, how to manipulate the values stored in those objects, and how to format those objects.

How to use the GregorianCalendar class to set dates and times

When you create dates and times, you usually use the GregorianCalendar class as shown in figure 13-1. Although you might think that a class named after a calendar would work mainly with dates, this class actually represents a point in time down to the millisecond.

This figure starts by showing four constructors of the GregorianCalendar class. The first constructor creates an object that contains the current date and time. The next three constructors create objects that contain values for a date and time that you specify. For instance, the second constructor creates a date and time using integer values for year, month, and day. In this case, Java sets the hour, minute, and second to 00. However, you can use the third or fourth constructors to set these values.

The statement in the first example shows how to get the current date and time. When you call this constructor, it sets the GregorianCalendar object equal to the current date and time. Java gets this date from your computer's internal clock. As a result, the date and time should be set correctly for your time zone.

The two statements in the second example show how to create a date using literals as arguments in the constructor of the GregorianCalendar class. Here, the first statement creates a GregorianCalendar object named startDate and sets the date to January 30, 2009. The second statement creates a GregorianCalendar object named startTime and sets it to 3:30 PM on July 20, 2012. Notice in both of these examples that the month is specified as an integer between 0 and 11, which might not be what you'd expect.

Like the first statement in the second example, the statement in the third example creates a GregorianCalendar object by supplying just a date. In this case, though, the year, month, and day are supplied as variables instead of literals.

When setting times, any values that you don't set will default to 0. The exception is if you use the first constructor shown in this figure, in which case the time is set to the current time. In addition, to set the hour, you must enter an integer between 0 and 23 where 0 is equal to midnight and 23 is equal to 11 PM. As a result, the first statement of example 2 and example 3 sets the time to midnight (12:00:00 AM). The second statement of example 2 sets the hours to 15, which represents 3:00 PM, and the minutes to 30.

The GregorianCalendar class

```
java.util.GregorianCalendar;
```

Common constructors of the GregorianCalendar class

Method	Description
`GregorianCalendar()`	Creates a GregorianCalendar object set to the current date and time.
`GregorianCalendar(year, month, day)`	Creates a GregorianCalendar object set to the specified date.
`GregorianCalendar(year, month, day, hour, minute)`	Creates a GregorianCalendar object set to the specified date and time.
`GregorianCalendar(year, month, day, hour, minute, second)`	Creates a GregorianCalendar object set to the specified date and time.

Example 1: A statement that gets the current date

```
GregorianCalendar now = new GregorianCalendar();
```

Example 2: Statements that create dates with literals

```
GregorianCalendar startDate = new GregorianCalendar(2009, 0, 30);
GregorianCalendar startTime = new GregorianCalendar(2012, 6, 20, 15, 30);
```

Example 3: A statement that creates a date with variables

```
GregorianCalendar birthDate =
        new GregorianCalendar(birthYear, birthMonth, birthDay);
```

Description

- Year must be a four-digit integer.
- Month must be an integer from 0 to 11 with 0 being January and 11 being December.
- Day must be an integer from 1 to 31.
- Hour must be an integer from 0 to 23, with 0 being 12 AM (midnight) and 23 being 11 PM.
- Minute and second must be integers from 0 to 59.

Figure 13-1 How to use the GregorianCalendar class to set dates and times

How to use the Calendar and GregorianCalendar fields and methods

The GregorianCalendar class is a subclass of the Calendar class. As a result, it inherits all the public and protected fields and methods of the Calendar class. Then, the GregorianCalendar class overrides some of the methods of the Calendar class.

Once you create an object from the GregorianCalendar class, you can use the fields and methods shown in figure 13-2 to work with the object. The examples in this figure show how to use several of these fields and methods. Although these examples show how to work with the date portion of a GregorianCalendar object, you can use the same skills to work with the time portion. You can also find other fields and methods for working with dates and times in the API documentation for the Calendar and GregorianCalendar classes.

The first example shows how to use the set, add, and roll methods to change the value that's stored in a GregorianCalendar object. As you can see, you can use the same arguments for the set method that you used for the constructors of the GregorianCalendar class. In addition, you can use fields from the Calendar class, such as JANUARY and FEBRUARY, to set the month. Notice that when you use the add method to add 14 months to the date, the year is also increased. In contrast, when you use the roll method to roll the current month forward by 14 months, the year isn't affected. As a result, it only changes the month from August to October.

When you manipulate dates and times, you need to make sure to supply values that make sense. For example, since there are only 30 days in November, it doesn't make sense to use 31 as the day argument. If you do that, Java sets the date to December 1.

The second example shows how to use the get method to return various integer values that are stored in the GregorianCalendar object. Here, the year is 2010, the month is 1 (February), the day is 4, the day of the week is 5 (Thursday), and the day of the year is 35 (the 31 days of January plus the 4 days of February).

The other two methods listed in this figure, setTime and getTime, work with Date objects. The setTime method sets a GregorianCalendar object to the date specified by a Date object, and the getTime method returns a Date object for a GregorianCalendar object. You'll learn more about Date objects in the next topic.

The Calendar class

```
java.util.Calendar;
```

Common fields of the Calendar class

```
DATE          DAY_OF_MONTH      DAY_OF_WEEK        DAY_OF_YEAR
HOUR          HOUR_OF_DAY       MINUTE             MONTH
SECOND        YEAR              MONDAY...SUNDAY    JANUARY...DECEMBER
```

Common methods of the Calendar and GregorianCalendar classes

Method	Description
`set(intYear, intMonth, ...)`	Sets the values for year, month, day, hour, minute, and second just as they are set in the constructor for the GregorianCalendar class.
`set(intField, intValue)`	Sets the specified field to the supplied value.
`setTime(Date)`	Sets the date and time values based on the supplied Date object.
`add(intField, intValue)`	Adds the supplied value to the specified field.
`roll(intField, intValue)`	Adds the supplied value to the specified field, but doesn't affect other fields.
`roll(intField, booleanValue)`	Increments the value of the specified field by 1 for true values and decrements the value of the field by 1 for false values.
`get(intField)`	Returns the int value of the specified field.
`getTime()`	Returns a Date object.

Example 1: Code that changes a GregorianCalendar object

```
GregorianCalendar endDate = new
   GregorianCalendar(2010, 0, 1);                    // January 1, 2010
endDate.set(2010, 2, 30);                            // March 30, 2010
endDate.set(2010, Calendar.MARCH, 30);               // March 30, 2010
endDate.set(Calendar.MONTH, Calendar.JANUARY);       // January 30, 2010
endDate.add(Calendar.MONTH, 5);                      // June 30, 2010
endDate.add(Calendar.MONTH, 14);                     // August 30, 2011
endDate.roll(Calendar.MONTH, 14);                    // October 30, 2011
endDate.roll(Calendar.MONTH, true);                  // November 30, 2011
endDate.roll(Calendar.DAY_OF_MONTH, false);          // November 29, 2011
```

Example 2: Code that accesses fields in a GregorianCalendar object

```
GregorianCalendar birthday = new
   GregorianCalendar(2010, Calendar.FEBRUARY, 4);   // Thurs, Feb 4, 2010
int year = birthday.get(Calendar.YEAR);              // year is 2010
int month = birthday.get(Calendar.MONTH);            // month is 1
int day = birthday.get(Calendar.DAY_OF_MONTH);       // day is 4
int dayOfWeek = birthday.get(Calendar.DAY_OF_WEEK); // dayOfWeek is 5
int dayOfYear = birthday.get(Calendar.DAY_OF_YEAR); // dayOfYear is 35
```

Note

- For more information about these and other fields and methods, look up the Calendar and GregorianCalendar classes in the documentation for the Java API.

Figure 13-2 How to use the Calendar and GregorianCalendar fields and methods

How to use the Date class

Figure 13-3 shows how to use the Date class. Unlike the GregorianCalendar class, the Date class doesn't have fields that represent the year, month, day, and so on. Instead, the Date class represents a point in time by the number of milliseconds since January 1, 1970 00:00:00 Greenwich Mean Time (GMT). You need to use Date objects when you want to format a date as shown in the next figure. You may also find Date objects useful when you want to perform arithmetic operations on dates like subtracting one date from another.

To create a Date object, you can invoke the getTime method of a GregorianCalendar object as shown in the first example in this figure. Since the getTime method returns a Date object, you don't need to call either of the Date constructors. However, you can also use either of the constructors in this figure to create a Date object. The first constructor creates a Date object for the current date and time while the second constructor creates a Date object based on the number of milliseconds that are passed to it. The second example shows how to use the first constructor to create a Date object for the current date and time.

The third example shows how to use the toString and getTime methods of the Date class. The toString method returns a readable string that displays the day of the week, month, date, time, time zone, and year. The getTime method returns a long integer that represents the number of milliseconds since January 1, 1970 00:00:00 GMT.

The fourth example shows how Date objects can be useful when you want to calculate the elapsed time between two dates. First, two GregorianCalendar dates are converted to Date objects using the getTime method of the GregorianCalendar class. Next, the Date objects are converted to milliseconds using the getTime method of the Date class. Then, the starting date in milliseconds is subtracted from the ending date in milliseconds to get the elapsed milliseconds, and that result is divided by the number of milliseconds in a day to get the elapsed days. This type of routine is useful in many business programs.

The Date class

```
java.util.Date;
```

Common constructors

Constructor	Description
`Date()`	Creates a Date object for the current date and time based on your computer's internal clock.
`Date(longMilliseconds)`	Creates a Date object based on the number of milliseconds that is passed to it.

Common methods

Method	Description
`getTime()`	Returns a long value that represents the number of milliseconds for the date.
`toString()`	Returns a String object that contains the date and time formatted like this: Wed Aug 04 08:31:25 PDT 2009.

Example 1: A statement that converts a GregorianCalendar object to a Date object

```
Date endDate = gregEndDate.getTime();
```

Example 2: A statement that gets a Date object for the current date/time

```
Date now = new Date();
```

Example 3: Statements that convert Date objects to string and long variables

```
String nowAsString = now.toString();     // converts to a string
long nowInMS = now.getTime();            // converts to milliseconds
```

Example 4: Code that calculates the number of days between two dates

```
Date startDate = gregStartDate.getTime();
Date endDate = gregEndDate.getTime();
long startDateMS = startDate.getTime();
long endDateMS = endDate.getTime();
long elapsedMS = endDateMS - startDateMS;
long elapsedDays = elapsedMS / (24 * 60 * 60 * 1000);
```

Description

- A Date object stores a date and time as the number of milliseconds since January 1, 1970 00:00:00 GMT (Greenwich Mean Time).
- You need to convert GregorianCalendar objects to Date objects when you want to use the DateFormat class to format them as shown in the next figure.
- Date objects are also useful when you want to calculate the number of milliseconds (or days) between two dates.

Figure 13-3 How to use the Date class

How to use the DateFormat class to format dates and times

Figure 13-4 shows how to use the DateFormat class to convert a Date object to a string that you can use to display dates and times. In addition, it shows how to control the format of these strings. Since this class works similarly to the NumberFormat class, you shouldn't have much trouble using it.

Before you can format a date, you need to use one of the static methods of the DateFormat class to create a DateFormat object that has a particular format. When you do that, you can choose to return the date only, the time only, or the date and time. If you don't specify a format, the DateFormat object will use the default format. However, you can use one of the four DateFormat fields to override the default date format. Once you've created a DateFormat object that has the format you want, you can use its format method to apply the specified format to a Date object.

The first example shows how to format a Date object with the default format. Here, the getDateTimeInstance method is used to return both date and time. Since no arguments are supplied for this method, it will return a string that contains the current date and time with the default format, which should look something like this:

```
Jan 30, 2010 12:10:10 PM
```

The second example shows how to format a GregorianCalendar object with the default date format. Here, you can see that you start by using the getTime method to convert the GregorianCalendar object to a Date object. Then, you use the getDateInstance method to return a format with the date only. Since no arguments are supplied for this method, it will return a string that contains this date:

```
Dec 31, 2010
```

The third example shows how you can use the fields of the DateFormat class to override the default date format. Here, you can see how to use the SHORT field, but the same skills apply to the other three fields. If you use the getDateTimeInstance method, you need to supply the first argument for the date and the second argument for the time. Since both of the arguments are specified as short in this example, they will return a date with a format something like this:

```
12/31/10 7:30 AM
```

When you use the LONG and FULL fields, the time portion of the date will end with an abbreviation for the current time zone. In this figure, the examples use the Pacific Standard Time (PST) time zone.

The DateFormat class

```
java.text.DateFormat;
```

Common static methods

Method	Description
`getDateInstance()`	Returns a DateFormat object with date, but not time.
`getTimeInstance()`	Returns a DateFormat object with time, but not date.
`getDateTimeInstance()`	Returns a DateFormat object with date and time.
`getDateInstance(intField)`	Same as above, but you can use the fields shown below to override the default date format.
`getTimeInstance(intField)`	Same as above, but you can use the fields shown below to override the default time format.
`getDateTimeInstance(intField, intField)`	Same as above, but you can use the fields shown below to override the default date and time formats.

Common fields

Style	Date example	Time example
`SHORT`	12/31/10	12:00 AM
`MEDIUM`	Dec 31, 2010	7:30:00 PM
`LONG`	December 31, 2010	7:30:00 AM PST
`FULL`	Saturday, December 31, 2010	7:30:00 AM PST

Common method

Method	Description
`format(Date)`	Returns a String object of the Date object with the format that's specified by the DateFormat object.

Example 1: Code that formats a Date object

```
Date now = new Date();
DateFormat defaultDate = DateFormat.getDateTimeInstance();
String nowString = defaultDate.format(now);
```

Example 2: Code that formats a GregorianCalendar object

```
GregorianCalendar gregEndDate = new GregorianCalendar(2010,11,31,7,30);
Date endDate = gregEndDate.getTime();
DateFormat defaultDate = DateFormat.getDateInstance();
String endDateString = defaultDate.format(endDate);
```

Example 3: Code that overrides the default date and time formats

```
DateFormat shortDate = DateFormat.getDateInstance(DateFormat.SHORT);
DateFormat shortTime = DateFormat.getTimeInstance(DateFormat.SHORT);
DateFormat shortDateTime =
    DateFormat.getDateTimeInstance(DateFormat.SHORT, DateFormat.SHORT);
```

Description

- You can use the DateFormat class to format Date objects in various ways.

Figure 13-4 How to use the DateFormat class to format dates and times

A DateUtils class that provides methods for handling dates

Although the date handling features of the Java API are powerful, they must frequently be used in combination to provide some of the most common operations needed by business applications. As a result, it's common for an application that uses dates to include a class like the one in figure 13-5. This class presents just a few of the date handling operations you may need to perform, but it should give you a good idea of what you can do with the date handling features.

In the DateUtils class, the getCurrentDate method returns a Date object that contains just the current date. To do that, it creates a GregorianCalendar object with the current date and time. Then, it uses the set method to set the hour, minute, and second to zero. Finally, it uses the getTime method to convert the GregorianCalendar object to a Date object. You might want to use a method like this to get a date that you can use to calculate the age of an invoice. In that case, you'll want to be sure that neither the invoice date or the current date contains a time so the age is calculated properly.

The createDate method provides a simple way to create a Date object for a specific date with the hour, minute, and second set to zero. This method starts by creating a GregorianCalendar object for the specified date. Then, it uses the getTime method to convert the GregorianCalendar object to a Date object.

The stripTime method strips the hour, minute, and second from a Date object. It works by setting a GregorianCalendar object to the date and time specified by the Date object so the hour, minute, and second can be accessed. Then, it sets these values to zero and converts the result back to a Date object.

The daysDiff method calculates the difference between two Date objects in days. To do that, it starts by calling the stripTime method to remove the time-of-day component from both Date objects. That's important when you're working with Date objects that include times, because you don't want the time of day to be considered in the calculation.

Next, the daysDiff method uses the getTime method to convert the Date objects to long values. Then, it subtracts these two values to get the difference, which is expressed in milliseconds. To convert that value to days, it divides it by the number of milliseconds in a day, which is represented by the constant named MILLS_IN_DAY that's defined at the top of the class.

The code example at the bottom of this figure shows how you might use the DateUtils class in a simple application. This example determines the number of days between the current date and Christmas. The first two lines get the current date and then extract the current year using the get method. Next, a Date object named currentDate is set to the current date and another Date object named Christmas is set to December 25 of the current year. Then, an int variable named daysToChristmas is calculated by calling the daysDiff method. The rest of the code formats and displays the result.

The code for the DateUtils class

```
import java.util.*;

public class DateUtils {
    static final int MILLS_IN_DAY = 24 * 60 * 60 * 1000;

    public static Date getCurrentDate() {
        GregorianCalendar currentDate = new GregorianCalendar();
        currentDate.set(Calendar.HOUR, 0);
        currentDate.set(Calendar.MINUTE, 0);
        currentDate.set(Calendar.SECOND, 0);
        return currentDate.getTime();
    }

    public static Date createDate(int year, int month, int day) {
        GregorianCalendar date = new GregorianCalendar(year, month, day);
        return date.getTime();
    }

    public static Date stripTime(Date date) {
        GregorianCalendar currentDate = new GregorianCalendar();
        currentDate.setTime(date);
        currentDate.set(Calendar.HOUR, 0);
        currentDate.set(Calendar.MINUTE, 0);
        currentDate.set(Calendar.SECOND, 0);
        return currentDate.getTime();
    }

    public static int daysDiff(Date date1, Date date2) {
        date1 = stripTime(date1);
        date2 = stripTime(date2);
        long longDate1 = date1.getTime();
        long longDate2 = date2.getTime();
        long longDiff = longDate2 - longDate1;
        return (int) (longDiff / MILLS_IN_DAY);
    }
}
```

Code that uses some of the DateUtils methods

```
GregorianCalendar currentGC = new GregorianCalendar();
int currentYear = currentGC.get(Calendar.YEAR);

Date currentDate = DateUtils.getCurrentDate();
Date christmas = DateUtils.createDate(currentYear, Calendar.DECEMBER, 25);
int daysToChristmas = DateUtils.daysDiff(currentDate, christmas);

DateFormat dateFormat = DateFormat.getDateInstance(DateFormat.LONG);
String formattedDate = dateFormat.format(currentDate);
System.out.println("Today is " + formattedDate);
System.out.println("There are " + daysToChristmas + " days until Christmas.");
```

Resulting output

```
Today is July 11, 2011
There are 166 days until Christmas.
```

Figure 13-5 A DateUtils class that provides methods for handling dates

An Invoice class that includes an invoice date

To show how you can use some of the date skills you just learned, figure 13-6 shows how to add a date to the Invoice class that was presented in chapter 12. The constructor for this class sets the invoice date, which is declared as a Date object, to the current date. To do that, it uses the getCurrentDate method of the DateUtils class so that the invoice date doesn't include a time.

Two methods have also been added to this class to provide access to the invoice date. The getInvoiceDate method simply returns the invoice date as a Date object. The getFormattedDate method applies a short date format to the invoice date and returns it as a string.

To make the date classes available to this class, the two import statements at the beginning of the class have been changed. Now, instead of just importing the NumberFormat class of the java.text package and the ArrayList class of the java.util package, they import all of the classes in these packages. That way, the DateFormat class is available from the java.text package, and the GregorianCalendar, Calendar, and Date classes are available from the java.util package.

Code that adds a date to the Invoice class

```
import java.text.*;
import java.util.*;

public class Invoice
{
    private ArrayList<LineItem> lineItems;
    private Date invoiceDate;

    public Invoice()
    {
        lineItems = new ArrayList<>();
        invoiceDate = DateUtils.getCurrentDate();
    }

    public ArrayList<LineItem> getLineItems()
    {
        return lineItems;
    }

    public void addItem(LineItem lineItem)
    {
        this.lineItems.add(lineItem);
    }

    public double getInvoiceTotal()
    {
        double invoiceTotal = 0;
        for (LineItem lineItem : this.lineItems)
        {
            invoiceTotal += lineItem.getTotal();
        }
        return invoiceTotal;
    }

    public String getFormattedTotal()
    {
        NumberFormat currency = NumberFormat.getCurrencyInstance();
        return currency.format(this.getInvoiceTotal());
    }

    public Date getInvoiceDate()
    {
        return invoiceDate;
    }

    public String getFormattedDate()
    {
        DateFormat shortDate = DateFormat.getDateInstance(DateFormat.SHORT);
        return shortDate.format(invoiceDate);
    }
}
```

Figure 13-6 An Invoice class that includes an invoice date

How to work with the String class

In section 1, you learned how to create a String object and how to use two methods of the String class that compare two strings. Now, you'll learn some new ways to create String objects, and you'll learn how to use more of the methods of the String class.

Constructors of the String class

Figure 13-7 shows three constructors of the String class. The first constructor provides another way to create an empty string, and the second and third constructors allow you to create a string from an array of char or byte types. Although none of these constructors are commonly used, the second and third constructors show that you can think of a string as an array of Unicode characters.

You may remember from chapter 3 that char is a primitive type that can hold a Unicode character with two bytes used for each character. That provides for over 65,000 unique characters. Now, you'll learn that a String variable can store an array of these Unicode characters.

Code examples that create strings

The first two examples in this figure show how to create a string. In example 1, the first statement uses the shorthand notation you learned how to use in chapter 2. Then, the second statement shows how to do the same task using a constructor of the String class. In example 2, the first statement initializes the new string from a string literal, and the second statement initializes it from a variable.

The third example creates a string from an array of characters. Here, the second statement converts the entire array of characters to a string named cityString1. Then, the third statement converts the first three characters in the array to a string named cityString2. Although there's little reason to create a string in this way, we included this example to demonstrate that an array of characters can be converted to a string. Note that literal char values must be enclosed in single quotes, not double quotes the way string literals are.

The fourth example creates a string from an array of bytes. Here, the first statement creates an array of bytes that represents the same characters as the characters that are used in the third example. That's because every character in the ASCII character set corresponds to a byte value. For example, the byte value of 68 represents the character *D*. Then, the second and third statements in this example work just like they did in the previous example.

The String class

```
java.lang.String;
```

Common constructors of the String class

Constructor	Description
`String()`	Creates an empty string ("").
`String(arrayName)`	Creates a string from an array of char or byte types.
`String(arrayName, intOffset, intLength)`	Creates a string from a subset of an array of char or byte types.

Example 1: Two ways to create an empty string

```
String name = "";
String name = new String();
```

Example 2: Two ways to create a string from another string

```
String title = "Murach's Beginning Java";
String title = bookTitle;
```

Example 3: Two ways to create a string from an array of characters

```
char cityArray[] = {'D','a','l','l','a','s'};
String cityString1 = new String(cityArray);
String cityString2 = new String(cityArray, 0, 3);
```

Example 4: Two ways to create a string from an array of bytes

```
byte cityArray[] = {68, 97, 108, 108, 97, 115};
String cityString1 = new String(cityArray);
String cityString2 = new String(cityArray, 0, 3);
```

Notes

- For the third constructor shown above, the characters referred to by the intOffset and intLength arguments must fall within the array. Otherwise, the constructor will throw an IndexOutOfBoundsException.
- A char data type contains a single Unicode character, which is stored in two bytes. When you use the second and third constructors above, you can construct a String object from an array of char types. To code a literal char value, you use single quotes instead of double quotes as shown in the third example.
- Because a byte data type can hold the Unicode value for every character in the ASCII character set, you can also construct a String object from an array of bytes as shown in the fourth example.
- Since String objects are immutable, they can't grow or shrink. Later in this chapter, you'll learn how to work with StringBuilder objects that can grow and shrink.

Figure 13-7 How to create strings

Methods of the String class

In chapters 2 and 4, you learned how to use the equals and equalsIgnoreCase methods of the String class to compare strings. Now, figure 13-8 reviews these methods and introduces you to 17 more methods that you can use to work with strings. In the next figure, you'll see some examples that use some of these methods. You can also get more information about any of these methods by looking up the String class in the documentation for the Java API.

As you can see, we divided the methods presented in this figure into two categories. The first table lists methods that are used to manipulate the value of the string in one way or another. The first five of these methods return int values. The length method returns the total number of characters in the string. The indexOf and lastIndexOf methods return a value that represents an index within the string. This index value works as if the string was an array of characters. In other words, the index value for the first character in a string is 0, the index value for the second character is 1, and so on.

The next four methods return String objects. Here, the trim method returns the string, but it removes any spaces from the beginning and end of the string. The substring methods allow you to return part of a string by specifying index values. The replace method replaces all occurrences of a specified character with another character.

The split method returns an array of String objects. This method splits the string up into individual strings based on the delimiter string you specify. Actually, the delimiter string can be any *regular expression*, which is a complicated expression that can contain wildcards and other special characters. If you want to learn more about regular expressions, you can search the web for "java regular expression." In most cases, however, the delimiter string will be a single character or an escape sequence such as "\t" for tabs or "\n" for returns.

When using methods that require an index, you must be careful to supply a valid index. If you supply an index argument that's negative or greater than the length of the string minus one, the method will throw a StringIndexOutOfBoundsException.

The second table in this figure lists methods that are useful for comparing string values. The first six of these methods return boolean values. You've already seen the equals and equalsIgnoreCase methods, which compare strings and return a true value if the strings are equal. The startsWith and endsWith methods check whether a string starts or ends with a certain combination of characters and return a true value if it does. And the isEmpty method checks whether the string is an empty string and returns a true value if it is.

The last two methods are used to compare two strings to see which one is greater according to the sort order of the strings. These methods return an int value that's negative if the string is less than the specified string, zero if the strings are equal, and positive if the string is greater than the specified string. These methods are useful because you can't use normal comparison operators (such as < and >) with String objects.

Methods for manipulating strings

Method	Description
`length()`	Returns an int value for the number of characters in this string.
`indexOf(String)`	Returns an int value for the index of the first occurrence of the specified string in this string. If the string isn't found, this method returns -1.
`indexOf(String, startIndex)`	Returns an int value for the index of the first occurrence of the specified string starting at the specified index. If the string isn't found, this method returns -1.
`lastIndexOf(String)`	Returns an int value for the index of the last occurrence of the specified string in this string.
`lastIndexOf(String, startIndex)`	Returns an int value for the index of the last occurrence of the specified string in this string starting at the specified index.
`trim()`	Returns a String object with any spaces removed from the beginning and end of this string.
`substring(startIndex)`	Returns a String object that starts at the specified index and goes to the end of the string.
`substring(startIndex, endIndex)`	Returns a String object that starts at the specified start index and goes to, but doesn't include, the end index.
`replace(oldChar, newChar)`	Returns a String object that results from replacing all instances of the specified old char value with the specified new char value.
`split(delimiter)`	Returns an array of String objects that were separated in the original string by the specified delimiter.
`charAt(index)`	Returns the char value at the specified index.

Methods for comparing strings

Method	Description
`equals(String)`	Returns a boolean true value if the specified string is equal to the current string. This comparison is case-sensitive.
`equalsIgnoreCase(String)`	Returns a boolean true value if the specified string is equal to the current string. This comparison is *not* case-sensitive.
`startsWith(String)`	Returns a boolean true value if this string starts with the specified string.
`startsWith(String, startIndex)`	Returns a boolean true value if this string starts with the specified string starting at the start index.
`endsWith(String)`	Returns a boolean true value if the string ends with the specified string.
`isEmpty()`	Returns a Boolean true value if this string contains an empty string. This method was introduced with Java 1.6.
`compareTo(String)`	Returns an int that's less than zero if the string is less than the specified string, greater than zero if the string is greater than the specified string, and zero if the strings are equal.
`compareToIgnoreCase(String)`	The same as compareTo, but the case of the strings is ignored.

Figure 13-8 Methods of the String class

Code examples that work with strings

Figure 13-9 shows some examples of how you can use the methods of the String class. The first example shows how to parse the first name from a string that contains a full name. Here, the first statement sets the string to a string literal that includes a first and last name, and the second statement uses the trim method to remove any spaces from the beginning or end of the string. Then, the third statement uses the indexOf method to get the index of the first space in the string, which is the space between the first and last names. Finally, the last statement uses the substring method to set the first name variable equal to the string that begins at the first character of the string and ends at the first space character in the string.

The second example shows how to parse a string that contains an address into the components of the address. In this case, tab characters separate each component of the address. Here, the second statement uses the trim method to remove any spaces that may have been included at the beginning or end of the string. Next, the split method is used to separate the string into its individual components. Then, simple assignment statements are used to assign the components to individual strings. Note that this code doesn't account for an improperly formatted address string. In an actual application, you'd want to at least check the length of the addressParts array to make sure the string was successfully parsed into four components.

The third example shows how to add dashes to a phone number. To do that, this example creates a second string. Then, it uses the substring method to parse the first string and add the dashes at the appropriate locations in the string. In figure 13-11, you'll learn an easier way to accomplish this task.

The fourth example shows how to remove the dashes from a phone number. To do that, this example creates a second string. Then, it uses a for loop to cycle through each character in the first string. The only statement within this loop uses the charAt method to add all characters in the first string that are not equal to a dash to the second string. As a result, the second string won't contain any dashes. You'll learn another way to accomplish this task in figure 13-11.

The fifth example shows how to compare two strings to determine which one comes first based on the string's sort order. Here, two strings are created. Then, the compareToIgnoreCase method of the first string is used to compare the strings. If the result is less than zero, a message is printed indicating that the first string comes first in sequence. If the result is zero, the message indicates that the strings are equal. And if the result is greater than zero, the message indicates that the second string comes first.

The sixth example shows how to use the isEmpty method that was introduced with Java 1.6 to check if a string contains an empty string. Here, the first statement creates a string variable named customerNumber that contains an empty string. Then, two commented out if statements show two ways that were commonly used to check for empty strings prior to Java 1.6. Although these statements will still work, the isEmtpy method that's used in the third if statement requires less typing and is easier to read.

Example 1: Code that parses a first name from a name string

```
String fullName = " Pamela Caldwell ";
fullName = fullName.trim();
int indexOfSpace = fullName.indexOf(" ");
String firstName = fullName.substring(0, indexOfSpace);
```

Example 2: Code that parses a string containing a tab-delimited address

```
String address = "805 Main Street\tDallas\tTX\t12345";
address = address.trim();
String[] addressParts = address.split("\t");
String street = addressParts[0];
String city = addressParts[1];
String state = addressParts[2];
String zip = addressParts[3];
```

Example 3: Code that adds dashes to a phone number

```
String phoneNumber1 = "9775551212";
String phoneNumber2 = phoneNumber1.substring(0, 3);
phoneNumber2 += "-";
phoneNumber2 += phoneNumber1.substring(3, 6);
phoneNumber2 += "-";
phoneNumber2 += phoneNumber1.substring(6);
```

Example 4: Code that removes dashes from a phone number

```
String phoneNumber3 = "977-555-1212";
String phoneNumber4 = "";
for(int i = 0; i < phoneNumber3.length(); i++)
{
   if (phoneNumber3.charAt(i) != '-')
      phoneNumber4 += phoneNumber3.charAt(i);
}
```

Example 5: Code that compares strings

```
String lastName1 = "Smith";
String lastName2 = "Lee";
int sortResult = lastName1.compareToIgnoreCase(lastName2);
if (sortResult < 0)
    System.out.println(lastName1 + " comes first.");
else if (sortResult == 0)
    System.out.println("The names are the same.");
else
    System.out.println(lastName2 + " comes first.");
```

Example 6: Code that uses the isEmpty method

```
String customerNumber = "";
//if (customerNumber.equals(""))        // old way
//if (customerNumber.length() == 0)     // old way
if (customerNumber.isEmpty())           // Java 1.6 and later
    System.out.println("customerNumber contains an empty string.");
```

Figure 13-9 Code examples that work with strings

How to work with the StringBuilder class

When you use the String class to work with strings, the string has a fixed length and you can't edit the characters that make up the string. In other words, the String class creates strings that are *immutable*. Then, when you assign a new value to a string variable, the original String object is deleted and it's replaced with a new String object that contains the new value.

If you want more flexibility when working with strings, you can use the StringBuilder class. When you use this class, you create strings that are *mutable*. In other words, you can add, delete, or replace the characters in a StringBuilder object. This makes it easier to write some types of routines, and it can improve the efficiency of your code in some situations.

Note that the StringBuilder class was introduced with Java 1.5. It's designed to be a more efficient replacement for the StringBuffer class that was used prior to Java 1.5. Because the API for the StringBuffer class is identical to the API for the StringBuilder class, you can easily switch between StringBuffer and StringBuilder.

Constructors and methods of the StringBuilder class

Figure 13-10 shows three constructors and thirteen methods of the StringBuilder class. In the next figure, you'll see some examples that use these constructors and methods. As always, you can find more information by looking up the StringBuilder class in the documentation for the Java API.

The first constructor in this figure creates an empty StringBuilder object with an initial capacity of 16 characters. Then, if you add more than 16 characters to this StringBuilder object, Java will automatically increase the capacity. To do that, it doubles the current capacity and adds 2.

Whenever possible, you should set the capacity to an appropriate value by using the second or third constructor shown in the figure. Otherwise, Java will have to allocate memory each time the capacity is exceeded, and that can cause your programs to run less efficiently. On the other hand, if you set a large capacity and use a small percentage of it, you waste memory.

Once you create a StringBuilder object, you can use the methods in this figure to work with the object. You can use the first three methods to check the capacity of the object or to check or set the length of the string. You can use the next six methods to add, edit, or delete strings or characters. And you can use the last four methods to return a String object or a character.

The StringBuilder class

```
java.lang.StringBuilder;
```

Constructors of the StringBuilder class

Constructor	Description
`StringBuilder()`	Creates an empty StringBuilder object with an initial capacity of 16 characters.
`StringBuilder(intLength)`	Creates an empty StringBuilder object with an initial capacity of the specified number of characters.
`StringBuilder(String)`	Creates a StringBuilder object that contains the specified string plus an additional capacity of 16 characters.

Methods of the StringBuilder class

Methods	Description
`capacity()`	Returns an int value for the capacity of this StringBuilder object.
`length()`	Returns an int value for the number of characters in this StringBuilder object.
`setLength(intNumOfChars)`	Sets the length of this StringBuilder object to the specified number of characters.
`append(value)`	Adds the specified value to the end of the string.
`insert(index, value)`	Inserts the specified value at the specified index pushing the rest of the string back.
`replace(startIndex, endIndex, String)`	Replaces the characters from the start index to, but not including, the end index with the specified string.
`delete(startIndex, endIndex)`	Removes the substring from the start index to, but not including, the end index.
`deleteCharAt(index)`	Removes the character at the specified index.
`setCharAt(index, character)`	Replaces the character at the specified index with the specified character.
`charAt(index)`	Returns a char value for the character at the specified index.
`substring(index)`	Returns a String object that contains the characters starting at the specified index to the end of the string.
`substring(startIndex, endIndex)`	Returns a String object that contains the characters from the start index to, but not including, the end index.
`toString()`	Returns a String object that contains the string that's stored in the StringBuilder object.

Description

- StringBuilder objects are *mutable*, which means you can modify the characters in the string. The capacity of a StringBuilder object is automatically increased if necessary.
- The append and insert methods accept primitive types, objects, and arrays of characters.
- The StringBuilder class was introduced with Java 1.5. It's designed to replace the older StringBuffer class, which has identical constructors and methods but isn't as efficient.

Figure 13-10 Constructors and methods of the StringBuilder class

Code examples that work with the StringBuilder class

Figure 13-11 presents some examples that show how you can use the constructors and methods of the StringBuilder class. In particular, this figure shows how to add characters to the end of a string, insert characters into the middle of a string, and delete characters from a string.

The first example shows how to use the append method of the StringBuilder class. Here, the first statement creates an empty StringBuilder object with the default capacity of 16 characters. Then, the next three statements use the append method to add 10 characters to the end of the string. As a result, the length of the string is 10 and the capacity of the StringBuilder object is 16. (You can do the same thing by using simple string concatenation, but Java must create a new String object for each statement since the length of a String object can't be increased. In contrast, when you use the append method of the StringBuilder class, a new StringBuilder object isn't created because the length of a StringBuilder object can be increased.)

The second example adds dashes to the string that was created in the first example. Here, the first statement uses the insert method to insert a dash after the first three characters. This pushes the remaining numbers back one index. Then, the second statement uses the insert method to insert a dash after the seventh character in the string, which was the sixth character in the original string. This pushes the remaining four numbers in the string back one index.

The third example shows how to remove dashes from a phone number. Here, a loop cycles through each character, using the charAt method to check if the current character is a dash. If so, the deleteCharAt method deletes it. Since this causes all characters to the right of the dash to move forward one index, it's necessary to decrement the counter so the loop doesn't skip any characters.

The fourth example shows how to use the substring method of the StringBuilder class to separate the area code, prefix, and suffix components of a phone number. Here, the first statement uses a constructor to create a StringBuilder object from a String literal. Then, the next three statements use the substring method to create three String objects from the StringBuilder object. For example, the second statement specifies a substring that goes from the first character up to, but not including, the fourth character. (Note that the substring method works the same for the String class as it does for the StringBuilder class, so the same thing could be done with a simple string.)

The fifth example shows how a StringBuilder object automatically increases its capacity as the length of the string increases. Here, the first statement creates an empty StringBuilder object with a capacity of 8 characters, and the second statement uses the capacity method to check the capacity. Next, the third statement appends a string of 17 characters to the empty string. Since this causes the capacity of the StringBuilder object to be exceeded, Java automatically increases the capacity. As a result, the capacity of the name string is increased from 8 to 18 characters. Then, the last two statements check the length and capacity of the modified StringBuilder object.

Example 1: Code that creates a phone number

```
StringBuilder phoneNumber = new StringBuilder();
phoneNumber.append("977");
phoneNumber.append("555");
phoneNumber.append("1212");
```

Example 2: Code that adds dashes to a phone number

```
phoneNumber.insert(3, "-");
phoneNumber.insert(7, "-");
```

Example 3: Code that removes dashes from a phone number

```
for(int i = 0; i < phoneNumber.length(); i++)
{
   if (phoneNumber.charAt(i) == '-')
      phoneNumber.deleteCharAt(i--);
}
```

Example 4: Code that parses a phone number

```
StringBuilder phoneNumber = new StringBuilder("977-555-1212");
String areaCode = phoneNumber.substring(0,3);
String prefix = phoneNumber.substring(4,7);
String suffix = phoneNumber.substring(8);
```

Example 5: Code that shows how capacity automatically increases

```
StringBuilder name = new StringBuilder(8);
int capacity1 = name.capacity();     // capacity1 is 8
name.append("Raymond R. Thomas");
int length = name.length();          // length is 17
int capacity2 = name.capacity();     // capacity2 is 18 (2 * capacity1 + 2)
```

Figure 13-11 Code examples that work with the StringBuilder class

Perspective

Now that you've finished this chapter, you should be able to use the classes provided by the Java API to work with dates, and you should be able to use the String and StringBuilder classes to work with strings. These are skills that you will use often as you develop Java applications.

Summary

- You can use the GregorianCalendar, Calendar, Date, and DateFormat classes to create, manipulate, and format dates and times.
- You can use methods of the String class to locate a string within another string, return parts of a string, and compare all or part of a string. However, String objects are *immutable*, so you can't add, delete, or modify individual characters in a string.
- StringBuilder objects are *mutable*, so you can use the StringBuilder methods to add, delete, or modify characters in a StringBuilder object. Whenever necessary, Java automatically increases the capacity of a StringBuilder object.

Exercise 13-1 Add a due date to the Invoice application

For this exercise, you'll modify the Invoice class that's shown in figure 13-6 so it contains methods that return a due date, calculated as 30 days after the invoice date. Then, you'll modify the Invoice application that was shown in chapter 12 to display the invoice date and due date for a batch of invoices.

1. Open the project named ch13_ex1_Invoice that's in the ex_starts directory. Then, review the code in the Invoice and InvoiceApp classes.
2. Add two methods named getDueDate and getFormattedDueDate to the Invoice class. The getDueDate method should calculate and return a Date object that's 30 days after the invoice date. The getFormattedDueDate method should return the due date in the short date format.
3. Modify the displayInvoices method in the InvoiceApp class so that the invoice display includes columns for the invoice date and the due date in addition to the invoice number and total. Then, run the application to make sure it works.

Exercise 13-2 Calculate the user's age

In this exercise, you'll write a program that accepts a person's birth date from the console and displays the person's age in years. To make that easier to do, we'll give you a class that contains the code for accepting the birth date. The console output for the program should look something like this:

```
Welcome to the age calculator.

Enter the month you were born (1 to 12): 5
Enter the day of the month you were born: 16
Enter the year you were born (four digits): 1959

Your birth date is May 16, 1959
Today's date is Feb 9, 2012
Your age is: 52
```

1. Open the project named ch13_ex2_AgeCalculator that's in the ex_starts directory. Then, review the code in the AgeCalculatorApp class.
2. Add code to this class that gets the current date and then uses the current year to validate the birth year the user enters. The user should not be allowed to enter a year after the current year or more than 110 years before the current year.
3. Add code to create, format, and print the user's birth date and to format and print the current date.
4. Add code to calculate and print the user's age.
5. Test this project with a variety of dates to be sure it works.

Exercise 13-3 Parse a name

In this exercise, you'll write an application that parses full names into first and last name or first, middle, and last name, depending on whether the user enters a string consisting of two or three words. The output for the program should look something like this:

```
Welcome to the name parser.

Enter a name: Joel Murach

First name:  Joel
Last name:   Murach
```

1. Open the project named ch13_ex3_NameParser that's in the ex_starts directory. Then, review the code in the NameParserApp class.
2. Add code that separates the name into two or three strings depending on whether the user entered a name with two words or three.

3. Display each word of the name on a separate line. If the user enters fewer than two words or more than three words, display an error message. Also, make sure the application works even if the user enters one or more spaces before or after the name.
4. Test the project to make sure it works correctly.

Exercise 13-4 Validate a social security number

In this exercise, you'll add a method named getSSN to the Validator class that was presented in chapter 7. Then, you'll use this method in a program to validate a social security number entered by the user.

1. Open the project named ch13_ex4_SSNValidator that's in the ex_starts directory. Then, open the SSNValidatorApp and Validator classes and review the code.
2. Add a method named getSSN to the Validator class that accepts and validates a social security number. This method should accept a Scanner object and a string that will be displayed to the user as a prompt. After it accepts the social security number, this method should check that the entry contains 11 characters. If it does, the method should validate the entry by checking that the first three characters are numeric digits, the fourth character is a hyphen, the fifth and sixth characters are numeric digits, the seventh character is a hyphen, and the eighth through eleventh characters are numeric digits. To check for a numeric digit, you can use a private method that tests if a character is equal to any of the numbers from 0 through 9. If the user's entry doesn't conform to this format, the method should display an error message and ask the user to enter the number again.
3. Modify the SSNValidatorApp class so it uses the getSSN method. Then, compile and run this class to make sure the validation works correctly.

14

How to handle exceptions

In chapter 5, you were introduced to the concept of exceptions and how to use the try statement to catch them. However, there's much more to exceptions than what was covered in that chapter. In this chapter, you'll learn the additional details you need to know to develop professional applications that handle all kinds of exceptions.

An introduction to exceptions

All applications encounter runtime errors. For example, a user may enter data that's not appropriate for the program, or a file that your program needs may get moved or deleted. These types of errors may cause a poorly-coded program to crash and cause the user to lose data. In contrast, when an error occurs in a well-coded program, the program will notify the user, save as much data as possible, clean up resources, and exit the program as smoothly as possible.

To help you handle errors, Java uses a mechanism known as *exception handling*. Before you learn how to handle errors, though, you need to learn about the exception hierarchy and the exception handling mechanism.

The exception hierarchy

In Java, an *exception* is an object that's created from the Exception class or one of its subclasses. An exception represents an error that has occurred, and it contains information about the error. All exception classes are derived from the Throwable class as shown by the diagram in figure 14-1.

As this diagram shows, two classes directly inherit the Throwable class: Error and Exception. The classes that inherit the Error class represent internal errors that you usually can't do anything about, such as problems with the Java runtime environment. As a result, you can ignore these errors most of the time. In contrast, you need to handle most of the exceptions that are derived from the Exception class.

The classes in the Exception hierarchy are divided into two categories: (1) exceptions that are derived from the RuntimeException class and (2) all other exceptions. The exceptions that are derived from the RuntimeException class are called *unchecked exceptions* because the compiler doesn't force you to explicitly handle them. On the other hand, the compiler requires that you explicitly handle all the other exceptions that are derived from the Exception class. As a result, these exceptions are known as *checked exceptions*.

Unchecked exceptions often occur because of coding errors. For example, if a program attempts to access an array with an invalid index, Java will throw an ArrayIndexOutOfBoundsException, which is a type of IndexOutOfBoundsException. If you're careful when you write your code, you can usually prevent these types of exceptions from being thrown.

Checked exceptions, on the other hand, usually occur due to circumstances that are beyond the programmer's control, such as a missing file or a bad network connection. Although you can't avoid these exceptions, you can write code that handles them when they occur.

The Throwable hierarchy

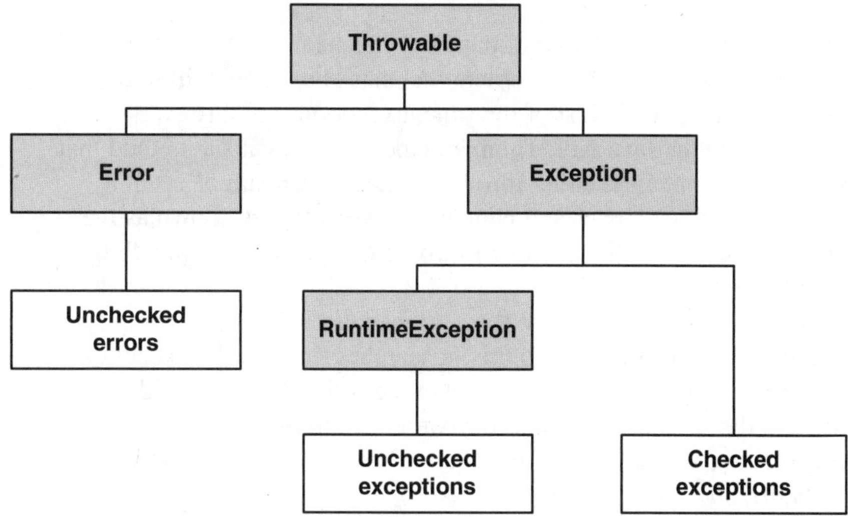

Common checked exceptions

```
ClassNotFoundException
IOException
    EOFException
    FileNotFoundException
NoSuchMethodException
```

Common unchecked exceptions

```
ArithmeticException
IllegalArgumentException
    NumberFormatException
IndexOutOfBoundsException
    ArrayIndexOutOfBoundsException
    StringIndexOutOfBoundsException
NullPointerException
InputMismatchException
```

Description

- An *exception* is an object of the Exception class or any of its subclasses. It represents a condition that prevents a method from successfully completing.
- The Exception class is derived from a class named Throwable. Two types of exceptions are derived from the Exception class: checked exceptions and unchecked exceptions.
- *Checked exceptions* are checked by the compiler. As a result, you must write code that handles all checked exceptions before you can compile your code.
- *Unchecked exceptions* are not checked by the compiler, but they can occur at runtime. It's generally considered a good practice to write code that handles unchecked exceptions. If an unchecked exception occurs and isn't handled by your code, your program will terminate.
- Like the Exception class, the Error class is also derived from the Throwable class. However, the Error class identifies internal errors that are rare and can't usually be recovered from. As a result, you can usually ignore the Error class.

Figure 14-1 The exception hierarchy

How exceptions are propagated

Figure 14-2 shows how the exception handling mechanism works in Java. To start, when a method encounters a problem that can't be solved within that method, it *throws* an exception. Most of the time, exceptions are thrown by methods from classes in the Java API. Then, any method that calls a method that throws a checked exception must either throw the exception again or catch it and handle it. The code that catches and handles the exception is known as the *exception handler*. You'll learn the details of throwing, catching, and handling exceptions in this chapter.

Once a method throws an exception, the runtime system begins looking for the appropriate exception handler. To do this, it searches through the execution *stack trace,* also called the *call stack*. The stack trace is the list of methods that have been called in the reverse order that they were called. In this diagram, for example, the stack trace when the code in MethodD executes is: MethodD, MethodC, MethodB, and MethodA.

This figure shows how MethodA calls MethodB, which calls MethodC, which calls MethodD. Here, MethodD may throw an exception. If it does, MethodD throws the exception up to MethodC, which throws it to MethodB, which throws it to MethodA, which catches it in a catch clause.

If you throw a checked exception all the way out of the program by coding a throws clause on each method in the call stack, including the main method, the program will terminate when the exception occurs. Then, Java will display information about the exception at the console.

Note that unchecked exceptions work the same way, except that you don't have to explicitly list unchecked exceptions in the throws clause of a method declaration. For example, suppose the try statement in MethodA also includes a catch clause that catches a runtime exception such as ArithmethicException. Then, if the code in MethodD throws ArithmeticException, the exception propagates up through MethodC and MethodB and is handled by the exception handler in MethodA, even though none of the method declarations include a throws clause that lists ArithmeticException.

How Java propagates exceptions

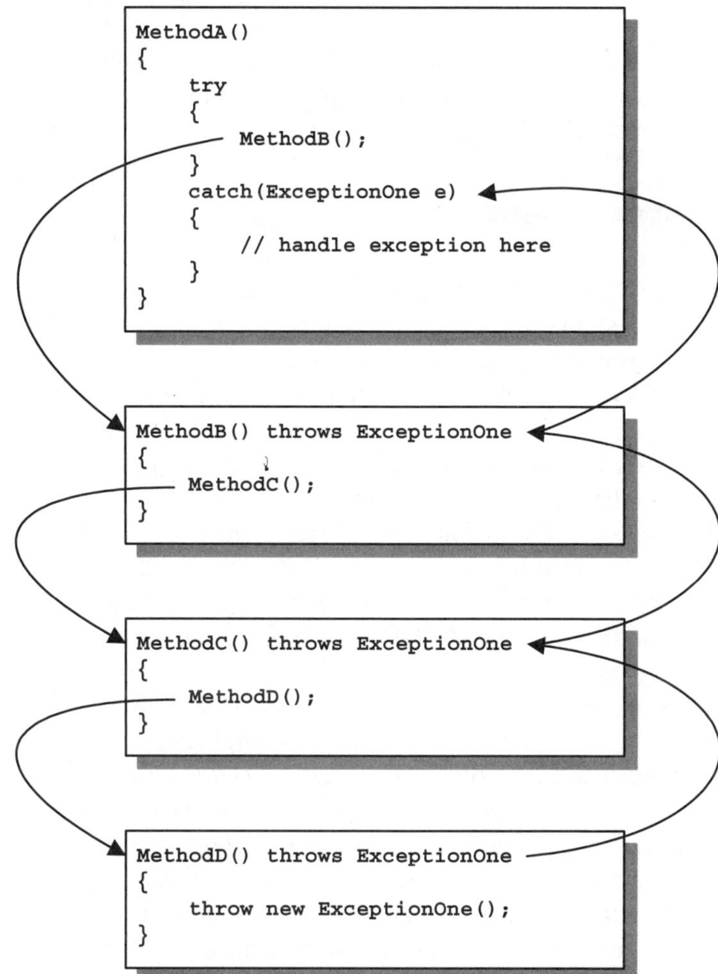

MethodA()
{
try
{
MethodB();
}
catch(ExceptionOne e)
{
// handle exception here
}
}
MethodB() throws ExceptionOne
{
MethodC();
}
MethodC() throws ExceptionOne
{
MethodD();
}
MethodD() throws ExceptionOne
{
throw new ExceptionOne();
}

Two ways to handle checked exceptions

- Throw the exception to the calling method
- Catch the exception and handle it

Description

- When a method encounters a condition it can't handle, that method should throw an exception. This allows users of the method to handle the exception in a way that's appropriate for their programs. Many methods in the Java API throw exceptions.
- When a method calls another method that throws a checked exception, the method must either throw the exception to its caller or catch the exception and handle it directly. Code that catches an exception is known as an *exception handler*.
- When an exception occurs, the runtime system looks for the appropriate exception handler. To do that, it looks through the *stack trace*, or *call stack*, which lists the methods that have been called until it finds a method that catches the exception.

Figure 14-2 How exceptions are propagated

How to work with exceptions

In the topics that follow, you'll learn some additional techniques for using the try statement. You'll also learn how to throw an exception and how to use some of the constructors and methods of the Throwable class.

How to use the try statement

Figure 14-3 starts by showing the syntax for coding a try statement that catches exceptions. This syntax shows that a *try statement* begins with a *try block* that's coded around any statements that may throw an exception. The try block is followed by a *catch block* for each type of exception that may be thrown in the try block.

When you add catch blocks, you should be sure to code them in sequence from the most specific class in the Throwable hierarchy to the least specific class. For example, the FileNotFoundException inherits IOException, so FileNotFoundException must be coded before IOException. Otherwise, the code won't compile. For exceptions that are at the same level in the exception hierarchy, such as FileNotFoundException and EOFException, the order doesn't matter.

After the catch blocks, you can code a *finally block* to free any system resources that are used by the try statement. For example, you might close files or release database connections in a finally block. The finally block is optional, but if you code it, it is always executed. This is true whether or not an exception has been thrown, and it's true even if a return statement has been executed.

The code example shows a method named readFirstLine that contains a try statement that includes two catch blocks and a finally block. This method accepts a String that specifies the path to a file, and it returns a String for the first line of the file. Within the body of the method, the first statement initializes a variable that can store a RandomAccessFile object. As you'll learn in chapter 18, this object lets you read and write data to a file.

Within the try block, the first statement creates a RandomAccessFile object for the file at the specified path. If the file doesn't exist, this constructor throws a FileNotFoundException, and program execution jumps into the first catch block. However, if the file exists, the second statement calls the readLine method of the RandomAccessFile object to read the first line of the file. If this method isn't able to read the first line, it throws an IOException and program execution jumps into the second catch block. Otherwise, the return statement in the try block returns a String object for the first line to the calling method.

Both catch blocks work similarly. To start, the first statement prints a message to the console that briefly describes the error. Then, the second statement returns a null value to the calling method. This return value is appropriate since the method was unable to read the first line of the file.

Within the finally block, the code attempts to close the RandomAccessFile object by calling its close method. Unfortunately, if the code in the try block

The syntax of the try statement

```
try {statements}
[catch (MostSpecificExceptionType e) {statements}] ...
[catch (LeastSpecificExceptionType e) {statements}]
[finally {statements}]
```

A method that catches two types of exceptions and uses a finally clause

```
public static String readFirstLine(String path)
{
    RandomAccessFile in = null;
    try
    {
        in = new RandomAccessFile(path, "r"); // may throw FileNotFound
        String line = in.readLine();          // may throw IOException
        return line;
    }
    catch (FileNotFoundException e)
    {
        System.out.println("File not found.");
        return null;
    }
    catch(IOException e)
    {
        System.out.println("I/O error occurred.");
        return null;
    }
    finally
    {
        try
        {
            if (in != null)
                in.close();                   // may throw IOException
        }
        catch (Exception e)
        {
            System.out.println("Unable to close file.");
        }
    }
}
```

Description

- You can code a *try block* around any statements that may throw an exception.
- You can code one *catch block* for each type of exception that may be thrown in the try block. You should code the catch clauses in sequence from the most specific class in the Throwable hierarchy to the least specific class.
- You can code a *finally block* to free any system resources that are used by objects created in the try block. The code in the finally block is always executed.

Figure 14-3 How to use the try statement

doesn't execute successfully, the RandomAccessFile object may contain a null value. As a result, this code checks that this object is not null before it calls its close method. In addition, the close method may throw an IOException, so you need to code a try statement within the finally block that catches this exception.

When you code try statements, it's often tempting to create empty catch clauses for checked exceptions just to get your code to compile. That's okay, as long as you remember to add appropriate exception handling code later. Unfortunately, it's all too easy to forget to do that, so the exception never gets handled. Instead, the empty catch clause catches the exception, then ignores it. This is sometimes called *swallowing an exception*, and it's rarely an acceptable coding practice.

How to use the try-with-resources statement

Prior to Java 1.7, you had to use a finally block to release system resources as you saw in the previous figure. That required including additional exception handling code in case the code in the finally block threw exceptions. Unfortunately, this exception handling code can complicate the logic of a program and make it more difficult to read and maintain.

That's why Java 1.7 introduced the *try-with-resources* statement that's described in figure 14-4. This is a special type of try statement that declares and instantiates one or more objects that use system resources and automatically closes those objects and releases the resources after the try statement finishes executing. This allows you to write less error handling code and to focus on the logic of your program. For example, the readFirstLine method in this figure accomplishes the same task as the method in the previous figure, but without the unwieldy finally clause. As a result, the code is easier to read and to maintain.

To use the try-with-resources statement, you begin by coding a set of parentheses after the try keyword but before the braces for the try block. Then, within the parentheses, you can code one or more statements that declare and instantiate objects that use system resources. In this figure, for example, the statement that creates the RandomAccessFile object is coded within these parentheses. To create more than one object, you just separate the statements that declare and instantiate them with a semicolon.

Note that you can only use the try-with-resources statement with objects that implement the java.lang.AutoCloseable interface. However, as of version 1.7 of Java, most of the classes in the Java API that work with system resources have been retrofitted to implement this interface. That includes all of the classes for working with files and databases that are described in section 5 of this book.

The syntax of the try-with-resources statement

```
try (statement[;statement] ...) {statements}
[catch (MostSpecificExceptionType e) {statements}] ...
[catch (LeastSpecificExceptionType e) {statements}]
```

A method that catches two types of exceptions and automatically closes the specified resource

```
public static String readFirstLine(String path)
{
    try (RandomAccessFile in = new RandomAccessFile(path, "r"))
    {
        String line = in.readLine();          // may throw IOException
        return line;
    }
    catch (FileNotFoundException e)
    {
        System.out.println("File not found.");
        return null;
    }
    catch(IOException e)
    {
        System.out.println("I/O error occurred.");
        return null;
    }
}
```

Description

- The *try-with-resources* statement is a special type of try statement that declares and instantiates one or more objects that use system resources and automatically closes those objects and releases the resources after the try statement finishes executing.
- The try-with-resources statement was introduced with version 1.7 of Java.
- Any object that implements the java.lang.AutoCloseable interface can be created on the try-with-resources statement.
- As of version 1.7 of Java, most of the classes in the Java API that use system resources have been retrofitted to implement the AutoCloseable interface.

Figure 14-4 How to use the try-with-resources statement

How to use the methods of an exception

Figure 14-5 shows how to use the methods of an exception to get more information about the exception. Since the Throwable class provides these methods, they are available to all exception objects.

The first example uses the first three methods in the table to print increasing amounts of information about an exception. In this case, the catch block catches an IOException object and assigns it to a variable named e. Within the catch block, the first statement uses the getMessage method to get the exception's message, and it prints this message to the console. Then, the second statement uses the toString method to get the exception's class and message, and it prints this data to the console. Next, the third statement uses the printStackTrace method to print the exception's class, message, and stack trace to the console.

When you write code that handles exceptions, you need to decide how much information is the right amount to display. For example, in some cases, you only want to use the getMessage method to display the exception's message. However, not all exceptions include messages. Because of that, it's often helpful to use the toString method to display the exception's class name and message. Other times, you may want to use the printStackTrace method to display a complete stack trace for the exception. This can help you debug your applications when you're testing them. However, it's generally considered a good practice to remove the printStackTrace method from production applications or replace it with a better way of logging exceptions.

In the first example, the statements in the catch block use the System.err object to print data to the standard error output stream. This works the same as using the System.out object to print data to the standard output stream. In NetBeans, for example, both of these objects print data to the Output window. However, the error output stream is displayed in red, which is consistent with how NetBeans displays exceptions. As a result, it's common to use the error output stream for displaying information about exceptions. You can also direct the standard output stream to one source (such as the console) and the standard error output stream to another source (such as a log file).

If you don't supply an argument for the printStackTrace method, it prints its data to the error output stream (System.err). However, if you want to print this data to another output stream such as the standard output stream (System.out), you can specify that output stream as an argument of the method. In this figure, for example, all of the statements in the second example print data to the standard output stream.

Four methods available from all exceptions

Method	Description
`getMessage()`	Returns the exception's message, if one is available.
`toString()`	Returns the exception's class name and message, if one is available.
`printStackTrace()`	Prints the exception's class name, message, and stack trace to the standard error output stream (System.err).
`printStackTrace(outputStream)`	Prints the exception's class name, message, and stack trace to the specified output stream.

Example 1: How to print exception data to the error output stream

```
catch(IOException e)
{
    System.err.println(e.getMessage() + "\n");
    System.err.println(e.toString() + "\n");
    e.printStackTrace();
    return null;
}
```

Resulting output for a FileNotFoundException

```
c:\murach\java\files\produx.txt (The system cannot find the
file specified)

java.io.FileNotFoundException: c:\murach\java\files\produx.txt
(The system cannot find the file specified)

java.io.FileNotFoundException: c:\murach\java\files\produx.txt
(The system cannot find the file specified)
  at java.io.RandomAccessFile.open(Native Method)
  at java.io.RandomAccessFile.<init>(RandomAccessFile.java:233)
  at java.io.RandomAccessFile.<init>(RandomAccessFile.java:118)
  at ProductApp.readFirstLine(ProductApp.java:70)
  at ProductApp.main(ProductApp.java:10)
```

Example 2: How to print exception data to the standard output stream

```
catch(IOException e)
{
    System.out.println(e.getMessage() + "\n");
    System.out.println(e.toString() + "\n");
    e.printStackTrace(System.out);
    return null;
}
```

Description

- The Throwable class provides methods that are available to all exceptions.
- The System.err object works like the System.out object, but it prints data to the standard error output stream instead of the standard output stream.
- It's generally considered a good practice to remove the printStackTrace method from production applications or replace it with a better way of logging exceptions.

Figure 14-5 How to use the methods of an exception

How to use a multi-catch block

Figure 14-6 shows how to use the *multi-catch block* feature that was introduced with version 1.7 of Java. This feature allows you to use a single catch block for multiple exceptions that are at the same level in the inheritance hierarchy. To do that, you separate the exceptions with a pipe character (|) as shown in the syntax at the top of this figure.

To illustrate how the multi-catch block works, the first example in this figure shows how you would catch both the FileNotFoundException and the EOFException prior to version 1.7 of Java. Here, a separate catch clause is coded for each exception. Because these exceptions are at the same level in the inheritance hierarchy, though, and because the code in the catch blocks for these exceptions are identical, you can catch them in a multi-catch block as shown in the second example.

On a related note, both FileNotFoundException and EOFException are subclasses of IOException. As a result, if you want to execute the same code for all three exceptions, you only need to code a catch block for the IOException like this:

```
try (RandomAccessFile in = new RandomAccessFile(path, "r"))
{
    String line = in.readLine();    // may throw IOException
    return line;
}
catch(IOException e)
{
    System.err.println(e.toString());
    return null;
}
```

In this case, the same code is excecuted for IOException and all of its subclasses, including the FileNotFoundException and EOFException. Although this technique doesn't provide as much flexibility as the multi-catch block feature, it's commonly used and works for all versions of Java.

The syntax of the multi-catch block

```
catch (ExceptionType | ExceptionType [| ExceptionType]... e) {statements}
```

A method that does not use a multi-catch block

```
public static String readFirstLine(String path)
{
    try (RandomAccessFile in = new RandomAccessFile(path, "r"))
    {
        String line = in.readLine();          // may throw IOException
        return line;
    }
    catch (FileNotFoundException e)
    {
        System.err.println(e.toString());
        return null;
    }
    catch (EOFException e)
    {
        System.err.println(e.toString());
        return null;
    }
    catch(IOException e)
    {
        e.printStackTrace();
        return null;
    }
}
```

A method that uses a multi-catch block

```
public static String readFirstLine(String path)
{
    try (RandomAccessFile in = new RandomAccessFile(path, "r"))
    {
        String line = in.readLine();          // may throw IOException
        return line;
    }
    catch (FileNotFoundException | EOFException e)
    {
        System.err.println(e.toString());
        return null;
    }
    catch(IOException e)
    {
        e.printStackTrace();
        return null;
    }
}
```

Description

- The *multi-catch block* allows you to use a single catch block for multiple exceptions that are at the same level in the inheritance hierarchy.
- The multi-catch block was introduced with version 1.7 of Java.

Figure 14-6 How to use a multi-catch block

How to use the throws clause

When you call a method from the Java API that throws a checked exception, you must either throw the exception or catch it. If you decide that you can't handle the exception properly in the method that you're coding, you code a throws clause on the method declaration as shown in figure 14-7. This throws the exception up to the calling method, which can handle it with an exception handler or throw it up to its calling method. If a method throws more than one exception, you can use commas to separate the exceptions in the throws clause.

The first example in this figure shows how to code a method named getFileLength that throws an IOException. Here, the first statement in this method calls the constructor of the RandomAccessFile class, which may throw a FileNotFoundException. Then, the next statement calls the length method of the RandomAccessFile object, which may throw an IOException. Since the FileNotFoundException class inherits the IOException class, a FileNotFoundException can be treated as an IOException. As a result, the declaration for the getFileLength method uses a throws clause to allow both of these exceptions to be thrown.

The second example shows how to code a method that catches the IOException that's thrown by the first example. To start, this method calls the getFileLength method shown in the first example. Then, it uses a try statement to catch and handle this exception.

Although it's not shown here, you should realize that if a method throws an exception and the code within that method throws a subclass of that exception, the calling method can catch either exception. For example, if a FileNotFoundException is thrown by the first method in this figure, the second method can catch that exception. That's true even though the throws clause on the first method doesn't include this exception.

The third example shows how to code a method that does not catch the exception that's thrown by the first example. Instead, this method throws the exception again. To start, the declaration for the method includes a throws clause that indicates that this method throws an IOException. As a result, the code for this method doesn't need to handle this exception even though it calls the getFileLength method shown in the first example.

This figure also shows an example of the type of error message that's generated by the compiler if you fail to catch or throw a checked exception. This error message would be generated if you didn't include the try statement in the second example. Similarly, this error message would be generated if you omitted the throws clause in the third example.

At this point, you may be wondering when you should throw an exception and when you should handle an exception. In general, you should throw exceptions early and catch them late. In other words, if you are at a low level in your program where you aren't able to handle the exception, you should throw it. Then, the exception will propagate up to a higher level where you can catch the exception and handle it in a way that makes sense for your program. For example, you can ask the user how to handle the exception. You can display a user-friendly error message. Or, if necessary, you can save data, close resources, and exit the program as gracefully as possible.

The syntax for the declaration of a method that throws exceptions

```
modifiers returnType methodName([parameterList]) throws exceptionList {}
```

Example 1: A method that throws an IOException

```
public static long getFileLength() throws IOException
{
    RandomAccessFile in = new RandomAccessFile(path, "r");
    long length = in.length();                      // may throw IOException
    return length;
}
```

Example 2: A method that catches the exception from example 1

```
public static int getRecordCount2()
{
    try
    {
        long length = getFileLength();              // may throw IOException
        int recordCount = (int) (length / RECORD_SIZE);
        return recordCount;
    }
    catch (IOException e)
    {
        System.err.println("An IO error occurred.");
        return 0;
    }
}
```

Example 3: A method that throws the exception from example 1

```
public static int getRecordCount3() throws IOException
{
    long length = getFileLength();                  // may throw IOException
    int recordCount = (int) (length / RECORD_SIZE);
    return recordCount;
}
```

Compiler error generated if you don't catch or throw a checked exception

```
C:\murach\java\netbeans\examples\ch14\src\ProductApp.java:12:
error: unreported exception IOException; must be caught or
declared to be thrown
        getRecordCount()
```

Description

- Any method that calls a method that throws a checked exception must either catch the exception or throw the exception. Otherwise, the program won't compile.
- To throw a checked exception, you code a throws clause in the method declaration. The throws clause must name each checked exception that's thrown up to the calling method.
- Although you can specify unchecked exceptions in the throws clause, the compiler doesn't force you to handle unchecked exceptions.

Figure 14-7 How to use the throws clause

How to use the throw statement

When you're coding a method, you may sometimes need to throw an exception. For example, you may need to throw an exception when a method encounters a problem that prevents it from completing its task, such as when the method is passed unacceptable argument values. You may also need to throw an exception to test an exception handler. Finally, you may need to throw an exception when you want to catch an exception, perform some processing, and then throw the exception again so it can be handled by the calling method.

To throw an exception, you code a throw statement that throws an object of an exception class as shown in figure 14-8. To do that, you usually use the new keyword to create an object from the exception class. Since all exception classes inherit the Throwable class, you can use either of the constructors shown in this figure to create an exception. If you use the first constructor, no message is assigned to the exception. If you use the second constructor, the message you specify is assigned to the exception.

The first example in this figure shows a method named calculateFutureValue that accepts three parameters and throws an IllegalArgumentException if any of these parameters are less than or equal to zero. In general, it's a good coding practice for any public method to throw an IllegalArgumentException if the method is passed any parameters that have unacceptable values.

The second example shows how you might throw an exception to test an exception handler. This technique is useful for exceptions that are difficult to force otherwise. For example, you can easily test a handler for FileNotFoundException by providing a file name that doesn't exist. But testing a handler for IOException can be difficult. Sometimes, the easiest way is to explicitly throw the exception at the point you would expect it to occur.

When you throw an exception for testing, the throw statement must be the last statement of the try clause, or it must be coded within an if statement. Otherwise, the code won't compile, and the compiler will display a message that indicates that the code contains unreachable statements. Because a statement is coded after the throw statement in the second example, for instance, the throw statement is coded within an if statement. Notice that this if statement is coded so its condition is always true, so the exception is always thrown. However, this if statement allows the code to compile.

The third example shows code that rethrows an exception after processing it. Here, the exception handler prints an error message that indicates an exception has occurred. Then, it rethrows the exception so the calling method can handle it. To do that, the throw statement throws the IOException object named e that was declared in the catch clause.

The syntax of the throw statement

```
throw throwableObject;
```

Common constructors of the Throwable class

Constructor	Description
`Throwable()`	Creates a new exception with a null message.
`Throwable(message)`	Creates a new exception with the specified message.

Example 1: A method that throws an unchecked exception

```
public double calculateFutureValue(double monthlyPayment,
        double monthlyInterestRate, int months)
{
    if (monthlyPayment <= 0)
        throw new IllegalArgumentException("Monthly payment must be > 0");
    if (monthlyInterestRate <= 0)
        throw new IllegalArgumentException("Interest rate must be > 0");
    if (months <= 0)
        throw new IllegalArgumentException("Months must be > 0");

    // code to calculate and return future value goes here
}
```

Example 2: Code that throws an IOException for testing purposes

```
try
{
    // code that reads the first line of a file

    if (true)
        throw new IOException("I/O exception test");

    return firstLine;
}
catch (IOException e)
{
   // code to handle IOException goes here
}
```

Example 3: Code that rethrows an exception

```
try
{
    // code that throws IOException goes here
}
catch (IOException e)
{
   System.out.println("IOException thrown in getFileLength method.");
   throw e;
}
```

Description

- You use the throw statement to throw an exception. You can throw any object that's created from a subclass of the Throwable class.
- You can use the constructors of the Throwable class to create a new exception. Then, you can throw that exception. To throw an existing exception, you must first catch it.

Figure 14-8 How to use the throw statement

How to work with custom exception classes

Although the Java API contains a wide range of exceptions, you may encounter a situation where none of those exceptions describes your exception accurately. If so, you can code a class that defines a custom exception as described in the following topics. Then, you can throw your exception just as you would throw any other exception.

How to create your own exception class

Figure 14-9 shows how to create your own custom exception class. To do that, you inherit the Exception class or one of its subclasses to create a checked exception. To illustrate, the first example in this figure shows an exception class named DAOException that inherits the Exception class. As a result, DAOException is a checked exception. However, you can also code a class that defines an unchecked exception by inheriting the RuntimeException class or one of its subclasses.

By convention, all exception classes should have a default constructor that doesn't accept any arguments and another constructor that accepts a string argument. That way, your exception class will behave like the rest of the exception classes in the Java API. You can see these two constructors in the first example. Notice that the second constructor calls the constructor of the Exception class, passing it the message that it received via the parameter.

The second example shows code that throws the custom DAOException. This example defines a method named getProduct, which calls a method named readProduct to retrieve a Product object for a specified product code. The readProduct method throws an IOException, which is caught by the catch clause. The catch clause then throws a DAOException.

The third example shows code that catches the custom exception. Here, the getProduct method is called in a try statement and the DAOException is caught by the catch clause. In the exception handler for the DAOException, an error message is displayed at the console.

At first glance, it might seem that the custom exception defined by these examples isn't necessary. After all, couldn't the getProduct method simply throw an IOException if an IO error occurs? Although it could, that would result in a poor design because it would expose too many details of the getProduct method's operation. An IOException can occur only when file I/O operations are used. As a result, throwing IOException would reveal that the getProduct method uses file I/O to access the product data.

What if the application is changed so the product data is kept in a database instead of a file? In that case, the getProduct method would throw some type of database exception instead of an IOException. Then, any methods that call the getProduct method would have to be changed to handle the new exception. By

Example 1: Code for the DAOException class

```
public class DAOException extends Exception
{
    public DAOException()
    {
    }

    public DAOException(String message)
    {
        super(message);
    }
}
```

Example 2: A method that throws the DAOException

```
public static Product getProduct(String productCode)
    throws DAOException
{
    try
    {
        Product p = readProduct(productCode);     // may throw IOException
        return p;
    }
    catch (IOException e)
    {
        throw new DAOException(
            "An error occurred while reading the product.");
    }
}
```

Example 3: Code that catches the DAOException

```
try
{
    Product p = getProduct("1234");
}
catch (DAOException e)
{
    System.out.println(e.getMessage());
}
```

When to define your own exceptions

- When a method requires an exception that isn't provided by any of Java's exception types
- When using a built-in Java exception would inappropriately expose details of a method's operation

Description

- To define a checked exception, inherit the Exception class or any of its subclasses.
- To define an unchecked exception, inherit the RuntimeException class or any of its subclasses.
- By convention, each exception class should contain a default constructor that doesn't accept any arguments and another constructor that accepts a string argument.

Figure 14-9 How to create your own exception class

creating a custom DAOException for the getProduct method, you can hide the details of how the getProduct method works from methods that call it. So even if the application is changed to use a database, the getProduct method can still throw DAOException if an error occurs while retrieving a product object.

How to use exception chaining

You'll often throw custom exceptions in response to other exceptions that occur. For example, in the previous figure, DAOException was thrown in response to IOException. Unfortunately, information about the underlying error that led to the DAOException is lost. And that information might prove invaluable to determining what caused the DAOException to occur.

Figure 14-10 shows how you can throw a custom exception without losing the details of the original exception that was thrown. This feature is called *exception chaining* because it lets you chain exceptions together. Whenever you create a custom exception type, it's a good practice to use exception chaining to avoid losing valuable debugging information.

To use exception chaining, you use an exception constructor that lets you specify an exception object as the cause for the new exception you're creating. Then, you can use the getCause method to retrieve the original exception object.

The first example in this figure shows a version of the DAOException class that lets you specify a cause via the constructor. As you can see, the second constructor accepts a Throwable object as a parameter. Then, it passes this parameter on to the Exception constructor.

The second example shows code that throws a DAOException in response to an IOException. Here, the IOException object is passed to the DAOException constructor as an argument. That way, all of the information contained in the original IOException will be saved as part of the DAOException object.

The third example shows code that catches a DAOException and displays information about the cause of the exception. Here, an error message is displayed to indicate that a DAOException has occurred. Then, the getCause method is used to retrieve the original exception, and the toString method is used to display information about the original exception. Notice here that the output from the toString method includes the class name and message. To include the message, I used a throw statement like the one in the second example in figure 14-8 to throw the IOException.

Constructors and methods of the Throwable class for exception chaining

Constructor	Description
`Throwable(cause)`	Creates a new exception with the specified exception object as its cause.
`Throwable(message, cause)`	Creates a new exception with the specified message and cause.
Method	**Description**
`getCause()`	Returns the exception object that represents this exception's cause.
`initCause(cause)`	Sets the exception's cause to the specified exception. Note that this method can be called only once. If you initialize the cause via the constructor, you can't call this method at all.

Example 1: A custom exception class that uses exception chaining

```
public class DAOException extends Exception
{
    public DAOException()
    {
    }

    public DAOException(Throwable cause)
    {
        super(cause);
    }
}
```

Example 2: Code that throws a DAOException with chaining

```
catch (IOException e)
{
    throw new DAOException(e);
}
```

Example 3: Code that catches a DAOException and displays the cause

```
catch (DAOException e)
{
    System.out.println("DAOException: Error reading the product");
    System.out.println(e.getCause().toString());
}
```

Resulting output

```
DAOException: Error reading the product
java.io.IOException: I/O exception test
```

Description

- *Exception chaining* lets you maintain exception information for exceptions that are caught when new exceptions are thrown. Exception chaining uses the cause field, which represents the original exception that caused the current exception to be thrown.

Figure 14-10 How to use exception chaining

How to work with assertions

An *assertion* is a type of statement that was introduced with version 1.4 of Java. It lets you test that a condition is true at a particular point in your application. And that can help you to be more confident that the application is working correctly.

Assertions work differently than most Java statements because they can be enabled or disabled. By default, assertions are disabled so your applications run efficiently. However, when you're testing and debugging an application, you can enable assertions so they're tested as the program executes.

How to code assert statements

Figure 14-11 shows how to code an assert statement. To start, you code the assert keyword followed by an expression that evaluates to true or false. Then, if you want to include a message that's displayed if the condition is false, you code a colon followed by a string expression.

The example in this figure shows an assert statement that specifies that the future value of a series of monthly investments should be greater than the sum of all of the investments. This is a reasonable assertion because the future value should include the investments plus the interest earned on those investments. Because the future value calculation isn't coded correctly in this figure, however, this condition evaluates to false. As a result, if assertions are enabled, the assert statement throws an AssertionError at runtime and prints information to the standard error stream as shown in this figure.

How to enable and disable assertions

Figure 14-11 also shows how to enable and disable assertions. The technique you use depends on the tool that you're using to work with Java. For NetBeans, you enable assertions by adding the –ea switch to the VM Options text box in the Project Properties dialog box. Then, assertions are enabled when you run that project, and they remain enabled until you remove this switch. Note that you should add this switch to the beginning of the options or it may not work correctly.

Since assertions can be enabled or disabled, it's critical that they only test a Boolean condition and don't perform any tasks. For example, you wouldn't want an assert statement to update a counter variable. If it did, the application would work differently depending on whether assertions were enabled or disabled.

The syntax of the assert statement

```
assert booleanExpression [: message ];
```

Code that makes a reasonable assertion about a calculation

```
for (int i = 1; i <= months; i++)
{
    futureValue =
        (futureValue + monthlyInvestment) * monthlyInterestRate;
}
// future value should be at least monthlyInvestment * months
assert (futureValue > monthlyInvestment * months) : "FV out of range";
```

The output that's displayed when an assertion exception is thrown

```
Exception in thread "main" java.lang.AssertionError: FV out of range
    at FutureValueApp.calculateFutureValue(FutureValueApp.java:152)
    at FutureValueApp.main(FutureValueApp.java:27)
```

NetBean's Project Properties dialog box with the -ea switch set

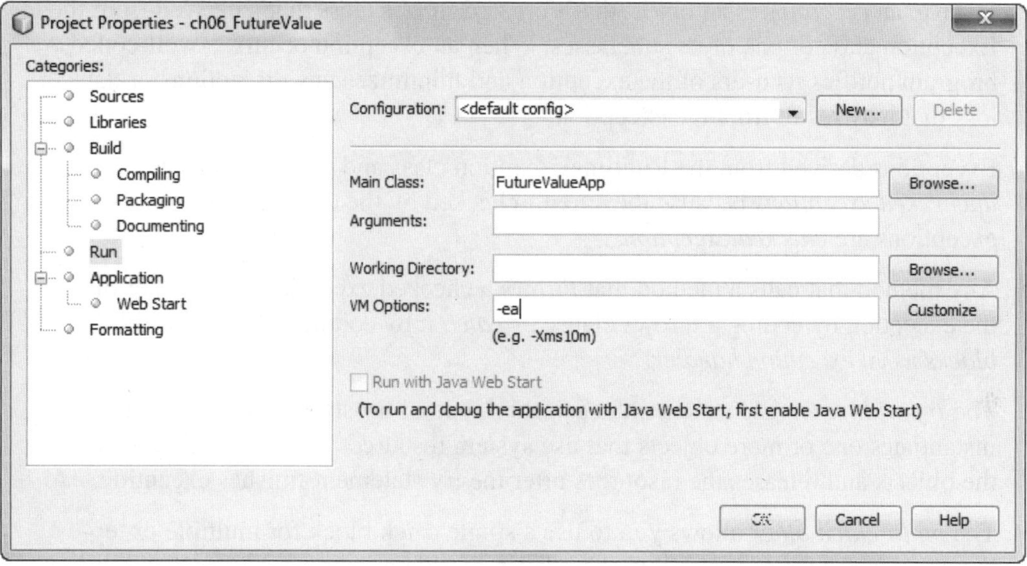

Description

- The assert statement was introduced with Java 1.4. You can use this statement to code an *assertion*, which is a condition that should be true at a particular point in your application.
- Assertions are disabled by default. To enable assertions from NetBeans, right-click on the project, choose the Properties command, select the Run group, and enter -ea in the VM Options text box.
- If assertions are enabled, the JRE evaluates assert statements and throws an AssertionError if the condition specified by the assert statement is false. If the assert statement specifies a message, the message is included in the AssertionError.
- An assert statement shouldn't include any code that performs a task. If it does, the program will run differently depending on whether assertions are enabled or disabled.

Figure 14-11 How to work with assertions

Perspective

In this chapter, you learned the most important techniques for handling exceptions in Java. Unfortunately, exception handling is one of the more troublesome aspects of any serious application development. The essential problem of exception handling is that exceptions are usually thrown at the lowest levels of an application, but should be handled at the highest levels. For example, a getProduct method that retrieves Product objects probably has no idea what should be done if an IO error occurs. So this low-level method throws an exception that's handled by a higher-level method, which can write the exception to an error log, display an error message, or even terminate the application. In short, exception handling usually affects every level of an application's design.

Summary

- In Java, an *exception* is an object that's created from a class that's derived from the Exception class or one of its subclasses. When an exception occurs, a well-coded program notifies its users of the exception and minimizes any disruptions or data loss that may result from the exception.
- Exceptions derived from the RuntimeException class and its subclasses are *unchecked exceptions* because they aren't checked by the compiler. All other exceptions are *checked exceptions*.
- Any method that calls a method that *throws* a checked exception must either throw the exception by coding a throws clause or *catch* it by coding *try/catch/finally blocks* as an *exception handler*.
- The *try-with-resources* statement is a special type of try statement that declares and instantiates one or more objects that use system resources and automatically closes the objects and releases the resources after the try statement finishes executing.
- The *multi-catch block* allows you to use a single catch block for multiple exceptions that are at the same level in the inheritance hierarchy.
- When coding your own methods, if you encounter a potential error that can't be handled within that method, you can code a *throw statement* that throws the exception to another method. If you can't find an appropriate exception class in the Java API, you can code your own exception class.
- You can create custom exception classes to represent exceptions your methods might throw. This is often useful to hide the details of how a method is implemented.
- When you create custom exceptions, you can use *exception chaining* to save information about the cause of an exception.
- An *assertion* lets you test that a condition is true at a specific point in an application.

Exercise 14-1 Throw and catch exceptions

In this exercise, you'll experiment with ways to throw and catch exceptions.

1. Open the project named ch14_ex1_ExceptionTester in the ex_starts directory. Then, open the ExceptionTesterApp class and review its code. Run this class to get a feel for how it works.
2. Add code to Method3 that throws an unchecked exception by attempting to divide an integer by zero. Compile and run the program and note where the exception is thrown.
3. Delete the code you just added to Method3. Then, add a statement to this method like the one in figure 14-7 that creates an object from the RandomAccessFile class, but use the string "products.ran" in place of the path variable. The constructor for this class throws a checked exception named FileNotFoundException. Note the error message that indicates that you haven't handled the exception. If this error message isn't shown, compile the class to display the error message.
4. Add throws clauses to all of the methods including the main method. Then, run the program to see how a checked exception can propagate all the way out of a program.
5. Add the code necessary to handle the FileNotFoundException in Method1. To do that, you'll need to remove the throws clauses from the main method and Method1, and you'll need to add a try statement to Method1 that catches the exception. The catch block should display an appropriate error message. Run the program to make sure the exception handler works.

Exercise 14-2 Release system resources

In this exercise, you'll get a chance to use try and a try-with-resources statements to release the system resources used by an object.

1. Open the project named ch14_ex2_ResourcesTester in the ex_starts directory. Then, open the ResourcesTesterApp class. Note that the main method calls two other methods that open a RandomAccessFile object but don't close it.
2. Modify the method named readLineWithResources so it uses a try-with-resources statement to close the RandomAccessFile object. Run the program to make sure it works correctly. If it does, the try-with-resources statement is working correctly too.
3. Modify the method named readLineWithFinally so it uses a finally block to close the RandomAccessFile object. To do that, you'll need to declare this object outside the try block. Add statements to the finally block that print information to the console to indicate whether the file was closed (this is typical for normal operations), never opened (which happens if the file can't be found), or unable to close (which happens only in rare cases).
4. Run the program to make sure the finally clause works as expected. To test what happens if the file is never opened, you can change the name of the file to cause

a FileNotFoundException. To test what happens if the close method doesn't work, you can throw an IOException just before the statement that closes the resource.

Exercise 14-3 Create a custom class

In this exercise, you'll experiment with custom classes and chained exceptions.

1. Open the project named ch14_ex3_CustomTester in the ex_starts directory. Then, create a custom checked exception class named TestException that contains two constructors: one that accepts no parameters and one that accepts a message.
2. Open the CustomTesterApp class. Then, add a statement to Method3 that throws a TestException without a message. Add the code necessary to catch this exception in Method2. The catch block should print a message of your choice at the console. Run the program to make sure it works correctly.
3. Modify your solution so that a custom message of your choice is passed to the TestException and is then displayed in the catch block. Run the program to make sure the custom message is displayed correctly.
4. Add another constructor to the TestException class that accepts a Throwable object as a parameter.
5. Add a try statement to Method3 of the CustomTesterApp class. The try clause should throw an IOException, and the catch clause should throw a TestException, passing the IOException to its constructor.
6. Modify the catch block in Method2 that catches the TestException so it includes two statements. The first statement should print a message that indicates that a TestException occurred, and the second statement should print a message that gives information about the underlying cause of the exception. Run the application to make sure it works correctly.

Exercise 14-4 Use the assert statement

In this exercise, you'll add an assert statement to the Invoice application of chapter 4 so you can see how it works.

1. Open the project named ch14_ex4_Invoice in the ex_starts directory. Then, open the InvoiceApp class. Note that the statement that calculates the invoice total has been changed so it adds the discount amount to the subtotal instead of subtracting it.
2. Add an assert statement that tests that the calculated invoice total is always less than or equal to the subtotal entered by the user. Include an appropriate message to be displayed if this assertion is false. Then, run the application to see that this statement isn't executed by default.
3. Enable assertions, and then run the program again. This time, an assertion error should occur and the message you specified should be displayed.

Section 4

GUI programming with Swing

So far in this book, all of the applications have been *console applications*. That means they interact with the user through a console window, one line at a time. Of course, console-style I/O was abandoned long ago in favor of *graphical user interfaces* (*GUIs*), such as the interface used by Microsoft Windows and the Macintosh operating system.

In this section, you'll learn how to develop GUI applications using the popular GUI library known as *Swing* and the popular *Swing GUI Builder* (formerly Project Matisse) that comes with NetBeans. First, chapter 15 shows how to develop a simple GUI application that provides for data validation. Then, chapter 16 shows how to use the most popular types of user interface controls, such as combo boxes and radio buttons, and it shows how to use some advanced event handling features.

Chapter 17 shows you how to develop a special type of application known as an *applet*. This type of application can be run within a web browser. To create the user interface for this type of program, you use the same skills as you do for creating a regular Swing application. For this reason, you should read at least chapter 15 before you read chapter 17.

Before you continue, you should know that there is a library other than Swing that's sometimes used to develop GUI applications. This library is known as the *Standard Widget Toolkit* (*SWT*), and it was created because of the performance problems with early versions of Swing. Fortunately, these performance problems have been solved to a large extent in later versions of Swing.

Although you can build powerful GUI applications with either library, Swing has two main advantages. First, it is part of the Java API so you don't have to add any additional libraries to your application. Second, it is completely portable so you know that it works the same on all operating systems. As a result, it makes sense for most programmers to learn Swing first. Then, if Swing isn't adequate for your applications, you can learn more about SWT.

15

How to develop a form

The NetBeans IDE provides an excellent tool for building graphical user interfaces (GUIs). This tool is known as the Swing GUI builder, and it is considered by many to be the leading tool for building GUIs using Swing components. In a moment, you'll learn how to use the Swing GUI builder to develop a GUI application. But first, you'll be introduced to some basic terminology related to graphical user interfaces.

An introduction to Swing

In this chapter, you'll learn how to create graphical user interfaces using classes from the javax.swing package. These classes are known as *Swing*, or the *Swing set*.

The user interface for the Future Value Calculator application

Figure 15-1 presents the graphical user interface for the Future Value Calculator application that's presented in this chapter. This shows some of the terminology that Java uses for working with GUIs. For example, Java calls a "decorated" window a *frame*, which is also known as a *form*. In other words, a frame (or form) is a window that contains a title bar with an icon, a title, a Minimize button, a Maximize button, and a Close button.

In this figure, the form contains ten controls: four *labels*, four *text fields* (also called text boxes), and two *buttons*. Here, the fourth text field has been modified so it can display output but it can't accept input from the user. In this chapter, you'll learn how to add these components to a form.

A user can use this application to calculate the future valuc of a monthly investment. To start, the user enters appropriate numbers into the first three text fields. Then, the user selects the Calculate button. One way to do that is to click on the button. Another way is to press the Alt key and the shortcut key for the button at the same time. In this figure, for example, the user can press Alt+C to select the Calculate button. (Notice that the letter C on this button is underlined.) Still another way is to press the Tab key to move the focus to the Calculate button and then press the spacebar. Whatever technique is used, the application displays the future value in the fourth text field.

By default, Swing components look and act the same on any platform. This is known as the *Metal look and feel*. However, these components look and act slightly different than the components that are native to a particular platform. For example, the user interface shown in this figure looks slightly different than a native Windows user interface. Although Swing provides classes that let programmers set the look and feel of a user interface to a particular platform, the Metal look and feel is appropriate for most programs. As a result, that's the look and feel that this book uses for all of its applications.

The user interface for the Future Value Calculator application

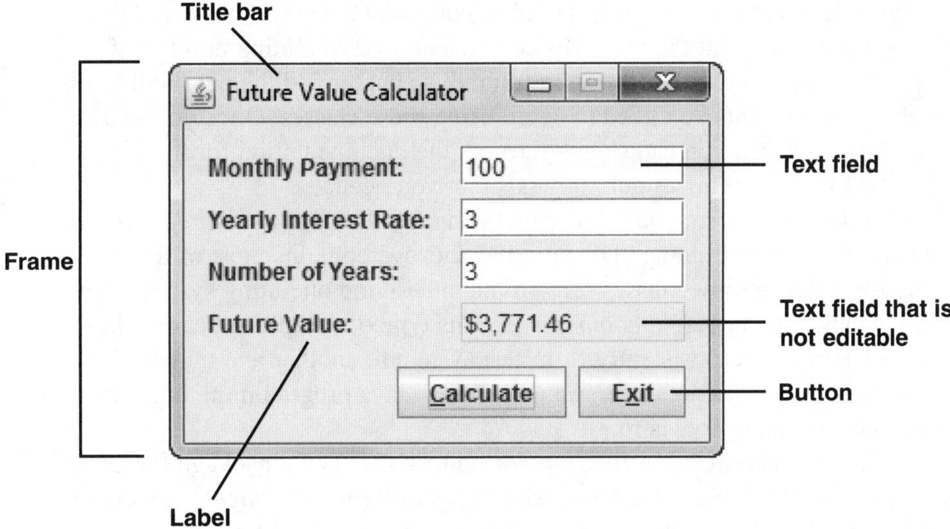

Description

- The window that contains the GUI is called a *frame*, or *form*.
- The form in this figure contains ten controls: four *labels*, four *text fields*, and two *buttons*.
- The last text field in this figure is not editable. As a result, this text field can display output, but the user can't enter data into it.
- To calculate a future value, the user enters or changes the monthly payment amount, the yearly interest rate, and the number of years. Then, the user selects the Calculate button.
- To exit the program, the user selects the Exit button.
- To select a button, the user can click on the button, press the Alt key and the shortcut key for the button at the same time, or use the Tab key to move the focus to the button and then press the spacebar.

Figure 15-1 The user interface for the Future Value Calculator application

The inheritance hierarchy for Swing components

Figure 15-2 presents a simplified inheritance hierarchy for user interface programming. Although the Java API contains an overwhelming number of classes and methods for GUI programming, this chapter and the next will teach you all of the concepts you need to begin using these classes. Once you understand these concepts, you can search through the documentation for the Java API to find the other classes and methods that you need.

When Java was first released, it contained only the *Abstract Window Toolkit* (*AWT*) for GUI programming. The java.awt package contains most of the classes for the AWT. Since these classes rely on the underlying operating system, they are often called *heavyweight components*. This type of component can make your code perform inconsistently from one system to another and thus difficult to debug. Instead of “write once, run anywhere,” Java programming becomes “write once, debug everywhere.”

That’s why version 1.2 of the JDK introduced the Swing package for GUI programming. The Swing classes consist of *lightweight components*, which are written entirely in Java and don’t rely on the underlying operating system as much. However, since Swing classes are derived from classes in the AWT, you need to understand how the AWT works. In fact, you need to use classes and methods from the AWT just to create a simple GUI like the one shown in this chapter.

The hierarchy shown in this figure includes a mixture of Swing and AWT classes. Many of the Swing classes shown in this figure also have corresponding AWT classes that aren’t shown. You can tell which of the classes in this figure are Swing classes because they all begin with the letter J. Thus, JComponent and JFrame are Swing classes as are the classes for the individual controls. In contrast, the Component, Container, Window, and Frame classes are AWT classes.

Although Swing frames are derived from the AWT Frame and Window classes, the other Swing components shown in this figure are derived from the JComponent class. In other words, Swing labels, text fields, and buttons all inherit JComponent.

The Component hierarchy

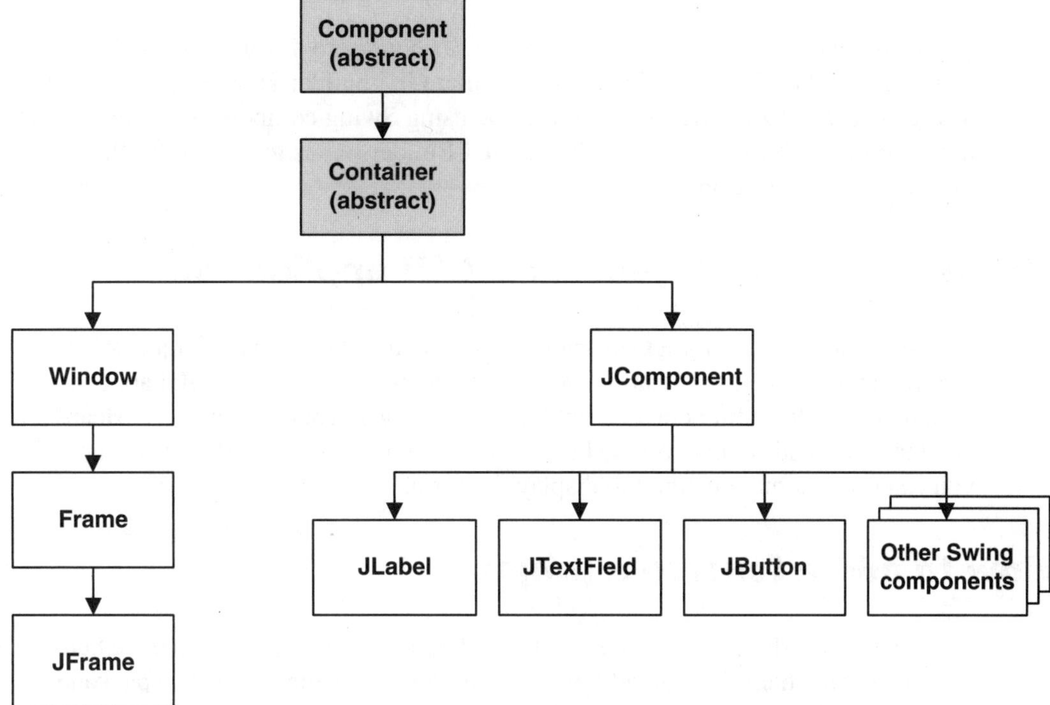

A summary of the classes

Class	Description
Component	An abstract base class that defines any object that can be displayed. For instance, frames, buttons, labels, and text fields are derived from this class.
Container	An abstract class that defines any component that can contain other components.
Window	The AWT class that defines a window without a title bar or border.
Frame	The AWT class that defines a window with a title bar and border.
JFrame	The Swing class that defines a window with a title bar and border.
JComponent	A base class for Swing components such as JButton, JLabel, and JTextField.

Description

- The *Abstract Window Toolkit* (*AWT*) is an older technology for creating GUIs that look and act a little different on different platforms. The AWT classes are stored in the java.awt package.
- *Swing* is a newer technology that creates GUIs that are consistent from platform to platform. The Swing classes are stored in the javax.swing package. All Swing classes begin with the letter J.
- The *Standard Widget Toolkit* (*SWT*) is another GUI library that isn't used as often as Swing and isn't described in this chapter.

Figure 15-2 The inheritance hierarchy for Swing components

How to design a form

Most developers use a tool known as a *GUI builder* to develop forms. As I mentioned earlier, NetBeans includes a popular GUI builder known as the *Swing GUI Builder* that lets you build GUIs using Swing components. In this topic, you'll learn how to use the Swing GUI Builder to design a form for the Future Value application.

How to create a project for a GUI application

To create a project for a GUI application, you use the same technique you use for any other Java application. When you create a project for a GUI application, though, you should create it without a main class. That's because NetBeans automatically adds a main method to a form that you add to the project. Then, you can use that main method to display the form.

How to add a form to a project

Figure 15-3 shows the dialog box for adding a form to a project. Notice here that the form, which I've named FutureValueFrame, is being stored in a package named murach.ui (ui stands for user interface). When you develop GUI applications, you'll typically store the forms for the application in a separate package. Before you add the first form to a project, then, you should create that package.

For most GUI applications, you base the form on the JFrame class. However, it's also possible to base a form on other classes. If, for example, you want to create a form that can be displayed in a browser, you can base the form on the JApplet class. You'll learn more about this class and how you use it to create applets in chapter 17 of this book.

The New JFrame Form dialog box

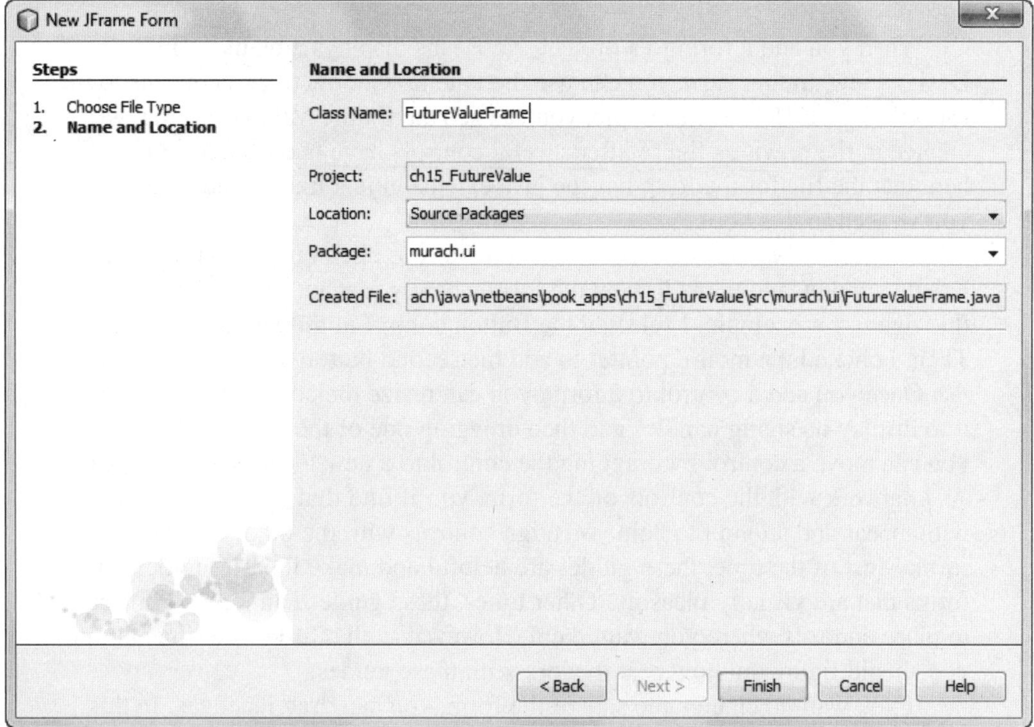

Description

- Before you add the first form to a project, you should create a package to hold the forms for the application.
- To add a form to a package, right-click on the package and select the New→JFrame Form command. Then, enter a class name in the resulting dialog box.

Notes

- When you create a project for a GUI application, you should create it without a main class. Then, you can use the class that defines the first form of the application as the main class.
- If the JFrame Form command isn't available from the New menu, the GUI Builder plugin may not be activated. To activate this plugin, select the Tools→Plugins command and display the Installed tab of the resulting dialog box. Then, locate the GUI Builder plugin, select the check box for this plugin, and click the Activate button.

How to add controls to a form

When you add a form to a project, NetBeans displays a blank form in Design view. In this view, you can use the Palette window to add controls to the form. In figure 15-4, for example, you can see the Future Value form that was created in the previous figure after several controls have been added to it. Notice here that the file for the form has the java extension just like all the other files you've seen in this book.

The easiest way to add a control to a form is to click on the control in the Palette window and then click on the form where you want to add the control. In this figure, for example, I selected the Button control in the Palette window. Then, I clicked the mouse pointer to add the second button to the form.

Once you add a control to a form, you can resize the control by clicking on it to display its sizing handles and then dragging one of the handles. Similarly, you can move a control by dragging the control to a new location on the form. As you work with the controls on the form, you'll find that alignment guides will appear and attempt to help you align controls with the other controls on the form. Most of the time, these guides are helpful and make it easier to develop forms that are visually pleasing. Other times, these guides can make it difficult to place controls where you want them. However, with a little experimentation, you should figure out how best to work with these guides.

If you want to change the size of the form, you can drag its edges. In this figure, for example, the form is too tall and too wide for the controls. As a result, it makes sense to drag the bottom and right sides of the form to make it smaller.

If you need to work with several controls at the same time, you can do that by holding down the Ctrl key as you click on the controls. Or, you can click on a blank spot in the form and drag an outline around the controls you want to select. Then, you can work with the selected controls as a group. For example, you can align a group of selected controls by clicking one of the alignment buttons in the toolbar at the top of the form window.

A form after some controls have been added to it

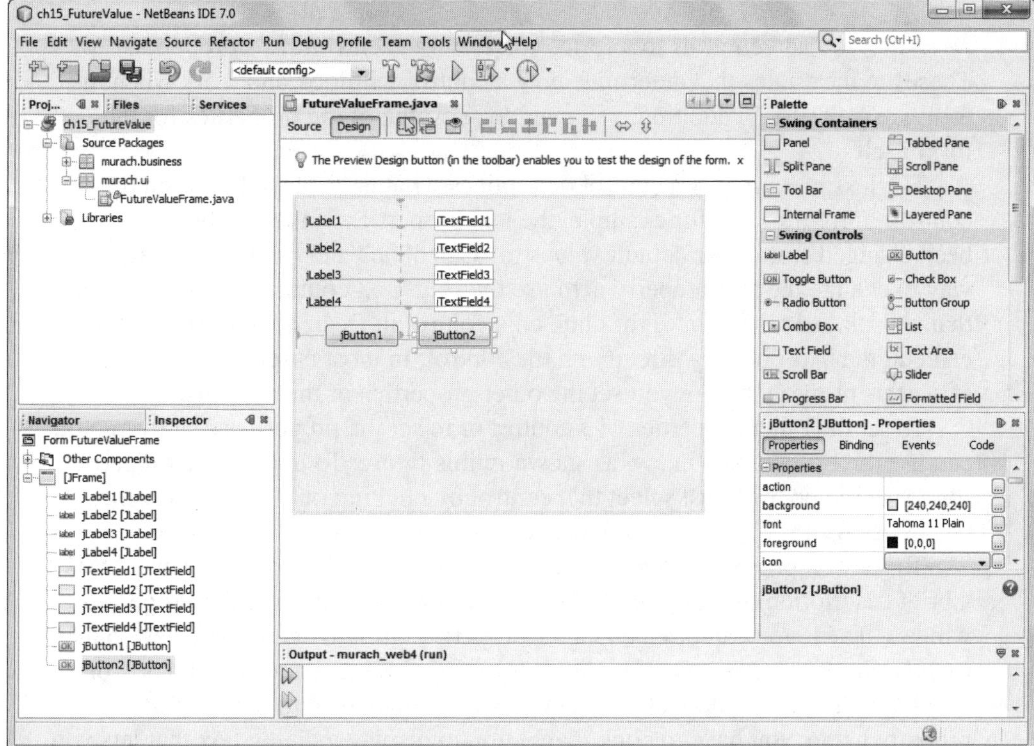

Description

- To open a form, double-click on the .java file for the form in the Projects window.
- You can display a form in two views in NetBeans. Design view shows a graphical representation of the form, and Source view shows the source code for the form.
- To switch between Design view and Source view, click on the Design and Source buttons in the toolbar at the top of the form window.
- To add a control to a form, select the control in the Palette window and then click on the form where you want to place the control. If the Palette window isn't displayed, you can display it by using the Window→Palette command.
- To select a control, click on it. To move a control, drag it. To size a control, select it and drag one of its handles. To change the size of the form, drag its edges.
- To select a group of controls, hold down the Ctrl key as you click on each control. Or, click on a blank spot in the form and drag an outline around the controls.
- To move a group of controls, drag one of them. To align a group of controls, use the buttons in the toolbar at the top of the form window.

How to set properties

After you add controls to a form, you can set each control's *properties*. These are the values that determine how a control will look and work when the form is displayed. In addition, you need to set some of the properties for the form itself.

The text property for a control determines what is displayed in or on the control. In figure 15-5, for example, the text properties of the two buttons have been changed from their default values to "Calculate" and "Exit." The easiest way to change the text property is to use the Edit Text command from the menu that's displayed when you right-click on a control in Design view. Then, you can edit the text property directly on the control. In most cases, it makes sense to set this property before you set the other properties of the controls.

To set the other properties of a control or to set the properties of a form, you can use the Properties window as shown in this figure. To display the properties for a specific control, just select that control by clicking on it. To display the properties for the form, click any blank area of the form.

To select a property in the Properties window, just click on it. When you do, a brief description of that property is displayed at the bottom of the Properties window. Then, you can often change a property setting by entering a new value to the right of the property name or by selecting a value from a combo box or check box. However, if an ellipsis button (...) is displayed to the right of the property name, you have to click that button to display a dialog box that lets you change the property.

As you work with properties, you'll find that most are set the way you want them by default. In addition, some properties are set interactively as you size and position the form and its controls in Design view. As a result, you usually need to change just a few properties for each control.

When you change a property from the default value, the property is displayed in bold in the Properties window. As a result, you can easily identify all properties that you've changed. In this figure, for example, the mnemonic and text properties for the Exit button have been changed from their defaults.

A form after the properties have been set

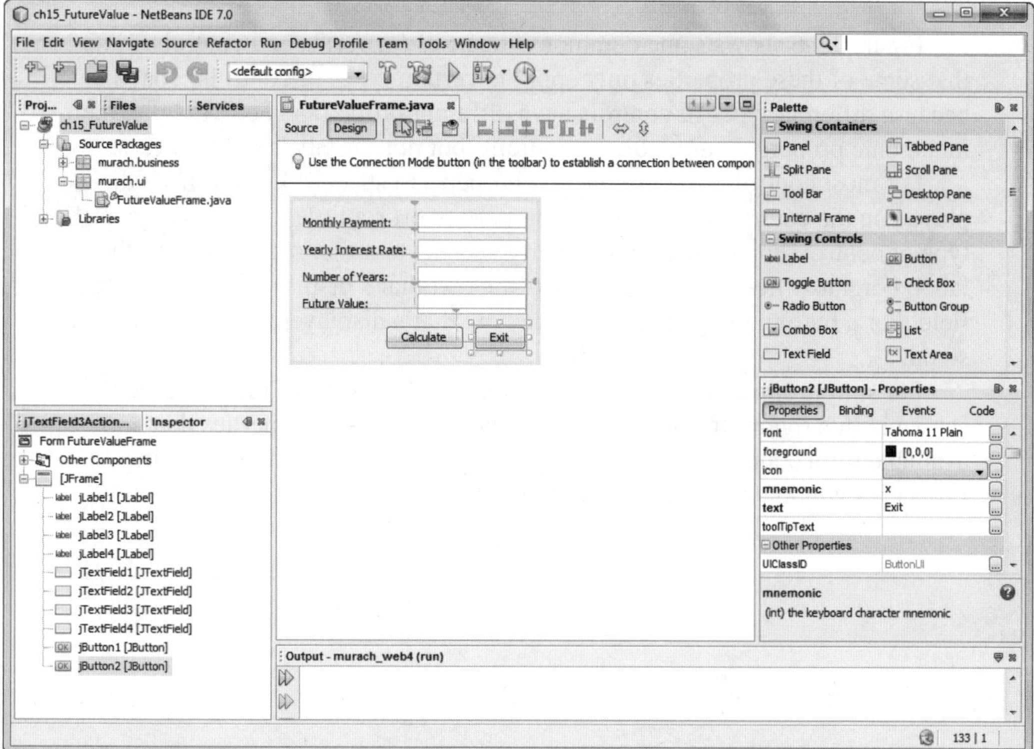

Description

- To set a property for a control, select the control and then use the Properties window to change the property.
- You can also change the text property for a control by right-clicking the control, selecting the Edit Text command, and entering new text for the control.
- To set a property for more than one control at the same time, select the controls and use the Properties window to change the property.
- To set a property for a form, click outside the controls to select the JFrame object.
- The properties that have been changed from their default values are displayed in bold in the Properties window.
- To sort the properties of a control by category or name, right-click in the Properties window and select the Sort by Category or Sort by Name command.
- To search for a specific property when the focus is in the Properties window, type the starting letter or letters of the property. This starts the Quick Search feature.
- A description of the currently selected property is normally displayed at the bottom of the properties window. If this description isn't shown, right-click in the Properties window and select Show Description Area.

Common properties for forms and controls

Figure 15-6 shows some common properties for forms and controls. Note that some of these properties only apply to certain types of controls. That's because different types of controls have different properties. For example, the mnemonic property is available for buttons, but not for labels or text fields.

For most controls, you use the text property to specify the text that's displayed on the control. However, this property works a little differently for each type of control. For a label, this property sets the text that's displayed by the label. For a text field, this property sets the text that's displayed within the text field. For a button, this property sets the text that's displayed on the button. And so on.

For simple applications, you'll probably need to use just the properties shown in this figure. If you want to learn about the other properties that are available for a control, though, you can select the control and then use the Properties window to review its properties.

Common properties for forms

Property	Description
`title`	Sets the text that's displayed in the title bar for the frame.
`defaultCloseOperation`	Sets the action that's performed when the user clicks on the Close button in the upper right corner of the frame. The default value, EXIT_ON_CLOSE, causes the application to exit.
`resizable`	Determines whether the user can resize the frame by dragging its edges.

Common properties for controls

Property	Description
`text`	Sets the text that's displayed on the control.
`editable`	Determines whether the user can edit the text that's stored in the control. Typically used for text fields and other controls that contain text.
`enabled`	Determines whether a control is enabled or disabled.
`focusable`	Determines whether the control accepts the focus when the user presses the Tab key to move the focus through the controls on the form.
`horizontalAlignment`	Determines how the text on a button or in a text field is aligned: left, right, center, trailing, or leading.
`mnemonic`	Specifies a keyboard character that allows the user to quickly access the control by holding down the Alt key and pressing the specified character. Typically used for buttons.
`preferredSize`	Sets the width and height in pixels for the control.

Description

- To learn about the properties that are available for a control, you can select the control, use the Properties window to scroll through its properties, and read the descriptions for each property.

Figure 15-6 Common properties for forms and controls

How to add code to a form

After you add controls to a form and set their properties, you can run the form and it should display properly. However, you won't be able to interact with the controls on the form until you add the required Java code. You'll learn how to do that in the topics that follow. But first, you'll learn how to set the variable names that you'll use to refer to controls in code.

How to set the variable name for a control

When you add a control to a form, NetBeans creates a generic variable name for the control. For example, it uses JTextField1 for the name of the first JTextField control you add to the form, JTextField2 for the name of the second JTextField control you add, and so on. Before you write code that uses any of the controls on a form, you should change these generic names to meaningful names that are easier to remember and use.

As figure 15-7 shows, you can set the variable name for a control using the Properties window. To do that, you select the control in Design view, click on the Code button at the top of the Properties window to access the properties that affect code generation, and then edit the default value for the Variable Name property. In this figure, for example, I changed the default value of JButton2 to exitButton.

A form after the variable names have been set for the controls

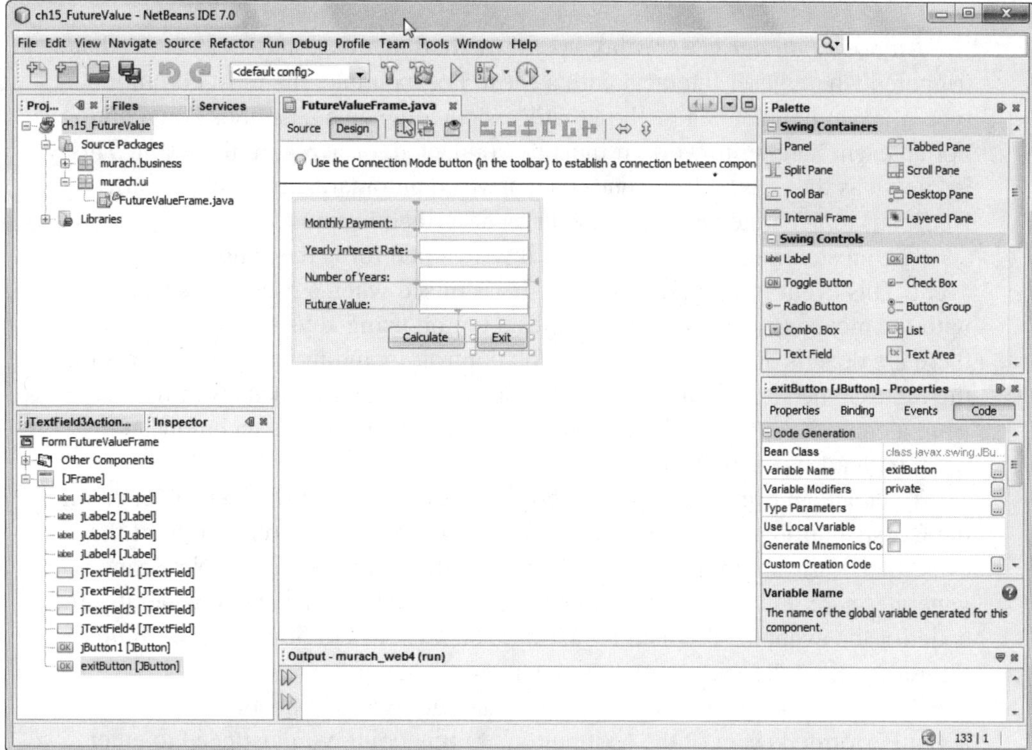

Typical variable names for controls

```
paymentTextField
calculateButton
messageLabel
```

Description

- When you add controls to a form, default variable names are given to the controls. If you're going to refer to a control in your Java code, you should change its name so it's easier to remember and use.
- To change the name of the variable that's used for a control, select the control, click the Code button in the Properties window, and then change the Variable Name property.

Figure 15-7 How to set the variable name for a control

How to create an event handler for a control

An *event handler* is a special type of method that responds to an *event* that's triggered when a user interacts with a form. For example, the most common type of event handler is a method that's executed when a user clicks on a button. For an event handler to work, it must be connected, or *wired*, to the event. This is known as the *event wiring*, and it's generated automatically when you use NetBeans to generate an event handler as described in figure 15-8.

The most common event that you'll write code for is the actionPerformed event. This event is a high-level event that's raised when a user clicks a button with the mouse or when a user activates a button using keystrokes. However, there are dozens of other events for each control, including low-level events like the focusGained and focusLost events that occur when the focus is moved to or from a control. As you will see, you can use the same general techniques to work with all types of events.

To create an event handler for a control, you can select the control, click on the Events button at the top of the Properties window, click to the right of the event that you want to handle, and then press the Enter key. Then, NetBeans generates a default name for the method that will handle the event, generates the code for the event handler and its wiring, and switches to Source view. In this figure, for example, NetBeans has generated the name exitButtonActionPerformed for the event handler that will handle the actionPerformed event of the Exit button. At this point, you just need to enter the code for that event handler.

If you don't want to use the generated name for an event handler, you can change it in the Properties window before you press the Enter key. If, for example, you want to create an event handler named textFieldFocusGained for the focusGained event of a text field, you can enter "textFieldFocusGained" to the right of the focusGained event and press the Enter key. Later, if you want to wire another text field to the event handler named textFieldFocusGained, you can enter that event handler name in the Properties window for the focusGained event of the text field. That way, the same event handler will be used for the same event of two different text fields.

When you generate event handlers, you should realize that they're added to your code in the sequence in which you generate them. Unfortunately, NetBeans doesn't let you change that sequence. If you want the event handlers for an application to appear in a specific sequence, then, you will need to generate them in that sequence.

Below the screen in this figure, you can see the code for the event handler that's generated for the Exit button on the Future Value form. Here, the name of the method is the name of the control (exitButton) followed by the name of the event (ActionPerformed). This shows that it's important to set the variable name for the control before you start an event handler for a control. That way, the variable name will be reflected in the name of the event handler.

This figure also shows the wiring for the event handler that's generated for the Exit button. This wiring is stored in a generated region of code, and you

The actionPerformed event for the Exit button

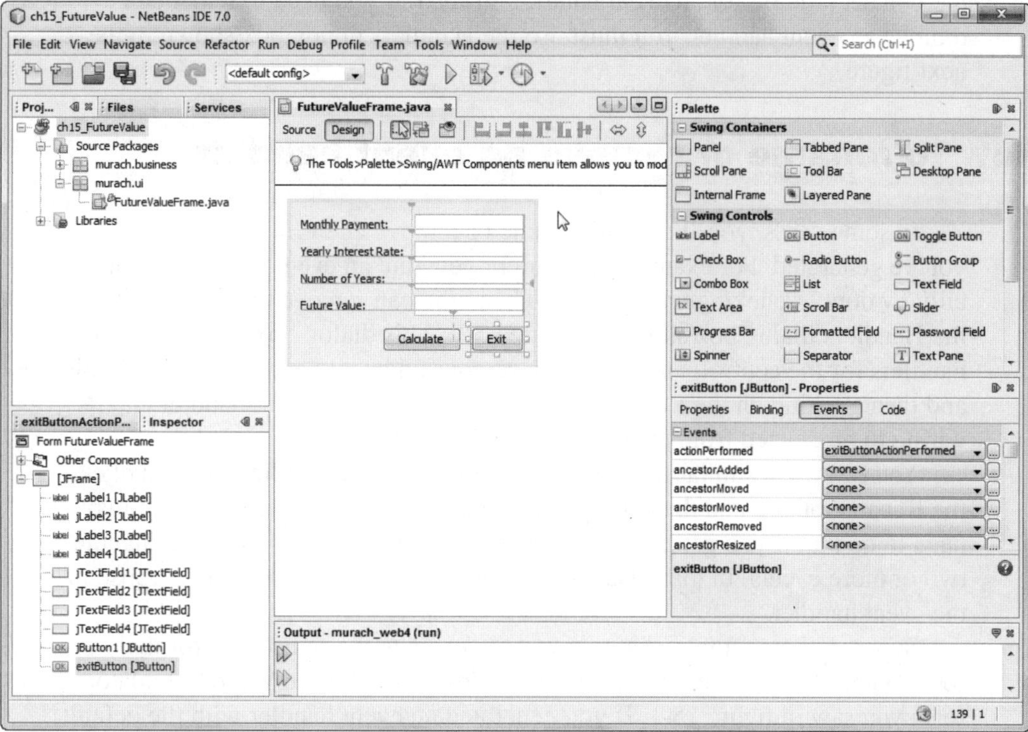

The code that's generated for the actionPerformed event of the Exit button

```
private void exitButtonActionPerformed(java.awt.event.ActionEvent evt) {
    // TODO add your handling code here:
}
```

The generated code that wires the event handler to the event

```
exitButton.addActionListener(new java.awt.event.ActionListener() {
    public void actionPerformed(java.awt.event.ActionEvent evt) {
        exitButtonActionPerformed(evt);
    }
});
```

Description

- To create an event handler for the default event of a control, double-click on the control.
- To create an event handler for other events, select the control, click the Events button in the Properties window, and select the name for the event handler from the combo box list.
- To create an event handler with a custom name, select the control, click the Events button in the Properties window, click in the combo box for the event that you want to handle, enter a custom name for the event handler, and press the Enter key.
- To wire an event to an existing event handler, enter the name of the event in the combo box for the event that you want to handle.

Figure 15-8 How to create an event handler for a control

can't edit it manually. In addition, you can't manually rename or remove the method declaration for an event handler. Instead, if you need to rename or remove an event handler, you must use the Handlers dialog box shown in the next figure.

How to rename or remove an event handler

In some cases, you'll need to rename or remove an event handler that you've generated. For example, you might generate an event handler accidentally by double-clicking on a control. Then, you can remove the handler using the Handlers dialog box shown in figure 15-9. This dialog box lists all the event handlers for the control, and it lets you remove an event handler by selecting it and then clicking on the Remove button. This causes the event handler and its wiring to be deleted from the source code for the form.

You can use a similar technique to rename an event handler, but you click the Rename button and then enter a new name for the event handler. You may need to do that if you generate an event handler that you want to use to handle two or more events. In that case, you'll want the name to reflect the purpose of the event handler.

Suppose, for example, that you want to execute the same code for the focusGained event of the first three text fields on the Future Value Calculator form you saw in figure 15-1. If you generated an event handler with the default name for the first text field, the event handler would be named monthlyPaymentTextFieldFocusGained. Then, you could rename this event handler to something like textFieldFocusGained to make it clear that it's used for all three text fields. Of course, you could also create the event handler with a custom name to begin with so you wouldn't have to rename it.

The Handlers dialog box

Description

- Since an event handler includes wiring code that's automatically generated and stored in a different location than the event handler code, you should always use the Handlers dialog box if you need to rename or remove an event handler. That way, both the event handler and its wiring are updated or removed in a single operation.
- To rename or remove an event handler, select the control, click on the Events button in the Properties window, and click on the ellipsis button to the right of the event that you want to work with. Then, use the Handlers dialog box to remove or rename the event handler.

Figure 15-9 How to rename or remove an event handler

How to enter the code for a form

Figure 15-10 shows how to enter the code for a form. To start, you should enter any import statements that you need for classes that are going to be used by the form. That way, you won't have to qualify these classes with their package names when you refer to them in code.

Next, you can enter the code for the event handlers that you've generated for the form. In this figure, for example, I have entered the code for the event handlers for the actionPerformed event of the Exit and Calculate buttons. As I entered the code, I used the variable names that refer to the text field controls. For example, I used the name "paymentTextField" to refer to the entry in the Monthly Payment text field.

Although the event handlers in this figure don't call any other methods, you can add methods to a form just as you would add methods to any other class. For example, this application could have included a method that calculates the future value. When you add a method like this to a form class, you typically place it near the event handlers that call it.

If you need to use code to initialize a control, you can add that code to the end of the constructor for the form class. In this figure, you can see that the constructor contains a single statement that calls the initComponents method. This method contains generated code that creates the controls on the form and sets the properties for the form and its controls so they're displayed correctly. If you want to set any additional properties, you can add that code after the call to the initComponents method. For example, you might want to load the items that will be displayed in a list box or combo box. You'll learn more about these controls in the next chapter.

The Generated Code region of a form contains the code that's generated as you create the form in Design view. Since you can't edit this code directly, you rarely need to view it. If you're curious, however, you can review this code to see how it works. To do that, just expand this region by clicking on the plus sign (+) that's displayed to its left.

The source code after two event handlers have been coded

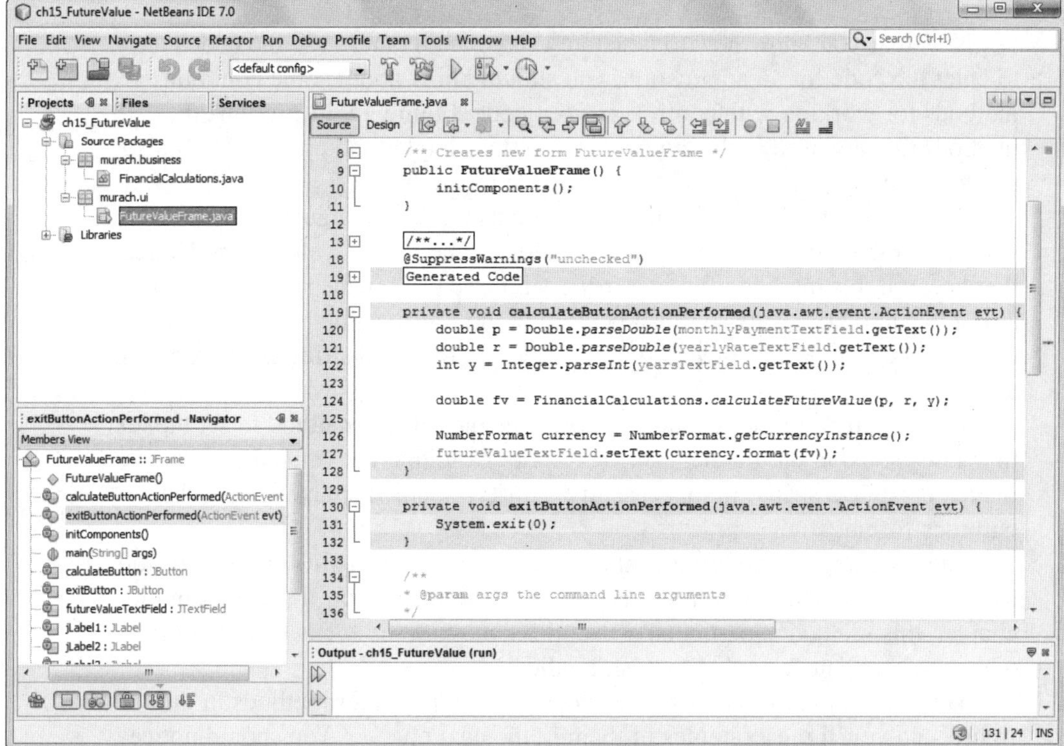

Description

- You can use the code editor to enter the code for an event handler just as you would enter any other code.
- To refer to the controls on the form, you use the variable names that you assigned to the controls. You can review these variable names in the Navigator window for the frame. You can also review the declarations for these variables at the end of the source code for the form.
- To import a class that will be used by the form, code an import statement after the package statement that's at the start of the form class just like you would for any other class.
- If you need to initialize a control, you can add code to the constructor for the class after the call to the initComponents method.
- You can also add methods other than event handlers to a form. When you do that, you typically place the methods following the event handlers that call them.
- NetBeans shades all generated code, and you can't manually edit this code. If you need to change this code, use Design view as described in previous topics.

Common methods for controls

Now that you know how to generate event handlers and use the code editor to enter the code for an application, you should know about some common methods for working with controls in your code. Figure 15-11 presents the methods that are used in the applications in this chapter and chapter 16. It also shows some examples that use some of these methods.

The first example includes three statements that use the getText method to get the text from the three enabled text fields on the Future Value form. Notice that because this method returns a string, all three statements must convert the string to a numeric value so it can be used in the future value calculation. Here, the first two strings are converted to doubles and the third string is converted to an int.

The statement in the second example uses the setText method to set the text that's displayed in the Future Value text field. Note that the value that's displayed must be a string. In this case, the future value is displayed using the currency format.

The statement in the last example uses the requestFocusInWindow method to move the focus to the Monthly Payment text field. As you'll see later in this chapter, this method is particularly useful for moving the focus to a control when the user enters a value that isn't valid.

You shouldn't have any trouble understanding the other methods in this figure, and you'll see examples of them in the next chapter. You should notice, though, that three of these methods—setEditable, setEnabled, and setFocusable—have property counterparts that you saw in figure 15-6. When I designed the Future Value form, for example, I set the editable property of the Future Value text field so the user can't edit the text in this field. Another way to do that would be to use the setEditable method in the constructor for the Future Value form like this:

```
futureValueTextField.setEditable(false);
```

Since the editable property doesn't change as the program executes, though, it's easier to set the editable property as you're designing the form. In contrast, if a property like this will change as the program executes, you can use the related method to change the setting in code.

Common methods for controls

Method	Description
`getText()`	Returns the text in the control as a string. Used for text fields and other controls that contain text.
`setText(String)`	Sets the text in the control to the specified string. Used for text fields and other controls that contain text.
`requestFocusInWindow()`	Moves the focus to the control.
`setEditable(boolean)`	If the boolean value is true, the control is editable. Otherwise, it's not. Used for text fields and other controls that contain text.
`setEnabled(boolean)`	If the boolean value is true, the control is enabled so the user can interact with it. Otherwise, it's disabled.
`setFocusable(boolean)`	If the boolean value is true, the control can receive the focus. Otherwise, it can't.
`selectAll()`	Selects all the text in a control. Used for text fields and other controls that contain text.

Example 1: Code that gets the text from three controls

```
double p = Double.parseDouble(monthlyPaymentTextField.getText());
double r = Double.parseDouble(yearlyInterestRateTextField.getText());
int y = Integer.parseInt(yearsTextField.getText());
```

Example 2: Code that sets the text in a control

```
futureValueTextField.setText(currency.format(futureValue));
```

Example 3: Code that moves the focus to a control

```
monthlyPaymentTextField.requestFocusInWindow();
```

Description

- To learn more about the methods that are available for a control, refer to the API documentation for the control.
- The getText, setText, setEditable, and selectAll methods are defined by the JTextComponent class. The setEnabled and requestFocusInWindow methods are defined by the JComponent class. And the setFocusable method is defined by the Component class.

Figure 15-11 Common methods for controls

How to display and center a form

Figure 15-12 starts by showing the main method that's generated by NetBeans for a form. Although this code may seem complicated, most of it works the way you want. As a result, you typically only need to make some minor changes to the statements within the run method. In this figure, for example, the generated code creates a new form and displays it using a single statement like this:

```
new FutureValueFrame().setVisible(true);
```

This displays the form in the upper left corner of the screen.

If you want to display the form in the center of the screen, you can do that as shown in the second example. Here, the run method starts by creating a FutureValueFrame object and assigning it to a variable named frame. Then, the setVisible method of that frame is used to display the frame, and the setLocationRelativeTo method is used to center the frame on the screen.

Most of the time, that's all you need to know about displaying a form. If you're curious about how the rest of this generated code works, though, you can review the notes at the bottom of this figure along with the information in the related chapters.

Two methods for displaying a form

Method	Description
setVisible(boolean)	Shows this component if the boolean value is true. Otherwise, this method hides the component.
setLocationRelativeTo(component)	Sets the location of this component relative to the specified component. If the component is null, this method centers the frame on the screen. Otherwise, it centers the frame on the specified component.

A main method for a form that's generated by NetBeans

```
public static void main(String args[]) {
    java.awt.EventQueue.invokeLater(new Runnable() {
        public void run() {
            new FutureValueFrame().setVisible(true);
        }
    });
}
```

A main method for a form that displays and centers the form

```
public static void main(String args[]) {
    java.awt.EventQueue.invokeLater(new Runnable() {
        public void run() {
            FutureValueFrame frame = new FutureValueFrame();
            frame.setVisible(true);
            frame.setLocationRelativeTo(null);
        }
    });
}
```

Description

- By default, NetBeans generates a main method for a form that creates the form and displays it in the upper left corner of the user's screen.
- You can modify this code to display the form in the center of the screen as shown in the second example above.

Notes

- The code that's generated by NetBeans for a form creates a new *thread* for the form, which is a single flow of execution through the program. To create this thread, the code creates a new class that implements the Runnable interface. This interface has a single method named run. For more information about working with threads, see chapter 22.
- The class that implements the Runnable interface is coded within the invokeLater method of the EventQueue class. As a result, this class is a type of inner class as described in chapter 10. Since this inner class doesn't have a name, it's known as an *anonymous class*.
- The invokeLater method of the EventQueue class puts the thread for the form in a queue. Then, it runs the thread when the thread reaches the front of the queue.

Figure 15-12 How to display and center a form

The code for the FutureValueFrame class

Figure 15-13 shows the code for a simple version of the FutureValueFrame class. To start, the package statement stores the class in the package named murach.ui. Then, the import statements import the NumberFormat class from the Java API and the FinancialCalculations class from the murach.business package.

After the import statements, the declaration for the class shows that the FutureValueFrame class inherits the JFrame class. Within the body of the FutureValueFrame class, the constructor calls the initComponents method to initialize the form and its controls. Although the declaration for this method is shown in this figure, this method is hidden by default and you shouldn't modify any of the code it contains directly. Instead, you can use Design view to adjust the properties of the form and its controls and NetBeans will automatically update the code in the initComponents method.

The calculateButtonActionPerformed method is the event handler for the actionPerformed event of the Calculate button. To start, this event handler gets the string that the user entered into the first text field on the form by calling the getText method of that control. Then, it converts this string to a double value named p. After that, this method performs similar processing for the next two text fields to get the interest rate and number of years. Next, this method calls the calculateFutureValue method of the FinancialCalculations class to calculate and return the future value. Finally, it uses the NumberFormat class to format the future value, and it displays the formatted value in the fourth text field on the form.

For this simple example, the calculateButtonActionPerformed event handler doesn't validate the data that's entered by the user. As a result, if the user enters an invalid value such as "xx", the application will print a stack trace to the error output stream. To prevent this, you can validate the data that's entered by the user as shown later in this chapter.

The exitButtonActionPerformed method is the event handler for the actionPerformed event of the Exit button. This method executes a single statement that exits the application with a status code of 0. By convention, a status code of 0 indicates that the application ended normally.

The code for the main method has been modified as described in the previous figure. As a result, it displays the form in the center of the screen.

The declarations for the control variables used by the class are shown at the end of the class. Although you shouldn't modify these declarations, you may want to take a look at them to see what classes the generated code uses. In particular, note that this code uses the JButton class for buttons, the JTextField class for text fields, and the JLabel class for labels. Also note that these classes are qualified with the javax.swing package that contains them. That's why the application doesn't include an import statement for this package. In the next chapter, you'll learn more about working with Swing components like these. For now, you just need to understand that Swing provides a class for each type of control.

The code for the FutureValueFrame class

```
package murach.ui;

import java.text.NumberFormat;
import murach.business.FinancialCalculations;

public class FutureValueFrame extends javax.swing.JFrame {

    public FutureValueFrame() {
        initComponents();
    }

    private void initComponents() {
        // Generated code - do not modify
    }

    private void calculateButtonActionPerformed(
    java.awt.event.ActionEvent evt) {
        double p = Double.parseDouble(monthlyPaymentTextField.getText());
        double r = Double.parseDouble(yearlyInterestRateTextField.getText());
        int y = Integer.parseInt(yearsTextField.getText());
        double futureValue = FinancialCalculations.calculateFutureValue(
            p, r, y);
        NumberFormat currency = NumberFormat.getCurrencyInstance();
        futureValueTextField.setText(currency.format(futureValue));
    }

    private void exitButtonActionPerformed(java.awt.event.ActionEvent evt) {
        System.exit(0);
    }

    /**
    * @param args the command line arguments
    */
    public static void main(String args[]) {
        java.awt.EventQueue.invokeLater(new Runnable() {
            public void run() {
            FutureValueFrame frame = new FutureValueFrame();
            frame.setVisible(true);
            frame.setLocationRelativeTo(null);
            }
        });
    }

    // Variables declaration - do not modify
    private javax.swing.JButton calculateButton;
    private javax.swing.JButton exitButton;
    private javax.swing.JTextField futureValueTextField;
    private javax.swing.JLabel jLabel1;
    private javax.swing.JLabel jLabel2;
    private javax.swing.JLabel jLabel3;
    private javax.swing.JLabel jLabel4;
    private javax.swing.JTextField monthlyPaymentTextField;
    private javax.swing.JTextField yearlyInterestRateTextField;
    private javax.swing.JTextField yearsTextField;
}
```

Figure 15-13 The code for the FutureValue Frame class

How to validate Swing input data

In chapter 5, you learned how to validate input data for console applications. Then, in chapter 7, you saw an example of a Validator class that uses static methods to help validate data for console applications. In the topics that follow, you'll see that you can use similar techniques to validate the input data for Swing applications.

How to display error messages

When you validate data in a Swing application, you need to be able to display an error message to inform the user that an invalid entry has been detected. The easiest way to do that is to display the error message in a separate dialog box as shown at the top of figure 15-14. To display a dialog box like this, you use the showMessageDialog method of the JOptionPane class as described in this figure.

The four parameters accepted by this method are the parent component that determines the location of the dialog box, the message displayed in the dialog box, the title of the dialog box, and the message type, which determines the icon that's displayed in the dialog box. The parent component can be the control that's being validated or the frame that contains the control. It can also be null, in which case the dialog box is centered on the screen.

The code example in this figure shows how to display a simple error message. To start, the first statement defines a string for the message to display in the dialog box, and the second statement defines a string for the title of the dialog box. Then, the third statement calls the showMessageDialog method. Here, the parent component argument is set to the this keyword, which causes the dialog box to be displayed within the current frame. For that to work, this code must appear in a class that inherits the Component class or a class derived from it, such as JFrame or JApplet. Finally, the message type argument is set to the ERROR_MESSAGE field of the JOptionPane class. This causes the dialog box to display an error icon.

An error message displayed in a JOptionPane dialog box

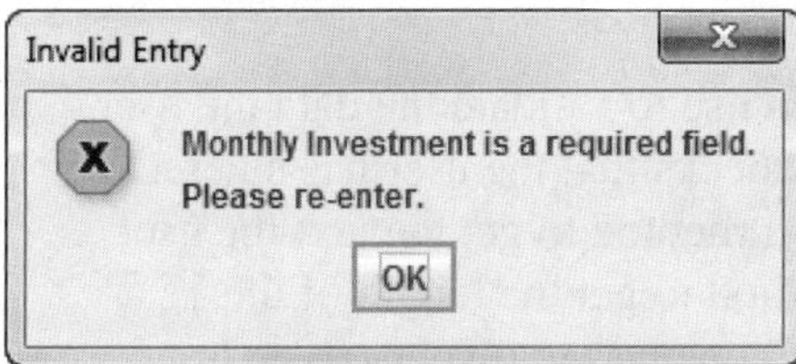

The showMessageDialog method of the JOptionPane class

Syntax

```
showMessageDialog(parentComponent, messageString,
                  titleString, messageTypeInt);
```

Arguments

Argument	Description
`parent`	An object representing the component that's the parent of the dialog box. If you specify null, the dialog box will appear in the center of the screen.
`message`	A string representing the message to be displayed in the dialog box.
`title`	A string representing the title of the dialog box.
`messageType`	An int that indicates the type of icon that will be used for the dialog box. You can use the fields of the JOptionPane class for this argument.

Fields used for the message type parameter

Icon displayed	Field
(none)	PLAIN_MESSAGE
(i)	INFORMATION_MESSAGE
⚠	WARNING_MESSAGE
(x)	ERROR_MESSAGE
?	QUESTION_MESSAGE

Code that displays the dialog box shown above

```
String message = "Monthly Investment is a required field.\n"
               + "Please re-enter.";
String title = "Invalid Entry";
JOptionPane.showMessageDialog(this,
    message, title, JOptionPane.ERROR_MESSAGE);
```

Description

- The showMessageDialog method is a static method of the JOptionPane class that is commonly used to display dialog boxes with error messages for data validation.
- To close a dialog box, the user can click the OK button or the close button in the upper right corner of the dialog box.
- You can also use the JOptionPane class to accept input from the user. For more information, see the API documentation for this class.

Figure 15-14 How to display error messages

How to validate the data entered into a text field

Figure 15-15 shows two techniques you can use to validate the data the user enters into a text field. The first code example checks that the user has entered data into the field. To do that, it uses the getText method to get the text the user entered as a string. Then, it uses the length method to get the length of the string. If the length is zero, it uses the JOptionPane class to display an error message in a dialog box. Then, it calls the text field's requestFocusInWindow method to move the focus to the text field after the user closes the dialog box.

The second example shows how to check that the user entered a numeric value. Here, the parseDouble method of the Double class is used to parse the text entered by the user to a double value. This conversion is placed within a try statement. Then, if a NumberFormatException occurs, the catch block catches the exception, displays an error message, and moves the focus to the text field.

Example 1: Code that checks if an entry has been made

```
if (monthlyPaymentTextField.getText().length() == 0)
{
    String message = "Monthly Investment is a required field.";
    String title = "Invalid Entry";
    JOptionPane.showMessageDialog(this, message,
        title, JOptionPane.ERROR_MESSAGE);
    monthlyPaymentTextField.requestFocusInWindow();
    return;
}
```

Example 2: Code that checks if an entry is a valid number

```
try
{
    double d = Double.parseDouble(monthlyPaymentTextField.getText());
}
catch (NumberFormatException e)
{
    String message = "Monthly Investment must be a valid number.";
    String title = "Invalid Entry";
    JOptionPane.showMessageDialog(this, message,
        title, JOptionPane.ERROR_MESSAGE);
    monthlyPaymentTextField.requestFocusInWindow();
    return;
}
```

Description

- Like console applications, GUI applications should validate all data entered by the user before processing the data.
- When an entry is invalid, the application can display an error message and give the user another chance to enter valid data.
- To test whether a value has been entered into a text field, you can use the getText method of the text field to get a string that contains the text the user entered. Then, you can check whether the length of that string is zero by using its length method.
- To test whether a text field contains valid numeric data, you can code the statement that converts the data in a try block and use a catch block to catch a NumberFormatException.

Figure 15-15 How to validate the data entered into a text field

The SwingValidator class

Figure 15-16 shows a class named SwingValidator that you can use to validate the data entered into a text component. Like the Validator class that was presented in chapter 7, this class uses methods to perform common validation functions. Unlike the Validator class, though, the SwingValidator class doesn't use static methods. As a result, you must create a SwingValidator object before you can use the methods in this class. That makes it easier to use the methods if the name of the object variable is shorter than the class name, and it makes it easier to change the class that's used for validation if that need arises.

Each of the three public methods in this class returns a boolean value to indicate whether or not the component passed the validation test. The private method is called to display an error message in a dialog box when an error is detected by one of the public methods.

Each of the public methods accepts two parameters. The first parameter is the control to be validated, and the second parameter is a string that contains the name of the field being validated. Notice that the first parameter is of type JTextComponent. Since the JTextField class is derived from the JTextComponent class, you can use this method with text fields.

The isPresent method determines whether or not the user has entered data into a text component. The code in this method is similar to the code you saw in the first example in the previous figure. The isInteger method determines whether the value entered is a valid integer, and the isDouble method determines whether the value is a valid double value. The code in these methods is similar to the code you saw in the second example in the previous figure. Of course, you can easily extend this class to perform other types of tests, such as checking for valid dates or checking that a number or date is within a valid range.

The code for the SwingValidator class

```
package murach.ui;

import javax.swing.*;
import javax.swing.text.JTextComponent;

public class SwingValidator
{
    public boolean isPresent(JTextComponent c, String fieldName)
    {
        if (c.getText().length() == 0)
        {
            showMessage(c, fieldName + " is a required field.");
            c.requestFocusInWindow();
            return false;
        }
        return true;
    }

    public boolean isInteger(JTextComponent c, String fieldName)
    {
        try
        {
            int i = Integer.parseInt(c.getText());
            return true;
        }
        catch (NumberFormatException e)
        {
            showMessage(c, fieldName + " must be an integer.");
            c.requestFocusInWindow();
            return false;
        }
    }

    public boolean isDouble(JTextComponent c, String fieldName)
    {
        try
        {
            double d = Double.parseDouble(c.getText());
            return true;
        }
        catch (NumberFormatException e)
        {
            showMessage(c, fieldName + " must be a valid number.");
            c.requestFocusInWindow();
            return false;
        }
    }

    private void showMessage(JTextComponent c, String message)
    {
            JOptionPane.showMessageDialog(c, message, "Invalid Entry",
                JOptionPane.ERROR_MESSAGE);
    }
}
```

Figure 15-16 The SwingValidator class

How to validate multiple entries

Figure 15-17 shows how you can create a single method to handle the validation testing for all of the controls on a form. The first two examples show two different ways to code this method, named isValidData. Both of these examples begin by creating a SwingValidator object named sv. Then, they use this object to call the methods of the SwingValidator class to perform the validation tests for each control.

The code in the first example uses a series of if statements to test each condition that must be met for the input data to be considered valid. For example, the first two if statements test that the user entered a value for the monthly investment and that the value is a double. Similarly, the last two if statements test that the user entered a value for the number of years and that the value was an int. If any of these validation tests fails, a false value is returned to the calling method. If all of the validation tests succeed, the last statement in the method returns a true value to the calling method.

The second example performs the same validation tests as the first example, but it uses a compound conditional expression in a single return statement. Here, the validation tests are combined using the && (and) operator. That way, this compound expression returns a true value only if each of the separate calls to the SwingValidator methods returns a true value. If any of the SwingValidator calls returns a false value, the expression returns a false value.

Note that it's important to use the short-circuit and operator (&&) rather than the normal and operator (&). That way, if one of the SwingValidator calls returns a false value, the rest of the conditions aren't tested. As a result, an error message is displayed only for the first validation test that fails.

The third example in this figure shows how to call the isValidData method from an event handler. As you can see, this method is called before the data is processed. That way, you can be sure that the data processing code will work correctly.

Example 1: Validate multiple entries with a series of if statements

```
private boolean isValidData()
{
    SwingValidator sv = new SwingValidator();

    if (!sv.isPresent(monthlyPaymentTextField, "Monthly Investment"))
        return false;
    if (!sv.isDouble(monthlyPaymentTextField, "Monthly Investment"))
        return false;

    if (!sv.isPresent(yearlyInterestRateTextField, "Interest Rate"))
        return false;
    if (!sv.isDouble(yearlyInterestRateTextField, "Interest Rate"))
        return false;

    if (!sv.isPresent(yearsTextField, "Number of Years"))
        return false;
    if (!sv.isInteger(yearsTextField, "Number of Years"))
        return false;

    return true;
}
```

Example 2: Validate multiple entries with a compound condition

```
private boolean isValidData()
{
    SwingValidator sv = new SwingValidator();
    return
        sv.isPresent(monthlyPaymentTextField, "Monthly Investment") &&
        sv.isDouble(monthlyPaymentTextField, "Monthly Investment") &&
        sv.isPresent(yearlyInterestRateTextField, "Interest Rate") &&
        sv.isDouble(yearlyInterestRateTextField, "Interest Rate") &&
        sv.isPresent(yearsTextField, "Number of Years") &&
        sv.isInteger(yearsTextField, "Number of Years");
}
```

Example 3: Code that calls the isValidData method

```
private void calculateButtonActionPerformed(java.awt.event.ActionEvent evt)
{
    if (isValidData())
    {
        // code that processes the data
    }
}
```

Description

- When more than one field needs to be validated, it is best to put all the validation logic in a separate method that returns a boolean value to indicate whether or not the data is valid.
- The first and second examples above show two alternatives for validating multiple entries. Both use the non-static methods of the SwingValidator class.

Figure 15-17 How to validate multiple entries

The Future Value application

In chapter 4, you were introduced to a console version of the Future Value application. Now, you're ready to see the code for a GUI version of the Future Value application. This application performs the same calculation as the console version, but it uses Swing components to display a graphical user interface.

The user interface

When the Future Value application starts, it displays a Future Value Calculator form like the one shown in figure 15-18. Then, the user can enter the monthly payment, yearly interest rate, and number of years. Next, the user can click on the Calculate button or press Alt+C to perform the calculation.

If the user enters invalid data, the application displays a dialog box like the ones shown in this figure. Then, after the user clicks on the OK button, the application moves the focus to the text field that contains the invalid data. This process continues until the user enters valid data into all three text fields. Then, the future value is calculated and displayed in the fourth text field.

At this point, the user can enter different values into the text fields and then select the Calculate button again. When the user is done performing calculations, he or she can click on the Exit button or press Alt+X to exit the application.

The code

Figure 15-19 shows the code for the Future Value application. Since this code is similar to the code for the FutureValueFrame class presented earlier in this chapter, you shouldn't have much trouble understanding it. The main difference is that this code uses the SwingValidator class shown in figure 15-16 to validate the input. Also, for the sake of completeness, this code listing shows the code for the FinancialCalculations class that contains the static method that calculates the future value.

The Future Value Calculator form

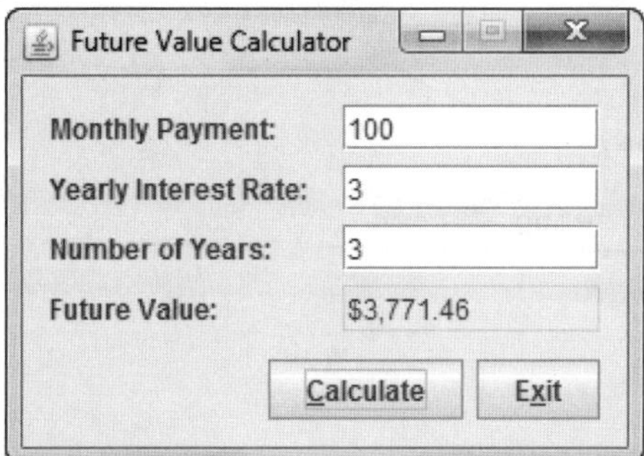

Typical dialog boxes displayed when invalid data is entered

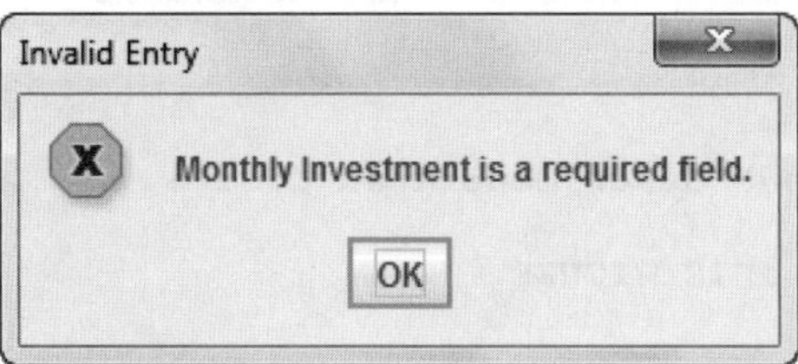

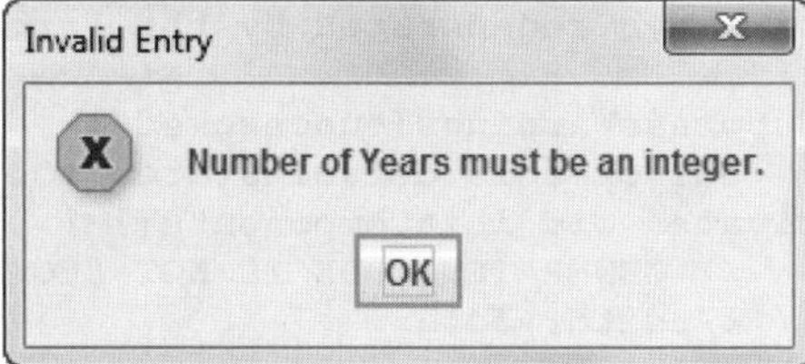

Description

- When the Future Value application starts, it displays the Future Value Calculator form.
- To perform a calculation, the user enters a monthly payment, yearly interest rate, and number of years and then clicks on the Calculate button or presses Alt+C. If the data is valid, the future value is formatted and displayed.
- If the user enters invalid data, the application displays a dialog box that describes the error. Then, after the user clicks the OK button, the application moves the focus to the text field that contains the invalid data.
- To exit the application, the user clicks on the Exit button or presses Alt+X.

Figure 15-18 The user interface for the Future Value application

The FutureValueFrame class — Page 1

```
package murach.ui;

import java.text.NumberFormat;
import murach.business.FinancialCalculations;

public class FutureValueFrame extends javax.swing.JFrame {

    /** Creates new form FutureValueFrame */
    public FutureValueFrame() {
        initComponents();
    }

    /** This method is called from within the constructor to
     * initialize the form.
     * WARNING: Do NOT modify this code. The content of this method is
     * always regenerated by the Form Editor.
     */
    @SuppressWarnings("unchecked")
    // <editor-fold defaultstate="collapsed" desc="Generated Code">
    private void initComponents() {
        // GENERATED CODE IS NOT SHOWN IN THIS FIGURE
    }// </editor-fold>

    private void calculateButtonActionPerformed(
    java.awt.event.ActionEvent evt) {
        if (isValidData())
        {
            double p = Double.parseDouble(monthlyPaymentTextField.getText());
            double r = Double.parseDouble(yearlyRateTextField.getText());
            int y = Integer.parseInt(yearsTextField.getText());

            double fv = FinancialCalculations.calculateFutureValue(p, r, y);

            NumberFormat currency = NumberFormat.getCurrencyInstance();
            futureValueTextField.setText(currency.format(fv));
        }
    }

    private void exitButtonActionPerformed(java.awt.event.ActionEvent evt) {
        System.exit(0);
    }

    private boolean isValidData()
    {
        SwingValidator sv = new SwingValidator();
        return
            sv.isPresent(monthlyPaymentTextField, "Monthly Investment") &&
            sv.isDouble(monthlyPaymentTextField, "Monthly Investment") &&
            sv.isPresent(yearlyInterestRateTextField, "Interest Rate") &&
            sv.isDouble(yearlyInterestRateTextField, "Interest Rate") &&
            sv.isPresent(yearsTextField, "Number of Years") &&
            sv.isInteger(yearsTextField, "Number of Years");
    }
```

The FutureValueFrame class

Page 2

```
    /**
    * @param args the command line arguments
    */
    public static void main(String args[]) {
        java.awt.EventQueue.invokeLater(new Runnable() {
            public void run() {
                FutureValueFrame frame = new FutureValueFrame();
                frame.setVisible(true);
                frame.setLocationRelativeTo(null);
            }
        });
    }

    // Variables declaration - do not modify
    private javax.swing.JButton calculateButton;
    private javax.swing.JButton exitButton;
    private javax.swing.JTextField futureValueTextField;
    private javax.swing.JLabel jLabel1;
    private javax.swing.JLabel jLabel2;
    private javax.swing.JLabel jLabel3;
    private javax.swing.JLabel jLabel4;
    private javax.swing.JTextField monthlyPaymentTextField;
    private javax.swing.JTextField yearlyRateTextField;
    private javax.swing.JTextField yearsTextField;
    // End of variables declaration
}
```

The FinancialCalculations class

```
package murach.business;

public class FinancialCalculations
{
    public static final int MONTHS_IN_YEAR = 12;

    public static double calculateFutureValue(double monthlyPayment,
    double yearlyInterestRate, int years)
    {
        int months = years * MONTHS_IN_YEAR;
        double monthlyInterestRate = yearlyInterestRate/MONTHS_IN_YEAR/100;
        double futureValue = 0;
        for (int i = 1; i <= months; i++)
        {
            futureValue = (futureValue + monthlyPayment) *
            (1 + monthlyInterestRate);
        }
        return futureValue;
    }
}
```

Figure 15-19 The code for the Future Value application (part 2 of 2)

Perspective

In this chapter, you learned how to use the Swing GUI builder that comes with NetBeans to build a GUI version of the Future Value application. This application uses some of the most common controls that are available from the Swing library including labels, text fields, and buttons. In the next chapter, you'll learn how to use more of the controls that are available from this library.

Summary

- A *GUI builder* is a graphical tool that a developer can use to generate the code that's used to display a graphical user interface and to write the code that makes the GUI work.
- The *Swing GUI builder* is one of the most popular GUI builders for Java developers, and it is available from the NetBeans IDE.
- The window that contains the GUI is called a *frame*, or *form*. Within a form, you add GUI controls such as *labels*, *text fields*, and *buttons*.
- The *Abstract Window Toolkit* (*AWT*) is an old technology for creating GUIs. *Swing* is a newer technology for creating GUIs. All Swing classes begin with the letter J and are stored in the javax.swing package.
- *Properties* are the values that determine how a form and its controls will look and work when the form is displayed.
- An *event handler* is a special type of method that responds to an *event* that's triggered when a user interacts with a form. NetBeans automatically generates the code that *wires* the method for an event handler to an event.

Exercise 15-1 Develop a GUI version of the Future Value application

This exercise guides you through the process of using NetBeans to develop the GUI version of the Future Value application presented in this chapter.

Add a form and its controls to the project

1. Open the project named ch15_ex1_FutureValue in the ex_starts directory. Note that it includes the FinancialCalculations and SwingValidator classes described in this chapter.
2. Add a form named FutureValueForm to the murach.forms package.
3. Add the 10 controls to the Future Value form, and set the text property for each control. Then, size and align the controls and size the form.
4. Change the variable names for the four text fields and two buttons so they can easily be referred to in your Java code.

5. Change any of the other properties for the form or controls so they will look and act the way you want.
6. Preview the form by clicking on the Preview Design button in the toolbar at the top of the form window. This shows that NetBeans has many features that aren't mentioned in this introductory chapter. Close the form by clicking on the Close button in its upper right corner.
7. Make any changes necessary to get the form to look the way it should, and then preview it again.

Review the code that was generated for the form

8. Switch to Source view, and review the code for the constructor of the FutureValueForm class. Note that it calls a method named InitComponents.
9. Click on the plus sign to the left of the Generated Code region to display the InitComponents method within this region. Then, scroll through this method and review its code. As you do, take a moment to consider how much work NetBeans has done for you.
10. View the main method near the end of the code, and note that it creates an instance of the FutureValueForm class, which in turn causes the constructor near the start of the class to be executed.
11. Review the declarations for the control variables at the end of the code.

Add code to the form class

12. Add import statements for the java.text.NumberFormat and murach.business.FinancialCalculations classes.
13. Switch back to Design view, and then double-click on the Exit button to generate the starting code and wiring for an event handler that handles the actionPerformed event of that button. Then, add code to this event handler that exits the application.
14. Use the Properties window to generate the starting code and wiring for an event handler that handles the actionPerformed event of the Calculate button. Then, add code to this event handler that gets the values the user entered in the form, calculates the future value using the calculateFutureValue method of the FinancialCalculations class, formats the result, and displays it in the Future Value text field.
15. Modify the code in the main method so it displays the form in the center of the screen.
16. Run the form by right-clicking on the .java file for the form in the Projects window and selecting Run File. Test the form to be sure it works with valid data. When you're done, click the form's Exit button.

Add validation to the form class

17. Add a private method named isValidData that uses the methods of the SwingValidator class to validate the data that's entered by the user.
18. Modify the code in the event handler for the actionPerformed event of the Calculate button so it only executes if the data is valid.

19. Run the form again. Test it to make sure it handles invalid entries in an appropriate way.

Exercise 15-2 Develop a GUI version of the Invoice application

In this exercise, you'll use NetBeans to develop a GUI version of the Invoice application you saw earlier in this book. When you're done, the user interface for this application should look something like this:

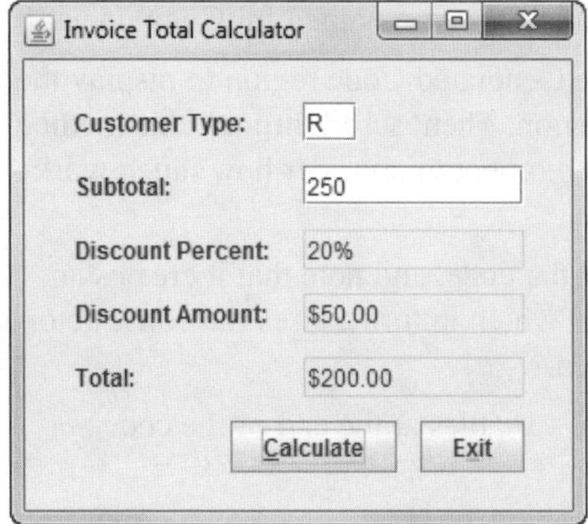

1. Open the project named ch15_ex2_Invoice in the ex_starts directory, and review the code for this project.
2. Add a form named InvoiceForm to the murach.forms package. Then, use Design view to add, size, and align the required controls, and set the control and form properties so they look as shown above.
3. Set the variable names for the controls that you'll need to access from the Java code. Then, display the form to make sure it looks the way it should.
4. Add import statements for the murach.business.InvoiceCalculations and java.text.NumberFormat classes.
5. Add an event handler for the actionPerformed event of the Calculate button. Add code to this event handler that gets the customer type and subtotal from the form, uses the calculateDiscountPct method in the InvoiceCalculations class to calculate the discount percent based on those values, calculates the discount amount and total, and formats and displays the values on the form.
6. Add an event handler for the actionPerformed event of the Exit button that exits the application. Then, run the form and test it to be sure it works with valid data.
7. Add code that uses the methods of the SwingValidator class to check that the user enters values in the Customer Type and Subtotal text fields and that the Subtotal text field is a double value.
8. Add code to the main method that centers the form when it's displayed. Then, run the form again to be sure it works properly.

16

How to work with controls and handle events

In the last chapter, you learned how to code a graphical user interface that uses the three most common controls. Now, you'll learn how to code a graphical user interface that uses more sophisticated controls. In addition, you'll learn how to handle low-level events such as focus events and keyboard events.

Two of the controls that are presented in this chapter require some knowledge of arrays and some of the examples use array lists. So if you haven't already read chapters 11 and 12, you may want to do that before you read this chapter.

How to work with components

In the last chapter, you learned how to work with three Swing components: labels, text fields, and buttons. Now, you'll learn how to use some other components to enhance the user interfaces you create.

How to work with text areas

A *text area* is similar to a text field, except that it lets you accept more than one line of input from the user. In fact, both the JTextField class and the JTextArea class extend the JTextComponent class, which provides many of the basic functions for both classes. For example, the getText and setText methods are defined by the JTextComponent class, so they're available to both text fields and text areas.

Figure 16-1 shows you how to use the JTextArea class to create a *text area*. After you use the Palette window to add a text area to a form, you can size the control to change the amount of text it can display. Then, if you want to display any initial text in the text area, you can set its text property.

The lineWrap and wrapStyleWord properties determine how the text wraps from one line to the next within a text area. By default, the text doesn't wrap. As a result, the user must press the Enter key to start a new line of text. If you want the text to wrap, you must select the lineWrap property. In addition, wrapped lines are split wherever the line reaches the end of the text area by default, even if that's in the middle of a word. To make sure that the text is wrapped between words, you must also select the wrapStyleWord property. In this figure, both the lineWrap and wrapStyleWord properties have been selected.

The code examples in this figure show how to use two of the methods presented in this figure. In the first example, the getText method is used to retrieve the text that's displayed in a text area as a string. In the second example, the setText method is used to set the text that's displayed in the text area. These methods work just as they do for text fields.

When you add a text area to a form, the NetBeans GUI builder automatically adds the text area to a *scroll pane*. A scroll pane is a control that provides scroll bars for the controls that it contains. As a result, if a text area contains more lines than can be displayed in the specified number of rows, the scroll pane displays a vertical scroll bar that allows the user to scroll up or down as shown in this figure. Similarly, if a text area contains more characters than can be displayed in the specified number of columns, the scroll pane displays a horizontal scroll bar that allows the user to scroll left or right. By default, the scroll pane only displays a vertical or horizontal scroll bar if that scroll bar is needed, which is often what you want. However, you can change how this works using the properties of the scroll pane shown in this figure.

A form with a text area

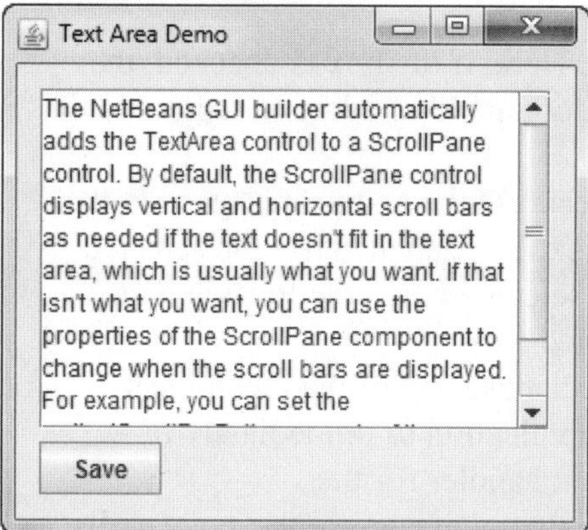

Common properties and methods of a text area

Property	Description
`text`	Specifies the text that's displayed in the text area.
`lineWrap`	Specifies whether a line that's too long wraps to the next line.
`wrapStyleWord`	If line wrapping is on and this property is on, lines will be separated between words.
Method	**Description**
`append(String)`	Appends the specified string to the text in the text area.
`getText()`	Returns the text in the text area as a string.
`setText(String)`	Sets the text in the text area to the specified string.

Common properties of a scroll pane

Property	Description
`verticalScrollBarPolicy`	Specifies when the vertical scroll bar is displayed (AS_NEEDED, NEVER, or ALWAYS).
`horizontalScrollBarPolicy`	Specifies when the horizontal scroll bar is displayed (AS_NEEDED, NEVER, or ALWAYS).

Code that gets the text stored in a text area

```
String comments = commentTextArea.getText();
```

Code that sets the text stored in a text area

```
commentTextArea.setText("Enter your comment here");
```

Description

- In contrast to a text field, a *text area* can be used to enter and display more than one line of text.
- By default, the GUI builder adds a text area to a *scroll pane*. A scroll pane can provide scroll bars for the text area.

Figure 16-1 How to work with text areas

How to work with check boxes

Figure 16-2 shows how to use a *check box*. Here, if the box is checked, the Address text area is enabled so the user can enter a mailing address. Otherwise, the Address text area is disabled.

After you add a check box to a form, you can use the text property to set the text that's displayed to the right of the check box. You can also use the selected property to determine if the check box will be selected when the form is first displayed. By default, a check box is not selected.

To select or deselect a check box, the user can use any of the techniques described in this figure. Then, if you want an application to immediately respond to the user action, you can create an event handler for the actionPerformed event of the check box. To do that, you can use the same skills you learned in the previous chapter. In this figure, for example, the code example shows a method that handles the actionPerformed event of the check box at the top of this figure. To start, this method uses an if statement to determine whether the check box is selected. If so, the code enables the text area for the address. Otherwise, the code disables that text area.

In many cases, you don't need to handle the actionPerformed event of a check box. Instead, you just need to use the isSelected method to check whether the check box is selected when the user triggers some other event on the form, such as the actionPerformed event of a button.

A form with a check box

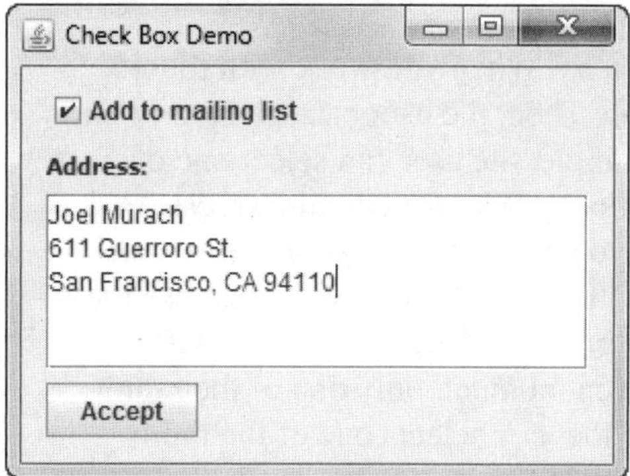

Common properties and methods of a check box

Property	Description
`text`	Specifies the label for the check box.
`selected`	Specifies whether the check box is selected.
Method	**Description**
`isSelected()`	Returns a true value if the check box is selected.
`setSelected(boolean)`	Checks or unchecks the check box depending on the boolean value.

Code that checks the status of the check box

```
private void mailingCheckBoxActionPerformed(java.awt.event.ActionEvent evt)
{
    if (mailingCheckBox.isSelected())
        addressTextArea.setEnabled(true);
    else
        addressTextArea.setEnabled(false);
}
```

Description

- A *check box* lets the user choose to turn an option on or off.
- To select or deselect a check box, the user can click on the check box, press the Alt key plus the shortcut key for the check box, or move the focus to the check box and then press the spacebar.

How to work with radio buttons

Figure 16-3 shows how to use *radio buttons*. When you work with these buttons, you must put them in a *button group*. Then, the user can select only one button from the group. In this figure, for example, the user can select one of three shipping methods: USPS (the Post Office), UPS, or Federal Express.

After you add a radio button to a form, you can use the text property to set the text that's displayed to the right of the button. In addition, you must use the button's buttonGroup property to add it to a group. A button group creates a logical grouping of radio buttons. At any given moment, only one of the radio buttons in a button group can be selected. If the user selects one of the radio buttons in a button group, all the other buttons in that group are deselected.

To create a button group, you add a Button Group control to the form and then set its variable name. Note that the button group doesn't have a visual interface, so it doesn't appear on the form. Instead, it's added to the drop-down list for the buttonGroup property of any radio buttons on the form.

Like a check box, a radio button is not selected by default. As a result, when you create a group of radio buttons, you typically use the selected property for one of the radio buttons so that button is selected when the form is first displayed.

The code example in this figure shows how to determine which of the three radio buttons is selected. To do that, it uses an if/else statement that tests the isSelected method of each button. Then, it assigns an appropriate string value to the shipVia variable.

When working with a group of radio buttons, it's usually a good idea to visually group the controls and provide a title for the group. That way, users can easily see which radio buttons belong to the group. To group radio buttons visually, you can use a panel. A *panel* is a control that can contain other controls such as radio buttons. Then, you can add the radio buttons to the panel, and you can use the border property of the panel to add a *border* to the panel.

The border property provides for several types of borders, including a plain line border, an etched border, a beveled border, and a titled border. If you select a titled border, you can specify a title that's displayed in the upper left corner of the panel. In this figure, for example, the form contains a panel with a title of Carrier that contains the three radio buttons.

A form with three radio buttons

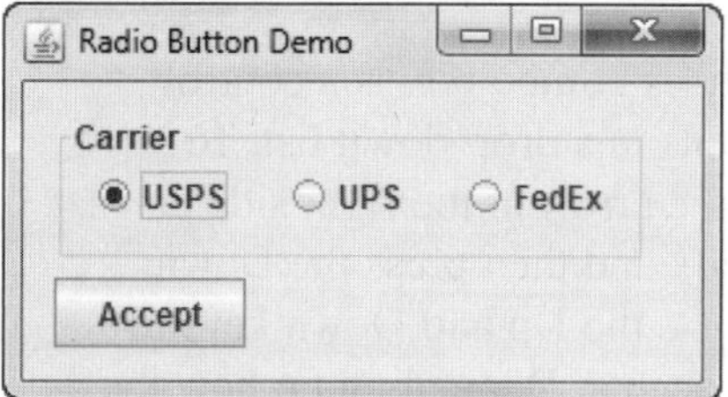

Common properties and methods of a radio button

Property	Description
`text`	Specifies the text for the radio button.
`selected`	Specifies whether the radio button is selected.
`buttonGroup`	Specifies the button group that the radio button belongs to.
Method	**Description**
`isSelected()`	Returns a true value if the radio button is selected.

A common property for a panel

Property	Description
`border`	Specifies the type of border that's used for the panel. If you select the Titled Border option, you can specify a title for the panel.

Code that determines which radio button is selected

```
String shipVia = "";
if (uspsRadioButton.isSelected())
    shipVia = "USPS";
else if (upsRadioButton.isSelected())
    shipVia = "UPS";
else if (fedexRadioButton.isSelected())
    shipVia = "Federal Express";
```

Description

- *Radio buttons* let the user choose one option from among several options. Selecting a radio button automatically deselects all other radio buttons in the same button group.
- A *panel* is a control that can contain other controls. A panel can have a *border* that's used to visually group controls such as radio buttons or to enhance the appearance of controls.
- Because a panel only groups controls visually, you must still use the buttonGroup property to group radio buttons logically. Before you can set the buttonGroup property, you must create a button group using the Button Group control in the Palette window.
- To select a radio button, the user can click on the button, press the Alt key plus the shortcut key for the button, or move the focus to the button and then press the spacebar.

Figure 16-3 How to work with radio buttons

How to work with combo boxes

Figure 16-4 shows how to create a *combo box*. A combo box is a control that lets the user choose from one of several options in a drop-down list. To display the drop-down list, the user can click on the arrow at the right side of the combo box or move the focus to the combo box and then press the Down key. To select an item, the user can click on it or use the Up and Down keys to highlight it and then press the Enter key or the spacebar. Depending on how the combo box is configured, the user may also be able to type data directly into the box. In effect, a combo box is a combination of a text field and a drop-down list.

When you add a combo box to a form, it contains three items by default (Item 1, Item 2, Item 3, and Item 4). If the combo box will contain a short list of items that won't change, you can change this default list of items using the model property of the combo box. Otherwise, you'll want to use this property to delete the list of default items. Then, you can use code like that shown in this figure to add items to the combo box.

The first code example in this figure declares a variable that stores an array list of Product objects. This variable is used by the second and third examples.

The second example shows the constructor for a frame that contains a combo box. Here, the first statement in the constructor calls the initComponents method, which initializes all of the controls for the form. Then, the next statement calls the getProducts method of the ProductDB class to return an ArrayList of Product objects and stores this ArrayList in the variable named products. After the array list is stored in the products variable, an enhanced for loop adds the description of each product to the combo box by calling the addItem method of the combo box. In most cases, that's all you need to do to initialize a combo box. However, you may also want to use the setSelectedIndex method to change the item that's selected when the list is first displayed. By default, the first item in the list is selected.

The third code example shows how to determine which product the user selected. To start, this method handles the itemStateChanged event of the combo box named productComboBox. This event is generated every time the user selects a new item from the combo box. Within the event handler for this event, the first statement uses the getSelectedIndex method to retrieve the index of the selected product. Then, the second statement uses this index to get the selected product from the products array list. Finally, the third statement displays the formatted price for the product in a text field.

By default, combo boxes aren't editable, so the user can't change the value that's in the combo box. Although that's usually what you want, you can use the editable property to make the combo box editable. Then, the user can type the text of an item into the combo box instead of selecting an item from the list. If you do this, keep in mind that the user might enter invalid data. As a result, you'll have to add some data validation code to prevent invalid entries.

Although the example shown in this figure adds String objects to the combo box, the addItem method lets you add any type of object. As a result, this

A form with a combo box

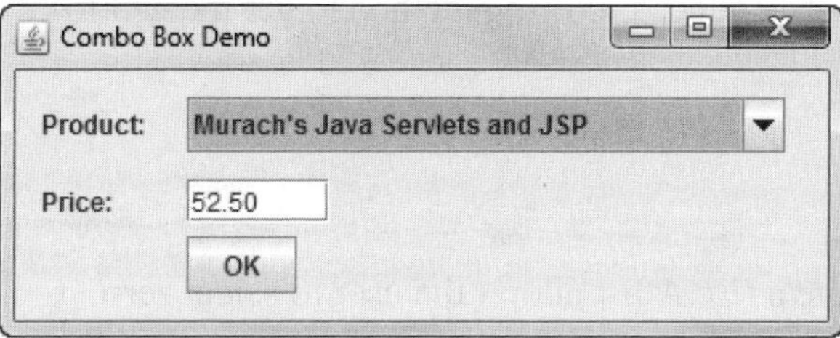

Common properties and methods of a combo box

Property	Description
`model`	Specifies the items that are displayed in the combo box list.
`editable`	Specifies whether the combo box can be edited.
Method	**Description**
`getSelectedItem()`	Returns an Object type for the selected item.
`getSelectedIndex()`	Returns an int value for the index of the selected item.
`setSelectedIndex(int)`	Selects the item at the specified index.
`getItemCount()`	Returns the number of items stored in the combo box.
`addItem(Object)`	Adds the specified item to the combo box.
`removeItemAt(int)`	Removes the item at the specified index from the combo box.
`removeItem(Object)`	Removes the specified item from the combo box.

Example 1: Code that declares a variable that stores products

```
private ArrayList<Product> products;
```

Example 2: Code that fills the combo box with products

```
public ComboBoxFrame() {
    initComponents();
    products = ProductDB.getProducts();
    for (Product p : products)
        productComboBox.addItem(p.getDescription());
}
```

Example 3: Code that gets the selected product

```
private void productComboBoxItemStateChanged(java.awt.event.ItemEvent evt) {
    int i = productComboBox.getSelectedIndex();
    Product p = products.get(i);
    priceTextField.setText(p.getFormattedPrice());
}
```

Description

- A *combo box* lets the user choose one of several items from a drop-down list.
- If a combo box will contain just a few items that won't change, you can use the Properties window to enter those items for the model property. Otherwise, you should use code to add items to the combo box as shown above.

Figure 16-4 How to work with combo boxes

example could have added the Product objects directly to the combo box. In that case, the combo box would call each product's toString method to get the text to display for the object.

How to work with lists

Figure 16-5 shows how to create a *list*. A list allows the user to select zero or more items. For example, the form at the top of this figure includes a list that displays products. Here, not all of the products can be displayed in the list at once, so a vertical scroll bar is needed to allow the user to scroll through the entries. As with a text area, NetBeans automatically stores a list within a scroll pane, so scroll bars appear when necessary.

By default, a list box contains five items (Item 1, Item 2, and so on). Like you can for a combo box, you can use the model property to change these items. However, you only want to do that for a short list of items that won't change. Otherwise, it makes sense to use code to add items to a list. You'll see how to do that in the next figure.

Unlike a combo box, a list allows a user to select more than one item by default. If necessary, the user can select multiple intervals of consecutive items. To do that, the user can hold down the Ctrl key while selecting items. Or, the user can select one item and then hold down the Shift key and click on another item to select a range of items that includes the first item through second item. To select another range of items, the user can hold down the Ctrl key and select the first item in the range and then hold down the Ctrl and Shift keys and select the last item in the range.

If you need to, you can use the selectionMode property to change the types of selections a user can make. For example, you can set this property so the user is limited to making a single selection. Or, you can set this property so the user can select a single interval of consecutive items.

A form that includes a list

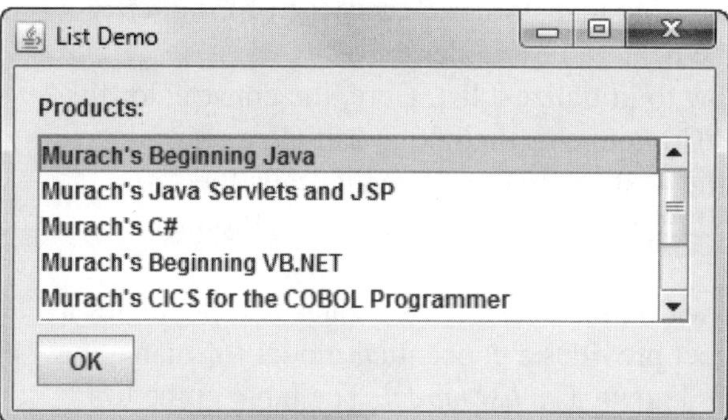

Common properties and methods of a list

Property	Description
`model`	Specifies the items that are displayed in the list.
`selectionMode`	Sets the selection mode. By default, the user can select multiple intervals of consecutive items (MULTIPLE_INTERVAL_SELECTION). However, you can change this so the user can only select a single item (SINGLE_SELECTION) or a single interval of consecutive items (SINGLE_INTERVAL_SELECTION).
Method	**Description**
`getSelectedValuesList()`	Returns a List<> type that contains the selected items.
`getSelectedIndices()`	Returns an array of int values for the indices of the selected items.
`getSelectedValue()`	Returns the selected item as an Object type.
`getSelectedIndex()`	Returns an int value for the index of the selected item.
`isSelectedIndex(int)`	Returns a true value if the item at the specified index is selected.
`setSelectedIndex(int)`	Selects the item at the specified index.
`setModel(listModel)`	Sets the model for the list that's defined by the DefaultListModel class.

Description

- A *list* allows the user to select zero or more items from a list of items.
- If a list will contain just a few items that won't change, you can use the Properties window to enter those items for the model property. Otherwise, you should use code to add items to the list as shown in the next figure.

The code examples in part 2 of figure 16-5 illustrate how you work with a list. The first example declares a variable that stores an array list of Product objects. This variable is used by the next two examples.

The second example shows how to initialize a list. Here, the constructor for the frame begins by calling the initComponents method to initialize all of the components for the frame. Then, the next group of statements calls the getProducts method of the ProductDB class to get an array list of Product objects.

The third group of statements within the constructor creates and populates a DefaultListModel object. This object provides a conceptual model for managing the items in the list. As a result, it's known as a *list model*. The table at the top of this figure presents some of the methods for working with a list model.

After creating the list model, an enhanced for loop populates the model with the product descriptions. To do that, it uses the addElement method of the list model object. Then, the setModel method of the list is used to associate the list model with the list. Finally, the setSelectedIndex method is used to set the initial selection to the first item in the list. That's necessary because the first item isn't selected by default like it is in a combo box.

The third example shows how to access the item or items that have been selected by the user. Here, the getSelectedValuesList method retrieves a list of selected values. Then, an enhanced for loop displays these values. Note that you can also use the getSelectedIndexes method to return the indexes of the selected items too if necessary. Similarly, if the list box only allows a single selection, you can use the getSelectedIndex or getSelectedValue method to get the selected index or value for the selected item.

Common methods for working with a list model

Method	Description
`addElement(Object)`	Adds the specified element to the list.
`contains(Object)`	Returns a true value if the list contains the specified object.
`get(int)`	Returns an Object type for the element at the specified position.
`removeElementAt(int)`	Removes the element at the specified position.
`size()`	Returns the number of elements in the list.
`clear()`	Removes all elements from the list.

Example 1: Code that declares a variable that stores products

```
private ArrayList<Product> products;
```

Example 2: Code that initializes the list

```
public ListFrame() {
    initComponents();

    products = ProductDB.getProducts();

    DefaultListModel<String> model = new DefaultListModel<>();
    for (Product p : products)
        model.addElement(p.getDescription());

    productList.setModel(model);
    productList.setSelectedIndex(0);
}
```

Example 3: Code that gets the selected items from the list

```
List<String> selections = productList.getSelectedValuesList();

String message = "You selected:\n";
for (String s : selections)
    message += s + "\n";
JOptionPane.showMessageDialog(this, message);
```

Description

- To modify the contents of a list using code, you must first create a *list model* that defines the data displayed by the list. The list model can be any object that implements the ListModel interface. The most commonly used model is the DefaultListModel class.
- When you use a list model, you should include an import statement for its class. The list model classes are in the javax.swing package.

The Payment application

Now that you understand how to work with different types of controls, you're ready to review a Payment application that uses some of these controls.

The user interface

Figure 16-6 shows the user interface for the Payment application. Here, the user can enter the data for a credit card by selecting the "Credit card" radio button and then using the other controls to enter the credit card data. Then, when the user clicks the Accept button, the application displays the credit card data in a dialog box.

Alternatively, the user can send a bill to the customer by selecting the "Bill customer" radio button. This disables the controls for entering credit card data. Then, the user can click the Accept button to display a message that indicates that the customer will be billed.

The code

Figure 16-7 shows the code for the Payment application. To start, after the constructor for the frame calls the initComponents method, it initializes the combo box that stores the list of years. To do that, this code gets the current year and then uses a for loop to add the current year and the next seven years to the combo box list. Notice that I didn't use code to initialize the items in the Card Type list or the combo box list that stores the list of months. Instead, I used the model property since these lists are short and unlikely to change.

In the event handler for the actionPerformed event of the radio button group, the first line of code checks if the "Credit card" radio button is selected. If so, this code passes a true value to the enableCreditCardControls method to enable the controls for entering the credit card data. On the other hand, if the "Bill customer" radio button is selected, this code disables the credit card controls.

In the event handler for the actionPerformed event of the Accept button, the first statement defines a variable that stores the message that's displayed. Then, this code gets the data entered by the user and formats it in a message. To do that, this code uses some of the methods described in this chapter. For example, it uses the getSelectedValue method of the list box. This works because this list box only allows the user to select a single item. Similarly, it uses the getSelectedItem method of the two combo boxes to get the selected expiration date. Since this method returns an Object type, this code casts the return values to String types.

After storing the appropriate message in the variable, this code displays the message in a dialog box. Then, it sets all of the controls to their default state. To do that, this code uses some of the methods described in this chapter. In particular, it uses the setSelectedIndex method of the list and combo boxes to select the first item in those controls. In addition, it passes a false value to the setSelected method of the check box to deselect that check box.

The user interface for the Payment application

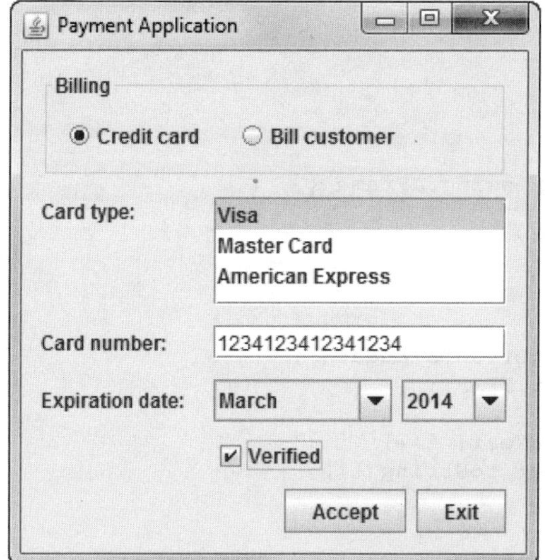

Typical dialog boxes displayed by the application

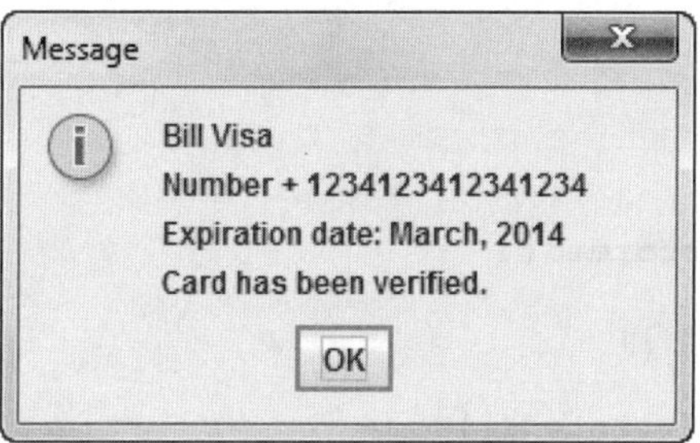

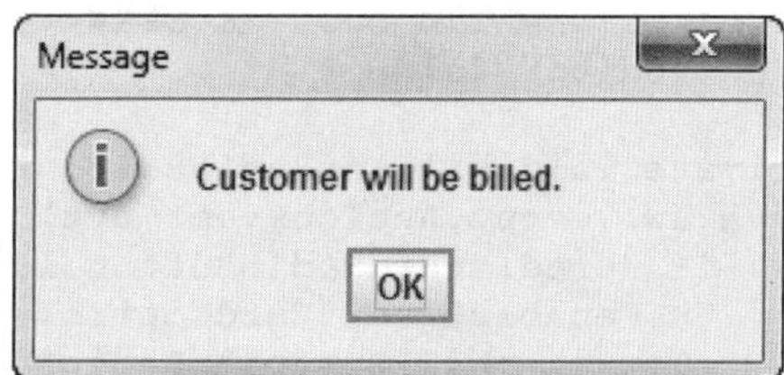

Description

- The Payment application uses some of the controls shown in this chapter to allow the user to enter information regarding a payment.
- To enter a credit card payment, the user selects the "Credit card" radio button, selects a card type from the list, enters a card number in the text field, and selects an expiration month and year from the combo boxes. If the credit card has been verified, the user can also select the check box. When the user clicks the Accept button, the application displays the credit card data that was entered in a dialog box.
- To send a bill to the customer, the user selects the "Bill customer" radio button. This disables the controls for entering credit card data. If the user clicks the Accept button, the application displays a dialog box with a message that indicates that the customer will be billed.
- To exit the application, the user clicks the Exit button.

Figure 16-6 The user interface for the Payment application

The code for the Payment application **Page 1**

```
package murach.ui;

import javax.swing.JOptionPane;
import java.util.Calendar;
import java.util.GregorianCalendar;

public class PaymentFrame extends javax.swing.JFrame {

    /** Creates new form PaymentFrame */
    public PaymentFrame() {
        initComponents();

        GregorianCalendar gc = new GregorianCalendar();
        int startYear = gc.get(Calendar.YEAR);
        int endYear = startYear + 8;
        for (int i = startYear; i < endYear; i++)
            yearComboBox.addItem(Integer.toString(i));
    }

    /** This method is called from within the constructor to
     * initialize the form.
     * WARNING: Do NOT modify this code. The content of this method is
     * always regenerated by the Form Editor.
     */
    private void initComponents() {
        // GENERATED CODE IS HERE
    }// </editor-fold>

    private void billingRadioButtonActionPerformed(
    java.awt.event.ActionEvent evt) {
        if (creditCardRadioButton.isSelected())
            enableCreditCardControls(true);
        else if (billCustomerRadioButton.isSelected())
            enableCreditCardControls(false);
    }

    private void enableCreditCardControls(boolean enable)
    {
        cardTypeList.setEnabled(enable);
        cardNumberTextField.setEnabled(enable);
        monthComboBox.setEnabled(enable);
        yearComboBox.setEnabled(enable);
        verifiedCheckBox.setEnabled(enable);
    }

    private void acceptButtonActionPerformed(java.awt.event.ActionEvent evt) {
        String msg = "";
        if (creditCardRadioButton.isSelected())
        {
            msg = "Bill " + (String)cardTypeList.getSelectedValue() +
                  "\nNumber + " + cardNumberTextField.getText() +
                  "\nExpiration date: " +
                  (String)monthComboBox.getSelectedItem() +
                   ", " + (String)yearComboBox.getSelectedItem();
```

Figure 16-7 The code for the Payment application (part 1 of 2)

The code for the Payment application **Page 2**

```
            if (verifiedCheckBox.isSelected())
                msg+= "\nCard has been verified.";
            else
                msg+= "\nCard has not been verified.";
        }
        else
        {
            msg = "Customer will be billed.";
        }
        JOptionPane.showMessageDialog(this, msg);
        cardTypeList.setSelectedIndex(0);
        cardNumberTextField.setText("");
        monthComboBox.setSelectedIndex(0);
        yearComboBox.setSelectedIndex(0);
        verifiedCheckBox.setSelected(false);
    }

    private void exitButtonActionPerformed(java.awt.event.ActionEvent evt) {
        System.exit(0);
    }

    public static void main(String args[]) {
        java.awt.EventQueue.invokeLater(new Runnable() {
            public void run() {
                PaymentFrame frame = new PaymentFrame();
                frame.setVisible(true);
                frame.setLocationRelativeTo(null);
            }
        });
    }

    // Variables declaration - do not modify
    private javax.swing.JButton acceptButton;
    private javax.swing.JRadioButton billCustomerRadioButton;
    private javax.swing.ButtonGroup buttonGroup1;
    private javax.swing.JTextField cardNumberTextField;
    private javax.swing.JList cardTypeList;
    private javax.swing.JRadioButton creditCardRadioButton;
    private javax.swing.JButton exitButton;
    private javax.swing.JLabel jLabel1;
    private javax.swing.JLabel jLabel2;
    private javax.swing.JLabel jLabel3;
    private javax.swing.JPanel jPanel1;
    private javax.swing.JScrollPane jScrollPane1;
    private javax.swing.JComboBox monthComboBox;
    private javax.swing.JCheckBox verifiedCheckBox;
    private javax.swing.JComboBox yearComboBox;
    // End of variables declaration

}
```

Figure 16-7 The code for the Payment application (part 2 of 2)

How to code low-level events

So far, you've learned how to handle the *semantic events* that are generated by controls, such as when the user clicks on a button or selects an item from a combo box. Now, you'll learn how to work with *low-level events*, such as a mouse being moved or the user pressing a key on the keyboard.

A summary of low-level events

The table in figure 16-8 presents a summary of some common low-level events. The first four types of events can occur on any component. In other words, any component can be wired to an event handler for a focus, key, mouse, or component event. On the other hand, a window event can only occur on a window such as a frame.

To understand how events work in Java, you need to know that every event class has a corresponding *listener* interface that defines the names of the events that can be handled. For example, the FocusEvent class has a corresponding interface named FocusListener that defines the focusGained and focusLost events. Similarly, the KeyEvent class has a corresponding KeyListener interface that defines the keyPressed, keyReleased, and keyTyped events.

In the next two figures, you'll learn how to work with the focus events and key events. Then, if you want to learn more about the rest of the low-level events, you can use NetBeans to view them, and you can experiment with them to figure out how they work. Or, you can look up the classes for these events in the documentation for the Java API. All of these classes are stored in the java.awt.event package.

Common low-level events and listeners

User action	Event class	Event name
Moving the focus	`FocusEvent`	`focusGained` `focusLost`

Pressing or releasing a key	`KeyEvent`	`keyPressed`
		`keyReleased`
		`keyTyped`

Moving, dragging, or clicking the mouse	`MouseEvent`	`mouseDragged`
		`mouseMoved`
		`mouseClicked`
		`mouseEntered`
		`mouseExited`
		`mousePressed`
		`mouseReleased`

Moving or sizing a component	`ComponentEvent`	`componentHidden`
		`componentMoved`
		`componentResized`
		`componentShown`

Working with the window	`WindowEvent`	`windowActivated`
		`windowClosed`
		`windowClosing`
		`windowDeactivated`
		`windowDeiconified`
		`windowIconified`
		`windowOpened`

Description

- A *semantic event* is an event that's related to a specific component like clicking on a button. In contrast, a *low-level event* is a less specific event like clicking the mouse.
- Every event class has a corresponding *listener* interface that defines the names of the events that can be handled.
- The classes for the events and their corresponding listeners are stored in the java.awt.event package.

Figure 16-8 A summary of low-level events

How to work with focus events

Figure 16-9 shows how to work with *focus events*. To start, this figure describes the two focus events. Then, it describes two methods you can use to get information about the FocusEvent object that's passed to the event handler for a focus event. Next, it describes the selectAll method of the JTextComponent class, which is inherited by the JTextField class that's used in the code example in this figure.

The code example shows an event handler for a focus event that selects the text in a text component that's receiving the focus. The declaration for this event handler is generated automatically when you use NetBeans to handle the focusGained event of a component. This event handler accepts a FocusEvent object as its only argument. In addition, this event handler has been given a generic name so it's appropriate for any text field on the form.

After the declaration for the event handler, the first line of code checks whether the component that generated this event is an instance of the JTextField class. If so, this method casts the component to a JTextField type and calls the component's selectAll method to select all of the text in the text field. In effect, this class causes the text field to automatically select all of its contents whenever it receives the focus. For some data entry applications, this can result in faster data entry.

Focus events

Event name	Description
`focusGained`	Invoked when a component gains the focus.
`focusLost`	Invoked when a component loses the focus.

Common methods of the FocusEvent class

Method	Description
`getComponent()`	Returns the component where the event occurred.
`getOppositeComponent()`	Returns the other component involved in the focus change.

A method of the JTextComponent class

Method	Description
`selectAll()`	Selects all of the text in the text component.

An event handler for a focus event

```
private void textFieldFocusGained(java.awt.event.FocusEvent evt)
{
    if (evt.getComponent() instanceof JTextField)
    {
        JTextField tf = (JTextField) evt.getComponent();
        tf.selectAll();
    }
}
```

Description

- A *focus event* occurs when the focus moves to or from a component.

Figure 16-9 How to work with focus events

How to work with keyboard events

Figure 16-10 shows how to work with *keyboard events* that result from keys being pressed. To start, this figure describes the three keyboard events. Then, it describes some of the methods of the KeyEvent class. Next, it describes the consume method of the InputEvent class, which is inherited by the KeyEvent class. As a result, this method is available from a KeyEvent object.

The code example shows an event handler for a keyboard event that prevents the user from entering non-numeric characters into a text field. The declaration for this event handler is generated automatically when you use NetBeans to handle the keyTyped event of a component. This event handler accepts a KeyEvent object as its only argument. In addition, this event handler has been given a generic name so it's appropriate for any text field on the form that accepts numeric data.

After the declaration, the first line of code calls the getKeyChar method of the KeyEvent object. This gets a character that represents the key that was pressed. Then, it checks whether the user pressed a key other than a numeral, a decimal point, or a plus or minus sign. If so, this code calls the consume method of the KeyEvent object to stop the event processing. For some data entry applications, this can help reduce data entry errors by preventing the user from entering non-numeric characters.

Keyboard events

Event	Description
`keyPressed`	Invoked when a key is pressed.
`keyReleased`	Invoked when a key is released.
`keyTyped`	Invoked when a key is pressed and released.

Common methods of the KeyEvent class

Method	Description
`getKeyCode()`	Returns an int that represents the key pressed.
`getKeyChar()`	Returns a char that represents the key pressed.
`isControlDown()`	Returns a boolean that indicates if the Ctrl key is down.
`isAltDown()`	Returns a boolean that indicates if the Alt key is down.
`isShiftDown()`	Returns a boolean that indicates if the Shift key is down.

A method of the InputEvent class

Method	Description
`consume()`	Stops further processing of the event.

An event handler for a keyboard event

```
private void numTextFieldKeyTyped(java.awt.event.KeyEvent evt)
{
    char c = evt.getKeyChar();

    if (c != '0' && c != '1' && c != '2' &&
        c != '3' && c != '4' && c != '5' &&
        c != '6' && c != '7' && c != '8' &&
        c != '9' && c != '.' && c != '+' && c != '-')
    {
        evt.consume();
    }
}
```

Description

- A *keyboard event* occurs when a user presses, releases, or presses and releases a key.

Figure 16-10 How to work with keyboard events

The Product Maintenance application

Now that you understand how the Payment application works and you've learned how to code low-level events, you're ready to review a GUI version of the Product Maintenance application. This application was first presented as a console application in chapter 9, and the GUI version uses many of the same classes as the console version.

However, there are two primary differences. First, the GUI version uses the ProductMaintFrame class instead of the ProductMaintApp class to get and display data. Second, the GUI version uses the SwingValidator class instead of the Validator class to validate data. If necessary, you can review chapter 8 for more information about how the rest of the classes in this application work.

The user interface

Figure 16-11 presents the user interface for the Product Maintenance application. As you can see, the main form for this application lets the user add, edit, or delete products.

To add a product, the user clicks the Add button. This causes the product code, description, and price text fields to be cleared and enabled so the user can enter data for the new product. In addition, the Add, Edit, and Delete buttons are disabled and the Accept and Cancel buttons are enabled. The user can then enter data for the new product and click the Accept button to add the product to the products data store as well as to the combo box. The user can also click the Cancel button to cancel the entry. Either way, the form reverts to its original state: the text fields are disabled, the Add, Edit, and Delete buttons are enabled, and the Accept and Cancel buttons are disabled.

To edit an existing product, the user selects the product from the combo box. Then, the product's data appears in the text fields, which are still disabled so they can't be changed. However, if the user clicks the Edit button, the application enables the description and price text fields (the application doesn't allow the user to change the product code), disables the Add, Edit, and Delete buttons, and enables the Accept and Cancel buttons. At this point, the user can edit the description or price and click the Accept button to save the changes to the products data store. The user can also click the Cancel button to cancel the changes.

To delete a product, the user selects the product from the combo box and clicks the Delete button. This deletes the product from the products data store and removes it from the combo box.

When the user moves the focus into an enabled text field, the application selects the text in that field. In this figure, for example, the user has selected a product and moved the focus into the Unit Price field. As a result, the application has selected the text in that field.

The user interface for the Product Maintenance application

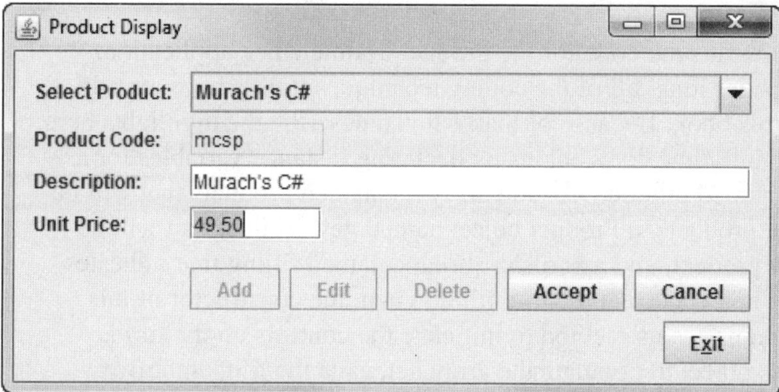

Typical dialog boxes displayed when invalid data is entered

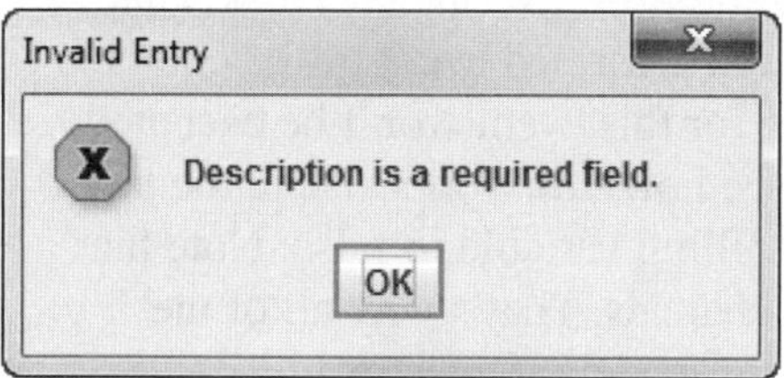

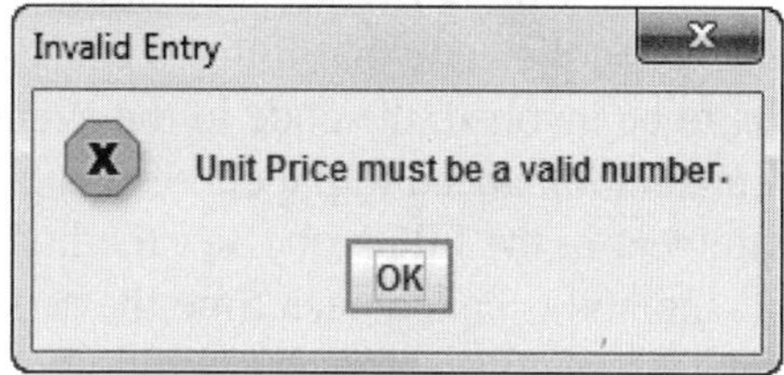

Description

- The Product Maintenance application lets the user add, edit, or delete products. It is similar to the Product Maintenance application that was presented in chapter 9, but it is a GUI application rather than a console application.
- To add a new product, the user clicks the Add button. This enables the Product Code, Description, and Unit Price text fields as well as the Accept and Cancel buttons. Then, the user enters the data for the new product and clicks the Accept button to accept the new product or the Cancel button to cancel the entry.
- To edit a product, the user selects the product from the combo box. This displays the data for the selected product in the text fields. Then, the user clicks the Edit button to enable the Description and Unit Price text fields. Finally, the user can enter any necessary changes and click the Accept button to accept the changes or the Cancel button to cancel the changes.
- To delete a product, the user selects the product from the combo box and then clicks the Delete button.
- When the user moves the focus into an enabled text field, the text within that field is automatically selected.

Figure 16-11 The user interface for the Product Maintenance application

The code

Figure 16-12 presents the code for the Product Maintenance application. Although it's five pages long, all of the coding techniques it uses have already been presented in this book. Because of that, I'll just describe the highlights here.

The ProductMaintFrame class begins by declaring instance variables for a data access object named productDAO, an array list named products that will be used to store all the products, a Product object named newProduct that will be used to store a new product, and a boolean variable named filling that indicates whether the combo box is currently being filled. Then, the constructor of this class calls the initComponents method to initialize the controls on the form, uses the data access object to populate the array list, calls the fillComboBox method to add the products to it, and calls the showProduct method to display the data for the first product.

The fillComboBox method starts by setting the filling variable to true. That way, when the code that follows causes the actionPerformed event of the combo box to be invoked, the code in the event handler for this event won't be executed. You can look ahead to page 3 of this listing to see how this works. Then, the last statement in the fillComboBox method sets the filling variable to false. Note that this method is called each time the product list changes. That's why all of the items are removed from the combo box before the current items are added.

The fillComboBox method is followed by a series of methods that are used by the event handlers of the frame. The selectProduct method selects an item in the combo box. The getCurrentProduct method gets a product from the combo box. And the showProduct method displays the code, description, and price for a specified product in the text fields.

The code for the Product Maintenance application Page 1

```
package murach.ui;

import javax.swing.JTextField;
import java.util.ArrayList;

import murach.business.Product;
import murach.db.*;

public class ProductMaintFrame extends javax.swing.JFrame {

    // declare global variables for the form
    ProductDAO productDAO;
    ArrayList<Product> products;
    Product newProduct = null;
    boolean filling = false;

    /** Creates new form ProductMaintenanceFrame */
    public ProductMaintFrame() {
        initComponents();

        // fill the products combo box
        productDAO = DAOFactory.getProductDAO();
        products = productDAO.getProducts();
        this.fillComboBox(products);
        this.showProduct(this.getCurrentProduct());
    }

    // <editor-fold defaultstate="collapsed" desc=" Generated Code ">
    private void initComponents()
    {
        // GENERATED CODE IS HERE
    }// </editor-fold>

    private void fillComboBox(ArrayList<Product> a) {
        filling = true;
        productComboBox.removeAllItems();
        for (Product p : a)
            productComboBox.addItem(p);
        filling = false;
    }

    private void selectProduct(Product p) {
        productComboBox.setSelectedItem(p);
    }

    private Product getCurrentProduct() {
        return (Product) productComboBox.getSelectedItem();
    }

    private void showProduct(Product p) {
        codeTextField.setText(p.getCode());
        descriptionTextField.setText(p.getDescription());
        priceTextField.setText(p.getFormattedPrice());
    }
```

Figure 16-12 The code for the Product Maintenance application (part 1 of 5)

The setAddMode, setEditMode, and setDisplayMode methods call the setEditable and setFocusable methods of the text fields, passing a value that depends on whether the user is adding, editing, or displaying a product. Similarly, the setAddEditMode method enables or disables the maintenance buttons depending on the operation that's being performed. It also enables or disables the combo box.

As I mentioned earlier, the code in the event handler for the actionPerformed event of the combo box is executed only if the combo box is not being filled. In other words, it's executed only if the user selects another

The code for the Product Maintenance application

Page 2

```
private void clearFields() {
    codeTextField.setText("");
    descriptionTextField.setText("");
    priceTextField.setText("");
}

// return a new Product object with the data in the text fields
private Product getProduct() {
    Product p = new Product();
    p.setCode(codeTextField.getText());
    p.setDescription(descriptionTextField.getText());
    p.setFormattedPrice(priceTextField.getText());
    return p;
}

private void setAddMode() {
    codeTextField.setEditable(true);
    codeTextField.setFocusable(true);
    codeTextField.requestFocusInWindow();
    descriptionTextField.setEditable(true);
    descriptionTextField.setFocusable(true);
    priceTextField.setEditable(true);
    priceTextField.setFocusable(true);
}

private void setEditMode() {
    descriptionTextField.setEditable(true);
    descriptionTextField.setFocusable(true);
    descriptionTextField.requestFocusInWindow();
    priceTextField.setEditable(true);
    priceTextField.setFocusable(true);
}

private void setDisplayMode() {
    codeTextField.setEditable(false);
    codeTextField.setFocusable(false);
    descriptionTextField.setEditable(false);
    descriptionTextField.setFocusable(false);
    priceTextField.setEditable(false);
    priceTextField.setFocusable(false);
}

private void setAddEditMode(boolean e) {
    addButton.setEnabled(!e);
    editButton.setEnabled(!e);
    deleteButton.setEnabled(!e);
    productComboBox.setEnabled(!e);
    acceptButton.setEnabled(e);
    cancelButton.setEnabled(e);
}
```

Figure 16-12 The code for the Product Maintenance application (part 2 of 5)

item from the list. Then, this event handler gets the current product from the combo box and displays the data for that product in the text fields.

The event handler for the actionPerformed event of the Add button starts by creating a new Product object and clearing the data entry fields. Then, it calls the setAddEditMode method so the appropriate controls are enabled, and it calls the setAddMode method so the user can enter data for a new product. Note that this event handler doesn't actually add a new product. That's done after the user enters the data for the product and clicks the Accept button.

The event handler for the actionPerformed event of the Edit button also calls the setAddEditMode method. Then, it calls the setEditMode method so the user can edit the product. Like the event handler for the actionPerformed event of the Add button, this event handler doesn't actually update the product. That's done when the user clicks the Accept button.

In contrast, the event handler for the actionPerformed event of the Delete button actually deletes the selected product. To do that, it starts by getting the current product. Then, it deletes the product from the data store, and it removes the product from the products array list. Next, it reloads the combo box so it doesn't contain the deleted product, it selects the first product in the combo box and displays the data for that product in the text fields, and it moves the focus to the combo box.

The event handler for the actionPerformed event of the Accept button begins by calling the isValidData method to validate the input data. Note that this method, shown on page 4 of this listing, checks the newProduct variable for a null value to determine if a product is being added or updated. If a product is being added, the product code field is validated. Otherwise, it isn't.

If the data is valid, this event handler either adds a new product or updates an existing product depending on whether newProduct is null. To add a new product, it starts by getting a product with the values the user entered. Then, it adds the object to the data store and the products array list, it refreshes the combo box so it includes the new product, and it selects that product. Finally, it sets newProduct to null to prepare for the next user action.

To update an existing product, this event handler gets the current product as well as a new product with the values the user entered. Then, it assigns the new description and price values to the existing product, updates the product in the data store, and updates the display. Finally, this event handler resets the controls on the form so the user can perform another operation.

The event handler for the actionPerformed event of the Cancel button starts by setting the newProduct variable to null. Then, it sets the controls to display mode, calls the showProduct method to redisplay the data for the current product, sets add/edit mode to false, and moves the focus to the combo box. This effectively discards any changes made by the user.

The event handler for the focusGained event is wired to all three text fields. As a result, if these fields are enabled and the user moves the focus into one of them, this event handler selects all of the existing text in that field.

The code for the Product Maintenance application **Page 3**

```
private void productComboBoxActionPerformed(
java.awt.event.ActionEvent evt) {
    if (!filling) {
        Product p = (Product) productComboBox.getSelectedItem();
        this.showProduct(p);
    }
}

private void addButtonActionPerformed(java.awt.event.ActionEvent evt) {
    newProduct = new Product();
    this.clearFields();
    this.setAddEditMode(true);
    this.setAddMode();
}

private void editButtonActionPerformed(java.awt.event.ActionEvent evt) {
    this.setAddEditMode(true);
    this.setEditMode();
}

private void deleteButtonActionPerformed(java.awt.event.ActionEvent evt) {
    Product p = this.getProduct();
    productDAO.deleteProduct(p);
    products.remove(p);
    this.fillComboBox(products);
    this.selectProduct(products.get(0));
    this.showProduct(products.get(0));
    this.productComboBox.requestFocusInWindow();
}

private void acceptButtonActionPerformed(java.awt.event.ActionEvent evt) {
    if (isValidData()) {
        if (newProduct != null) {
            newProduct = this.getProduct();
            productDAO.addProduct(newProduct);
            products.add(newProduct);
            this.fillComboBox(products);
            this.selectProduct(newProduct);
            newProduct = null;
        }
        else {
            Product cp = this.getCurrentProduct();
            Product p = this.getProduct();
            cp.setDescription(p.getDescription());
            cp.setPrice(p.getPrice());
            productDAO.updateProduct(cp);
            this.fillComboBox(products);
            this.selectProduct(cp);
            this.showProduct(this.getCurrentProduct());
        }
        this.setDisplayMode();
        this.setAddEditMode(false);
        this.productComboBox.requestFocusInWindow();
    }
}
```

Figure 16-12 The code for the Product Maintenance application (part 3 of 5)

The code for the Product Maintenance application **Page 4**

```
private boolean isValidData() {
    SwingValidator sv = new SwingValidator();
    if (newProduct != null)
        return
            sv.isPresent(this.codeTextField, "Product Code") &&
            sv.isPresent(this.descriptionTextField, "Description") &&
            sv.isPresent(this.priceTextField, "Unit Price") &&
            sv.isDouble(this.priceTextField, "Unit Price");
    else
        return
            sv.isPresent(this.descriptionTextField, "Description") &&
            sv.isPresent(this.priceTextField, "Unit Price") &&
            sv.isDouble(this.priceTextField, "Unit Price");
}

private void cancelButtonActionPerformed(java.awt.event.ActionEvent evt) {
    if (newProduct != null) {
        newProduct = null;
    }
    this.setDisplayMode();
    this.showProduct(this.getCurrentProduct());
    this.setAddEditMode(false);
    this.productComboBox.requestFocusInWindow();
}

private void textBoxFocusGained(java.awt.event.FocusEvent evt)
{
    if (evt.getComponent() instanceof JTextField) {
        JTextField t = (JTextField) evt.getComponent();
        t.selectAll();
    }
}

private void exitButtonActionPerformed(java.awt.event.ActionEvent evt) {
    System.exit(0);
}

/**
 * @param args the command line arguments
 */
public static void main(String args[]) {
    java.awt.EventQueue.invokeLater(new Runnable() {
        @Override
        public void run() {
            ProductMaintFrame frame = new ProductMaintFrame();
            frame.setVisible(true);
            frame.setLocationRelativeTo(null);
        }
    });
}
```

Figure 16-12 The code for the Product Maintenance application (part 4 of 5)

The code for the Product Maintenance application **Page 5**

```
    // Variables declaration - do not modify
    private javax.swing.JButton acceptButton;
    private javax.swing.JButton addButton;
    private javax.swing.JButton cancelButton;
    private javax.swing.JTextField codeTextField;
    private javax.swing.JButton deleteButton;
    private javax.swing.JTextField descriptionTextField;
    private javax.swing.JButton editButton;
    private javax.swing.JButton exitButton;
    private javax.swing.JLabel jLabel1;
    private javax.swing.JLabel jLabel2;
    private javax.swing.JLabel jLabel3;
    private javax.swing.JLabel jLabel4;
    private javax.swing.JTextField priceTextField;
    private javax.swing.JComboBox productComboBox;
    // End of variables declaration

}
```

Figure 16-12 The code for the Product Maintenance application (part 5 of 5)

Perspective

In this chapter, you learned how to work with some new components, and you learned how to handle low-level events such as focus events and keyboard events. If you understand the Product Maintenance application that's presented at the end of this chapter, you've come a long way. Once you master the data access skills that are presented in the next section, you'll have a solid set of skills for developing Java applications at a professional level.

Summary

- A *text area* lets the user enter one or more lines of text. You can use many of the same techniques to work with text fields and text areas.
- A *scroll pane* can provide scroll bars for controls. By default, NetBeans automatically adds a text area to a scroll pane since text areas often need scroll bars.
- *Radio buttons* let the user select one option from a group of options in a *button group*. A *check box* lets the user select or deselect a single option.
- When working with radio buttons and other related controls, you can visually group them by adding them to a *panel* that has a *border*.
- A *combo box* lets a user select one item from a drop-down list of items, and a *list* lets a user select one or more items from a list of items.
- A *semantic event* is an event that's related to a specific component like selecting a button. In contrast, a *low-level event* is a less specific event.
- Two types of low-level events are *focus events* such as moving the focus to a control and *keyboard events* such as pressing or releasing a key.

Exercise 16-1 Modify the Future Value application

For this exercise, you'll modify the Future Value application presented in chapter 15 so that it uses a combo box and a list. When you're done, the user interface should look something like this:

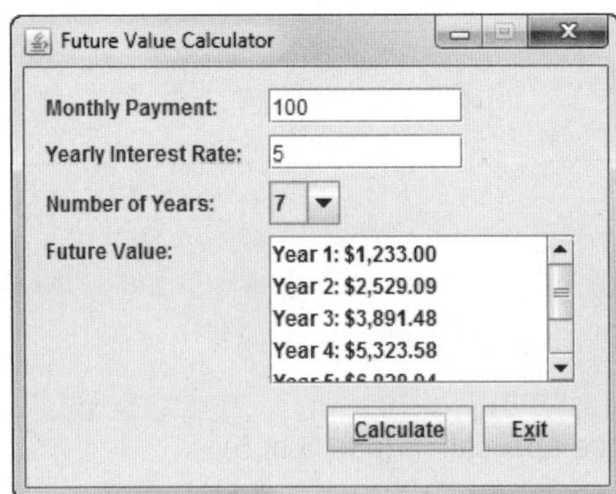

1. Open the project named ch16_ex1_FutureValue in the ex_starts directory. Then, review the design and code for the form.
2. Replace the Number of Years text field with a combo box. Then, code a method that fills this combo box with the values 1 through 20, and call this method from the constructor for the frame. Make any other necessary changes to provide for the combo box. Test the project to be sure it works correctly.
3. Replace the Future Value text field with a list that displays five rows and uses a vertical scroll bar but no horizontal scroll bar.
4. Modify the actionPerformed event for the Calculate button so that instead of calculating a single value, it calculates the future value for each year up to the year selected via the combo box and adds a string showing the calculation for each year to the list.
5. Test the project to be sure it works correctly.

Exercise 16-2 Create a Pizza Calculator application

For this exercise, you'll develop an application that calculates the price of a pizza based on its size and toppings. The user interface for this application should look something like this:

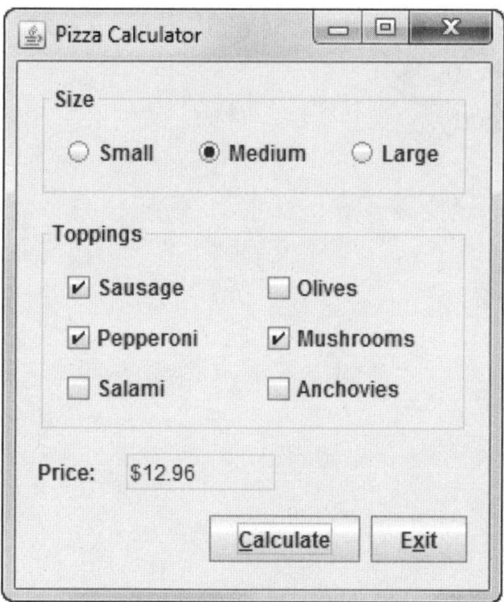

1. Open the project named ch16_ex2_PizzaOrder in the ex_starts directory. This project contains an empty form.
2. Add the controls and code necessary to implement this application. When the user selects a size and toppings for the pizza and clicks the Calculate button, the application should calculate the price of the pizza and display that price in the text field. To calculate the price of the pizza, add the price of the selected toppings to the base price of the pizza:

Item	Price
Small pizza	$6.99
Medium pizza	$8.99
Large pizza	$10.99
Sausage	$1.49
Pepperoni	$1.49
Salami	$1.49
Olives	$0.99
Mushrooms	$0.99
Anchovies	$0.99

3. Test the project to be sure it works correctly.

Exercise 16-3 Add low-level events to the Future Value application

1. Open the project named ch16_ex3_FutureValue in the ex_starts directory. Review the code for this application.
2. Add low-level event handlers that prevent the user from entering non-numeric characters into the text fields.
3. Add low-level event handlers that automatically select the characters in each text field when the text field receives the focus.
4. Test the project to be sure it works correctly.

17

How to develop and deploy applets

In this chapter, you'll learn how to develop and deploy an applet, a special type of application that can be downloaded from an Internet or intranet server and run on a client computer within a web browser. Applets are unique to Java, and they helped fuel the remarkable growth of Java in its early days. In recent years, though, other technologies such as DOM scripting, Adobe Flash, JavaFX, AJAX, Microsoft Silverlight, and HTML 5 have taken over many of the tasks that used to be performed with applets. Nevertheless, applets are still commonly used for some types of applications such as online games.

An introduction to applets

This topic begins by showing a simple applet. Then, it discusses some security issues that apply to applets. Finally, it gives an overview of the classes and methods that you use to work with applets.

The Future Value Calculator applet

Figure 17-1 shows the Future Value Calculator application that was presented in chapter 15 after it has been converted to an *applet*. The main difference between this applet and the application is that an applet can be stored on a web server. Then, anyone with a web browser can run this applet within their browser. Another difference is that the applet doesn't include an Exit button. That's because it runs in a web page within a browser, not in a frame. As a result, you exit from the applet by closing the browser or by navigating to another page.

A brief history of applets

Applets were introduced with version 1.0 of the JDK, which was released in 1996. In the early days of applets, both major browsers (Internet Explorer and Netscape) included versions of the *Java Runtime Environment* (*JRE*). Because the JRE provides for running compiled programs in Java, this allowed applets to be run within the browser. However, the version of the JRE that was included with Microsoft's Internet Explorer differed slightly from the version of the JRE that was included with the Netscape browser. Worse, after version 1.1 of the JDK, Microsoft stopped upgrading its version of the JRE. As a result, when later versions of the JDK became available, Internet Explorer couldn't run applets that used any of the newer Java features, including Swing.

To get around these problems, Sun developed the *Java Plug-in*. This piece of software is similar to other browser plug-ins such as Apple QuickTime that extend the browser's capabilities. It allows the browser to run a current and standard version of the JRE. Before the user can run an applet for the first time, the JRE, which includes the Java Plug-in, must be downloaded and installed. Fortunately, the JRE is downloaded and installed automatically in most cases.

In 2007, Microsoft stopped including its version of the JRE in Internet Explorer. Similarly, some of the newer web browsers (such as Firefox, Chrome, Safari, and Opera) don't include a version of the JRE. However, all of these browsers can use the Java Plug-in to run applets.

The Future Value Calculator applet

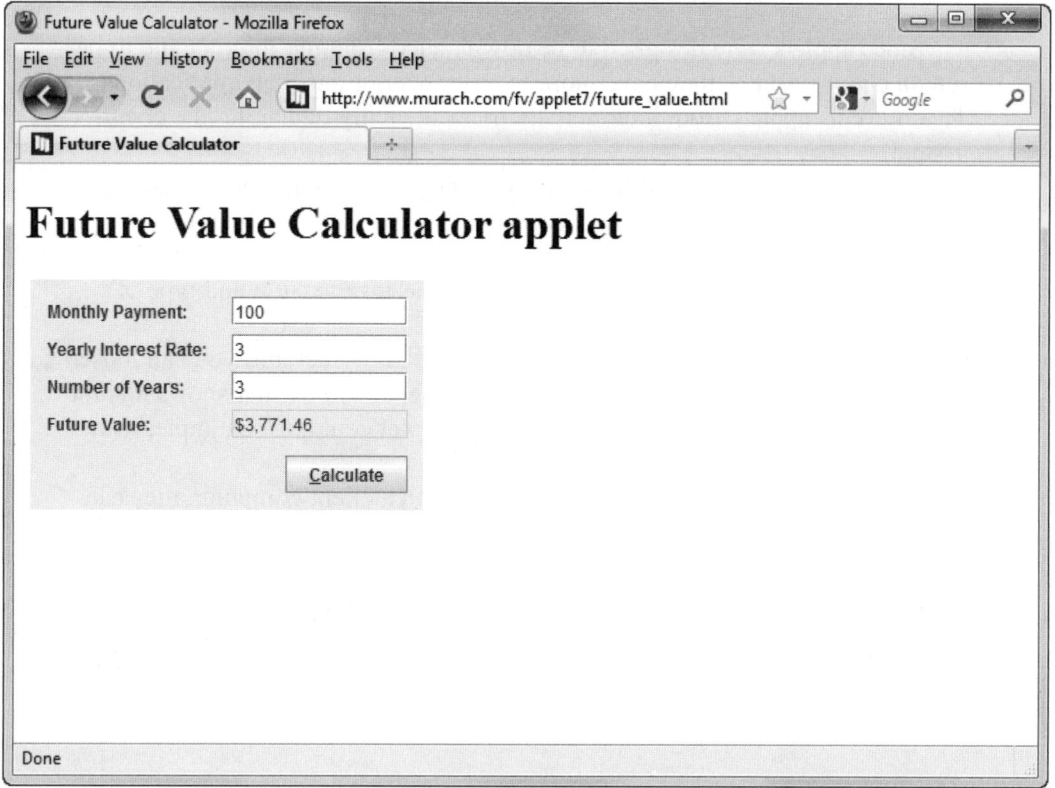

Description

- An *applet* is a special type of application that can be downloaded from an Internet or intranet server and run on the client's computer within a web browser.
- The *Java Plug-in* is a browser plug-in that allows a web browser to use the Java Runtime Environment to run an applet.
- The *Java Runtime Environment* (*JRE*) is the Java interpreter that lets you run compiled programs in Java. The Java plug-in is included as part of the JRE.
- For a client machine to run applets, a current version of the JRE and Java Plug-in must be installed on the client.
- When you install the current version of the JDK, the current version of the JRE is automatically installed on your machine.
- If a user attempts to run an applet without first installing the required version of the JRE, the JRE will be downloaded automatically, and the user will be prompted to install it.
- The JRE and Java Plug-in can be downloaded from www.java.com. If necessary, you can provide a link to this site from your web page.

Figure 17-1 How applets work

Applet security issues

Since applets were designed to be downloaded from the Internet and to be run on client systems, they have more security restrictions than applications. This prevents applets from intentionally or accidentally damaging the client system.

Figure 17-2 lists some of these security restrictions. This shows that an applet can't access any files or databases on the client system, and it can't access much information about the client system. In fact, an applet can only access the information it needs to run, such as the Java version and type of operating system that's used by the client.

Although applets have tight security restrictions by default, you can loosen these restrictions. To do that, you can create a *signed applet* that shows that the applet comes from a trusted source. Then, an applet could, for example, read files from the client system's hard drive.

Although applets can't read and write files on a client computer, they can read and write files on Internet, intranet, and network servers. To do that, an applet can send and receive data from other programs located on the host server. This way, another program can read and write files and transfer the data back and forth to the applet. However, this requires some networking techniques that aren't presented in this book. That's why this chapter focuses on applets that don't work with files or databases.

What an applet can't do

- Read, write, or delete files or databases on the client system.
- Access information about the files or databases on the client system.
- Run programs on the client system.
- Access system properties for the client system except the Java version, the name and version of the operating system, and the characters used to separate directories, paths, and lines.
- Make network connections to other servers available to the client system.

What an applet can do

- Display user interface components and graphics.
- Send keystrokes and mouse clicks back to the applet's server.
- Make network connections to the applet's server.
- Call public methods from other applets on the same web page.

Description

- To prevent applets from damaging a client system or from making it possible to damage a client system, security restrictions limit what an applet can do.
- To overcome these security restrictions, you can create a *signed applet*. This indicates that the applet comes from a trusted source. Then, you can add rights to the signed applet.

Figure 17-2 Applet security issues

The inheritance hierarchy for applets

Figure 17-3 begins by presenting the inheritance hierarchy for the JApplet class that's stored in the javax.swing package. In figure 17-5, you'll learn how to extend this class to define an applet that uses Swing components.

The JApplet class inherits the older Applet class that's stored in the java.applet package. This class contains the methods that control the execution of an applet.

The JApplet class also inherits the Component, Container, and Panel classes. As a result, you can call methods of these classes to work with the applet, to place other components on the applet, and to handle the events that are generated for the applet. Since you've already learned how to use these classes, you should already have most of the skills that you need for developing applets.

Four methods of an applet

Figure 17-3 also introduces the four methods of the Applet class that are used to control the execution of any applet. Since the browser automatically calls these methods, you don't need to call them explicitly. However, when you write the code for an applet, you need to override one or more of these methods to provide the functionality of your applet. In figure 17-5, for example, you'll see how to override the init method to initialize an applet.

The inheritance hierarchy for a Swing applet

```
java.awt.Component
    java.awt.Container
        java.awt.Panel
            java.applet.Applet
                javax.swing.JApplet
```

Four methods of the Applet class

Method	Description
`public void init()`	Called when the browser first loads the applet.
`public void start()`	Called after the init method and every time the user moves to the web page for the applet.
`public void stop()`	Called before the destroy method and every time the user moves to another web page.
`public void destroy()`	Called when the user exits the browser.

Description

- To create a Swing applet, you define a class that extends the JApplet class. This class is stored in the javax.swing package, and it inherits the Applet class in the java.applet package.
- Once you define a class that extends the JApplet class, you can override any of the four methods of the Applet class. These methods are called automatically by the browser as indicated above, and they control the execution of the applet.
- The JApplet class also inherits the Component, Container, and Panel classes. As a result, you can call methods of these classes when you code an applet.

Figure 17-3 The inheritance hierarchy and methods of an applet

How to develop applets

In this topic, you'll learn how to develop and test an applet. More specifically, you'll learn how to develop the user interface for an applet, how to write the code for an applet, and how to test an applet using a tool that comes with the JDK.

How to develop a panel for an applet

To develop an applet in NetBeans, you start by using the Swing GUI Builder to create a *panel* that contains the controls and code for the applet. Fortunately, the skills for developing a panel are similar to the skills for developing a frame. In figure 17-4, for example, you can see the panel for a Future Value applet. The only difference between this panel and the Future Value frame that was presented in chapter 15 is that the panel doesn't include an Exit button. That's because the applet will run within a browser.

The code for the panel is also similar to the code for the Future Value frame. In fact, the only difference is that the panel doesn't include code for the ActionPerformed event of the Exit button since the panel doesn't include an Exit button. As a result, if you understand how to develop the Future Value frame, you shouldn't have any trouble developing a Future Value panel like the one shown in this figure.

After you create the panel for an applet, you can add that panel to an applet and then run and test the applet on your computer. You'll learn how to do that in the next figure.

The FutureValuePanel class in Design view

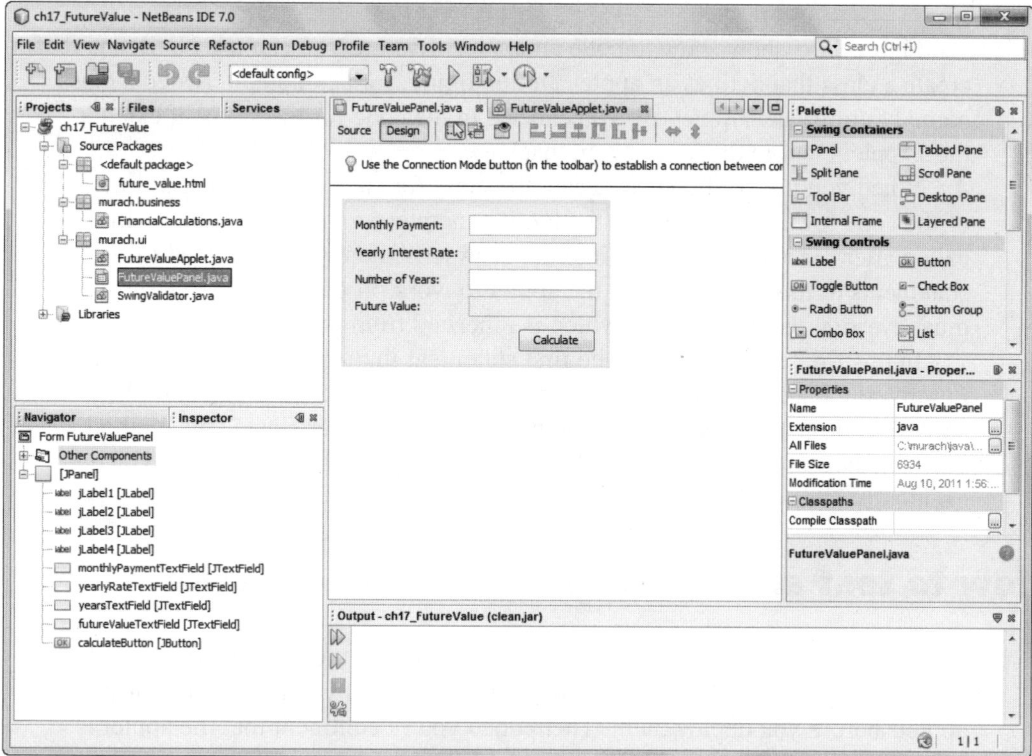

Description

- To create a class that defines a panel, right-click on the package where you want to add the panel. Then, select the New→JPanel Form command and use the resulting dialog box to enter a name for the class.
- You can use the same skills for developing a JPanel class for a form as you do for developing a JFrame class for a form.
- The form for an application often includes an Exit button. Since an applet runs within a browser, the form for an applet should not include an Exit button.

How to code an applet

Figure 17-5 shows how to code an applet. To start, you can use NetBeans to create a class that defines an applet. In this figure, for example, I created a class named FutureValueApplet. As you can see in the code for this class, it extends the JApplet class in the javax.swing package.

When you use NetBeans to create the class for an applet, it generates most of the code for the applet. In particular, it generates an init method that will be called after the applet is loaded into the browser. Often, you only need to add statements to this method to get the applet to work properly. To do that, you must override the init method, which is inherited from the Applet class.

In this figure, for example, the first statement in the init method creates a FutureValuePanel object. Then, the second statement adds that object to the applet. To do that, it uses the add method of the Container class. This method is available because the FutureValuePanel class inherits the JPanel class, which eventually inherits the Container class.

How to test an applet with the Applet Viewer

Figure 17-5 also shows how to test an applet with the Applet Viewer. The Applet Viewer is a tool that's included in the JDK, and you can use it to test applets before you deploy them. Then, once you're confident that the applet is working correctly, you can deploy it and use a web browser to do the final testing.

An applet in the Applet Viewer

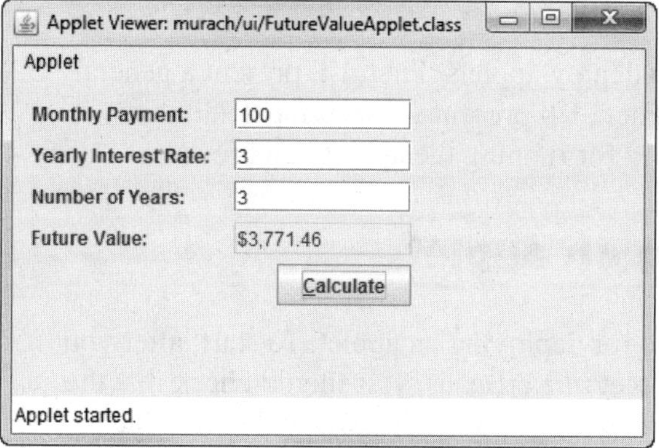

The FutureValueApplet class

```
package murach.ui;

import javax.swing.JApplet;

public class FutureValueApplet extends JApplet
{
    @Override
    public void init()
    {
        FutureValuePanel panel = new FutureValuePanel();
        this.add(panel);
    }
}
```

A method that you can use to add a panel to a container such as an applet

Method	Description
`add(Component)`	Adds a component to the container.

Description

- To create a class that defines an applet, right-click on the package where you want to add the applet and select the New→Other command to display the New File dialog box. Then, select the Java category, select the JApplet file type, and click the Next button. Finally, enter a class name for the applet in the New JApplet dialog box that's displayed.
- Most of the code for an applet is generated by NetBeans when you create the class for the applet. Then, you can add code to the init method of the applet class that adds the appropriate panel to the applet.
- The Applet Viewer lets you test an applet before you deploy it. The Applet Viewer is included in the JDK.
- To run an applet in the Applet Viewer, right-click on the java file for the applet and select the Run File command. If necessary, resize the Applet Viewer window so it's the correct size for the applet.

How to deploy applets

In this topic, you'll learn how to deploy applets. First, I'll present a general procedure for deploying an applet. Then, I'll present some of the details for creating a web page for the applet and for running the applet in a browser.

A procedure for deploying an applet

Figure 17-6 presents a procedure for deploying an applet. To start, after you open the project that contains the applet in NetBeans, you should check that the Source/Binary Format option is set the way you want it. This will determine what version of the JRE will need to be installed on clients that run the applet. Typically, you'll want to set this option to the version before the most recent version. If the most recent version of the JRE is version 7, for example, you'll want to set this option to JDK 6.

After you set the Source/Binary Format option, you build the project to create a JAR file for the applet. This file is stored in the dist subfolder of the project folder by default. Note, though, that you can't see this folder in NetBeans.

Next, you create an HTML file for the web page that contains the applet. You'll learn how to do that in the next figure. As you'll see in that figure, the HTML file refers to the JAR file for the applet. Because of that, these two files must be in the same folder. An easy way to do that during development is to copy the HTML file to the dist subfolder of the project, since that's where the JAR file is stored. An alternative is to create a new folder and then copy both files into that folder. In either case, you'll need to use the program for your operating system that lets you work with the files on your computer. For the Windows operating system, for example, you can use Windows Explorer.

After you create the HTML file and place it in the same folder as the JAR file, you can display the HTML file in a browser so you can test the applet. Then, if the applet works correctly, you can store the JAR and HTML files on a web server. If you're deploying the applet to a web server on an intranet, you can typically do that by simply copying the files to the appropriate folder on the server. If you're deploying the applet to the Internet, however, you'll need to use an FTP application to upload the files to the server. Then, the applet will be available to any client computer that has a web browser and security clearance to view the HTML page.

Note that if the client computer doesn't have the specified minimum version of the JRE installed, it will be download automatically. Then, a dialog box will prompt the user to install the Java Plug-in. If the user agrees to install it, the browser downloads the JRE from www.java.com and launches the installer.

A procedure for deploying an applet

1. Open the project that contains the applet in NetBeans and be sure you have the Source/Binary Format option for the project set the way you want it.
2. Build the project to create a JAR file that contains the class files and resources for the applet.
3. Create an HTML file for the web page that contains the applet. See figure 17-7 for details.
4. Place the JAR and HTML files in the same folder.
5. Display the HTML file for the applet in a browser to view and test the applet.
6. Copy the JAR and HTML files to a server to make them accessible to users.

Description

- To display the Source/Binary Format option in NetBeans, right-click on the project, select the Properties command, and then select the Sources category in the resulting dialog box. See chapter 1 for more information on this option.
- By default, NetBeans stores the JAR file for a project in the project's dist subfolder when you build the project.
- To place the JAR and HTML files in the same folder, you can copy the HTML file to the project's dist subfolder. Or, you can create a new folder and then copy both files into that folder. The folder does not have to be part of the project.
- Because a JAR file stores the files it contains in a compressed format, storing the files for an applet in a JAR file can dramatically improve the download time for the applet.
- Before you can display an applet in a web browser, you must create a web page for the applet. Then, when you display the web page in a browser, the applet is downloaded and displayed.
- If you will be deploying an applet to an intranet, you can simply copy the JAR and HTML files to the web server. If you will be deploying an applet to the Internet, you can use an FTP program to copy the files to the web server. See chapter 23 for more information on using an FTP program.

Figure 17-6 A procedure for deploying an applet

How to create an HTML document for an applet

To define the web page for an applet, you use the *Hypertext Markup Language* (*HTML*) to create an *HTML document*. In this topic, I'll present an overview of HTML and show you how to use it to include an applet in a web page. If you're interested in learning more about HTML, we recommended one of our books on HTML and CSS.

To create an HTML document in NetBeans, you use the New→HTML File command and then enter the name for the file in the resulting dialog box. When you do, NetBeans generates starting code for the document, and it stores this document in a file with the .html file extension. Typically, you create this file in the default package for the project.

An HTML document consists of *HTML elements*. Most HTML elements start with an *opening tag* that names the element, followed by content and a *closing tag*. In figure 17-7, for example, <html> is the opening tag for the document and </html> is the closing tag. Everything between these two tags is the element's content.

In this case, the content consists of additional elements. For example, the <head> element contains information about the web page, and the <body> element defines the content of the page. Then, additional elements are nested within these elements. It's often necessary to nest elements within an HTML document like this.

You can also include *attributes* within the opening tag for an element. An attribute provides information about the element. The first <script> element in this figure, for example, includes an attribute named src. This attribute specifies the URL of a JavaScript library that's used by the second <script> element.

When the first script element is processed by the browser, the browser loads the JavaScript library. This library, called the *JavaScript Deployment Toolkit*, includes functions that can help you deploy an applet so it will work consistently in any browser and on any operating system. You can also use it to check that the required version of the JRE is installed on a client.

The second <script> element includes JavaScript code that uses the deployJava object that's exposed by the Deployment Toolkit. To start, this code defines four attributes for the applet. The code attribute specifies the class file for the applet, including its package. Then, the archive attribute specifies the name of the JAR file that contains all the files needed by the applet. Finally, the width and height attributes specify the size of the applet in pixels. You may need to experiment with the values for these attributes to determine the appropriate size.

Next, this code specifies an empty array for the parameters since no parameters are required. Then, it specifies 1.6 as the minimum version of the JRE that's required by the applet. This indicates that the applet can use Java 6 or later. Finally, this code executes the runApplet function of the deployJava object using the specified attributes, parameters, and JRE version. This causes the applet to be downloaded and displayed in the browser.

An HTML document that includes the Future Value applet

```
<!DOCTYPE html>
<html>
    <head>
        <title>Future Value Calculator</title>
        <meta http-equiv="Content-Type" content="text/html; charset=UTF-8">
    </head>
    <body>
        <h1>Future Value Calculator applet</h1>
        <script src="http://www.java.com/js/deployJava.js"></script>
        <script>
            var attributes = {
                code:'murach.ui.FutureValueApplet.class',
                archive:'ch17_FutureValue.jar',
                width:280,
                height:160
            };
            var parameters = {};
            var version = '1.6'
            deployJava.runApplet(attributes, parameters, version);
        </script>
    </body>
</html>
```

Some attributes for working with the Deployment Toolkit library

Attribute	Description
`code`	Specifies the class name for the applet.
`archive`	Specifies the JAR file that contains the applet.
`width`	Specifies the width of the applet in pixels.
`height`	Specifies the height of the applet in pixels.

Description

- The *Hypertext Markup Language* (*HTML*) is the language that's used to create web pages. An *HTML document* contains *HTML elements* that define the content and structure of the web page.
- Most HTML elements have three parts: an *opening tag* that includes the tag name, a *closing tag* that includes the tag name preceded by a forward slash, and the content between the opening and closing tags.
- Within an opening tag, you can code *attributes* to provide optional values. To code an attribute, you code the name of the attribute, an equals sign, and the value for the attribute enclosed in quotes.
- The <head> element of a document contains information about the web page. For example, the <title> element specifies the text that's displayed in the browser's title bar.
- The <body> element of a document defines the content of the web page. Within this element, you can code <script> elements to run the applet.
- The first <script> element loads the *JavaScript Deployment Toolkit*. Then, the second <script> element calls a JavaScript function that's stored in this toolkit.
- To create an HTML document in NetBeans, use the New→HTML File command.

Figure 17-7 How to create an HTML document for an applet

How to run an applet within a web browser

When you install the JDK on your computer, the Java Plug-in is automatically installed in your browser. Because of that, you can run an applet simply by displaying the HTML file that contains it. To do that, you enter the address of the HTML file into your browser as shown in figure 17-8. Here, I entered the address of the HTML file for the Future Value applet. Note that I did not enter the characters "file:///" that appear at the beginning of this address. These characters were added by the browser.

Once you display the applet, you can test it to be sure it works correctly. If you tested the applet thoroughly using the Applet Viewer, though, you shouldn't run into any problems.

An applet with the Java Console displayed

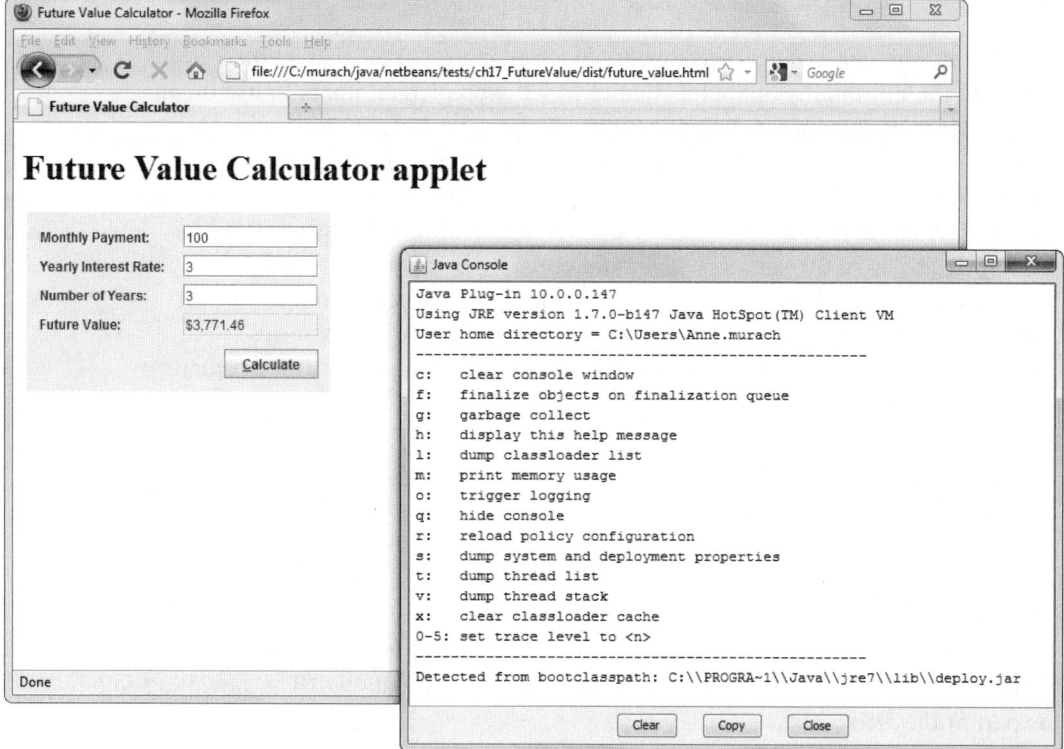

Description

- To run an applet in a web browser, start the browser and then enter the address of the HTML page that contains the applet. When the HTML file is processed, the applet is downloaded and displayed.
- If you're using Internet Explorer, it may display its Information Bar and prevent the applet from running. To continue, you can click on the Information Bar and select the Allow Blocked Content command.
- Once the applet is displayed in the browser, you can test it to be sure it works correctly.

Figure 17-8 How to run an applet within a web browser

Perspective

In this chapter, you learned how to develop applets. You also learned about some of the limitations of applets that have led web programmers to use other methods for developing web applications. As a result, before you begin developing a project that relies heavily on applets, you should review this technology to make sure that it's appropriate for your project.

In particular, if you want to develop web applications that store data in a file or database on the server, you should consider using servlets and Java Server Pages (JSP). Then, all processing is done on the server and the server returns standard HTML to the browser. The second book in this series, *Murach's Java Servlets and JSP*, shows how to use servlets and JSP to create web applications.

Summary

- An *applet* is a special type of application that's stored on a web server and runs within a web browser on a client machine.
- To view an applet, the client computer must have the appropriate version of the *Java Runtime Environment* (*JRE*) and the *Java Plug-in* installed. The Java Plug-in is part of the JRE.
- Since applets are downloaded from remote servers and run on client machines, they have stricter security restrictions than applications. To get around these restrictions, it's possible to create a *signed applet*.
- You can use the JApplet class to create an applet from a *panel* that contains the Swing controls and code for the applet.
- You can use the Applet Viewer to test an applet before you deploy it.
- You can use a *Java Archive* (*JAR*) file to store all of the Java classes and resources for an applet.
- You can create a *Hypertext Markup Language* (*HTML*) *document* that displays an applet. Within the HTML file, you can use a JavaScript library to start the applet.
- To test an applet after it has been deployed, you view the HTML page in a web browser.

Exercise 17-1 Develop a Payment applet

In this exercise, you'll modify the Payment application described in chapter 16 so it can be run as an applet.

1. Open the project named ch17_ex1_Payment that's in the ex_starts directory. Then, review the design and code of the PaymentFrame class.
2. Create a class named PaymentPanel in the murach.ui package that inherits the JPanel class. Then, use the Swing GUI Builer to provide all of the same controls as the ones that are available from the frame for the Payment application. However, don't include an Exit button.
3. Add the code that's required by this panel. To do that, you can generate the starting code for the event handlers and then cut and paste the remaining code from the PaymentFrame class to the PaymentPanel class.
4. Create a class named PaymentApplet in the murach.ui package that inherits the JApplet class. Then, add code to the init method of this class that displays an instance of the PaymentPanel class.
5. Build the project to create the JAR file for the project.
6. Use the Applet Viewer to test the applet. When you're done, close the browser window to end the applet.
7. Create an HTML file named Payment in the default package. Modify the <title> element so it will display "Payment Application" in the browser's title bar. Then, add an <h1> element within the <div> element that's nested within the <body> element. (The <div> element was omitted from the HTML document in figure 17-7 because it's not required.) The content of the <h1> element should be "Payment applet". Finally, add the two <script> elements for the applet.
8. Copy the HTML file into the same folder as the JAR file.
9. Use your web browser to run and test the applet. Since the JRE and Java Plug-in were automatically installed on your system when you installed the JDK, the applet should work properly. If the size you specified for the applet isn't right, though, change it and then run the applet again.
10. If you have access to a computer that doesn't have the current version of Java installed, test the applet on this system to see what happens.

Section 5

Data access programming with Java

In the last section, you learned how to create graphical user interfaces that get input from the user. But unless you save that data to a file or database, the data is lost when the program ends. That's why Java provides classes that let you work with files and databases. You'll learn about those classes in this section.

In chapter 18, you'll learn how to work with the data in text files and binary files. In chapter 19, you'll learn how to work with data using XML. In chapter 20, you'll learn how to use the Derby database that's included as part of the JDK. In chapter 21, you'll learn how to work with the data in any database.

Since the chapters in this section have been designed as independent modules, you can read them in any order you like. For example, if you want to learn how to use XML right away, you can jump to chapter 19. Or, if you want to learn how to work with a Derby database, you can jump to chapter 20. However, chapter 21 assumes that you understand the basics of working with a database as described in chapter 20. As a result, you should read chapter 20 before you read chapter 21.

18

How to work with text and binary files

In this chapter, you'll learn how to work with two types of files: text files and binary files. Although binary files are used more often in business applications, text files are appropriate for some applications. For random access, though, you have to use binary files.

When you work with files, you frequently use arrays and collections (chapters 11 and 12). You need to be able to handle the exceptions thrown by I/O operations (chapter 14). And you may need to parse strings for some applications (chapter 13). As a result, you may want to review those chapters as you progress through this chapter.

Introduction to directories and files

Prior to Java SE 7, it was common to use the File class from the java.io package to perform some basic operations on directories and files. However, this class has many limitations. That's why Java SE 7 introduced the java.nio.file package (also known as NIO.2). This package provides an improved way to access the default file system. As a result, it's generally considered a best practice to use the classes and interfaces of this package to work with directories and files.

A package for working with directories and files

Figure 18-1 begins by presenting the static get method of the Paths class in the java.nio.file package. You can pass one or more strings to this method to return a Path object that represents a path to a directory or a file. A Path object includes *name elements* that represent the directories and file in the path. For example, the path

```
c:\murach\java\files\products.txt
```

includes name elements for three directories and one file. In addition, it includes the root component "c:".

Once you have a Path object, you can use the methods of the Path interface to get information about the path. For example, you can use the getName method to get a Path object for the name element at the specified index. The index refers to the position of the name element in the path, where the first element is at index 0.

You can also use the static methods of the Files class to get information about a path. For example, you can use the first four methods to check whether a path exists and whether you can read from or write to a path. Similarly, you can use the next two methods to test whether the path refers to a directory or a file. Finally, if the path refers to a file, you can use the size method to return the number of bytes in the file.

To display the contents of a directory, you can use the newDirectoryStream method with a Path object. This method returns a DirectoryStream<Path> object. Then, you can use this object to loop through all of the subdirectories and files within that directory. You'll see an example of how this works in the next figure.

Finally, you can use the last four methods of the Files class to create and delete directories and files. If these methods aren't able to create or delete a file or directory, they throw exceptions that should give you a good idea of why they failed. For example, if you try to create a file that already exists, you will get a FileAlreadyExistsException. Similarly, if you try to delete a directory that contains files, you will get a DirectoryNotEmptyException.

As you review these methods, you should know that they're only some of the most commonly used methods of the java.nio.file package. So, if you need to perform other file-handling tasks, you can consult the Java API documentation for this package.

A package for working with directories and files

`java.nio.file`

A static method of the Paths class

Method	Description
`get(String[, String]...)`	Returns a Path object for the string or series of strings that specify the path.

Methods of the Path interface

Method	Description
`getFileName()`	Returns a Path object for the name of the file or directory.
`getName(int)`	Returns a Path object for the element at the specified index.
`getNameCount()`	Returns an int value for the number of name elements in the path.
`getParent()`	Returns a Path object for the parent path if one exists. Returns a null value if a parent does not exist.
`getRoot()`	Returns a Path object for the root component of the path. Returns a null value if a root does not exist.
`toAbsolutePath()`	Returns a Path object for the absolute path to the file or directory.
`toFile()`	Returns a File object for the path.

Static methods of the Files class

Method	Description
`exists(Path)`	Returns a true value if the path exists.
`notExists(Path)`	Returns a true value if the path does not exist.
`isReadable(Path)`	Returns a true value if the path exists and is readable.
`isWritable(Path)`	Returns a true value if the path exists and is writable.
`isDirectory(Path)`	Returns a true value if the path exists and refers to a directory.
`isRegularFile(Path)`	Returns a true value if the path exists and refers to a regular file.
`size(Path)`	Returns a long value for the number of bytes in the file.
`newDirectoryStream(Path)`	Returns a DirectoryStream<Path> object that you can use to loop through all files and subdirectories of the directory.
`createFile(Path)`	Creates a new file for the specified Path object if one doesn't already exist. Returns a Path object for the file.
`createDirectory(Path)`	Creates a new directory for the specified Path object if the directory doesn't already exist and all parent directories do exist. Returns a Path object for the directory.
`createDirectories(Path)`	Creates a new directory represented by the specified Path object including any necessary but non-existent parent directories. Returns a Path object for the directory.
`delete(Path)`	Deletes the file or directory represented by the Path object. A directory can only be deleted if it's empty.

Description

- To work with a directory or file, you use a Path object. A Path object can include a root component as well as directory names and a file name.

Figure 18-1 A package for working with directories and files

Code examples that work with directories and files

The first example in figure 18-2 shows how to create a new directory. To do this, the first statement creates a string that refers to a directory. In this case, the directory is murach\java\files on the C drive. Then, the second statement uses the Paths class to get a Path object for this directory. Finally, an if statement checks whether this directory already exists. If it doesn't, the last statement calls the static createDirectories method of the Files class to create the directory and any necessary parent directories.

The second example shows how to create a new file. To do this, the first statement creates a string that contains the name of the file. Then, the second statement gets a Path object that refers to the directory and file. In this case, the file is named products.txt and the directory is c:\murach\java\files. If the file doesn't already exist, the last statement calls the static createFile method of the Files class to create the file.

Notice that the get method of the Paths class in this example includes two arguments: one for the directory and one for the file. When you code the get method like this, the arguments are joined together and separated by a separator character. In most cases, the separator character is the same as the character that's used to separate the name elements in the arguments. In this case, the separator character will be a front slash.

In this example, the Path object contains an *absolute path name*. In other words, this example specifies the entire path and file name for the file. However, if you want to create a Path object that refers to a file that's in the same directory as the application, you can use a *relative path name*. To do that, you just specify the name of the file.

The third example shows how to get information about the Path object that was created in the previous example. The output below this example shows the result of the three statements. First, the getFileName method returns the name of the file. Then, the toAbsolutePath method returns a Path object for the full path. Finally, the static isWritable method of the Files class returns a true value to show that the file is not read-only, which is the default.

The fourth example shows how to list the names of the files in a directory. To start, an if statement checks whether the path exists and whether it is a directory. If both are true, the first statement in the if block prints the name of the directory to the console, and the second statement prints a string to the console. Then, the static newDirectoryStream method of the Files class returns a DirectoryStream<Path> object. Finally, this code loops through all of the Path objects in this stream, checks if the Path object is a file, and prints the file name to the console if it is.

If you're used to working with Windows, you may be surprised to find that you use a front slash instead of a backslash to separate the parts of a path. That's because Java uses the backslash to identify escape characters. This makes it cumbersome to use backslashes when specifying paths. However, using a front slash works equally well for both Windows and other operating systems such as Linux. The output for these examples shows that the Java API automatically converts the front slash to a backslash when necessary.

Example 1: Code that creates a directory if it doesn't already exist

```
String dirString = "c:/murach/java/files";
Path dirPath = Paths.get(dirString);
if (Files.notExists(dirPath)) {
    Files.createDirectories(dirPath);
}
```

Example 2: Code that creates a file if it doesn't already exist

```
String fileString = "products.txt";
Path filePath = Paths.get(dirString, fileString);
if (Files.notExists(filePath)) {
    Files.createFile(filePath);
}
```

Example 3: Code that displays information about a file

```
System.out.println("File name:      " + filePath.getFileName());
System.out.println("Absolute path:  " + filePath.toAbsolutePath());
System.out.println("Is writable:    " + Files.isWritable(filePath));
```

Resulting output

```
File name:      products.txt
Absolute path:  c:\murach\java\files\products.txt
Is writable:    true
```

Example 4: Code that displays the files in a directory

```
if (Files.exists(dirPath) && Files.isDirectory(dirPath))
{
    System.out.println("Directory: " + dirPath.toAbsolutePath());
    System.out.println("Files: ");
    DirectoryStream<Path> dirStream = Files.newDirectoryStream(dirPath);
    for (Path p: dirStream) {
        if (Files.isRegularFile(p))
            System.out.println("    " + p.getFileName());
    }
}
```

Description

- Java SE 7 introduced the java.nio.file package (also known as NIO.2). This package provides an improved way to access the default file system and is designed to replace the functionality that was available from the java.io.File class.
- The java.nio.file package provides support for many features that aren't provided by the java.io.File class.
- When coding paths, you can use a front slash to separate directory names. This works equally well for Windows and other operating systems.
- To identify the name and location of a file, you can use an *absolute path name* to specify the entire path for a file. You can also use a *relative path name* to specify the path of the file relative to the directory that contains the class that identifies the path.

Figure 18-2 Code examples that work with directories and files

Introduction to file input and output

This topic introduces the types of files and streams that you can use for file input and output. Then, it presents an example that introduces the code that's needed to perform input and output operations on a file. Finally, it shows how to handle the exceptions that occur most frequently when you perform input and output operations.

How files and streams work

Figure 18-3 presents the two types of files and the two types of streams that you use when you perform *I/O operations* (or *file I/O*). In a *text file*, all of the data is stored as characters with one character per byte on disk. Often, the fields and records in this type of file are separated by delimiters like tabs and new line characters. In this figure, for example, the fields in the text file are separated by tabs and the records by new line characters.

In contrast, the data in a *binary file* is stored in a different format that can read and write the primitive data types. In this figure, for example, some of the bytes in this format can't be read by a text editor. Here, two non-character bytes are written before the code and description fields of each product record, and the price field is written in a non-character format that isn't readable by a text editor. Also, since the records in a binary file don't end with new line characters, all records are displayed on a single line when a binary file is opened by a text editor.

To handle I/O operations, Java uses *streams*. You can think of a stream as the flow of data from one location to another. For instance, an *output stream* can flow from the internal memory of an application to a disk file, and an *input stream* can flow from a disk file to internal memory. When you work with a text file, you use a *character stream*. When you work with a binary file, you use a *binary stream*.

Although this chapter shows you how to use streams with disk files, Java also uses streams with other types of devices. For instance, you can use an output stream to send data to the console or to a network connection. In fact, the System.out and System.err objects are the standard output streams that are used for printing data to the console. Similarly, you can use an input stream to read data from a source like a keyboard or a network connection. In fact, the System.in object that's used by the Scanner class is a standard input stream that is used for reading data from the keyboard.

When you save a text or binary file, you can use any extension for the file name. In this book, we have used *txt* as the extension for all text files, *bin* for binary files that are accessed sequentially, and ran for binary files that are accessed randomly. For instance, the text file in this figure is named products.txt, and the binary file is named products.bin.

A text file that's opened by a text editor

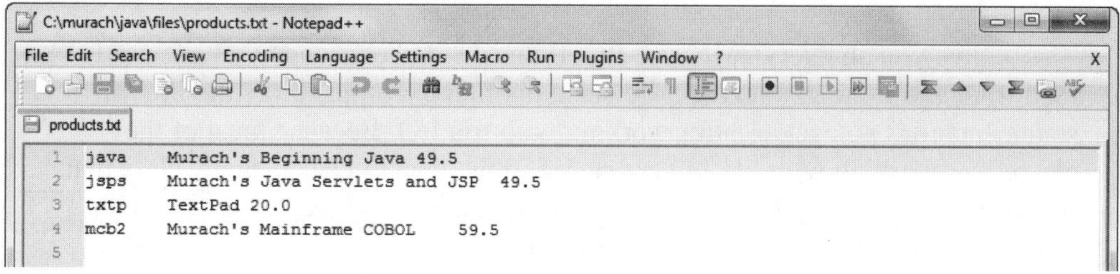

A binary file that's opened by a text editor

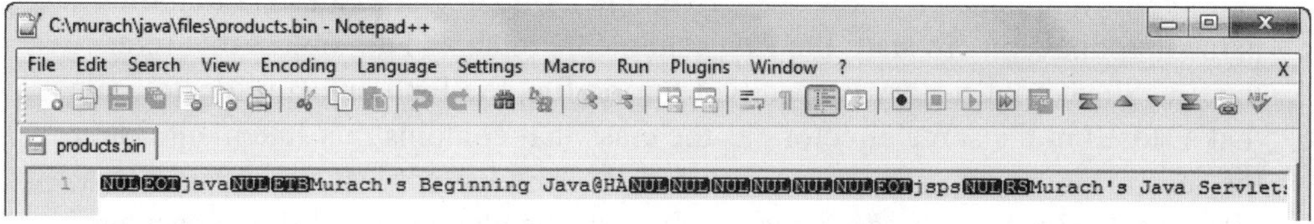

Two types of files

File	Description
Text	A file that contains characters. The fields and records in this type of file are often delimited by special characters like tab and new line characters.
Binary	A file that may contain characters as well as other non-character data types that can't be read by a text editor.

Two types of streams

Stream	Description
Character	Used to transfer text data to or from an I/O device.
Binary	Used to transfer binary data to or from an I/O device.

Description

- An *input file* is a file that is read by a program; an *output file* is a file that is written by a program. Input and output operations are often referred to as *I/O operations* or *file I/O*.
- A *stream* is the flow of data from one location to another. To write data to a file from internal storage, you use an *output stream*. To read from a file into internal storage, you use an *input stream*.
- To read and write *text files*, you use *character streams*. To read and write *binary files*, you use *binary streams*.
- Streams are not only used with disk devices, but also with input devices like keyboards and network connections and output devices like PC monitors and network connections.

Figure 18-3 How files and streams work

A file I/O example

To give you an overview of file I/O, figure 18-4 shows code you can use to read from and write to a text file. To start, the first example shows the import statements for two packages for working with file I/O. Because most of the classes for working with file I/O are stored in the java.io package, any class that works with file I/O typically imports all of the classes in this package. In addition, the import statement for the java.nio.file package is typically included to make it easy to work with the classes (Paths and Files) and interfaces (Path) described in the previous figures.

The second example shows how to create a File object that refers to a file named products.txt. To start, the first statement creates a Path object that refers to the file. Since no directory is specified for the file, the Path object refers to a file that's stored in the same directory as the class that contains this statement. Then, the second statement calls the toFile method of the Path object to convert it to a File object. This is necessary because many of the classes in the file.io package were created before the Path object was introduced. As a result, they are designed to work with a File object and don't work directly with a Path object.

The third example shows how to write data to a file. To start, you create an output stream. In this example, the output stream is created in the try clause of a try-with-resources statement.

To create a stream that has all the functionality that you need for an application, you can *layer* two or more streams into a single stream. To layer streams in Java, you use an object of one class as the argument for the constructor of another class. In this example, a BufferedWriter object is used as the argument of the PrintWriter constructor, and a FileWriter object is used as the argument of the BufferedWriter constructor.

The BufferedWriter object adds a block of internal memory known as a *buffer* to the stream. This causes the data in the stream to be stored in a buffer before it is written to the output device. Then, when the buffer is full or the stream is closed, all of the data in the buffer is *flushed* to the disk file in a single I/O operation. Similarly, when you use a buffer for input, a full buffer of data is read in a single I/O operation.

The benefit of buffering is that it reduces the number of I/O operations that are done by a disk device. If, for example, a buffer can hold 4000 bytes of data, only one write or read operation is required to flush or fill the buffer. In contrast, if the data is written or read one field at a time, 4000 bytes might require hundreds of I/O operations. For each I/O operation, the disk has to rotate to the starting disk location. Since this rotation is extremely slow relative to internal operations, buffering dramatically improves the performance of I/O operations. That's why you should use buffers for all but the most trivial disk operations.

After creating the output stream, the statement in the try block uses the println method of the output stream to write the data to a file. Then, when the try block finishes executing, the try-with-resources statement automatically closes the stream and flushes any data that's in the buffer to the file.

The fourth example reads the data that was written by the third example. To start, it uses the try clause of a try-with-resources statement to create a buffered

Example 1: Import all necessary packages

```
import java.io.*;
import java.nio.file.*;
```

Example 2: Get a Path object for the file

```
Path productsPath = Paths.get("products.txt");
File productsFile = productsPath.toFile();
```

Example 3: Write data to the file

```
try (PrintWriter out = new PrintWriter(
                       new BufferedWriter(
                       new FileWriter(productsFile))))
{
    out.println("java\tMurach's Beginning Java\t49.50");
}
catch (IOException e)
{
    System.out.println(e);
}
```

Example 4: Read data from the file

```
try (BufferedReader in = new BufferedReader(
                         new FileReader(productsFile)))
{
    String line = in.readLine();
    System.out.println(line);
}
catch (IOException e)
{
    System.out.println(e);
}
```

Resulting output

```
java    Murach's Beginning Java         49.50
```

Description

- The java.io package contains dozens of classes that can be used to work with different types of streams that have different functionality.
- To get the functionality you need for a stream, you often need to combine, or *layer*, two or more streams. You'll learn more about how this works as you progress through this chapter.
- To make disk processing more efficient, you can use a *buffered stream* that adds a block of internal memory called a *buffer* to the stream.
- When working with buffers, you often need to *flush* the buffer. This sends all data in the buffer to the I/O device. One way to do that is to use a try-with-resources statement to automatically close the I/O stream after you use it.

Figure 18-4 A file I/O example

input stream for the products file. Within the try block, the two statements read the first line of that file and print that line to the console. Finally, once the try-with-resources statement finishes executing, it automatically closes the input stream, which flushes the buffer and frees all system resources associated with the input stream.

Because this figure is only intended to give you an idea of how file I/O works, you shouldn't worry if you don't understand it completely. As you progress through this chapter, you'll learn about all of the classes and methods shown here in more detail.

How to work with I/O exceptions

If you've read chapter 14, you know the basic skills for handling exceptions. In fact, you have already been introduced to some of the exceptions that are thrown by I/O operations. Now, figure 18-5 summarizes three types of checked exceptions that must be handled when you're working with file I/O. It also shows a typical way to prevent or handle these types of exceptions. You'll see other examples like this throughout this chapter.

All exceptions that are thrown by classes that perform file I/O operations inherit the IOException class. In particular, an EOFException may be thrown when a program attempts to read beyond the end of a file, and a FileNotFoundException is thrown when a program attempts to open a file that doesn't exist.

To prevent a FileNotFoundException, you can use code like that shown in this figure. To start, this code gets a Path object for a file. Then, it uses the exists method of the Files class to check if a file exists for that path. If so, the code within the if block executes.

The first statement within the if block converts the Path object to a File object. Then, the try statement creates an input stream for the file. The code within the try block starts by reading the first record in the file. Then, it uses a while loop to display the current record and read the next record. This continues as long as the string that's returned isn't null. If the string is null, it indicates that the end of the file has been reached and the loop ends. This prevents the EOFException from occurring.

To handle any other unknown I/O exceptions that might occur as the file is read, the statements that create the input stream and read the file are coded within a try-with-resources statement. Here, the catch clause catches the IOException and prints it to the console.

A subset of the IOException hierarchy

```
IOException
    EOFException
    FileNotFoundException
```

Common I/O exceptions

Exception	Description
`IOException`	Thrown when an error occurs in I/O processing.
`EOFException`	Thrown when a program attempts to read beyond the end of a file.
`FileNotFoundException`	Thrown when a program attempts to open a file that doesn't exist.

Code that handles I/O exceptions

```
Path productsPath = Paths.get("products.txt");
if (Files.exists(productsPath))  // prevent the FileNotFoundException
{
    File productsFile = productsPath.toFile();
    try (BufferedReader in = new BufferedReader(
                             new FileReader(productsFile)))
    {
            String line = in.readLine();

            while(line != null)
            {
                System.out.println(line);
                line = in.readLine();
            }
    }
    catch (IOException e)
    {
        System.out.println(e);
    }
}
else
{
    System.out.println(
        productsPath.toAbsolutePath() + " doesn't exist");
}
```

Figure 18-5 How to work with I/O exceptions

How to work with text files

When working with text files, you need to layer two or more classes to create a character input or output stream. You'll learn how to do that in the topics that follow. In addition, you'll learn how to use the methods of these classes to work with text files. Then, you'll see a complete class that you can use to read and write Product objects to a text file.

How to connect a character output stream to a file

Before you can write to a text file, you need to create a character output stream, and you need to connect that stream to a file. To do that, you must layer two or more of the classes in the Writer hierarchy as shown in figure 18-6. Then, you use the methods of the PrintWriter class to write data to the output stream, you use the BufferedWriter class to create a buffer for the output stream, and you use the FileWriter class to connect the stream to a file.

Although it's typically a good coding practice to use a buffer, the first example in this figure shows how to connect to a file without using a buffer. Here, the first statement creates a FileWriter object by passing a String object for a path name to the constructor of the FileWriter class. Alternately, this statement could pass a File object for a file to this constructor. Either way, the second statement creates a PrintWriter object by passing the FileWriter object to the constructor of the PrintWriter class.

The second example shows a more concise way to write the first example. Here, you don't assign the FileWriter object to a named variable. Instead, you nest the call to the constructor of the FileWriter class within the constructor of the PrintWriter class. You can align these nested constructor calls any way you like. In this example, the whole statement is coded on one line, but it's often easier to read if each constructor call is coded on a separate line as shown in the next three examples.

The third example shows how to include a buffer in the output stream. To do that, you use a BufferedWriter object in addition to a FileWriter and PrintWriter object.

The fourth example shows how to append data to an existing file. To do that, you set the second argument of the FileWriter constructor to true. If you don't code a value for this argument, the existing data in the file is overwritten.

By default, the data in an output stream is flushed from the buffer to the disk when the buffer is full. However, if you set the second argument of the PrintWriter constructor to true, the *autoflush feature* is turned on. Then, the buffer is flushed each time the println method is executed.

The constructors in this figure should help you understand how to layer output streams. Here, the PrintWriter constructor accepts any class derived from the Writer class. As a result, you can supply a BufferedWriter object or a FileWriter object as an argument of the PrintWriter constructor. Similarly, since the BufferedWriter constructor also accepts any Writer object, you can supply a FileWriter object as an argument of the BufferedWriter constructor.

A subset of the Writer hierarchy

```
Writer <<abstract>>
    BufferedWriter
    PrintWriter
    OutputStreamWriter
        FileWriter
```

Classes used to connect a character output stream to a file

PrintWriter	contains the methods for writing data to a text stream
→BufferedWriter	creates a buffer for the stream
→FileWriter	connects the stream to a file

Constructors of these classes

Constructor	Throws
`PrintWriter(Writer[, booleanFlush])`	None
`BufferedWriter(Writer)`	None
`FileWriter(File[, booleanAppend])`	IOException
`FileWriter(StringPathName[, booleanAppend])`	IOException

Example 1: How to connect without a buffer (not recommended)

```
FileWriter fileWriter = new FileWriter("products.txt");
PrintWriter out = new PrintWriter(fileWriter);
```

Example 2: A more concise way to code example 1

```
PrintWriter out = new PrintWriter(new FileWriter("products.txt"));
```

Example 3: How to connect to a file with a buffer

```
PrintWriter out = new PrintWriter(
                  new BufferedWriter(
                  new FileWriter("products.txt")));
```

Example 4: How to connect for an append operation

```
PrintWriter out = new PrintWriter(
                  new BufferedWriter(
                  new FileWriter("products.txt", true)));
```

Example 5: How to connect with the autoflush feature turned on

```
PrintWriter out = new PrintWriter(
                  new BufferedWriter(
                  new FileWriter("products.txt")), true);
```

Description

- The Writer class is an abstract class that's inherited by all of the classes in the Writer hierarchy. To learn more about the Writer hierarchy, see the Java API documentation.
- If the output file doesn't exist when the FileWriter object is created, it's created automatically. If it does exist, it's overwritten by default. If that's not what you want, you can specify true for the second argument of the constructor to append data to the file.
- If you specify true for the second argument of the PrintWriter constructor, the *autoflush feature* flushes the buffer each time the println method is called.

Figure 18-6 How to connect a character output stream to a file

How to write to a text file

Figure 18-7 shows how to write to a text file. To do that, you use the print and println methods to send data to the file. These methods work like the print and println methods of the System.out object, but they print data to the output stream instead of printing data to the console.

As you saw earlier in this chapter, you can use a try-with-resources statement to create a stream. Then, the stream is automatically flushed and closed when the try statement ends. If you don't use a try-with-resources statement, though, you can use the close method to manually close the output stream. This flushes the buffer and frees any system resources that are being used by the output stream. Or, if you want to keep the output stream open, you can use the flush method to flush all the data in the stream to the file. Either way, you need to throw or catch the IOException that can be thrown by these methods.

The first example in this figure shows how to append a string and an object to a text file named log.txt. To start, the FileWriter constructor creates a FileWriter object that can append data to the file. If no file named log.txt exists in the current directory, this statement will create the file. Then, the print method prints a string, and the println method prints a Date object that represents the current date and time. For this to work, the toString method of the Date object is called automatically to convert the date to a string.

The second example in this figure shows how to write the data that's stored in a Product object to a *delimited text file*. In this type of file, one type of *delimiter* is used to separate the *fields* (or *columns*) that are written to the file, and another type of delimiter is used to separate the *records* (or *rows*). In this example, the tab character (\t) is used as the delimiter for the fields, and the new line character is used as the delimiter for the records. That way, the code, description, and price for one product are stored in the same record separated by tabs. Then, the new line character ends the data for that product, and the data for the next product can be stored in the next record.

Common methods of the PrintWriter class

Method	Throws	Description
`print(argument)`	None	Writes the character representation of the argument type to the file.
`println(argument)`	None	Writes the character representation of the argument type to the file followed by the new line character. If the autoflush feature is turned on, this also flushes the buffer.
`flush()`	IOException	Flushes any data that's in the buffer to the file.
`close()`	IOException	Flushes any data that's in the buffer to the file and closes the stream.

Example 1: Code that appends a string and an object to a text file

```
// open an output stream for appending to the text file
PrintWriter out = new PrintWriter(
                  new BufferedWriter(
                  new FileWriter("log.txt", true)));

// write a string and an object to the file
out.print("This application was run on ");
Date today = new Date();
out.println(today);

// flush data to the file and close the output stream
out.close();
```

Example 2: Code that writes a Product object to a delimited text file

```
// open an output stream for overwriting a text file
PrintWriter out = new PrintWriter(
                  new BufferedWriter(
                  new FileWriter(productsFile)));

// write the Product object to the file
out.print(product.getCode() + "\t");
out.print(product.getDescription() + "\t");
out.println(product.getPrice());

// flush data to the file and close the output stream
out.close();
```

Description

- To write a character representation of a data type to an output stream, you use the print and println methods of the PrintWriter class. If you supply an object as an argument, these methods will call the toString method of the object.
- To create a *delimited text file*, you delimit the *records* in the file with one *delimiter*, such as a new line character, and you delimit the *fields* of each record with another delimiter, such as a tab character.
- To flush all data to the file, you can use a try-with-resources statement to automatically close the stream when you're done using it.You can also use the flush or close methods of the stream to manually flush all data to the file.

Figure 18-7 How to write to a text file

How to connect a character input stream to a file

Before you can read characters from a text file, you must connect the character input stream to the file. Figure 18-8 shows how to do that with a buffer and a File object. As you can see in the example in this figure, you supply the FileReader class as the argument of the constructor of the BufferedReader class. This creates a stream that uses a buffer and has methods that you can use to read data.

If you look at the constructors for the BufferedReader and FileReader classes, you can see why this code works. Since the constructor for the BufferedReader object accepts any object in the Reader hierarchy, it can accept a FileReader object that connects the stream to a file. However, the BufferedReader object can also accept an InputStreamReader object, which can be used to connect the character input stream to the keyboard or to a network connection rather than to a file.

A subset of the Reader hierarchy

```
Reader <<abstract>>
    BufferedReader
    InputStreamReader
        FileReader
```

Classes used to connect to a file with a buffer

BufferedReader contains the methods for reading data from the stream

→FileReader connects the stream to a file

Constructors of these classes

Constructor	Throws
`BufferedReader(Reader)`	None
`FileReader(File)`	FileNotFoundException
`FileReader(StringPathName)`	FileNotFoundException

How to connect a character input stream to a file

```
BufferedReader in = new BufferedReader(
                    new FileReader("products.txt"));
```

Description

- The Reader class is an abstract class that's inherited by all of the classes in the Reader hierarchy. To learn more about the Reader hierarchy, check the documentation for the Java API. All classes in the java.io package that end with Reader are members of the Reader hierarchy.
- Although you can read files with the FileReader class alone, the BufferedReader class improves efficiency and provides better methods for reading character input streams.

Figure 18-8 How to connect a character input stream to a file

How to read from a text file

The two examples in figure 18-9 show how to read the two text files that are written by the examples in figure 18-7. In the first example, the first statement uses the readLine method to read the first record in the log file. Then, a while loop prints the current record to the console and reads the next record. When the readLine method attempts to read past the end of the file, it returns a null, which causes the while loop to end. Then, the close method is called to flush the buffer and close the input stream.

The second example shows how to read a record from the products file. To do that, it uses the readLine method. Then, because this file is a delimited text file, it parses the string into its individual columns. To do that, it uses the split method of the String class to split the string into an array. In this example, the tab character is supplied as the argument of the split method since this is the character that's used to divide the fields in the record. (If you're not familiar with how the split method works, please see chapter 13.)

This example continues by creating a Product object from the data in the columns array. Since the product code and description are strings, the columns that contain these values can be passed directly to the constructor of the Product object. However, the price column must be converted from a String object to a double value. In this example, the parseDouble method of the Double class is used to do that.

The last statement in this example calls the close method. That flushes the buffer and frees any system resources.

Although you can also use the read method to read a text file, that's not common. That's because it reads a single character, and it returns an int value that represents the ASCII code for the character. Then, to get the character, you must cast the return type to a char value.

If you know the structure of the data in the input stream that you're working with, you may occasionally need to skip a specific number of characters. To do that, you can use the skip method. When you call this method, it tries to move forward in the file the specified number of characters without reading new characters into the stream. However, if this method encounters the end of the file or can't continue for some other reason, it returns the actual number of characters that were skipped.

Common methods of the BufferedReader class

Method	Throws	Description
`readLine()`	IOException	Reads a line of text and returns it as a string.
`read()`	IOException	Reads a single character and returns it as an int that represents the ASCII code for the character. When this method attempts to read past the end of the file, it returns an int value of -1.
`skip(longValue)`	IOException	Attempts to skip the specified number of characters, and returns an int value for the actual number of characters skipped.
`close()`	IOException	Closes the input stream and flushes the buffer.

Example 1: Code that reads the records in a text file

```
// read the records of the file
String line = in.readLine();
while(line != null)
{
    System.out.println(line);
    line = in.readLine();
}

// close the input stream
in.close();
```

Sample output

```
This application was run on Mon Oct 19 09:21:42 PDT 2009
This application was run on Tue Oct 20 10:14:12 PDT 2009
```

Example 2: Code that reads a Product object from a delimited text file

```
// read the next line of the file
String line = in.readLine();

// parse the line into its columns
String[] columns = line.split("\t");
String code = columns[0];
String description = columns[1];
String price = columns[2];

// create a Product object from the data in the columns
Product p = new Product(code, description, Double.parseDouble(price));

// print the Product object
System.out.println(p);

// close the input stream
in.close();
```

Sample output

```
Code:        java
Description: Murach's Beginning Java
Price:       $49.50
```

Figure 18-9 How to read from a text file

An interface for working with file I/O

In chapter 9, you saw a ProductDAO interface that defines I/O methods and constants for a data access object. Now, figure 18-10 presents a similar interface that you can use to access data. As you can see, this interface extends the ProductReader, ProductWriter, and ProductConstants interfaces. Since these interfaces are similar to the interfaces that were presented in chapter 9, you shouldn't have trouble understanding how they work. In fact, the only difference is that the ProductReader interface shown here uses an array list to store Product objects instead of using a string to store the product data. In the next figure, you'll see an example of a class that implements this interface for a text file.

To start, the ProductReader interface defines two methods that you can use to get product data from a file or database. Here, the getProduct method returns a single Product object for the product with the specified product code, and the getProducts method returns an ArrayList object that contains Product objects for all the products in a file or database.

The ProductWriter interface defines three methods that you can use to write product data to a file or database. Each of these methods accepts a Product object and returns a boolean value that indicates whether or not the operation was successful.

Finally, the ProductConstants interface defines two constants. Here, the CODE_SIZE constant specifies the maximum number of characters in a product's code, and the DESCRIPTION_SIZE constant specifies the maximum number of characters in a product's description.

As you learned in chapter 9, you must implement all five methods defined by the ProductReader and ProductWriter interfaces when you code a class that implements the ProductDAO interface. In addition, you have the option of using the constants stored in the ProductConstants interface. In this chapter, you'll see two examples of file I/O classes that implement the ProductDAO interface. The first example, shown in the next figure, doesn't use any constants from the ProductConstants interface. However, the second example, shown in the last figure, does use these constants.

The ProductDAO interface

```
public interface ProductDAO
    extends ProductReader, ProductWriter, ProductConstants {}
```

The ProductReader interface

```
import java.util.ArrayList;

public interface ProductReader
{
    Product getProduct(String code);
    ArrayList<Product> getProducts();
}
```

The ProductWriter interface

```
public interface ProductWriter
{
    boolean addProduct(Product p);
    boolean updateProduct(Product p);
    boolean deleteProduct(Product p);
}
```

The ProductConstants interface

```
public interface ProductConstants
{
    int CODE_SIZE = 4;
    int DESCRIPTION_SIZE = 40;
}
```

Figure 18-10 An interface for working with file I/O

A class that works with a text file

Figure 18-11 shows a complete class named ProductTextFile that can be used to read and write products to a text file. This class implements the ProductDAO interface shown in figure 18-10. As a result, it includes all five public methods defined by the ProductReader and ProductWriter interfaces. In addition, it includes some private methods that are used by these methods.

To start, this class defines three instance variables and a constant. Here, the ArrayList variable named products will store a list of Product objects for the products in the file, the Path object named productsPath will be used to define the path to the file, and the File object named productsFile will be used to connect the input and output streams to the file. Then, the FIELD_SEP constant defines the tab character as the character that's used to separate the columns in the products file.

The constructor for the ProductTextFile class initializes the instance variables. To do that, it creates a Path object for a file named products.txt that's stored in the same directory as the ProductTextFile class. As a result, if the ProductTextFile class is stored in the java\files directory, the products.txt file will be stored in that directory too. Then, the constructor uses the toFile method of the Path object to convert the Path object to a File object. Finally, it calls the getProducts method to load the products array list.

The getProducts method returns an ArrayList of all the Product objects in the products file. This method starts by checking whether the products array list has been created. If so, it returns that array list. This increases efficiency by reading the file only when necessary.

If the ArrayList of Products hasn't been created, this code creates an empty ArrayList of Product objects. Then, it checks if the products file exists, and it uses a try-with-resources statement to create a buffered input stream if it does.

To create the Product objects, this method starts by reading the first line from the products file into a string variable. Then, it uses a while loop to process the lines in the file until the end of the file is reached. As you learned earlier in this chapter, you can test for an end-of-file condition by checking the string that's returned by the readLine method for a null.

Within the while loop, the first statement uses the FIELD_SEP constant to split the line into its three columns (code, description, and price). Then, this loop creates a Product object from the values in these columns and adds the Product object to the array list. Finally, this loop reads the next line in the file.

If an IOException is thrown somewhere in the getProducts method, this method returns a null. That way, any method that calls the getProducts method can test whether it executed successfully by checking the array list it returns for a null. Whether or not an exception is thrown, the try-with-resources statement automatically closes the input stream.

In this class, the catch clauses in the getProducts method and the saveProducts method you'll see in a minute print the error message to the console. This is useful when you're testing and debugging a program, but it might not be appropriate when you put a program into production. As a result, before putting a class like this into a production environment, you might want to

The code for the ProductTextFile class

Page 1

```
import java.util.*;
import java.io.*;
import java.nio.file.*;

public final class ProductTextFile implements ProductDAO
{
    private ArrayList<Product> products = null;
    private Path productsPath = null;
    private File productsFile = null;

    private final String FIELD_SEP = "\t";

    public ProductTextFile()
    {
        productsPath = Paths.get("products.txt");
        productsFile = productsPath.toFile();
        products = this.getProducts();
    }

    public ArrayList<Product> getProducts()
    {
        // if the products file has already been read, don't read it again
        if (products != null)
            return products;

        products = new ArrayList<>();

        if (Files.exists(productsPath))  // prevent the FileNotFoundException
        {
            try (BufferedReader in =
                     new BufferedReader(
                     new FileReader(productsFile)))
            {
                // read all products stored in the file into the array list
                String line = in.readLine();
                while(line != null)
                {
                    String[] columns = line.split(FIELD_SEP);
                    String code = columns[0];
                    String description = columns[1];
                    String price = columns[2];

                    Product p = new Product(
                        code, description, Double.parseDouble(price));
                    products.add(p);

                    line = in.readLine();
                }
            }
            catch(IOException e)
            {
                System.out.println(e);
                return null;
            }
        }
        return products;
    }
```

Figure 18-11 A class that works with a text file (part 1 of 2)

change the way that exceptions are handled. For example, you might want to write an error message to a log file. Or, you might want to throw a custom exception that indicates that a generic access error has occurred. For more information on how to create a custom exception, see chapter 14.

The getProduct method returns a Product object for a product that matches the specified product code. To search for the product, this method loops through each product in the products array list until it finds one with the specified product code. Finally, it returns that product. If no product is found with the specified code, this method returns a null.

The saveProducts method accepts an ArrayList object that contains Product objects, and it writes all of these Product objects to the file. If this operation is successful, it returns a true value. If an IOException is thrown, this method returns a false value to indicate that the save operation wasn't successful.

The saveProducts method starts by creating a buffered output stream that connects to the products file. Then, this method uses a loop to write each product in the array list to the file. To do that, it uses the FIELD_SEP constant to separate each field in a product record, and it uses the println method to insert a new line character at the end of each product record.

The addProduct method starts by calling the add method of the ArrayList class to add the product to the array list. Then, it calls the saveProducts method to save the modified array list to the products file so that the array list and the file contain the same data. Notice that the addProduct method returns the boolean value that's returned by the saveProducts method. That way, if the saveProducts method returns a true value, the addProduct method will also return true.

The deleteProduct method is similar. It starts by calling the getProducts method to return a products array list. Then, it calls the remove method of the ArrayList class to remove the product from the array list. Finally, it calls the saveProducts method to save the array list to the products file, and it returns the boolean value that's returned by that method.

The updateProduct method works a little differently. This method updates the data for an existing product with the data in a new Product object. To start, this method uses the getProduct method to get the old Product object with the same product code as the new Product object. Then, it gets the index for the old product, and it removes that product from the array list. Next, it inserts the new product into the array list where the old product used to be. Finally, it calls the saveProducts method to save the array list to the products file, and it returns a value that indicates whether the save operation was successful.

As you review this code, you should realize that this class won't work correctly for multiple users. For example, suppose that both user A and user B read the products file, and user A modifies that file. Then, suppose user B also modifies the file. At this point, user B's changes overwrite user A's changes. This is known as a *concurrency problem*.

One way to reduce concurrency problems would be to read the data from the file each time the getProducts, getProduct, addProduct, updateProduct, and deleteProduct methods are called. That way, the data is more likely to be current. However, this would be inefficient, particularly if the file contained thousands of records. That's why developers typically use databases to store data that's going to be accessed by multiple users.

The code for the ProductTextFile class

Page 2

```
    public Product getProduct(String code)
    {
        for (Product p : products)
        {
            if (p.getCode().equals(code))
                return p;
        }
        return null;
    }

    private boolean saveProducts()
    {
        try (PrintWriter out = new PrintWriter(
                               new BufferedWriter(
                               new FileWriter(productsFile))))
        {
            // write all products in the array list to the file
            for (Product p : products)
            {
                out.print(p.getCode() + FIELD_SEP);
                out.print(p.getDescription() + FIELD_SEP);
                out.println(p.getPrice());
            }
        }
        catch(IOException e)
        {
            System.out.println(e);
            return false;
        }

        return true;
    }

    public boolean addProduct(Product p)
    {
        products.add(p);
        return this.saveProducts();
    }

    public boolean deleteProduct(Product p)
    {
        products.remove(p);
        return this.saveProducts();
    }

    public boolean updateProduct(Product newProduct)
    {
        // get the old product and remove it
        Product oldProduct = this.getProduct(newProduct.getCode());
        int i = products.indexOf(oldProduct);
        products.remove(i);

        // add the updated product
        products.add(i, newProduct);

        return this.saveProducts();
    }
}
```

Figure 18-11 A class that works with a text file (part 2 of 2)

How to work with binary files

To connect a binary stream to a binary file, you use a technique that's similar to the technique you use to connect a character stream to a text file. However, the methods you use to read and write binary data are different from the methods you use to read and write character data. In the topics that follow, you'll learn how to work with the data that's stored in a binary file.

How to connect a binary output stream to a file

To create a binary output stream that's connected to a file, you can layer three streams in the OutputStream hierarchy as shown in figure 18-12. Here, both examples use a string to refer to a binary file named products.bin. Note, however, that these examples could use a File object. This works just like it does for a text file.

Both examples create a buffered stream and connect to the specified binary file. In the first example, the code creates an output stream that will create the file if it doesn't exist or delete all the data in the file if it does exist. Then, the second example shows how you can append data to the end of a file. To do that, you set the second argument of the FileOutputStream constructor to true.

The constructors shown in this figure should help you understand how to layer binary output streams. Here, you can see that the DataOutputStream constructor accepts any class in the OutputStream hierarchy. As a result, you can supply a BufferedOutputStream object as an argument of the DataOutputStream constructor. Similarly, since the BufferedOutputStream constructor also accepts any OutputStream object, you can supply a FileOutputStream object as an argument of the BufferedOutputStream constructor. Then, to create a FileOutputStream object, you can supply a File object or a String object that refers to a binary file.

A subset of the OutputStream hierarchy

```
OutputStream <<abstract>>
    FileOutputStream
    FilterOutputStream
        BufferedOutputStream
        DataOutputStream <<implements DataOutput interface>>
```

Classes used to connect a binary output stream to a file

DataOutputStream	writes data to the stream
→BufferedOutputStream	creates a buffer for the stream
→FileOutputStream	connects the stream to a file

Constructors of these classes

Constructor	Throws
`DataOutputStream(OutputStream)`	None
`BufferedOutputStream(OutputStream)`	None
`FileOutputStream(File[, booleanAppend])`	FileNotFoundException
`FileOutputStream(StringPathName[, booleanAppend])`	FileNotFoundException

Example 1: How to connect to a file with a buffer

```
DataOutputStream out = new DataOutputStream(
                       new BufferedOutputStream(
                       new FileOutputStream("products.bin")));
```

Example 2: How to connect for an append operation

```
DataOutputStream out = new DataOutputStream(
                       new BufferedOutputStream(
                       new FileOutputStream("products.bin", true)));
```

Description

- The OutputStream class is an abstract class that's inherited by all of the classes in the OutputStream hierarchy. To learn more about the OutputStream hierarchy, check the documentation for the Java API.
- All classes in the java.io and java.util.zip packages that end with OutputStream are members of the OutputStream hierarchy.
- The FilterOutputStream class is a superclass of all classes that filter binary output streams.
- If the output file doesn't exist when the FileOutputStream object is created, it's created automatically. If it does exist, it's overwritten by default. If that's not what you want, you can specify true for the second argument of the constructor to append data to the file.
- Although a buffer isn't required, it makes output operations more efficient.

Figure 18-12 How to connect a binary output stream to a file

How to write to a binary file

If you look back at figure 18-12, you can see that the DataOutputStream class implements the DataOutput interface. As a result, you can call any of the methods of the DataOutput interface from an output stream that includes a DataOutputStream object. Some of the most commonly used methods of this interface are summarized in figure 18-13.

You can use the first four methods in this figure to write primitive data types to a binary output stream. For example, you can use the writeInt method to write an int value to a binary output stream. To read these data types, you sometimes need to know how many bytes each data type uses. That's why we've included the number of bytes used by each data type in this figure.

You can use the writeChars and writeUTF methods to write strings to a binary output stream. When you use the writeChars method, it writes two bytes per character. When you use the writeUTF method, it starts by writing a two-byte number that indicates the length of the string. Then, it writes the *UTF* (*Universal Text Format*) representation of the string. Although this usually writes each ASCII character as one byte, it may write some Unicode characters as two or three bytes. In general, you can use the writeUTF method whenever it's okay to write strings with lengths that vary. But when you need to write strings that have equal lengths, you need to use the writeChars method. Later in this chapter, you'll learn why.

This figure also summarizes the size, flush, and close methods of the DataOutputStream class. You can use these methods if you need to check the number of bytes that have been written to the stream, or if you need to flush data from the buffer. As always, you should use the close method to close the stream when you're done working with it. Of course, if you use a try-with-resources statement to open the stream, that statement automatically closes the stream when it's done executing.

The example in this figure shows how to write the data that's stored in a Product object to a binary file. To start, the writeUTF method is used to write the product's code and description, which are String objects. Then, the writeDouble method is used to write the product's price to the file. Finally, the last statement closes the output stream, which flushes all data to the file and releases the resources that were used by the stream object.

Note that all of the methods shown here except for size can throw an IOException. As a result, you must either throw or catch this exception when you use these methods. Otherwise, you won't be able to compile your code.

Common methods of the DataOutput interface

Method	Throws	Description
`writeBoolean(boolean)`	IOException	Writes a 1-byte boolean value to the output stream.
`writeInt(int)`	IOException	Writes a 4-byte int value to the output stream.
`writeDouble(double)`	IOException	Writes an 8-byte double value to the output stream.
`writeChar(int)`	IOException	Writes a 2-byte char value to the output stream.
`writeChars(String)`	IOException	Writes a string using 2 bytes per character to the output stream.
`writeUTF(String)`	IOException	Writes a 2-byte value for the number of bytes in the string followed by the UTF representation of the string, which typically uses 1 byte per character.

Methods of the DataOutputStream class

Method	Throws	Description
`size()`	None	Returns an int for the number of bytes written to this stream.
`flush()`	IOException	Flushes any data that's in the buffer to the file.
`close()`	IOException	Flushes any data that's in the buffer to the file and closes the stream.

Code that writes data to a binary file

```
// write a Product object to the file
out.writeUTF(product.getCode());
out.writeUTF(product.getDescription());
out.writeDouble(product.getPrice());

// flush data to the file and close the output stream
out.close();
```

Description

- Since the DataOutputStream class implements the DataOutput interface, you can call any of the methods shown above from a DataOutputStream object.
- The writeUTF method writes a two-byte number that indicates the number of bytes in the string. Then, it writes the characters using the *Universal Text Format* (*UTF*). For most strings, UTF uses one byte per character.

How to connect a binary input stream to a file

To create a binary input stream, you can layer three streams from the InputStream hierarchy as shown in figure 18-14. The example in this figure shows how you do that. Here, a String object is used to identify the binary file. Alternately, a File object could be used.

The constructors of the classes shown here explain how you can layer these streams. For example, the DataInputStream constructor accepts an InputStream object. As a result, you can use an object created from any class in the InputStream hierarchy as an argument. Similarly, since the BufferedInputStream constructor also accepts any object of the InputStream hierarchy, it can accept a FileInputStream object. Finally, the FileInputStream constructor accepts a File object or a String object.

Notice in the InputStream hierarchy that the DataInputStream implements the DataInput interface. As a result, you can call any of the methods of this interface from an input stream that includes a DataInputStream object. You'll see how this works in the next figure.

A subset of the InputStream hierarchy

```
InputStream {abstract}
    FileInputStream
    FilterInputStream
        BufferedInputStream
        DataInputStream {implements DataInput interface}
```

Classes used to connect a binary input stream to a file

DataInputStream	reads data from the stream
→BufferedInputStream	creates a buffer for the stream
→FileInputStream	connects the stream to the file

Constructors of these classes

Constructor	Throws
`DataInputStream(InputStream)`	None
`BufferedInputStream(InputStream)`	None
`FileInputStream(File)`	FileNotFoundException
`FileInputStream(StringPathName)`	FileNotFoundException

How to connect a binary input stream to a file

```
DataInputStream in = new DataInputStream(
                     new BufferedInputStream(
                     new FileInputStream("products.bin")));
```

Description

- The InputStream class is an abstract class that's inherited by all of the classes in the InputStream hierarchy. To learn more about the InputStream hierarchy, check the documentation for the Java API.
- All classes in the java.io and java.util.zip packages that end with InputStream are members of the InputStream hierarchy.
- The FilterInputStream class is a superclass of all classes that filter binary input streams.
- Although a buffer isn't required, it makes input operations more efficient.

Figure 18-14 How to connect a binary input stream to a file

How to read from a binary file

Figure 18-15 starts by summarizing some of the most commonly used methods of the DataInput interface that's implemented by the DataInputStream class. You can use the first four methods in this figure to read primitive data types from a binary input stream. For example, you can use the readInt method to read an int value from a binary input stream. To read these data types, you sometimes need to know how many bytes each data type uses. That's why the number of bytes used by each data type is included in this figure.

You can use the readUTF method to read binary data that's stored in the Universal Text Format that was described earlier in this chapter. Usually, that means that you'll use the readUTF method to read data that was written with the writeUTF method.

You can use the skipBytes method to skip a specified number of bytes in an input stream. If for some reason it can't skip that number of bytes, though, the method skips as many bytes as it can and returns an int value for the actual number that it skipped. This can happen, for example, if the method reaches the end of the file before it skips the specified number of bytes.

Although the read methods in this figure correspond to the write methods shown earlier in this chapter, there is no corresponding read method for the writeChars method. As a result, to read strings written by the writeChars method, you need to create a loop that reads in each character using the readChar method. The next figure shows an example of how to do this.

When working with a binary input stream, you can also use some methods from the DataInputStream class. In particular, you can use the available method to return the number of bytes in the file that haven't been read, and you can use the close method to close the input stream and release any resources it's using.

The example in this figure shows how to read the data for Product objects from a binary file. To start, the while loop uses the available method to determine when the end of the file has been reached. Then, the first two statements in the while loop use the readUTF method to read the product's code and description. This will only work if these fields were written using the writeUTF method as shown in figure 18-13. Then, the third statement uses the readDouble method to read the product's price. Again, this will only work if the product's price was written using the writeDouble method.

Once the three fields have been read, the fourth statement uses the fields to create a Product object. Notice that, unlike the example that works with a text file, this example doesn't convert the price from a string to a double value. That's because the price was written to the file and read from the file as a double value. Finally, after the loop finishes, the last statement uses the close method to close the file. As always, if you use a try-with-resources statement to initialize the stream, you don't need to explicitly call this method.

Note that all of the methods shown in this figure can throw an IOException that's checked by the compiler. As a result, you must either throw or catch this exception. Otherwise, you won't be able to compile your code.

Common methods of the DataInput interface

Method	Throws	Description
`readBoolean()`	EOFException	Reads 1 byte and returns a boolean value.
`readInt()`	EOFException	Reads 4 bytes and returns an int value.
`readDouble()`	EOFException	Reads 8 bytes and returns a double value.
`readChar()`	EOFException	Reads 2 bytes and returns a char value.
`readUTF()`	EOFException	Reads and returns the string encoded with UTF.
`skipBytes(int)`	EOFException	Attempts to skip the specified number of bytes, and returns an int value for the actual number of bytes skipped.

Common methods of the DataInputStream class

Method	Throws	Description
`available()`	IOException	Returns the number of bytes remaining in the file.
`close()`	IOException	Closes the stream.

Code that reads Product objects from a binary file

```
while (in.available() > 0)
{
    // read product data from a file
    String code = in.readUTF();
    String description = in.readUTF();
    double price = in.readDouble();

    // create the Product object from its data
    Product p = new Product(code, description, price);
}

// close the input stream
in.close();
```

Description

- Since the DataInputStream class implements the DataInput interface, you can call any of the methods shown above from an object of this class.
- The readUTF method reads characters that were written with the Universal Text Format.

Figure 18-15 How to read from a binary file

Two ways to work with binary strings

Figure 18-16 illustrates two ways you can read and write binary strings. First, you can use the readChar and WriteChars methods to read and write strings using two bytes per character. Second, you can use the readUTF and writeUTF methods to read and write strings with one byte per character using the Universal Text Format.

The first example shows how the writeUTF method differs from the writeChars method. This example starts by creating a string that contains 23 characters (22 regular characters plus one new line character). Then, the first group of statements starts by calling the writeUTF method to write the string to the stream. Then, it calls the size method to return the number of bytes that were written, and it prints the number of bytes that were written to the console. As you can see, the writeUTF method wrote 25 bytes: two bytes that indicate the length of the string and one byte for each of the 23 characters in the string.

The next group of statements starts by calling the writeChars method to write the same string. Then, it calculates the number of bytes that were written to the stream. To do that, it subtracts the number of bytes written by the writeUTF method from the total number of bytes written to the stream. Finally, it prints the number of bytes that were written to the console. In this case, 46 bytes, or two bytes per character, were written to the stream. If you open this test file in a text editor as shown here, you can see the difference between how these two strings are stored.

The second example reads the strings that were written by the writeUTF and writeChars methods. To start, the first statement in this example calls the available method to get the total number of bytes in the file. Then, the first group of statements calls the readUTF method to read the string that was written by the writeUTF method. After the string has been read, the next statement calculates the total number of bytes that were read. To do that, it subtracts the number of bytes that are left in the file from the total number of bytes in the file. Then, the last statement in this group prints a message to the console that indicates the number of bytes that were read. In this case, 25 bytes were read, which is the same number of bytes that were written by the writeUTF method.

The second group of statements uses the readChar method within a loop to read the string that was written by the writeChars method. Before the loop is executed, the number of bytes left in the file is divided by 2 to determine the number of characters in the string. Then, the loop is executed once for each character. Within the loop, the first statement appends the char value that's read from the binary file to the String variable named string2. Then, the second statement keeps a running count of the number of bytes that have been read (2 bytes per character) so it can be printed to the console when the loop ends.

For many applications, you can use the writeUTF and readUTF methods to write and read string data. However, if you need to make sure that each string has the same length, you have to use the writeChars and readChar methods. You'll see an example of how to do that later in this chapter.

Example 1: Two ways to write a binary string

```
// create a test string
String testString = "This is a test string.\n";

// use the writeUTF method
out.writeUTF(testString);
int writeSize1 = out.size();
System.out.println("writeUTF writes " + writeSize1 + " bytes.");

// use the writeChars method
out.writeChars(testString);
int writeSize2 = out.size() - writeSize1;
System.out.println("writeChars writes " + writeSize2 + " bytes.\n");

out.close();
```

Resulting output

```
writeUTF writes 25 bytes.
writeChars writes 46 bytes.
```

The file opened in a text editor

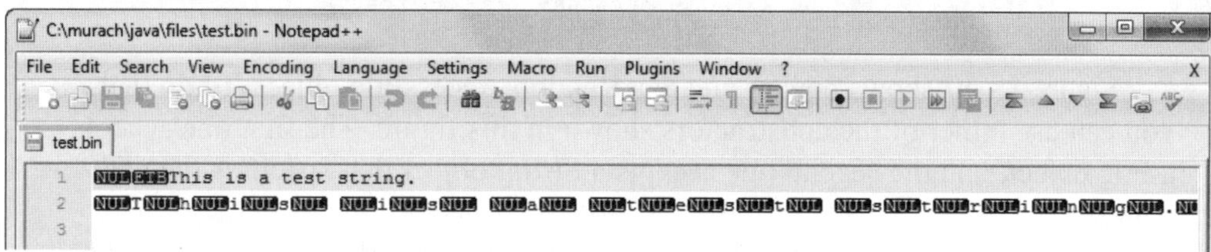

Example 2: Two ways to read a binary string

```
// get total bytes
int totalBytes = in.available();

// use the readUTF method
String string1 = in.readUTF();
int readSize1 = totalBytes - in.available();
System.out.println("readUTF reads " + readSize1 + " bytes.");

// use the readChar method
int readSize2 = 0;
String string2 = "";
int charCount = in.available() / 2;
for (int i = 0; i < charCount; i++)
{
    string2 += in.readChar();
    readSize2 += 2;
}
System.out.println("readChar reads " + readSize2 + " bytes.\n");
```

Resulting output

```
readUTF reads 25 bytes.
readChar reads 46 bytes.
```

Figure 18-16 Two ways to work with binary strings

How to work with random-access files

So far in this chapter, you've learned how to use streams to read and write files sequentially. That means that you read or write one record after another, from the first record in a file to the last. As a result, you have to read the first 49 records in a file before you can read the 50th record in the file. Files that you access sequentially are known as *sequential-access files* (or just *sequential files*).

Now, you'll learn how to access a binary file randomly using a RandomAccessFile object. A binary file that you access randomly is known as a *random-access file*. This type of file lets you move a *pointer* (or *cursor*) to any location in the file. Then, you can read or write from that point, which means you can read the 50th record in a file without reading the first 49 records in the file. This type of access is far more efficient than sequential access for many types of business applications.

How to connect to a random-access file

Figure 18-17 shows how to create a RandomAccessFile object. To do that, you can use either of the constructors shown in this figure. The first one accepts a File object, and the second one accepts a String object that specifies the path name.

Both constructors accept a second argument that specifies the mode for the random-access file. Here, you can specify "r" to open the file in read-only mode, "rw" to open the file in read-write mode, and "rws" or "rwd" to open the file in one of the synchronized read-write modes. The difference between the two synchronized modes is that the rws mode updates the data stored in the file as well as the *metadata* for the file, while the rwd mode updates just the data. The metadata includes information about the file such as its size and the date it was last modified. Since updating the metadata requires an additional file I/O operation, the rws mode isn't as efficient as the rwd mode.

You should use one of the synchronized modes when your program needs to allow two or more users to update the same random-access file at the same time. That way, one user won't be able to update the file while another user is updating the same part of the file. In practice, though, you'll probably want to use a database for any program that needs to allow two or more users to update the same data. That's because databases provide features that make it easier to handle this type of problem.

Notice that when you work with a random-access file, you can't use a buffer. That's because you normally read or write just one record at a time. As a result, buffering isn't as critical as it is for working with sequential-access files where you often need to read and write the entire file.

Constructors of the RandomAccessFile class

Constructor	Throws
`RandomAccessFile(File, stringMode)`	FileNotFoundException
`RandomAccessFile(StringPathName, StringMode)`	FileNotFoundException

Access mode values

Value	Description
`r`	Open for reading only.
`rw`	Open for reading and writing. If the file doesn't already exist, an attempt will be made to create it.
`rws`	Open for reading and writing and also require that every update to the data stored in the file or the metadata for the file be written synchronously to the underlying storage device.
`rwd`	Open for reading and writing and also require that every update to the data stored in the file be written synchronously to the underlying storage device.

Example 1: How to create a read-write RandomAccessFile object

```
RandomAccessFile productsFile = new RandomAccessFile("products.ran", "rw");
```

Example 2: How to create a read-only RandomAccessFile object

```
RandomAccessFile productsFile = new RandomAccessFile("products.ran", "r");
```

Example 3: How to create a synchronized read-write object

```
RandomAccessFile productsFile = new RandomAccessFile("products.ran", "rws");
```

Description

- You can use the classes in the OutputStream and InputStream hierarchies to read and write files sequentially. A file you access sequentially is called a *sequential-access file*. When you work with a sequential-access file, you read from the beginning of the file to the end of the file, and you can add data only at the end of the file.
- You can use the RandomAccessFile class to read and write files randomly. A file you access randomly is called a *random-access file*. When you work with a random-access file, you can move a *pointer* to any point in the file. Then, you can read and write data starting at that point. This lets you modify part of a file without affecting the rest of the file.
- If you use one of the synchronized read-write modes, only one user at a time can update the file. Since the rwd mode doesn't update the metadata with each operation, it reduces the number of IO operations and runs slightly faster than the rws mode.
- The *metadata* for a file includes information about the file such as its size, the date it was last modified, and so on.

Figure 18-17 How to connect to a random-access file

How to read to and write from a random-access file

Figure 18-18 shows how to read and write random-access files. To start, it shows that this class implements both the DataOutput and DataInput interfaces you saw in figures 18-13 and 18-15. As a result, you can call the methods of those interfaces to write and read random-access files.

In addition, you can use the four methods summarized in this figure that are specific to random-access files. Of these four methods, the seek method makes random access possible. This method lets you move the pointer to any location in the file without reading the records before that point. To use this method, you supply a long value that specifies the number of bytes from the beginning of the file that you want to move the pointer to. This lets you move the pointer forward or backward through the file. If you try to move the pointer beyond the end of the file, the pointer will be moved just beyond the last byte in the file so you can write a record at the end of the file.

The other three methods let you work with the length of a file and close a file. For instance, you can use the length method to return a long value that indicates the length of a file in bytes. You can also use the setLength method to change the length of a random-access file. If you use this method to make a random-access file shorter, it will truncate the file, thus deleting any data stored after the new length. When you're done working with a RandomAccessFile object, you can use the close method to close it and free the resources that are used by this object.

When you write data to a random-access file, each field of a record should have the same length as the same field in other records so that each record will have the same length. That way, you can easily calculate the number of bytes that marks the beginning of the field or record that you want to access. Then, you can use the seek method to move the pointer to that field or record.

To illustrate, the first example in this figure shows how to use a RandomAccessFile object to write three records that contain two fields. Here, the first statement opens a random-access file in read-write mode. Then, a loop writes each record to the file using methods provided by the DataOutput interface. Within this loop, the first statement uses the writeChars method to write a string using two bytes per character. Since each string has four characters, this statement always writes eight bytes. Then, the second statement writes a double value, which always uses eight bytes.

The second example shows how to read the third record in the random-access file that was written by the first example. Here, the first statement initializes a constant that specifies the record length. Then, the second statement opens the file in read-only mode. The next two statements specify the record to read (the third record) and use the seek method to move the pointer to the beginning of that record. After that, the next group of statements reads the data of the third record. To do that, the readChar method is called four times from within a loop to read all four characters of the first field, and the readDouble method is called to read the double value of the second field.

Two interfaces implemented by the RandomAccessFile class

`DataOutput`	(see figure 18-13)
`DataInput`	(see figure 18-15)

Methods of the RandomAccessFile class used for input and output

Method	Throws	Description
`seek(long)`	IOException	Sets the pointer to the specified number of bytes from the beginning of the file. If the pointer is set beyond the end of the file, the pointer will be moved to the end of the file.
`length()`	IOException	Returns a long for the number of bytes in the file.
`setLength(long)`	IOException	Sets the length of the file to the specified number of bytes.
`close()`	IOException	Closes the file.

Example 1: Code that writes data to a file

```
RandomAccessFile productsFile = new RandomAccessFile("products.ran", "rw");

// write 3 records that contain codes and prices to the file
String[] codes = {"java", "jsps", "txtp"};
double[] prices = {49.5, 49.5, 20.0};
for (int i = 0; i < codes.length; i++)
{
    productsFile.writeChars(codes[i]);
    productsFile.writeDouble(prices[i]);
}

productsFile.close();
```

Example 2: Code that reads data from a file

```
final int RECORD_LENGTH = 16;  // 4 chars @ 2 bytes per char +
                               // 1 double @ 8 bytes

RandomAccessFile productsFile = new RandomAccessFile("products.ran", "r");

// move the pointer to the third record
int recordNumber = 3;
productsFile.seek((recordNumber - 1) * RECORD_LENGTH);

// read the third record
String code = "";
for (int i = 0; i < 4; i++)
    code += productsFile.readChar();
double price = productsFile.readDouble();

productsFile.close();
```

Description

- When writing to a random-access file, it's a common coding practice to write each record with the same number of bytes. This makes it possible to move the file pointer to the start of each record in the file.

Figure 18-18 How to read to and write from a random access file

How to read and write fixed-length strings

When you write strings to a random-access file, you need to write each string with a fixed number of characters. In other words, you need to write *fixed-length strings*. If, for example, you want to create a field that stores last names, you might decide to use 20 characters for that field. Then, when you write a last name that has fewer than 20 characters, you can pad the field so it contains 20 characters. One way to do that is to add Unicode zeros to the end of the field. Then, when you read the field, you read characters until the first Unicode zero is encountered.

To illustrate, figure 18-19 shows how to code a class named IOStringUtils. This class contains two static methods that you can use for writing and reading fixed-length strings. Then, the next figure shows how you can call these methods from another class.

Within the IOStringUtils class, the writeFixedString method contains code that writes a fixed-length string. This method accepts three arguments and throws an IOException. The first argument is a DataOutput object, which is usually a RandomAccessFile object. The second argument is an int value that specifies the length of the fixed-length string. The third argument is a String object that contains the string to be written. Within the method, a loop writes each character of the string to the file. If the string is shorter than the specified length, the method writes Unicode zeros until it reaches the specified length.

Conversely, the readFixedString method reads the fixed-length strings that were written by the writeFixedString method, discarding any Unicode zeros. This method acccpts two arguments and throws an IOException. The first argument is a DataInput object, which can be either a RandomAccessFile object or a DataInputStream object. The second argument is an int value that specifies the length of the fixed-length string. Within the method, the code reads characters and builds a string. If it reads a Unicode zero, it stops adding characters to the string. Otherwise, it reads until it reaches the specified length. Then, it returns the string.

A class that writes and reads fixed-length strings

```
import java.io.*;

public class IOStringUtils
{
    public static void writeFixedString(DataOutput out, int length,
    String s) throws IOException
    {
        for (int i = 0; i < length; i++)
        {
            if (i < s.length())
                out.writeChar(s.charAt(i)); // write char
            else
                out.writeChar(0);           // write Unicode zero
        }
    }

    public static String readFixedString(DataInput in, int length)
    throws IOException
    {
        StringBuilder sb = new StringBuilder();
        for (int i = 0; i < length; i++)
        {
            char c = in.readChar();
            // if char is not Unicode zero add to string
            if (c != 0)
                sb.append(c);
        }
        return sb.toString();
    }
}
```

Description

- When you write strings to a random-access file, you need to write *fixed-length strings*. That way, the length of the strings won't vary from one record to another, and all of the record lengths in the file will be the same.
- You can create a class like the IOStringUtils class shown above that contains static methods to write and read fixed-length strings.
- The writeFixedString method writes the characters of an input string to an output file followed by Unicode zeros for any unused positions in the fixed-length output string.
- The readFixedString method reads a string written by the writeFixedString method, but stops appending characters to the StringBuilder object when the first Unicode zero is read.

Figure 18-19 How to read and write fixed-length strings

A class that works with a random-access file

Figure 18-20 presents the complete code for the ProductRandomFile class. Like the ProductTextFile class, this class implements the ProductDAO interface shown in figure 18-10.

To start, this class declares two instance variables. The first instance variable defines a RandomAccessFile object named productsFile, and the second instance variable defines an ArrayList object named productCodes.

Next, this class defines three constants that are available to the entire class. The PRICE_SIZE constant indicates that the size of the price field is 8 bytes since it is a double value. Then, the RECORD_SIZE constant calculates the size of each record in the file. To do that, it uses the CODE_SIZE and DESCRIPTION_SIZE constants that are stored in the ProductConstants interface shown in figure 18-10, along with the PRICE_SIZE constant. After that, the DELETION_CODE constant defines a string that's used to indicate that a product has been marked for deletion. In this case, the string contains four spaces. In other words, if a product has a code of four spaces, it has been marked for deletion.

The constructor for the ProductRandomFile class initializes the two instance variables of the class. The first statement initializes the productsFile variable by opening a random-access file named products.ran in read-write mode. Then, the second statement initializes the productCodes variable by calling the getCodes method that's coded later in this class. Since the constructor of the RandomAccessFile class can throw a FileNotFoundException, these statements are coded within a try statement. Then, the catch clause that catches this exception prints the exception to the console.

The next four methods in this class are private methods that are used to read records from the products file. The first method, getRecordCount, returns the number of records in the file. To do that, it calculates the number of records in the file by dividing the total number of bytes in the file by the number of bytes in each record. Since the length method returns a long value, the result of this calculation must be cast to an int value.

The getRecordNumber method accepts a string that contains a product code and returns the record number for that product code. To do that, it compares each string in the productCodes array list with the specified product code. If it finds a match, it returns the current position in the array. Otherwise, it returns a value of -1 to indicate that the record wasn't found.

The code for the ProductRandomFile class

Page 1

```
import java.io.*;
import java.util.*;

public class ProductRandomFile implements ProductDAO
{
    private RandomAccessFile productsFile = null;
    private ArrayList<String> productCodes = null;

    private final int PRICE_SIZE = 8;  // doubles are 8 bytes
    private final int RECORD_SIZE =
        CODE_SIZE * 2 +             // from the ProductConstants interface
        DESCRIPTION_SIZE * 2 +      // from the ProductConstants interface
        PRICE_SIZE;
    private final String DELETION_CODE = "    ";

    public ProductRandomFile()
    {
        try
        {
            productsFile = new RandomAccessFile("products.ran", "rw");
            productCodes = this.getCodes();
        }
        catch(IOException e)
        {
            System.out.println(e);
        }
    }

    //***************************************************
    // Private methods for reading products
    //***************************************************

    private int getRecordCount() throws IOException
    {
        int recordCount = (int) productsFile.length() / RECORD_SIZE;
        return recordCount;
    }

    private int getRecordNumber(String productCode)
    {
        for (int i = 0; i < productCodes.size(); i++)
        {
            String code = productCodes.get(i);
            if (productCode.equals(code))
                return i;
        }
        return -1;  // no record matches the product code
    }
```

Figure 18-20 A class that works with a random-access file (part 1 of 4)

The getRecord method accepts an int value that specifies the record number for a record and returns a Product object for that record. To start, this method checks if the record number is greater than or equal to zero and less than the total number of records. If so, the record number is valid and the method continues by creating a Product object from the data that's stored in the record and returning it to the calling method. Otherwise, the method returns a null to indicate that no product exists for that record number.

To create the Product object, the getRecord method uses the seek method to position the pointer at the beginning of the specified record. Then, the readFixedString method of the IOStringUtils class is used to read the product's code and description, and the readDouble method is used to read the product's price. Finally, these values are passed to the constructor of the Product class to create a Product object.

The getCodes method creates an array list that contains every product code that's stored in the file. To start, this method declares an array list of strings. Then, it uses a loop to read each product code from the file into the array. To do that, this method uses the getRecordCount method to return the number of records in the file, it uses the seek method to skip to the beginning of each record, and it uses the static readFixedString method of the IOStringUtils class to read the string for the product code. When the loop completes, the array list is returned to the calling method. If an exception is encountered as the product codes are read, however, the exception is printed to the console and a null is returned to indicate that the getCodes method did not complete successfully.

The code for the ProductRandomFile class

Page 2

```
private Product getRecord(int recordNumber) throws IOException
{
    if (recordNumber >= 0 && recordNumber < this.getRecordCount())
    {
        productsFile.seek(recordNumber * RECORD_SIZE);

        String code = IOStringUtils.readFixedString(
            productsFile, CODE_SIZE);
        String description = IOStringUtils.readFixedString(
            productsFile, DESCRIPTION_SIZE);
        double price = productsFile.readDouble();

        Product product = new Product(code, description, price);
        return product;
    }
    else
    {
        return null;
    }
}

private ArrayList<String> getCodes()
{
    try
    {
        ArrayList<String> codes = new ArrayList<>();
        for (int i = 0; i < getRecordCount(); i++)
        {
            productsFile.seek(i * RECORD_SIZE);
            codes.add(IOStringUtils.readFixedString(
                productsFile, CODE_SIZE));
        }
        return codes;
    }
    catch(IOException e)
    {
        System.out.println(e);
        return null;
    }
}
```

Figure 18-20 A class that works with a random-access file (part 2 of 4)

The next two methods in this class are public methods that return Product objects. Both of these methods catch any IOException that might be thrown. This prevents any of the implementation details of this class (such as the type of exceptions) from being exposed to other classes, and it makes it easier for programmers to use these methods since they don't have to handle these exceptions.

If either of these methods encounter an IOException, its catch clause executes two statements. The first statement prints the exception to the console, which can help the programmer who is coding this class determine the cause of the error during the testing and debugging phase. Then, the second statement returns a null. This indicates to the programmer who is using this class that the operation wasn't completed successfully.

The getProducts method returns an array list that contains all the Product objects in the file that haven't been marked for deletion. To do that, this method begins by creating an ArrayList object named products that can store Product objects. Then, it uses a loop to create a Product object for each record. Within the loop, an if statement checks if the product code for the record is equal to the DELETION_CODE constant. If not, the product has not been marked for deletion. Then, the getRecord method is called to get the Product object for the record, and the Product object is added to the array list.

The getProduct method accepts a product code. If the random-access file contains a record with this product code, this method returns a Product object that contains the data that's stored in that record. To do that, it calls the getRecordNumber method to get the record number of the record with the specified product code. Then, it calls the getRecord method to get the record with that number, and it creates a Product object from the data in that record.

Note that if a record with the specified product code isn't found, the getRecordNumber method returns –1. Then, the getRecord method returns a null because –1 is an invalid record number. In that case, the Product object that's returned to the calling method is null.

The code for the ProductRandomFile class **Page 3**

```
//*****************************************************
// Public methods for reading products
//*****************************************************

public ArrayList<Product> getProducts()
{
    ArrayList<Product> products = new ArrayList<>();
    try
    {
        for (int i = 0; i < productCodes.size(); i++)
        {
            // if record has been marked for deletion,
            // don't add to products array list
            if (!productCodes.get(i).equals(DELETION_CODE))
            {
                Product product = this.getRecord(i);
                products.add(product);
            }
        }
    }
    catch(IOException e)
    {
        System.out.println(e);
        return null;
    }
    return products;
}

public Product getProduct(String productCode)
{
    try
    {
        int recordNumber = this.getRecordNumber(productCode);
        Product product = this.getRecord(recordNumber);
        return product;
    }
    catch(IOException e)
    {
        System.out.println(e);
        return null;
    }
}
```

Figure 18-20 A class that works with a random-access file (part 3 of 4)

The next method in this class is a private method named writeProduct that's used to write the data for a product to the file. This method accepts a Product object and a record number. It uses the record number to move the pointer to the position in the file where the record is to be written. Then, it writes the data in the Product object to the file. To write the product code and description fields, it uses the writeFixedString method of the IOStringUtils. To write the price field, it uses the writeDouble method. If an exception is thrown by any of these statements, this method prints the exception and returns a false value.

The next three methods are public methods that can be used to add, update, and delete the products stored in the products file. All three of these methods accept a Product object as an argument.

The addProduct method writes the data in the Product object that's passed to it to the end of the random-access file. To do that, it adds the product code to the productCodes array list. Then, it calls the getRecordNumber method to get the record number of the new product. Finally, it calls the writeProduct method to write the new product at the position indicated by the record number, which should be at the end of the file. If the writeProduct method executes successfully, it returns a true value. That value is then returned to the method that called the addProduct method.

The updateProduct method writes the data that's stored in the Product object that's passed to it over the record that has the same product code. To do that, it starts by calling the getRecordNumber method to get the record number for the product. If this record number isn't equal to –1, which indicates that the product was found, this method calls the writeProduct method to write the data for the specified Product object over the data for the current record. However, if the product code isn't found, this method returns a false value and doesn't update the record.

The deleteProduct method marks the specified Product object for deletion. To do that, the first statement gets the record number for the Product by calling the getRecordNumber method. If this method returns a value other than –1, indicating that the product was found, the set method of the productCodes array list is used to set the product code of the specified product to the value that's stored in the DELETION_CODE constant. Then, the product code for the product is set to the DELETION_CODE constant. Finally, the deleteProduct method calls the writeProduct method to write the Product object to the file. If this write operation is successful, this method returns a true value. If this operation isn't successful, or if the product wasn't found, this method returns a false value.

Since the deleteProduct method doesn't actually delete the record from the file, you may want to include another method in this class that deletes all the records that have been marked for deletion. Then, you can run that method periodically to remove unnecessary data from the file. To do that, this method could use the getProducts method to read all the products that haven't been marked for deletion. Then, it could write all of these products to the file, overwriting any existing records. Finally, it could use the setLength method of the RandomAccessFile class to set the length of the file based on the number of records that remain, which would truncate any leftover data at the end of the file.

The code for the ProductRandomFile class **Page 4**

```
//************************************************
//* Private method for writing products
//************************************************
private boolean writeProduct(Product product, int recordNumber)
{
    try
    {
        productsFile.seek(recordNumber * RECORD_SIZE);
        IOStringUtils.writeFixedString(
            productsFile, CODE_SIZE, product.getCode());
        IOStringUtils.writeFixedString(
            productsFile, DESCRIPTION_SIZE, product.getDescription());
        productsFile.writeDouble(product.getPrice());
        return true;
    }
    catch(IOException e)
    {
        System.out.println(e);
        return false;
    }
}

//************************************************
//* Public methods for writing products
//************************************************

public boolean addProduct(Product product)
{
    productCodes.add(product.getCode());
    int recordNumber = getRecordNumber(product.getCode());
    return writeProduct(product, recordNumber);
}

public boolean updateProduct(Product product)
{
    int recordNumber = getRecordNumber(product.getCode());
    if (recordNumber != -1)
        return writeProduct(product, recordNumber);
    else
        return false;
}

public boolean deleteProduct(Product product)
{
    int recordNumber = getRecordNumber(product.getCode());
    if (recordNumber != -1)
    {
        productCodes.set(recordNumber, DELETION_CODE);
        product.setCode(DELETION_CODE);  // mark record for deletion
        return writeProduct(product, recordNumber);
    }
    else
        return false;
}
}
```

Figure 18-20 A class that works with a random-access file (part 4 of 4)

Perspective

In this chapter, you learned how to read and write text files sequentially, and you learned how to read and write binary files sequentially and randomly. If you've already read the chapters in section 4, this means that now at last you can see how all of the classes and methods in a business application work together. That includes presentation classes like JFrame and JPanel classes, business classes like Product and Invoice classes, and data access classes like the ProductTextFile and ProductRandomFile classes.

Now that you've seen how to work with text files and binary files, you might want to take a moment to consider the advantages and disadvantages of each. For example, since you don't need to convert int and double values to strings and back, binary files make it easier to work with numbers. However, text files often make it easier to share data with other programs. For example, the data in a text file can be viewed in a text editor or a web browser.

As you work with files, remember that they are only one option for storing data. Another option is to store data in a database. Because databases provide sophisticated features for organizing and managing data, they're used for most serious applications. You'll learn how to work with databases in chapter 20. But first, the next chapter will show you how to work with data using XML.

Summary

- A *text file* stores data as characters. A *binary file* stores data in a binary format.
- In a *delimited text file*, *delimiters* are used to separate the *fields* and *records* of the file.
- You use *character streams* to read and write text files and *binary streams* to read and write binary files. To get the functionality you need, you can *layer* two or more streams.
- A *buffer* is a block of memory that is used to store the data in a stream before it is written to or after it is read from an I/O device. When an output buffer is full, its data is *flushed* to the I/O device.
- When you work with I/O operations, you'll need to catch or throw three types of checked exceptions: IOException, FileNotFoundException, and EOFException.
- To identify a file when you create a File object, you can use an *absolute path name* or a *relative path name*.
- The java.nio.file package provides classes and interfaces that you can use to check whether a file or directory exists, to get information about a path, to create or delete directories and files, and to create a File object.
- You can use the classes in the Writer and Reader hierarchies to work with a text file. You can use the classes in the OutputStream and InputStream hierarchies to

work with a binary file. You can also use the methods of the DataOutput and DataInput interfaces to work with binary files.

- You can use the RandomAccessFile class to access a binary file randomly rather than sequentially. When you use a *random-access file*, you can position a *pointer* to any location in the file.
- When you work with random-access files, you store string values as *fixed-length strings*. That way, the files have the same number of bytes for each field within each record.

About the exercises for this chapter

In the exercises for this chapter, you'll work with maintenance applications that use the factory pattern you learned about in chapter 9. That makes it easy to switch from a class that processes one type of file to a class that processes a different type of file. If you need to refresh your memory about how the factory pattern works, you can review the Product Maintenance application in figures 9-10 through 9-13.

Exercise 18-1 Work with a text file

In this exercise, you'll add code to a Customer Maintenance application for reading and writing data from a text file named customers.txt. Each record in this file contains three fields with the customer's first name, last name, and email. The fields are separated by a tab character, and the records are separated by a new line character.

Open the application and review its code

1. Open the project named ch18_ex1_CustomerMaint that's in the ex_starts directory.
2. Open the Customer class and review its code.
3. Open the CustomerTextFile class, and notice the three class variables that will store the array list of Customer objects, a Path object for the file, and a File object for the file. Add code to the constructor that initializes these variables.
4. Add code to the getCustomers method that loads the array list variable with the Customer objects that are created from the data in the customers.txt file. Be sure to check that this file exists, and if it does, use a try-with-resources statement to open the input stream. If an IOException occurs when the input stream is opened, print the exception to the console and return a null to the calling method.
5. Add code to the saveCustomers method that writes the data in each Customer object in the array list to a record in the customers file. Be sure to delimit the fields and records with the appropriate character. If an IOException is thrown

when the output stream is opened, print the exception to the console and return false to the calling method.

6. Run the application, and test the list, add, and delete functions to be sure they work.

Exercise 18-2 Work with a binary file

In this exercise, you'll enhance the Product Maintenance application so it can use a binary file.

1. Open the project named ch18_ex2_ProductMaint that's in the ex_starts directory.
2. Use the Refactor→Rename command to change the name of the ProductTextFile.java file to ProductBinaryFile.java. This will automatically change any occurrences of "ProductTextFile" in the project to "ProductBinaryFile". That includes the statement in the DAOFactory class that creates the ProductDAO object.
3. Display the code for the ProductBinaryFile class, and modify this class so it uses a binary file named products.bin. Be sure to store the product code and description as UTF characters.
4. Run the ProductMaintApp application to see how it works with a binary file, but leave at least 3 product records in the file.

Exercise 18-3 Improve the exception handling

In this exercise, you'll improve the way that exceptions are handled by the ProductMaintApp and ProductTextFile classes.

1. Open the project named ch18_ex3_ProductMaint that's in the ex_starts directory.
2. Open the ProductMaintApp class, and modify the displayAllProducts method so it displays an error message and exits the application if the getProducts method returns a null.
3. Open the ProductTextFile class, and notice that the saveProducts method doesn't use a try-with-resources statement. That way, you can test the processing for an IOException before the output stream is opened and the data in the products file is deleted.
4. Comment out the line in the catch clause of the getProducts method that prints the exception to the console. Then, add a statement like this at the beginning of the try block in this that method throws an IOException:

```
if (true)
    throw new IOException();
```

5. Test these changes to make sure they're working correctly. To do that, run the application and enter the list command. If this works, comment out the

statement you added that throws the IOException.

6. Modify the ProductMaintApp class so it responds appropriately if the addProduct or deleteProduct method in the ProductTextFile class returns a false value. Test this exception by commenting out the line in the catch clause of the saveProducts method that displays the exception and adding a statement at the beginning of the try block in this method that throws an IOException. Test these changes.
7. Modify the ProductTextFile class so it writes exceptions to a text file named errorLog.txt instead of printing them to the console. To do that, add a method named printToLogFile that accepts an IOException as an argument. This method should append two records to the log file: one that indicates the date and time the exception occurred and one that contains information about the exception.
8. Modify the getProducts and saveProducts methods so they call the printToLogFile method when an error occurs. Test these changes. When you're sure this works correctly, comment out the statement you added that throws the IOException and save the file.

Exercise 18-4 Enhance the random-access processing

In this exercise, you'll modify the ProductRandomFile class so it works more efficiently. In addition, you'll add a method to this class that can be used to permanently delete the records in the products.ran file that have been marked for deletion. Then, you'll write the code to call this method.

1. Open the project named ch18_ex4_ProductMaint that's in the ex_starts directory.
2. Display the DAOFactory class, and modify it so the application will use the products.ran file.
3. Open the ProductRandomFile class and review its code. Note that the getProducts method works by looping through the productCodes array list and then calling the getRecord method for each product to retrieve the record for that product randomly.
4. Modify the getProducts method so it uses a buffered DataInputStream to read each product in the products.ran file sequentially, creates a Product object for each product that isn't marked for deletion, and adds the Product object to the products array list. Be sure to check that the file exists before you process it.
5. Run the application and test this change by entering the list command.
6. Add a method named commitDeletions to the ProductRandomFile class. This method should delete all the records from the products.ran file that are marked for deletion and return the number of records that were deleted. (If an

IOException occurs, it should return –1.) To do that, you can load the products array with all the records that haven't been deleted, write all the products in the products array list to the file, and use the setLength method to set the file to the appropriate length. To make this code work, you'll need to close the RandomAccessFile object so the new file length is applied. Also, be sure to reopen the file for random access, and reinitialize the productCodes array so it contains only the current products.

7. Display the ProductMaintApp class and add a commit command to the menu. When the user enters this command, a method named commitDeletions should be executed. Add the code for this method so it creates a new ProductRandomFile object and then calls the commitDeletions method of this object. If the commit operation is successful, it should display the number of records that were deleted. Otherwise, it should display an appropriate error message.
8. Test this code to be sure it works correctly. To do that, start by deleting one or more records. Then, commit the deletions.

19

How to work with XML

XML provides a standard way of storing data. Although XML is often used to exchange data between applications, particularly web-based applications, it can also be used to store structured data in a file. In this chapter, you'll learn the basics of creating XML documents, and you'll learn how to store those documents in a file. Because the class that's presented at the end of this chapter uses an array list, you may want to review chapters 11 and 12 before you read this chapter.

Introduction to XML

The topics that follow introduce you to the basics of XML. Here, you'll learn what XML is, how it is used, and the rules you must follow to create a simple XML document.

An XML document

XML (*Extensible Markup Language*) provides a standard way to structure data by using *tags* that identify each data element. In some ways, XML is similar to HTML, the markup language that's used to format HTML documents on the web. As a result, if you're familiar with HTML, you'll have no trouble learning how to create *XML documents*.

Figure 19-1 shows a simple XML document that contains data for three products. Each product has a code, description, and price. In the next two figures, you'll learn how the tags in this XML document work. But even without knowing those details, you can pick out the code, description, and price for each of the three products represented by this XML document.

You can also use XML files as an alternative to the text and binary files described in chapter 18. Later in this chapter, for example, you'll see a ProductXMLFile class that uses an XML file. You can use this class with the Product Maintenance application you first saw in chapter 9.

Data for three products

Code	Description	Price
java	Murach's Beginning Java	49.50
jsps	Murach's Java Servlets and JSP	49.50
zjcl	Murach's OS/390 and z/OS JCL	62.50

The products.xml document

```
<?xml version="1.0" encoding="utf-8" ?>
<!--Product data-->
<Products>
  <Product Code="java">
    <Description>Murach's Beginning Java</Description>
    <Price>49.50</Price>
  </Product>
  <Product Code="jsps">
    <Description>Murach's Java Servlets and JSP</Description>
    <Price>49.50</Price>
  </Product>
  <Product Code="zjcl">
    <Description>Murach's OS/390 and z/OS JCL</Description>
    <Price>62.50</Price>
  </Product>
</Products>
```

Description

- *XML*, which stands for *Extensible Markup Language*, is a method of structuring data using special *tags*.
- The *XML document* in this figure contains data for three products. Each product has an *attribute* named Code and *elements* named Description and Price. You'll learn more about attributes and elements in the next two figures.
- XML can be used to exchange data between different systems, especially via the Internet.
- XML documents that are stored in a file can be used as an alternative to binary files, text files, or even database systems for storing data.
- When XML is stored in a file, the file name usually has an extension of xml.

Figure 19-1 An XML document

XML tags, declarations, and comments

Figure 19-2 shows how XML uses tags to structure the data in an XML document. Here, each XML tag begins with the < character and ends with the > character. As a result, the first line in the XML document in this figure contains a complete XML tag. Similarly, the next three lines also contain complete tags. In contrast, the fifth line contains two tags, <Description> and </Description>, with a text value in between.

The first tag in any XML document is an *XML declaration.* This declaration identifies the document as an XML document and indicates which XML version the document conforms to. In this example, the document conforms to XML version 1.0. In addition, the declaration usually identifies the character set that's being used for the document. In this example, the character set is UTF-8, the most common one used for XML documents in English-speaking countries.

An XML document can also contain comments. These are tags that begin with <!-- and end with -->. Between the tags, you can type anything you want. For instance, the second line in this figure is a comment that indicates what type of data is contained in the XML document. It's often a good idea to include similar comments in your own XML documents.

XML elements

Elements are the building blocks of XML. Each element in an XML document represents a single data item and is identified by two tags: a *start tag* and an *end tag*. The start tag marks the beginning of the element and provides the element's name. The end tag marks the end of the element and repeats the name, prefixed by a slash. For example, <Description> is the start tag for an element named Description, and </Description> is the corresponding end tag.

It's important to realize that XML does not provide a pre-defined set of element names the way HTML does. Instead, you create your own element names to describe the contents of each element. Also, since XML names are case-sensitive, <Product> and <product> are not the same.

A complete element consists of the element's start tag, its end tag, and the *content* between the tags. For example, <Price>49.50</Price> indicates that the content of the Price element is 49.50. And <Description>Murach's Beginning Java</Description> indicates that the content of the Description element is *Murach's Beginning Java*.

Besides content, elements can contain other elements, known as *child elements*. This lets you add structure to a *parent element*. For example, a parent product element can have child elements that provide details about each product, such as the product's description and price. In this figure, for example, you can see that the start tag, end tag, and values for the Description and Price elements are contained between the start and end tags for the Product element. As a result, Description and Price are children of the Product element, and the Product element is the parent of both the Description and Price elements.

An XML document

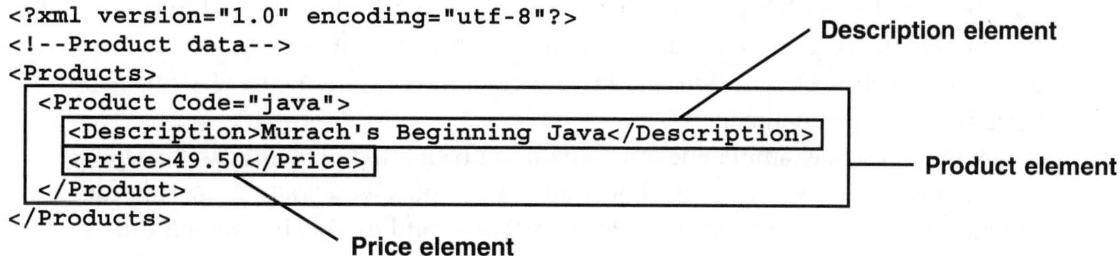

<?xml version="1.0" encoding="utf-8"?>
<!--Product data-->
<Products>
<Product Code="java">
<Description>Murach's Beginning Java</Description>
<Price>49.50</Price>
</Product>
</Products>
Description element
Product element
Price element

XML tags, declarations, and comments

- Each XML tag begins with < and ends with >.
- The first line in an XML document is an *XML declaration* that indicates which version of the XML standard is being used for the document. In addition, the declaration usually identifies the standard character set that's being used. For documents in English-speaking countries, UTF-8 is the character set that's commonly used.
- You can use the <!-- and --> tags to include comments in an XML document.

Elements

- An *element* is a unit of XML data that begins with a *start tag* and ends with an *end tag*. The start tag provides the name of the element and contains any attributes assigned to the element (see figure 19-3 for details on attributes). The end tag repeats the name, prefixed with a slash (/). You can use any name you want for an XML element.
- The text between an element's start and end tags is called the element's *content*. For example, <Description>Murach's Beginning Java</Description> indicates that the content of the Description element is the string *Murach's Beginning Java.*
- Elements can contain other elements. An element that's contained within another element is known as a *child element*. The element that contains a child element is known as the child's *parent element.*
- Child elements can repeat within a parent element. For instance, in the example above, the Products element can contain more than one Product element. Similarly, each Product element could contain repeating child elements.
- The highest-level parent element in an XML document is known as the *root element*. An XML document can have only one root element.

Figure 19-2 XML tags, declarations, comments, and elements

As the XML document in figure 19-1 shows, an element can occur more than once within an XML document. In this case, the document has three Product elements, each representing a product. Since each of these Product elements contains Description and Price elements, these elements also appear three times in the document.

Although this example doesn't show it, a given child element can also occur more than once within a parent. For example, suppose you want to provide for products that have more than one category. You could do this by using a Category child element to indicate the category of a product. Then, for a product that belongs to multiple categories, you simply include multiple Category child elements within the Product element for that product.

The highest-level parent element in an XML document is known as the *root element*, and an XML document can have only one root element. In the examples in figures 19-1 and 19-2, the root element is Products. For XML documents that contain repeating data, it is common to use a plural name for the root element to indicate that it contains multiple child elements.

XML attributes

As shown in figure 19-3, *attributes* are a concise way to provide data for XML elements. In the products XML document, for example, each Product element has a Code attribute that provides an identifying code for the product. Thus, <Product Code="java"> contains an attribute named Code whose value is *java*.

Here again, XML doesn't provide a set of pre-defined attributes. Instead, you create attributes as you need them, using names that describe the content of the attributes. If an element has more than one attribute, you can list the attributes in any order you wish. However, you must separate the attributes from each other with one or more spaces. In addition, each attribute can appear only once within an element.

When you plan the layout of an XML document, you will often need to decide whether to use elements or attributes to represent each data item. In many cases, either one will work. In the products document, for example, I could have used a child element named Code rather than an attribute to represent each product's code. Likewise, I could have used an attribute named Description rather than a child element for the product's description.

Because attributes are more concise than child elements, it's often tempting to use attributes rather than child elements. Keep in mind, though, that an element with more than a few attributes soon becomes unwieldy. As a result, most designers limit their use of attributes to certain types of data, such as identifiers like product codes or customer numbers.

An XML document

Code attribute

```
<?xml version="1.0" encoding="utf-8" ?>
<!--Product data-->
<Products>
  <Product Code="java">
    <Description>Murach's Beginning Java</Description>
    <Price>49.50</Price>
  </Product>
</Products>
```

Description

- You can include one or more *attributes* in the start tag for an element. An attribute typically consists of an attribute name, an equal sign, and a string value in quotes.
- If an element has more than one attribute, the order in which the attributes appear doesn't matter, but the attributes must be separated by one or more spaces.

When to use attributes instead of child elements

- When you design an XML document, you can use either child elements or attributes to represent the data for an element. The choice of whether to implement a data item as an attribute or as a separate child element is often a matter of preference.
- Two advantages of attributes are that they can appear in any order and they are more concise because they do not require end tags.
- Two advantages of child elements are that they are easier for people to read and they are more convenient for long string values.

Figure 19-3 XML attributes

An introduction to DTDs

By now, you can begin to see that XML provides a flexible way to store structured data. However, the XML standard provides for other tools that you can use to work with an XML document. One of the most useful is a *schema*, which you can use to define a list of conditions that an XML document must follow. For example, figure 19-4 shows how to use a *Document Type Definition (DTD)* to define the conditions for the products.xml document shown in figure 19-1.

Although a DTD is optional, you can use a DTD to make sure that various XML documents use the same format. For example, if various suppliers were sending you information about their products, you could supply them with a DTD to make sure that they all used a compatible format. This provides a way to create a standard set of tags for a certain application.

In a DTD, each XML element is declared in an ELEMENT declaration. If an element has children, that element must declare the children by listing the names in order, separated by commas. For example, the Product element DTD in this figure contains Description and Price elements in that order.

To specify that a child element may occur zero or one time, you can code a question mark after the element name. To specify that a child element may occur zero or more times, you can code an asterisk after the element name. And to specify that an element must occur one or more times, you can code a plus sign after the element name. If you don't code any of these characters after an element name, the element must occur one and only one time.

If an element contains text, you code the #PCDATA (parsed character data) keyword for that element. In this figure, for example, you can see that this keyword is coded for both the Description and Price elements.

To specify the attributes for an element, you use the ATTLIST declaration. This declaration specifies the element to which the attribute belongs, the name of the attribute, and the attribute type. If an attribute contains character data, you code the CDATA keyword. (Notice that you don't prefix this keyword with the # character.) In addition, an attribute declaration can include the #REQUIRED keyword to show that the attribute is required. In this figure, the Code attribute of the Product element is required, and it can store character data.

This figure also shows an XML document that uses a DOCTYPE declaration to refer to a DTD that's stored in an external file. Here, the DOCTYPE declaration is coded after the XML declaration but before the start tag of the root element, and this declaration points to a DTD file named products.dtd. (Because a path isn't specified for this file, it must be stored in the same directory as the products.xml file.) That way, you can easily validate this XML document against the specified DTD.

Rules for the products.xml document

- The document must contain one and only one Products element.
- The document can contain multiple Product elements. Each of these Product elements must contain two elements named Description and Price.
- Each Product element must contain one attribute named Code that holds a string.
- The Description and Price elements can contain text data, but they can't contain child elements.

A DTD that implements these rules

```
<?xml version="1.0" encoding="UTF-8"?>
<!-- DTD for the products.xml file. -->
<!ELEMENT Products (Product*)>
<!ELEMENT Product (Description, Price)>
<!ATTLIST Product
          Code CDATA #REQUIRED
>
<!ELEMENT Description (#PCDATA)>
<!ELEMENT Price (#PCDATA ) >
```

How to specify a DTD file in an XML document

```
<?xml version="1.0" encoding="UTF-8"?>
<!DOCTYPE Products SYSTEM "products.dtd">
<Products>
    <Product Code="java">
        <Description>Murach's Beginning Java</Description>
        <Price>49.5</Price>
    </Product>
    <Product Code="jsps">
        <Description>Murach's Java Servlets and JSP</Description>
        <Price>49.5</Price>
    </Product>
</Products>
```

Description

- XML allows you to set conditions that must be enforced on an XML document. To define these conditions, you use a *schema language* to create a *schema*. *Document Type Definition (DTD)* is a schema language that's part of standard XML.
- You use the ELEMENT declaration in a DTD to define the names of the elements and the types of data they will contain. You use the ATTLIST declaration to define the names of the attributes and the types of data they will contain.
- By default, each child element must occur one time. To specify that a child element can occur zero or one time, code a question mark after the name of a child element on the parent element declaration. To specify that the child element can occur zero or more times, code an asterisk. And to specify that a child element can occur one or more times, code a plus sign.
- In an XML document, you can use a DOCTYPE declaration to refer to a DTD that's stored in a DTD file.

Figure 19-4 An introduction to DTDs

How to view and edit an XML file

When working with XML files, you often need to view or edit the data they contain. To view the data that's stored in an existing XML file, you can use a web browser. To enter or edit the data that's stored in an XML file, you can use a text editor.

How to view an XML file

The browser shown in figure 19-5 displays the XML document that's stored in a file named products.xml. This shows that a browser is able to read the XML tags and display an XML document in a structured format that's easy to read. When you view an XML document in a browser, you can click on the minus sign (-) to the left of an element to collapse the element. Then, you can click on the plus sign (+) to expand the element.

To view an XML file that's available on a local drive in a browser, you can use your operating system to navigate to that file and then double-click on it. Note that for this to work, the operating system must associate the .xml file extension with a browser. Alternatively, you can enter the path and file name directly into the browser. If the XML file is stored on an intranet or the Internet, you can open the file by entering its web address in the browser.

How to edit an XML file

To edit an XML file, you can open it with a text editor. Then, you can enter new tags and data, or you can edit the existing tags and data. Although you can use any text editor to work with an XML file, it usually makes send to use a text editor that's designed for working with XML. For example, you can use the XML text editor that's included with NetBeans as shown in figure 19-5.

The XML editor provided by NetBeans makes it easy to edit XML documents. For example, tags, content, attributes, values, and comments are color-coded so you can easily tell them apart. After you type a start tag, you can use the XML editor to automatically add the end tag and position the cursor between the start and end tags. In addition, this text editor makes it easier to indent your child elements.

A good XML editor such as the one that's included with NetBeans also contains features that make it easy to create and work with DTD files. For example, NetBeans includes a Validate XML command that checks an XML file to make sure it adheres to the rules specified by the DTD. If so, NetBeans displays a message like the one shown in the Output window in this figure. Otherwise, it displays an error message that can help you find and fix the invalid XML.

Often, you want to work with an XML or DTD file that isn't stored with the source code for a NetBeans project. In that case, you can use NetBean's File→Open File command to open a single file.

An XML document in a browser

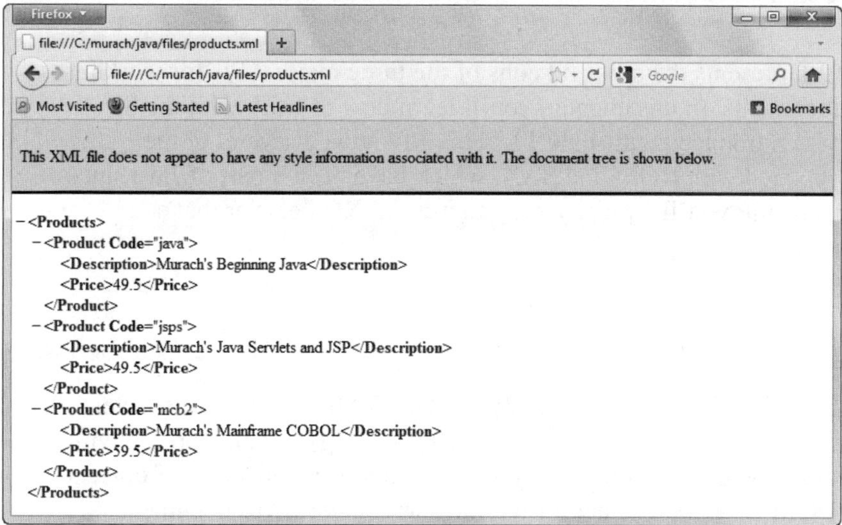

An XML document in a text editor

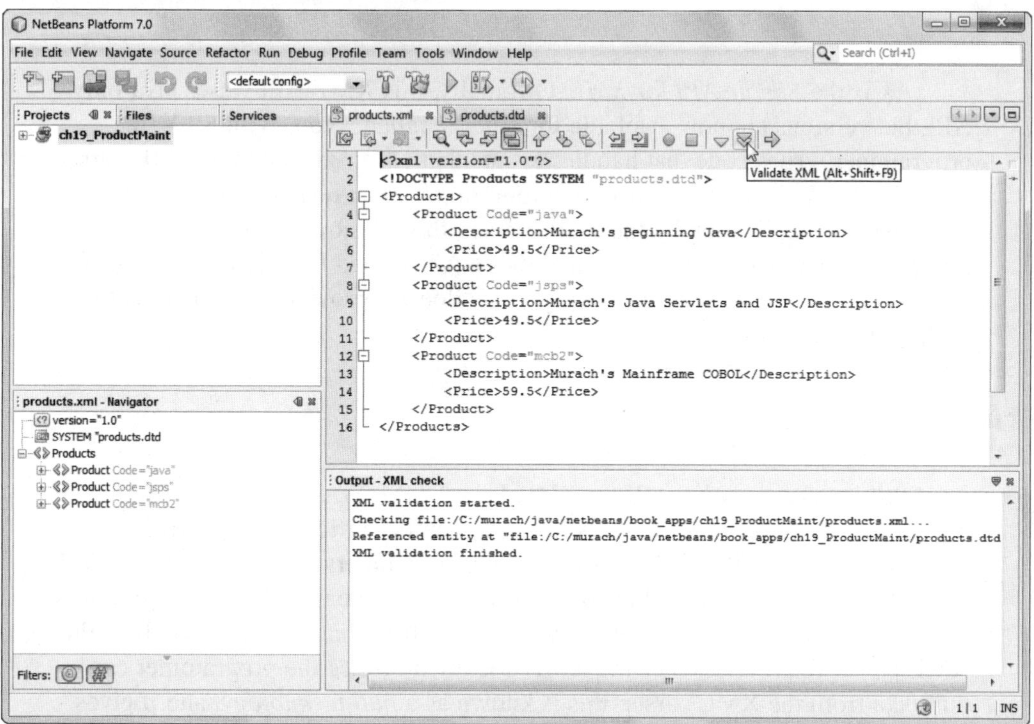

Description

- You can display an XML document in a browser. You can edit an XML document in a text editor like the one that comes with NetBeans.

An introduction to three XML APIs

Figure 19-6 presents the pros and cons of the three major APIs for working with XML documents. In this chapter, you'll learn how to work with the StAX API, which was introduced with JDK 1.6. This API solved several of the problems associated with DOM and SAX, which have been a part of Java since JDK 1.4. As a result, you'll typically want to use StAX whenever that's possible.

DOM

DOM stands for *Document Object Model*. This XML standard was developed by the World Wide Web Consortium (www.w3c.org). When working with DOM, the entire XML document is stored in memory as a collection of objects. As a result, DOM isn't appropriate for working with large XML documents.

SAX

SAX is the *Simple API for XML*. Originally, this XML API was a Java-only API, but versions are now available for other languages too. With SAX, the programmer writes code that handles events that are fired when the XML parser reads the XML document. Since the programmer must respond to data that is pushed to the application by the XML parser, this is known as a *push technology*. Although this approach allows SAX to read large XML documents quickly and to use memory efficiently, SAX doesn't provide a mechanism for writing documents.

StAX

StAX is the *Streaming API for XML*. Like DOM, StAX can be used to read or write XML. Like SAX, StAX is fast and memory efficient when working with small or large files. In addition, many programmers feel that the StAX API is designed better than DOM or SAX, which makes it easier for the programmer to use. With StAX, the programmer writes code that controls when and how the XML parser reads and writes the XML document. Since the programmer can pull data from the XML parser, this is known as a *pull technology*, and it gives the programmer more flexibility for working with XML.

DOM is

- Memory intensive
- Read-write
- Typically used for working with documents smaller than 10 megabytes

SAX is

- Memory efficient
- Read-only
- Typically used for working with documents larger than 10 megabytes

StAX is

- Memory efficient
- Read-write
- Appropriate for documents of all sizes.
- Easier to use than DOM or SAX

Description

- The *Document Object Model* (*DOM*) and the *Simple API for XML* (*SAX*) are two older XML APIs. Both of these APIs have been supported since JDK 1.4.
- The *Streaming API for XML* (*StAX*) is a newer API that was introduced with JDK 1.6.
- When you use DOM, the entire XML document structure is read into memory.
- When you use SAX or StAX, you can read only the parts of the XML document that you need.
- With SAX, the programmer writes code that handles events that are fired when the XML parser reads the elements of the XML document. This is known as a *push technology*.
- With StAX, the programmer writes code that controls when and how the XML parser reads and writes the XML document. This is known as a *pull technology*.

Figure 19-6 An introduction to three XML APIs

How to use StAX to work with XML

Now that you've been introduced to some of Java's APIs for working with XML, you're ready to learn how to use StAX to work with an XML document. You can find all of the classes and interfaces needed to work with StAX in one convenient package: the javax.xml.stream package. As a result, you'll want to code an import statement for this package before you begin working with StAX.

How to create an XMLStreamWriter object

Before you can write an XML document, you need to create an object that implements the XMLStreamWriter interface. To do that, you can use the XMLOutputFactory class as shown in figure 19-7. First, you call the static newFactory method of the XMLOutputFactory class to create an XMLOutputFactory object. Then, you call the createXMLStreamWriter method from that object to create the XMLStreamWriter object. Once you do that, you can use the XMLStreamWriter object to write an XML document as described in the next figure.

When you call the createXMLStreamWriter method, you must supply an argument that connects the XMLStreamWriter to an output stream. If you want to write XML to a file, you can supply a FileWriter object as the argument. In this figure, for example, the first statement within the try block creates a FileWriter object that specifies a file named products.xml. This works because the FileWriter class implements the Writer interface, and the Writer interface is a valid argument for the createXMLStreamWriter method.

If you want to write XML to an output stream, you can supply any object that implements the abstract OutputStream class as the argument. In this figure, for example, the last code example shows how to write an XML document to the console. This works because the System.out object implements the OutputStream class, and the abstract OutputStream class is a valid argument for the createXMLStreamWriter method.

Since the createXMLStreamWriter method throws an XMLStreamException, you must handle this exception whenever you create an XMLStreamWriter object. In addition, if you create a FileWriter object, you must handle the IOException that's thrown by the constructor of the FileWriter class. In this figure, for example, a multi-catch statement handles these exceptions by printing the exception to the console.

Classes for creating an XMLStreamWriter object

```
javax.xml.stream.XMLOutputFactory
javax.xml.stream.XMLStreamException
```

An interface for creating an XMLStreamWriter object

```
javax.xml.stream.XMLStreamWriter
```

Common methods of the XMLOutputFactory class

Method	Description
`newFactory()`	A static method that returns an XMLOutputFactory object.
`createXMLStreamWriter(out)`	Returns an XMLStreamWriter object for the specified Writer or OutputStream object. This method throws an XMLStreamException.

Code that creates an XMLStreamWriter object that writes to a file

```
// create the XMLOutputFactory object
XMLOutputFactory outputFactory = XMLOutputFactory.newFactory();

try
{
    // create XMLStreamWriter object
    FileWriter fileWriter =
        new FileWriter("products.xml");
    XMLStreamWriter writer =
        outputFactory.createXMLStreamWriter(fileWriter);

    // Write XML data here
}
catch (IOException | XMLStreamException e)
{
    System.out.println(e);
}
```

Code that creates an XMLStreamWriter object that writes to the console

```
    XMLStreamWriter writer =
        outputFactory.createXMLStreamWriter(System.out);
```

Description

- You can use the XMLOutputFactory class to create an XMLStreamWriter object. Then, you can use the XMLStreamWriter object to write an XML document to a stream as described in the next figure.
- To write XML to a file, you can supply a FileWriter object as the argument for the createXMLStreamWriter method. For more information about the FileWriter object, please see chapter 18.
- To write XML to an output stream, such as the console, you can supply any stream that implements the abstract OutputStream class as the argument for the createXMLStreamWriter method.

Figure 19-7 How to create an XMLStreamWriter object

How to write XML

Once you've created an XMLStreamWriter object as described in the last figure, you can use its methods to write XML as shown in figure 19-8. Although additional methods are available for writing XML, the methods presented in this figure are the ones that you'll need for writing most XML documents.

To start, you can use the writeStartDocument method to write the XML declaration. Here, you supply a string argument that indicates the version of XML that you'll be using. In this figure, for example, the code specifies version 1.0 of XML.

Then, you can use the writeStartElement, writeAttribute, writeCharacters, and writeEndElement methods to write the start tags, data, and end tags for the elements in your XML document. In this figure, for example, the writeStartElement method writes the start tag for the Products element before the for statement loops through the collection of Product objects. Within the loop, the various write methods are used to write the tags and data for the Product, Description, and Price elements that correspond with the Product objects in the collection. Since all of the write methods work with strings, this code must convert the product price from a double value to a string before writing it. Finally, after the loop, the writeEndElement method writes the end tag for the Products element.

If you want to include comments in your XML document, you can use the writeComment method. In this figure, for example, a comment that says "Product data" is written after the XML declaration but before the Products element. Similarly, if you want to include a DTD in your XML document, you can use the writeDTD method to write a DTD section.

When you're done writing the XML, you can call the flush method to write any cached data that's left in the stream to the underlying output mechanism. In addition, you can call the close method to close the XMLStreamWriter object and free any resources associated with it.

Because XML uses the less than and greater than signs to identify start and end tags, they can't be stored as the text within an element. For example, a string that says "Java > C#" can't be stored as the text for the Description element. If you try to use the XMLStreamWriter object to write this string as text for an element, it will automatically substitute the escape characters shown in this figure for the greater than sign. Similarly, it will substitute the other escape characters shown in this figure whenever they're necessary. In addition, the XMLStreamReader object described later in this chapter will automatically convert these escape characters back to the original characters when you read them. As a result, you don't need to worry about this substitution when you're using StAX. However, if you view the XML file in an XML editor, you will see the escape characters instead of the original characters.

Common methods of the XMLStreamWriter interface

Method	Description
`writeStartDocument(version)`	Writes the XML declaration.
`writeStartElement(name)`	Writes the start tag for an element.
`writeAttribute(name, value)`	Writes an attribute for the current element.
`writeCharacters(value)`	Writes characters.
`writeComment(value)`	Writes an XML comment.
`writeDTD(value)`	Writes a DTD section.
`writeEndElement()`	Writes the end tag for the current element.
`flush()`	Writes any cached data to the underlying output mechanism.
`close()`	Closes the XMLStreamWriter object and frees any resources associated with it.

Code that writes an XML document to a stream

```
writer.writeStartDocument("1.0");
writer.writeComment("Product data");
writer.writeStartElement("Products");
for (Product p : products)
{
    writer.writeStartElement("Product");
    writer.writeAttribute("Code", p.getCode());

    writer.writeStartElement("Description");
    writer.writeCharacters(p.getDescription());
    writer.writeEndElement();

    writer.writeStartElement("Price");
    double price = p.getPrice();
    writer.writeCharacters(Double.toString(price));
    writer.writeEndElement();

    writer.writeEndElement();  // for the Product element
}
writer.writeEndElement();      // for the Products element
writer.flush();
writer.close();
```

Escape characters used by the writeCharacters method

Character	Escape	Description
<	<	less than
>	>	greater than
&	&	ampersand

Description

- Since these methods throw an XMLStreamException, you must handle this exception when working with these methods.

Figure 19-8 How to write an XML document to a stream

How to create an XMLStreamReader object

Before you can write an XML document, you need to create an object that implements the XMLStreamReader interface. To do that, you can use the XMLInputFactory class as shown in figure 19-9. Since this works similarly to the code presented in figure 19-7, you shouldn't have much trouble understanding how it works.

To start, you call the static newFactory method of the XMLInputFactory class to create an XMLInputFactory object. Then, you call the createXMLStreamReader method from that object to create the XMLStreamReader object. Once you do that, you can use the XMLStreamReader object to read an XML document as described in the next figure.

When you call the createXMLStreamReader method, you must supply an argument that connects the XMLStreamReader to an input stream. If you want to read XML from a file, you can supply a FileReader object as the argument. This works because the FileReader class implements the Reader interface, and the Reader interface is a valid argument for the createXMLStreamReader method. If, on the other hand, you want to read XML from an input stream, you can supply any object that implements thc abstract InputStream class as the argument.

Since the createXMLStreamReader method throws an XMLStreamException, you must handle this exception whenever you create an XMLStreamReader object. In addition, if you create a FileReader object, you must handle the IOException that's thrown by the constructor of the FileReader class. In this figure, for example, the multi-catch block handles these exceptions by printing the exception to the console.

Classes for creating an XMLStreamReader object

```
javax.xml.stream.XMLInputFactory
javax.xml.stream.XMLStreamException
```

An interface for creating an XMLStreamReader object

```
javax.xml.stream.XMLStreamReader
```

Common methods of the XMLInputFactory class

Method	Description
`newFactory()`	A static method that returns an XMLInputFactory object.
`createXMLStreamReader(in)`	Returns an XMLStreamReader object for the specified Reader or InputStream object. This method throws an XMLStreamException.

Code that creates an XMLStreamReader object

```
// create the XMLInputFactory object
XMLInputFactory inputFactory = XMLInputFactory.newFactory();
try
{
    // create an XMLStreamReader object
    FileReader fileReader =
        new FileReader("products.xml");
    XMLStreamReader reader =
        inputFactory.createXMLStreamReader(fileReader);

    // Read XML here
}
catch (IOException | XMLStreamException e)
{
    System.out.println(e);
}
```

Description

- You can use the XMLInputFactory class to create an XMLStreamReader object. Then, you can use the XMLStreamReader object to read an XML document from a stream as described in figure 19-10.
- To read XML from a file, you can supply a FileReader object as the argument for the createXMLStreamReader method. For more information about the FileReader object, please see chapter 18.

How to read XML

Once you've created an XMLStreamReader object as described in the last figure, you can use the methods and constants shown figure 19-10 to read XML. Although additional methods and constants are available for reading XML, the ones presented in this figure are the ones that you'll need most of the time.

To begin reading an XML document, you can use the hasNext method to check if there are any parsing events to process. In part 2 of this figure, for example, the while loop uses the hasNext method to determine whether the loop should be executed.

When the XML parser is positioned on a parsing event, you can call the getEventType method to return an int value that corresponds with one of the constants defined by the XMLStreamConstants interface. Then, you can use a switch statement to handle any parsing events that you want. In part 2 of this figure, for example, the code only handles two events: the START_ELEMENT event and the END_ELEMENT event. However, if necessary, this code could easily be modified to handle the events that are raised when the parser reads other types of events, such as the COMMENT event that's raised when the parser reads a comment.

If you experiment with the constants and methods shown in this figure, you'll find that some of the methods that work with the START_ELEMENT event read the next event in the stream. For example, the getElementText method reads the CHARACTERS event. Similarly, the getAttributeValue method reads the ATTRIBUTE event. As a result, if you use these methods and then try to use the getText method to read the text stored in the ATTRIBUTE or CHARACTERS event, it won't work since that event has already been read from the stream.

Common methods of the XMLStreamReader interface

Method	Description
`hasNext()`	Returns true if there are more parsing events and false if there are no more events.
`next()`	Gets the next parsing event.
`getEventType()`	Returns an int value that indicates the type of the parsing event. This int value corresponds with the constants defined by the XMLStreamConstants interface.
`getLocalName()`	Returns the name of the current element.
`getAttributeValue(index)`	Returns a string value for the attribute stored at the index.
`getAttributeCount()`	Returns a count of attributes for this element.
`getAttributeLocalName(index)`	Returns the name of the attribute at the specified index.
`getElementText()`	Reads the value of a text-only element. An exception is thrown if the element isn't a text-only element.
`getText()`	Reads the value of a COMMENT, DTD, CHARACTERS, CDATA, or SPACE parsing event.

Common constants defined by the XMLStreamConstants interface

Constant	Description
`START_ELEMENT`	The event is a start element.
`END_ELEMENT`	The event is an end element.
`ATTRIBUTE`	The event is an attribute.
`CHARACTERS`	The event is character data.
`COMMENT`	The event is a comment.
`SPACE`	The event is whitespace.
`DTD`	The event is a DTD.

Description

- If the called method isn't valid for the current event, an XMLStreamException is thrown. As a result, you must handle the XMLStreamException when you work with these methods.
- If the called method isn't valid for the event, an IllegalStateException is thrown. Since an IllegalStateException is an unchecked exception, you don't have to handle it. If possible, though, it's a good practice to write your code so it prevents this type of exception from being thrown.

Figure 19-10 How to read an XML document from a file (part 1 of 2)

When you handle a START_ELEMENT, you can use the getLocalName method to get the name of the element that corresponds with the start tag that's being processed. Then, you can use an if statement to process each element.

If an element has attributes, you can use the getAttributeValue method to get the string value that's stored in the attribute at the specified index. In this figure for example, the getAttributeValue method is used to retrieve the string value that's stored for the first attribute of the Product element. Since the Product element only has a single attribute, the Code attribute, this returns a string for the code.

If an element contains text, you can use the getElementText method to get that text. In this figure, for example, the getElementText method is used to retrieve the string value that's stored in the Description and Price elements. Since this method returns a string for the product's price, this code converts the price string to a double value before storing it in the Product object.

When you handle an END_ELEMENT, you can use the getLocalName method to get the name of the element that corresponds with the end tag that's being processed. Then, you can check the name and provide the appropriate processing. In this figure, for example, the Product object is added to the products collection after the end tag for the Product element is processed.

If you review the code in the first example, you'll realize that it only works because you know the structure of the XML document. In particular, you know that each Product element will contain one Code attribute, one Description element, and one Price element. When you work with XML documents, you will often know the structure of the document. In addition, if you use a DTD, it's possible to validate the XML document against the DTD before you begin processing the file.

Even if you don't know the structure of the XML document, you can still use StAX to read the document. To do that, though, you may need to use some methods and parsing events that aren't presented in this figure. Of course, the less you know about the structure of the XML document, the more difficult it is to read.

If you call a method that isn't valid for the event, an IllegalStateException will be thrown at runtime. For example, this exception will be thrown if you call the getAttributeValue method on an END_ELEMENT parsing event. Similarly, this exception will be thrown if you call the getElementText method on the START_ELEMENT parsing event for an element that contains other sub elements, such as the Product element.

Since an IllegalStateException is an unchecked exception, you don't have to handle it at compile time, and you typically won't want to. Instead, you should write your code to prevent this exception from being thrown at runtime. To do that, you may need to write extra code that does more checking before you attempt to read data. In this figure, for instance, the second example uses the getAttributeCount and getAttributeLocalName methods to check that the attribute is named Code before reading the attribute. As a result, this code will work even if the Product element contains multiple attributes and the Code attribute isn't the first attribute. This code will also work if the Code attribute doesn't exist.

Code that reads all Product elements into a products array list

```
ArrayList<Product> products = new ArrayList<>();
Product p = null;

while (reader.hasNext())
{
    int eventType = reader.getEventType();
    switch (eventType)
    {
        case XMLStreamConstants.START_ELEMENT:
            String elementName = reader.getLocalName();
            if (elementName.equals("Product"))
            {
                p = new Product();
                String code = reader.getAttributeValue(0);
                p.setCode(code);
            }
            if (elementName.equals("Description"))
            {
                String description = reader.getElementText();
                p.setDescription(description);
            }
            if (elementName.equals("Price"))
            {
                String priceString = reader.getElementText();
                double price = Double.parseDouble(priceString);
                p.setPrice(price);
            }
            break;
        case XMLStreamConstants.END_ELEMENT:
            elementName = reader.getLocalName();
            if (elementName.equals("Product"))
            {
                products.add(p);
            }
            break;
        default:
            break;
    }
    reader.next();
}
```

A safer and more flexible way to read attributes

```
int count = reader.getAttributeCount();
for (int i = 0; i < count; i++)
{
    if (reader.getAttributeLocalName(i).equals("Code"))
    {
        String code = reader.getAttributeValue(i);
    }
}
```

Figure 19-10 How to read an XML document from a file (part 2 of 2)

A class that works with an XML file

Figure 19-11 presents the complete code for the ProductXMLFile class. If you've read chapter 18, you'll see that, like the ProductTextFile and ProductRandomFile classes presented in that chapter, this class implements the ProductDAO interface. If you haven't read chapter 18, you may want to review figure 18-10 to see how this interface is defined.

The ProductXMLFile class starts by declaring and initializing two instance variables. The first instance variable, named productsPath, is a Path object that will refer to the XML file that stores the products. The second instance variable, named products, is an ArrayList of Product objects that will store one Product object for each Product element in the file.

The instance variables are followed by a constructor that assigns values to the variables. The first statement uses the get method of the Paths class to get a Path object for the products.xml file. Note that since the path specifies only the file name for the XML file, the Path object refers to a file in the same directory as the ProductXMLFile class. The second statement in the constructor calls the getProducts method to load the products array list. You'll see the code for this method in a minute.

The private saveProducts method writes the products in the array list to the XML file. To start, this method creates an XMLOutputFactory object that will be used later in the method to create the XMLStreamWriter object. Then, this method creates an XMLStreamWriter object that's used to write the XML to the products file. To do that, this method creates a FileWriter object for the file. Then, it passes this object as an argument to the createXMLStreamWriter method of the XMLOutputFactory object. Note that the IOException that's thrown by the constructor of the FileWriter class is caught by the multi-catch block that handles the IOException and the XMLStreamException.

Once the XMLStreamWriter object has been created, the saveProducts method uses it to write the XML file. To start, it writes the XML declaration and the start element for the Products element. Then, it loops through the array list and uses the various write methods of the XMLStreamWriter object to write the XML tags and data for each product to the XML file. After the loop, the method finishes by writing the end tag for the Products element and by calling the flush and close methods to make sure that all characters in the stream have been written and to free any resources associated with the stream.

If you call one of the methods of the XMLStreamWriter object in the wrong context, it won't work correctly and may throw an XMLStreamException. In that case, the multi-catch block that catches this exception prints the exception to the console and returns a false value to indicate that the save operation wasn't successful. If the saveProducts method is successful, however, it returns a true value, which is usually what happens with code that has been tested and debugged.

The code for the ProductXMLFile class

Page 1

```
import java.util.*;
import java.io.*;
import java.nio.file.*;
import javax.xml.stream.*;  // StAX API

public class ProductXMLFile implements ProductDAO
{
    private Path productsPath = null;
    private ArrayList<Product> products = null;

    public ProductXMLFile()
    {
        productsPath = Paths.get("products.xml");
        products = this.getProducts();
    }

    private boolean saveProducts()
    {
        // create the XMLOutputFactory object
        XMLOutputFactory outputFactory = XMLOutputFactory.newFactory();
        try
        {
            // create XMLStreamWriter object
            FileWriter fileWriter =
                new FileWriter(productsPath.toFile());
            XMLStreamWriter writer =
                outputFactory.createXMLStreamWriter(fileWriter);

            //write the products to the file
            writer.writeStartDocument("1.0");
            writer.writeStartElement("Products");
            for (Product p : products)
            {
                writer.writeStartElement("Product");
                writer.writeAttribute("Code", p.getCode());
                writer.writeStartElement("Description");
                writer.writeCharacters(p.getDescription());
                writer.writeEndElement();
                writer.writeStartElement("Price");
                double price = p.getPrice();
                writer.writeCharacters(Double.toString(price));
                writer.writeEndElement();
                writer.writeEndElement();
            }
            writer.writeEndElement();
            writer.flush();
            writer.close();
        }
        catch (IOException | XMLStreamException e)
        {
            System.out.println(e);
            return false;
        }
        return true;
    }
```

Figure 19-11 A class that works with an XML file (part 1 of 3)

The getProducts method returns an ArrayList object that contains Product objects that are created from the Product elements stored in the XML document. This method starts by checking whether the array list does not contain a null. If it doesn't, the XML file has already been read. As a result, this method returns that array list and exits. This prevents the class from reading the XML file unnecessarily.

However, if the array list is null, this code must read the XML file. To do that, it initializes the array list so it can store Product objects, and it declares and initializes a Product object. Then, this method checks whether the XML file exists. If so, it creates an XMLStreamReader object that can be used to read the products from the file.

After it creates the XMLStreamReader object, the getProducts method uses a loop to create a Product object from each Product element in the XML document and to add each Product object to the array list. Within the loop, the first statement returns an int value that corresponds to one of the constants defined in the XMLStreamConstants interface. Then, a switch statement is used to process the start tags for the Product, Description, and Price elements of the XML document and the end tag for the Product element.

If a start tag for the Product element is encountered, this code creates a new Product object and uses the getAttributeValue method to get a string value for the Code attribute of that element. Then, when the start tags for the Description and Price elements are encountered, this code uses the getElementText method to get the string value that's stored in those elements. Finally, it uses the appropriate method to store these values in the Product object.

Since the Price element stores the price as a string, this string must be converted to a double value before it can be stored in the Product object. To do that, this code uses the parseDouble method of the Double class.

After the start tags for the Product, Description, and Price elements have been processed. The end tag for the Product element is processed. This code adds the Product object to the array list.

The code for the ProductXMLFile class Page 2

```
public ArrayList<Product> getProducts()
{
    // if the XML file has already been read, don't read it again
    if (products != null)
        return products;

    products = new ArrayList<>();

    Product p = null;
    if (Files.exists(productsPath))  // prevent the FileNotFoundException
    {
        // create the XMLInputFactory object
        XMLInputFactory inputFactory = XMLInputFactory.newFactory();
        try
        {
            // create a XMLStreamReader object
            FileReader fileReader =
                new FileReader(productsPath.toFile());
            XMLStreamReader reader =
                inputFactory.createXMLStreamReader(fileReader);

            // read the products from the file
            while (reader.hasNext())
            {
                int eventType = reader.getEventType();
                switch (eventType)
                {
                    case XMLStreamConstants.START_ELEMENT:
                        String elementName = reader.getLocalName();
                        if (elementName.equals("Product"))
                        {
                            p = new Product();
                            String code = reader.getAttributeValue(0);
                            p.setCode(code);
                        }
                        if (elementName.equals("Description"))
                        {
                            String description = reader.getElementText();
                            p.setDescription(description);
                        }
                        if (elementName.equals("Price"))
                        {
                            String priceText = reader.getElementText();
                            double price = Double.parseDouble(priceText);
                            p.setPrice(price);
                        }
                        break;
                    case XMLStreamConstants.END_ELEMENT:
                        elementName = reader.getLocalName();
                        if (elementName.equals("Product"))
                        {
                            products.add(p);
                        }
                        break;
```

Figure 19-11 A class that works with an XML file (part 2 of 3)

The getProduct, addProduct, deleteProduct, and updateProduct methods work the same as to the methods presented figure 18-11. As a result, if you read chapter 18, you should understand these methods. In case you didn't read that chapter, though, I'll describe these methods again in the paragraphs that follow.

The getProduct method returns a Product object for a product that matches the specified product code. To search for the product, the getProduct method loops through each product in the products array list until it finds one with the specified product code. Then, it returns that product. If no product is found with the specified code, this method returns a null.

The addProduct method calls the add method of the ArrayList class to add the product that's passed to it to the array list. Then, it calls the saveProducts method to save the modified products array list to the products file so the array list and the file contain the same data. Notice that the addProduct method returns the boolean value that's returned by the saveProducts method. That way, if the saveProducts method returns a true value, the addProduct method will also return a true value.

The deleteProduct method is similar. It calls the remove method of the ArrayList class to remove the product from the array list. Then, it calls the saveProducts method to save the array list to the products file, and it returns the boolean value that's returned by that method.

The updateProduct method works a little differently. This method updates the data for an existing product with the data in a new Product object. To start, it uses the getProduct method to get the old Product object with the same product code as the new Product object. Then, it gets the index for the old product, and it removes that product from the array list. Next, it inserts the new product into the array list where the old product used to be. Finally, it calls the saveProducts method to save the array list to the products file, and it returns a value that indicates whether the save operation was successful.

The code for the ProductXMLFile class

Page 3

```
                        default:
                            break;
                    }
                    reader.next();
                }
            }
            catch (IOException | XMLStreamException e)
            {
                System.out.println(e);
                return null;
            }
        }
        return products;
    }

    public Product getProduct(String code)
    {
        for (Product p : products)
        {
            if (p.getCode().equals(code))
                return p;
        }
        return null;
    }

    public boolean addProduct(Product p)
    {
        products.add(p);
        return this.saveProducts();
    }

    public boolean deleteProduct(Product p)
    {
        products.remove(p);
        return this.saveProducts();
    }

    public boolean updateProduct(Product newProduct)
    {
        // get the old product and remove it
        Product oldProduct = this.getProduct(newProduct.getCode());
        int i = products.indexOf(oldProduct);
        products.remove(i);

        // add the updated product
        products.add(i, newProduct);

        return this.saveProducts();
    }
}
```

Figure 19-11 A class that works with an XML file (part 3 of 3)

Perspective

In this chapter, you learned the basic concepts and terms for working with XML. In addition, you learned how to use the XMLStreamReader and XMLStreamWriter interfaces to read and write XML documents. With that as background, you should be able to read and write XML documents of all types and sizes.

However, the StAX API provides two other interfaces that can also be used to read and write XML documents: the XMLEventReader and XMLEventWriter interfaces. You can use the XMLEventFactory class to create objects that implement these interfaces. Since this works similarly to the techniques presented in this chapter, you shouldn't have too much trouble using these interfaces if necessary. The main advantage is that the XMLEventReader interface includes a peek method that allows you to look at the next XML event without reading it from the stream.

Finally, if you want or need to learn how to work with the DOM, SAX, or other XML API, you can find more information on the Java web site.

Summary

- *XML* provides a standard way to structure data by using *tags* that identify data items.
- An *element* begins with a *start tag* and ends with an *end tag*. An element can contain data in the form of *content* that appears between the tags. It can also contain *child elements*.
- An *attribute* consists of a name and value that appear within an element's start tag.
- A *DTD* (*Documentation Type Definition*) is a *schema* that defines the structure of an XML document. This schema can be enforced when a document is read or written.
- You can use a web browser to view XML data, and you can use any text editor to edit an XML file, but it's helpful to use a text editor that's designed for working with XML.
- *DOM* (the *Document Object Model*) is an API that can be used to build a DOM tree, work with the nodes of a tree, read an XML document from a file, and write an XML document to a file.
- *SAX* (the *Simple API for XML*) can be used to read an XML document.
- *StAX* (the *Streaming API for XML*) is appropriate for reading or writing XML documents of all sizes.

Exercise 19-1 Work with an XML file

In this exercise, you'll write code that works with an XML document that's stored in a file. When you complete this exercise, the console output should look like this:

```
Products list:
java    Murach's Beginning Java                    $49.50
jsps    Murach's Java Servlets and JSP             $49.50

XML Tester has been added to the XML document.

Products list:
java    Murach's Beginning Java                    $49.50
jsps    Murach's Java Servlets and JSP             $49.50
test    XML Tester                                 $77.77

XML Tester has been deleted from the XML document.

Products list:
java    Murach's Beginning Java                    $49.50
jsps    Murach's Java Servlets and JSP             $49.50
```

1. Use a web browser to view the products.xml file in the ex_starts\ch19_ex1_XMLTester directory. Then, collapse and expand some of the elements.
2. Open the project named ch19_ex1_XMLTester that's stored in the ex_starts directory. Then, open the XMLTesterApp class and review its code. Finally, run this project to see how it works. At this point, it prints three messages to the console, but it doesn't work with the XML file.
3. Add code to the readProducts method that reads an XML document from the products.xml file and stores it in an array list. Be sure to catch any exceptions that may be thrown. Then, test the class. At this point, the application should print three identical product lists, and those lists should match the data that's stored in the products.xml file.
4. Add code to the writeProducts method that writes the XML document to the products.xml file. Then, remove the comments from the code in the main method that adds and removes a product from the list. Finally, test the application again. When you do, it should display the messages shown above.

20

How to work with a Derby database

Since Java SE 6, Java has included an open-source, all-Java database known as Derby that provides the features of a true relational database management system (RDMS). Since this database is already installed on your computer, it's a convenient way to learn about how relational database management systems work. In addition, if you need to embed a database in a client application, Derby might be exactly what you need.

To start, this chapter teaches you some basic concepts for working with a relational database. Then, it shows you some specific skills for working with a Derby database.

How a relational database is organized

In 1970, Dr. E. F. Codd developed a model for a new type of *database* called a *relational database*. This type of database eliminated some of the problems that were associated with earlier types of databases like hierarchical databases. By using the relational model, you can reduce data redundancy, which saves disk storage and leads to more efficient data retrieval. You can also view and manipulate data in a way that is both intuitive and efficient. Today, relational databases are the de facto standard for database applications.

How a table is organized

A relational database stores data in *tables*. Each table contains *rows* and *columns* as shown in figure 20-1. In practice, rows and columns are often referred to by the traditional terms, *records* and *fields*. That's why this book uses these terms interchangeably.

In a relational database, a table has one column that's defined as the *primary key*. The primary key uniquely identifies each row in a table. That way, the rows in one table can easily be related to the rows in another table. In this table, the ProductCode column is the primary key.

The software that manages a relational database is called the *database management system* (*DBMS*) or *relational database management system* (*RDBMS*). The DBMS provides features that let you design the database. After that, the DBMS manages all changes, additions, and deletions to the database. Three of the most popular database management systems are Oracle, Microsoft's SQL Server, and IBM's DB2. In recent years, MySQL has also become popular. This DBMS is fast, easy-to-use, and free for most purposes.

The Products table

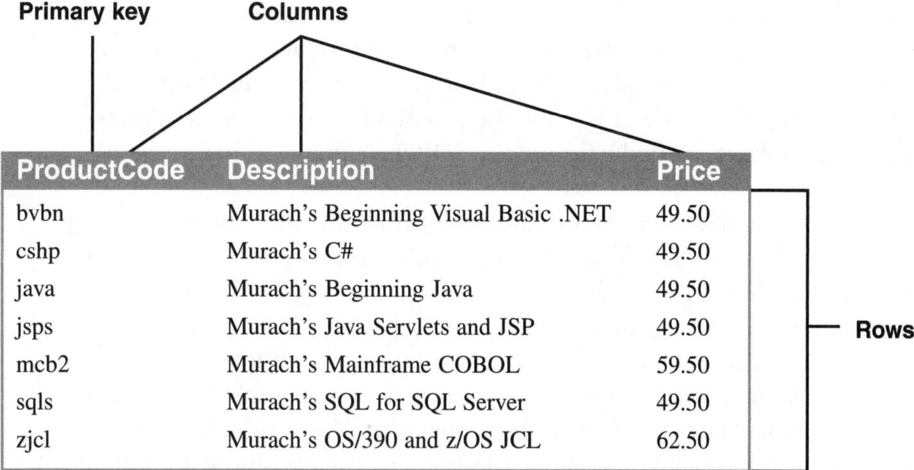

ProductCode	Description	Price
bvbn	Murach's Beginning Visual Basic .NET	49.50
cshp	Murach's C#	49.50
java	Murach's Beginning Java	49.50
jsps	Murach's Java Servlets and JSP	49.50
mcb2	Murach's Mainframe COBOL	59.50
sqls	Murach's SQL for SQL Server	49.50
zjcl	Murach's OS/390 and z/OS JCL	62.50

Description

- A *relational database* uses *tables* to store and manipulate data. Each table contains one or more *records*, or *rows*, that contain the data for a single entry. Each row contains one or more *fields*, or *columns*, with each column representing a single item of data.
- Most tables contain a *primary key* that uniquely identifies each row in the table.
- The software that manages a relational database is called a *database management system* (*DBMS*). Four popular database management systems today are Oracle, Microsoft's SQL Server, IBM's DB2, and MySQL.

Figure 20-1 How a table is organized

How the tables in a database are related

Figure 20-2 shows how a relational database uses the values in the primary key column to relate one table to another. Here, each ProductCode column in the LineItems table contains a value that identifies one row in the Products table. Since the ProductCode column in the LineItems table points to a primary key in another table, it's called a *foreign key*. Often, a table will have several foreign keys.

In this figure, each row in the Products table relates to one or more rows in the LineItems table. As a result, the Products table has a *one-to-many relationship* with the LineItems table. Although a one-to-many relationship is the most common type of relationship between tables, you can also have a *one-to-one relationship* or a *many-to-many relationship*. However, a one-to-one relationship between two tables is rare since the data can be stored in a single table. In contrast, a many-to-many relationship between two tables is typically implemented by using a third table that has a one-to-many relationship with both of the original tables.

Incidentally, the primary key in the LineItems table is the LineItemID column. It is automatically generated by the DBMS when a new row is added to the database. This type of primary key is often appropriate for tables like Invoice and Customer tables.

The relationship between the Products and LineItems tables

Primary key

ProductCode	Description	Price
bvbn	Murach's Beginning Visual Basic .NET	49.50
cshp	Murach's C#	49.50
java	Murach's Beginning Java	49.50
jsps	Murach's Java Servlets and JSP	49.50
mcb2	Murach's Mainframe COBOL	59.50
sqls	Murach's SQL for SQL Server	49.50
zjcl	Murach's OS/390 and z/OS JCL	62.50

LineItemID	InvoiceID	ProductCode	Quantity
1	1	java	5
2	1	jsps	5
3	2	mcb2	1
4	4	cshp	1
8	4	zjcl	2
9	6	sqls	1
10	6	java	1
11	7	mcb2	5

Foreign key

Description

- The tables in a relational database are related to each other through their key columns. For example, the ProductCode column is used to relate the Products and LineItems tables. The ProductCode column in the LineItems table is called a *foreign key* because it identifies a related row in the Products table.
- Three types of relationships can exist between tables. The most common type is a *one-to-many relationship* as illustrated above. However, two tables can also have a *one-to-one relationship* or a *many-to-many relationship*.

How the columns in a table are defined

Figure 20-3 shows how a DBMS defines a column in a table. In particular, it shows how the DBMS defines a name and data type for each column, which are required by all relational databases. In addition, most modern relational databases let you set other properties for each column in the database such as a default value for new rows, whether the column can contain null values, and so on.

This figure shows the names and data types for the columns in the Products table. Here, the ProductCode and Description columns are defined with the VARCHAR data type, which maps to the String type in Java. In addition, the ProductCode column can store a maximum of 10 characters, while the Description column can store a maximum of 40 characters. In contrast, the Price column is defined with the DOUBLE data type, which maps to the double type in Java.

When the definition for a column indicates that the column can't contain *null values*, an application must provide a value for the column when it tries to add a row to the database. The exception is if the column is defined with a *default value*. Then, if the application tries to add a new row without specifying a value for the column, the DBMS will use the default value.

The design of the Products table

Column name	Data type
ProductCode	VARCHAR(10)
Description	VARCHAR(40)
Price	DOUBLE

Description

- A database management system requires a name and data type for each column in a table. Depending on the data type, the column definition can include other properties such as the column's size.
- Each column definition also indicates whether or not the column can contain *null values*. A null value indicates that the value of the column is not known.
- A column can be defined with a *default value*. Then, that value is used for the column if another value isn't provided when a row is added to the table.

Figure 20-3 How the columns in a table are defined

How to use SQL to work with the data in a database

Structured Query Language (*SQL*) is a standard language that you can use to communicate with any modern DBMS. This language can be divided into two parts. The *Data Definition Language* (*DDL*) lets you define the tables in a database. The *Data Manipulation Language* (*DML*) lets you manipulate the data that's stored in those tables.

Since you'll normally use database software to define the tables in a database, this topic will focus on the four SQL statements that you can use to manipulate the data in a database: the SELECT, INSERT, UPDATE, and DELETE statements. These are the statements that you will use in your Java applications.

How to query a single table

Figure 20-4 shows how to use a SELECT statement to *query* a single table in a database. The SELECT statement is the most commonly used SQL statement. It returns a *result set* (or *result table*) that contains the rows and columns that are specified by the SELECT statement.

In the syntax summary for this statement, the capitalized words are SQL keywords and the lowercase words represent the items that you must supply. To separate the items in a statement, you can use one or more spaces, and you can use indentation whenever it helps improve the readability of a statement. Unlike Java, SQL is not case-sensitive. As a result, you can use whatever capitalization you like when referring to SQL keywords. In this chapter, we capitalize all SQL keywords to make it easy to tell the difference between these keywords and other parts of the SQL language such as column names. In practice, though, many programmers use lowercase for SQL keywords when writing SQL statements.

The first example in this figure shows how to retrieve three columns from the Products table. Here, the SELECT clause identifies the three columns and the FROM clause identifies the table. Then, the WHERE clause limits the number of rows that are retrieved by specifying that the statement should only retrieve rows where the value in the Price column is greater than 50. Last, the ORDER BY clause indicates that the retrieved rows should be sorted in ascending order (from A to Z) by the ProductCode column.

The result set is a logical table that's created temporarily within the database. Then, the *current row pointer*, or *cursor*, keeps track of the current row. If you make a change to the data in a result set, the change is also made to the table that the result set was created from.

As you might guess, queries can have a significant effect on the performance of a database application. The more columns and rows that a query returns, the more traffic the network has to bear. As a result, when you design queries, you should try to keep the number of columns and rows to a minimum.

SELECT syntax for selecting from one table

```
SELECT column-1 [, column-2] ...
FROM table-1
[WHERE selection-criteria]
[ORDER BY column-1 [ASC|DESC] [, column-2 [ASC|DESC]] ...]
```

A SELECT statement that gets selected columns and rows

```
SELECT ProductCode, Description, Price
FROM Products
WHERE Price > 50
ORDER BY ProductCode ASC
```

The result set defined by the SELECT statement

ProductCode	Description	Price
mcb2	Murach's Mainframe COBOL	59.5
zjcl	Murach's OS/390 and z/OS JCL	62.5

A SELECT statement that returns all columns and rows

```
SELECT * FROM Products
```

Description

- The SELECT statement is used to perform a *query* that retrieves rows and columns from a database.
- The *result set* (or *result table*) is the set of rows that are retrieved by a query.
- The *current row pointer*, or *cursor*, identifies the current row in a result set. You can use this pointer to identify the row you want to update or delete from a result set. Any change to the result set is reflected in the table that the result set is based on.
- To select all of the columns in a table, you can code an asterisk (*) instead of coding column names.
- For efficiency, you should code your queries so the result set has as few rows and columns as possible.

Figure 20-4 How to query a single table

How to join data from two or more tables

Figure 20-5 shows how to use the SELECT statement to retrieve data from two tables. Since the data from the two tables is joined together into a single result set, this type of operation is known as a *join*. In this figure, for example, the SELECT statement joins data from the Products and LineItems tables into a single result set.

An *inner join* is the most common type of join. When you use an inner join, which is sometimes called an *equi-join*, the rows from the two tables in the join are included in the result set only if their related columns match. These matching columns are specified in the SELECT statement. In this figure, for example, rows from the Products and LineItems tables are included only if the value of the ProductCode column of the Products table is equal to the ProductCode column of the LineItems table. In other words, if there isn't any data in the LineItems table for a product, that Product won't be included in the result set.

In this SELECT statement, the last column in the query, the Total column, is calculated by multiplying Price and Quantity. In other words, a column by the name of Total doesn't actually exist in the database. This type of column is called a *calculated column*, and it exists only in the results of the query.

In the FROM clause, this query assigns a variable name known as an *alias* to each table. For example, it assigns an alias of p to the Products table and an alias of li to the LineItems table. Then, it uses these aliases to qualify the names of the columns in the rest of the query. This is necessary because some columns such as the ProductCode column have the same name in both tables.

Another type of join is an *outer join*. With this type of join, all of the rows in one of the tables are included in the result set whether or not the other table contains matching rows. In a *left outer join*, all of the rows in the first table (the one on the left) are included in the result set. In a *right outer join*, all of the rows in the second table are included. To illustrate, assume that the SELECT statement in this figure had used a left outer join. In that case, all of the rows in the Products table whose price is greater than 50 would have been included in the result set...even if no matching row was found in the LineItems table.

Although this figure only shows how to join data from two tables, you can extend this syntax to join data from additional tables. If, for example, you want to create a result set that includes data from three tables named Customers, Invoices, and LineItems, you could code the FROM clause of the SELECT statement like this:

```
FROM Customers c
    INNER JOIN Invoices i
        ON c.CustomerID = i.CustomerID
    INNER JOIN LineItems li
        ON i.InvoiceID = li.InvoiceID
```

Then, you could include any of the columns from the three tables in the column list of the SELECT statement.

This figure also shows an alternate SQL syntax that lets you join two tables by using the WHERE clause instead of the FROM clause. Using this syntax, the FROM clause lists all of the tables in the result set. Then, the WHERE clause

SELECT syntax for joining two tables

```
SELECT column-1 [, column-2] ...
FROM table-1
   {INNER | LEFT OUTER | RIGHT OUTER} JOIN table-2
   ON table-1.column-1 {=|<|>|<=|>=|<>} table-2.column-2
[WHERE selection-criteria]
[ORDER BY column-1 [ASC|DESC] [, column-2 [ASC|DESC]] ...]
```

A SELECT statement that retrieves data from the Products and LineItems tables

```
SELECT p.ProductCode, p.Price, li.Quantity,
       p.Price * li.Quantity AS Total
FROM Products p
   INNER JOIN LineItems li
   ON p.ProductCode = li.ProductCode
WHERE p.Price > 50
ORDER BY p.ProductCode ASC;
```

Another way to write the SELECT statement shown above

```
SELECT p.ProductCode, p.Price, li.Quantity,
       p.Price * li.Quantity AS Total
FROM Products p, LineItems li
WHERE p.ProductCode = li.ProductCode AND p.Price > 50
ORDER BY p.ProductCode ASC;
```

The result set defined by the SELECT statement

ProductCode	Price	Quantity	Total
mcb2	59.50	1	59.50
mcb2	59.50	5	297.50
zjcl	62.50	2	125.00

Description

- A *join* lets you combine data from two or more tables into a single result set.
- An *inner join*, or *equi-join*, returns rows from both tables only if their related columns match. An *outer join* returns rows from one table in the join (the LEFT or RIGHT table) even if the rows aren't matched by rows in the other table.

Figure 20-5 How to join data from two or more tables

identifies the join by using the AND keyword to connect all of the selection criteria that must be satisfied. This is an older syntax for joins that is still used by some database management systems.

How to add, update, and delete data in a table

Figure 20-6 shows how to use the INSERT, UPDATE, and DELETE statements to add, update, and delete one or more rows in a database. To start, you can use the INSERT statement to add one row to a database. To do that, the first INSERT statement supplies the names of the columns that are going to receive values in the new row, followed by the values for those columns. When you insert a row, you can specify the list of column names if you don't want to specify every column or if you want to specify the columns in a different sequence than they occur in the table. However, if you are going to specify all column names in the same sequence as they occur in the table, you can omit the column list as shown by the second example.

Although you typically use the INSERT statement to add a single row, you can use the UPDATE statement to update a single row or multiple rows. In the first UPDATE example, the UPDATE statement updates the Description and Price columns in a single row where ProductCode is equal to "casp". In the second example, the Price column is updated to 49.95 in all of the rows where Price is equal to 49.50.

Similarly, you can use the DELETE statement to delete a single row or a group of rows. Here, the first example deletes the row from the Products table where the ProductCode equals "casp". Since each row contains a unique value in the ProductCode column, this deletes a single row. However, in the second example, many rows in the Invoices table may have an AmountDue column that equals 0. As a result, this statement deletes all invoices whose balance has been paid in full. That way, the Invoices table will only contain unpaid invoices.

In the third example, the DELETE statement doesn't include a WHERE clause. As a result, it deletes all rows in the table. Although this is often useful when you're setting up and testing a database, you typically want to make sure to include a WHERE clause for your DELETE statements once the database has been set up correctly.

When you issue an UPDATE or DELETE statement from a Java application, you usually work with one row at a time. You'll see this illustrated by the ProductsDB class shown later in this chapter. UPDATE and DELETE statements that affect more than one row are typically used by database administrators and programmcrs using tools provided by the DBMS.

How to add rows

INSERT syntax for adding a single row

```
INSERT INTO table-name [(column-list)]
VALUES (value-list)
```

A statement that adds a row with a column list

```
INSERT INTO Products (ProductCode, Description, Price)
VALUES ('casp', 'ASP.NET Web Programming with C#', 54.50)
```

A statement that adds a row without a column list

```
INSERT INTO Products
VALUES ('casp', 'ASP.NET Web Programming with C#', 54.50)
```

How to update rows

UPDATE syntax

```
UPDATE table-name
SET expression-1 [, expression-2] ...
[WHERE selection-criteria]
```

A statement that updates a single row

```
UPDATE Products
SET Description = 'Murach''s ASP.NET Web Programming with C#',
    Price = 49.50
WHERE ProductCode = 'casp'
```

A statement that updates multiple rows

```
UPDATE Products
SET Price = 49.95
WHERE Price = 49.50
```

How to delete rows

DELETE syntax

```
DELETE FROM table-name
[WHERE selection-criteria]
```

A statement that deletes a single row

```
DELETE FROM Products WHERE ProductCode = 'casp'
```

A statement that deletes multiple rows

```
DELETE FROM Invoices WHERE AmountDue = 0
```

A statement that deletes all rows

```
DELETE FROM Invoices
```

Figure 20-6 How to add, update, and delete data in a table

An introduction to Derby

Apache Derby is an open-source, Java-based relational database management system (RDBMS) that can be embedded in Java applications that run on a client machine or run as the database server for a networked client/server system. Oracle has distributed this database as part of the JDK ever since Java SE 6. This distribution of Derby is marketed as *Java DB*. Although the Java DB distribution is used throughout this chapter, the Derby name is still used by the JAR files and classes. As a result, I'll use the Derby name to refer to this database throughout this chapter.

An overview of Derby

Figure 20-7 lists some of the advantages and disadvantages of using Derby. To start, since Derby is open-source, it's free. Since Derby is written in Java, it runs on all modern operating systems. Since Derby is based on established *JDBC* (*Java Database Connectivity*) and SQL standards, it works well with any other applications that rely on these standards. Since Derby only requires about 2.8 MB of memory, it can easily be run on most computers, including client machines. And finally, since Derby can be embedded within a client application or run on a server in a client/server system, it can be used for a wide range of applications.

When Derby is embedded in a client application, it's known as an *embedded database*, and it runs in the same process as the client application. On the other hand, when Derby is run in a separate process on a server and accessed by multiple client applications, it's known as a *networked database*. Other popular databases that are typically run as networked databases include Oracle, MySQL, DB2, and SQL Server. Although versions of these databases can also run on the client, the database runs in a process separate from the applications that use it. If you want the database to run in the same process as the client application, you have to use an embedded database like Derby.

So, what's the downside of working with Derby? To start, unlike the other database systems mentioned previously in this chapter, Derby doesn't provide a GUI tool for viewing and working with the database. Instead, you must use a command-line tool that you'll learn about in this chapter. In addition, Derby isn't designed to work with large, enterprise databases. Nevertheless, Derby can be a good choice if you're working with a small- to medium-sized database, especially if you want to use an embedded database.

The Apache Derby website

```
http://db.apache.org/derby/
```

Pros

- Is inexpensive (free).
- Is platform-independent.
- Is based on the Java, JDBC, and SQL standards.
- Is included as part of the JDK.
- Doesn't use much memory (about 2.6 MB).
- Can be run on the client and embedded in a Java application.
- Can be run on a server and accessed by multiple clients.

Cons

- Doesn't provide easy-to-use GUI tools.
- Not designed for large, enterprise databases.

Description

- *Apache Derby* is an open-source, Java-based relational database management system (RDBMS) that can be embedded in Java applications or run in a networked client/server system.
- Starting with JDK 6, Java includes Oracle's distribution of the Derby database. This distribution of Derby is known as *Java DB*.
- When a database runs in the same process as the application, it's known as an *embedded database*. When a database runs on a server and is accessed by clients, it's known as a *networked database*.
- A Derby database that's embedded in a client application can be completely transparent to the user of the application.
- *JDBC* (*Java Database Connectivity*) is a Java API that provides for querying and updating the data in a database. See chapter 21 for details on using JDBC.

Mac OS X note

- Derby isn't included as part of the JDK for Mac OS X, so you have to install it separately. For more information, see appendix B.

Figure 20-7 An overview of Derby

How to configure your system to work with a Derby database

Figure 20-8 shows how to configure a Windows system for working with a Derby database. Derby is included in the Java SE download in the db subdirectory of the JDK directory. Within the db directory, the lib directory contains the JAR files for the Derby database. Of these JAR files, the derby.jar file contains the database engine that's needed to work with any Derby database, and the derbytools.jar file contains the classes that are needed to run the interactive JDBC tool described in the next figure.

Since these JAR files aren't included as part of the JRE, you must include them in the *class path* before you can work with Derby. The class path is the path that your system uses to look for the Java classes. If you're using Windows, you can do that by following the procedures shown in this figure. If you're using another operating system, you can search the Internet for details on how to add these JAR files to your class path.

In addition, if you want to work with Derby in a networked client/server environment as described at the end of this chapter, you'll need to add the derbynet.jar and derbyclient.jar files to your class path. That way, you can use a class in the derbynet.jar file to start the Derby server. Then, you can use the derbyclient.jar file to allow a client to connect to the derby server.

If you're using a Mac, Derby is not included as part of the JDK. As a result, you must download and install Derby as described in appendix B. To do that, you download the four JAR files shown in this figure and place them in the correct directory. This automatically sets the class path.

A typical Derby installation directory

```
C:\Program Files\Java\jdk1.7.0\db
```

Three important JAR files in the db\lib directory

Filename	Description
derby.jar	Needed to work with any Derby database.
derbytools.jar	Needed to run the ij tool described in the next figure.
derbynet.jar	Needed to start the server for a networked Derby database.
derbyclient.jar	Needed to allow a client to connect to a networked Derby database.

A class path that contains the current directory and four Derby JAR files

```
.;
C:\Program Files\Java\jdk1.7.0\db\lib\derby.jar;
C:\Program Files\Java\jdk1.7.0\db\lib\derbytools.jar;
C:\Program Files\Java\jdk1.7.0\db\lib\derbynet.jar;
C:\Program Files\Java\jdk1.7.0\db\lib\derbyclient.jar;
```

How to set the class path for Windows 7 and Vista

1. Display the System section of the Control Panel. To do that, press the Windows key and the Pause/Break key at the same time. Or, display the Control Panel, select the System and Security (Windows 7) or System and Maintenance (Vista) link, and select the System link.
2. Select the Advanced System Settings link to display the System Properties dialog box. If necessary, enter the password for an administrator account.
3. In the System Properties dialog box, select the Advanced tab and click on the Environment Variables button.
4. Use the Environment Variables dialog box to add or edit the system variable named CLASSPATH. If this variable contains other entries, type a semicolon and the path to the JAR file to the far right of the list of paths.

How to set the class path for Windows XP

1. Display the System Properties dialog box. To do that, press the Windows key and the Pause/Break key at the same time. Or, right-click on the My Computer icon that's available from the desktop or the Start menu and select the Properties command.
2. Follow steps 3 and 4 from the Windows 7 and Vista procedure shown above.

Description

- The *class path* tells the JRE where to find the .class files needed to run a program. To allow your application to work with Derby, you must include the necessary JAR files in the class path.
- To include the current directory in the class path, just code a period for the directory followed by a semicolon at the start of the list of paths as shown above.
- After you change the class path, you may need to close and reopen the command prompt before the new class path takes effect. Or, in some cases, you may need to reboot your computer.

Figure 20-8 How to configure your system to work with a Derby database

How to use the ij tool to work with a Derby database

Before you can work with a database, you need to run the SQL statements that create the database. In addition, as you develop JDBC code that works with the database, you often need a quick way to test your SQL statements. When you work with a Derby database, you can use the *interactive JDBC tool* (*ij tool*) to perform these tasks.

How to start and stop the ij tool

Since the ij tool runs from the console, or command prompt, you must start the command prompt for your operating system before you can begin using this tool. Although this chapter shows how to use the command prompt for the Windows operating system, the same principles apply to all operating systems including Mac OS X, Linux, and Solaris.

By default, the ij tool looks for the Derby database in the current directory. As a result, it usually makes sense to use the cd command to change the current directory to the directory that contains the database. In figure 20-9, for example, the first command changes the current directory to the directory that's used to store the database that's presented in this chapter.

Once you've changed the current directory, you can start the ij tool by using the java command to run the ij class that's stored in the derbytools.jar file. To do that, you enter the java command followed by the package and class for the ij tool as shown in this figure. Since this involves a lot of typing, you may want to create a script to run this command. That's why the source code for this book includes script files in the directory shown in this figure.

For Windows, the script is a batch file named ij.bat. For Mac OS X, the script is a Bash shell script named ij.sh. Once you set the current directory to the one shown in this figure, you can execute the batch file by entering "ij". To execute the Bash file, you can enter "sh ij.sh". Or, you can use your operating system to locate the script file and then double-click on it to open a command prompt. Note that a Bash file must be configured properly for this to work.

After you start the ij tool, the command prompt changes from a standard command prompt to an ij prompt. At this point, you can stop the ij tool and return to the command prompt by entering the exit command. Like all of the commands that you enter when the ij tool is running, you must type a semicolon after the command. If you don't, pressing the Enter key will start a new line instead of executing the command. In that case, you can type a semicolon on the new line and press Enter to execute the command.

How to connect to and disconnect from a database

If a Derby database is available on your system, you can use the connect command to connect to it. To do that, enter the connection string enclosed in single quotes. Here, the connection string should specify the protocol (jdbc), the subprotocol (derby), and a URL that specifies the name and location of the

How to connect to an existing database

```
C:\Users\Joel>cd \murach\java\db

C:\murach\java\db>java org.apache.derby.tools.ij
ij version 10.8
ij> connect 'jdbc:derby:MurachDB';
ij> disconnect;
ij> exit;

C:\murach\java\db>
```

The error message that's displayed if the database doesn't exist

```
C:\murach\java\db>java org.apache.derby.tools.ij
ij version 10.8
ij> connect 'jdbc:derby:MurachDB';
ERROR XJ004: Database 'MurachDB' not found.
ij> exit;
```

How to create a database and connect to it

```
C:\Users\Joel>cd \murach\java\db

C:\murach\java\db>java org.apache.derby.tools.ij
ij version 10.8
ij> connect 'jdbc:derby:MurachDB;create=true';
ij> disconnect;
ij> exit;

C:\murach\java\db>
```

Description

- You can use the *ij (interactive JDBC) tool* to interactively work with a Derby database.
- By default, the ij tool looks for the Derby database within the current directory. As a result, it usually makes sense to use the cd command to change the current directory to the directory that contains the database.
- To start the ij tool, use the java command to run the ij class that's stored in the derbytools.jar file.
- To stop the ij tool, enter the exit command.
- To connect to a database, enter the connect command followed by the connection string enclosed in single quotes. The connection string should specify the protocol (jdbc), the subprotocol (derby), and a URL that specifies the name and location of the database.
- To disconnect from a database, enter the disconnect command.
- To create a database, append ";create=true" to the end of the connection string.
- You must enter a semicolon at the end of each command.

Figure 20-9 How to use the ij tool to create and connect to a database

database. In figure 20-9, for instance, the first example uses the jdbc:derby protocol to connect to the database named MurachDB that's stored in the current directory.

If you try to connect to a database and the database isn't found, Derby will display an error message like the one shown in the second example in figure 20-9. In this case, you may need to exit the ij tool, use the cd command to change the current directory, and start the ij tool again. Or, you may need to create the database as described in the next topic. When you're done working with a database, you can use the disconnect command to free any resources that are used by the connection to the database.

How to create a database and connect to it

When working with the ij tool, you can use the connect command to create a new database and connect to it. To do that, append ";create=true" to the end of the connection string. In figure 20-9, for instance, the third example shows how to create the MurachDB database and connect to it. When you create a database, it creates an empty database that doesn't contain any tables. As a result, you typically continue by using SQL statements to create the tables of the database.

How to run SQL statements

After you use the ij tool to connect to a database, you can run any SQL statement by entering the statement followed by a semicolon. In figure 20-10, for example, you can see how to enter a SQL statement that creates a Products table that has three columns, a SQL statement that inserts a row into this table, and a SQL statement that selects all rows from this table. To make these SQL statements easier to read, I pressed the Enter key at the ij prompt to insert a blank line before each SQL statement. In addition, I used the Enter key and the spacebar to split these statements onto multiple lines and to indent them appropriately.

Of these three statements, the only statement you weren't introduced to earlier in this chapter is the CREATE TABLE statement. This statement is a standard SQL statement that's used to create the tables of a database. In this figure, for example, this statement creates a table named Products that has three columns. The first column is named ProductCode and stores a string with a variable number of characters up to a maximum of 10 characters. The second column is named Description and stores a string with a variable number of characters up to a maximum of 40 characters. And the third column is named Price and stores a double value.

When you're using the ij tool to test a SQL statement, you may encounter an error. In that case, you'll often want to edit the SQL statement and run it again. To do that, you can use the up and down arrows to scroll through previously entered statements. Then, when you find the statement you want, you can use the left and right arrows and the other keys to edit the statement. And finally, you can press the Enter key to run the statement again.

How to run SQL statements against a database

```
C:\murach\java\db>java org.apache.derby.tools.ij
ij version 10.8
ij> connect 'jdbc:derby:MurachDB';
ij>

CREATE TABLE Products
(
    ProductCode VARCHAR(10),
    Description VARCHAR(40),
    Price DOUBLE
);
0 rows inserted/updated/deleted
ij>

INSERT INTO Products
VALUES ('java', 'Murach''s Beginning Java', 49.50);
1 row inserted/updated/deleted
ij>

SELECT * FROM Products;
PRODUCTC&|DESCRIPTION                                |PRICE

-----------------------------------------------------------
java     |Murach's Beginning Java                    |49.5

1 row selected
ij> exit;

C:\murach\java\db>
```

Description

- To run a SQL statement, enter the statement at the ij prompt followed by a semi-colon. When you do, the ij tool will display a message that shows the result of the SQL statement.
- To quickly reenter a previous statement, you can use the up and down arrows to scroll through previously entered statements. Then, you can edit the statement and run it again.
- You can use capitalization, line breaks, and spacing to make the SQL statement easy to read.
- When you use the ij tool to run a SELECT statement, the data in the returned rows and columns are displayed in a table that uses the column names as the column headers. If a column name has more characters than the column has, the column header is truncated and ends with the & character.
- If the table you're working with is stored in a *schema*, you have to identify that schema to access the table using the ij tool. To do that, you can use this command:

  ```
  ij> set schema AppUser;
  ```

  Or, you can qualify the name of the table with the schema like this:

  ```
  ij> SELECT * FROM AppUser.Products;
  ```

Figure 20-10 How to use the ij tool to run SQL statements

When you use the ij tool, you should realize that a table can be stored in a *schema*, which is a container that stores tables and other database objects. If a table is stored in a schema, you have to identify that schema to work with the table using the ij tool. You can do that using one of the two techniques shown in figure 20-10. First, you can use the set schema command to identify the schema. In this figure, this command is used to set the schema to AppUser. Then, the ij tool will assume that any tables you refer to in any SQL statements you enter are stored in that schema. Second, you can qualify the name of a table in a SQL statement with the schema. Then, the ij tool only uses the schema for that statement.

How to run SQL scripts from the ij prompt

Although being able to use the ij tool to interactively execute SQL statements can help you test new SQL statements, you also need to be able to run SQL statements that have been saved in files. These files are known as *SQL scripts*. For example, a SQL script is often used to store the SQL statements that are used to create a database.

You can run a SQL script for a Derby database in two ways. To start, you can run a SQL script from the ij prompt as shown in figure 20-11. If you need to run several scripts, this is usually the best way to do it. However, you can also run a SQL script from the command prompt as shown in the figure 20-12. The advantage of that approach is that it allows you to use an operating system script file to run the SQL script. As a result, a user can typically run the script by double-clicking on the appropriate .bat or .sh file.

The top of figure 20-11 shows the SQL scripts that are used to create the Products table and to insert data into this table. Here, the first script is stored in the ProductsTableCreate.sql file. This script contains a single SQL statement that's used to create the Products table. The second script is stored in the ProductsTableInsert.sql file. This script contains two SQL statements that are used to insert two rows into the Products table. Here, a semicolon is coded to identify the end of each SQL statement.

To run a SQL script from the ij prompt, you begin by starting the ij tool and using it to connect to a database. Then, you enter the run command followed by the name of the script. Here, you must enclose the name of the script in single quotes. If the script is in the current directory, you don't need to enter a path for the script. Otherwise, you need to enter the full path for the script.

In this figure, for example, both of the scripts are in the current directory. As a result, the path for these scripts isn't necessary. When it is necessary, though, you can enter a full path like this:

```
run 'C:/MyDBScripts/ProductsTableCreate.sql'
```

In this case, Derby runs the script stored in the ProductsTableCreate.sql file that's in the MyDBScripts directory of the C drive.

The SQL statement stored in the ProductsTableCreate.sql file

```
CREATE TABLE Products
(
    ProductCode VARCHAR(10),
    Description VARCHAR(40),
    Price DOUBLE
)
```

The SQL statements stored in the ProductsTableInsert.sql file

```
INSERT INTO Products
VALUES ('java', 'Murach''s Beginning Java', 49.50);

INSERT INTO Products
VALUES ('jsps', 'Murach''s Java Servlets and JSP', 49.50);
```

How to run SQL scripts from the ij prompt

```
C:\murach\java\db>java org.apache.derby.tools.ij
ij version 10.8
ij> connect 'jdbc:derby:MurachDB';
ij> run 'ProductsTableCreate.sql';
ij> CREATE TABLE Products
(
        ProductCode VARCHAR(10),
        Description VARCHAR(40),
        Price DOUBLE
);
0 rows inserted/updated/deleted
ij> run 'ProductsTableInsert.sql';
ij> INSERT INTO Products
VALUES ('java', 'Murach''s Beginning Java', 49.50);
1 row inserted/updated/deleted
ij> INSERT INTO Products
VALUES ('jsps', 'Murach''s Java Servlets and JSP', 49.50);
1 row inserted/updated/deleted
ij> disconnect;
ij> exit;
```

Description

- To run a SQL script from the ij prompt, you can start the ij tool, connect to the database, and use the run command to run the script. Here, you must enclose the name of the script in single quotes.
- If the script is in the root directory for the database, you don't need to enter a path for the script. Otherwise, you need to enter the full path for the script.

How to run SQL scripts from the command prompt

The top of figure 20-12 shows part of the SQL script that's used to create the MurachDB database. To start, this script uses a connect command to connect to the MurachDB database, creating it if necessary. Then, this script creates the Products table and inserts seven rows into it. Finally, this script selects all rows and columns from the Products table so you can make sure that the rows have been added successfully.

Note that you need to include the connect command at the beginning of any scripts that you intend to run from the command prompt. If you don't, Derby will display an error message that indicates that it couldn't connect to the database.

To run a SQL script from the command prompt, you can enter the name of the script after you use the java command to run the ij class that's stored in the derbytools.jar file. In this figure, for example, the command that's entered at the command prompt runs the script stored in the MurachDBCreate.sql. Since this file is stored in the current directory, it isn't necessary to enter a path for the file.

As mentioned earlier, the main advantage of running a script from the command prompt is that you can create an operating system script file to make it easier to run the SQL script. This figure, for example, shows a .bat file that you can run from Windows. However, the same principles apply to an .sh file that you can run from Mac OS X and Linux.

The MurachDBCreate.bat file contains three DOS commands that make it easy to run the MurachDBCreate.sql script. To start, the cd command is used to change the current directory to the root directory for the MurachDB database. Then, the second command uses the ij tool to run the script that's stored in the MurachDBCreate.sql file. Finally, the third command causes the command prompt to pause so you can view the results of running the batch file. This causes the "Press any key to continue…" message to be displayed at the bottom of the Command Prompt window. After you view the results displayed in the Command Prompt window, you can press any key to close it.

To run a batch file that executes a SQL script, you can use Windows Explorer to locate the batch file and double-click on it. Or, you can enter the name of the batch file at the command prompt. For this to work, you may need to use the cd command to change the current directory to the directory that contains the batch file. Although this requires some typing, it requires less typing than entering the java command shown in this figure.

Some of the SQL statements stored in the MurachDBCreate.sql file

```
CONNECT 'jdbc:derby:MurachDB;create=true';

CREATE TABLE Products
(
    ProductCode VARCHAR(10),
    Description VARCHAR(40),
    Price DOUBLE
);

INSERT INTO Products VALUES
('bvbn', 'Murach''s Beginning Visual Basic .NET', 49.50);
INSERT INTO Products VALUES
('cshp', 'Murach''s C#', 49.50);
INSERT INTO Products VALUES
('java', 'Murach''s Beginning Java', 49.50);
INSERT INTO Products VALUES
('jsps', 'Murach''s Java Servlets and JSP', 49.50);
INSERT INTO Products VALUES
('mcb2', 'Murach''s Mainframe COBOL', 59.50);
INSERT INTO Products VALUES
('sqls', 'Murach''s SQL for SQL Server', 49.50);
INSERT INTO Products VALUES
('zjcl', 'Murach''s OS/390 and z/OS JCL', 62.50);

SELECT * FROM Products;
```

How to run a script from the command prompt

```
C:\murach\java\db>java org.apache.derby.tools.ij MurachDBCreate.sql
```

The DOS commands stored in the MurachDBCreate.bat file

```
cd \murach\java\db
java org.apache.derby.tools.ij MurachDBCreate.sql
pause
```

Description

- To run a SQL script from the command prompt, you can enter the name of the script after you use the java command to run the ij class that's stored in the derbytools.jar file. For this to work, the script must begin with a connect command that connects to the database.
- If the script is in the root directory for the database, you don't need to enter a path for the script. Otherwise, you need to enter the full path for the script.
- To run a DOS batch file that executes a SQL script, you can use Windows Explorer to locate the batch file and double-click on it. Or, you can enter the name of the batch file at the command prompt.

Figure 20-12 How to run SQL scripts from the command prompt

How to start and stop the Derby database server

Although Derby is commonly used to embed a database in a Java application that runs on a client, you can also run the Derby database server on a server. Then, multiple client applications can connect to the server and work with the same database. When you use this approach, you must start the Derby database server so it can listen for requests from the clients. Typically, you leave the Derby database server running so the database is always available to its clients. However, you can stop the Derby server whenever that's necessary.

How to start the server

Figure 20-13 begins by showing how to start the Derby network server. To test how this works, you can start it on your own computer. However, for a real client-server system, you start the Derby server on a networked server computer. Then, multiple clients can connect to the Derby server and use JDBC to work with the databases on the server. For this to work, the derbyclient.jar file must be installed on the client machines.

To start the Derby network server, you use the java command to pass the start argument to the NetworkServerControl class. When you start the Derby server from a command prompt on a Windows system, this displays a message like the one shown in this figure. This message indicates that the server has been started and is ready to accept connections on port 1527, which is the default port for the Derby server. Note that a command prompt isn't displayed after this message, so you can't enter any additional commands in this window.

Once you've started to the server, you can use the ij tool to connect to a database. To do that, you have to include the server name and port number in the connection string as shown in the next chapter. After you connect to the database, you can run SQL statements and scripts against the database using the same techniques you use for an embedded database.

How to stop the server

For a real client-server system, you will rarely need to stop the Derby server. However, if you need to do that, you must start a new command prompt. Then, you can stop the Derby network server by using the java command to pass the shutdown argument to the NetworkServerControl class as shown in figure 20-13. When you do, the Command Prompt window will display a message that indicates that the Derby server has been shut down.

Just like starting and stopping the ij tool, starting and stopping the server can involve a lot of typing. As a result, if you plan to work with a networked Derby server, you can create script files for your operating system to start and stop the server. That's why the downloadable files for this book include script files that can be used to start and stop the Derby server. By default, these script files are stored in the c:\murach\java\db directory.

The command to start the Derby server

```
java org.apache.derby.drda.NetworkServerControl start
```

The window that's displayed when the Derby server is running

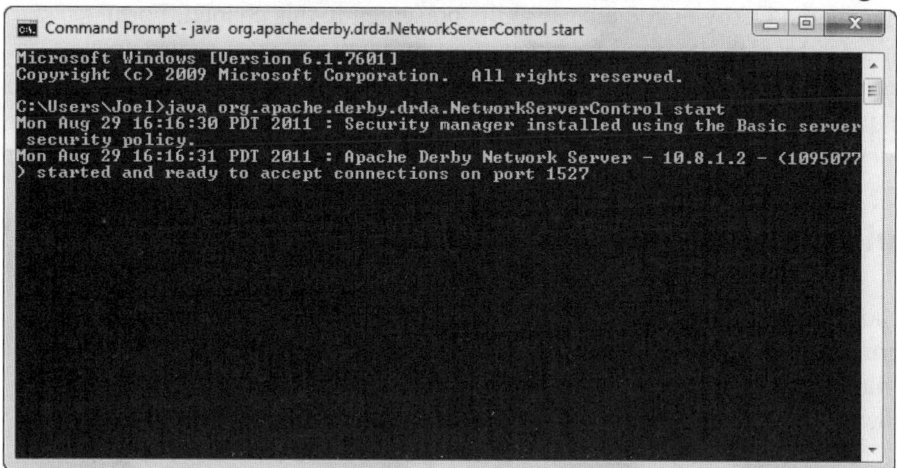

The command to stop the Derby server

```
java org.apache.derby.drda.NetworkServerControl shutdown
```

The message that's displayed when the Derby server is stopped

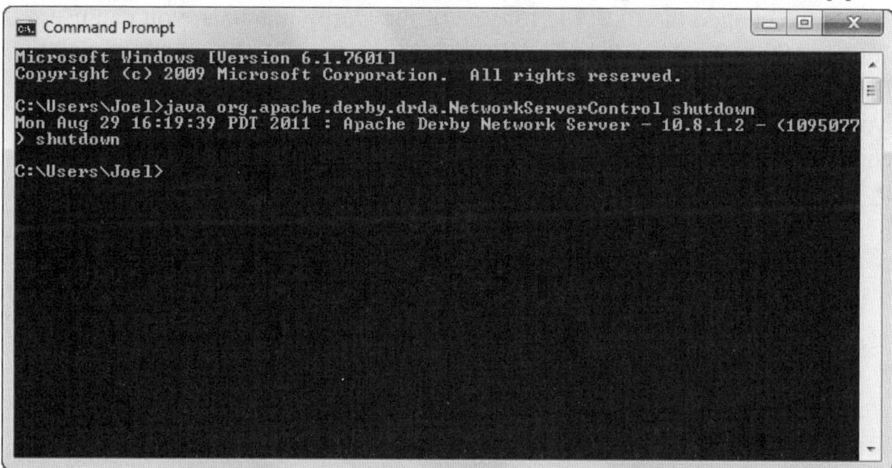

Description

- To start the Derby network server, use the java command to pass the start argument to the NetworkServerControl class that's stored in the derbynet.jar file. For this to work, the derbynet.jar file must be included in the class path.
- Once you start the server, you can use the ij tool to connect to a database and run SQL statements and scripts. For this to work, the derbyclient.jar file must be included in the class path.
- To stop the Derby network server, use the java command to pass the shutdown argument to the NetworkServerControl class that's stored in the derbynet.jar file.

Figure 20-13 How to start and stop the Derby server

How to learn more about Derby

If you plan to develop a serious application that uses Derby, you'll need to learn more about Derby than the basic skills presented in this chapter. Fortunately, the Derby web site provides a wealth of in-depth and easy-to-use documentation. To start, figure 20-14 shows the URL for a page on the Derby web site that provides links to a handful of Derby manuals that are available for Derby developers and administrators.

How to view the Derby documentation

Although the Derby manuals are available in HTML and PDF format, the PDF format makes it especially easy to view the Derby documentation. To view a PDF file for one of the Derby manuals, go to the Derby web site and use your web browser to navigate to the PDF file for the documentation. Then, if you want to, you can save the PDF file to your computer so you can view it even when you aren't connected to the Internet.

How to navigate through the documentation

Once you've opened the PDF file for one of the Derby manuals, you can use the contents on the left side of the window to navigate through the documentation. Or, you can use the search feature to look for specific topics. If, for example, you want to learn more about the CREATE TABLE statement that's used in this chapter, you can search the Derby Reference Manual for that statement.

The Derby documentation

`http://db.apache.org/derby/manuals/`

The Derby manuals that are available online

- Getting Started with Derby
- Derby Reference Manual
- Derby Developer's Guide
- Tuning Derby
- Derby Server and Administration Guide
- Derby Tools and Utilities Guide

A page from the Derby Reference Manual

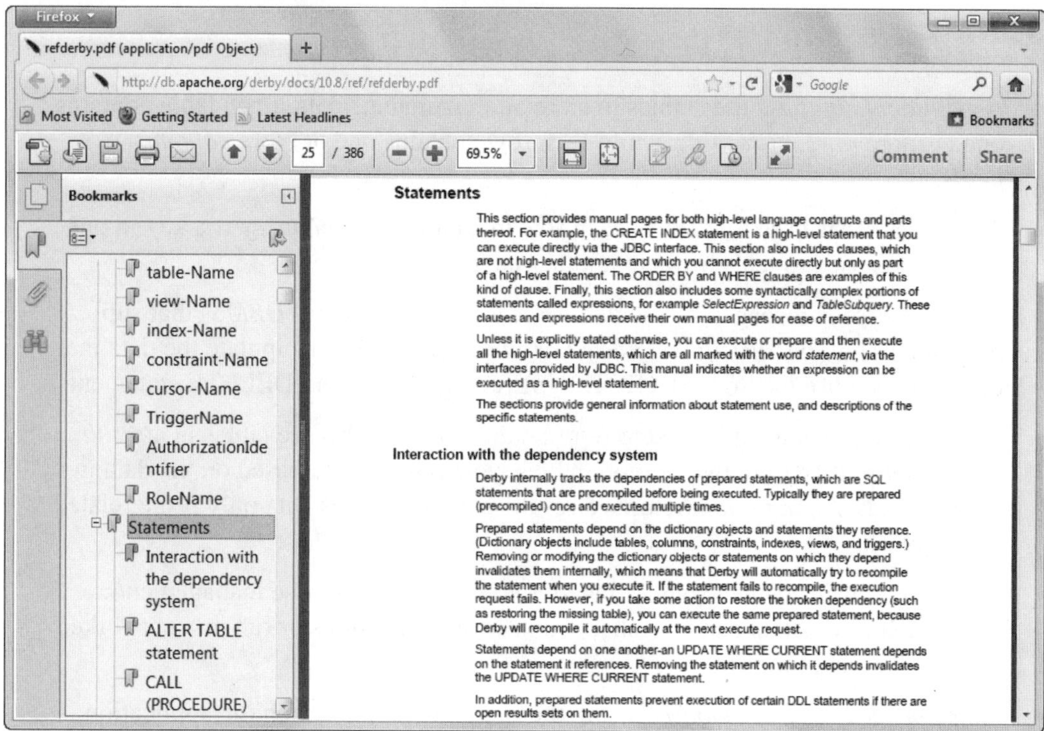

Description

- To view the Derby documentation, go to the Derby website and use your web browser to navigate to the PDF file for the documentation. If you want to, you can save the PDF file to your computer so you can view it without connecting to the Internet.
- To navigate through the documentation, you can expand, collapse, or select the topics in the table of contents in the left panel of the window. Or, you can use the search feature to search the documentation for a word or phrase.

Figure 20-14 How to learn more about Derby

Perspective

Now that you've finished this chapter, you have some basic skills for working with a Derby database. Please note, however, that this chapter is only an introduction to the use of Derby databases. To learn more, you can refer to the extensive documentation that's available from the Derby web site.

If you want to create an application that allows multiple clients to access a database that's running on a server, you might consider using a database such as MySQL that's specifically designed to work in a client-server environment. Like Derby, MySQL is open-source and available for free. However, MySQL provides more features than Derby, including GUI tools that make it easier to work with your databases.

Summary

- A *relational database* uses tables to store and manipulate data. Each table contains one or more *rows*, or *records*, while each row contains one or more *columns*, or *fields*.
- A *primary key* is used to identify each row in a table. A *foreign key* is a key in one table that is used to relate rows to another table.
- Each database is managed by a *database management system* (*DBMS*) that supports the use of the *Structured Query Language* (*SQL*). To manipulate the data in a database, you use the SQL SELECT, INSERT, UPDATE, and DELETE statements.
- The SELECT statement is used to return data from one or more tables in a *result set*. To return data from two or more tables, you *join* the data based on the data in related fields. An *inner join* returns a result set that includes data only if the related fields match.
- *Apache Derby* is an open-source, Java-based relational database management system (RDBMS) that can be embedded in Java applications or run in a networked client/server environment.
- An *embedded Derby database* runs in the same process in which the application that uses the database runs.
- A *networked Derby database* runs on a network server so the database can be accessed by two or more clients.
- The JDK includes a distribution of Derby known as *Java DB*. This is the version of Derby that's included in the db directory of Java SE.
- To work with a Derby database, you can use the *ij tool* (*interactive JDBC tool*) to connect to a database and execute SQL statements.
- SQL statements that have been saved in files are known as *SQL scripts*. You can run these scripts from the ij prompt or the command prompt.

Exercise 20-1 Work with a Derby database

In this exercise, you'll use the ij tool to work with an existing Derby database and to create a new Derby database.

Work with an existing Derby database

1. Add the derby.jar and derbytools.jar files to the class path as described in figure 20-8.
2. Use your operating system to view the files in the murach\java\db directory. Note that this directory includes a subdirectory that stores the files for the MurachDB database.
3. Start a command prompt and change the current directory to the murach\java\db directory.
4. Use the ij tool to connect to the MurachDB database that's stored in this directory.
5. Run a SELECT statement that selects all rows from the Products table.
6. Run an INSERT statement that adds a row to the Products table. Then, select all rows in the Products table again to make sure the INSERT statement worked correctly.
7. Run a SELECT statement that only selects the row you just added to the Products table.
8. Run a DELETE statement to delete the row you added to the Products table. Then, select all rows in the Products table again to make sure the DELETE statement worked correctly.
9. Disconnect from the database and exit the ij tool.

Use a SQL script to create a new Derby database

10. Use your operating system to view the files in the ch20_db directory that's in the ex_starts directory. Note that this directory does not contain a directory for the MurachDB database. However, it should contain a SQL script for creating this database and an operating system script for starting the ij tool.
11. Open the MurachDBCreate.sql script in a text editor. Note that it has all of the SQL statements necessary to create a database named MurachDB that contains a Products table.
12. Modify this script so it inserts an additional row that has a product code of "test", description of "Test Product", and price of 99.99.
13. Use the appropriate script for your operating system to start the ij tool. Note that this changes the current directory to the ch20_db directory.
14. Use the ij tool to run the MurachDBCreate.sql script. Review the output of the script. This output should include messages that indicate that the table was created and the rows were inserted. In addition, it should display the data that's stored in the Products table.

21

How to use JDBC to work with databases

In the last chapter, you learned how to use the ij tool to work with a Derby database. In this chapter, you'll learn how to use Java code to work with data that's stored in a database. As you will see, databases provide data management features that aren't offered with files. That's why databases are used for most serious business applications.

An introduction to Java database drivers

When you use *JDBC* (*Java Database Connectivity*) to work with a database, you need to use a database driver to communicate with the database.

The four driver types

Figure 21-1 shows four ways a Java application can access a database. To start, the Java application uses the JDBC driver manager to load a *database driver*. Then, the Java application can use one or more of the driver types to connect to the database and manipulate the data.

You can use a type-1, *JDBC-ODBC bridge driver* to connect to a database through *ODBC* (*Open Database Connectivity*), a standard way to access databases. Since ODBC drivers exist for most modern databases, a type-1 driver provides a way to connect Java with almost any type of database. And since a type-1 driver is included with the JDK, it's available to all Java programmers. However, for a type-1 driver to work, an ODBC data source must be registered on the client machine. Since this is often a tedious process that varies from one operating system to another, you'll want to avoid this type of driver whenever possible.

You can use a type-2, *native protocol partly Java driver* to connect to a database without using ODBC. Like ODBC, however, this driver requires that some binary code be installed on each client machine. As a result, you'll want to use a type-3 or type-4 driver if you plan to distribute the application on multiple client machines.

You can use a type-3, *net protocol all Java driver* to connect to a database by converting JDBC calls to an independent net protocol that's used by a specific vendor. Then, the vendor's middleware software, which runs on a server, converts the net protocol into calls in the native protocol that's used by the DBMS. Since the middleware software can typically convert the net protocol into the native DBMS protocol for multiple databases, this solution is the most flexible.

You can also use a type-4, *native protocol all Java driver* to connect to a database. This type of driver, which runs on a server, converts JDBC calls directly to the native DBMS protocol. Since most DBMS protocols are proprietary, these types of drivers are typically available from the database vendors. For example, type-4 drivers are available for Derby, MySQL, Oracle, IBM DB2, and Microsoft SQL Server.

For any serious application, you'll want to use a type-3 or type-4 driver. You can download type-4 drivers for most databases from the database vendor's web site. Or, you can search the Internet for a type-3 or type-4 driver for your database. The documentation for these drivers typically shows how to install and configure the driver.

Four ways to access a database

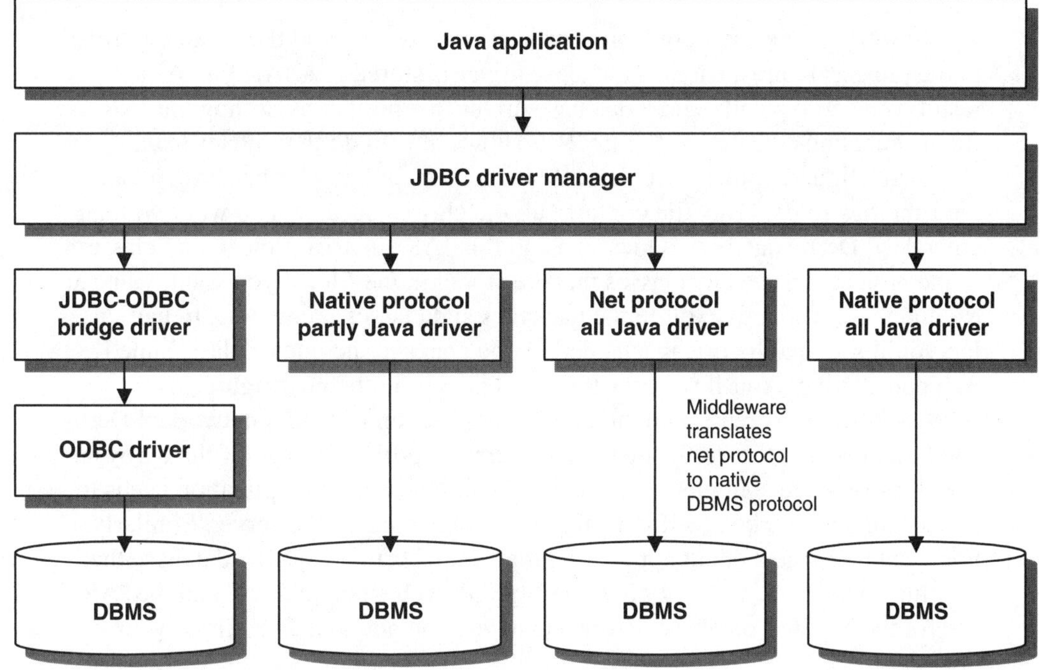

The four types of Java drivers

Type 1 A *JDBC-ODBC bridge driver* converts JDBC calls into ODBC calls that access the DBMS protocol. This data access method requires that the ODBC driver be installed on the client machines.

Type 2 A *native protocol partly Java driver* converts JDBC calls into calls in the native DBMS protocol. Since this conversion takes place on the client, some binary code must be installed on the client machine.

Type 3 A *net protocol all Java driver* converts JDBC calls into a net protocol that's independent of any native DBMS protocol. Then, middleware software running on a server converts the net protocol to the native DBMS protocol. Since this conversion takes place on the server side, no installation is required on the client machine.

Type 4 A *native protocol all Java driver* converts JDBC calls into a native DBMS protocol. Since this conversion takes place on the server side, no installation is required on the client machine.

Notes

- To get information about the drivers that are currently available, search the database vendor's web site or the Internet.
- Since type-1 and type-2 drivers require some client-side installation, they're not a good solution for most applications, especially Internet applications.

Figure 21-1 The four driver types

How to add a database driver to a project

To work with a database from a project, you have to add the database driver to the project. In most cases, a database driver is stored in a JAR file. As a result, you can typically add a database driver to a project by adding the JAR file that contains the driver. Figure 21-2 shows how to do that in NetBeans.

In this figure, you can see that a JAR file named derby.jar has been added to the Libraries folder. This file contains all the classes necessary to work with an embedded Derby database. Once you add this JAR file to a project, any classes in the project can use any classes that are stored in the file. If you want, you can expand the JAR file to explore the packages and classes it contains. In particular, you'll see that the org.apache.derby.jdbc package includes a class named EmbeddedDriver. You'll see how this class is used in the next figure.

If you want to create a client application that connects to a networked Derby database, you add the derbyclient.jar file to your project instead of the derby.jar file. This JAR file contains the database driver that a client application needs to connect to a networked Derby database that's running on the server. Similarly, if you want to create a client application that connects to a MySQL database that's running on a server, you can go to the MySQL web site and download the JAR file for the MySQL database driver. Then, you can add that JAR file to your project.

A project after the Derby database driver has been added

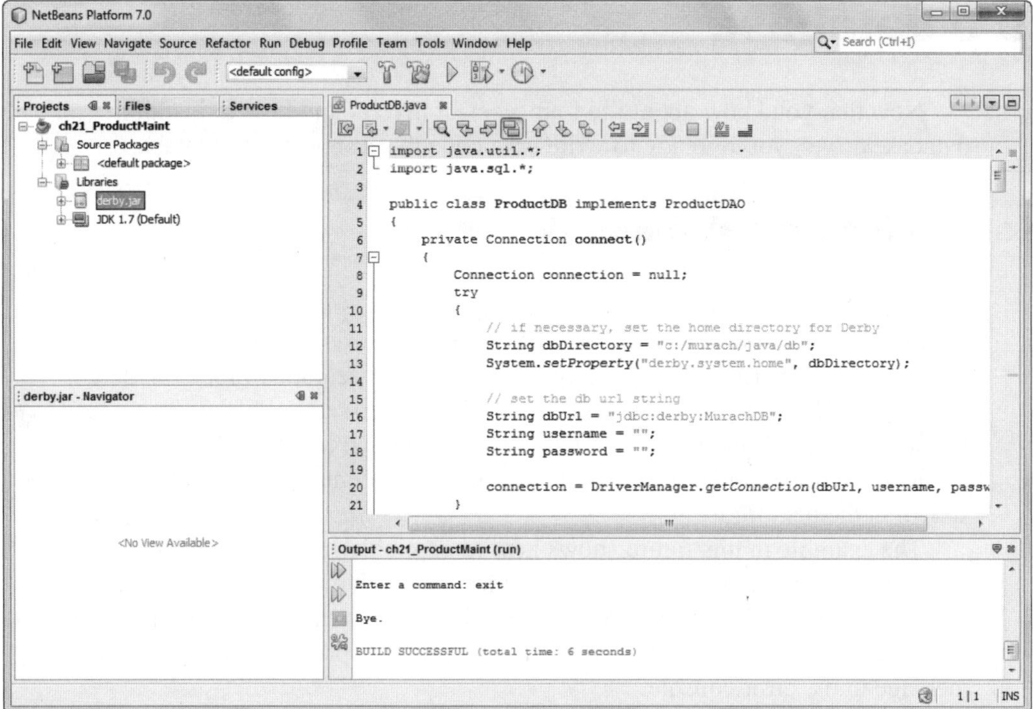

Description

- A database driver is a class that's typically stored in a JAR file.
- To add a database driver to a NetBeans project, right-click on the Libraries folder for the project, select the Add JAR/Folder command, and use the resulting dialog box to select the JAR file that contains the driver.
- After you add the JAR file that contains a database driver to a project, the JRE can find and run the class for the driver.
- To remove a database driver from a project, right-click on the JAR file that contains the driver and select the Remove command.

How to use Java to connect to a database

Now that you know about the four types of drivers and how to install a database driver, you're ready to write Java code that connects to a database.

How to load a database driver

JDBC 4.0 (JDK 1.6) introduced a feature known as *automatic driver loading*. This feature loads the database driver automatically. As a result, when you're using JDK 1.6 or later, you typically won't write code to load the database driver. However, if you're working with an older version of Java, you need to use the forName method of the Class class as shown in figure 21-3 to explicitly load the driver. Otherwise, you won't be able to connect to the database as shown in the next figure.

The example in this figure shows how to explicitly load the embedded Derby driver that comes with Java SE. Since the forName method throws a ClassNotFoundException, you also have to handle this exception. In this figure, for example, the catch block handles the exception by printing an appropriate message to the error console.

Although you can use the forName method to explicitly load a driver even if you're using JDK 1.6 or later, it usually makes sense to let JDBC load the driver automatically. That way, less code is required to connect to the database. In addition, the name of the database driver isn't included in the code. As a result, you can typically upgrade a database driver by swapping in a new JAR file for the driver as shown in the previous figure.

How to load a database driver prior to JDBC 4.0

```
try
{
    // load the driver for an embedded Derby database
    Class.forName("org.apache.derby.jdbc.EmbeddedDriver");
}
catch(ClassNotFoundException e)
{
    System.err.println("Database driver not found.");
}
```

Description

- Prior to JDBC 4.0 (JDK 1.6), you needed to use the forName method of the Class class to load the driver.
- With JDBC 4.0 (JDK 1.6) and later, the database driver is loaded automatically. This feature is known as *automatic driver loading*.

Figure 21-3 How to load a database driver

How to connect to an embedded database

An embedded Derby database runs in the same process as the application. When you connect to an embedded Derby database, the Derby database engine starts automatically. This engine continues to run until you disconnect from the database as shown in the next figure.

Figure 21-4 presents a method named getConnection that connects to an embedded database using a type-4 driver. The first two statements in the try block of this method use the setProperty method of the System class to set the derby.system.home property to the directory that contains the database. In this case, this property is set to the /murach/java/db directory. If you don't set this property, Derby looks for the database in the current directory, which is the directory where the Java class that uses the database is stored.

After setting the default directory, the try block creates a string that stores the database URL. Note that this URL is the same as the URL you use when you connect to an embedded database using Derby's ij tool.

After creating the database URL, this code specifies the username and password that are used to connect to the database. Here, the username and password are hard-coded values that are appropriate for any user of an application. However, if the database is set up so that only users with specific usernames and passwords can access the database, you'll want to have the user enter these values instead of hard-coding them. Alternatively, you could use the getProperty method of the System class to get the username.

After you create these variables, you can connect to the database by passing them to the getConnection method of the DriverManager class. If this method executes successfully, a Connection object is returned to the calling method. Otherwise, this method throws a SQLException and a null value is returned.

In chapter 14, you learned how to use exception chaining to maintain information for exceptions that are caught when new exceptions are thrown. With JDBC 4.0 (JDK 1.6) and later, exception chaining is used to maintain information about the exceptions that caused a SQLException to be thrown. Then, because the SQLException class implements the Iterable interface, you can use an enhanced for statement to loop through the chained exceptions as shown in this figure. This for loop retrieves a Throwable object named t for each chained exception. Then, it prints the stack trace for this exception. This works because the Throwable class is the superclass for all exceptions, and a Throwable object is returned by the iterator for the SQLException class.

When you connect to an embedded Derby database, you aren't required to supply a username and password. As a result, you can often omit this code. If you specify a username, though, you should know that by default, any tables you create with that connection are stored in a *schema* that corresponds to the username. For example, if you use the connection in this figure to create a Products table and you don't explicitly specify a different schema for the table, that table is stored in the AppUser schema of the MurachDB database. Often, this is what you want since it allows any code that connects to the database with a username of AppUser to create and use objects within the AppUser schema of the MurachDB database.

How to connect with a type-4 driver

```
private Connection getConnection()
{
    Connection connection = null;
    try
    {
        // if necessary, set the home directory for Derby
        String dbDirectory = "/murach/java/db";
        System.setProperty("derby.system.home", dbDirectory);

        // create and return the connection
        String dbUrl = "jdbc:derby:MurachDB";
        String username = "AppUser";
        String password = "sesame!";
        connection = DriverManager.getConnection(dbUrl, username, password);
        return connection;
    }
    catch (SQLException e)
    {
        for (Throwable t : e)
            e.printStackTrace();
        return null;
    }
}
```

The URL for connecting to a database named MurachDB

```
String dbUrl = "jdbc:derby:MurachDB";
```

The URL for creating a database named MurachDB if it doesn't exist

```
String dbUrl = "jdbc:derby:MurachDB;create=true";
```

Description

- All of the interfaces, classes, and exceptions for using JDBC that are presented in this chapter are stored in the java.sql package.
- By default, Derby looks for the specified database in the directory where the Java class is stored. If the database is stored in another directory, you can use the setProperty method of the System class to set the derby.system.home property to that directory.
- To connect to an embedded Derby database, you can call the getConnection method of the DriverManager class to pass a database URL that indicates the protocol to be used and the name of the database. You can also pass the username and password that are used to connect to the database.
- The getConnection method uses automatic driver loading to load the right driver for the database. In this example, that driver is the embedded Derby JDBC driver.
- The getConnection method throws a SQLException if the connection fails. With JDBC 4.0 (JDK 1.6) and later, the SQLException class implements the Iterable interface. As a result, you can use an enhanced for statement to loop through any chained exceptions.
- If necessary, you can use the getProperty method of the System class to get the default directory for the database or to get the username for the current user.

Figure 21-4 How to connect to an embedded database

How to disconnect from an embedded database

When your Java application connects to an embedded database, it automatically starts the Derby database engine. As a result, when the Java application is done working with the database, it's a good programming practice to disconnect from the database and shut down the database engine. That way, the Derby database engine can shut down cleanly and release the resources that it's using. This allows your application to start more quickly the next time it runs, since Derby won't have to run any recovery code.

Figure 21-5 shows a disconnect method that uses JDBC to disconnect from all databases and shut down the database engine. To start, the first statement creates a database URL that indicates that Derby should be shut down. Then, the second statement passes this database URL to the getConnection method of the DriverManager class. Since a successful shutdown throws a SQLException, the catch block for this exception checks the message that's stored in the SQLException object to make sure that Derby has been shut down. If so, it returns a true value. Otherwise, the last statement in this method returns a false value.

If you just want to disconnect from a specific database and free any resources associated with it, you can use the last URL shown in this figure as the parameter for the getConnection method. However, this doesn't shut down the Derby database engine, which is usually what you want to do when working with embedded databases. As a result, you'll typically use the URL that disconnects from all databases.

How to disconnect from all databases and shut down the database engine

```
public boolean disconnect()
{
    try
    {
        // On a successful shutdown, this throws an exception
        String shutdownURL = "jdbc:derby:;shutdown=true";
        DriverManager.getConnection(shutdownURL);
    }
    catch (SQLException e)
    {
        if (e.getMessage().equals("Derby system shutdown."))
            return true;
    }
    return false;
}
```

The URL for disconnecting from all databases

```
String shutdownURL = "jdbc:derby:;shutdown=true";
```

The URL for disconnecting from a specific database

```
String shutdownURL = "jdbc:derby:MurachDB;shutdown=true";
```

Description

- To disconnect from all databases and shut down the Derby database engine, you can call the getConnection method of the DriverManager class with a parameter that indicates the protocol to be used and that the database engine should be shut down.
- To disconnect from a specific database, you can call the getConnection method of the DriverManager class with a parameter that indicates the protocol to be used, the name of the database, and that one database should be shut down.
- When you disconnect from a specific database, the Derby database engine isn't shut down since other databases could be connected to it. If an application works with a single database, you should use the technique for disconnecting from all databases so the database engine is shut down.
- Since a successful shutdown throws a SQLException, you need to handle this exception.

Figure 21-5 How to disconnect from an embedded database

How to connect to a networked database

If you run a networked Derby database on a server, you can connect to it from a client application. To do that, you can use the database driver that's stored in the derbyclient.jar file. In addition, you can use the syntax for the database URL that's shown in figure 21-6.

In the first example, the database URL starts with "jdbc" to indicate that the connection is using JDBC. Then, it specifies a subprotocol of "derby" to work with a Derby database. Next, it specifies the server and path of the database. To do that, it uses two front slashes, the name of the server, a colon, and the port that Derby is using. Here, the URL uses the localhost keyword to indicate that the local computer is being used as the server, and it uses 1527 as the port number because that's the default port for a Derby database. Then, it specifies a database named MurachDB. For this to work, the database must be stored in the same directory as the NetworkServerControl class. If the database is stored in a different directory, you can include that directory in the URL as shown in the second example.

To connect to a server over a network, you include the name of the database server in the URL as shown in the third example. Here, the URL specifies DBSERVER as the name of the server and 1527 as the port. Notice in this example that the database must be stored in the Databases directory on the server.

It's also common to use JDBC to work with MySQL and Oracle databases. Before you do that, of course, you must add the appropriate database driver to the project as described in figure 21-2. In addition, you should know that you almost always need to supply a username and password when connecting to one of these databases since security is critical.

To connect to a MySQL database, you use a URL like the one you use for a Derby database, except you use port 3306. This is illustrated in the fourth example. Here, the URL will connect to a database server that's running on the client, but you can also connect to a database server that's running on a network server by replacing the localhost keyword with the name of the server.

To connect to an Oracle database on a local computer, you use a URL like the one in the fifth example. This URL uses a second subprotocol to indicate that JDBC should use the thin version of the database driver, which requires less overhead and is appropriate for most clients. In addition, it uses the @ symbol to identify the location of the server. In this case, the server is running on the client, so the localhost keyword is used. Finally, this URL uses XE (short for Express Edition) to specify the name of the server instance. Notice that it isn't necessary to specify the database name. That's because Oracle uses the username to automatically connect to the correct database schema.

The last example shows how to connect to an Oracle database on a server. This URL uses ORCL instead of XE to refer to an instance of one of the full editions of Oracle. It also uses two front slashes between the @ symbol and the name of the database server. These two slashes are optional, though.

In practice, connecting to the database is often the most time consuming and frustrating part of working with a database. So if some of your colleagues have already made a connection to the database you need to use, by all means get help from them. That can save you hours of frustration.

URL syntax

```
jdbc:subprotocolName:databasePath
```

Example 1: A Derby database on a local computer in the default directory

```
jdbc:derby://localhost:1527/MurachDB
```

Example 2: A Derby database on a local computer in a specific directory

```
jdbc:derby://localhost:1527/murach/java/db/MurachDB
```

Example 3: A Derby database on a server in the default directory

```
jdbc:derby://DBSERVER:1527/Databases/MurachDB
```

Example 4: A MySQL database on a local computer

```
jdbc:mysql://localhost:3306/MurachDB
```

Example 5: An Oracle database on a local computer

```
jdbc:oracle:thin:@localhost:1521/XE
```

Example 6: An Oracle database on a server

```
jdbc:oracle:thin:@//DBSERVER:1521/ORCL
```

Description

- By default, the Derby client attempts to connect to the database that's in the directory where the NetworkServerControl class is stored. To connect to a database in a different directory, include that directory in the database path.
- To connect to a database server that's running on the client, use the localhost keyword followed by the port number.
- To connect to a database server that's running on a network server, specify the server name followed by the port number.
- By default, the Derby database uses port number 1527. In contrast, MySQL uses port number 3306, and Oracle uses port number 1521.
- The database server for a networked database is always running. As a result, there's no need to shut down the server when you disconnect from the database.

Figure 21-6 How to connect to a networked database

How to use Java to work with a database

Now that you know how to connect to a database, you're ready to learn how to use JDBC to work with the data that's stored in that database. Once you have a connection to a database with a driver that supports JDBC, this code works the same regardless of the type of database.

To work with a database, you start by retrieving a result set. Then, you can use that result set to insert, update, and delete records in the database. For this to work, you need to make sure that your driver supports all the features JDBC provides for working with result sets. For example, an old driver might not be able to support the features that were added to more recent versions of JDBC. In addition, even the latest drivers don't always implement the JDBC features the same way. As a result, if your driver isn't working correctly with JDBC, you may need to use a newer or better driver. Or, you may need to avoid using the JDBC features that are causing the problems.

How to return a result set

Figure 21-7 shows how to use Statement objects to return ResultSet objects. The first example shows how to create a forward-only, read-only result set. Here, the createStatement method is called from a Connection object to return a Statement object. Then, the executeQuery method is called from the Statement object to execute an SQL SELECT statement that's coded as a string. This SELECT statement selects all columns and rows from the Products table.

The second example shows how to create a scrollable, updateable result set. To do this, the code supplies two arguments for the createStatement method of the Connection object.

The first argument uses a field from the ResultSet class to specify the type of result set. In this example, the argument specifies that the result set should be scrollable, and it should display changes that have been made by other users to the data that's in the result set. Although this is the most flexible type of result set, it also requires the most system resources. In contrast, a scrollable result set that isn't sensitive to changes requires fewer resources.

The second argument in this example specifies the concurrency of the result set. Here, the concurrency has been set to updateable. That means that you can update the values in the result set, and those values will be stored in the database.

How to create a forward-only, read-only result set

```
Statement statement = connection.createStatement();
ResultSet rs = statement.executeQuery("SELECT * FROM Products");
```

How to create a scrollable, updateable result set

```
Statement statement = connection.createStatement(
    ResultSet.TYPE_SCROLL_SENSITIVE,
    ResultSet.CONCUR_UPDATABLE);

String query = "SELECT ProductCode, Description, Price "
             + "FROM Products ORDER BY ProductCode ASC";

ResultSet rs = statement.executeQuery(query);
```

Five ResultSet fields that set type and concurrency

Constant	Description
TYPE_FORWARD_ONLY	Creates a result set where the cursor can only move forward (default).
TYPE_SCROLL_INSENSITIVE	Creates a result set where the cursor can scroll through the result set but won't display changes made by others to the result set.
TYPE_SCROLL_SENSITIVE	Creates a result set where the cursor can scroll through the result set and display changes made by others to the result set.
CONCUR_READ_ONLY	Creates a read-only result set (default).
CONCUR_UPDATABLE	Creates an updateable result set.

Description

- The createStatement method of a Connection object creates a Statement object. Then, the executeQuery method of the Statement object executes a SELECT statement that returns a ResultSet object.
- By default, the createStatement method creates a forward-only, read-only result set. However, you can set the type and concurrency of a Statement object by coding the fields above for the two arguments of the createStatement method.
- Both the createStatement and executeQuery methods throw an exception of the SQLException type. As a result, any code that returns a result set needs to catch or throw this exception.

Figure 21-7 How to return a result set

How to move the cursor through a result set

Figure 21-8 shows how to move the cursor through a result set. To start, this figure shows some methods of the ResultSet object. Some database drivers may not support all of these methods, especially the ones for working with scrollable result sets.

If the result set is a forward-only result set, you'll only be able to use the next method to move through the result set as shown in the first example. In this example, the next method is coded as the condition for a while loop. This works because the next method returns a boolean value that indicates if the next row exists. As a result, the first time the next method is called, it attempts to move the pointer to the first row in the result set. If it is successful, it returns a true value. Within the loop, you can write code like the code shown in the next figure that works with the current row. Once the loop has moved through all of the rows in the result set, the next method returns a false value and the loop ends.

If the result set is scrollable, you can use the next, previous, first, last, absolute, and relative methods to move the cursor through the result set as shown in the second example. Here, the first statement moves the cursor to the first row in the result set, and the second statement moves the cursor to the last row. Then, the first if statement moves the cursor to the previous row if the cursor isn't on the first row, and the second if statement moves the cursor to the next row if the cursor isn't on the last row. Finally, the fifth statement moves the cursor to the fourth row in the result set; the sixth statement moves the cursor back two rows; and the seventh statement moves the cursor forward three rows.

Like the next method, all of these methods return a boolean value that indicates whether the cursor has been moved to a valid row. For example, the previous method returns a true value until it reaches the first row of the result set or until it hits a row that's invalid for other reasons. Since all of these methods throw an exception of the SQLException type, you either need to throw or catch this exception when you're working with these methods.

Methods of a ResultSet object that work with a result set

Method	Description
`beforeFirst()`	Moves the cursor before the first row in this result set.
`afterLast()`	Moves the cursor after the last row in this result set.
`first()`	Moves the cursor to the first row in this result set.
`previous()`	Moves the cursor to the previous row in this result set.
`next()`	Moves the cursor to the next row in this result set.
`last()`	Moves the cursor to the last row in this result set.
`absolute(intRow)`	Moves the cursor to the row specified by the int value where 1 is the first row, 2 is the second row, and so on.
`relative(intRow)`	Moves the cursor the number of rows specified relative to the current row.
`isBeforeFirst()`	Returns a true value if the cursor is positioned before the first row.
`isAfterLast()`	Returns a true value if the cursor is positioned after the last row.
`isFirst()`	Returns a true value if the cursor is positioned on the first row.
`isLast()`	Returns a true value if the cursor is positioned on the last row.
`close()`	Releases the result set's JDBC and database resources.
`getRow()`	Returns an int value that identifies the current row of the result set.

How to work with a forward-only result set

```
while(rs.next())
{
    // code that works with each row
}
rs.close();
```

How to work with a scrollable result set

```
rs.first();
rs.last();

if (rs.isFirst() == false)
   rs.previous();

if (rs.isLast() == false)
   rs.next();

rs.absolute(4);
rs.relative(-2);
rs.relative(3);
```

Description

- When you create a result set, the cursor is positioned before the first row. As a result, the first time you call the next method, it moves to the first row in the result set.
- The first, previous, next, last, absolute, and relative methods all return a true value if the new row exists and a false value if the new row doesn't exist or the result set is empty.
- All of the methods in this figure throw an exception of the SQLException type.

Figure 21-8 How to move the cursor through a result set

How to return data from a result set

Figure 21-9 shows how to return data from the current row in a result set. In particular, it shows how to use the getString and getDouble methods of the ResultSet object to return strings and double values. However, the same principles can be used for any of the get methods of the ResultSet object.

The four methods in this figure show the two types of arguments accepted by the get methods. The first and third get methods accept an int value that specifies the number of the column in the result set, where 1 is the first column, 2 is the second column, and so on. The second and fourth get methods accept a string value that specifies the name of the column in the result set. Although the get methods that specify the column index require less typing, using the get methods that specify the column name can be more flexible. For example, these methods work regardless of the sequence in which the columns are returned.

The first example shows how to use column indexes to return data from a result set named rs. Here, the first two statements use the getString method to return the code and description for the current product, while the third statement uses the getDouble method to return the price of the product. Since these methods use column indexes, the first column in the result set must contain the product code, the second column must contain the description, and the third column must contain the price.

The second example shows how to use column names to return data from a result set. Since this code uses the column names, the order of the columns in the result set doesn't matter. However, the column names must exist in the result set. If a column doesn't exist, a SQLException is thrown indicating that the column wasn't found.

The third example shows how you can use the get methods to create a Product object from a row in a result set. Here, the constructor for the Product object uses three values that are returned by the get methods to create a new Product object. Since objects are often created from data that's stored in a database, code like this is used frequently.

If you look up the ResultSet interface in the documentation for the API, you'll see that get methods exist for all of the primitive types as well as for other types of data. For example, get methods exist for the Date, Time, and Timestamp classes that are a part of the java.sql package. In addition, they exist for *BLOB objects* (*Binary Large Objects*) and *CLOB objects* (*Character Large Objects*). These types of objects are used for storing large objects such as multimedia files in databases.

Methods of a ResultSet object that return data from a result set

Method	Description
`getString(intColumnIndex)`	Returns a String from the specified column number.
`getString(StringColumnName)`	Returns a String from the specified column name.
`getDouble(intColumnIndex)`	Returns a double value from the specified column number.
`getDouble(StringColumnName)`	Returns a double value from the specified column name.

Code that uses column indexes to return fields from the Products result set

```
String code = rs.getString(1);
String description = rs.getString(2);
double price = rs.getDouble(3);
```

Code that uses column names to return the same fields

```
String code = rs.getString("ProductCode");
String description = rs.getString("Description");
double price = rs.getDouble("Price");
```

Code that creates a Product object from the result set

```
Product p = new Product(rs.getString("ProductCode"),
                        rs.getString("Description"),
                        rs.getDouble("Price"));
```

Description

- The get methods of a ResultSet object can be used to return all eight primitive types. For example, the getInt method returns the int type and the getLong method returns the long type.
- The get methods of a ResultSet object can also be used to return some objects such as dates and times. For example, the getDate, getTime, and getTimestamp methods return objects of the Date, Time, and Timestamp classes of the java.sql package.
- The getBlob and getClob methods can be used to return *BLOB objects* (*Binary Large Objects*) and *CLOB objects* (*Character Large Objects*).
- The get methods accept an argument that specifies the number or name of the column in the result set. The column numbers begin with 1.

Figure 21-9 How to return data from a result set

How to modify data in a database

Figure 21-10 shows how to use Java to modify the data in a database. First, it shows how to use the executeUpdate method of a Statement object to execute SQL statements that add, update, and delete data. This method has been available since JDBC 1.0 and is supported by virtually all database drivers. Then, this figure shows how to use methods that were introduced with JDBC 2.0 (JDK 1.4). These JDBC methods don't always work as you would expect for all JDBC drivers.

To use the executeUpdate method, you pass a SQL statement to the database. In these examples, the code adds, updates, and deletes a product in the Products table. To do that, the code combines data from a Product object with the appropriate SQL statement. For the UPDATE and DELETE statements, the SQL statement uses the product's code in the WHERE clause to select a single product.

When you work with the methods that were introduced with the JDBC 2.0 API, you don't have to use SQL statements. Instead, you just call methods of the ResultSet object to add, update, and delete rows from the current result set. In these examples, you can assume that the ResultSet object named rs contains three columns and many rows.

To add a row, you call the moveToInsertRow method to move the cursor to a special buffer area that's used to construct a new row. Then, you call the appropriate update method for each column in the row. For example, you call the updateString method for a string or the updateDouble method for a double value. Here, the first argument specifies the name of the column and the second argument specifies the value of the column. When you're done providing values for all of the columns in the row, you call the insertRow method to commit the changes to the database. Then, you can call the moveToCurrentRow method to move back to the row that you were on before you called the moveToInsertRow method.

To update or delete a row, you start by moving to that row using the methods that were described earlier in this chapter. Then, you can update the row by calling the appropriate update method for any of the columns that you wish to update and by calling the updateRow method after that. Or, you can delete a row by calling the deleteRow method.

Depending on the driver that you're using, the modifications that you make to a result set may cause some problems. For example, when you add a row, you may not be able to move to that row. Worse, when you delete a row, an invalid row may remain in the result set where the deleted row used to be. Then, if you try to move to that row, your application will throw a SQLException. The best way to solve these problems is to get a better driver or change the way your program retrieves data. However, you can sometimes solve these problems by closing the result set and opening it again. Although that isn't efficient, it often refreshes all the rows in the result set.

How to use the executeUpdate method to modify data

How to add a record

```
String insertStatement =
    "INSERT INTO Products (ProductCode, Description, Price) " +
    "VALUES ('" + p.getCode() + "', " +
            "'" + p.getDescription() + "', " +
                  p.getPrice() + ")";
int count = statement.executeUpdate(insertStatement);
```

How to update a record

```
String updateStatement =
    "UPDATE Products SET " +
        "ProductCode = '" + p.getCode() + "', " +
        "Description = '" + p.getDescription() + "', " +
        "Price = " + p.getPrice() + " " +
    "WHERE ProductCode = '" + p.getCode() + "'";
int count = statement.executeUpdate(updateStatement);
```

How to delete a record

```
String deleteStatement =
    "DELETE FROM Products " +
    "WHERE ProductCode = '" + p.getCode() + "'";
int count = statement.executeUpdate(deleteStatement);
```

How to use methods from JDBC 2.0 (JDK 1.4) and later to modify data

How to add a record

```
rs.moveToInsertRow();
rs.updateString("ProductCode", p.getCode());
rs.updateString("Description", p.getDescription());
rs.updateDouble("Price", p.getPrice());
rs.insertRow();
rs.moveToCurrentRow();
```

How to update a record

```
rs.updateString("ProductCode", p.getCode());
rs.updateString("Description", p.getDescription());
rs.updateDouble("Price", p.getPrice());
rs.updateRow();
```

How to delete a record

```
rs.deleteRow();
```

Description

- The executeUpdate method returns an int value that identifies the number of records that were affected by the update.
- The executeUpdate method works with most JDBC drivers. The other methods shown in this figure may not work properly with all JDBC drivers.
- In some cases, you may need to refresh the result set after a modification by closing it and reopening it.

Figure 21-10 How to modify data in a database

How to work with prepared statements

Figure 21-11 shows how to use a prepared SQL statement to return a result set or to modify data. When you use a *prepared statement*, you include placeholders in the statement for parameters whose values will vary. Then, before you execute the statement, you set the values of those parameters.

Prepared statements provide two main benefits. First, because the database can cache and reuse prepared statements, they execute faster than regular statements. Second, prepared statements are more secure since they prevent SQL injection attacks, which can be used by hackers to view and modify data. (For more information on SQL injection attacks, you can search the Internet.) Because of these benefits, you should use prepared statements whenever possible.

The first example in this figure shows how to use a prepared statement to create a result set that contains a single product. Here, the first statement uses a question mark (?) placeholder to identify the parameter for the SELECT statement, which is the code for the product. The second statement uses the prepareStatement method of the Connection object to return a PreparedStatement object. The third statement uses a set method (the setString method) of the PreparedStatement object to set a value for the first parameter in the SELECT statement. And the fourth statement uses the executeQuery method of the PreparedStatement object to return a ResultSet object. Note that this is the same method you use to execute a Statement object that contains a SELECT statement.

By default, the prepareStatement method of the Connection object creates a forward-only, read-only result set. However, you can set the type and concurrency of a PreparedStatement object just as you can for Statement objects as shown in figure 21-7. That way, you can create a scrollable, updateable result set from a prepared statement.

The second example shows how to use a prepared statement to execute an UPDATE query that requires three parameters. Here, the first statement uses three question marks (?) to identify the three parameters of the UPDATE statement, and the second statement creates the PreparedStatement object. Then, the next three statements use set methods to set the three parameters in the order that they appear in the UPDATE statement. The last statement uses the executeUpdate method of the PreparedStatement object to execute the UPDATE statement. The third and fourth examples show how to insert and delete records with prepared statements. Notice that all three of these examples use the executeUpdate method to execute the PreparedStatement object. This is the same method that's used to execute a Statement object that contains an INSERT, UPDATE, or DELETE statement.

The executeUpdate method returns an int value that indicates the number of records that were successfully updated. In this example, the SQL statements only modify a single record, so this value isn't that useful. However, if a SQL statement modifies multiple records, this count is more useful.

How to use a prepared statement

To return a result set

```
String selectProduct =
    "SELECT ProductCode, Description, Price " +
    "FROM Products " +
    "WHERE ProductCode = ?";
PreparedStatement ps = connection.prepareStatement(selectProduct);
ps.setString(1, p.getCode());
ResultSet rs = ps.executeQuery();
```

To update a record

```
String updateProduct =
    "UPDATE Products " +
    "SET Description = ?, Price = ? " +
    "WHERE ProductCode = ?";
PreparedStatement ps = connection.prepareStatement(updateProduct);
ps.setString(1, p.getDescription());
ps.setDouble(2, p.getPrice());
ps.setString(3, p.getCode());
int count = ps.executeUpdate();
```

To insert a record

```
String insertProduct =
    "INSERT INTO Products (ProductCode, Description, Price) " +
    "VALUES (?, ?, ?)";
PreparedStatement ps = connection.prepareStatement(insertProduct);
ps.setString(1, p.getCode());
ps.setString(2, p.getDescription());
ps.setDouble(3, p.getPrice());
int count = ps.executeUpdate();
```

To delete a record

```
String deleteProduct =
    "DELETE FROM Products " +
    "WHERE ProductCode = ?";
PreparedStatement ps = connection.prepareStatement(deleteProduct);
ps.setString(1, p.getCode());
int count = ps.executeUpdate();
```

Description

- To specify a placeholder for a parameter in the SQL statement, type a question mark (?).
- To supply values for the parameters in a prepared statement, use the set methods of the PreparedStatement interface. For a complete list of set methods, look up the PreparedStatement interface of the java.sql package in the documentation for the Java API.
- To execute a SELECT statement, use the executeQuery method. To execute an INSERT, UPDATE, or DELETE statement, use the executeUpdate method.

Figure 21-11 How to work with prepared statements

Two classes for working with databases

In chapters 18 and 19, you learned how to code classes that implement the ProductDAO interface (see figure 18-10) so you can use that interface to store data in files. Now, you'll learn how to code a ProductDB class that implements the ProductDAO interface so you can use that interface to store data in a database. But first, you'll be introduced to a utility class that you can use to solve a common problem that you may encounter when using a Statement object to store strings in a database.

A utility class for working with strings

In a SQL statement that specifies column values, you use the single quote (') to identify the beginning and end of the data for each column. As a result, if you try to insert a string that contains a single quote as shown in the first example of figure 21-12, the database interprets that quote as the end of the string. Then, an exception is thrown when the database isn't able to interpret the rest of the SQL statement. To fix this problem, you can prefix the single quote with another single quote as shown in the second example. In other words, you can code two single quotes to tell the database that you want to include a single quote in the string, not end the string.

The DBUtil class shown in this figure contains a method named fixDBString that you can use to fix the single quotes for any string that's passed to it. If the string that's passed to this method is null, the method returns a null and ends. This prevents a NullPointerException. Otherwise, this method loops through each character in the string. Then, each time it finds a single quote, it adds another single quote immediately before that single quote. When it's done, it returns the resulting string.

To use the fixDBString method, you can use code like that shown at the bottom of this figure. This code creates a statement that inserts a row into the Products table. Because the product description can contain single quotes, the fixDBString method is used to process this string.

If you use prepared statements as shown in figure 21-11, this problem is handled for you automatically. As a result, you only need to use code like the code in this figure if you aren't using prepared statements. This is yet another reason to use prepared statements.

A SQL statement that causes an error

```
"INSERT INTO Products (ProductCode, Description, Price) " +
"VALUES ('java', 'Murach's Beginning Java 2', 49.50)";
```

A SQL statement that works

```
"INSERT INTO Products (ProductCode, Description, Price) " +
"VALUES ('java', 'Murach''s Beginning Java 2', 49.50)";
```

A utility class for working with strings

```
public class DBUtils
{
    // handle strings that contain one or more apostrophes (')
    private static String fixDBString(String s)
    {
        // if the string is null, return it
        if (s == null)
            return s;

        // add an apostrophe before each existing apostrophe
        StringBuilder sb = new StringBuilder(s);
        for (int i = 0; i < sb.length(); i++)
        {
            char ch = sb.charAt(i);
            if (ch == 39)  //39 is the ASCII code for an apostrophe
                sb.insert(i++, "'");
        }
        return sb.toString();
    }
}
```

Code that uses this class

```
Statement statement = connection.createStatement();
String insert =
    "INSERT INTO Products (ProductCode, Description, Price) " +
    "VALUES ('" + p.getCode() + "', " +
            "'" + DBUtils.fixDBString(p.getDescription()) + "', " +
                  p.getPrice() + ")";
statement.executeUpdate(insert);
```

Description

- SQL uses single quotes to indicate the beginning and end of the value of a column. If you need to store a single quote in a column value, you have to code two consecutive single quotes if you're using a Statement object. Alternately, you can use a prepared statement to store a single quote in a column value.

Figure 21-12 A utility class for working with strings

A class that works with a database

Figure 21-13 presents the complete code for the ProductDB class. This class works with the data in the Products table of the MurachDB database. Like the ProductTextFile and ProductRandomFile classes presented in chapter 18 and the ProductXMLFile class presented in chapter 19, this class implements the ProductDAO interface shown in figure 18-10. If you have already read chapter 18 or 19, you shouldn't have any trouble understanding how a class that implements the ProductDAO interface works.

To start, this class declares a private method named getConnection that returns a Connection object that provides a connection to the database. To create a Connection object, the getConnection method starts by setting the home directory for Derby, which contains the database named MurachDB. Then, this method sets the URL for the database to MurachDB, and it sets the default username and password to empty strings. Next, this method uses the static getConnection method of the DriverManager class to automatically load the appropriate database driver and connect to the database. If this method is successful, the Connection object is returned to the calling method. Otherwise, an appropriate error message is printed to the console and a null value is returned.

The getProducts method returns an ArrayList object that contains all of the Product objects that are stored in the Products table of the MurachDB database. This method starts by creating a string that contains a SQL statement that selects the ProductCode, Description, and Price fields from the Products table and sorts them in ascending order. Then, it creates an ArrayList object that can store Product objects. Next, it uses a try-with-resources statement to create the Connection, PreparedStatement, and ResultSet objects that are needed by this method. That way, these objects are automatically closed when the try block ends.

Once the ResultSet object has been created, the getProducts method uses a loop to read each row in the result set. Within the loop, the first two statements use the getString method of the ResultSet object to return strings for the ProductCode and Description columns of the result set. Then, the third statement uses the getDouble method of the ResultSet object to return a double value for the Price column. Finally, this loop creates the Product object and adds it to the products array list.

If a SQLException is thrown anywhere in the try block, this method returns a null value. Otherwise, the getProducts method returns the products array list. That way, any method that calls the getProducts method can determine if the method executed successfully by checking for a null value.

The code for the ProductDB class **Page 1**

```
import java.util.*;
import java.sql.*;

public class ProductDB implements ProductDAO
{
    private Connection getConnection()
    {
        Connection connection = null;
        try
        {
            // if necessary, set the home directory for Derby
            String dbDirectory = "c:/murach/java/db";
            System.setProperty("derby.system.home", dbDirectory);

            // set the db url, username, and password
            String url = "jdbc:derby:MurachDB";
            String username = "";
            String password = "";
            connection = DriverManager.getConnection(url, username, password);
            return connection;
        }
        catch(SQLException e)
        {
            System.err.println(e);
            return null;
        }
    }

    public ArrayList<Product> getProducts()
    {
        String sql = "SELECT ProductCode, Description, Price "
                   + "FROM Products ORDER BY ProductCode ASC";
        ArrayList<Product> products = new ArrayList<>();

        try (Connection connection = getConnection();
             PreparedStatement ps = connection.prepareStatement(sql);
             ResultSet rs = ps.executeQuery())
        {
            while(rs.next())
            {
                String code = rs.getString("ProductCode");
                String description = rs.getString("Description");
                double price = rs.getDouble("Price");

                Product p = new Product(code, description, price);
                products.add(p);
            }
            return products;
        }
        catch(SQLException e)
        {
            System.err.println(e);
            return null;
        }
    }
```

Figure 21-13 A class that works with a database (part 1 of 3)

The getProduct method returns a Product object for a product that matches the specified product code. To do that, it uses a prepared SQL statement to return a result set. Then, it calls the next method of the result set to attempt to move the cursor to the first row in the result set. If successful, this method continues by reading the description and price fields from the row and creating a Product object from these fields. Then, it closes the result set and returns the Product object.

Note that, unlike the getProducts method, the result set used by the getProduct method can't be created in the try-with-resources statement. That's because before the result set can be opened, the value of the parameter in the prepared statement must be set. However, the connection and prepared statement can still be created in the try-with-resources statement, which means that they don't have to be closed explicitly.

If no product record contains a product code that matches the specified code, this method returns a null to indicate that the product couldn't be found. In addition, if a SQLException is thrown anywhere in this method, this method returns a null to indicate that it was not successful.

As you review the getProduct method, note that if the try block throws a SQLException, the result set isn't explicitly closed. In most cases, that's not a problem because the result set will be automatically closed when the prepared statement that was used to create the result set is closed. If you wanted to close the result set explicitly, though, you could do that by adding a finally clause to the try statement.

The addProduct method begins by creating a prepared statement that can be used to insert values into the three columns of the Products table. Then, it sets the values of the three parameters in the prepared statement to the values stored in the Product object that's passed to it. Finally, it executes the executeUpdate method of the prepared statement. If this update is successful, the addProduct method returns a true value. However, if a SQLException is thrown anywhere in this method, it returns a false value to indicate that it was not successful.

The code for the ProductDB class

Page 2

```
    public Product getProduct(String code)
    {
        String sql =
            "SELECT ProductCode, Description, Price " +
            "FROM Products " +
            "WHERE ProductCode = ?";
        try (Connection connection = getConnection();
             PreparedStatement ps = connection.prepareStatement(sql))
        {
            ps.setString(1, code);
            ResultSet rs = ps.executeQuery();
            if (rs.next())
            {
                String description = rs.getString("Description");
                double price = rs.getDouble("Price");
                Product p = new Product(code, description, price);
                rs.close();
                return p;
            }
            else
            {
                rs.close();
                return null;
            }
        }
        catch(SQLException e)
        {
            System.err.println(e);
            return null;
        }
    }

    public boolean addProduct(Product p)
    {
        String sql =
            "INSERT INTO Products (ProductCode, Description, Price) " +
            "VALUES (?, ?, ?)";
        try (Connection connection = getConnection();
             PreparedStatement ps = connection.prepareStatement(sql))
        {
            ps.setString(1, p.getCode());
            ps.setString(2, p.getDescription());
            ps.setDouble(3, p.getPrice());
            ps.executeUpdate();
            return true;
        }
        catch(SQLException e)
        {
            System.err.println(e);
            return false;
        }
    }
```

Figure 21-13 A class that works with a database (part 2 of 3)

The deleteProduct method uses a prepared SQL statement to delete the product record that has the same product code as the Product object that's passed to it. Like the addProduct method, the deleteProduct method returns a true value if the operation is successful, and it returns a false value if a SQLException is thrown anywhere in the method.

The updateProduct method uses a prepared SQL statement to update an existing product in the Products table with the data that's stored in the Product object that's passed to it. Note that this method only works if the Product object has a product code that exists in the Products table. Like the addProduct and deleteProduct methods, this method returns a boolean value that indicates whether the operation was successful.

The code for this class only uses methods from JDBC 1.0. That's because this is still the most common way to use JDBC to work with databases. The downside of this technique is that you must understand SQL. However, SQL is easy to learn, and most programmers who work with databases already know how to use it. In fact, some programmers prefer using SQL so they have direct control over the SQL statement that's sent to the database.

Each method in this class that needs a connection opens the connection, does its processing, and automatically closes the connection. The advantage of this approach is that all the resources used by the Connection object are freed as soon as the connection is no longer needed. This is helpful if your application is used by a large number of users and the number of open database connections is an issue. The disadvantage of this approach is that opening a database connection can be a relatively time-consuming process. Because of that, this may have a negative impact on the performance of your application. However, it's probably acceptable for most applications.

Note that the ProductDB class does not include a disconnect method like the one shown in figure 21-5. As a result, this class doesn't provide a way to shut down the Derby engine. Although applications can still use this class to work with a Derby database, the database might not shut down cleanly. As a result, you typically include a disconnect method if you're using an embedded database like the Derby database. To do that, you can follow the steps in exercise 21-2 at the end of this chapter.

The code for the ProductDB class

Page 3

```
    public boolean deleteProduct(Product p)
    {
        String sql = "DELETE FROM Products " +
                     "WHERE ProductCode = ?";
        try (Connection connection = getConnection();
             PreparedStatement ps = connection.prepareStatement(sql))
        {
            ps.setString(1, p.getCode());
            ps.executeUpdate();
            return true;
        }
        catch(SQLException e)
        {
            System.err.println(e);
            return false;
        }
    }

    public boolean updateProduct(Product p)
    {
        String sql = "UPDATE Products SET " +
                         "Description = ?, " +
                         "Price = ? " +
                     "WHERE ProductCode = ?";
        try (Connection connection = getConnection();
             PreparedStatement ps = connection.prepareStatement(sql))
        {
            ps.setString(1, p.getDescription());
            ps.setDouble(2, p.getPrice());
            ps.setString(3, p.getCode());
            ps.executeUpdate();
            return true;
        }
        catch(SQLException e)
        {
            System.err.println(e);
            return false;
        }
    }
}
```

Figure 21-13 A class that works with a database (part 3 of 3)

An introduction to working with metadata

When you work with a result set, you can get data about the definition of the result set. This type of information is known as *metadata*. For example, the metadata of a result set includes the number of columns, names of the columns, and the data type that's stored in each column. Although working with metadata is an advanced skill that you don't need for normal business applications, this topic gives you a taste of what you can do with it.

How to work with metadata

Figure 21-14 shows the basic skills for working with metadata. First, this figure shows how to return a ResultSetMetaData object from a ResultSet object. Then, it shows five methods that are commonly used to work with metadata.

When you use the last four methods in this figure, you use an integer value to specify the column, where 1 is the first column, 2 is the second column, and so on. The difference between the second and third methods is that the second method returns the *name* that the DBMS uses to identify the column while the third method returns the *label* that's used as a heading for GUIs and reports. If a label hasn't been defined for a column, the DBMS often uses the column name as a default. The difference between the fourth and fifth methods is that the fourth method returns an int type that represents an SQL data type while the fifth method returns the name of the SQL data type.

The first example shows a static method that returns the column names for a result set. This method accepts a ResultSet object as a parameter and returns an ArrayList object that contains all of the column names. To do that, the first statement creates an ArrayList object that can store strings. Then, the second statement gets the ResultSetMetaData object from the result set that has been passed to the method, and the third statement uses the getColumnCount method to get the column count. After that, a for loop cycles through all of the columns in the result set and uses the getColumnName method to add each column name to the array list. The last statement in this method returns the array list.

The second example shows a static method that returns the data for each row in a result set. This method also accepts a ResultSet object as a parameter and returns an ArrayList object. However, the array list that's returned in this example is a two-dimensional array list. That way, the outer array list can store one inner array list for each row in the result set. To do that, this method uses a while loop to cycle through all of the rows in the result set. Inside the outer loop, the inner loop cycles through each column in the result set using the getColumnType method to check the data type for the column. Depending on the data type, the appropriate get method is used to add the data to the inner array list. In this example, the code uses the fields of the Types class to check for the VARCHAR, INTEGER, and DOUBLE types.

How to use the getMetaData method to create a ResultSetMetaData object

```
ResultSetMetaData metaData = resultSet.getMetaData();
```

Methods of a ResultSetMetaData object for working with metadata

Method	Description
`getColumnCount()`	Returns the number of columns in this ResultSetMetaData object as an int type.
`getColumnName(intColumn)`	Returns the name of this column as a String object.
`getColumnLabel(intColumn)`	Returns the label of this column as a String object.
`getColumnType(intColumn)`	Returns an int type for the SQL data type of the column.
`getColumnTypeName(intColumn)`	Returns a string for the name of the SQL data type of the column.

A method that returns the column names of a result set

```
public static ArrayList<String> getColumnNames(ResultSet results)
throws SQLException
{
    ArrayList<String> columnNames = new ArrayList<>();
    ResultSetMetaData metaData = results.getMetaData();
    int columnCount = metaData.getColumnCount();
    for (int i = 1; i <= columnCount; i++)
        columnNames.add(metaData.getColumnName(i));
    return columnNames;
}
```

A method that returns the rows of a result set

```
public static ArrayList<ArrayList> getRows(ResultSet results)
throws SQLException
{
    ArrayList<ArrayList> rows = new ArrayList<>();
    ResultSetMetaData metaData = results.getMetaData();
    while (results.next())
    {
        ArrayList<Object> row = new ArrayList<>();
        for (int i = 1; i <= metaData.getColumnCount(); i++)
        {
            if (metaData.getColumnType(i) == Types.VARCHAR)
                row.add(results.getString(i));
            else if (metaData.getColumnType(i) == Types.INTEGER)
                row.add(new Integer(results.getInt(i)));
            else if (metaData.getColumnType(i) == Types.DOUBLE)
                row.add(new Double(results.getDouble(i)));
        }
        rows.add(row);
    }
    return rows;
}
```

Description

- You can use the fields of the Types class of the java.sql package to specify an int value for a SQL data type.

Figure 21-14 How to work with metadata

How SQL data types map to Java data types

Figure 21-15 shows how some of the most common SQL data types map to the Java data types. Some of these conversions are intuitive. For example, the SQL INTEGER type corresponds to the Java int type. However, some of these conversions aren't as intuitive. For example, the SQL REAL type maps to the Java float type.

When you write code that converts SQL types to Java types, you can use the constants in the Types class of the java.sql package to refer to the SQL types as shown in the previous figure. And if a constant doesn't exist for the data type, you can use an int value to refer to the data type. To get the int value for a data type in your result set, you can use the getColumnType method described in the previous figure. This is particularly useful for databases that use non-standard data types. Then, you can use the getColumnType method with a column that you know contains the non-standard type to get the int value for that data type. Then, you can use that value to test the data types of other columns. You can also use the getColumnTypeName method to get the name of the data type.

How SQL data types map to Java data types

SQL data type	Java data type
VARCHAR, LONGVARCHAR	String
BIT	boolean
TINYBIT	byte
SMALLINT	short
INTEGER	int
BIGINT	long
REAL	float
DOUBLE	double
VARBINARY, LONGVARBINARY	byte[]
NUMERIC	java.math.BigDecimal
DATE	java.sql.Date
TIME	java.sql.Time
TIMESTAMP	java.sql.Timestamp

Description

- To get the SQL data type that's used in the column of a result set, you can use the getColumnType and getColumnTypeName methods of the ResultSetMetaData class.

Figure 21-15 How SQL data types map to Java data types

Perspective

Now that you've finished this chapter, you should understand how to use JDBC to store data in a database and to retrieve data from a database. Although there's much more to learn about working with databases, those are the essential skills. To enhance your database skills, you can learn more about SQL, database management systems like MySQL or Oracle, and other JDBC features.

Summary

- With JDBC 4.0 (JDK 1.6) and later, the *database driver* that's used to connect the application to a database is loaded automatically. This is known as *automatic driver loading*. With JDBC 4.0 and later, you can also loop through any exceptions that are nested within the SQLException object.
- A Java program can use one of four driver types to access a database. *Type-1* and *type-2 drivers* run on the client's machine, while *type-3* and *type-4 drivers* can run on a server machine.
- If you connect to a Derby database with a username and create a table in a database, that table is stored in a *schema* that corresponds to the username. Then, to access that table, you need to connect to the database with the same username or qualify any reference to that table with the username.
- You can use JDBC to execute SQL statements that select, add, update, or delete one or more records in a database. You can also control the location of the *cursor* in the result set.
- You can use *prepared statements* to supply parameters to SQL statements. Since prepared statements provide better performance and security than regular statements, you should use them whenever possible.
- You can return a list of the column names and types in a result set by using *metadata*. To do this, you may need to convert SQL data types to Java data types.

Exercise 21-1 Work with JDBC

In this exercise, you'll write JDBC code that works with the Derby database named MurachDB that was described in the previous chapter.

1. Open the project named ch21_ex1_DBTester that's in the ex_starts directory. Add the derby.jar file to the Libraries folder for this project.
2. Review the code in the source files and run the project. It should print all of the records in the Products table to the console three times with some blank product lines in between.

3. Write the code for the printFirstProduct method. Use column names to retrieve the column values. Then, test the project. You can tell if this method is working correctly if it prints the first product in the list of products that's printed by the printProducts method.
4. Write the code for the printLastProduct method. To move to the last product in the result set, you can use a scrollable result set. Then, test the project.
5. Write the code for the printProductByCode method. Use a prepared statement to create the result set, and use indexes to retrieve the column values. Then, test the project.
6. Write the code for the insertProduct method. This method should begin by checking if a product with the specified product code exists in the database. If so, this method should display an error message. Otherwise, it should add the product to the database and print the product that was added to the console.
7. Test the insertProduct method. To do that, you need to run the project twice. The first time, the product should be added to the database. The second time, the product should appear in the list of products, but then an error message should be displayed indicating that the product already exists.
8. Write the code for the deleteProduct method. This method should delete the product that was added by the insertProduct method. Then, test the project.

Exercise 21-2 Use a Derby database with the Product Maintenance application

This exercise has you enhance a Product Maintenance application that uses the Derby database described in chapter 20 to store the product data. To work with that data, this application uses the ProductDB class that's presented in this chapter.

Review the code and test the application

1. Open the project named ch21_ex2_ProductMaint that's in the ex_starts directory.
2. Open the DAOFactory class. Note that the getProductDAO method has been changed so this application uses the methods in the ProductDB class to work with the Derby database.
3. Open the ProductDB class and review its code. This is the code that's presented in this chapter.
4. Open the ProductMaintApp class and review its code. Then, run this application. It should work the same as it did earlier in this book, but now it stores the data in a Derby database.

Add a disconnect method to the ProductDB class

5. Add a public method to the ProductDB class named disconnect that shuts

down the Derby database engine and returns a boolean value that indicates if the shutdown was successful.

6. Switch to the ProductMaintApp class and try to add a statement that calls the disconnect method from the ProductDB class when the application ends. Note that you can't access this method because it's being called from a static context.
7. Now, try to call the disconnect method from the ProductDAO object. This time, you won't be able to access this method because it isn't available from the ProductDAO interface.
8. Create an interface named EmbeddedDB and add a method named disconnect to it.
9. Modify the ProductDAO interface so it inherits the EmbeddedDB interface.
10. Modify the ProductMaintApp class so it calls the disconnect method from the ProductDAO object when the application ends. Then, test the application to make sure it works correctly.

Section 6

Advanced Java skills

If you have read the first 5 sections of this book, you have all the skills you need to develop console or GUI applications that work with files and databases. So far, all of these applications have run in a single thread. Now, you'll learn how to use multiple threads in a Java application whenever that's necessary. Then, you'll learn how to deploy a Java application so your users can run it.

22

How to work with threads

When you run a program in Java, the program runs in one or more threads. So far in this book, all of the programs have run within a single thread. In this chapter, you'll learn how to develop programs that run in two or more threads that perform separate tasks. For example, you can use one thread to retrieve data from a database while another thread makes a complicated calculation. Then, the program can alternate between the two tasks so it runs more efficiently.

An introduction to threads

Before you learn how to develop applications that use two or more threads, you need to understand how threads work and when you would typically use them. You also need to be familiar with the classes and interfaces you use when you work with threads, and you need to understand the life cycle of a thread. That's what you'll learn in the topics that follow

How threads work

As figure 22-1 explains, a *thread* is a single flow of execution through a program. By default, Java applications use a single thread, called the *main thread*. This thread begins executing with the first statement of a program's main method and continues executing statements in sequence until the main method exits. The program may create additional objects and call additional methods, but the flow of control is always sequential, one statement at a time.

In some cases, single-threaded execution can be inefficient. For example, imagine a program that performs two independent tasks. To accomplish the first task, the program must read data from a file, and this task spends most of its time waiting for file I/O operations to complete. As a result, the second task must wait too, even though it doesn't require any I/O operations.

The first diagram in this figure shows how this program might work when executed as a single thread. First, the program performs the first task. In this case, the CPU is idle while it waits for the I/O operations required by this task. When the first task is complete, the program runs the second task.

The second diagram shows how this program could benefit from being split into two threads, one to perform each task. As you can see, using two threads allows the two tasks to overlap, so the second task is executed while the first task waits on I/O operations. The result is that the two tasks finish sooner than they would if they were executed as a single thread.

Applications that perform several tasks that aren't dependent on one another benefit the most from *multithreading*. For example, the second task shown in this figure can only be overlapped with the first task if the second task doesn't depend on the results of the first task. If the second task depends on the results of the first task, some overlap may still be possible. But the two tasks must communicate with each other so they can coordinate their operations. As you'll learn later in this chapter, managing this sort of coordination can be challenging.

Typical uses for threads

In addition to showing the basics of how threads work, figure 22-1 lists three of the most common uses for threads. The first is to improve the performance of I/O operations. Any application that performs extensive I/O can benefit from multithreading. That's because I/O operations are thousands of times slower than CPU operations. So any program that reads data from a disk spends almost all of its time waiting for that information to be retrieved.

How using threads can improve performance

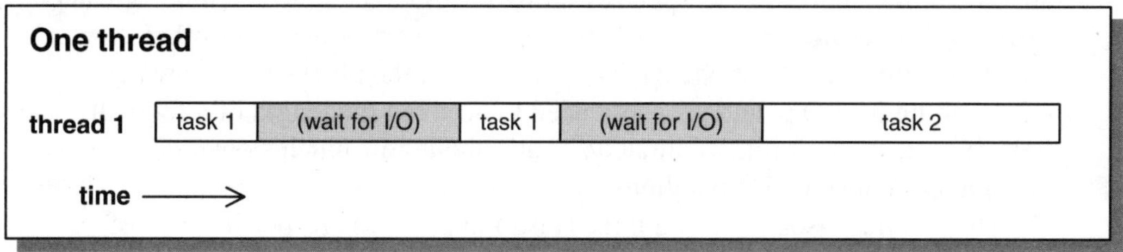

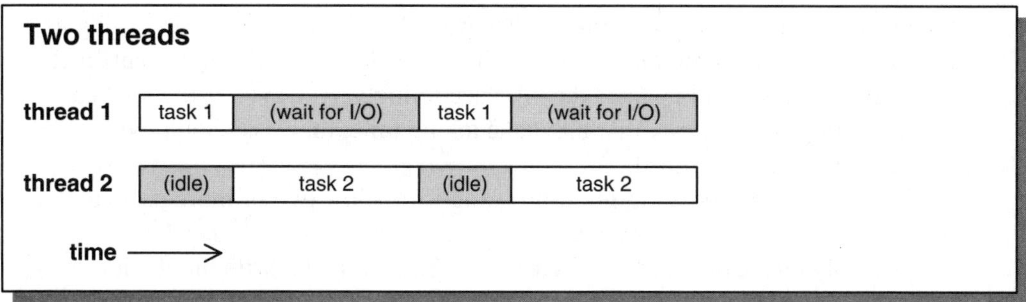

Typical uses for threads

- To improve the performance of applications with extensive I/O operations
- To improve the responsiveness of GUI applications
- To allow two or more users to run server-based applications simultaneously

Description

- A *thread* is a single sequential flow of control within a program. A thread often completes a specific task.
- By default, a Java application uses a single thread, called the *main thread*. However, some programs can benefit by using two or more threads to allow different parts of the program to execute simultaneously.
- On a computer that has just one *central processing unit*, or *CPU*, the threads don't actually execute simultaneously. Instead, a part of the Java virtual machine called the *thread scheduler* alternately lets portions of each thread execute. This gives the appearance that all of the tasks are running at the same time, and this can make an application work more efficiently.

Figure 22-1 How threads work

To give you some perspective on this, you should realize that the actual amount of time that the CPU spends waiting for I/O to complete is much greater than what's indicated in figure 22-1. In fact, since each of the blocks that show task 1 executing are about one half of an inch long, the blocks that show the CPU waiting for I/O would probably need to be about the length of a football field to show the wait time accurately. That's about how much slower disk operations are than CPU operations.

The second reason for using threads is to improve the responsiveness of programs that use graphical user interfaces. For example, when a user clicks a toolbar button, he or she expects the program to respond immediately, even if the program is busy doing something else. A GUI application that uses Swing as described in section 4 automatically runs in a thread that handles the events that are fired by the user and updates the GUI accordingly. However, if the application needs to perform a task that may take a long time, this task should be performed in a second thread.

The final reason for using multithreading is to allow two or more users to run server-based applications simultaneously. For example, Java *servlets* automatically create one thread for each user. You learned a little bit about servlets in chapter 1, and you can learn more about them in our book, *Murach's Java Servlets and JSP*. For now, you should just realize that each person who uses a servlet runs it in a separate thread. As a result, when you write servlet code, you must make sure that the code is thread-safe.

Classes and interfaces for working with threads

Figure 22-2 presents two classes and an interface that you can use to create and work with threads and summarizes the key methods they provide. As you can see, the Thread class inherits the Object class, which means it has access to all of its public and protected methods. In addition, the Thread class implements the Runnable interface. Because the Runnable interface declares a single method named run, that means that the Thread class must implement this method.

To create a thread, you can use one of two techniques. First, you can define a class that inherits the Thread class. This class should override the run method so it contains the code to be executed by the thread. Then, you can instantiate this class to create a thread.

The second way to create a thread is to define a class that implements the Runnable interface. To do that, this class must implement the run method. Then, you pass an instance of this class to a constructor of the Thread class. This creates a thread that executes the Runnable object by calling its run method.

If these two techniques seem confusing right now, don't worry. They will become clearer when you see examples later in this chapter. For now, you just need to know that the Thread class defines a thread, but the code that's executed by the thread can be provided by any class that implements the Runnable interface.

The Object class also has some methods that can be used for threading. These methods are used to enable threads to easily communicate with each other. You'll learn about them later in this chapter.

Classes and interfaces used to create threads

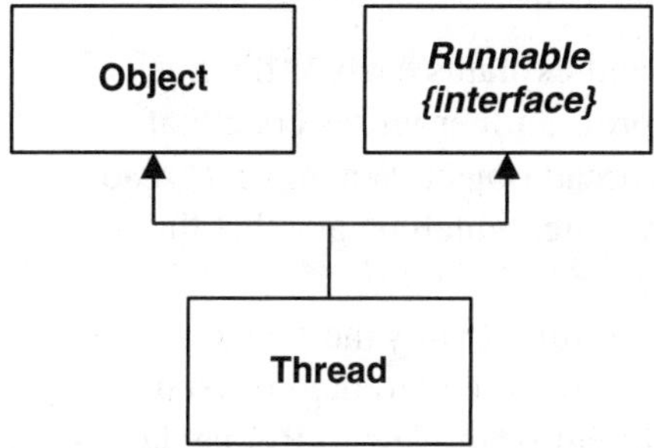

Summary of these classes and interfaces

Class/Interface	Description
Thread	A class that defines a thread. This class inherits the Object class and implements the Runnable interface.
Runnable	An interface that must be implemented by any class whose objects are going to be executed by a thread. The only method in this interface is the run method.
Object	The Object class has several methods that are used for threading. These methods are described in figure 22-10.

Key methods of the Thread class, Runnable interface, and Object class

Method	Class/Interface	Description
`start`	Thread	Registers this thread with the thread scheduler so it's available for execution.
`run`	Runnable, Thread	An abstract method that's declared by the Runnable interface and implemented by the Thread class. The thread scheduler calls this method to run the thread.
`sleep`	Thread	Causes the current thread to wait (sleep) for a specified period of time so the CPU can run other threads.
`wait`	Object	Causes the current thread to wait until another thread calls the notify or notifyAll method for the current object.
`notify`	Object	Notifies one arbitrary thread that's waiting on this object that it can resume execution.
`notifyAll`	Object	Notifies all the threads that are waiting on this object that they can resume execution.

Two ways to create a thread

- Inherit the Thread class.
- Implement the Runnable interface, then pass a reference to the Runnable object to the constructor of the Thread class. This is useful if the thread needs to inherit a class other than the Thread class.

Description

- After you create a Thread object, you can call its start method so the thread scheduler can run the thread. Then, you can use the other methods shown above to manage the thread.

Figure 22-2 Classes and interfaces for working with threads

The life cycle of a thread

Figure 22-3 shows the life cycle of a thread and explains each of the five states a thread can be in. To create a thread, the programmer writes code that defines a class for the thread and instantiates a Thread object. When the Thread object is first instantiated, it is placed in the New state, which means that the thread has been created but is not yet ready to be run.

When the program is ready for the thread to be run, it calls the thread's start method. Although you might think that this causes the thread to begin execution, all it really does is change the state of the thread from New to Runnable. Once it's in the Runnable state, the thread joins a list of any other threads that are also in the Runnable state. Then, a component of the Java virtual machine called the *thread scheduler* selects one of the Runnable threads to be executed.

Note that Java doesn't have a separate state for the thread that's running. The state of the thread that's running, as well as all other threads that are eligible to be running, is Runnable. Also, the thread scheduler may at any time decide that the thread that's currently running has been running long enough. Then, the thread scheduler interrupts that thread and lets one of the other Runnable threads run. This doesn't change the state of either thread.

A thread enters the Blocked state if a condition occurs that makes the thread temporarily not runnable. For example, a thread becomes Blocked when it is waiting for an I/O operation to complete. The thread automatically returns to the Runnable state when the I/O operation completes. A thread that's in Blocked state can't be selected for execution by the thread scheduler.

The Waiting state comes into play when threads need to coordinate their activities. You'll learn more about how this works later in this chapter. For now, just realize that a thread can voluntarily enter the Waiting state by calling the wait method. While in the Waiting state, the thread can't run. It remains in Waiting state until another thread calls the notify or notifyAll method to let the thread know that it can resume.

Finally, when the run method of a thread finishes execution, the thread's state is changed to Terminated. Once a thread has entered the Terminated state, it remains there until the application ends.

The life cycle of a thread

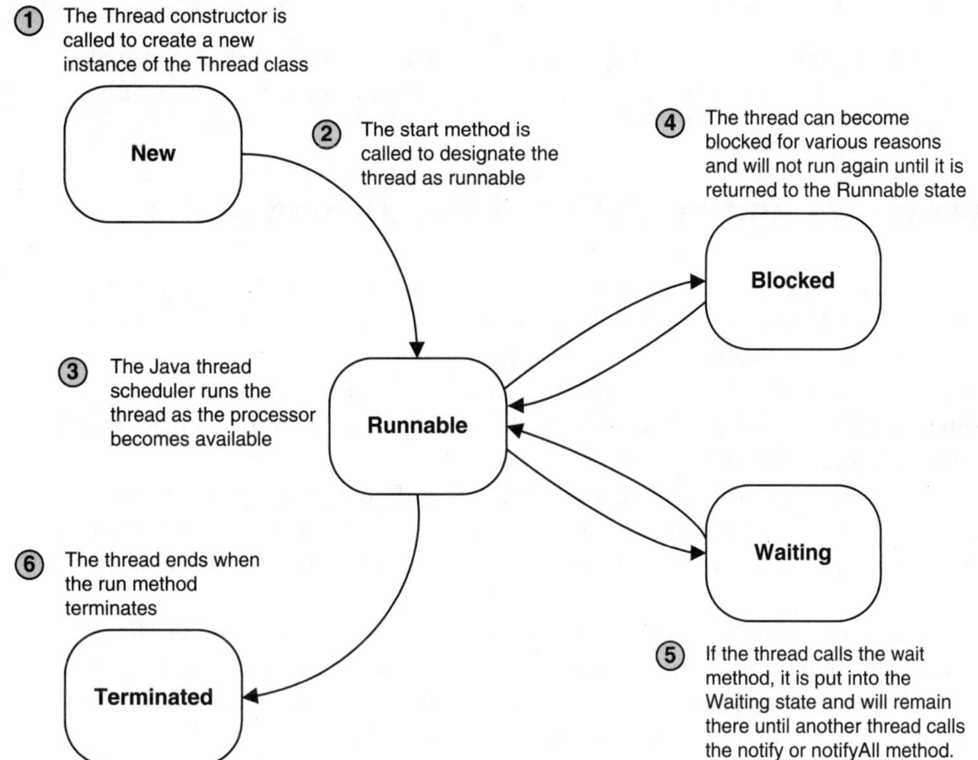
1 The Thread constructor is called to create a new instance of the Thread class
New
2 The start method is called to designate the thread as runnable
4 The thread can become blocked for various reasons and will not run again until it is returned to the Runnable state
Blocked
3 The Java thread scheduler runs the thread as the processor becomes available
Runnable
Waiting
6 The thread ends when the run method terminates
Terminated
5 If the thread calls the wait method, it is put into the Waiting state and will remain there until another thread calls the notify or notifyAll method.

Thread states

State	Description
New	The thread has been created (its constructor has been called), but not yet started.
Runnable	The thread's start method has been called and the thread is available to be run by the thread scheduler. A thread in Runnable state may actually be running, or it may be waiting in the thread queue for an opportunity to run.
Blocked	The thread has been temporarily removed from the Runnable state so it can't be executed. This can happen if the thread's sleep method is called, if the thread is waiting on I/O, or if the thread requests a lock on an object that's already locked. When the condition changes (for example, the I/O operation completes), the thread is returned to the Runnable state.
Waiting	The thread has called its wait method so that other threads can access an object. The thread remains in the Waiting state until another thread calls the notify or notifyAll method.
Terminated	The thread's run method has ended.

Description

- All threads have a life cycle that can include five states: New, Runnable, Blocked, Waiting, and Terminated.

Figure 22-3 The life cycle of a thread

How to create threads

In the topics that follow, you'll learn two ways to create a thread. But first, you'll learn more about the Thread class, which you must use regardless of how you create a thread.

Constructors and methods of the Thread class

The first table in figure 22-4 summarizes some of the constructors you can use to create Thread objects. The first constructor is used by default when you instantiate a class that inherits the Thread class. (Of course, you can also overload this constructor or define other constructors just as you can for any subclass.) The second constructor is used to create a thread from an object that implements the Runnable interface.

The third and fourth constructors let you specify the name of the thread that's created. By default, threads are named numerically (Thread-0, Thread-1, etc.). Since you don't typically refer to threads by name, the defaults are usually acceptable.

The second table in this figure presents some of the methods of the Thread class. You can use these methods to get information about a thread and to control when a thread runs and when it waits. Although most of these methods are self-explanatory, two require further explanation. First, you can use the setDaemon method to create a subordinate thread known as a *daemon thread* (pronounced *dee*-mon, not *day*-mon). When you create a daemon thread, that thread ends when the thread that started it ends. If you don't use this method to explicitly create a daemon thread, the thread is considered a *user thread*. User threads continue running even if the thread that created them ends.

Second, although it may seem like you could use the yield method to allow another thread to run, this method only provides a hint to the thread scheduler that the current thread is willing to yield to other threads. Often, the thread scheduler ignores this hint. In addition, the thread scheduler is implemented differently on each platform. As a result, the yield method works a little differently on each platform.

Even on the same platform, the yield method may work differently each time you test the application. That's because it depends on the load that's currently on the processor. Since you can't rely on the yield method to behave in a particular way, you will rarely ever want to use this method. If you do use it, you should test it thoroughly to make sure it gives the desired results on all systems.

The Thread class

```
java.lang.Thread;
```

Common constructors of the Thread class

Constructor	Description
`Thread()`	Creates a default Thread object.
`Thread(Runnable)`	Creates a Thread object from any object that implements the Runnable interface.
`Thread(String)`	Creates a Thread object with the specified name.
`Thread(Runnable, String)`	Creates a Thread object with the specified name from any object that implements the Runnable interface.

Common methods of the Thread class

Method	Description
`run()`	Implements the run method of the Runnable interface. This method should be overridden in all subclasses to provide the code that's executed by a thread.
`start()`	Places a thread in the Runnable state so it can be run by the thread scheduler.
`getName()`	Returns the name of a thread.
`currentThread()`	A static method that returns a reference to the currently executing thread.
`setDaemon(boolean)`	If the boolean value is true, marks a thread as a daemon thread. This means it's a subordinate thread that ends when the thread that created it ends.
`sleep(long)`	A static method that places the currently executing thread in the Blocked state for the specified number of milliseconds so other threads can run.
`interrupt()`	Interrupts a thread.
`isInterrupted()`	Returns a true value if a thread has been interrupted.
`yield()`	A static method that gives a hint to the thread scheduler that the current thread is willing to yield so other threads can run. The thread scheduler may or may not use this hint. As a result, any use of this method should be thoroughly tested to make sure it provides the desired results on all systems.

Description

- By default, the threads that you create explicitly are named numerically. If that's not what you want, you can specify the name on the constructor of the thread.
- By default, a thread is independent of the thread that created it. This is called a *user thread*. Or, you can use the setDaemon method to create a *daemon thread*.
- The sleep method throws InterruptedException. Because this is a checked exception, you must throw or catch this exception when you use the sleep method.

Figure 22-4 Constructors and methods of the Thread class

How to create a thread by extending the Thread class

Figure 22-5 presents a procedure for creating a thread by extending the Thread class. To illustrate this procedure, this figure presents two classes. The Main class contains the main method that's run when the application starts, and the IOThread class defines a thread that simulates an I/O operation.

The IOThread class starts by inheriting the Thread class. Then, it overrides the run method to provide the code that's executed when the thread is run. Within this method, the first statement prints the name of the thread. Then, the run method uses the static sleep method to place the thread in Blocked state for 2000 milliseconds (2 seconds). After 2 seconds expire, the thread is returned to Runnable state so the thread scheduler can resume its execution.

Because the sleep method can throw InterruptedException, that exception must be either caught or thrown. As you'll learn in figure 22-8, this exception indicates that some other thread is attempting to interrupt the current thread while it is sleeping. How you deal with this exception depends on the application. In this case, the application simply ignores any attempts to interrupt the thread by catching the exception but not providing any code to process it. Normally, "swallowing" an exception like this is not a good programming practice. In this case, however, it's appropriate.

If you use the sleep method, you should also realize that it doesn't guarantee that the thread will start running after the amount of time you specify. Instead, it simply guarantees that the thread will be returned to the Runnable state after that amount of time. It's up to the thread scheduler to decide when the thread will resume execution. Because of that, you shouldn't use the sleep method for applications that require precise timing.

The Main class contains the main method for the application. Within this method, the first statement calls the currentThread method of the Thread class and assigns the Thread object that's returned to a variable named t1. Then, the second statement uses the println method to display a message that indicates that the thread has started. To include the name of the thread in this message, this code uses the getName method to get the name of the current thread.

The third statement creates the IOThread object and assigns it to a Thread variable named t2. Then, the fourth statement starts the thread by calling its start method. This places the thread in the Runnable state so the thread scheduler can run it. The fifth statement prints a message indicating that the main thread has started the second thread. And the sixth statement prints a message indicating that the main thread has finished.

The first three lines of the output shown at the bottom of this figure are printed by the main method, which runs in a thread named "main". Then, the next two lines are printed by the thread that's created from the IOThread class, named "Thread-0". The first line is printed at the beginning of the run method to indicate that the thread has started, and the second line is printed at the end of the run method to indicate that the thread has finished. This output shows that the main thread can continue executing while the code in the second thread executes. In other words, the statements in the main method don't have to wait for the statements in the run method of the second thread to finish.

A procedure for creating a thread from the Thread class

1. Create a class that inherits the Thread class.
2. Override the run method to perform the desired task.
3. Create the thread by instantiating an object from the class.
4. Call the start method of the thread object.

A Main class that starts a thread

```
public class Main
{
    public static void main(String[] args)
    {
        Thread t1 = Thread.currentThread();
        System.out.println(t1.getName() + " started.");

        Thread t2 = new IOThread();    // create the IO thread
        t2.start();                    // start the IO thread
        System.out.println(t1.getName() + " starts " + t2.getName() + ".");

        System.out.println(t1.getName() + " finished.");
    }
}
```

A class named IOThread that defines a thread

```
public class IOThread extends Thread
{
    @Override
    public void run()
    {
        System.out.println(this.getName() + " started.");

        try
        {
            Thread.sleep(2000);    // Sleep for 2 seconds to simulate
                                   // an IO task that takes a long time
        }
        catch(InterruptedException e) {}

        System.out.println(this.getName() + " finished.");
    }
}
```

Sample output

```
main started.
main starts Thread-0.
main finished.
Thread-0 started.
Thread-0 finished.
```

Figure 22-5 How to create a thread by extending the Thread class

How to create a thread by implementing the Runnable interface

Figure 22-6 shows a procedure for creating a thread by implementing the Runnable interface. Although this method of creating threads requires a little more code, it's also more flexible because it lets you define a thread that inherits a class other than the Thread class. As a result, it's used more often than the technique you saw in the previous figure.

If you compare this code to the code in the previous figure, you'll notice several differences. First, because the IOTask class doesn't inherit the Thread class, you can't create a Thread object directly from it. Instead, you have to create a Runnable object and pass it to the constructor of the Thread class. This is shown in the third statement of the main method.

Second, the IOTask class differs in several ways from the IOThread class. To start, the IOTask class implements the Runnable interface rather than extending the Thread class. Then, within the run method of the IOTask class, the first statement calls the static currentThread method of the Thread class to get a reference to the thread that's currently executing. That way, the getName method can be used to get the name of this thread.

A procedure for creating a thread using the Runnable interface

1. Create a class that implements the Runnable interface.
2. Implement the run method to perform the desired task.
3. Create the thread by supplying an instance of the Runnable class to the Thread constructor.
4. Call the start method of the thread object.

A Main class that starts a thread using the Runnable interface

```
public class Main
{
    public static void main(String[] args)
    {
        Thread t1 = Thread.currentThread();
        System.out.println(t1.getName() + " started.");

        Thread t2 = new Thread(new IOTask());      // create the new thread
        t2.start();                                // start the new thread
        System.out.println(t1.getName() + " starts " + t2.getName() + ".");

        System.out.println(t1.getName() + " finished.");
    }
}
```

An IOTask class that implements the Runnable interface

```
public class IOTask implements Runnable
{
    @Override
    public void run()
    {
        Thread ct = Thread.currentThread();
        System.out.println(ct.getName() + " started.");

        try
        {
            Thread.sleep(2000);    // Sleep for 2 seconds to simulate
                                   // an IO task that takes a long time
        }
        catch(InterruptedException e) {}

        System.out.println(ct.getName() + " finished.");
    }
}
```

Note

- The output from this code is similar to the output shown in figure 22-5.

Figure 22-6 How to create a thread by implementing the Runnable interface

How to manipulate threads

Once you've created a thread, Java provides several methods you can use to control how the thread executes. The most common way to control how a thread executes is to use the sleep method as shown in the previous figures. Now, this topic presents some other methods of the Thread class that you can use to manipulate threads.

How to set a thread's priority

Figure 22-7 shows how to prioritize threads. When a thread is created, it's given a priority value between 1 and 10, where 10 is the highest priority and 1 is the lowest priority. Then, the thread scheduler takes these priorities into account when it determines which of several Runnable threads should be run next.

However, depending on the operating system and Java version, thread priorities may be handled differently. In some cases, they might not have any effect at all. In other cases, they might not work as you would intuitively expect. Although you can still set thread priorities, you shouldn't rely on them to coordinate thread tasks. To do that, you can use the wait and notifyAll methods as described later in this chapter.

In the example in this figure, the main method sets the priority of the IOTask thread to the minimum priority. On some systems, this may cause the thread scheduler to only run the IOTask thread when no other threads are running, which may be what you want. On other systems, the thread scheduler may schedule these threads differently. The only way to make sure this yields the desired result is to thoroughly test it on all platforms.

The setPriority method of the Thread class

Method	Description
`setPriority(int)`	Changes this thread's priority to an int value from 1 to 10. This provides a hint to the thread scheduler about the thread's priority. However, the thread scheduler may or may not use this hint.

Fields of the Thread class used to set thread priorities

Field	Description
`MAX_PRIORITY`	The maximum priority of any thread (an int value of 10).
`MIN_PRIORITY`	The minimum priority of any thread (an int value of 1).
`NORM_PRIORITY`	The default priority of any thread (an int value of 5).

A Main class that sets the priority of a thread

```
public class Main
{
    public static void main(String[] args)
    {
        Thread t1 = new Thread(new IOTask());
        t1.setPriority(Thread.MIN_PRIORITY);
        t1.start();
        .
        .
        .
    }
}
```

Description

- By default, every thread is given the priority of the thread that created it. If a thread is created from the main thread, it's given a priority of 5 by default.
- Since thread scheduling relies on the underlying system, the result of setting a thread's priority may vary depending on the platform.

Figure 22-7 How to set a thread's priority

How to interrupt a thread

In some cases, you may need to interrupt the thread that's currently executing. To do that, you use the interrupt method of the Thread class as shown in figure 22-8.

The application in this figure defines a thread named Counter that counts one-second intervals. This thread continues counting until the user presses the Enter key. To accomplish this, the main method starts the Counter thread and then enters a while loop that uses the next method of the Scanner class to wait for the user to press the Enter key. When that happens, the main method calls the Counter thread's interrupt method to interrupt the thread.

In the Counter thread's run method, several statements are required to properly detect that the thread has been interrupted. First, notice that the while loop repeats as long as the isInterrupted method of the thread returns a value of false. All threads maintain an internal flag that indicates whether the thread has been interrupted. If another thread calls the current thread's interrupt method, that flag is set to true. You can use the isInterrupted method to determine the setting of this flag.

Unfortunately, the isInterrupted method only works if the other thread (in this case, the main thread) calls the Counter thread's interrupt method while the Counter thread is executing. If the Counter thread is interrupted while it is in the Blocked state (for example, because it has called the sleep method), the thread's interrupted flag isn't set. Instead, InterruptedException is thrown. To allow the thread to be interrupted while it is sleeping, the sleep method shown in this figure is coded within a try/catch block. Then, when the catch clause catches the InterruptedException, it uses a break statement to terminate the while loop.

The output shown in this figure illustrates how this application works. Once the main method starts the Counter thread, this thread begins displaying numbers on the console at one-second intervals. Meanwhile, the main thread waits for the user to press the Enter key at the console. When the user presses the Enter key, the main method calls the Counter thread's interrupt method. The Counter thread detects this, either by seeing that isInterrupted returns true or by catching the InterruptedException. In either case, the Counter thread terminates.

If you code a sleep method within a loop as shown in this figure, NetBeans marks that statement with a warning. NetBeans does this because calling the sleep method repeatedly within a loop can cause poor performance for the thread. In this figure, though, the code is supposed to run slowly to illustrate a point. As a result, you can ignore this warning or suppress it. To do that, you can move the cursor into the statement that contains the sleep method, press the Alt+Enter keystroke, and respond to the resulting prompt.

A Main class that interrupts a thread

```
import java.util.Scanner;

public class Main
{
    public static void main(String[] args)
    {
        System.out.println("Press the Enter key to stop counting.");
        Thread counter = new Thread(new Counter());
        counter.start();                    // start the counter thread
        Scanner sc = new Scanner(System.in);
        String s = "start";
        while (!s.equals(""))               // wait for the user to press Enter
            s = sc.nextLine();
        counter.interrupt();                // interrupt the counter thread
    }
}
```

A Counter class that defines a task that can be interrupted

```
public class Counter implements Runnable
{
    @Override
    public void run()
    {
        Thread ct = Thread.currentThread();
        int count = 1;
        while (!ct.isInterrupted())
        {
            System.out.println(ct.getName() + " count " + count);
            count++;
            try
            {
                Thread.sleep(1000);    // Sleep for 1 second
            }
            catch(InterruptedException e)
            {
                break;
            }
        }
        System.out.println(ct.getName() + " interrupted.");
    }
}
```

Sample output

```
Press the Enter key to stop counting.
Thread-0 count 1
Thread-0 count 2
Thread-0 count 3

Thread-0 interrupted.
```

Description

- If a thread is interrupted while it is sleeping, InterruptedException is thrown. In this case, the isInterrupted method won't indicate that the thread has been interrupted.

Figure 22-8 How to interrupt a thread

How to synchronize threads

So far, the threads you've seen execute independently of each other. These types of threads are known as *asynchronous threads*. In the next two topics, you'll learn how to work with threads that share resources and must be synchronized. These types of threads are known as *synchronous threads*.

How to create synchronized threads

Whenever you create an application that uses more than one thread, you need to think about any *concurrency* issues that the application might face. Concurrency issues result from conflicts that can occur when two or more threads attempt to access the same object at the same time. For example, suppose you create a multithreaded application that includes a method named calculateFutureValue that calculates future values using a for loop. If you then created a single instance of this object and let multiple threads call the calculateFutureValue method at the same time, the calculations would interfere with one another. Then, the results of most, if not all, of the threads would be inaccurate.

To solve this type of problem, you can synchronize the threads that have access to the object. To do that, you use the synchronized keyword as shown in figure 22-9. As you can see, you can code this keyword on a method declaration. Then, the Java virtual machine guarantees that when a thread calls the method, no other thread can call it until the first thread is done with it.

The first example in this figure shows a synchronized version of the calculateFutureValue method. Because the synchronized keyword is used, this method can be used safely in a multithreaded application.

The second example shows that a method doesn't have to be long or complicated to require the synchronized keyword. Here, the method consists of a single statement that increments a variable and returns the incremented value. You might be tempted to think that this method wouldn't have to be synchronized. After all, if two threads call it at the same time, won't the first thread execute the method's single statement and exit before the second thread has a chance to execute the same statement? Not necessarily. The problem is that even a single statement like this can be compiled to several Java bytecode instructions. Because of that, the thread scheduler could switch to another thread between any of these instructions.

The synchronized keyword works by *locking* the object. Once the object is locked, no other thread can obtain a lock on the object until the synchronized method ends and the lock is released. Note that it is the object itself that's locked, not the synchronized method. As a result, when a thread calls a synchronized method, other threads are prevented from running any of the object's synchronized methods, not just the method called by the first thread. However, other threads aren't prevented from running unsynchronized methods. That's because an object's lock isn't checked when an unsynchronized method is called.

The syntax for creating a synchronized method

```
public|private synchronized returnType methodName([parameterList])
{
   statements
}
```

Example 1: A synchronized method that calculates future values

```
public synchronized double calculateFutureValue(double monthlyPayment,
double yearlyInterestRate, int years)
{
    int months = years * 12;
    double monthlyInterestRate = yearlyInterestRate/12/100;
    double futureValue = 0;
    for (int i = 1; i <= months; i++)
    {
        futureValue = (futureValue + monthlyPayment) *
                      (1 + monthlyInterestRate);
    }
    return futureValue;
}
```

Example 2: A synchronized method that increments an instance variable

```
public synchronized int getInvoiceNumber()
{
    return invoiceNumber++;
}
```

Description

- Whenever two or more threads can access an object, *concurrency* is an important issue. Concurrency problems can result because a thread running a method may be interrupted in the middle of the method so control can be given to another thread that runs the same method. When that happens, the intermediate results from the first thread can affect the accuracy of the second thread.
- The synchronized keyword assures that only one thread at a time is allowed to execute any *synchronized method* of an object by *locking* the object. Any other thread that attempts to run any synchronized method for the object is blocked until the first thread releases the lock by exiting the synchronized method.
- A thread can run an unsynchronized method of an object even if the object is locked. That's because the object isn't checked for a lock unless a synchronized method is executed.
- You should use synchronized methods whenever two or more threads might execute the same method. Even methods with just one line of code typically need to be synchronized.

Figure 22-9 How to create synchronized threads

How to communicate among threads

When you use synchronized methods in a multithreaded application, you sometimes need a way for the threads to communicate with each other so they can coordinate their operations. For example, imagine an application in which two or more threads add orders to a queue, and two or more threads retrieve orders from the queue so they can be processed. For this application, the threads that add orders to the queue might need a way to notify the threads that retrieve the orders that an order is ready for processing.

As figure 22-10 shows, Java provides three methods you can use to accomplish this: wait, notify, and notifyAll. The wait method is used in a synchronized method to temporarily release the lock it holds on the current object. This places the thread object in the Waiting state until another method calls the notify or notifyAll method to return it to the Runnable state. (Although the notify and notifyAll methods perform similar functions, in practice, the notify method is rarely used. I'll explain why in a moment.)

To understand how this works, the first example in this figure shows code that might be used in a thread that retrieves orders from a queue. This code causes the thread to wait until an order is available in the queue before it retrieves the order. Here, a while loop tests the value returned by the queue's count method. If it is zero, meaning that no orders are available, the wait method is called. This places the thread in the Waiting state, allowing other threads to execute.

The second example shows code that might be used by a thread that adds orders to the queue. Here, the first statement adds an order to the queue. Then, the second statement calls the notifyAll method of the thread. This restores all the waiting threads to the Runnable state. That way, one of the threads can retrieve and process the order.

I mentioned previously that the notifyAll method is usually preferred over the notify method. The problem with the notify method is that it only restores one waiting thread to the Runnable state, and it doesn't guarantee that this thread will be able to process the order. That's why it's better to call notifyAll to restore all waiting threads to the Runnable state. Then, each of these threads can determine whether they can process the order.

This is also why the wait method is placed in a while loop in the first example. Since all waiting threads are returned to the Runnable state when notifyAll is called, each thread must again test the condition it is waiting for (in this case, that at least one order is in the queue) before proceeding. If the condition has not been met, the thread should wait again.

If you're having trouble understanding the examples shown in this figure, don't worry. The rest of this chapter presents a complete version of an order queuing application. Once you see this complete application, the wait and notifyAll methods should become clear.

Methods of the Object class for thread communication

Method	Description
`wait()`	Places the current thread in the Waiting state until another thread calls the notify or notifyAll method of the current object. This relinquishes the lock on the object so that other blocked threads can run. Throws InterruptedException.
`notify()`	Returns an arbitrary thread to the Runnable state.
`notifyAll()`	Returns all threads to the Runnable state so the scheduler can select one to run.

Example 1: Code that waits on a condition

```
while (orderQueue.count() == 0)        // if there are no orders ready, wait
{
    try
    {
        wait();
    }
    catch (InterruptedException e) {}
}
```

Example 2: Code that satisfies the condition and notifies other threads

```
orderQueue.add(order);                // add an order to the queue
notifyAll();                          // notify other threads
```

Description

- In some multithreaded applications, it's important for threads to inform one another when certain events have occurred or conditions have been met. The wait, notify, and notifyAll methods provide for this type of communication.
- The wait method releases the lock on the current object so other threads can execute synchronized methods. The effect of the wait method is to interrupt the current thread until another thread calls the notify or notifyAll method.
- The notifyAll method restores all the threads that are waiting for the current object's lock to the Runnable state. The Java thread scheduler then selects one of the threads for execution.
- The notify method is similar to the notifyAll method, but it restores only one arbitrarily selected thread to the Runnable state. Since this thread may not be able to perform its function, the notifyAll method is typically used instead.
- The wait, notify, and notifyAll methods can only be used in synchronized methods. If you call one of these methods from an unsynchronized method, IllegalMonitorStateException is thrown.

Figure 22-10 How to communicate among threads

The Order Queue application

The following topics present a multithreaded application that demonstrates many of the threading concepts presented in this chapter. Before I present the code for this application, I'll present an overview of the application and its operation. Then, I'll summarize the various classes used by the application.

The operation

Figure 22-11 presents the operation of the Order Queue application. The diagram at the top of this figure shows how the application uses multiple OrderTaker threads to create orders and add them to the queue and multiple OrderHandler threads to remove orders from the queue and process them. The queue itself is managed by a class named OrderQueue that runs in its own thread (the main thread).

So you can focus on the threading aspects of this application, each order is represented by an Order object that consists of just an order number. Obviously, a more realistic Order object would include additional details, such as customer, product, and payment information.

The OrderTaker and OrderHandler classes are also simplified. In this application, the OrderTaker class simply creates a specified number of orders at one-second intervals, displaying a message on the console as each order is created. Similarly, the OrderHandler class retrieves an order from the queue, displays it on the console, and then waits two seconds before retrieving another order. In a more realistic application, the OrderTaker class would get input from a user about each order, and the OrderHandler class would print invoices, update customer information, and so on.

If you study the console output shown in this figure, you'll see that the Order Queue application begins by displaying information about the OrderTaker and OrderHandler threads. The number of OrderTaker and OrderHandler threads can easily be changed, as can the number of orders to be created by each OrderTaker thread. For this example, the application creates three OrderTaker threads, each of which creates three orders. As a result, a total of nine orders are created. In addition, the application creates two OrderHandler threads.

After displaying this initial information, the application starts the OrderTaker and OrderHandler threads. Each OrderTaker thread displays a message when it creates an order, and each OrderHandler thread displays a message when it processes an order. As you can see, nine orders are created by the three OrderTaker threads, and nine orders are eventually processed by the two OrderHandler threads.

Incidentally, the design of the Order Queue application is based on a commonly-used design pattern called the *producer/consumer pattern*. This design pattern uses a queue to coordinate *producers*—objects that create items that need to be processed—with *consumers*—objects that process the items created by the producers.

The operation of the Order Queue application

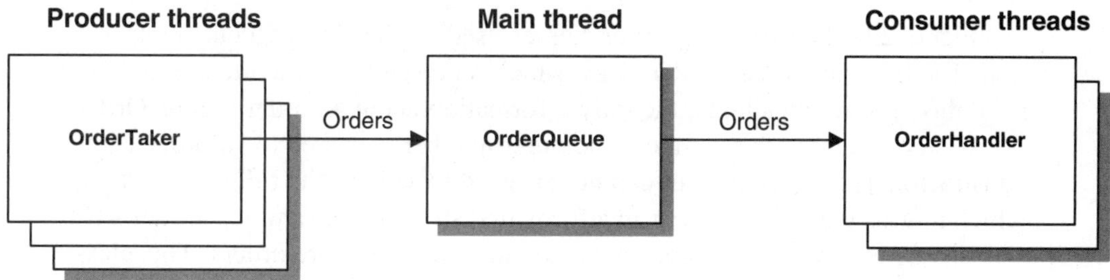

Sample output from the Order Queue application

```
Starting the order queue.
Starting 3 order taker threads, each producing 3 orders.
Starting 2 order handler threads.

     OrderTaker threads               OrderHandler threads
============================     =============================
Order #1 created by Thread-1
Order #2 created by Thread-2
                                 Order #1 processed by Thread-3
                                 Order #2 processed by Thread-4
Order #3 created by Thread-0
Order #4 created by Thread-1
Order #5 created by Thread-2
Order #6 created by Thread-0
                                 Order #3 processed by Thread-3
                                 Order #4 processed by Thread-4
Order #7 created by Thread-1
Order #8 created by Thread-2
Order #9 created by Thread-0
                                 Order #5 processed by Thread-3
                                 Order #6 processed by Thread-4
                                 Order #7 processed by Thread-3
                                 Order #8 processed by Thread-4
                                 Order #9 processed by Thread-3
```

Description

- This application simulates a multithreaded ordering application in which multiple order takers, each running the application in a separate thread, generate orders that are added to a queue that runs in the application's main thread. The orders are then handled by multiple order-handling threads, which remove orders from the queue and display them on the console.
- This application is an example of a common design pattern called *producer/ consumer*. With this pattern, threads that produce objects place them in a queue so the objects can later be retrieved by threads that consume them.

Figure 22-11 The operation of the Order Queue application

The classes

Figure 22-12 describes the four classes used by the Order Queue application. The first class is the Order class, which represents an individual order. To keep this application simple, the only information about an order that an Order object stores is the order number. The order number is passed to an order via its constructor. Then, this number can be retrieved by calling the toString method, which returns the order number in a formatted string (for example, "Order #1").

The OrderQueue class represents the queue used to store orders. This class uses a linked list internally to store the Order objects. It has two methods, both of which are synchronized. The pushOrder method adds an order to the queue, and the pullOrder method retrieves an order from the queue.

The OrderTaker class creates orders by adding them to the queue. It sleeps for one second between each order it creates. This class is designed to be run as a thread, so it extends the Thread class and implements the run method. Unlike the other thread classes you've seen, the OrderTaker class includes a constructor that accepts two parameters. The first parameter indicates how many orders the thread should create before ending. The second parameter holds a reference to the OrderQueue object that the orders should be added to.

The OrderHandler class retrieves orders from the order queue. It too is designed to run as a thread, so it extends the Thread class and defines its operations in the run method. It also includes a constructor that accepts a parameter that refers to the OrderQueue object that the orders should be retrieved from.

The Order class

Constructor	Description
Order(int number)	Creates an Order object with the specified number.
Method	**Description**
toString()	Returns a string in the form "Order #*n*," where *n* is the order number.

The OrderQueue class

Method	Description
pushOrder(Order order)	Adds the specified order to the queue.
Order **pullOrder**()	Retrieves the first available order from the queue.

The OrderTaker class

Constructor	Description
OrderTaker(int orderCount, OrderQueue queue)	Creates a new order taker that adds the specified number of orders to the queue.
Method	**Description**
run()	Adds the number of orders specified by the constructor to the queue specified by the constructor. A message is displayed on the console for each order added, and the thread sleeps for one second between orders.

The OrderHandler class

Constructor	Description
OrderHandler(OrderQueue queue)	Creates a new order handler that reads orders from the specified queue.
Method	**Description**
run()	Retrieves orders from the queue specified by the constructor. A message is displayed on the console for each order retrieved, and the thread sleeps for two seconds between orders.

Description

- An Order object represents an order.
- An OrderQueue object uses a linked list to store orders created by the OrderTaker threads so they can be retrieved by the OrderHandler threads.
- An OrderTaker object runs in a separate thread, creates orders at one-second intervals, and adds them to a queue. The constructor lets you specify how many orders to create before the thread terminates.
- An OrderHandler object runs in a separate thread and removes orders from the queue at two-second intervals.

Figure 22-12 The classes used by the Order Queue application

The OrderQueueApp class

The three parts of figure 22-13 show the code for the classes that make up the Order Queue application. To start, you can see the OrderQueueApp class, which contains the application's main method. This method begins by declaring three constants that store the number of OrderTaker threads to create, the number of orders to be created by each OrderTaker thread, and the number of OrderHandler threads to create. If you want, you can experiment with this application by varying these values and observing the effect your changes have on how the application runs.

Next, the main method creates an instance of the OrderQueue class and assigns it to a variable named queue. Then, it displays the starting information you saw in figure 22-11. Next, it uses two for loops to create and start the OrderTaker and OrderHandler threads. The first for loop creates the number of OrderTaker threads indicated by the TAKER_COUNT constant, and the second for loop creates the number of OrderHandler threads indicated by the HANDLER_COUNT constant. Note that the queue variable is passed to each OrderTaker and OrderHandler constructor so these objects have access to the order queue. Also, the ORDER_COUNT constant is passed to the OrderTaker constructor so those objects know how many orders to create.

The Order class

Part 1 of figure 22-13 also presents the Order class. To keep this application simple, this class just defines an instance variable named number, a constructor that accepts an order number as an argument, and a toString method that returns the order number in a displayable format. Otherwise, it would provide all the variables and methods related to an order.

The code for the OrderQueueApp class

```
public class OrderQueueApp
{
    public static void main(String[] args)
    {
        final int TAKER_COUNT = 3;    // number of OrderTaker threads
        final int ORDER_COUNT = 3;    // number of orders per OrderTaker thread
        final int HANDLER_COUNT = 2;  // number of OrderHandler threads

        OrderQueue queue = new OrderQueue();       // create the order queue

        System.out.println("Starting the order queue.");

        System.out.println("Starting " + TAKER_COUNT + " order takers, "
            + "each producing " + ORDER_COUNT + " orders.");

        System.out.println("Starting " + HANDLER_COUNT
            + " order handlers.\n");

        String s
          = "     OrderTaker threads               OrderHandler threads    \n"
          + "============================  ============================";
        System.out.println(s);

        for (int i = 0; i < TAKER_COUNT; i++)    // create the Taker threads
        {
            OrderTaker t = new OrderTaker(ORDER_COUNT, queue);
            t.start();
        }

        for (int i = 0; i < HANDLER_COUNT; i++) // create the Handler threads
        {
            OrderHandler h = new OrderHandler(queue);
            h.start();
        }
    }
}
```

The code for the Order class

```
public class Order
{
    private int number;

    public Order(int number)
    {
        this.number = number;
    }

    @Override
    public String toString()
    {
        return "Order #" + number;
    }
}
```

Figure 22-13 The code for the Order Queue application (part 1 of 3)

The OrderTaker class

The OrderTaker class shown in part 2 of figure 22-13 begins by declaring a static variable named orderNumber. This variable is used to supply the order numbers for the orders that are created by this class. As you can see, the private method named getOrderNumber returns this variable and then increments its value. This method is synchronized so that if two threads call it at the same time, each receives a unique order number.

The constructor for the OrderTaker class accepts the order count and order queue as parameters and saves these values in instance variables. Then, the run method consists primarily of a while loop that creates the correct number of orders. The code within this loop creates a new Order object using the result of the getOrderNumber method as the order number. Then, it calls the pushOrder method of the order queue to add the order to the queue. Finally, it calls the sleep method to place the thread in Blocked state for at least one second before creating another order.

The code for the OrderTaker class

```
public class OrderTaker extends Thread
{
    private static int orderNumber = 1;

    private int count = 0;
    private int maxOrders;
    private OrderQueue orderQueue;

    public OrderTaker(int orderCount, OrderQueue orderQueue)
    {
        this.maxOrders = orderCount;          // number of orders to create
        this.orderQueue = orderQueue;         // order queue
    }

    @Override
    public void run()
    {
        Order order;
        while (count < maxOrders)
        {
            order = new Order(getOrderNumber());
            orderQueue.pushOrder(order);      // add order to the queue
            System.out.println(order.toString() + " created by "
                + this.getName());
            count++;
            try
            {
                Thread.sleep(1000);           // delay one second
            }
            catch (InterruptedException e)
            {}                                // ignore interruptions
        }
    }

    private static synchronized int getOrderNumber()
    {
        return orderNumber++;
    }
}
```

Figure 22-13 The code for the Order Queue application (part 2 of 3)

The OrderHandler class

Part 3 of figure 22-13 starts by presenting the OrderHandler class. As you can see, this class is simpler than the OrderTaker class. Its constructor accepts a reference to the order queue and saves it in an instance variable. Then, the run method consists of a never-ending while loop that calls the order queue's pullOrder method to get an order. The order is then displayed on the console, and the sleep method is called to place the thread in the Blocked state for at least two seconds before trying to retrieve another order.

The OrderQueue class

The OrderQueue class is also shown in part 3 of figure 22-13. To store the orders that are taken, this class uses a linked list. If you don't remember how to work with a linked list, you may want to refer to chapter 12 to refresh your memory.

As you can see, the pushOrder method is synchronized so only one thread can add an order to the queue at a time. It adds the order to the queue, and then calls the notifyAll method to wake up any threads that might be waiting to process orders.

The pullOrder method, which is also synchronized, uses a while loop to wait until the size method of the linked list indicates that there's at least one order available to be processed. Within the while loop, the wait method is called to place the OrderHandler thread in the Waiting state if an order isn't available. It remains in that state until one of the OrderTaker threads calls the pushOrder method, which in turn calls the notifyAll method to return the threads to the Runnable state.

Keep in mind that once an OrderHandler thread is returned to the Runnable state, the pullOrder method of the OrderQueue class is still in the while loop. So before an order is pulled from the queue, the size of the queue is checked to make sure that an order is still available. If it is, the loop ends and the order is retrieved from the linked list and returned to the calling thread. If it isn't, it means that another thread has already processed the order, so the wait method is called again.

When you execute an application that uses threads, you should realize that the application doesn't end until all of its threads end. In this case, though, because the run method of the OrderHandler class contains a never-ending while loop, the OrderHandler threads never end. Because of that, you have to end the application explicitly by closing the console window. In NetBeans, you can do that by clicking on the Stop button in the Output window.

The code for the OrderHandler class

```
public class OrderHandler extends Thread
{
    private OrderQueue orderQueue;

    public OrderHandler(OrderQueue orderQueue)
    {
        this.orderQueue = orderQueue;
    }

    @Override
    public void run()
    {
        Order order;
        while (true)
        {
            order = orderQueue.pullOrder();    // get next available order
            System.out.println(
                "                              " + order.toString() +
                " processed by " + this.getName());
            try
            {
                Thread.sleep(2000);            // delay two seconds
            }
            catch (InterruptedException e) {}  // ignore interruptions
        }
    }
}
```

The code for the OrderQueue class

```
import java.util.LinkedList;

public class OrderQueue
{
    private LinkedList<Order> orderQueue = new LinkedList<>();

    public synchronized void pushOrder(Order order)
    {
        orderQueue.addLast(order);
        notifyAll();                           // notify any waiting threads
    }

    public synchronized Order pullOrder()
    {
        while (orderQueue.size() == 0)         // if no orders in queue, wait
        {
            try
            {
                wait();
            }
            catch (InterruptedException e) {}  // ignore interruptions
        }
        return orderQueue.removeFirst();
    }
}
```

Figure 22-13 The code for the Order Queue application (part 3 of 3)

Perspective

In this chapter, you learned the essential skills for working with threads. Frankly, threading is one of the most challenging topics in this book. So don't be too worried if you don't understand every detail of how it works. The best way to learn how to work with threads is to develop multithreaded applications. You'll get a chance to do that in the exercises that follow.

You should be aware that several threading features were introduced with JDK 1.4 and 1.5. We didn't cover those features in this chapter, though, because they're used for more advanced aspects of multithreaded programming. For example, JDK 1.4 introduced a new variable modifier called *volatile* that lets you share access to variables in unsynchronized methods. And JDK 1.5 introduced a set of classes (java.util.concurrent, java.util.concurrent.atomic, and java.util.concurrent.locks) that provide more advanced threading features. You can refer to the Java documentation if you want to find out more about these features.

Summary

- A *thread* is a single sequential flow of control within a program that often completes a specific task.
- A *multithreaded application* consists of two or more threads whose execution can overlap.
- Since a processor can only execute one thread at a time, the *thread scheduler* determines which thread to execute.
- *Multithreading* is typically used to improve the performance of applications with I/O operations, to improve the responsiveness of GUI operations, and to allow two or more users to run server-based applications simultaneously.
- You can create a thread by extending the Thread class and then instantiating the new class. Or, you can implement the Runnable interface and then pass a reference to the Runnable object to the constructor of the Thread class.
- You can use the methods of the Thread class to start a thread, to control when a thread runs, and to control when other threads are allowed to run.
- *Asynchronous threads* execute independently of each other.
- *Synchronized methods* can be used to ensure that two threads don't run the same method of an object simultaneously. When a thread calls a synchronized method, the object that contains that method is *locked* so other threads can't access it.

Exercise 22-1 Create a Number Finder application

In this exercise, you'll create an application that generates a random number between 0 and 999 and uses four threads to search for the number. When one of the threads finds the number, it should print a message on the console. The output from this application should look like this:

```
The number is 784
Target number 784 found by Thread-3
```

1. Open the project named ch22_ex1_NumberFinder in the ex_starts directory. Review the code for the Main class and note that it generates a random number between 0 and 999 and then displays it as shown in the first line above.
2. Add a class named FinderThread that extends the Thread class.
3. Add a constructor that accepts three parameters: the number to search for, the number where the search should begin, and the number where the search should end. Store these parameters in private variables.
4. Add a run method that searches for the number. This method should use a for loop to check each value in the specified range to determine if it matches the target value. If a match is made, the thread should display a message like the second line shown above and terminate by exiting from the for loop.
5. In the Main class, add code to the main method to create and start the four threads. The threads should check the following ranges: Thread-0, 0-249; Thread-1, 250-499; Thread-2, 500-749; and Thread-3, 750-999.
6. Test the application two or more times to be sure it works correctly.

Exercise 22-2 Use the Runnable interface and the sleep method

In this exercise, you'll create an application that's similar to the one that you created in exercise 22-1. However, in this exercise, you'll implement the Runnable interface instead of extending the Thread class.

1. Open the project named ch22_ex2_NumberFinderApp in the ex_starts directory. Then, review the code for the Main class.
2. Add a class named Finder that implements the Runnable interface. This class should work like the FinderThread class created in exercise 22-1. If you did exercise 22-1, you can copy in much of this code. Otherwise, you can complete steps 3 and 4 of exercise 22-1.
3. In the Main class, add code to the main method to create and start the four Finder threads. The threads should check the following ranges: Thread-0, 0-249; Thread-1, 250-499; Thread-2, 500-749; and Thread-3, 750-999.
4. Test the application two or more times to be sure it works correctly.

5. Modify the Finder class so its run method uses the sleep method to cause the thread to sleep for 1 millisecond every ten times through the loop. If an InterruptedException occurs, display the exception at the console.
6. Test the application to be sure it still works correctly.

Exercise 22-3 Add a Monitor thread to the Number Finder application

In this exercise, you'll create an application that's similar to the one that you created in exercise 22-2. However, in this exercise, you'll include code so the thread that finds the number notifies a Monitor thread, which then interrupts all of the Finder threads. When a Finder thread is interrupted, it should display a line indicating that it has been interrupted and then end. The resulting output should look like this:

```
The number is 20
Target number 20 found by Thread-1
Thread-2 interrupted
Thread-3 interrupted
Thread-4 interrupted
```

1. Open the project named ch22_ex3_NumberFinder in ex_starts directory. Review the code in the Main class.
2. If you haven't already done exercise 22-2, do steps 2 and 3 to create a class named Finder that implements the Runnable interface and then create and run four Finder threads from the main method.
3. Add a class named Monitor to the project. This class should define a thread by extending the Thread class. Then, code a method named addThread that adds a thread to a private array list of Thread objects.
4. In the Monitor class, add a synchronized method named foundNumber that interrupts each thread in the threads collection. This method should also set a boolean instance variable to true to indicate that the number has been found.
5. In the Monitor class, add a run method that tests the boolean variable within an infinite loop.
6. In the Main class, modify the main method so it creates and starts the Monitor thread, passes a reference to the Monitor thread to the Finder threads, and adds the four Finder threads to the Monitor thread.
7. In the Finder class, modify its constructor so it accepts a reference to the Monitor thread.
8. Modify the run method so it calls the Monitor thread's foundNumber method if it finds the target number. Also, modify this method so a message is displayed when the thread is interrupted.
9. Test the application to be sure that it works correctly. If necessary, stop the Monitor thread after the number is found.

23

How to deploy an application

Once you're done creating and testing an application, you need to deploy the application so your users can run it. You can use several techniques to do that. This chapter starts by briefly describing three of the best techniques. Then, it provides a more detailed explanation for the first two.

An introduction to deployment

Figure 23-1 lists three techniques you can use to deploy a Java application. Each of these techniques has its advantages and disadvantages.

How executable JAR files work

The easiest way to deploy a Java application is to create an *executable JAR (Java Archive) file* that has all of the classes and resources needed by your application. Then, you can manually distribute this file to your users and show them how to run it.

Although this way of deploying an application is adequate for simple applications with just a few users, it doesn't provide a way to automatically install prerequisite files (such as the JRE that's needed to run Java applications), and it doesn't provide a way to automatically update the application. As a result, you'll only want to use this deployment option when you are prepared to help your users install the JRE and when you are willing to manually redistribute a new executable JAR file any time you have critical updates to your application.

How Java Web Start works

The second way to deploy an application is known as *Java Web Start* (*JWS*). This type of deployment lets the user install and start a Java application by clicking on a link from a web page.

Although it requires a little more work to set up Web Start, the advantages of this type of deployment are often worth the effort. That's because Java Web Start automates the process of installing the correct version of the JRE, and it can automatically update your application whenever you make an updated version available. However, since Java Web Start allows users to download the application from the web, the application has some significant security restrictions by default. These security restrictions are similar to those of applets. For example, an application can't read or write files from the user's file system. As with applets, you can get around these restrictions by creating a signed JAR file, but this can be difficult to set up.

How an installer program works

The third way to deploy an application is to use an *installer program* such as InstallAnywhere to create an install file for the application. Then, you can make this install file available to your users, and they can install your application just as they would install other professional applications.

Although this is a huge advantage for a professional application, this technique also has several disadvantages. First, most installer programs are expensive commercial products. Second, most installer programs require more work to set up and configure. Third, most installer programs don't provide any way to automatically update the application after it has been installed.

Executable JAR file

An *executable JAR (Java Archive) file* stores all the classes and resources needed by your application. You can manually distribute this file to your users and show them how to run it.

Pros

- There are no significant security restrictions.

Cons

- The correct version of the JRE is *not* installed automatically, so you or your users must install it.
- The code is *not* automatically updated, so if the application changes, you must redistribute it.

Web Start

Java Web Start (JWS) allows users to download an application from the web, cache the application locally, and start it.

Pros

- The correct version of Java is automatically installed.
- The code is automatically updated.

Cons

- There are some significant security restrictions.

Installer program

An *installer program* allows you to create an install file for every operating system that you want your application to run on. Then, users can use the install file for their operating system to install the application just as they would install any other application.

Pros

- The application installs and runs like a professional desktop application.
- The correct version of Java can be installed as part of the installation process.
- There are no significant security restrictions.

Cons

- The code is *not* automatically updated after the program is installed.
- Most installer programs are expensive commercial products.
- This approach requires more work to set up and configure.

Figure 23-1 An introduction to deployment

How to use an executable JAR file

You can use an executable JAR file to deploy an application just by making that file available to your users. Then, if the application is a GUI application, users can run the application by double-clicking on the JAR file. However, if the application is a console application, it usually makes sense to create a script file to run the application. Then, your users can double-click on the script file to run the console application.

How to create an executable JAR file

Figure 23-2 shows how to create an executable JAR file. Fortunately, if you're using NetBeans, all you need to do is to build the project. When you do, NetBeans automatically creates an executable JAR file for the project and stores that JAR file in the project's dist directory.

If you want to review the options for the JAR file that's created for a project, you can display the Project Properties dialog box for the project and then click on the Packaging category. This category shows the name and location of the JAR file, along with its properties. By default, the JAR file includes the .class files for the project, but does not include the .java and .form files that contain the source code for the project. That makes sense because you typically don't want to make the source code available to users. The JAR file also contains any other files necessary to run the application, including any Java libraries that are needed by the application.

In addition to the class files and libraries, a JAR file always contains a *manifest file*. This file stores additional information about the files in the JAR file, including which .class file contains the main method for the application.

Although it's possible to distribute the files for an application without storing them in a JAR file, it's almost always better to use a JAR file. This makes it easier to manage the files of the application. In addition, since a JAR file uses a compressed format, it can dramatically improve the download time for an application that's deployed to the web.

The properties for building a project

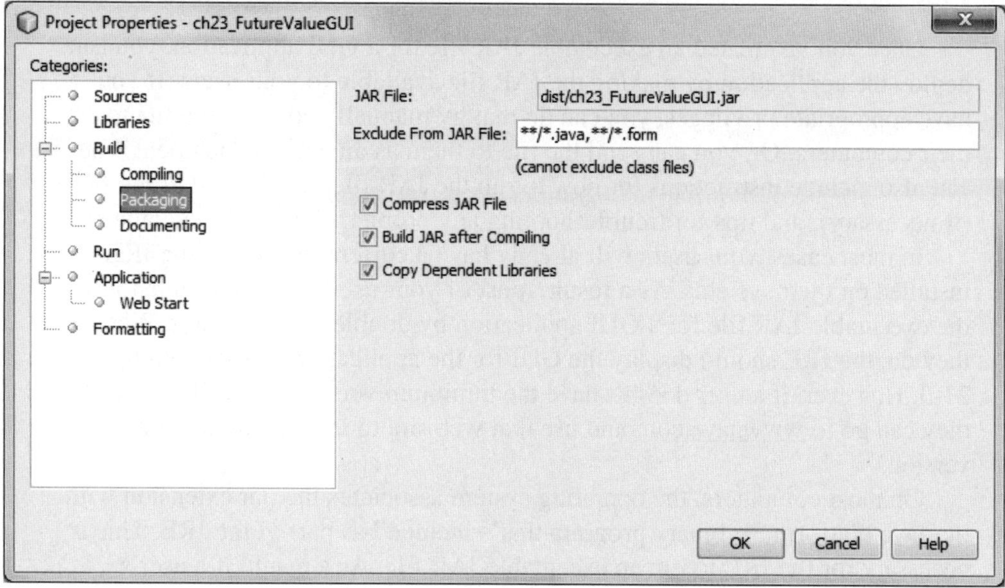

Description

- When you build a project, NetBeans creates an executable JAR file and stores it in the project's dist directory by default.
- The executable JAR file contains all of the files necessary to run the application, including any Java libraries that are needed by the application.
- The executable JAR file also contains a *manifest file* that stores information about the files that the JAR file contains, including which .class file contains the main method for the application.
- Because a JAR file uses a compressed format, it can dramatically improve the download time for an application that's deployed to the web.

Figure 23-2 How to create an executable JAR file

How to deploy a GUI application

Once you've created an executable JAR file for a GUI application, you can deploy the application by making the JAR file available to your users. If you have appropriate privileges, you can do that by manually copying the file to their computers. Or, you can send the file to them as an email attachment. You can also include instructions for how to run the JAR file, how to install the JRE (if necessary), and tips for troubleshooting any problems they may encounter.

In most cases, your users will already have a current version of the JRE installed on their systems. As a result, most of your users should be able to run the executable JAR file for a GUI application by double-clicking on it. When they do, the JRE should display the GUI for the application as shown in figure 23-3. However, if a user doesn't have the minimum version of the JRE installed, they can go to www.java.com and use that web site to install a more current version.

On most computers, the operating system associates the .jar extension with the Java Platform SE binary program that's included as part of the JRE. This is necessary for the JRE to run an executable JAR file. As a result, if a user's operating system isn't attempting to use Java to run the JAR file, you may need to modify the user's system so it works correctly with executable JAR files.

A GUI application running outside of NetBeans

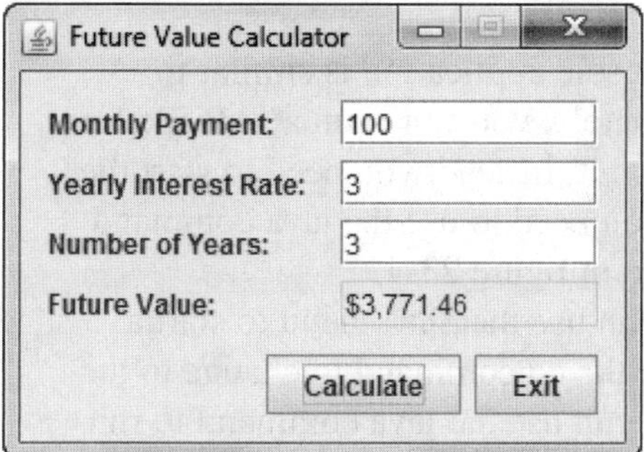

Description

- Once you've created an executable JAR file for a GUI application, you can deploy it by making the JAR file available to your users.
- To run an executable JAR file, the user can double-click on it.
- The JRE has to be installed on the user's computer for the user to run an executable JAR file.
- To install the JRE on a system other than one running Mac OS X, the user can go to www.java.com.
- The JRE is installed on systems running Mac OS X by default. To install a newer version, the user can use the Software Update feature that's available from the Apple menu.
- For an operating system to run an executable JAR file, it must associate the .jar extension with the Java Platform SE binary program that's included as part of the JRE.

Figure 23-3 How to deploy an executable JAR file for a GUI application

How to deploy a console application

Deploying an executable JAR file for a console application is similar to deploying one for a GUI application. Unfortunately, you can't run a JAR file for a console application just by double-clicking on it. Instead, you need to start the console for the operating system first. Then, you need to use the java command to run the JAR file for the application as shown in figure 23-4.

On a Windows system, for example, you can use the Start menu to start a Command Prompt window. Then, you can use the cd command to change to the directory that contains the JAR file. Next, you can use the java command to run the executable JAR file. Although the details are slightly different, you can use a similar technique to run a console application on other operating systems such as Mac OS X or Linux.

To make it easier for users to run a console application, you can create a script file that starts the console and runs the application. In Windows, for example, you can create a batch (.bat) file that changes to the appropriate directory and executes the appropriate java command. Then, the user can start your application by double-clicking on the .bat file. On a Mac OS X or Linux system, you can create a bash (.sh) file that works similarly.

In some cases, the operating system won't be able to find the java command. That's typically because the java command isn't in the system path. To fix this problem, you can specify an absolute path to the java command as shown in the figure. Or, you can modify the system's Path variable so it includes the bin directory for the JRE. To change the Path variable on a Windows system, you can use the same technique you use to change the CLASSPATH variable. For more information, see figure 20-8 in chapter 20.

Once you've created a script file, you can make both the script file and the JAR file available to your users. Then, your users can run the console application by double-clicking on the script file. For this to work, however, you need to store the JAR file in the directory that's specified by the script file. Otherwise, the script file won't be able to locate the JAR file.

A console application running outside of NetBeans

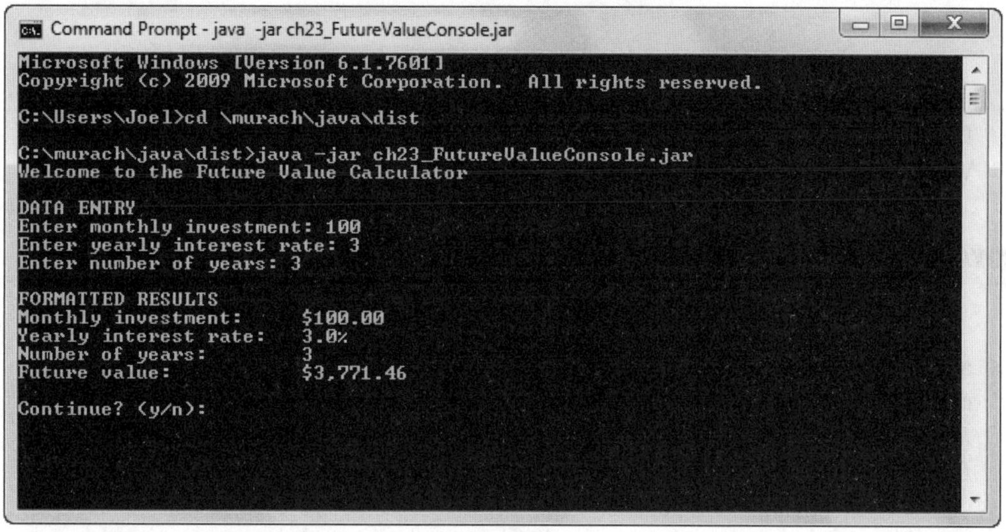

```
Command Prompt - java -jar ch23_FutureValueConsole.jar
Microsoft Windows [Version 6.1.7601]
Copyright (c) 2009 Microsoft Corporation.  All rights reserved.

C:\Users\Joel>cd \murach\java\dist

C:\murach\java\dist>java -jar ch23_FutureValueConsole.jar
Welcome to the Future Value Calculator

DATA ENTRY
Enter monthly investment: 100
Enter yearly interest rate: 3
Enter number of years: 3

FORMATTED RESULTS
Monthly investment:       $100.00
Yearly interest rate:     3.0%
Number of years:          3
Future value:             $3,771.46

Continue? (y/n):
```

Syntax to run an executable JAR file

```
java -jar JarName.jar
```

A batch (.bat) file that runs a console application on Windows

```
:: Change to the directory that stores the JAR file
cd \murach\java\dist

:: Use the java command to run the JAR file
java -jar ch23_FutureValueConsole.jar
```

A bash (.sh) file that runs a console application on Mac OS X or Linux

```
#!/bin/bash

# Change to the directory that stores the JAR file
cd /murach/java/dist

#Use the java command to run the JAR file
java -jar ch23_FutureValueConsole.jar
```

Description

- Once you've created an executable JAR file for a console application, you can deploy it by making the JAR file available to your users.
- To run an executable JAR file, the user starts a console and then uses the java command. This command is case-sensitive.
- For Windows, you can create a batch (.bat) file to start the console and execute the java command. For Mac OS X or Linux, you can create a bash (.sh) file.
- If a system can't find the java command, you can specify an absolute path to the command. For Windows, for example, the path will look like this:

  ```
  "C:\Program Files\Java\jre7\bin\java"
  ```

  Or, you can modify the system's Path variable so it includes the bin directory for the JRE.

Figure 23-4 How to deploy an executable JAR file for a console application

How to use Java Web Start

Java Web Start lets you deploy a GUI application to an intranet or the Internet. Then, your users can install and run the application by clicking on a link that's available from a web page. Unfortunately, Java Web Start doesn't work for console applications.

A procedure for using Java Web Start

Figure 23-5 shows a procedure for using Java Web Start to deploy an application. To start, you create an executable JAR file for the application as described earlier in this chapter. Then, you create a *Java Network Launch Protocol* (*JNLP*) file for the application, and you create a *Hypertext Markup Language* (*HTML*) file that includes a link to the JNLP file. You'll learn how to create these two files in the figures that follow.

Once you've created the necessary files, you can test them on your local system. To do that, you must put the files in the appropriate directories. That usually means putting the files in the same directory. As you'll see in a minute, though, the HTML file identifies the location of the JNLP file, and the JNLP file identifies the location of the JAR file. So it's also possible to store these files in different directories. Then, to test the application, you display the HTML file and click on the link to the JNLP file. If these files are coded correctly, the application should launch.

If the JNLP and HTML files work correctly on your local system, you can modify them so they'll work correctly on a remote web server. You'll learn how to do that in a minute. Then, if you're deploying an application to an intranet, you can use your operating system to copy the JAR, JNLP, and HTML files to the appropriate directories on the server. However, if you're deploying an application to the Internet, you can use an FTP program to copy the files to the web server as described later in this chapter. Finally, you can test the HTML and JNLP files on the remote server just as you did on the local server.

A procedure for using Web Start

1. Build the project to create a JAR file that contains the class files and resources for the application. See figure 23-2 for details.
2. Create a JNLP file for the application. See figure 23-6 for details.
3. Create an HTML file that includes a link to the JNLP file. See figure 23-7 for details.
4. Place the JAR, JNLP, and HTML files in the appropriate directories.
5. Display the HTML file in a browser and click on the link to the JNLP file to make sure it launches the application.
6. Modify the JNLP and HTML files as necessary so they will run on a remote web server.
7. Copy the JAR, JNLP, and HTML files to the appropriate directories on the web server to make them accessible to users.
8. Display the HTML file in a browser and click on the link to the JNLP file to make sure it launches the application.

Description

- The *Java Network Launch Protocol* (*JNLP*) can be used to launch Java applications that have been deployed on a network such as an intranet or the Internet.
- *Hypertext Markup Language* (*HTML*) can be used to create a web page that includes a link to a JNLP file.
- If you are deploying an application to an intranet, you can copy the JAR, JNLP, and HTML files to the appropriate directory on the server.
- If you are deploying an application to the Internet, you can use an FTP program to copy the files to the web server. See figure 23-8 for details.

Figure 23-5 A procedure for using Java Web Start

How to create a JNLP file

In chapter 19, you learned how to work with XML files. A JNLP file is a specific type of XML file. The elements and attributes of a JNLP file provide information about how a Java application should be launched from across a network.

The easiest way to create a JNLP file for an application is to copy a JNLP file for an existing application and then modify its elements and attributes. For example, if you download the code for this book, you can use the JNLP file that's included with the Future Value GUI application for this chapter as a starting point. In most cases, you only need to modify the elements and attributes shown in figure 23-6.

To start, you can use the codebase attribute of the <jnlp> element to specify the URL for the base location for all relative URLs in the rest of the file. Then, the href attribute of the <jnlp> element specifies the relative path to the JNLP file. In this case, the JNLP file is named future_value.jnlp and is stored on the Internet in the fv/app directory of the murach.com domain. However, if you have a local web server, you can use the localhost keyword to refer to the domain for that server. Or, if you're using Windows, you can test an application without using a web server by leaving this attribute blank.

The required <title> and <vendor> elements specify the name of the application and its vendor. The optional, self-closing <offline-allowed/> element specifies that the application should be available even if the user is not connected to the Internet. This element also controls how Java Web Start checks for an update to an application. If you include this element, the application can be run offline, but Java Web Start still checks whether an update is available. If you are connected to the Internet with a fast enough connection, Java Web Start usually updates the application, but this isn't guaranteed. If the connection is too slow or doesn't exist, Java Web Start runs a cached version of the application if one is available.

If you don't include the <offline-allowed/> element, the application can't be run offline. In that case, Java Web Start always uses the Internet connection to check whether an update is available. If so, it automatically updates and launches the application. As a result, you can be sure that your users always run the most current version of your application.

The <j2se> element specifies the minimum version of Java and a URL where the JRE can be automatically downloaded and installed. In this figure, this element specifies Java SE 6 or later.

The <jar> element specifies the path to the JAR file and indicates whether this file includes a main class. Note that the href attribute is relative to the codebase attribute of the <jnlp> element. In this case, the JAR file is stored in the same directory specified by the codebase attribute.

The <application-desc> element specifies that the JNLP file launches an application. This element is required because JNLP files can also be used to launch applets.

The <update> element indicates the application's preference for how Web Start checks for application updates. This element is optional, so you only need

A JNLP file for the Future Value application

```
<?xml version="1.0" encoding="UTF-8"?>
<jnlp spec="1.0+"
      codebase="http://www.murach.com/fv/app"
      href="future_value.jnlp">
    <information>
        <title>Future Value Calculator</title>
        <vendor>Mike Murach & Associates</vendor>
        <offline-allowed/>
    </information>
    <resources>
        <!-- Application Resources -->
        <j2se version="1.6+"
              href="http://java.sun.com/products/autodl/j2se"/>
        <jar href="ch23_FutureValueGUI.jar" main="true" />
    </resources>
    <application-desc></application-desc>
    <update check="background"
            policy="prompt-run" />
</jnlp>
```

Some elements and attributes for a JNLP file

Element	Description
`<jnlp>`	The codebase attribute specifies the URL for the base location for all relative URLs in the rest of the file. This attribute can be left blank to test the JNLP file under Windows without using a web server. The href attribute specifies the path to the JNLP file.
`<title>`	Specifies the name of the application.
`<vendor>`	Specifies the vendor that created the application.
`<offline-allowed/>`	A self-closing tag that specifies that the application should be available even if the user is not connected to the Internet.
`<j2se>`	The version attribute specifies the minimum version of Java that's needed to run the application. The href attribute specifies the URL where Web Start can automatically download the correct version of Java.
`<jar>`	The href attribute specifies the path to the JAR file. The main attribute specifies whether the JAR file contains a main class.
`<application-desc>`	Specifies that the JNLP file is launching an application, not an applet.
`<update>`	This element is optional. Its check attribute specifies how Web Start checks for updates of the application's code (always, background, or timeout). Its policy attribute specifies when and how Web Start installs updates (always, prompt-update, or prompt-run).

Description

- A JNLP file is a type of XML file that specifies all the information that Web Start needs to launch an application across a network such as the Internet.
- To create a JNLP file, copy an existing JNLP file and modify its elements and attributes so they're appropriate for your application.
- To test a JNLP file, double-click on the file. If your JNLP file is coded correctly, this should launch your application.

Figure 23-6 How to create a JNLP file for an application

to include it if the default settings aren't working adequately. In that case, you can experiment with the various options until you get the updating to work the way you want it to work.

Once you finish coding your JNLP file, you can test it by double-clicking on it. If your JNLP file is coded correctly and stored in the correct directory, this should launch your application. Otherwise, you'll get an error message that may provide some details to help you troubleshoot the problem.

Keep in mind that this figure only covers a starting set of JNLP elements and attributes. Other elements and attributes are available that let you provide an icon for the application, control how shortcuts are created, remove security restrictions, and so on. For more information about JNLP, you can search the Internet for its documentation.

How to create an HTML document that launches an application

Once you have your JNLP file working correctly, it's easy to create an HTML document that launches your application. To do that, you include a link to the JNLP file as shown in figure 23-7.

An *HTML document* contains *HTML elements* that are similar to the elements of an XML file. Like the elements of an XML file, the elements of an HTML document can include *attributes*. If you've read chapter 19, then, you shouldn't have much trouble understanding how to create an HTML document. The biggest difference between an HTML document and an XML file is that HTML uses predefined elements and attributes.

Within an HTML document, the <head> element contains other elements that provide information about the document. In particular, the <title> element provides the text that's displayed in the web browser's title bar. The <body> element of an HTML document defines the content of the web page. In this figure, for example, the <h1> element defines the level-1 heading that's displayed on the page. Then, the <a> element defines the link to the JNLP file for the application. The href attribute of this element identifies the JNLP file, and the element's content determines how the link is displayed on the page. In this case, the link will appear with the text "Launch application." When the user clicks on this link, the application is launched.

An HTML document that launches the Future Value application

```
<!DOCTYPE html>
<html>
    <head>
        <title>Future Value Calculator</title>
        <meta http-equiv="Content-Type" content="text/html; charset=UTF-8">
    </head>
    <body>
        <h1>Future Value Calculator application</h1>
        <a href="future_value.jnlp">Launch application</a>
    </body>
</html>
```

Description

- The *Hypertext Markup Language* (*HTML*) is the language that's used to create web pages.
- An *HTML document* contains *HTML elements* that define the content and structure of the web page. This works similarly to an XML file, except that the names of the HTML elements as well as any *attributes* they contain are predefined.
- The <head> element of a document provides information about the document, such as the text that's displayed in the browser's title bar.
- The <body> element of a document defines the content of the web page. Within this element, you can code an <a> element with an href attribute that defines a link to the JNLP file for the application. The content of this element determines what's displayed for the link on the page. When the user clicks on this link, the application is launched.

Figure 23-7 How to create an HTML document that launches an application

How to deploy an application to a remote web server

Figure 23-8 shows how to use an FTP program called FileZilla to deploy the files for an application to a web server. FileZilla is an open-source program that you can download for free from the Internet. It has an easy-to-use interface that lets you navigate through the files on both the local and remote system and upload and download files.

When you first start FileZilla, the left pane of the main window will show a directory tree for the local system. Then, you can use this program to connect to a remote web server. When you do, the right pane of the main window will display the directory tree for the remote system.

To display the contents of a subdirectory in the lower pane of the main window for either the local or remote system, just click on it in the directory tree. You can also double-click on a subdirectory in the lower pane to display its contents in that pane, and you can display the parent directory for the directories and files in the lower pane by double-clicking on the first directory in that pane (the one that's identified by two dots).

To transfer one or more files or directories from your local system to the remote system, you can use the technique described in this figure. This is known as *uploading* files. You can use a similar technique to transfer files from the remote site to your local site, which is known as *downloading* files. Note that before you upload files, you must navigate to the directory on the remote system where you want to store the files. Similarly, before you download files, you must navigate to the directory on the local system where you want to store the files.

FileZilla when it is connected to a web host

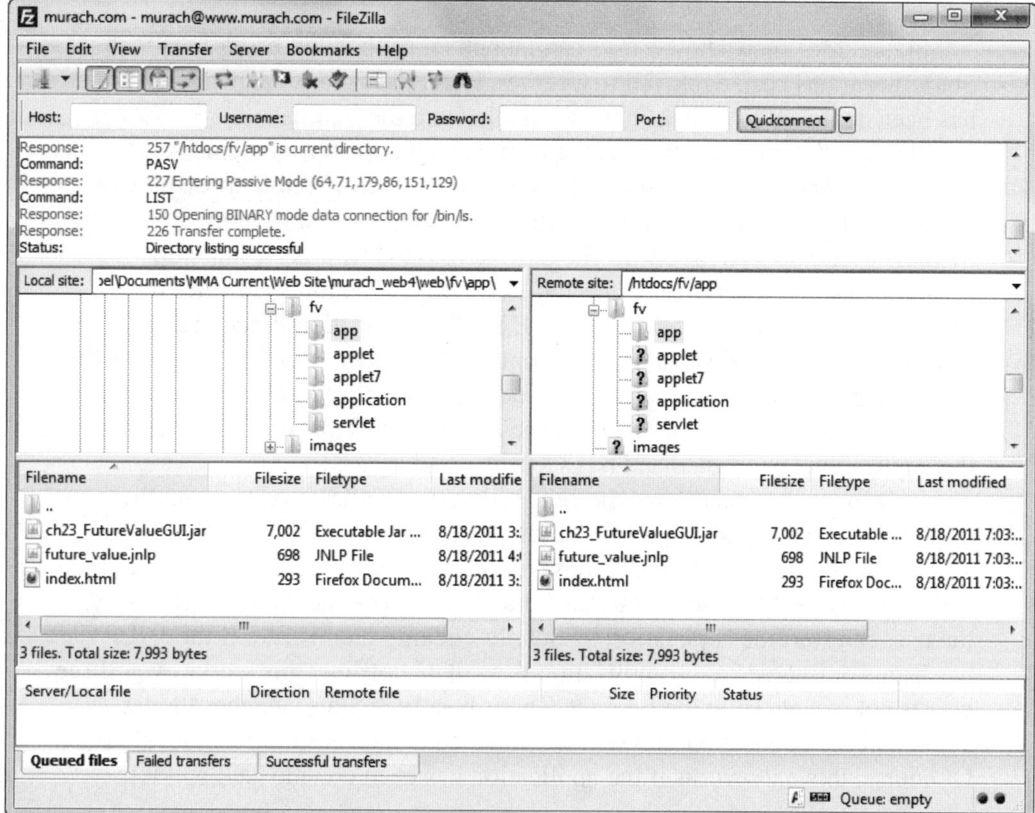

Description

- To deploy files to a remote web server, you can use an FTP program such as FileZilla, which is free and open-source. After you start FileZilla, you can use it to connect to your web server.
- The top left pane of the main FileZilla window shows the directory structure of the local system, and the top right pane shows the directory structure of the remote system.
- If you select a directory in either directory tree, the subdirectories and files in that directory are displayed in the lower pane of the main window. Then, you can use that pane to navigate through the directories.
- The directory that's identified by two dots at the top of each lower pane represents the parent directory.
- To *upload* a file or directory to the remote site, right-click on the file or directory in the local site and select the Upload command from the resulting menu.
- To *download* a file or directory from the remote site, right-click on the file or directory in the remote site and select the Download command from the resulting menu.
- You can also upload or download multiple files and directories by selecting them and then using the Upload or Download command.

Figure 23-8 How to deploy an application to a remote web server

How to launch an application

Figure 23-9 shows how a user can launch an application using Java Web Start after it has been deployed to a server. Here, the Future Value application has been deployed to a URL that's available from the Internet.

To start, the user navigates to the web page that includes the link for the application. Then, when the user clicks on the link, Java Web Start displays a dialog box like the one shown in the first screen in this figure. From this dialog box, the user can open the JNLP file or to save it to his or her computer.

If the user chooses to open the JNLP file, Java Web Start launches the application. This installs the correct JRE for the application if necessary, and it downloads an updated version of the application if necessary. Then, it starts the application as shown in the second screen. Notice the small warning icon that's displayed near the top right corner of the application. This icon indicates that the application is unsigned and has security restrictions.

If the user chooses to save the JNLP file on a Windows system, another dialog box is displayed that lets the user specify where the file will be saved. (On a Mac, the file is automatically saved in your Downloads directory.) In that case, it's common for the user to save the JNLP file on the desktop. That way, the user can start the application by double-clicking on this file. If the JNLP file has been configured so the application is available offline, this works even if the user is not connected to the Internet. Then, Java Web Start launches the last version of the application that was downloaded, which is stored in a local cache. Of course, this only works if the application has been downloaded previously.

How to fix a common problem

When the web server returns the JNLP file to the browser, it must include the correct header so the browser knows to use Java Web Start to open the JNLP file. By default, the Apache web server includes the correct header for a JNLP. As a result, Java Web Start usually works fine if an application is deployed to an Apache web server.

However, if your web server doesn't include the correct header, Java Web Start won't work correctly. In that case, you need to add a Multipurpose Internet Mail Extensions (MIME) type for the JNLP file to your web server. To do that, you can add the MIME type

```
application/x-java-jnlp-file
```

to the list of MIME types that are supported by your web server. Since the procedure for doing this varies depending on the web server, you can search the Internet for details for your specific server.

The Future Value application as it is being launched

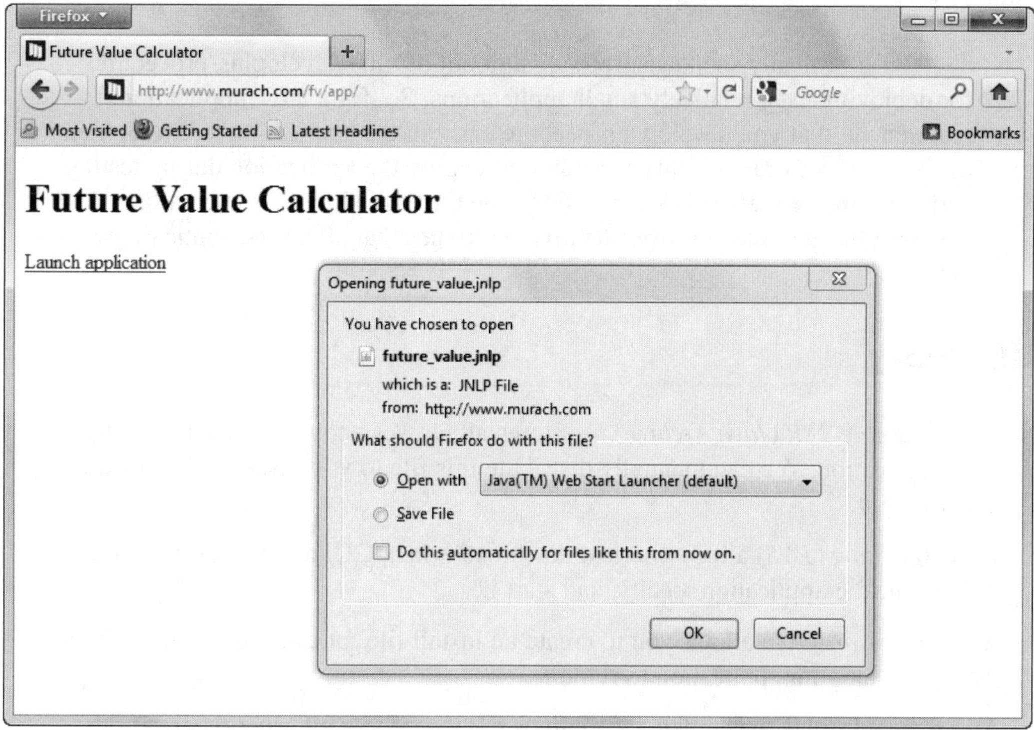

The Future Value application after it has been launched

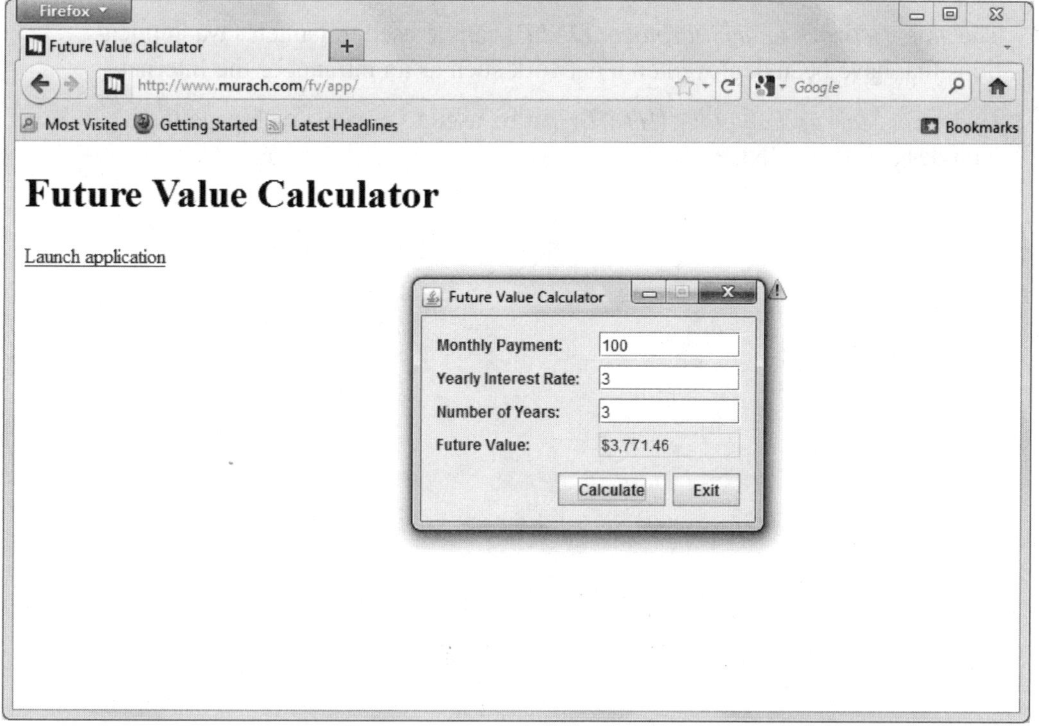

Figure 23-9 How to launch an application

Perspective

You'll probably spend a surprising amount of time developing procedures for deploying even relatively small applications. So, for a large application, I recommend that you develop a procedure early in the application's development cycle. Then, you can use this procedure to deploy the application during testing, and you can use that experience to fine-tune the procedure as you go along. As a side benefit, you may discover deployment issues that affect the application's design.

Summary

- An *executable JAR (Java Archive) file* stores all classes and resources needed by your application. You can manually distribute this file to your users and show them how to run it.
- *Java Web Start* (*JWS*) allows users to download a Java GUI application from the web, cache the application locally, and start it.
- An *installer program* allows you to create an install file for every operating system that you want your application to run on.
- An executable JAR file contains a *manifest file* that stores information about the files that are stored within the JAR file, including the file that contains the main method for the application.
- The *Java Network Launch Protocol* (*JNLP*) can be used to launch Java applications that have been deployed on a network such as an intranet or the Internet.
- *Hypertext Markup Language* (*HTML*) can be used to create a web page that includes a link to a JNLP file.

Appendix A

How to set up your PC for this book

This appendix shows how to install and configure the software that we recommend for developing Java applications on a PC. This software includes the Java Development Kit (JDK) and the NetBeans IDE. This appendix also shows how to install the source code and create the databases for this book.

Please note that this appendix is designed for a PC that's running the Windows operating system. For directions on setting up a Mac, see appendix B.

As you read this appendix, please remember that most web sites are continually updated. As a result, some of the procedures in this appendix may have changed since this book was published. Nevertheless, these procedures should still be good guides to installing the software. And if there are significant changes to these setup instructions, we will post updates on our web site (www.murach.com).

How to install the JDK

Figure A-1 shows how to install the Java Development Kit (JDK). To start, you download the exe file for the setup program for the most recent version of the JDK from the Java web site. Then, you navigate to the directory that holds the JDK, run the setup file, and respond to the resulting dialog boxes.

Since the Java web site may change after this book is printed, we've kept the procedure shown in this figure somewhat general. As a result, you may have to do some searching to find the current version of the JDK. In general, you can start by searching the Internet for the download for Java SE. Then, you can find the most current version of the JDK for your operating system.

By the way, all of the examples in this book have been tested against version 7.0.0 of the JDK. Since Java has a good track record of being backwards compatible, however, these examples should work equally well with later versions of the JDK.

How to install NetBeans

Figure A-1 also shows how to install the NetBeans IDE for Java. Since this works like most installation programs, you shouldn't have any trouble with this procedure. If you encounter any problems, you can view the documentation that's available from the NetBeans web site and consult the troubleshooting tips.

The download page for Java SE

```
http://www.oracle.com/technetwork/java/javase/downloads/index.html
```

How to install the JDK

1. Go to the download page for Java SE. If necessary, you can search the Internet to find this page.
2. Click on the Download button for JDK 7 and follow the instructions for your operating system.
3. Save the setup program to your hard disk. For Windows, this program is an exe file.
4. Run the setup program and respond to the resulting dialog boxes. When you're prompted for the JDK directory, use the default directory. For most Windows systems, the default directory for Java SE 7 is C:\Program Files\Java\jdk1.7.0.

The download page for the NetBeans IDE

```
http://netbeans.org/downloads/index.html
```

How to install the NetBeans IDE

1. Go to the download page for NetBeans. If necessary, you can search the Internet to find this page.
2. Download the version of the NetBeans IDE that's appropriate for you. For this book, you should download a version that supports Java SE 7.
3. Save the setup program to your hard disk. For Windows, this program is an exe file.
4. Run the setup program and respond to the resulting dialog boxes. When you're prompted to verify the JDK, make sure the setup program is pointing to the correct directory for JDK 7.

Notes

- For more information about installing the JDK, you can refer to the Oracle web site.
- For more information about installing NetBeans, you can refer to the NetBeans web site.

Figure A-1 How to install the JDK and NetBeans

How to install the source code for this book

Figure A-2 shows how to download and install the source code for this book. This includes the source code for the applications that are presented in this book and the source code for the starting points for the exercises.

When you finish this procedure, the book applications and exercise starts should be in the directories that are shown in this figure. Then, you can review the applications that are presented in this book, and you'll be ready to do the exercises in this book.

The Murach web site

```
www.murach.com
```

The directories for the book applications and exercise starts

```
C:\murach\java\netbeans\book_apps
C:\murach\java\netbeans\ex_starts
```

How to download and install the files for this book

1. Go to www.murach.com, and go to the page for *Murach's Java Programming*.
2. Click the link for "FREE download of the book applications." Then, click the "All book files" link for the self-extracting zip (exe) file. This should download a file named javp_allfiles.exe to your C drive.
3. Use Windows Explorer to find the exe file on your C drive. Then, double-click this file and respond to the dialog boxes that follow. This installs the files for this book in directories that start with C:\murach\java.

How to use a zip file instead of a self-extracting zip file

- Although we recommend using the self-extracting zip file (javp_allfiles.exe) to install the downloadable files as described above, some systems won't allow self-extracting zip files to run. In that case, you can download a regular zip file (javp_allfiles.zip) from our web site. Then, you can extract the files stored in this zip file into the C:\murach directory. If the C:\murach directory doesn't already exist, you will need to create it.

Notes for other versions of the JDK

- If you're using JDK 1.7 (Java SE 7) or later, you should be able to compile and run all of these applications.
- If you're using an earlier version of the JDK, you can still view the source code, but you won't be able to compile and run applications that use the features of Java introduced with later versions of the JDK. To solve this problem, you can download and install JDK 1.7 as described in figure A-1.

Figure A-2 How to install the source code for this book

Appendix B

How to set up your Mac for this book

This appendix shows how to install and configure the software that we recommend for developing Java applications on a Mac. This software includes the Java Development Kit (JDK), the NetBeans IDE, and the Apache Derby database. This appendix also shows how to install the source code for this book. This includes the files and databases that are used by the applications presented in this book.

Please note that this appendix is designed for a Mac that's running the OS X operating system. For directions on setting up a PC, see appendix A.

As you read this appendix, please remember that most web sites are continually updated. As a result, some of the procedures in this appendix may have changed since this book was published. Nevertheless, these procedures should still be good guides to installing the software. And if there are significant changes to these setup instructions, we will post updates on our web site (www.murach.com).

How to install the JDK

As this book goes to press, Apple includes an official version of JDK 1.6 with Mac OS X. However, it has not yet released an official version of JDK 1.7. Once it does, you should be able to install JDK 1.7 by using the Software Update feature as described in figure B-1.

If JDK 1.7 is not yet available through the Software Update feature, you can install an unofficial build of the OpenJDK as described in this figure. This JDK is similar to the Oracle JDK that's available to Windows users, and all of the examples in this book have been tested against OpenJDK 1.7. However, as this book goes to press, this JDK still contains some bugs that cause minor problems with some of the applications. For example, some applications aren't able to display the dollar sign character ($) correctly. These bugs should be fixed in later versions of OpenJDK and will surely be fixed before Apple releases the official version of JDK 1.7. In the meantime, to minimize these bugs, you can use JDK 1.6 for applications that don't use JDK 1.7 features. Of course, you must use JDK 1.7 or later for applications that use features that were introduced with JDK 1.7.

Since Java has a good track record of being backwards compatible, all of the examples in this book should work equally well with later versions of the JDK. For example, when JDK 1.8 becomes available, you should be able to use it for all examples in this book.

Since the web site shown in this figure may change after this book is printed, we've kept the procedure shown in this figure somewhat general. As a result, you may have to do some searching to find the current version of the JDK. In general, you can start by searching the Internet for "Mac OS X JDK 7 download". Then, you can find the most current version of the JDK for your operating system.

How to install the official JDK

1. Select the Software Update command from the Apple menu and respond to the resulting dialog boxes.
2. You can check which official versions of the JDK are installed on your system by using the Finder to view the contents of this directory:

   `/System/Library/Java/JavaVirtualMachines`

   If JDK 1.7 isn't shown in this directory, it isn't officially supported yet. In that case, you can install an unofficial build of JDK 1.7 as described below.

A download page for unofficial builds of OpenJDK for Mac OS X

`http://code.google.com/p/openjdk-osx-build/downloads/list`

The web page for the Apple Java Developer Preview

`https://connect.apple.com/cgi-bin/WebObjects/MemberSite.woa/wa/getSoftware?bundleID=20920`

How to install an unofficial build of JDK 1.7

1. Go to the download page for unofficial builds of OpenJDK 1.7. If necessary, you can search the Internet to find this page.
2. Follow the link on that page to the Apple Java Developer Preview for your version of Mac OS X and download the disk image (dmg) file. For example, for version 10.7, you can download Java Developer for 10.7. To do this, you need to log in to the Apple Developer center. If you don't already have an account, you'll need to create one.
3. Double-click on the disk image file, double click on the package (pkg) file, and respond to the resulting dialog boxes. This should install the Java Developer prerequisites.
4. Download the disk image (dmg) file for the OpenJDK 1.7. You typically want to select the most recent "universal" build.
5. Double-click on the disk image file, double-click on the package (pkg) file, and respond to the resulting dialog boxes. This should install JDK 1.7.

Notes

- When Apple makes an official version of JDK 1.7 available for the Mac, you can install it by using the Software Update feature. Until then, you can install an unofficial build of OpenJDK 1.7.
- For more information about installing the JDK on Mac OS X, you can search the Internet.

Figure B-1 How to install the JDK

How to install NetBeans

Figure B-2 shows how to install the NetBeans IDE for Java. Since this works like most installation programs, you shouldn't have any trouble with this procedure. If you encounter any problems, you can view the documentation that's available from the NetBeans web site and consult the troubleshooting tips.

Once you install NetBeans, you can start it and check which versions of the JDK are available to NetBeans as described in step 4 of this procedure. If JDK 1.7 or later is *not* available, you can make JDK 1.7 or later available as described in step 5.

Once JDK 1.7 or later is available to NetBeans, you can set the Java version for a project as shown in figure 1-11 of chapter 1. If the Java version for a project isn't set correctly, NetBeans will display errors, and you won't be able to compile or run the project.

How to install Derby

Although the Windows version of the JDK includes the JAR files for the Apache Derby database, the Mac version of the JDK does not include these files. As a result, if you want to use Derby as described in chapters 20 and 21, you must install it separately as described in figure B-2. The easiest way to do that is to copy the four JAR files named in this figure to the directory shown in this figure. Since this directory is automatically included in the class path, this saves you the trouble of having to modify the class path variable.

The download page for the NetBeans IDE

`http://netbeans.org/downloads`

How to install the NetBeans IDE

1. Go to the download page for NetBeans. If necessary, you can search the Internet to find this page.
2. Download the disk image (dmg) file for a version of the NetBeans IDE that's appropriate for you. For this book, you should download a version that supports Java SE 7.
3. Double-click on the disk image file, double-click on the make package (mpkg) file that's displayed, and respond to the resulting dialog boxes.
4. Start NetBeans. Then, select the Java Platforms command from the Tools menu. This should show the versions of the JDK that are available to NetBeans. If JDK 1.7 or later is available, you can skip the next step.
5. Click the Add Platform button. Then, navigate to the Home directory for JDK 1.7. On most systems, you can do that by setting the variable to a directory like this one:

   `/Library/Java/JavaVirtualMachines/1.7.0.jdk/Contents/Home`

   Here, you must Ctrl-click the JDK directory and select the Show Package Contents command to display the Contents directory.

The web page for the Apache Derby database

`http://db.apache.org/derby`

How to install Apache Derby

1. Go to the Apache Derby web site and click on the Downloads tab.
2. Download the zip file for the most recent version of Derby.
3. Extract the files from the zip file.
4. Copy the derby.jar, derbytools.jar. derbynet.jar, and derbyclient.jar files into this directory:

   `/System/Library/Java/Extensions`

Notes

- The JDK for the Mac doesn't include Derby. As a result, if you want to use Derby as described in chapters 20 and 21, you must install it separately.
- For more information about installing NetBeans or Derby on Mac OS X, you can search the Internet.

Figure B-2 How to install NetBeans and Derby

How to install the source code for this book

Figure B-3 shows how to download and install the source code for this book. This includes the source code for the applications that are presented in this book and the source code for the starting points for the exercises.

When you finish this procedure, the book applications and exercise starts should be in the directories that are shown in this figure. Then, you can review the applications that are presented in this book, and you'll be ready to do the exercises in this book.

Some of these book applications and exercise starts require JDK 1.7 or later. If the default JDK on your system is 1.6, NetBeans displays these projects in red when you open them, and it doesn't allow you to compile or run them. If you have installed JDK 1.7 as described in the previous figure, you can fix this problem by selecting JDK 1.7 as the Java platform as described in figure 1-11 of chapter 1.

As you read this book, you'll notice that it often instructs you to right-click, which is a common technique on PCs. However, on a Mac, right-clicking is not enabled by default. Instead, you can hold down the Ctrl key and click. Or, if you prefer, you can enable right-clicking by editing the system preferences for your mouse. Then, you can follow the instructions in this book more closely.

The Murach web site

www.murach.com

The directories for the book applications and exercise starts

```
/murach/java/netbeans/book_apps
/murach/java/netbeans/ex_starts
```

How to download and install the source code

1. Go to the Murach web site.
2. Find the page for *Murach's Java Programming*.
3. Click the link for "FREE download of the book applications." Then, click the "All book files (Mac)" link for the regular zip file. This will download a zip file named javp_allfiles_mac.zip onto your hard drive.
4. Use Finder to browse to this file and double-click on it to unzip it. This creates the java directory and its subdirectories.
5. Use Finder to create the murach directory directly on the Mac hard drive.
6. Use Finder to move the java directory into the murach directory.

Notes for other versions of the JDK

- If you're using JDK 1.7 (Java SE 7) or later, you should be able to compile and run all of these applications.
- If you're using an earlier version of the JDK, you can still view the source code, but you won't be able to compile and run applications that use the features of Java introduced with later versions of the JDK. To solve this problem, you can install JDK 1.7 as described in figure B-1 and configure NetBeans as described in figure B-2.

A note about right-clicking

- This book often instructs you to right-click, because that's common on PCs. On a Mac, right-clicking is not enabled by default. Instead, you can use the Ctrl-click instead of the right-click. Or, if you prefer, you can enable right-clicking by editing the system preferences for your mouse.

Figure B-3 How to install the source code for this book

Index

B

C

D

E

F

G

H

I

J

K

L

M

N

O

P

Q

R

S

T

U

V

W

X

Y

What software you need for this book

- Java SE 7 (JDK 1.7) or later. You can download this software for free and install it as described in appendix A (PC) or appendix B (Mac).
- NetBeans IDE 7.0 or later. You can download this software for free from netbeans.org and install it as described in appendix A (PC) or appendix B (Mac).
- Apache Derby 10.8 or later. This software is included as part of Java SE 7 on a PC. On a Mac, you can download it for free and install it as described in appendix B.

The downloadable files for this book

- Complete source code for the applications presented in this book so you can view, compile, and run the code for the applications as you read each chapter.
- Starting source code for the exercises presented at the end of each chapter so you can get more practice in less time.

How to download the files for this book

- Go to www.murach.com and navigate to the page for ***Murach's Java Programming.***
- Click the link for "FREE download of the book applications." Then, for Windows, download the self-extracting zip file that contains the source code for all book applications. For Mac, download the regular zip file.
- Double-click the downloaded file and respond to the dialog boxes that follow. For more details, see appendix A (PC) or appendix B (Mac).